Milestone Documents in African American History

Second Edition

Milestone Documents in African American History

Second Edition

Volume 4
1965–2017

Editors
Echol Nix, Jr.
Keturah C. Nix

SCHLAGER GROUP

GREY HOUSE PUBLISHING

Cover image Washington, DC, USA - October 10, 2012: Memorial to Dr. Martin Luther King. The memorial is America's 395th national park. http://www.istockphoto.com/portfolio/hanusst

Copyright © 2017, by Schlager Group, Inc., and Grey House Publishing. All rights reserved. No part of this work may be used or reproduced in any manner whatsoever or transmitted in any form or by any means, electronic or mechanical, including photocopy, recording, or any information storage and retrieval system, without written permission from the copyright owner. For information contact:

Schlager Group, Inc.	Grey House Publishing
325 N. Saint Paul, Suite 3425	4919 Route 22, PO Box 56
Dallas, TX 75201	Amenia, NY 12501
http://www.schlagergroup.com	http://www.greyhouse.com

Milestone Documents, 2017, published by Grey House Publishing, Inc., Amenia, NY.

∞ The paper used in these volumes conforms to the American National Standard for Permanence of Paper for Printed Library Materials, Z39.48 1992 (R2009).

Publisher's Cataloging-In-Publication Data
(Prepared by The Donohue Group, Inc.)

Names: Nix, Echol Lee, editor. | Nix, Keturah C., editor.

Title: Milestone documents in African American history / editors, Echol Nix, Jr., Keturah C. Nix.
Other Titles: Milestone documents.

Description: Second edition. | Dallas, TX : Schlager Group ; Amenia, NY : Grey House Publishing, [2017] | Includes bibliographical references and index. | Contents: Volume 1. 1619-1852 — Volume 2. 1853-1900 — Volume 3. 1901-1964 — Volume 4. 1965-2017.

Identifiers: ISBN 978-1-68217-579-8 (set) | ISBN 978-1-68217-870-6 (v.1) | ISBN 978-1-68217-871-3 (v.2) | ISBN 978-1-68217-872-0 (v.3) | ISBN 978-1-68217-873-7 (v.4)

Subjects: LCSH: African Americans—History—Sources. | Civil rights—United States—History—Sources. | Slavery—United States—History—Sources. | United States—Race relations—History—Sources.

Classification: LCC E184.6 .M55 2017 | DDC 305.896073—dc23

Contents

Publisher's Note IX
Editors' Introduction to the Second Edition XI
Editor's Introduction to the First Edition XV
Contributors XIX

Volume 1: 1619–1852

John Rolfe's Letter to Sir Edwin Sandys 1
Virginia's Act XII: Negro Women's Children to Serve according to the Condition of the Mother 13
Virginia's Act III: Baptism Does Not Exempt Slaves from Bondage 21
"A Minute against Slavery, Addressed to Germantown Monthly Meeting" 29
Daniel Horsmanden: *The New-York Conspiracy* 39
John Woolman's *Some Considerations on the Keeping of Negroes* 51
Lord Dunmore's Proclamation 65
Petition of Prince Hall and Other African Americans to the Massachusetts General Court 73
An Act for the Gradual Abolition of Slavery 83
Thomas Jefferson's *Notes on the State of Virginia* 95
Slavery Clauses in the U.S. Constitution 107
Alexander Falconbridge: *An Account of the Slave Trade on the Coast of Africa* 123
Benjamin Banneker's Letter to Thomas Jefferson 135
Fugitive Slave Act of 1793 143
Richard Allen: "An Address to Those Who Keep Slaves, and Approve the Practice" 153
Prince Hall: *A Charge Delivered to the African Lodge* 161
Ohio Black Code 171
Act to Prohibit the Importation of Slaves 181
Peter Williams, Jr.'s "Oration on the Abolition of the Slave Trade" 195
Samuel Cornish and John Russwurm's First *Freedom's Journal* Editorial 207
David Walker: *Appeal to the Coloured Citizens of the World* 217
State v. Mann 233
William Lloyd Garrison's First *Liberator* Editorial 243
The Confessions of Nat Turner 251
United States v. Amistad 267
Prigg v. Pennsylvania 281
Henry Highland Garnet: "An Address to the Slaves of the United States of America" 303

First Editorial of the *North Star* 315
William Wells Brown's "Slavery As It Is" 325
Roberts v. City of Boston 341
Fugitive Slave Act of 1850 355
Narrative of the Life of Henry Box Brown, Written by Himself 367
Sojourner Truth's "Ain't I a Woman?" 379
Frederick Douglass: "What, to the Slave, Is the Fourth of July" Speech 387
Martin Delany: *The Condition, Elevation, Emigration, and Destiny of the Colored People of the United States* 405

Volume 2: 1853–1900

Twelve Years a Slave: Narrative of Solomon Northup 423
Dred Scott v. Sandford 435
John S. Rock's "Whenever the Colored Man Is Elevated, It Will Be by His Own Exertions" 451
Virginia Slave Code 463
Harriet Jacobs's *Incidents in the Life of a Slave Girl* 477
Osborne P. Anderson: *A Voice from Harper's Ferry* 491
Emancipation Proclamation 511
Thomas Morris Chester's Civil War Dispatches 519
William T. Sherman's Special Field Order No. 15 533
Black Code of Mississippi 543
Thirteenth Amendment to the U.S. Constitution 553
Testimony Before the Joint Committee on Reconstruction on Atrocities in the South Against Blacks 563
Fourteenth Amendment to the U.S. Constitution 581
Henry McNeal Turner's Speech on His Expulsion from the Georgia Legislature 589
Fifteenth Amendment to the U.S. Constitution 601
Ku Klux Klan Act 611
United States v. Cruikshank 621
Richard Harvey Cain's "All That We Ask Is Equal Laws, Equal Legislation, and Equal Rights" 635
Civil Rights Cases 649
T. Thomas Fortune: "The Present Relations of Labor and Capital" 685
Anna Julia Cooper's "Womanhood: A Vital Element in the Regeneration and Progress of a Race" 695
John Edward Bruce's "Organized Resistance Is Our Best Remedy" 715
John L. Moore's "In the Lion's Mouth" 723
Josephine St. Pierre Ruffin's "Address to the First National Conference of Colored Women" 733
Booker T. Washington's Atlanta Exposition Address 747
Plessy v. Ferguson 757
Mary Church Terrell: "The Progress of Colored Women" 777
Ida B. Wells-Barnett's "Lynch Law in America" 791

Volume 3: 1901–1964

George H. White's Farewell Address to Congress 805
W. E. B. Du Bois: *The Souls of Black Folk* 817
W. E. B. Du Bois and Monroe Trotter: Niagara Movement Declaration of Principles 837
Theodore Roosevelt's Brownsville Legacy Special Message to the Senate 849
Act in Relation to the Organization of a Colored Regiment in the City of New York 865
Monroe Trotter's Protest to Woodrow Wilson 875
Guinn v. United States 883
William Pickens: "The Kind of Democracy the Negro Expects" 899
Thirty Years of Lynching in the United States 909
Cyril Briggs's *Summary of the Program and Aims of the African Blood Brotherhood* 927
Walter F. White: "The Eruption of Tulsa" 937
Marcus Garvey: "The Principles of the Universal Negro Improvement Association" 949
Alain Locke's "Enter the New Negro" 957
James Weldon Johnson's "Harlem: The Culture Capital" 971
Alice Moore Dunbar-Nelson: "The Negro Woman and the Ballot" 985
John P. Davis: "A Black Inventory of the New Deal" 995
Robert Clifton Weaver: "The New Deal and the Negro: A Look at the Facts" 1007
Charles Hamilton Houston's "Educational Inequalities Must Go!" 1019
Walter F. White's "U.S. Department of (White) Justice" 1031
Richard Wright: "Blueprint for Negro Writing" 1041
Mary McLeod Bethune's "What Does American Democracy Mean to Me?" 1055
A. Philip Randolph's "Call to Negro America to March on Washington" 1063
Executive Order 9983 1073
Ralph J. Bunche: "The Barriers of Race Can Be Surmounted" 1083
To Secure These Rights 1095
Sweatt v. Painter 1113
Haywood Patterson and Earl Conrad's *Scottsboro Boy* 1125
Brown v. Board of Education 1145
Marian Anderson's *My Lord, What a Morning* 1159
Roy Wilkins: "The Clock Will Not Be Turned Back" 1173
George Wallace's Inaugural Address as Governor 1183
Martin Luther King, Jr.: Letter from a Birmingham Jail 1195
John F. Kennedy: Report to the American People on Civil Rights 1209
Fannie Lou Hamer's Testimony at the Democratic National Convention 1217

Volume 4: 1965–2017

Malcolm X: "After the Bombing"	1229
Bond v. Floyd	1245
Stokely Carmichael: "Black Power"	1261
South Carolina v. Katzenbach	1279
Martin Luther King, Jr.: "Beyond Vietnam: A Time to Break Silence"	1297
Loving v. Virginia	1315
Kerner Commission Report Summary	1325
Eldridge Cleaver: "Education and Revolution"	1351
Jesse Owens: *Blackthink: My Life as Black Man and White Man*	1365
Clay v. United States	1379
Angela Davis's "Political Prisoners, Prisons, and Black Liberation"	1395
Jackie Robinson: *I Never Had It Made*	1413
FBI Report on Elijah Muhammad	1431
Final Report of the Tuskegee Syphilis Study Ad Hoc Advisory Panel	1447
Shirley Chisholm: "The Black Woman in Contemporary America"	1459
Jesse Jackson's Democratic National Convention Keynote Address	1471
Anita Hill's Opening Statement at the Senate Confirmation Hearing of Clarence Thomas	1489
Colin Powell's Commencement Address at Howard University	1501
Louis Farrakhan's Million Man March Pledge	1511
One America in the 21st Century	1519
Clarence Thomas's Concurrence/Dissent in *Grutter v. Bollinger*	1529
Barack Obama: "A More Perfect Union"	1545
U.S. Senate Resolution Apologizing for the Enslavement and Racial Segregation of African Americans	1559
Michelle Alexander: *The New Jim Crow*	1567
Shelby County v. Holder	1575
Movement for Black Lives—Vision for Black Lives	1591
Investigation of the Ferguson Police Department—Report Summary	1607
Cooper v. Harris	1617
Teachers' Activity Guide	1627
List of Documents by Category	1634
Acknowledgements	1637
Index	1639

Milestone Documents in African American History

Second Edition

Malcolm X before a 1964 press conference. By Marion S. Trikosko. U.S. News & World Report Magazine

Malcolm X: "After the Bombing"

1965

"So we saw that the first thing to do was to unite our people, not only unite us internally, but we have to be united with our brothers and sisters abroad."

Overview

On February 14, 1965, the African American activist Malcolm X addressed a crowd consisting primarily of college students at the Henry and Edsel Ford Auditorium in Detroit, Michigan, in what would be his final speech. The occasion of his speech was an event that had taken place the night before: the firebombing of his house in Queens, New York. He used this opportunity to address a wide range of issues of concern to him and to the African American community.

Born Malcolm Little in 1925, Malcolm X had witnessed racism firsthand as a child. He turned to a life of crime and was eventually convicted and incarcerated. While he was in prison, he converted to the religion known as the Nation of Islam. Throughout the 1950s and early 1960s, he was second only to the Nation of Islam's leader, Elijah Muhammad, as the public face of that organization. The Nation of Islam advocated African American separatism and pan-African unity and denounced nonviolence as a workable tactic for the civil rights movement. In 1964, though, Malcolm X broke with Muhammad but continued to speak out against racism and oppression worldwide. He converted to Sunni Islam, which he believed offered a path to racial harmony without requiring black separatism. The speech delivered at the Ford Auditorium in 1965 reflected this post–Nation of Islam viewpoint, especially with respect to Malcolm X's view of colonialism and the need for unity between Africans and African Americans as well as his insistence that sometimes victims of oppression must resist "by any means necessary." His break with the Nation of Islam had resulted in death threats and the firebombing of his house. Just a week after his speech, Malcolm X was assassinated by members of the Nation of Islam.

Context

Malcolm X's final speech was given in the context of troubled times, with civil rights issues, the Vietnam War, and assassinations making the headlines and in the forefront of Americans' minds. The last years of Malcolm X's life corresponded with the heyday of the civil rights movement in the United States. While its roots extend back to the formation of the Republic, the modern civil rights movement can be said to have begun in May 1954 with the U.S. Supreme Court's decision in *Brown v. Board of Education*. This decision brought about the desegregation of public education nationwide by striking down the separate-but-equal doctrine that had been enshrined in the Court's *Plessy v. Ferguson* decision issued in 1896. After the *Brown* decision, events in the civil rights movement unfolded rapidly, beginning with Rosa Parks's refusal to give up her seat on a bus to a white man, an event that sparked the Montgomery, Alabama, bus boycott of 1955 and 1956. It was this event that brought the Reverend Martin Luther King, Jr., to national prominence and made him the face of the civil rights movement.

In 1957 the nation's conscience was pricked when troops from the 101st Airborne Division had to protect black students who were trying to enroll at Central High School in Little Rock, Arkansas, after the state's governor, Orval Faubus, had resisted a federal order to integrate the school. Later, in 1963, Alabama Governor George Wallace tried to prevent the integration of the University of Alabama, going so far as to physically block the path of two black students who wanted to register for classes. The sit-in became a tool in the civil rights arsenal after college students in Greensboro, North Carolina, in 1960 peaceably sat at a segregated lunch counter at a Woolworth's store. The Freedom Rides of 1961, in which blacks and whites rode buses throughout the South and integrated restrooms, bus terminals, and drinking fountains, often led to violence when the Freedom Riders were attacked.

Voter registration drives, too, prompted violence in the South; in an infamous incident in June 1964, three civil rights workers were murdered by the Ku Klux Klan in Mississippi. In the spring of 1963, Americans were shocked by the heavy-handed tactics of Eugene "Bull" Connor, the commissioner of public safety in Birmingham, Alabama, after Martin Luther King. Jr., and the Southern Christian Leadership Conference, a civil rights organization, organized a movement to integrate public facilities and places of business in the city's downtown. After King had led a march on the Birmingham city hall, he was arrested and briefly imprisoned; it was then that he wrote his famous "Letter from Birmingham Jail." Later that year, in September, four girls were killed in a Klan bombing of Birmingham's Sixteenth Street Baptist Church. Also in 1963, Medgar Evers, a prominent civil rights leader, was murdered outside his home in Mississippi by a Klan member, dying just hours after President John F. Kennedy had delivered a major televised national address on civil rights. This address prefigured the Civil Rights Act of 1964, which was passed during the presidency of Lyndon B. Johnson after Kennedy's assassination in November 1963.

Also on the nation's mind was the deepening American involvement in Vietnam. In early August 1964, two U.S. naval destroyers in the Gulf of Tonkin reported having been attacked by Communist North Vietnamese forces. On August 5, Congress passed the Gulf of Tonkin Resolution by a unanimous vote in the House of Representatives and with just two nays in the Senate. This resolution (based on what seems to have been a false report) gave President Johnson the authority to send combat troops to South Vietnam. Less than one month after Malcolm X's death in February 1965, the first U.S. combat troops—thirty-five hundred Marines—joined twenty-three thousand U.S. military advisers already in Vietnam. By the end of 1965, nearly two hundred thousand American troops would be in Vietnam.

To some extent, turmoil within the Nation of Islam reflected the turmoil within U.S. society. The Nation of Islam had been formed in Detroit in 1930 by Wallace D. Fard, also known as Wallace D. Fard Muhammad. After Fard's disappearance in 1934, leadership of the Nation of Islam was assumed by one of his disciples, Elijah Poole, who later took the name Elijah Muhammad. One of the central tenets of the Nation of Islam was that African American youth were being put at a disadvantage by the nation's schools. Accordingly, the Nation of Islam established its own schools in various cities, often placing themselves at odds with state and local authorities because the schools were unaccredited. Although the Nation of Islam's members professed to be Muslims, they departed from traditional Islam in a number of important respects, notably in their belief that Fard was not only the Messiah of Christianity but also the Mahdi, or redeemer, of Islam. The Nation of Islam's teachings emphasized resistance to white supremacy. The organization argued that slavery and the African diaspora had been designed to deprive Africans of knowledge of their history, that blacks were the original humans, and that black separatism was the only hope for black Americans.

Throughout the late 1950s and early 1960s, Malcolm X was one of the Nation of Islam's most prominent spokesmen. He was also a highly controversial figure because of his belief that blacks were genetically superior to whites and for his provocative statements such as his remark that the white man was a "blue-eyed devil." That comment came at a time when he was fully under the influence of Elijah Muhammad and his belief that all whites were evil, a position Malcolm X would renounce after his conversion to Sunni Islam. Perhaps he referred to whites by reference to eye color rather than skin color because of his own lighter-than-average skin, a result of the fact that his mother was half white. Regardless of his skin tone, he became famous in large part through his inflammatory speeches and his public persona as an angry black man. He was critical of mainstream civil rights leaders such as Martin Luther King, rejecting King's doctrine of nonviolence and the Christian religion that was the source of King's inspiration.

In contrast to more radical groups such as the Black Panthers, Malcolm X did not preach revolution but rather a doctrine of self-help. He and his followers resisted confrontations with the police, arguing that the black community should police itself. He spoke with such power and eloquence that he was able to attract followers and supporters from outside the Nation of Islam, and it was this that had led to tensions between him and Elijah Muhammad and the Nation of Islam at large. When Malcolm X discovered that Muhammad had been having affairs with his secretaries, he became disillusioned with Muhammad and began to modify some of his positions. In particular, his travels in the Middle East convinced him that black separatism was not the path to racial equality and that Sunni Islam could provide a source of unity for peoples of all colors. Thus, just as King was growing more militant because of his opposition to the Vietnam War, Malcolm X was moving toward some of King's earlier positions. All of these strands of thought underpinned Malcolm X's final speech at Ford Auditorium in February 1965.

About the Author

Malcolm X was born Malcolm Little on May 19, 1925, in Omaha, Nebraska. Early in his life, he was exposed to issues of race and racism. His father, Earl Little, was a Baptist preacher and a supporter of Marcus Garvey, the flamboyant founder of the Universal Negro Improvement Association. The elder Little moved the family first to Milwaukee, Wisconsin, and then to Lansing, Michigan, to avoid death threats, but in 1929 the family's Lansing house was burned. Then, in 1931, Earl Little was killed by a streetcar in what authorities ruled was an accident. Malcolm, who was six at the time, believed that white supremacists had murdered Earl Little and made it appear to have been an accident.

Malcolm's mother, Louise Little, was half Scottish, and he had inherited light skin and reddish hair from her—traits that troubled him throughout his life. Louise's mental condition deteriorated after Earl's death, and several years later she was declared insane; Malcolm and his six siblings were then sent to foster homes. Initially a good student, Malcolm dropped out of school in the eighth grade after a white teacher told him that his goal of becoming a lawyer was unrealistic for an African American. After living in several foster homes, Malcolm moved to Boston to live with an older sister in 1941. He drifted through various jobs in various cities, but in 1943 he landed in New York City's Harlem, where he became involved in a variety of criminal activities. He returned to Boston, where he continued his involvement in illegal enterprises. He was arrested and in early 1946 sentenced to eight to ten years at the Massachusetts State Prison on charges of larceny and breaking and entering. Although he was initially hostile to all religion, while in prison he became acquainted with Elijah Muhammad's Nation of Islam. He corresponded with Elijah Muhammad and by 1948, while still in prison, had become a member of the Nation of Islam.

When Malcolm was released in 1952, he visited Elijah Muhammad in Chicago and changed his last name from Little to X. As he stated in his autobiography, "For me, my 'X' replaced the white slavemaster name of 'Little' which some blue-eyed devil named Little had imposed upon my paternal forebears." In 1953, a year that also marked the beginning of the Federal Bureau of Investigation's surveillance of Malcolm X, he became an assistant minister at Temple No. 1 in Detroit (Nation of Islam temples were numbered in the order in which they were founded). He rose rapidly in the Nation of Islam through his tireless work and convincing rhetorical style. In his speeches, he advocated separatism for African Americans and rejected the more mainstream civil rights movement's call for nonviolence. His mesmerizing speeches helped increase membership in the Nation of Islam dramatically.

Shortly after the death of President John F. Kennedy in 1963, Malcolm X delivered a speech he had prepared titled "God's Judgment of White America," which expressed his familiar theme based on the biblical statement "As you sow, so shall you reap." His point was that white America would be punished by God for its racism and hypocrisy. Thus, when asked after the speech about the Kennedy assassination, he made an easy transition from the biblical quote to the more colloquial expression of the same meaning, about the "chickens coming home to roost," a remark he later said he delivered "without a second thought." Angry whites, he believed, had not stopped at killing innocent blacks but had killed their own president as well. He believed that many people around the world agreed with the notion that America's "climate of hate" had caused the assassination, but controversy sparked when the media seized on his remarks—unfairly, he contended. Nonetheless, he was censured by the Nation of Islam and told he could not speak publicly for ninety days as a result of the remark.

That incident represented growing tension between Malcolm X and the Nation of Islam. In 1964 he broke with Elijah Muhammad after his discovery that Muhammad had engaged in a series of affairs with his secretaries. Malcolm X then founded Muslim Mosque, Inc., a religious organization, and, on the secular side, the Organization of Afro-American Unity. He also converted to the Sunni branch of Islam and made a pilgrimage to Mecca, Saudi Arabia, that spring. This pilgrimage led to an epiphany of sorts, for he came to believe that Islam could be a means to eliminate racial divisions. After the pilgrimage, he traveled throughout Africa, where he met with many prominent African leaders, and also visited Europe.

As Malcolm X continued his speaking engagements in the United States, he began receiving death threats from members of the Nation of Islam, which also sued to recover the New York City house in the borough of Queens in which he and his family were living. The Nation won the suit, but a hearing was scheduled for February 14, 1965, to argue for a postponement of his eviction date. However, the house was firebombed in the early-morning hours of that day. That evening, he delivered his "After the Bombing" address. This would prove to be his last speech, for on February 21, 1965, as he was speaking at a meeting of the Organization of Afro-American Unity, he was attacked by three men and shot to death. The three men, all members of the Nation of Islam, were convicted in the shooting.

Explanation and Analysis of the Document

Malcolm X's final speech, a portion of which is reproduced here, ranged over a broad variety of topics. But his first remarks place the speech in context. He begins, "Distinguished guests, brothers and sisters, ladies and gentlemen, friends and enemies." Although the FBI had opened a file on Malcolm X and monitored his activities, at this point he had more reason to be concerned about Black Muslims, who had made death threats against him and were the likely suspects in the firebombing of his house. Since he escaped the firebombing with literally the clothes on his back, he asks his audience to excuse his appearance.

♦ Colonialism and the African Revolution
Malcolm X then turns to the substantive points of his speech. First, he addresses the independence movements in Africa, arguing that the United States, along with Great Britain and France, was more worried about these movements than similar ones in Latin America and Asia because of the large number of African Americans in the United States. This statement reflects one of his persistent themes:

stressing the unity of all persons of African origin, whether they were still in Africa or were part of the African diaspora in the United States and elsewhere. At the time, Africa and other portions of the world were throwing off colonialism. India had achieved independence from Great Britain in 1948, Algeria had begun to free itself from French influence with the Proclamation of the Algerian National Front in 1954, Patrice Lumumba had issued the Proclamation of Congolese Independence in 1960, and the Palestinian National Charter was adopted in May 1964. These and other events signaled a profound shift in the relationships between former colonial powers and nations in the developing world.

Malcolm X then castigates the African Americans he had seen while in Africa, arguing that they were "just socializing, [that] they had turned their back on the cause over here." He compares those African Americans unfavorably to people of African heritage in countries such as Ghana or Tanzania. He then goes on to describe his organizational efforts throughout Africa, in particular the establishment of a branch of the Organization of Afro-American United. Later, he organized a similar group in Paris.

♦ The Power Structure

Malcolm X points to what he regards as the fear of the colonial powers, arguing that colonialism and imperialism are not just confined to the United States, which, he says, is "in cahoots" with Britain and France. He sees this alignment as an effort to "suppress the masses of dark-skinned people all over the world and exploit them of their natural resources." He argues that "the newly awakened people all over the world pose a problem for what's known as Western interests ... imperialism, colonialism, racism, and all these other negative isms or vulturistic isms." He then expresses his advocacy for a coalition of Africans, African Americans, Arabs, and Asians, which he says could be perceived as threatening by Western powers. In this context, he speaks of his meetings with Presidents Julius K. Nyerere of Tanzania, Jomo Kenyatta of Kenya, Nnamdi Azikiwe of Nigeria, Kwame Nkrumah of Ghana, and Ahmed Sékou Touré of Guinea, all of whom were major national figures in African independence movements who also supported the advancement of African Americans. Malcolm X also speaks of his meeting with Gamal Abdel Nasser of Egypt, who recently had challenged the West by nationalizing the Suez Canal, provoking an international crisis and threatening to cut off oil exports. He notes, too, the plight of "dark-skinned people in the Western Hemisphere," including people in Venezuela, Honduras, and other Central American countries, as well as the United States and Canada.

♦ Racism and Religion

Malcolm X then turns to issues of racism and religion, stating: "I don't believe in any form of racism. I don't believe in any form of discrimination or segregation. I believe in Islam. I am a Muslim." He stresses the unity of the three monotheistic religions—Judaism, Christianity, and Islam— and asserts that all believe in the same God and that Muhammad of Islam was simply the last in a line of prophets that stretched back to Abraham and had included Moses and Jesus. This theme of religious unity had started to appear in his speeches after his break with the Nation of Islam and his pilgrimage to Mecca ("Makkah" in the document). He goes on to observe that the religious beliefs espoused by the Nation of Islam were not "the real religion of Islam." He states that in reality Islam "doesn't teach anyone to judge another human being by the color of his skin" but rather judges people by their deeds. He indicates his rejection of the Black Muslim movement because it "didn't have the real religion of Islam." He comments favorably on his experience in Mecca, where "white" was simply an adjective. "White," he says, is a different thing in America, an indication of presumed racial superiority.

♦ Nonviolence

Malcolm X then articulates his position on violence in a "society ... controlled primarily by racists and segregationists," the government of which has continued to perpetrate violence in such places as Saigon and Hanoi (in Vietnam) and the Congo. He states that he has "never advocated any violence" but adds that African Americans should defend themselves from violence perpetrated by the Ku Klux Klan and other groups. In contrast, Malcolm X views the efforts of those African Americans who have attempted to overcome violence solely with the "capacity to love" as disgraceful and even encouraging of further acts of violence against blacks. He points out the hypocrisy of the position of nonviolence, noting that governments perpetrate violence in many places in the world but then urge blacks to remain nonviolent in the face of lynchings. He also takes the mass media to task for creating the impression that he advocates violence.

At this point in his speech, Malcolm X builds to perhaps his most notorious statement. He discusses the "language" that racists understand, the language of "brute force," which cannot be met merely with overtures of peace. He states that since the Klan knows "one language," victims of the Klan's oppression need to "start learning a new language" that the Klan understands. He characterizes the Klan as a "cowardly outfit" that has been able to remain safe only by making blacks afraid. He then quotes the words of Christ as he was being crucified—"Forgive them, Lord, they know not what they do"—while bitterly noting how some blacks might have uttered something similar as the lynch rope was being placed around their necks. Unlike Christ's persecutors, the lynch mobs, says Malcolm, have very much known what they've been doing and have had plenty of practice at it. He then observes that, because the federal government is unwilling to take action, it is the duty of African Americans to organize themselves and stop the actions of the Klan. He concludes this portion of the speech by repeating his statement that he does not believe in violence, which is why he wants to stop violence. Violence cannot be stopped with love but only by "vigorous action in self-defense." That

Malcolm X at a 1964 press conference. By Herman Hiller, World Telegram staff photographer [Public domain], via Wikimedia Commons.

action, he says, is to be initiated "by any means necessary." In the view of many observers, this statement was a call to arms—literally. This remark was taken out of context and was later used to accuse Malcolm X and his followers of having advocated violence.

Audience

Although Malcolm X enjoyed speaking before college audiences and was not averse to speaking to white and mixed audiences after his conversion from the Nation of Islam to Sunni Islam, he most often spoke in large cities in the Northeast, Midwest, and West before audiences of African Americans, many of whom may have been part of the civil rights movement but were discouraged with the speed of change the movement had thus far realized. With respect to the audience, then, his last speech, taking place in Detroit, Michigan, was typical—northern, urban, and primarily though not exclusively black. The audience would not have contained any members of the Nation of Islam, as members of that organization were forbidden to attend his speeches, but would have included members of his Organization of Afro-American Unity.

Impact

Malcolm X's speeches, whether delivered for the Nation of Islam or later, like this one, on his own, always had significant effects on his audience. He was a forceful speaker who always drew listeners to his cause. His "After the Bombing" speech is well remembered and often used in anthologies because it was his last, but the main points could have been taken from many of the speeches he delivered in the final period of his life. He forcefully advocated community action paired with African American self-help; the rejection of tobacco, alcohol, drugs, and promiscuity; and, in his later years, unity regardless of race or religion. He also refused to forswear violence, though condoning it only in self-defense. In this respect he served as a counterbalance to Martin Luther King, Jr.'s nonviolent positions.

Indeed, Malcolm X's impact was in part based on his distinction from other black leaders. He specifically rejected the nonviolence of King and his followers, who advocated a civil rights movement that looked to the gradual integration of African Americans into American society. He also took issue with black churches and the role of Christianity in thwarting the hopes of African Americans. But by 1965 Malcolm X had evolved beyond his role as a Black Muslim dissenter and rejected the black separatism of the Nation of Islam. The change he underwent was seen less in his public speeches and more in his autobiography, in which he examines his life as a spiritual and political pilgrimage that in the end led him to question his radicalism and his views about revolution and the white power structure. Published after his death, *The Autobiography of Malcolm X* inspired and continues to inspire African Americans and others and remains required reading in many high schools and colleges.

Despite some softening of his positions, Malcolm X became no less assertive in his determination to secure freedom for black America. As an outspoken black leader who had abandoned the politics of black nationalism, he became a symbol of the individual's role in interpreting and making history. Historically, though, Malcolm X exemplified one extreme of black protest. In the 1950s and early 1960s the public saw him as the opposite of King, but through his evolution as a thinker and public leader, his critique of American culture in part began to converge with King's. Beyond that, the self-criticism with which Malcolm X infused the discussion of African American lives makes him a figure who transcends the particular views he expressed in his speeches, including "After the Bombing." One can only speculate what he might have done and said given more time to evolve his views. His was an independent mind searching the world over for a version of truth.

Further Reading

♦ Books

Asante, Molefi Kete. *100 Greatest African Americans: A Biographical Encyclopedia*. Amherst, N.Y.: Prometheus Books, 2003.

Breitman, George. *The Last Year of Malcolm X: The Evolution of a Revolutionary*. New York: Pathfinder Press, 1970.

———, ed. *Malcolm X Speaks: Selected Speeches and Statements*. New York: Grove Weidenfeld, 1990.

Dyson, Michael Eric. *Making Malcolm: The Myth and Meaning of Malcolm X*. New York: Oxford University Press, 1995.

Jenkins, Robert L., and Mfanya Donald Tryman. *The Malcolm X Encyclopedia*. Westport, Conn.: Greenwood Press, 2002.

Joseph, Peniel E. *Waiting 'til the Midnight Hour: A Narrative History of Black Power in America*. New York: Henry Holt, 2006.

Malcolm X, and Alex Haley. *The Autobiography of Malcolm X*. New York: Grove Press, 1965.

Marable, Manning, Nishani Frazier, and John Campbell McMillan, eds. *Freedom on My Mind: The Columbia Documentary History of the African American Experience*. New York: Columbia University Press, 2003.

♦ **Web Sites**

"The Detroit Speeches of Malcolm X." Malcolm Web site. http://www.brothermalcolm.net/.

Malcolm-X.org Web site. http://www.malcolm-x.org/.

The Malcolm X Project at Columbia University Web site. http://www.columbia.edu/cu/ccbh/mxp/.

The Official Web Site of Malcolm X. http://www.cmgww.com/historic/malcolm/home.php.

——*Keith E. Sealing*

Time Line		
1925	May 19	■ Malcolm X is born Malcolm Little in Omaha, Nebraska.
1931	September 28	■ Earl Little, Malcolm's father, dies in what authorities call an accident but many consider to be murder by white supremacists.
1938	December	■ Louise Little, Malcolm's mother, has a nervous breakdown and is committed to a mental institution; Malcolm and six siblings begin living in foster homes.
1943		■ Malcolm moves to New York City and begins a life of crime.
1946	February 27	■ Malcolm begins serving an eight-year prison sentence in Massachusetts.
1948		■ Malcolm converts to the Nation of Islam.
1952	August 7	■ Malcolm is released from prison and becomes active in the Nation of Islam; soon, he will change his name from Malcolm Little to Malcolm X.
1963		■ *Malcolm X begins writing his autobiography with Alex Haley; unfinished at the time of his assassination, it will be completed by Haley in late 1965.*
1964	March 8	■ Malcolm X publicly breaks from the Nation of Islam.
	April 13	■ Malcolm X, now a Sunni Muslim, embarks on a hajj, or pilgrimage, to Mecca, Saudi Arabia.
	June 28	■ Malcolm X founds the Organization of Afro-American Unity, a civil rights group.
1965	February 14	■ Malcolm X's house is firebombed in the early morning hours, allegedly by members of the Nation of Islam; later that day he delivers his final speech.
	February 21	■ Malcolm X is assassinated by three Black Muslims.

Essential Quotes

"And I might point out right here that colonialism or imperialism, as the slave system of the West is called, is not something that's just confined to England or France or the United States.... It's an international power structure. And this international power structure is used to suppress the masses of dark-skinned people all over the world and exploit them of their natural resources."

"The newly awakened people all over the world pose a problem for what's known as Western interests ... imperialism, colonialism, racism, and all these other negative isms or vulturistic isms. Just as the external forces pose a grave threat, they can now see that the internal forces pose an even greater threat. But the internal forces pose an even greater threat only when they have properly analyzed the situation and know what the stakes really are."

"So we saw that the first thing to do was to unite our people, not only unite us internally, but we have to be united with our brothers and sisters abroad."

"I don't believe in any form of racism. I don't believe in any form of discrimination or segregation. I believe in Islam. I am a Muslim."

"This society is controlled primarily by racists and segregationists ... who are in Washington, D.C., in positions of power. And from Washington, D.C., they exercise the same forms of brutal oppression against dark-skinned people in South and North Vietnam, or in the Congo, or in Cuba, or in any other place on this earth where they're trying to exploit and oppress."

"So, we only mean vigorous action in self-defense, and that vigorous action we feel we're justified in initiating by any means necessary."

Questions for Further Study

1. At the time, Malcolm X was regarded as a bit of a frightening figure by mainstream America—and perhaps he still is. Why do you think this was so? Based on his speech, how "frightening" do you think Malcolm X really was?

2. Why did Malcolm X break with the Nation of Islam and black nationalism? To what extent do you think his defection weakened that organization?

3. On what basis did Malcolm X castigate American blacks he encountered in Africa?

4. Malcolm X was often regarded as a foil to Martin Luther King, Jr., and the two men were seen as standing on opposite poles of the civil rights movement. On what basis did people think this? Do you believe that this is an accurate comparison? Explain.

5. Imagine that Malcolm X had not been assassinated. What impact do you think he might have had on the civil rights and antiwar movements of the late 1960s and into the 1970s?

"After the Bombing"

The full text of Malcolm X's speech.

Distinguished guests, brothers and sisters, ladies and gentlemen, friends and enemies:

I want to point out first that I am very happy to be here this evening and I'm thankful [to the Afro-American Broadcasting Company] for the invitation to come here to Detroit this evening. I was in a house last night that was bombed, my own. It didn't destroy all my clothes, not all, but you know what happens when fire dashes through—they get smoky. The only thing I could get my hands on before leaving was what I have on now.

It isn't something that made me lose confidence in what I am doing, because my wife understands and I have children from this size on down, and even in their young age they understand. I think they would rather have a father or brother or whatever the situation may be who will take a stand in the face of any kind of reaction from narrow-minded people rather than to compromise and later on have to grow up in shame and in disgrace.

So I just ask you to excuse my appearance. I don't normally come out in front of people without a shirt and a tie. I guess that's somewhat a holdover from the "Black Muslim" movement, which I was in. That's one of the good aspects of that movement. It teaches you to be very careful and conscious of how you look, which is a positive contribution on their part. But that positive contribution on their part is greatly offset by too many other liabilities....

Tonight one of the things that has to be stressed is that which has not only the United States very much worried but which also has France, Great Britain, and most of the powers, who formerly were known as colonial powers, worried also, and that primarily is the African revolution. They are more concerned with the revolution that's taking place on the African continent than they are with the revolution in Asia and in Latin America. And this is because there are so many people of African ancestry within the domestic confines or jurisdiction of these various governments.

There are four different types of people in the Western Hemisphere, all of whom have Africa as a common heritage, common origin, and that's the—those of our people in Latin America, who are Black, but who are in the Spanish-speaking areas. Many of them ofttimes migrate back to Spain, the only difference being Spain has such bad economic conditions until many of the people from Latin America don't think it's worthwhile to migrate back there. And then the British and the French had a great deal of control in the Caribbean, in the West Indies. And so now you have many people from the West Indies migrating to both London—rather both England and France. The people from the British West Indies go to London, and those from the French West Indies go to Paris. And it has put France and England since World War II in the precarious position of having a sort of a commonwealth structure that makes it easy for all of the people in the commonwealth territories to come into their country with no restrictions. So there's an increasing number of dark-skinned people in England and also in France.

When I was in Africa in May, I noticed a tendency on the part of the Afro-Americans to, what I call lollygag. Everybody else who was over there had something on the ball, something they were doing, something constructive. For instance, in Ghana, just to take Ghana as an example. There would be many refugees in Ghana from South Africa. But those who were in Ghana were organized and were serving as pressure groups, some were training for military— some were being trained in how to be soldiers, but others were involved as a pressure group or lobby group to let the people of Ghana never forget what's happening to the brother in South Africa. Also you'd have brothers there from Angola and Mozambique. But all of the Africans who were exiles from their particular country and would be in a place like Ghana or Tanganyika, now Tanzania, they would be training. Their every move would still be designed to offset what was happening to their people back home where they had left.

The only difference on the continent was the American Negro. Those who were over there weren't even thinking about these over here. This was the basic difference. The Africans, when they escaped from their respective countries that were still colonized, they didn't try and run away from the problem. But as soon as they got where they were going, they then began to organize into pressure groups to get governmental support at the international level against the injustices they were experiencing back home.

And as I said, the American Negro, or the Afro-American, who was in these various countries, some working for this government, some working for that government, some just in business—they were just socializing, they had turned their back on the cause over here, they were partying, you know.

And when I went through one country in particular, I heard a lot of their complaints and I didn't make any move on them.

But when I got to another country, I found the Afro-Americans there were making the same complaints. So we sat down and talked and we organized a branch in this particular country, a branch of the OAAU, Organization of Afro-American Unity. That one was the only one in existence at that time. Then during the summer, when I went back to Africa, I was able in each country that I visited, to get the Afro-American community together and organize them and make them aware of their responsibility to those of us who are still here in the lion's den.

They began to do this quite well, and when I got to Paris and London—there are many Afro-Americans in Paris, and many in London. And in December—no, November—we organized a group in Paris and just within a very short time they had grown into a well-organized unit. And they, in conjunction with the African community, invited me to Paris, Tuesday, to address a large gathering of Parisians and Afro-Americans and people from the Caribbean and also from Africa who were interested in our struggle in this country and the rate of progress that we have been making.

But since the French government and the British government and this government here, the United States, know that I have been almost fanatically stressing the importance of the Afro-American uniting with the African and working as a coalition, especially in areas which are of mutual benefit to all of us. And the governments in these different places were frightened because they know that the Black revolution that's taking place on the outside of their house.

And I might point out right here that colonialism or imperialism, as the slave system of the West is called, is not something that's just confined to England or France or the United States. But the interests in this country are in cahoots with the interests in France and the interests in Britain. It's one huge complex or combine, and it creates what's known as not the American power structure or the French power structure, but it's an international power structure. And this international power structure is used to suppress the masses of dark-skinned people all over the world and exploit them of their natural resources.

So that the era in which you and I have been living during the past ten years most specifically has witnessed the upsurge on the part of the Black man in Africa against the power structure.

He wants his freedom.

Now, mind you, the power structure is international, and as such, its own domestic base is in London, in Paris, in Washington, D.C., and so forth. And the outside or external phase of the revolution, which is manifest in the attitude and action of the Africans today is troublesome enough. The revolution on the outside of the house, or the outside of the structure, is troublesome enough. But now the powers that be are beginning to see that this struggle on the outside by the Black man is affecting, infecting the Black man who is on the inside of that structure. I hope you understand what I'm trying to say.

The newly awakened people all over the world pose a problem for what's known as Western interests, which is imperialism, colonialism, racism, and all these other negative isms or vulturistic isms. Just as the external forces pose a grave threat, they can now see that the internal forces pose an even greater threat. But the internal forces pose an even greater threat only when they have properly analyzed the situation and know what the stakes really are.

Just by advocating a coalition of Africans, Afro-Americans, Arabs, and Asians who live within the structure, it automatically has upset France, which is supposed to be one of the most liberal—heh!—countries on earth, and it made them expose their hand. England the same way. And I don't have to tell you about this country that we are living in now.

So when you count the number of dark-skinned people in the Western Hemisphere you can see that there are probably over 100 million. When you consider Brazil has two-thirds what we call colored, or nonwhite, and Venezuela, Honduras and other Central American countries, Cuba and Jamaica, and the United States and even Canada—when you total all these people up, you have probably over 100 million. And this 100 million on the inside of the power structure today is what is causing a great deal of concern for the power structure itself.

Not a great deal of concern for all white people, but a great deal of concern for most white people.

Document Text

See, if I said "all white people" then they would call me a racist for giving a blanket condemnation of things.

And this is true; this is how they do it. They take one little word out of what you say, ignore all the rest, and then begin to magnify it all over the world to make you look like what you actually aren't. And I'm very used to that.

So we saw that the first thing to do was to unite our people, not only unite us internally, but we have to be united with our brothers and sisters abroad. It was for that purpose that I spent five months in the Middle East and Africa during the summer. The trip was very enlightening, inspiring, and fruitful. I didn't go into any African country, or any country in the Middle East for that matter, and run into any closed door, closed mind, or closed heart. I found a warm reception and an amazingly deep interest and sympathy for the Black man in this country in regards to our struggle for human rights.

While I was traveling, I had a chance to speak in Cairo, or rather Alexandria, with President [Gamal Abdel-]Nasser for about an hour and a half. He's a very brilliant man. And I can see why they're so afraid of him, and they are afraid of him—they know he can cut off their oil. And actually the only thing power respects is power. Whenever you find a man who's in a position to show power against power then that man is respected. But you can take a man who has power and love him all the rest of your life, nonviolently and forgivingly and all the rest of those ofttime things, and you won't get anything out of it.

So I also had a chance to speak to President [Julius K.] Nyerere in Tanganyika, which is now Tanzania, and also [President Jomo] Kenyata—I know that all of you know him. He was the head of the Mau Mau, which really brought freedom to many of the African countries. This is true. The Mau Mau played a major role in bringing about freedom for Kenya, and not only for Kenya but other African countries. Because what the Mau Mau did frightened the white man so much in other countries until he said, "Well I better get this thing straight before some of them pop up here." This is good to study because you see what makes him react: Nothing loving makes him react, nothing forgiving makes him react. The only time he reacts is when he knows you can hurt him, and when you let him know you can hurt him he has to think two or three times before he tries to hurt you. But if you're not going to do nothing but return that hurt with love—why good night! He knows you're out of your mind.

And also I had an opportunity to speak with President [Nnamdi] Azikiwe in Nigeria, President [Kwame] Nkrumah in Ghana, and President Sekou Toure in Guinea. And in all of these people I found nothing but warmth, friendship, sympathy, and a desire to help the Black man in this country in fighting our problem. And we have a very complex problem.

Before I get involved in anything nowadays, I have to straighten out my own position, which is clear. I am not a racist in any form whatsoever. I don't believe in any form of racism. I don't believe in any form of discrimination or segregation. I believe in Islam. I am a Muslim. And there's nothing wrong with being a Muslim, nothing wrong with the religion of Islam. It just teaches us to believe in Allah as the God. Those of you who are Christians probably believe in the same God, because I think you believe in the God who created the universe. That's the One we believe in, the one who created the universe, the only difference being you call Him God and I—we call Him Allah. The Jews call him Jehovah. If you could understand Hebrew, you'd probably call him Jehovah too. If you could understand Arabic, you'd probably call him Allah.

But since the white man, your "friend," took your language away from you during slavery, the only language you know is his language. You know, your friend's language. So you call for the same God he calls for. When he's putting a rope around your neck, you call for God and he calls for God. And you wonder why the one you call on never answers you.

So that once you realize that I believe in the Supreme Being who created the universe, and believe in him as being one—I also have been taught in Islam that one God only has one religion, and that religion is called Islam, and all of the prophets who came forth taught that religion— Abraham, Moses, Jesus, Mohammed, all of them. And by believing in one God and one religion and all of the prophets, it creates unity. There's no room for argument, no need for us to be arguing with each other.

And also in that religion, of the real religion of Islam—when I was in the Black Muslim movement, I wasn't—they didn't have the real religion of Islam in that movement. It was something else. And the real religion of Islam doesn't teach anyone to judge another human being by the color of his skin. The yardstick that is used by the Muslim to measure another man is not the man's color but the man's deeds, the man's conscious behavior, the man's intentions. And when you use that as a standard of measurement or judgment, you never go wrong.

But when you just judge a man because of the color of his skin, then you're committing a crime, because that's the worst kind of judgment. If you judged him just because he was a Jew, that's not as bad as judging him because he's Black. Because a Jew can hide his religion. He can say he's something else—and which a lot of them do that, they say they're something else. But the Black man can't hide. When they start indicting us because of our color that means we're indicted before we're born, which is the worst kind of crime that can be committed. The Muslim religion has eliminated all tendencies to judge a man according to the color of his skin, but rather the judgment is based upon his deeds.

And when, prior to going into the Muslim world, I didn't have any— Elijah Muhammad had taught us that the white man could not enter into Makkah in Arabia, and all of us who followed him, we believed it. And he said the reason he couldn't enter was because he's white and inherently evil, it's impossible to change him. And the only thing that would change him is Islam, and he can't accept Islam because by nature he's evil. And therefore by not being able to accept Islam and become a Muslim, he could never enter Makkah. This is how he taught us, you know.

So when I got over there and went to Makkah and saw these people who were blond and blue-eyed and pale-skinned and all those things, I said, "Well!" But I watched them closely. And I noticed that though they were white, and they would call themselves white, there was a difference between them and the white one over here. And that basic difference was this: in Asia or the Arab world or in Africa, where the Muslims are, if you find one who says he's white, all he's doing is using an adjective to describe something that's incidental about him, one of his incidental characteristics; so there's nothing else to it, he's just white.

But when you get the white man over here in America and he says he's white, he means something else. You can listen to the sound of his voice—when he says he's white, he means he's a boss. That's right. That's what "white" means in this language. You know the expression, "free, white, and twenty-one." He made that up. He's letting you know all of them mean the same. "White" means free, boss. He's up there. So that when he says he's white he has a little different sound in his voice. I know you know what I'm talking about.

This was what I saw was missing in the Muslim world. If they said they were white, it was incidental. White, black, brown, red, yellow, doesn't make any difference what color you are. So this was the religion that I had accepted and had gone there to get a better knowledge of it.

But despite the fact that I saw that Islam was a religion of brotherhood, I also had to face reality. And when I got back into this American society, I'm not in a society that practices brotherhood. I'm in a society that might preach it on Sunday, but they don't practice it on no day—on any day. And so, since I could see that America itself is a society where there is no brotherhood and that this society is controlled primarily by racists and segregationists—and it is—who are in Washington, D.C., in positions of power. And from Washington, D.C., they exercise the same forms of brutal oppression against dark-skinned people in South and North Vietnam, or in the Congo, or in Cuba, or in any other place on this earth where they're trying to exploit and oppress. This is a society whose government doesn't hesitate to inflict the most brutal form of punishment and oppression upon dark-skinned people all over the world.

To wit, right now what's going on in and around Saigon and Hanoi and in the Congo and elsewhere. They are violent when their interests are at stake. But all of that violence that they display at the international level, when you and I want just a little bit of freedom, we're supposed to be nonviolent. They're violent. They're violent in Korea, they're violent in Germany, they're violent in the South Pacific, they're violent in Cuba, they're violent wherever they go. But when it comes time for you and me to protect ourselves against lynchings, they tell us to be nonviolent.

That's a shame. Because we get tricked into being nonviolent, and when somebody stands up and talks like I just did, they say, "Why, he's advocating violence!" Isn't that what they say? Every time you pick up your newspaper, you see where one of these things has written into it that I'm advocating violence. I have never advocated any violence. I've only said that Black people who are the victims of organized violence perpetrated upon us by the Klan, the Citizens' Council, and many other forms, we should defend ourselves. And when I say that we should defend ourselves against the violence of others, they use their press skillfully to make the world think that I'm calling on violence, period. I wouldn't call on anybody to be violent without a cause. But I think the Black man in this country, above and beyond people all over the world, will be more justified when he stands up and starts to protect himself, no matter how many necks he has to break and heads he has to crack.

I saw in the paper where they—on the television where they took this Black woman down in Selma, Alabama, and knocked her right down on the ground, dragging her down the street. You saw it, you're trying to pretend like you didn't see it 'cause you knew you should've done something about it and didn't. It showed the sheriff and his henchmen throwing this Black woman on the ground—on the ground.

And Negro men standing around doing nothing about it saying, "Well, let's overcome them with our capacity to love." What kind of phrase is that? "Overcome them with our capacity to love." And then it disgraces the rest of us, because all over the world the picture is splashed showing a Black woman with some white brutes, with their knees on her holding her down, and full-grown Black men standing around watching it. Why, you are lucky they let you stay on earth, much less stay in the country.

When I saw it I dispatched a wire to Rockwell; Rockwell was one of the agitators down there, Rockwell, this [George] Lincoln Rockwell [leader of the American Nazi Party].

And the wire said in essence that this is to warn him that I am no longer held in check from fighting white supremacists by Elijah Muhammad's separatist "Black Muslim" movement. And that if Rockwell's presence in Alabama causes harm to come to Dr. King or any other Black person in Alabama who's doing nothing other than trying to enjoy their rights, then Rockwell and his Ku Klux Klan friends would be met with maximum retaliation from those of us who are not handcuffed by this nonviolent philosophy. And I haven't heard from Rockwell since.

Brothers and sisters, if you and I would just realize that once we learn to talk the language that they understand, they will then get the point. You can't ever reach a man if you don't speak his language. If a man speaks the language of brute force, you can't come to him with peace. Why, good night! He'll break you in two, as he has been doing all along. If a man speaks French, you can't speak to him in German. If he speaks Swahili, you can't communicate with him in Chinese. You have to find out what does this man speak. And once you know his language, learn how to speak his language, and he'll get the point. There'll be some dialogue, some communication, and some understanding will be developed.

You've been in this country long enough to know the language the Klan speaks. They only know one language. And what you and I have to start doing in 1965—I mean that's what you have to do, because most of us already been doing it—is start learning a new language. Learn the language that they understand. And then when they come up on our doorstep to talk, we can talk. And they will get the point. There'll be a dialogue, there'll be some communication, and I'm quite certain there will then be some understanding. Why? Because the Klan is a cowardly outfit. They have perfected the art of making Negroes be afraid. As long as the Negro's afraid, the Klan is safe. But the Klan itself is cowardly. One of them will never come after one of you. They all come together. Sure, and they're scared of you.

And you sit there when they're putting the rope around your neck saying, " Forgive them, Lord, they know not what they do." As long as they've been doing it, they're experts at it, they know what they're doing!

No, since the federal government has shown that it isn't going to do anything about it but talk, it is a duty, it's your and my duty as men, as human beings, it is our duty to our people, to organize ourselves and let the government know that if they don't stop that Klan, we'll stop it ourselves. And then you'll see the government start doing something about it. But don't ever think that they're going to do it just on some kind of morality basis, no. So I don't believe in violence—that's why I want to stop it. And you can't stop it with love, not love of those things down there, no. So, we only mean vigorous action in self-defense, and that vigorous action we feel we're justified in initiating by any means necessary.

Glossary

Abraham, Moses: two of the major Jewish patriarchs of the Christian Old Testament

"Black Muslim" movement: the movement centered on the Nation of Islam

British West Indies: the island nations in the Caribbean that were part of the British Empire, including such nations as the Bahamas and Jamaica

Citizens' Council: the White Citizens' Council, also called the Citizens' Council of America, a white supremacist organization

Congo: probably a reference to the Democratic Republic of the Congo, where Patrice Lumumba led a nationalist movement beginning in 1960; possibly a reference to the Republic of the Congo, which gained independence from the French in 1960

Elijah Muhammad: the Nation of Islam leader who attracted Malcolm X to the organization

"Forgive them, Lord …": words spoken by Jesus at the time of his Crucifixion

French West Indies: the island nations in the Caribbean that were (and in some instances still are) part of the French empire, including, for example, Guadeloupe and Martinique

Klan: the Ku Klux Klan, a white supremacist organization

Makkah: usually spelled Mecca, a city in Saudi Arabia and Islam's holiest site

Mau Mau: the name given to an insurgency in Kenya against British colonial rule from 1952 to 1960, often called the Mau Mau Uprising

Mohammad: usually spelled Muhammad, the seventh-century founder of Islam

Organization of Afro-American Unity: a civil rights group Malcolm X founded in 1964

Saigon and Hanoi: the capitals of South Vietnam and North Vietnam, respectively, and thus a reference to the Vietnam War

A portrait of Julian Bond by Eduardo Montes-Bradley. By Eduardo Montes-Bradley (Own work) [CC BY-SA 4.0 (http://creativecommons.org/licenses/by-sa/4.0)], via Wikimedia Commons

Bond v. Floyd

"The manifest function of the First Amendment ... requires that legislators be given the widest latitude to express their views."

Overview

Argued on November 10, 1966, and decided on December 5, 1966, the case of *Bond v. Floyd* is probably best known for its result: stopping the Georgia House of Representatives from refusing to seat Julian Bond, an elected representative, based on his opposition to the Vietnam War. However, its import far outstrips its result. The opinion holds that legislators enjoy all of the First Amendment protections that citizens enjoy, including the right to dissent, and that their exercise of those rights allows constituents to know whether they are properly representing the constituents' interests. The U.S Supreme Court's conception of the role of the First Amendment in fostering a healthy relationship between legislator and constituent led to its judgment that legislatures are not allowed to refuse to seat a dissenter merely because the other members of the legislature do not like what the dissenting legislator says. This opinion guaranteed that candidates for office and elected legislators, including African Americans, who were just beginning to be elected in reasonable numbers at the time, could openly dissent on issues of foreign and domestic policy without worrying about whether they could be blocked from taking their seats because of their political views.

Context

The broad context of *Bond v. Floyd* involves the way in which dissent on American foreign policy by legislators is tolerated and how legislators may treat fellow legislators who dissent from the prevailing views. Legislators may be treated poorly by fellow legislators and by their constituents as a result of their dissenting views. However, it was unclear at the time whether a legislature could use its power to judge the qualifications of its members in order to refuse to seat a duly elected member merely for his or her opposition to war and dissent on foreign policy.

The narrow context of *Bond v. Floyd* involved the convergence of three powerful forces in 1960s America: the civil rights movement, anti–Vietnam War sentiment, and the push toward equally populous districts that would lead to the election of African American candidates in significant numbers for the first time since Reconstruction. Julian Bond, a leader in the Student Nonviolent Coordinating Committee (SNCC)—a major civil rights organization in the 1960s—endorsed SNCC's anti–Vietnam War statements and was consequently denied a seat in the Georgia legislature after being elected to a district that was created as a result.

War and civil rights had been linked for many generations prior to *Bond v. Floyd*. Whether the war at issue was the Civil War, World War I, or World War II, some discussion of the need for adequate civil rights for African American soldiers and African Americans in general had taken place. In these earlier wars, the demand for equal civil rights accompanied support for the war. The Vietnam War was different. Many who fought for civil rights at home questioned whether it made sense for African Americans to fight in the war when they did not have equal rights at home, particularly given that the Vietnam War was ostensibly being fought to keep or make Vietnam free. The linkage between support of civil rights and dissent on American war policy allowed some to renew their contempt for civil rights and for those who supported equality. Others thought that civil rights supporters should stick to advocating for civil rights and should not comment on war or foreign policy.

The struggle for Vietnam had been ongoing for years before the United States committed substantial emotional and physical resources in 1964. The escalation of America's role occurred in the wake of the Gulf of Tonkin resolution, which authorized President Lyndon Johnson to use force in Vietnam. Over the next year, President Johnson ordered significant aerial bombing of Vietnam, sent tens of thousands of troops to Vietnam, and authorized many tens of thousands more.

This escalation came at a momentous time for the civil rights movement. The Civil Rights Act of 1964, the most sweeping civil rights bill since Reconstruction, had been passed in no small measure because of President Johnson's support. Through a series of cases, the Supreme Court had declared that one-man, one-vote was required under the Constitution, leading to the redrawing of district lines to guarantee that districts would consist of equal populations. This redistricting promised that—if African Americans were allowed to vote—areas with high concentrations of African American citizens would be able to elect representatives to their liking for the first time in many years, if ever. The eventual passage of the Voting Rights Act of 1965 helped ensure that African Americans would be allowed to vote in areas of the country where their electoral voices had been stifled for years. American life was becoming relatively more equal and democratic. However, civil rights organizations, their leaders, and many others recognized that the United States had far to go before its citizens would become truly equal. This is why the U.S. claim that the war was being fought to guarantee freedom to the people of Vietnam struck a discordant note to some in civil rights organizations and triggered dissent. Some dissenters were philosophically opposed to war. Others were opposed to this particular war. In sum, the dissent was significant.

In August 1965 Martin Luther King, Jr., spoke out against U.S. involvement in the Vietnam War. Although some might have thought that the 1964 Nobel Peace Prize winner would understandably speak out against war, others argued that he should stick to civil rights rather than opine on American foreign policy. Nonetheless, King specifically linked civil rights and the war in Vietnam. His outspokenness was not appreciated by President Johnson or by some of his own supporters. Undaunted, King continued to oppose the war. Other civil rights leaders and organizations would speak out against the war when they deemed the time was right. In early 1966 SNCC did just that. It was their statement opposing the war that led directly to *Bond v. Floyd*.

When private citizens dissented with respect to the Vietnam War in particular and American foreign policy in general, legislators could do little to stop them. The First Amendment clearly protected the right to dissent. Indeed, legislators arguably had little reason to pay attention to the dissenters as long as the dissent did not involve violence. However, legislators could take additional interest if those dissenters were going to become colleagues. Julian Bond's criticism of American foreign policy and the Vietnam War as he was about to take office put him in the category of potential legislator-dissenter.

Julian Bond was elected to the Georgia legislature in 1965 in a special election that was required when Georgia had to redraw its electoral districts as a result of the Supreme Court's one-man, one-vote jurisprudence. Before he was sworn in, he noted his support for an official statement made by SNCC in January 1966 regarding opposition to the Vietnam War. Bond was the communications director of SNCC and a supporter from the organization's early days, but he had not drafted the statement. The statement was issued in response to the murder of Samuel Younge, Jr. (misspelled "Young" in the document), a member of SNCC and a Tuskegee Institute student who was killed in January 1966 for using the segregated bathroom at a Tuskegee gas station. The statement indicated SNCC's disapproval of American foreign policy as expressed in the country's involvement in the Vietnam War. The statement linked freedom at home with freedom abroad, suggesting that the U.S. government's claims to fight for freedom overseas appeared to be at odds with its refusal to fight for freedom at home. The statement also linked Younge's struggle for freedom and his ultimate death with the Vietnamese peasants' fight for freedom and potential death. SNCC's statement ultimately suggested that Americans ought to be allowed to avoid the military draft by working with organizations in the United States that sought to build democracy here.

A number of members of the Georgia legislature wanted to refuse to seat Bond because of his support for the statement and his opposition to the Vietnam War. It could be argued that the legislators merely claimed that Bond could not honestly take the oath of office and therefore could not be seated. However, whether Bond could profess support for the U.S. Constitution and the Georgia constitution, as required by the oath, was inextricably linked to the substance of the debate about the Vietnam War. The Court decided that whether a legislator could sincerely take an oath was to be decided by the legislator alone, not by the legislator's peers.

Time Line

1960	February 1	■ Sit-ins begin in Greensboro, North Carolina, to protest segregation.
	April 17	■ The Student Nonviolent Coordinating Committee is founded by hundreds of students, including Julian Bond.
1961	May	■ Integrated Freedom Rides throughout the South seek to demonstrate the possibility of integrated interstate bus travel.
1962	October 1	■ James Meredith is the first African American to attend the University of Mississippi.
1963	August 28	■ Martin Luther King, Jr., delivers his "I Have a Dream" speech during the March on Washington.
	November 22	■ President John F. Kennedy is assassinated in Dallas, Texas; Lyndon B. Johnson becomes president.
1964	June 15	■ *Reynolds v. Sims* is decided, leading to the requirement that state legislative districts have equal populations.
	July 2	■ President Johnson signs the Civil Rights Act of 1964.
	August 7	■ The Gulf of Tonkin resolution is passed, giving President Johnson the explicit authority to use force in Vietnam.
1965		■ The Selma voting rights campaign, led by SNCC since 1963, intensifies when the Southern Christian Leadership Conference becomes involved in the campaign.
	June 15	■ Julian Bond is elected to the Georgia legislature.
	August 6	■ The Voting Rights Act of 1965 is signed.
	August 12	■ King begins to speak out against the Vietnam War, specifically linking the war and civil rights in his speech at the Southern Christian Leadership Conference annual meeting.

Time Line

1966	January 6	■ SNCC issues a statement in opposition to the Vietnam War, tying opposition to war with support for democracy and human rights in the United States. Julian Bond endorses this statement.
	December 5	■ The U.S. Supreme Court decides *Bond v. Floyd*, ruling unanimously that legislators and private citizens enjoy the same free speech right to dissent and that legislators may need to exercise that right to represent their constituents properly. 1967
		Congress refuses to seat Representative Adam Clayton Powell in the U.S. House, citing financial improprieties.
1969	June 16	■ The U.S. Supreme Court decides *Powell v. McCormack*, noting that in excluding members Congress is limited to basing such action on the qualifications listed in the U.S. Constitution.
1975	April	■ The Vietnam War ends.

About the Author

Born on March 19, 1891, in Los Angeles, California, Earl Warren was chief justice of the United States from 1953 to 1969. Warren grew up in Bakersfield, California, the son of parents who were born in Scandinavia and raised in the United States. During his youth, Warren worked for the Southern Pacific Railroad as a call boy rounding up crews for the railroad. That experience exposed him to working men and labor issues in a way that some have suggested shaped his thoughts on the law, if not his entire outlook on life. After graduating from high school in 1908, he attended the University of California at Berkeley and its law school, Boalt Hall. Despite his discomfort with the narrowness of its curriculum, he graduated from Boalt Hall in 1914.

After practicing in the legal department of an oil company in San Francisco and with a small firm in Oakland, Warren joined the U.S. Army during World War I. He served stateside and left active duty at the end of the war. After clerking for the California legislature and working in Oakland's city attorney's office and as a deputy district attorney for Alameda County, California, Warren was appointed district attorney of the county. He was then elected to the post and served as district attorney for thirteen years before being elected attorney general of California in 1938. As attorney general, Warren played a significant role in the tragic and ill-conceived decision of the U.S. government to relocate Japanese and Japanese Americans during World War II. He later expressed regret for his role in the affair. After serving one term as attorney general of California, Warren was elected governor of California in 1942. He was reelected in 1946 and 1950, serving as governor until he was appointed to the Supreme Court in 1953.

Warren was also active in national politics. In 1948, during his second term as governor, Warren ran for the vice presidency as Republican Thomas Dewey's running mate. Warren sought the Republican Party's nomination for president in 1952, losing to Dwight Eisenhower. In early 1953, Warren accepted the post of solicitor general. However, following the death of Chief Justice Fred Vinson, Warren was appointed chief justice of the United States. After serving for several months, Warren was confirmed by the Senate on March 1, 1954. Although the Warren Court has been cheered by many and derided by others, the decisions issued during Warren's tenure as chief justice changed fundamental aspects of American law. Many of those seminal decisions were authored by Chief Justice Warren himself, including *Brown v. Board of Education* (1954) and its sequel, commonly called *Brown II* (1955); *Reynolds v. Sims* (1964); *Miranda v. Arizona* (1966); *Loving v. Virginia* (1967); and *Terry v. Ohio* (1968).

In the wake of the assassination of President John F. Kennedy, Warren served as the chair of the President's Commission on the Assassination of President Kennedy, commonly known as the Warren Commission. That commission's most famous conclusion—that Lee Harvey Oswald acted alone in assassinating President Kennedy—has been debated and challenged since the commission's report was issued in 1964. Earl Warren retired in 1969 at the close of the Court's term and died on July 9, 1974.

Explanation and Analysis of the Document

Chief Justice Warren begins the opinion by stating the question that the Court must answer: whether the Georgia House of Representatives could exclude Julian Bond based on statements Bond had made criticizing the war in Vietnam and the operation of the draft. In stating the question as such, Warren arguably asks simply whether elected officials enjoy the constitutional protection of freedom of speech. Warren suggests that the question might not be as straightforward as it seemed, but he ultimately would determine that the First Amendment fairly clearly protects Bond's right to free speech.

Before analyzing the issue, Warren sets the case in context. However, he omits some facts that might appear important to understanding the significance of the moment and precisely why Bond acted as he did. For example, Warren notes that Bond was elected from a district where more than 90 percent of the voters were African American, but he does not comment that the district and the election were direct results of the Court's one-man, one-vote jurisprudence.

♦ SNCC's Statement in Opposition to Vietnam War and Bond's Statement of Support

Warren then provides the immediate circumstances that triggered the litigation: a statement issued by SNCC on January 6, 1966, opposing the war in Vietnam and remarks made by Bond, SNCC's communications director, in support of the statement. SNCC's statement noted that the organization opposed U.S. involvement in the Vietnam War and indicated the basis for its opposition: The U.S. government had neither sought nor supported freedom for people of color. The statement said that SNCC found a rough equivalence in the U.S. treatment of people of color in the southern United States and of people of color in Vietnam, with rights guaranteed by law ignored if enforcing those rights ran counter to U.S. interests. The killing of Samuel Younge, in Tuskegee, Alabama, was cited as proof that the United States was not willing to protect its citizens' rights any more than it was willing to protect the rights of the Vietnamese. In addition, the statement suggested that the right to free elections ensured by the Civil Rights Act of 1964 and the Voting Rights Act of 1965 was illusory, because those laws were not being fully implemented. Additionally, the U.S. government's commitment to free elections in other countries was questioned. The statement reasoned that, for many, it would not be sensible to fight for freedom abroad when freedom at home was impossible to achieve. Consequently, SNCC stated that "work[ing] in the civil rights movement and with other human rights organizations is a valid alternative to the draft" and urged those who agreed to embrace the alternative even though that embrace could cost them their lives.

SNCC's statement was issued the day after Samuel Younge, Jr., a member of the organization, a navy veteran, and a student at Tuskegee Institute, was murdered when he attempted to use a segregated restroom at a gas station in Tuskegee. After quoting portions of SNCC statement (but passing over the context in which it was made), the Court's opinion notes and quotes Bond's remarks. In an interview about the statement on the day it was released, Bond endorsed it, though he had not written it. Bond commented that as a pacifist he opposed all wars and felt it to be his duty to encourage others to oppose war in general, the Vietnam War in particular, and the draft. He also observed that the statement correctly noted the hypocrisy of the U.S. government in encouraging freedom in foreign countries but not within its own borders. Consequently, Bond indicated that "as a second-class citizen" he did not feel compelled to support the war and that he did feel obliged to challenge situations he thought wrong. Bond's views on the war led to his belief "that people ought [not] to participate in it" and to his opposition to the draft. Nonetheless, Bond stated that he felt that his views on the war and American foreign policy did not conflict with his taking the oath of office under the Georgia constitution.

◆ **Bond's Exclusion from the Georgia Legislature**

The opinion then details the firestorm that led to Bond's exclusion from the Georgia House of Representatives. In the wake of Bond's comments supporting SNCC's statement, many members of the Georgia legislature filed protests against Bond's taking his seat. The petitions claimed that "Bond's statements gave aid and comfort to the enemies of the United States and Georgia, violated the Selective Service laws, and tended to bring discredit and disrespect on the House." In addition, the petitions argued that Bond could not take the oath necessary to be seated, which required that the taker swear to support the Constitution of the United States. The clerk of the legislature refused to give Bond the oath until the challenge petitions were resolved.

Bond responded by arguing that the petitions were racially motivated and had been filed to restrict his First Amendment rights. Given how the Court resolved the case, it never reached the question of whether the petitions were racially motivated. A special committee of the Georgia legislature was convened to resolve the dispute, with the only testimony being Bond's, during which he defended his support for SNCC's statement. Bond explained that he had voiced support for those who had the courage to do what they believed to be right even when they faced serious harm for doing so. He denied that he ever had suggested that laws should be broken or draft cards should be burned, noting that he carried his own draft card in his pocket. The special committee also considered Bond's statements made after the clerk of the legislature refused to administer the oath. Bond indicated that he was being forced to defend his statements about a matter of public concern when others had not been asked to do so as a prerequisite to being seated. He spoke directly to his constituents, reiterating that he did not advocate violating the law but that he favored extending the recognized justifications for avoiding the draft to "building democracy at home." He explained that he had no plans to stop speaking out on matters of public concern as a legislator, even when his views were at odds with the views of others, and he reiterated that he planned to take the customary oath required of Georgia legislators.

The special legislative committee considered Bond's statements as proof that he could not honestly swear to support the constitutions of Georgia and the United States. In addition, it found that Bond's statements proved that he gave aid and comfort to the enemies of Georgia and the United States, violated the selective service laws, and would likely "bring discredit to and disrespect of" the legislature. Consequently, the committee determined that Bond would not be allowed to take the oath and would not be seated as a representative.

◆ **Procedural Background of the Case**

The opinion next describes the legal proceedings that brought the case to the Supreme Court. In the wake of being excluded from the Georgia legislature, Bond filed suit seeking judgment that Georgia was not authorized to deny him a seat and that his First Amendment rights had been violated. The three-judge panel that heard the suit determined that Georgia law allowed the legislature to require qualifications of its members in addition to those specified in the Georgia constitution. The panel then determined that Bond's constitutional rights had not been violated. The legislature had satisfied procedural due process by providing a proper hearing in front of the special legislative committee. Similarly, according to the panel, substantive due process was satisfied because Bond's statements gave the legislature a reasonable basis for determining that Bond could not take the oath of office required of him. Two judges agreed that Bond's call to action to challenge the draft, rather than his dissent regarding policy, provided a basis for the legislature to believe that Bond "could not in good faith take an oath to support the State and Federal Constitutions." One judge dissented, arguing that barring Bond based on qualifications not in the Georgia constitution was beyond the legislature's authority under Georgia law.

The opinion notes that in the wake of the panel's decision and while Bond's appeal to the Supreme Court was pending, the governor of Georgia had ordered a special election to fill Bond's vacant seat. Bond won that election, and the legislature again refused to seat him. Bond also won the 1966 regular election to fill the seat.

◆ **Legal Analysis of Case**

The opinion next analyzes the substance of the case, noting the specific qualifications listed in the Georgia constitution that could be required of its legislators without constitutional concern. Thus, the various eligibility requirements for Georgia's legislators, such as age and residency qualifications, were legitimate. In addition, the exclusion of those who have been convicted of various crimes or suffer from certain mental infirmities was acceptable. Indeed, even the requirement that legislators take an oath affirming support for the Georgia and U.S. constitutions and act in the best interests of Georgia was acceptable. However, the opinion then analyzes whether the Georgia legislature is limited to requiring that the oath be taken or whether it can opine on the sincerity of the legislator who takes the oath.

The opinion addresses the Georgia legislature's claim that the formal requirement of an oath allowed the House of Representatives to determine whether the legislator planned to take the oath "with sincerity" and that the sincerity requirement would merely qualify as an additional acceptable qualification for office. The legislature argued that it had the ability to establish the qualifications of its members under the Georgia constitution. Although it conceded that it could not exclude a member based on race or other unconstitutional bases, it argued that ascertaining the sincerity of a legislator in taking the required oath was at the core of determining a member's qualification and should not be subject to judicial review. The opinion rejects the suggestion that the Court did not have jurisdiction, noting that the issue was whether the decision violated Bond's First Amendment rights. That question, the opinion notes, was a matter for the Supreme Court to decide.

After noting its jurisdiction over the matter, the opinion reaches the key question: Did the Georgia legislature's action violate Bond's First Amendment rights? The Georgia House of Representatives claimed that Bond's statements called for violations of the law and that even if a private citizen could have uttered those statements without repercussions, the state could hold its legislators to higher standards of loyalty than it held the public. The opinion agrees that Georgia could require that its legislators take an oath swearing fidelity to the U.S. Constitution and the Georgia constitution consistent with First Amendment principles, but it rejects the implications that the Georgia legislature suggested came with the oath requirement. The oath requirement did not limit the legislator's First Amendment rights. First, contrary to the Georgia legislature's claim, the Court found Bond's statements to be lawful expressions of dissent to American policy, rather than a call for lawless action. Any citizen would have been allowed to say what Bond said without repercussions. Second, the Court notes that the Constitution does not allow the state to restrict a legislator's rights to free expression any more than it can restrict an ordinary citizen's rights.

♦ **The Representative's Obligation of Open and Free Expression**

The opinion takes the issue one step further in discussing the role of the First Amendment in public discourse. The Georgia legislature had sought to limit Bond's rights to free expression because he was to become a legislator. The Court suggested that Bond's rights needed to be protected precisely because he was about to become a legislator. Rather than being limited by their elected positions, legislators are supposed to be free to speak at least as broadly and forcefully about national policy as ordinary citizens are. Indeed, their role in deciding issues of public policy makes it necessary for legislators to communicate their positions to their constituents through expressions of opinions on matters of public interest. If that opinion is dissent regarding state or national policy, it ought to be known to those who elected a legislator, so they could take it into account when deciding whether that legislator is a proper representative. Consequently, the Court held "that the disqualification of Bond from membership in the Georgia House because of his statements violated Bond's right of free expression under the First Amendment."

Audience

When the Supreme Court speaks on the breadth of constitutional rights and the fostering of democracy through representative-constituent dialogue, the entire country is its broad audience. *Bond v. Floyd* is no different with respect to its general views on the subjects. The public was told to expect candor from their representatives because candor was necessary for representatives to communicate with and adequately represent constituents. However, the narrower, more legalistic portions of the opinion were arguably addressed to a narrower segment of the populace: those legislators and legislatures that would seek to make orthodoxy king and would root out dissent wherever it could be found. Federal and state legislators were encouraged to take notice that their prerogatives regarding when they could decline to seat members were to be limited and that they had no right to stifle dissent regarding policy through the exercise of their power to judge the qualifications of other members.

Impact

Bond v. Floyd guaranteed that a legislator's admission to a legislature was to be validated by qualifications and election by the citizenry, not by that person's ability to convince other legislators that his or her views were sufficiently orthodox. Consequently, candidates for office were free to explain their views and encouraged to present those views to their constituents to ensure that those candidates would make appropriate representatives for their constituents. In addition, the decision freed candidates who might have come out of civil rights protest organizations and antiwar organizations to express themselves fully and run for office without fear that they might not be able to take the seats they had won. The list of legislators in state legislatures and the halls of Congress who fit this description is much longer than it would have been without *Bond v. Floyd*.

Questions for Further Study

1. How would you describe the relationship between the civil rights movement and the antiwar movement in the 1960s? How did the two movements overlap?

2. Why was opposition to the war in Vietnam so intense in the 1960s and early 1970s? What was different about this war and, say, World War I or World War II?

3. Compare this document with Martin Luther King, Jr.'s "Beyond Vietnam: A Time to Break Silence." Taken together, how do the two documents paint a picture of opposition to the Vietnam War and the intersection of race and national policy during this time period?

4. On what basis did the Warren Court conclude that the Georgia legislature had to seat Bond?

5. Very often, the outcome of a legal case affects only the parties involved and, by extension, others who could be involved in similar circumstances. What argument could be made that the Court's decision in Bond v. Floyd had very much a national audience and that the outcome of the case affected all Americans?

Essential Quotes

"The question presented in this case is whether the Georgia House of Representatives may constitutionally exclude appellant Bond, a duly elected Representative, from membership because of his statements, and statements to which he subscribed, criticizing the policy of the Federal Government in Vietnam and the operation of the Selective Service laws."

"The manifest function of the First Amendment in a representative government requires that legislators be given the widest latitude to express their views on issues of policy."

"Legislators have an obligation to take positions on controversial political questions so that their constituents can be fully informed by them, and be better able to assess their qualifications for office; also so they may be represented in governmental debates by the person they have elected to represent them."

♦ Books

Bond, Julian. *A Time to Speak, a Time to Act.* New York: Simon & Schuster, 1972.

Davidson, Chandler, and Bernard Grofman, eds. *Quiet Revolution in the South.* Princeton, N.J.: Princeton University Press, 1994.

Forman, James. *The Making of Black Revolutionaries.* Seattle: University of Washington Press, 1997.

Lawson, Steven F. *Running for Freedom: Civil Rights and Black Politics in America since 1941.* 3rd ed. Chichester, U.K.: Wiley-Blackwell, 2008.

♦ Web Sites

African-American Involvement in the Vietnam War Web site. http://www.aavw.org.

SNCC 1960–1966 Web site. http://www.ibiblio.org/sncc/index.html.

—Henry J. Chambers, Jr.

Bond v. Floyd

Mr. Chief Justice Warren delivered the opinion of the Court.

The question presented in this case is whether the Georgia House of Representatives may constitutionally exclude appellant Bond, a duly elected Representative, from membership because of his statements, and statements to which he subscribed, criticizing the policy of the Federal Government in Vietnam and the operation of the Selective Service laws. An understanding of the circumstances of the litigation requires a complete presentation of the events and statements which led to this appeal.

Bond, a Negro, was elected on June 15, 1965, as the Representative to the Georgia House of Representatives from the 136th House District. Of the District's 6,500 voters, approximately 6,000 are Negroes. Bond defeated his opponent, Malcolm Dean, Dean of Men at Atlanta University, also a Negro, by a vote of 2,320 to 487.

On January 6, 1966, the Student Nonviolent Coordinating Committee, a civil rights organization of which Bond was then the Communications Director, issued the following statement on American policy in Vietnam and its relation to the work of civil rights organizations in this country:

> The Student Nonviolent Coordinating Committee has a right and a responsibility to dissent with United States foreign policy on an issue when it sees fit. The Student Nonviolent Coordinating Committee now states its opposition to United States' involvement in Viet Nam on these grounds: [385 U.S. 119]
>
> We believe the United States government has been deceptive in its claims of concern for freedom of the Vietnamese people, just as the government has been deceptive in claiming concern for the freedom of colored people in such other countries as the Dominican Republic, the Congo, South Africa, Rhodesia and in the United States itself.
>
> We, the Student Nonviolent Coordinating Committee, have been involved in the black people's struggle for liberation and self-determination in this country for the past five years. Our work, particularly in the South, has taught us that the United States government has never guaranteed the freedom of oppressed citizens, and is not yet truly determined to end the rule of terror and oppression within its own borders.
>
> We ourselves have often been victims of violence and confinement executed by United States government officials. We recall the numerous persons who have been murdered in the South because of their efforts to secure their civil and human rights, and whose murderers have been allowed to escape penalty for their crimes.
>
> The murder of Samuel Young in Tuskegee, Ala., is no different than the murder of peasants in Viet Nam, for both Young and the Vietnamese sought, and are seeking, to secure the rights guaranteed them by law. In each case, the United States government bears a great part of the responsibility for these deaths.
>
> Samuel Young was murdered because United States law is not being enforced. Vietnamese are murdered because the United States is pursuing an aggressive policy in violation of international law. The United States is no respecter of persons or law [385 U.S. 120] when such persons or laws run counter to its needs and desires.
>
> We recall the indifference, suspicion and outright hostility with which our reports of violence have been met in the past by government officials.
>
> We know that, for the most part, elections in this country, in the North as well as the South, are not free. We have seen that the 1965 Voting Rights Act and the 1964 Civil Rights Act have not yet been implemented with full federal power and sincerity.
>
> We question, then, the ability and even the desire of the United States government to guarantee free elections abroad. We maintain that our country's cry of "preserve freedom in the world" is a hypocritical mask behind which it squashes liberation movements which are not bound, and refuse to be bound, by the expediencies of United States cold war policies.
>
> We are in sympathy with, and support, the men in this country who are unwilling to respond to a military draft which would compel them to contribute their lives to United States aggression in Viet Nam in the name of the "freedom" we find so false in this country.
>
> We recoil with horror at the inconsistency of a supposedly "free" society where responsibility to freedom is equated with the responsibility to

Document Text

lend oneself to military aggression. We take note of the fact that 16 percent of the draftees from this country are Negroes called on to stifle the liberation of Viet Nam, to preserve a "democracy" which does not exist for them at home.

We ask, where is the draft for the freedom fight in the United States? [385 U.S. 121]

We therefore encourage those Americans who prefer to use their energy in building democratic forms within this country. We believe that work in the civil rights movement and with other human relations organizations is a valid alternative to the draft. We urge all Americans to seek this alternative, knowing full well that it may cost their lives—as painfully as in Viet Nam.

On the same day that this statement was issued, Bond was interviewed by telephone by a reporter from a local radio station, and, although Bond had not participated in drafting the statement, he endorsed the statement in these words:

Why, I endorse it, first, because I like to think of myself as a pacifist, and one who opposes that war and any other war, and eager and anxious to encourage people not to participate in it for any reason that they choose, and secondly, I agree with this statement because of the reason set forth in it—because I think it is sorta hypocritical for us to maintain that we are fighting for liberty in other places and we are not guaranteeing liberty to citizens inside the continental United States.

Well, I think that the fact that the United States Government fights a war in Viet Nam, I don't think that I, as a second class citizen of the United States, have a requirement to support that war. I think my responsibility is to oppose things that I think are wrong if they are in Viet Nam or New York, or Chicago, or Atlanta, or wherever.

When the interviewer suggested that our involvement in Vietnam was because "if we do not stop Communism [385 U.S. 122] there, that it is just a question of where will we stop it next," Bond replied:

Oh, no, I'm not taking a stand against stopping World Communism, and I'm not taking a stand in favor of the Viet Cong. What I'm saying that is, first, that I don't believe in that war. That particular war. I'm against all war. I'm against that war in particular, and I don't think people ought to participate in it. Because I'm against war, I'm against the draft. I think that other countries in the World get along without a draft—England is one—and I don't see why we couldn't, too.

… I'm not about to justify that war, because it's stopping International Communism, or whatever—you know, I just happen to have a basic disagreement with wars for whatever reason they are fought … fought to stop International Communism, to promote International Communism, or for whatever reason. I oppose the Viet Cong fighting in Viet Nam as much as I oppose the United States fighting in Viet Nam. I happen to live in the United States. If I lived in North Viet Nam, I might not have the same sort of freedom of expression, but it happens that I live here—not there.

The interviewer also asked Bond if he felt he could take the oath of office required by the Georgia Constitution, and Bond responded that he saw nothing inconsistent between his statements and the oath. Bond was also asked whether he would adhere to his statements if war were declared on North Vietnam and if his statements might become treasonous. He replied that he did not know "if I'm strong enough to place myself in a position where I'd be guilty of treason." [385 U.S. 123]

Before January 10, 1966, when the Georgia House of Representatives was scheduled to convene, petitions challenging Bond's right to be seated were filed by 75 House members. These petitions charged that Bond's statements gave aid and comfort to the enemies of the United States and Georgia, violated the Selective Service laws, and tended to bring discredit and disrespect on the House. The petitions further contended that Bond's endorsement of SNCC statement is totally and completely repugnant to and inconsistent with the mandatory oath prescribed by the Constitution of Georgia for a Member of the House of Representatives to take before taking his seat.

For the same reasons, the petitions asserted that Bond could not take an oath to support the Constitution of the United States. When Bond appeared at the House on January 10 to be sworn in, the clerk refused to administer the oath to him until the issues raised in the challenge petitions had been decided.

Bond filed a response to the challenge petitions in which he stated his willingness to take the oath and argued that he was not unable to do so in good faith. He further argued that the challenge against his seating had been filed to deprive him of his First Amendment rights, and that the challenge was racially motivated. A special committee was appointed to report on the challenge, and a hearing was held to determine exactly what Bond had said and the intentions with which he had said it.

Document Text

At this hearing, the only testimony given against Bond was that which he himself gave the committee. Both the opponents Bond had defeated in becoming the Representative of the 136th District testified to his good character and to his loyalty to the United States. A recording of the interview which Bond had given to the reporter after SNCC statement was played, and Bond was called to the stand for cross-examination. He there admitted his statements and elaborated his views. He [385 U.S. 124] stated that he concurred in SNCC statement "without reservation," and, when asked if he admired the courage of persons who burn their draft cards, responded:

> I admire people who take an action, and I admire people who feel strongly enough about their convictions to take an action like that knowing the consequences that they will face, and that was my original statement when asked that question.
>
> I have never suggested or counseled or advocated that any one other person burn their draft card. In fact, I have mine in my pocket, and will produce it if you wish. I do not advocate that people should break laws. What I simply tried to say was that I admired the courage of someone who could act on his convictions knowing that he faces pretty stiff consequences.

Tapes of an interview Bond had given the press after the clerk had refused to give him the oath were also heard by the special committee. In this interview, Bond stated:

> I stand before you today charged with entering into public discussion on matters of National interest. I hesitate to offer explanations for my actions or deeds where no charge has been levied against me other than the charge that I have chosen to speak my mind and no explanation is called for, for no member of this House, has ever, to my knowledge, been called upon to explain his public statements for public postures as a prerequisite to admission to that Body. I therefore, offer to my constituents a statement of my views. I have not counseled burning draft cards, nor have I burned mine. I have suggested that congressionally outlined alternatives to military service be extended to [385 U.S. 125] building democracy at home. The posture of my life for the past five years has been calculated to give Negroes the ability to participate in formulation of public policies. The fact of my election to public office does not lessen my duty or desire to express my opinions even when they differ from those held by others. As to the current controversy, because of convictions that I have arrived at through examination of my conscience, I have decided I personally cannot participate in war.
>
> I stand here with intentions to take an oath—that oath they just took in there—that will dispel any doubts about my convictions or loyalty.

The special committee gave general approval in its report to the specific charges in the challenge petitions that Bond's endorsement of SNCC statement and his supplementary remarks showed that he " does not and will not" support the Constitutions of the United States and of Georgia, that he "adheres to the enemies of the ... State of Georgia" contrary to the State Constitution, that he gives aid and comfort to the enemies of the United States, that his statements violated the Universal Military Training and Service Act, §12, 62 Stat. 622, 50 U.S.C. App. §462, and that his statements "are reprehensible, and are such as tend to bring discredit to and disrespect of the House." On the same day, the House adopted the committee report without findings and without further elaborating Bond's lack of qualifications, and resolved by a vote of 184 to 12 that

> Bond shall not be allowed to take the oath of office as a member of the House of Representatives and that Representative-Elect Julian Bond shall not be seated as a member of the House of Representatives.

Bond then instituted an action in the District Court for the Northern District of Georgia for injunctive relief[385 U.S. 126] and a declaratory judgment that the House action was unauthorized by the Georgia Constitution and violated Bond's rights under the First Amendment. A three-judge District Court was convened under 28 U.S.C. §2281. All three members of the District Court held that the court had jurisdiction to decide the constitutionality of the House action because Bond had asserted substantial First Amendment rights. On the merits, however, the court was divided.

Judges Bell and Morgan, writing for the majority of the court, addressed themselves first to the question of whether the Georgia House had power under state law to disqualify Bond based on its conclusion that he could not sincerely take the oath of office. They reasoned that separation of powers principles gave the Legislature power to insist on qualifications in addition to those specified in the State Constitution. The

Document Text

majority pointed out that nothing in the Georgia Constitution limits the qualifications of the legislators to those expressed in the constitution.

Having concluded that the action of the Georgia House was authorized by state law, the court considered whether Bond's disqualification violated his constitutional right of freedom of speech. It reasoned that the decisions of this Court involving particular state political offices supported an attitude of restraint in which the principles of separation of powers and federalism should be balanced against the alleged deprivation of individual constitutional rights. On this basis, the majority below fashioned the test to be applied in this case as being whether the refusal to seat Bond violated procedural or what it termed substantive due process. The court held that the hearing which had been given Bond by the House satisfied procedural due process. As for [385 U.S. 127] what it termed the question of substantive due process, the majority concluded that there was a rational evidentiary basis for the ruling of the House. It reasoned that Bond's right to dissent as a private citizen was limited by his decision to seek membership in the Georgia House. Moreover, the majority concluded, SNCC statement and Bond's related remarks went beyond criticism of national policy and provided a rational basis for a conclusion that the speaker could not in good faith take an oath to support the State and Federal Constitutions:

> A citizen would not violate his oath by objecting to or criticizing this policy or even by calling it deceptive and false, as the statement did.
>
> But the statement does not stop with this. It is a call to action based on race; a call alien to the concept of the pluralistic society which makes this nation. It aligns the organization with "... colored people in such other countries as the Dominican Republic, the Congo, South Africa, Rhodesia...." It refers to its involvement in the black people's "struggle for liberation and self-determination...." It states that "Vietnamese are murdered because the United States is pursuing an aggressive policy in violation of international law." It alleges that Negroes, referring to American servicemen, are called on to stifle the liberation of Viet Nam.
>
> The call to action, and this is what we find to be a rational basis for the decision which denied Mr. Bond his seat, is that language which states that SNCC supports those men in this country who are unwilling to respond to a military draft.

Chief Judge Tuttle dissented. He reasoned that the question of the power of the Georgia House under the [385 U.S. 128] State Constitution to disqualify a Representative under these circumstances had never been decided by the state courts, and that federal courts should construe state law, if possible, so as to avoid unnecessary federal constitutional issues. Since Bond satisfied all the stated qualifications in the State Constitution, Chief Judge Tuttle concluded that his disqualification was beyond the power of the House as a matter of state constitutional law.

Bond appealed directly to this Court from the decision of the District Court under 28 U.S.C. §1253. While this appeal was pending, the Governor of Georgia called a special election to fill the vacancy caused by Bond's exclusion. Bond entered this election and won overwhelmingly. The House was in recess, but the Rules Committee held a hearing in which Bond declined to recant his earlier statements. Consequently, he was again prevented from taking the oath of office, and the seat has remained vacant. Bond again sought the seat from the 136th District in the regular 1966 election, and he won the Democratic primary in September, 1966, and won an overwhelming majority in the election of November 8, 1966.

The Georgia Constitution sets out a number of specific provisions dealing with the qualifications and eligibility of state legislators. These provide that Representatives shall be citizens of the United States, at least 21 years of age, citizens of Georgia for two years, and residents for one year of the counties from which elected. The [385 U.S. 129] Georgia Constitution further provides that no one convicted of treason against the State, or of any crime of moral turpitude, or of a number of other enumerated crimes, may hold any office in the State. Idiots and insane persons are barred from office, and no one holding any state or federal office is eligible for a seat in either house. The State Constitution also provides:

> Election, returns, etc.; disorderly conduct.—Each House shall be the judge of the election, returns and qualifications of its members and shall have power to punish them for disorderly behavior, or misconduct, by censure, fine, imprisonment, or expulsion; but no member shall be expelled, except by a vote of two-thirds of the House to which he belongs.

These constitute the only stated qualifications for membership in the Georgia Legislature, and the State concedes that Bond meets all of them. The

Georgia Constitution also requires Representatives to take an oath stated in the Constitution:

> Oath of members.—Each senator and Representative, before taking his seat, shall take the following oath, or affirmation, to-wit: "I will support the Constitution of this State and of the United States, and on all questions and measures which may come before me, I will so conduct myself, as will, in my judgment, be most conducive to the interests and prosperity of this State." [385 U.S. 130]

The State points out in its brief that the latter part of this oath, involving the admonition to act in the best interests of the State, was not the standard by which Bond was judged.

The State does not claim that Bond refused to take the oath to support the Federal Constitution, a requirement imposed on state legislators by Art. VI, cl. 3, of the United States Constitution:

> The Senators and Representatives before mentioned, and the Members of the several State Legislatures, and all executive and judicial Officers, both of the United States and of the several States, shall be bound by Oath or Affirmation, to support this Constitution; but no religious Tests shall ever be required as a Qualification to any Office or public Trust under the United States.

Instead, it argues that the oath provisions of the State and Federal Constitutions constitute an additional qualification. Because, under state law, the legislature has exclusive jurisdiction to determine whether an elected Representative meets the enumerated qualifications, it is argued that the legislature has power to look beyond the plain meaning of the oath provisions, which merely require that the oaths be taken. This additional power is said to extend to determining whether a given Representative may take the oath with sincerity. The State does not claim that it should be completely free of judicial review whenever it disqualifies an elected Representative; it admits that, if a State Legislature excluded a legislator on racial or other clearly unconstitutional grounds, the federal (or state) judiciary would be justified in testing the exclusion by federal constitutional standards. But the State argues that there can be no [385 U.S. 131] doubt as to the constitutionality of the qualification involved in this case, because it is one imposed on the State Legislatures by Article VI of the United States Constitution. Moreover, the State contends that no decision of this Court suggests that a State may not ensure the loyalty of its public servants by making the taking of an oath a qualification of office. Thus, the State argues that there should be no judicial review of the legislature's power to judge whether a prospective member may conscientiously take the oath required by the State and Federal Constitutions.

We are not persuaded by the State's attempt to distinguish, for purposes of our jurisdiction, between an exclusion alleged to be on racial grounds and one alleged to violate the First Amendment. The basis for the argued distinction is that, in this case, Bond's disqualification was grounded on a constitutional standard—the requirement of taking an oath to support the Constitution. But Bond's contention is that this standard was utilized to infringe his First Amendment rights, and we cannot distinguish, for purposes of our assumption of jurisdiction, between a disqualification under an unconstitutional standard and a disqualification which, although under color of a proper standard, is alleged to violate the First Amendment.

We conclude, as did the entire court below, that this Court has jurisdiction to review the question of whether the action of the Georgia House of Representatives deprived Bond of federal constitutional rights, and we now move to the central question posed in the case—whether Bond's disqualification because of his statements violated the free speech provisions of the First Amendment as applied to the States through the Fourteenth Amendment.

The State argues that the exclusion does not violate the First Amendment because the State has a right, under Article VI of the United States Constitution, to insist on loyalty to the Constitution as a condition of office. A legislator, of course, can be required to swear to support the Constitution of the United States as a condition of holding office, but that is not the issue in this case, as the record is uncontradicted that Bond has repeatedly expressed his willingness to swear to the oaths provided for in the State and Federal Constitutions. Nor is this a case where a legislator swears to an oath *pro forma* while declaring or manifesting his disagreement with or indifference to the oath. Thus, we do not quarrel with the State's contention that the oath provisions of the United States and Georgia Constitutions do not violate the First Amendment. But this requirement does not authorize a majority of state legislators to test the sincerity with which another duly elected legislator can swear to uphold the Constitution. Such a power could be utilized to restrict the right of legis-

Document Text

lators to dissent from national or state policy or that of a majority of their colleagues under the guise of judging their loyalty to the Constitution. Certainly there can be no question but that the First Amendment protects expressions in opposition to national foreign policy in Vietnam and to the Selective Service system. The State does not contend otherwise. But it argues that Bond went beyond expressions of opposition, and counseled violations of the Selective Service laws, and that advocating violation of federal law demonstrates a lack of support for the Constitution. The State declines to argue that Bond's statements would violate any law if made by a private citizen, but it does argue that, even though such [385 U.S. 133] a citizen might be protected by his First Amendment rights, the State may nonetheless apply a stricter standard to its legislators. We do not agree.

Bond could not have been constitutionally convicted under 50 U.S.C. App. §462(a), which punishes any person who "counsels, aids, or abets another to refuse or evade registration." Bond's statements were, at worst, unclear on the question of the means to be adopted to avoid the draft. While SNCC statement said "We are in sympathy with, and support, the men in this country who are unwilling to respond to a military draft," this statement alone cannot be interpreted as a call to unlawful refusal to be drafted. Moreover, Bond's supplementary statements tend to resolve the opaqueness in favor of legal alternatives to the draft, and there is no evidence to the contrary. On the day the statement was issued, Bond explained that he endorsed it

> because I like to think of myself as a pacifist and one who opposes that war and any other war and eager and anxious to [385 U.S. 134] encourage people not to participate in it for any reason that they choose.

In the same interview, Bond stated categorically that he did not oppose the Vietnam policy because he favored the Communists; that he was a loyal American citizen, and supported the Constitution of the United States. He further stated "I oppose the Viet Cong fighting in Viet Nam as much as I oppose the United States fighting in Viet Nam." At the hearing before the Special Committee of the Georgia House, when asked his position on persons who burned their draft cards, Bond replied that he admired the courage of persons who "feel strongly enough about their convictions to take an action like that knowing the consequences that they will face." When pressed as to whether his admiration was based on the violation of federal law, Bond stated:

> I have never suggested or counseled or advocated that any one other person burn their draft card. In fact, I have mine in my pocket, and will produce it if you wish. I do not advocate that people should break laws. What I simply try to say was that I admired the courage of someone who could act on his convictions knowing that he faces pretty stiff consequences.

Certainly this clarification does not demonstrate any incitement to violation of law. No useful purpose would be served by discussing the many decisions of this Court which establish that Bond could not have been convicted for these statements consistently with the First Amendment. See, e.g., *Wood v. Georgia*, 370 U.S. 375 (1962); *Yates v. United States*, 354 U.S. 298 (1957); *Terminiello v. Chicago*, 337 U.S. 1 (1949). Nor does the fact that the District Court found the SNCC statement to have racial overtones constitute a reason for holding it outside [385 U.S. 135] the protection of the First Amendment. In fact, the State concedes that there is no issue of race in the case.

The State attempts to circumvent the protection the First Amendment would afford to these statements if made by a private citizen by arguing that a State is constitutionally justified in exacting a higher standard of loyalty from its legislators than from its citizens. Of course, a State may constitutionally require an oath to support the Constitution from its legislators which it does not require of its private citizens. But this difference in treatment does not support the exclusion of Bond, for while the State has an interest in requiring its legislators to swear to a belief in constitutional processes of government, surely the oath gives it no interest in limiting its legislators' capacity to discuss their views of local or national policy. The manifest function of [385 U.S. 136] the First Amendment in a representative government requires that legislators be given the widest latitude to express their views on issues of policy. The central commitment of the First Amendment, as summarized in the opinion of the Court in *New York Times Co. v. Sullivan*, 376 U.S. 254, 270 (1964), is that "debate on public issues should be uninhibited, robust, and wide-open." We think the rationale of the New York Times case disposes of the claim that Bond's statements fell outside the range of constitutional protection. Just as erroneous statements must be

Document Text

protected to give freedom of expression the breathing space it needs to survive, so statements criticizing public policy and the implementation of it must be similarly protected. The State argues that the *New York Times* principle should not be extended to statements by a legislator because the policy of encouraging free debate about governmental operations only applies to the citizen-critic of his government. We find no support for this distinction in the *New York Times* case or in any other decision of this Court. The interest of the public in hearing all sides of a public issue is hardly advanced by extending more protection to citizen critics than to legislators. Legislators have an obligation to take positions on controversial political questions so that their constituents can be fully informed by them, and be better able to assess their qualifications for office; also so they may be represented in governmental debates [385 U.S. 137] by the person they have elected to represent them. We therefore hold that the disqualification of Bond from membership in the Georgia House because of his statements violated Bond's right of free expression under the First Amendment. Because of our disposition of the case on First Amendment grounds, we need not decide the other issues advanced by Bond and the *amici*.

The judgment of the District Court is *Reversed*.

Glossary

amici: a reference to *amici curiae* briefs, or "friends of the court" briefs filed by people who are not directly involved in the case but have an interest in supporting one side or the other

burning draft cards: a common, public way of opposing the Vietnam War in the 1960s

cold war: the state of tension between the United States and its allies and the Soviet Union and its satellite states in the decades following World War II

declaratory judgment: a judge's statement about someone's rights

Idiots: a clinical term used at the time to refer to a particular class of mentally disabled persons

injunctive relief: a court order requiring someone to do something or refrain from doing something

***pro forma*:** from the Latin for "as a matter of form," used to describe something done in a perfunctory or purely formal way

procedural due process: the legal doctrine that ensures fairness in the application of rules, laws, and regulations

Samuel Young: Samuel Younge, Jr., a member of the Student Nonviolent Coordinating Committee and a Tuskegee Institute student killed in January 1966 for using the segregated bathroom at a Tuskegee gas station

Selective Service laws: the military draft, including the obligation to register for the draft

SNCC: an acronym for the Student Nonviolent Coordinating Committee, pronounced "snick"

substantive due process: the legal doctrine that ensures that the fundamental rights of people are protected in the outcome of a case

Viet Cong: a name derived from Vietnamese for "Vietnamese Communist" and referring to the National Liberation Front, which fought the United States and the South Vietnamese government in the Vietnam War

"Stokley Carmichael expounds 'black power' theory." By Michigan State University (photographer not identified) (1967 Wolverine (Michigan State yearbook), page 49), via Wikimedia Commons

Stokely Carmichael: "Black Power"

"We were never fighting for the right to integrate, we were fighting against white supremacy."

Overview

On October 29, 1966, Stokely Carmichael addressed an audience consisting primarily of college students at the open-air Greek Theater at the University of California at Berkeley in a speech that has become known as "Black Power"—although he gave other speeches that stressed the same theme and sometimes have been referred to by that same title. Carmichael was a leading spokesperson for the American civil rights movement as well as for international human rights and the relationship between the two movements; he was also an outspoken critic of the Vietnam War. He had first become known as a representative of the Student Nonviolent Coordinating Committee, or SNCC, commonly pronounced "snick." After breaking with SNCC in 1967, Carmichael became affiliated with the more militant Black Panther Party. Finally, after breaking with the Black Panthers, he spoke from his own platform during a period of self-imposed exile before his death in the Republic of Guinea. Carmichael touched on a broad range of issues in his "Black Power" speech, including SNCC's condemnation of white America's "institutional racism" (a term he has been credited with coining) and fear of the term "Black Power." He also discussed the relationship between the American civil rights movement and unrest in much of the postcolonial world, the need for white activists to organize in white communities, nonviolence versus self-defense in the face of racial oppression, and the evil of the Vietnam War.

Carmichael was talking to an audience of largely left-leaning students on one of the most liberal, even radical, campuses in the country at a time when the civil rights movement had begun to hit its stride. He was speaking as a representative of SNCC and cited the positions taken as those of SNCC, whose platform he was largely responsible for developing and articulating. Although SNCC espoused nonviolence at the time and included whites in its membership, Carmichael was already moving away from white inclusion in SNCC, calling instead for whites to organize nonracist whites in their own communities. He was also questioning the workability of nonviolence in the face of violence against peaceful African American demonstrators by whites in positions of power. It would be these two issues that caused Carmichael to separate himself from SNCC—which would itself move away from its dedication to nonviolence in the coming years—and join the more radical Black Panther Party.

Context

The year 1966 was pivotal for both of Carmichael's major concerns: civil rights and the Vietnam War. His address was delivered at a time when the political and social climate of the country was being shaped by the assassinations of three major figures. President John F. Kennedy had been assassinated on November 22, 1963, and the black civil rights activist Malcolm X had been killed on February 21, 1965. Eighteen months after the UC Berkeley speech, on April 4, 1968, the Reverend Martin Luther King, Jr., would be murdered in Memphis, Tennessee. Several months before the UC Berkeley speech, Carmichael had taken part in the March against Fear from Memphis, Tennessee, to Jackson, Mississippi. The march had been organized by James Meredith, the first African American student at the University of Mississippi, where he had been subject to constant harassment. After graduation he organized the march, which began on June 5, 1966, in order to bring attention to black voting rights issues in the South and to help blacks overcome fear of violence. During the march he was shot in an assassination attempt by Aubrey James Norvell, but he survived. Several civil rights leaders, including Carmichael, joined the march after the shooting. Carmichael was arrested in Greenwood, Mississippi, while participating in the march. When he rejoined the marchers, he galvanized them with a speech at a rally; this speech has also been referred to as his "Black Power" speech.

At the time of his speech at UC Berkeley, Carmichael was still not only a member of SNCC but also in many ways its public face and certainly its most charismatic speaker. He was particularly highly regarded as a speaker on college campuses. SNCC, formed in 1960, was a major force in the civil rights movement. It organized voter registration drives throughout the South and events such as the 1963 March on Washington. Leaders of the organization included such notables of the civil rights movement as Julian Bond, John Lewis, Marion Barry, and Carmichael's successor as chairman, H. Rap Brown (later known as Jamil Abdullah Al-Amin). In addition to its "Black Power" focus, SNCC was also involved in protests against the Vietnam War.

On March 9, 1965, the Reverend Martin Luther King, Jr., arrived in Selma, Alabama, to lead a nonviolent march of activists, both black and white, to the state capital at Montgomery. The march had already begun two days earlier, but its participants had encountered violent resistance from state troopers and local law enforcement at the Edmund Pettus Bridge on Selma's outskirts. On March 25, the marchers, under King's leadership and the protection of National Guard troops authorized by President Lyndon Johnson, arrived in Montgomery. The march had attracted over twenty-five thousand participants in its final days, but its triumph would soon be overshadowed by other events. In August of that same year, riots erupted in the Watts section of Los Angeles. During the five days of disturbances, over fourteen thousand National Guard troops were sent to South Central Los Angeles. When the dust settled, thirty-four had died (most of them black), more than one thousand had been injured, and property damage had amounted to an estimated $40 million, possibly much more. During the following months up to the time of Carmichael's UC Berkeley speech, violent conflict involving blacks and local law enforcement swept through cities across the nation. These events prompted SNCC's leadership to begin to move away from strict adherence to the principle of nonviolence.

Also on the nation's mind was the deepening American involvement in Vietnam. In August 1964 the Communist North Vietnamese attacked two U.S. naval destroyers. In response, Congress passed the Gulf of Tonkin Resolution (unanimously in the House of Representatives and with just two nays in the Senate), which gave President Lyndon Johnson the authority to send combat troops to South Vietnam. In March 1965, the first U.S. combat troops—thirty-five hundred Marines—joined twenty-three thousand U.S. advisers and special forces already in Vietnam. By the end of that year nearly two hundred thousand American troops would be in Vietnam. Antiwar sentiment was strongly felt on many college campuses in the mid-1960s, but the liberal UC Berkeley campus was a hotbed of student protest. In the spring of 1965, the Vietnam Day Committee—a coalition of student groups, political groups, labor organizations, and churches—was formed on the campus by the activists Jerry Rubin, Abbie Hoffman, and others. A campus protest on May 21 and 22 of that year, during which President Johnson was burned in effigy, attracted some thirty-five thousand people. In his speech at UC Berkeley in 1966, Carmichael would have been speaking before a highly receptive audience.

About the Author

Stokely Carmichael, later in life known also as Kwame Ture, was born on June 29, 1941, in Port-of-Spain, Trinidad and Tobago. His parents left him in the care of his grandparents at an early age and immigrated to New York City, where they worked in blue-collar jobs. Carmichael eventually joined his parents in New York and attended the Bronx High School of Science. In 1960 he began attending Howard University, where he became involved with the newly formed SNCC. While he was a member of SNCC in 1965, Carmichael established his effectiveness as an organizer when he played a lead role in increasing the number of registered black voters in Lowndes County, Alabama, from seventy to twenty-six hundred. There he worked with the Lowndes County Freedom Organization. Coincidentally for the future member of the California-based Black Panther organization, the Lowndes County Freedom Organization had as its mascot a black panther, which it used in juxtaposition with the white-controlled Democratic Party's local mascot, a white rooster instead of the nationwide symbol of the donkey. As a representative of the militant wing of SNCC, Carmichael rose to become the organization's chairman in 1966.

Carmichael was at first supportive of the work of Martin Luther King. He joined with King in 1966 to continue James Meredith's March against Fear from Memphis, Tennessee, to Jackson, Mississippi, after Meredith had been shot by a white sniper. Carmichael would later repudiate King's nonviolent stance, although as late as April 15, 1967, he joined King in speaking out against the Vietnam War. Through the force of his rhetoric, Carmichael became a celebrity, but others in SNCC resented his prominence. He was replaced as chairman of SNCC by H. Rap Brown in 1967 and was soon formally expelled from the organization. That year, Carmichael joined the more militant Black Panther Party. As "honorary prime minister" of the Panthers, he became an even more forceful critic of the Vietnam War and lectured throughout the world and the United States, often on college campuses. However, Carmichael never rose to become the official spokesperson for the Panthers. Eventually, he broke with the Panthers over the issue of whether whites should be allowed to become members.

After the assassination of King on April 4, 1968, Carmichael was in Washington, D.C., and, although he was no longer officially a member of SNCC, led members of that organization in trying to maintain order. In 1969 he left the United States and the Panthers to live in the Republic of

Guinea, which had gained independence from France in 1958. There he changed his name to Kwame Ture in honor of two figures: Guinea's president, Ahmed Sékou Touré, who ruled the country from its liberation until his death in 1984; and Kwame Nkrumah, the former president of Ghana, who, after he had been overthrown, was offered refuge by Touré. From his base in Guinea, Carmichael wrote and spoke, advocating pan-Africanism and Socialism.

Carmichael died of prostate cancer on November 15, 1998, at the age of fifty-seven, Before his death, he had claimed that the Federal Bureau of Investigation had infected him with a strain of cancer in order to assassinate him. It was later learned that he had been the subject of surveillance by the FBI and the Central Intelligence Agency since 1968.

Explanation and Analysis of the Document

Carmichael begins his speech at UC Berkeley with a mocking dig at his audience, in which he describes the university and its environs as the "white intellectual ghetto of the West." Continuing in this edgy but humorous vein, he announces that, based upon SNCC's successes at voter registration, he would be running for president, although he notes next that he is ineligible because he was not born in the United States. He then states that he would not get caught up in questions about the meaning of "Black Power"—leaving that to the press—though he mocks reporters, calling them "advertisers."

◆ Condemnation

Carmichael then turns to his first major point, the question of "whether or not a man can condemn himself." In breaking down this question, he turns to the thought of three intellectuals. Albert Camus and Jean-Paul Sartre were both French intellectuals and writers of the early- to mid-twentieth century. Camus, born in Algeria to parents of French and Spanish origin, was the first African-born writer to win the Nobel Prize. Although his name was often linked with existentialism, Camus rejected this label and thought of himself as an absurdist. He was also associated with the European Union movement and opposition to totalitarianism. Jean-Paul Sartre was a French existentialist and Communist who opposed French rule in Algeria. Frantz Fanon was a writer, philosopher, and revolutionary who was born in Martinique and whose books—*The Wretched of the Earth, Black Skin, White Masks,* and *A Dying Colonialism*—were key documents in the anticolonial movement and would likely have been familiar to many in Carmichael's UC Berkeley audience. Carmichael asserts that SNCC's leaders also believed that man cannot condemn himself. Carmichael's point is that since "white America cannot condemn herself," SNCC has condemned it. He then mentions Sheriff Lawrence Rainey in Neshoba County, Mississippi; this is a reference to the notorious murder in 1964 of three civil rights workers, two of them white and one black, through the collusion of local law enforcement agencies and the Ku Klux Klan.

◆ White Supremacy

With paragraph 6, Carmichael takes up the issue of white supremacy. He begins by arguing that integration is an "insidious subterfuge" that in fact maintains white supremacy. He compares integration to thalidomide, a drug given to pregnant women that infamously had turned out to cause severe birth defects. He makes reference to Ross Barnett, who had been the segregationist governor of Mississippi, and Jim Clark, the sheriff of Dallas County, Alabama, who had been responsible for authorizing the violent assaults and arrests of activists during the Selma-to-Montgomery march of 1965. He argues that American institutions are racist (Carmichael has been credited with having coined the term *institutional racism*) and then asks rhetorically what whites who are not racists can do to change the system.

Carmichael rejects the idea that whites can give anybody their freedom. "A man is born free" and then enslaved, so whites must stop denying freedom, rather than trying to "give" freedom. He then states that it follows logically that civil rights legislation, passed by white people, is ultimately for the benefit of white people. Laws regarding public accommodations and the right to vote, he argues, show white people that African Americans have certain rights; however, African Americans should already be aware that they are entitled to those rights. Voting, for example, is a right, not a privilege.

Carmichael next discusses white failures at democracy in the international sphere, citing Vietnam, South Africa, the Philippines, South America, and Puerto Rico. He states, in paragraph 11:

> We not only condemn the [United States] for what it's done internally, but we must condemn it for what it does externally. We see this country trying to rule the world, and someone must stand up and start articulating that this country is not God, and cannot rule the world.

In this vein he condemns missionary work in Africa as a component of white supremacy, arguing that missionary work was premised on the belief that Africans were uncivilized. He also portrays missionaries as exchanging Bibles for natives' land. Carmichael then links domestic endeavors such as Head Start to the same agenda. He rejects the notion that people are poor simply because they do not work. If this were actually the criterion for poverty, then such people as Nelson Rockefeller (the governor of New York and heir to the Standard Oil fortune), Bobby Kennedy (the brother of president John F. Kennedy), President Johnson and his wife, Lady Bird Johnson, and other powerful Americans should be poor, for in Carmichael's view, they do not work.

◆ Black Power

Carmichael then argues, in paragraph 16, that the debate over the use of the term *Black Power* is part of a psychological struggle over whether African Americans can use terms without white approval. He states that black Americans are often put in the position of having to defend their actions and maintains that it is time for white America to be put in the position of having to defend its actions—"defending themselves as to why they have oppressed and exploited us." He draws attention to the extent of segregation by noting that only 6 percent of black children are enrolled in integrated schools. Although the particular source that gave him this statistic is uncertain, a number of contemporary documents cited such a figure, including the decision in *United States v. Jefferson County Board of Education* (1966) by Justice John Minor Wisdom of the U.S. Court of Appeals for the Fifth Circuit, a judge who wrote a number of influential opinions on school desegregation. In paragraph 21, Carmichael draws his listeners' attention to the heavy-handed police presence in Oakland, California, and then asks what the nation's political parties can do to create institutions that "will become the political expressions of people on a day-to-day basis."

♦ White Activism

Carmichael then discusses true integration as being a two-way street. He argues that white activists must organize in the white community to change white society. He rejects the idea of whites working in the African American community as damaging on a psychological basis and concludes that his position on this is not "reverse racist." In this light, he alludes to the gubernatorial race in California; the election was held just over one week after his speech. The "two clowns" to whom he refers are the Democratic candidate and then-incumbent governor Edmund G. "Pat" Brown and the Republican candidate and future president Ronald Reagan, who would soon win by a margin of 15 percentage points. Interestingly, Carmichael asserts that SNCC did not believe that the Democratic Party represents the needs of black people. He argues that what was needed was a new coalition of voters who would start building new political and social institutions that would meet the needs of all people. After a reference to the nineteenth-century African American leader Frederick Douglass, Carmichael calls for a new generation of leaders in the black community, declaring, in paragraph 26, that "black people must be seen in positions of power, doing and articulating for themselves."

♦ The Vietnam War

Carmichael then turns to an attack on the Vietnam War as an "illegal and immoral war" and rhetorically asks the audience how it could be stopped. His answer is resistance to the draft. He refers to U.S. Secretary of Defense Robert McNamara as a "racist" and calls President Johnson a "buffoon" and describes American troops as "hired killers." The peace movement, he argues, has been ineffective because it consists of college students who are exempt from the draft anyway. A draft board classification of II-S ("2S" in the speech) gives deferred military service for students actively engaged in study. He calls attention to the irony of referring to black militancy as violent when black militant groups were fighting for human rights and the end of violence in places like Vietnam. As for African American soldiers who had been drafted and were fighting in Vietnam, he characterizes them as black mercenaries.

♦ Student Activism and Politics

Carmichael next challenges students on university campuses. He notes, in paragraph 34, that it is impossible for whites and blacks to form "human relationships" given the nature of the country's institutions. He refers to the "myths" about the United States, calling them "downright lies." He suggests that a form of social hypocrisy has become manifest in the economic insecurity of many African Americans and the unwillingness of most affluent whites to share their relative economic security with the black community. He calls on his listeners to examine "the histories that we have been told" and observes that in countries around the world students have led revolutions. He goes on to characterize American college students—essentially his audience—as "perhaps the most politically unsophisticated students in the world" and says that they, unlike many students throughout the rest of the world, have been unable or unwilling to become revolutionaries. Once again he lambastes the Democratic political establishment, including such people as Johnson, Bobby Kennedy, Wayne Morse (a U.S. senator from Oregon who, ironically, was one of only two U.S. senators who voted against the Gulf of Tonkin Resolution), James Eastland (a conservative U.S. senator from Mississippi), and George Wallace (the segregationist governor of Alabama). Carmichael states that it would be impossible to reach a common moral ground with these political figures, all of them at the time Democrats. Only the seizure of power by revolution would put these and other members of the political establishment out of business.

♦ SNCC

Carmichael then turns specifically to a discussion of SNCC. He states, in paragraph 42, that he does not want a "part of the American pie" and notes that a central purpose of SNCC was to raise questions. One of these questions was how the United States had come to be a world power and the world's wealthiest nation. He thus segues into a discussion of nonviolence at a time when he was coming to reject his initial stance—and that of SNCC—in favor of advocating violent social change. Groups like SNCC and the Quakers are not the ones who need to espouse nonviolence, he argues; rather, white supremacists in small Mississippi towns such as Cicero and Grenada need to be persuaded to act without violence toward peaceful demonstrators.

Once again Carmichael returns to the relationship between the American civil rights struggle and the international movement against postcolonialism, that is, Western domination of a postcolonial world largely inhabited by people of color. Again, he condemns the Peace Corps, as did Malcolm X, as a method of stealing nations' natural resources while teaching their citizens to read and write. He makes glancing references to hot spots in the world other than Vietnam. Among them are Santo Domingo (the capital of the Dominican Republic), South Africa (still in the grip of apartheid, or systematic segregation), and Zimbabwe (a former British colony then known as Rhodesia, which had recently declared its independence but was under white minority rule). He notes that the United States had tolerated oppression in these and other places as a way of opposing Communist expansion and aggression. He again alludes to the theft of smaller countries' natural resources through organizations like the Peace Corps, and again he urges (in paragraph 51) the white community "to have the courage to go into white communities and start organizing them." He then discusses the emergence of the organizational precursor to the Black Panther Party in Lowndes County, Alabama, as well as the fear that many white people have of anything black and the association of blackness with evil. Once more he stresses the double standard of urging nonviolence while the United States was "bombing the hell out [of] Vietnam." He sees a further irony in comments by the president and vice president (at the time, Hubert Humphrey) about looting during urban race riots, when the United States was in effect looting Vietnam. Carmichael challenges his listeners to consider whether Ho Chi Minh, the leader of Communist North Vietnam, would agree with him about America's illegal looting of Vietnam. He concludes his speech by stating that the chief issue facing African Americans was the psychological battle to define themselves and organize themselves as they saw fit. An important question related to this issue was how white activists could build new political institutions to destroy the old racist ones.

Audience

Stokely Carmichael's audience consisted of students at the University of California at Berkeley. At the time, the school was a major center of student activism; a large percentage of its students were, if not strident activists, opposed to the war in Vietnam and proponents of civil rights. Indeed, UC Berkeley was the home of the radical antiwar *Berkeley Barb*, and on October 16, 1965, the campus had been the starting point of a massive antiwar march to Oakland, one of the earliest mass protests in the antiwar movement.

Carmichael somewhat humorously attacks his audience as "the white intellectual ghetto of the West." The audience would have been primarily, though not exclusively, white. Carmichael plays off the left-wing leanings of his audience as well, with references to Albert Camus, Jean-Paul Sartre, and Frantz Fanon, all icons of the student left. His address has survived and has come to be regarded as a key document in the civil rights movement.

Impact

Although he was already questioning the direction of SNCC at the time of his UC Berkeley speech, Carmichael was then at the height of his prominence as SNCC's representative speaker both on and off college campuses. Along with King and Malcolm X, he was a leading figure in both the civil rights and the antiwar movements. All three men saw these movements as linked with issues of international human rights, yet there would be much debate over the successes and failures of the civil rights and antiwar movements as well as the extent of their broader influence. The year after the UC Berkeley speech, President Lyndon Johnson would name the first African American Supreme Court justice, Thurgood Marshall, but on April 4, 1968, King would be assassinated. Long before SNCC disbanded in the 1970s (a new branch, however, has recently been established at the University of Louisville), Carmichael would move to a more militant stance as a member of the Black Panther Party.

On October 15, 1966, two weeks before Carmichael's UC Berkeley speech, the Black Panther Party was formed in Oakland, California, by Bobby Seale and Huey P. Newton with the goal of protecting African American neighborhoods from police brutality. Carmichael's comments on the absurdity of counseling nonviolence to African Americans rather than to the white supremacists who constantly perpetrated violence against black people were indicative of the Black Panthers' stance on condoning violence in self-defense. The Panthers originally espoused black nationalism but ultimately came to reject that view and favor Socialism without race consciousness. The organization was known for its Ten-Point Program and its demand that African American men be exempted from the draft. In addition to Seale and Newton, the best known of the Panthers was Eldridge Cleaver, who edited its newspaper, raising circulation to two hundred fifty thousand. The Panthers quickly grew to national prominence, but its chapters in cities across the country became subject to extensive police harassment and federal surveillance ordered by FBI Director J. Edgar Hoover. At least two dozen members of the Panthers died at the hands of law enforcement agencies before the group faded out of existence in the 1970s.

Regardless of the fate of the Black Panther Party, the Black Power movement, in which Carmichael was a major leader, was a significant chapter in American history. On the international front, efforts to stop the Vietnam War were ongoing and growing—with the elevating attention of the public reflecting Carmichael's association of the anti–Vietnam War movement with the broader international human rights and anticolonialist movements—prompting President Johnson to announce that he would not run for reelection in 1968. Meanwhile, both the war and the antiwar movement continued to escalate until the years of conflict at last drew to a close: the shootings of unarmed antiwar protesters by National Guard troops at Kent State University in Ohio took place on May 4, 1970; the last American was helicoptered off the roof of the U.S. embassy in Saigon, South Vietnam, marking the end of the Vietnam War, on April 29, 1975.

Questions for Further Study

1. Compare Carmichael's comments on the Democratic Party in this document with Fannie Lou Hamer's Testimony at the Democratic National Convention. What were the problems that some, perhaps many, African Americans had with the Democratic Party at that time, particularly in the South?

2. Do you agree with Carmichael that many people were afraid of Black Power primarily because of the word black and that if the movement had had a different name, people might have responded to it more favorably? Why or why not?

3. Compare Stokely Carmichael's opposition to the war in Vietnam with that of Martin Luther King, Jr., in "Beyond Vietnam: A Time to Break Silence." On what grounds did the two men oppose the war? Did they have differing reasons for opposing the war?

4. Carmichael was speaking to an audience of primarily university students. In what ways did he tailor his remarks to appeal to the interests and concerns of students at that time?

5. Carmichael refers to voting as a right, and he is correct. But is there not a sense in which voting is also a privilege? Agree or disagree, and explain.

Essential Quotes

"We were never fighting for the right to integrate, we were fighting against white supremacy."

"Now, then, in order to understand white supremacy we must dismiss the fallacious notion that white people can give anybody their freedom. No man can give anybody his freedom. A man is born free."

"I knew that I could vote and that that wasn't a privilege; it was my right. Every time I tried I was shot, killed or jailed, beaten or economically deprived."

"In order for America to really live on a basic principle of human relationships, a new society must be born. Racism must die, and the economic exploitation of this country of non-white peoples around the world must also die."

Essential Quotes

"I maintain, as we have in SNCC, that the war in Vietnam is an illegal and immoral war. And the question is, What can we do to stop that war?... The only power we have is the power to say, 'Hell no!' to the draft."

"I do not want to be a part of the American pie. The American pie means raping South Africa, beating Vietnam, beating South America, raping the Philippines, raping every country you've been in. I don't want any of your blood money."

"The only time I hear people talk about nonviolence is when black people move to defend themselves against white people."

Further Reading

♦ **Books**

Asante, Molefi Kete. *100 Greatest African Americans: A Biographical Encyclopedia*. Amherst, N.Y. Prometheus Books, 2002.

Carmichael, Stokely. *Stokely Speaks: Black Power Back to Pan-Africanism*. New York, Random House, 1971.

———, and Charles V. Hamilton. *Black Power: The Politics of Liberation in America*. New York: Random House, 1967.

———, and Ekwueme Michael Thelwell. *Ready for Revolution: The Life and Struggles of Stokely Carmichael*. New York: Scribner, 2003.

Carson, Clayborne. *In Struggle: SNCC and the Black Awakening of the 1960s*. Cambridge, Mass. Harvard University Press, 1981.
Cwiklik, Robert. *Stokely Carmichael and Black Power*. Brookfield, Conn. Millbrook Press, 1993.

Johnson, Jacqueline. *Stokely Carmichael: The Story of Black Power*. Englewood Cliffs, N.J. Silver Burdett, 1990.

Marable, Manning, Nishani Frazier, and John Campbell McMillan. *Freedom on My Mind: The Columbia Documentary History of the African American Experience*. New York: Columbia University Press, 2003.

Sellers, Cleveland, and Robert Terrell. *The River of No Return: The Autobiography of a Black Militant in the Life and Death of SNCC*. New York: Morrow, 1973.

Zinn, Howard. *SNCC: The New Abolitionists*. Boston: Beacon Press, 1964.

♦ **Web Sites**

Kaufman, Michael T. "Stokely Carmichael, Rights Leader Who Coined 'Black Power,' Dies at 57." *New York Times*, November 16, 1998. http://www.interchange.org/Kwameture/nytimes111698.html

"Stokely Carmichael." Federal Bureau of Investigation Web site. http://foia.fbi.gov/foiaindex/carmichael_stokely.htm

———Keith E. Sealing

"Black Power"

Full text of speech.

Thank you very much. It's a privilege and an honor to be in the white intellectual ghetto of the West. We wanted to do a couple of things before we started. The first is that, based on the fact that SNCC, through the articulation of its program by its chairman, has been able to win elections in Georgia, Alabama, Maryland, and by our appearance here will win an election in California, in 1968 I'm going to run for President of the United States. I just can't make it, 'cause I wasn't born in the United States. That's the only thing holding me back.

We wanted to say that this is a student conference, as it should be, held on a campus, and that we're not ever to be caught up in the intellectual masturbation of the question of Black Power. That's a function of people who are advertisers that call themselves reporters. Oh, for my members and friends of the press, my self-appointed white critics, I was reading Mr. Bernard Shaw two days ago, and I came across a very important quote which I think is most apropos for you. He says, "All criticism is a[n] autobiography." Dig yourself. Okay.

The philosophers Camus and Sartre raise the question whether or not a man can condemn himself. The black existentialist philosopher who is pragmatic, Frantz Fanon, answered the question. He said that man could not. Camus and Sartre does not. We in SNCC tend to agree with Camus and Sartre that a man cannot condemn himself. Were he to condemn himself, he would then have to inflict punishment upon himself. An example would be the Nazis. Any prisoner who—any of the Nazi prisoners who admitted, after he was caught and incarcerated, that he committed crimes, that he killed all the many people that he killed, he committed suicide. The only ones who were able to stay alive were the ones who never admitted that they committed crimes against people—that is, the ones who rationalized that Jews were not human beings and deserved to be killed, or that they were only following orders.

On a more immediate scene, the officials and the population—the white population—in Neshoba County, Mississippi—that's where Philadelphia is—could not—could not condemn [Sheriff] Rainey, his deputies, and the other fourteen men that killed three human beings. They could not because they elected Mr. Rainey to do precisely what he did and that for them to condemn him will be for them to condemn themselves.

In a much larger view, SNCC says that white America cannot condemn herself. And since we are liberal, we have done it: You stand condemned. Now, a number of things that arises from that answer of how do you condemn yourselves. Seems to me that the institutions that function in this country are clearly racist, and that they're built upon racism. And the question, then, is how can black people inside of this country move? And then how can white people who say they're not a part of those institutions begin to move? And how then do we begin to clear away the obstacles that we have in this society, that make us live like human beings? How can we begin to build institutions that will allow people to relate with each other as human beings? This country has never done that, especially around the country of white or black.

Now, several people have been upset because we've said that integration was irrelevant when initiated by blacks, and that in fact it was a subterfuge, an insidious subterfuge, for the maintenance of white supremacy. Now we maintain that in the past six years or so, this country has been feeding us a "thalidomide drug of integration" and that some negroes have been walking down a dream street talking about sitting next to white people and that that does not begin to solve the problem, that when we went to Mississippi we did not go to sit next to Ross Barnett; we did not go to sit next to Jim Clark; we went to get them out of our way and that people ought to understand that; that we were never fighting for the right to integrate, we were fighting against white supremacy.

Now, then, in order to understand white supremacy we must dismiss the fallacious notion that white people can give anybody their freedom. No man can give anybody his freedom. A man is born free. You may enslave a man after he is born free, and that is in fact what this country does. It enslaves black people after they're born, so that the only acts that white people can do is to stop denying black people their freedom; that is, they must stop denying freedom. They never give it to anyone.

Document Text

Now we want to take that to its logical extension, so that we could understand, then, what its relevancy would be in terms of new civil rights bills. I maintain that every civil rights bill in this country was passed for white people, not for black people. For example, I am black. I know that. I also know that while I am black I am a human being, and therefore I have the right to go into any public place. White people didn't know that. Every time I tried to go into a place they stopped me. So some boys had to write a bill to tell that white man, "He's a human being; don't stop him." That bill was for that white man, not for me. I knew it all the time. I knew it all the time.

I knew that I could vote and that that wasn't a privilege; it was my right. Every time I tried I was shot, killed or jailed, beaten or economically deprived. So somebody had to write a bill for white people to tell them, "When a black man comes to vote, don't bother him." That bill, again, was for white people, not for black people; so that when you talk about open occupancy, I know I can live anyplace I want to live. It is white people across this country who are incapable of allowing me to live where I want to live. You need a civil rights bill, not me. I know I can live where I want to live.

So that the failures to pass a civil rights bill isn't because of Black Power, isn't because of the Student Nonviolent Coordinating Committee; it's not because of the rebellions that are occurring in the major cities. It is incapability of whites to deal with their own problems inside their own communities. That is the problem of the failure of the civil rights bill.

And so in a larger sense we must then ask, How is it that black people move? And what do we do? But the question in a greater sense is, How can white people who are the majority—and who are responsible for making democracy work—make it work? They have miserably failed to this point. They have never made democracy work, be it inside the United States, Vietnam, South Africa, Philippines, South America, Puerto Rico. Wherever American has been, she has not been able to make democracy work; so that in a larger sense, we not only condemn the country for what it's done internally, but we must condemn it for what it does externally. We see this country trying to rule the world, and someone must stand up and start articulating that this country is not God, and cannot rule the world.

Now, then, before we move on we ought to develop the white supremacy attitudes that were either conscious or subconscious thought and how they run rampant through the society today. For example, the missionaries were sent to Africa. They went with the attitude that blacks were automatically inferior. As a matter of fact, the first act the missionaries did, you know, when they got to Africa was to make us cover up our bodies, because they said it got them excited. We couldn't go bare-breasted anymore because they got excited.

Now when the missionaries came to civilize us because we were uncivilized, educate us because we were uneducated, and give us some literate studies because we were illiterate, they charged a price. The missionaries came with the Bible, and we had the land. When they left, they had the land, and we still have the Bible. And that has been the rationalization for Western civilization as it moves across the world and stealing and plundering and raping everybody in its path. Their one rationalization is that the rest of the world is uncivilized and they are in fact civilized. And they are un-civil-ized.

And that runs on today, you see, because what we have today is we have what we call "modern-day Peace Corps missionaries," and they come into our ghettos and they Head Start, Upward Lift, Bootstrap, and Upward Bound us into white society, 'cause they don't want to face the real problem which is a man is poor for one reason and one reason only: 'cause he does not have money—period. If you want to get rid of poverty, you give people money—period.

And you ought not to tell me about people who don't work, and you can't give people money without working, 'cause if that were true, you'd have to start stopping Rockefeller, Bobby Kennedy, Lyndon Baines Johnson, Lady Bird Johnson, the whole of Standard Oil, the Gulf Corp, all of them, including probably a large number of the Board of Trustees of this university. So the question, then, clearly, is not whether or not one can work; it's Who has power? Who has power to make his or her acts legitimate? That is all. And that in this country, that power is invested in the hands of white people, and they make their acts legitimate. It is now, therefore, for black people to make our acts legitimate.

Now we are now engaged in a psychological struggle in this country, and that is whether or not black people will have the right to use the words they want to use without white people giving their sanction to it; and that we maintain, whether they like it or not, we gonna use the word "Black Power"—and

Document Text

let them address themselves to that; but that we are not going to wait for white people to sanction Black Power. We're tired waiting; every time black people move in this country, they're forced to defend their position before they move. It's time that the people who are supposed to be defending their position do that. That's white people. They ought to start defending themselves as to why they have oppressed and exploited us.

Now it is clear that when this country started to move in terms of slavery, the reason for a man being picked as a slave was one reason—because of the color of his skin. If one was black one was automatically inferior, inhuman, and therefore fit for slavery; so that the question of whether or not we are individually suppressed is nonsensical, and it's a downright lie. We are oppressed as a group because we are black, not because we are lazy, not because we're apathetic, not because we're stupid, not because we smell, not because we eat watermelon and have good rhythm. We are oppressed because we are black.

And in order to get out of that oppression one must wield the group power that one has, not the individual power which this country then sets the criteria under which a man may come into it. That is what is called in this country as integration: "You do what I tell you to do and then we'll let you sit at the table with us." And that we are saying that we have to be opposed to that. We must now set up criteria and that if there's going to be any integration, it's going to be a two-way thing. If you believe in integration, you can come live in Watts. You can send your children to the ghetto schools. Let's talk about that. If you believe in integration, then we're going to start adopting us some white people to live in our neighborhood.

So it is clear that the question is not one of integration or segregation. Integration is a man's ability to want to move in there by himself. If someone wants to live in a white neighborhood and he is black, that is his choice. It should be his rights. It is not because white people will not allow him. So vice versa: If a black man wants to live in the slums, that should be his right. Black people will let him. That is the difference. And it's a difference on which this country makes a number of logical mistakes when they begin to try to criticize the program articulated by SNCC.

Now we maintain that we cannot afford to be concerned about 6 percent of the children in this country, black children, who you allow to come into white schools. We have 94 percent who still live in shacks. We are going to be concerned about those 94 percent. You ought to be concerned about them too. The question is, Are we willing to be concerned about those 94 percent? Are we willing to be concerned about the black people who will never get to Berkeley, who will never get to Harvard, and cannot get an education, so you'll never get a chance to rub shoulders with them and say, "Well, he's almost as good as we are; he's not like the others"? The question is, How can white society begin to move to see black people as human beings? I am black, therefore I am; not that I am black and I must go to college to prove myself. I am black, therefore I am. And don't deprive me of anything and say to me that you must go to college before you gain access to X, Y, and Z. It is only a rationalization for one's oppression.

The political parties in this country do not meet the needs of people on a day-to-day basis. The question is, How can we build new political institutions that will become the political expressions of people on a day-to-day basis? The question is, How can you build political institutions that will begin to meet the needs of Oakland, California? And the needs of Oakland, California, is not 1,000 policemen with submachine guns. They don't need that. They need that least of all. The question is, How can we build institutions where those people can begin to function on a day-to-day basis, where they can get decent jobs, where they can get decent houses, and where they can begin to participate in the policy and major decisions that affect their lives? That's what they need, not Gestapo troops, because this is not 1942, and if you play like Nazis, we playing back with you this time around. Get hip to that.

The question then is, How can white people move to start making the major institutions that they have in this country function the way it is supposed to function? That is the real question. And can white people move inside their own community and start tearing down racism where in fact it does exist? Where it exists. It is you who live in Cicero and stop us from living there. It is white people who stop us from moving into Grenada. It is white people who make sure that we live in the ghettos of this country. it is white institutions that do that. They must change. In order for America to really live on a basic principle of human relationships, a new society must be born. Racism must die, and the economic exploitation of this country of non-white peoples around the world must also die—must also die.

Document Text

Now there are several programs that we have in the South, most in poor white communities. We're trying to organize poor whites on a basis where they can begin to move around the question of economic exploitation and political disfranchisement. We know—we've heard the theory several times—but few people are willing to go into there. The question is, Can the white activist not try to be a Pepsi generation who comes alive in the black community, but can he be a man who's willing to move into the white community and start organizing where the organization is needed? Can he do that? The question is, Can the white society or the white activist disassociate himself with two clowns who waste time parrying with each other rather than talking about the problems that are facing people in this state? Can you dissociate yourself with those clowns and start to build new institutions that will eliminate all idiots like them.

And the question is, If we are going to do that when and where do we start, and how do we start? We maintain that we must start doing that inside the white community. Our own personal position politically is that we don't think the Democratic Party represents the needs of black people. We know it don't. And that if, in fact, white people really believe that, the question is, if they're going to move inside that structure, how are they going to organize around a concept of whiteness based on true brotherhood and based on stopping exploitation, economic exploitation, so that there will be a coalition base for black people to hook up with? You cannot form a coalition based on national sentiment. That is not a coalition. If you need a coalition to redress itself to real changes in this country, white people must start building those institutions inside the white community. And that is the real question, I think, facing the white activists today. Can they, in fact, begin to move into and tear down the institutions which have put us all in a trick bag that we've been into for the last hundred years?

I don't think that we should follow what many people say that we should fight to be leaders of tomorrow. Frederick Douglass said that the youth should fight to be leaders today. And God knows we need to be leaders today, 'cause the men who run this country are sick, are sick. So that can we on a larger sense begin now, today, to start building those institutions and to fight to articulate our position, to fight to be able to control our universities—we need to be able to do that—and to fight to control the basic institutions which perpetuate racism by destroying them and building new ones? That's the real question that faces us today, and it is a dilemma because most of us do not know how to work, and that the excuse that most white activists find is to run into the black community.

Now we maintain that we cannot have white people working in the black community, and we mean it on a psychological ground. The fact is that all black people often question whether or not they are equal to whites, because every time they start to do something, white people are around showing them how to do it. If we are going to eliminate that for the generation that comes after us, then black people must be seen in positions of power, doing and articulating for themselves, for themselves.

That is not to say that one is a reverse racist; it is to say that one is moving in a healthy ground; it is to say what the philosopher Sartre says: One is becoming an "antiracist racist." And this country can't understand that. Maybe it's because it's all caught up in racism. But I think what you have in SNCC is an anti-racist racism. We are against racists. Now if everybody who is white see themself [sic] as a racist and then see us against him, they're speaking from their own guilt position, not ours, not ours.

Now then, the question is, How can we move to begin to change what's going on in this country. I maintain, as we have in SNCC, that the war in Vietnam is an illegal and immoral war. And the question is, What can we do to stop that war? What can we do to stop the people who, in the name of our country, are killing babies, women, and children? What can we do to stop that? And I maintain that we do not have the power in our hands to change that institution, to begin to recreate it, so that they learn to leave the Vietnamese people alone, and that the only power we have is the power to say, "Hell no!" to the draft.

We have to say to ourselves that there is a higher law than the law of a racist named McNamara. There is a higher law than the law of a fool named Rusk. And there's a higher law than the law of a buffoon named Johnson. It's the law of each of us. It's the law of each of us. It is the law of each of us saying that we will not allow them to make us hired killers. We will stand pat. We will not kill anybody that they say kill. And if we decide to kill, we're going to decide who we going to kill. And this country will only be able to stop the war in Vietnam when the young men who are made to fight it begin to say, "Hell, no, we ain't going."

Document Text

Now then, there's a failure because the Peace Movement has been unable to get off the college campuses where everybody has a 2S and not going to get drafted anyway. And the question is, How can you move out of that into the white ghettos of this country and begin to articulate a position for those white students who do not want to go. We cannot do that. It is something, sometimes ironic that many of the peace groups [are] beginning to call us violent and say they can no longer support us, and we are in fact the most militant organization [for] peace or civil rights or human rights against the war in Vietnam in this country today. There isn't one organization that has begun to meet our stance on the war in Vietnam, 'cause we not only say we are against the war in Vietnam; we are against the draft. We are against the draft. No man has the right to take a man for two years and train him to be a killer. A man should decide what he wants to do with his life.

So the question then is it becomes crystal clear for black people because we can easily say that anyone fighting in the war in Vietnam is nothing but a black mercenary, and that's all he is. Any time a black man leaves the country where he can't vote to supposedly deliver the vote for somebody else, he's a black mercenary. Any time a black man leaves this country, gets shot in Vietnam on foreign ground, and returns home and you won't give him a burial in his own homeland, he's a black mercenary, a black mercenary.

And that even if I were to believe the lies of Johnson, if I were to believe his lies that we're fighting to give democracy to the people in Vietnam, as a black man living in this country I wouldn't fight to give this to anybody. I wouldn't give it to anybody. So that we have to use our bodies and our minds in the only way that we see fit. We must begin like the philosopher Camus to come alive by saying "No!" That is the only act in which we begin to come alive, and we have to say "No!" to many, many things in this country.

This country is a nation of thieves. It has stole everything it has, beginning with black people, beginning with black people. And that the question is, How can we move to start changing this country from what it is—a nation of thieves. This country cannot justify any longer its existence. We have become the policeman of the world. The marines are at our disposal to always bring democracy, and if the Vietnamese don't want democracy, well dammit, "We'll just wipe them the hell out, 'cause they don't deserve to live if they won't have our way of life."

There is then in a larger sense, What do you do on your university campus? Do you raise questions about the hundred black students who were kicked off campus a couple of weeks ago? Eight hundred? Eight hundred? And how does that question begin to move? Do you begin to relate to people outside of the ivory tower and university wall? Do you think you're capable of building those human relationships, as the country now stands? You're fooling yourself. It is impossible for white and black people to talk about building a relationship based on humanity when the country is the way it is, when the institutions are clearly against us.

We have taken all the myths of this country and we've found them to be nothing but downright lies. This country told us that if we worked hard we would succeed, and if that were true we would own this country lock, stock, and barrel—lock, stock, and barrel—lock, stock, and barrel. It is we who have picked the cotton for nothing. It is we who are the maids in the kitchens of liberal white people. It is we who are the janitors, the porters, the elevator men; we who sweep up your college floors. Yes, it is we who are the hardest workers and the lowest paid, and the lowest paid.

And that it is nonsensical for people to start talking about human relationships until they're willing to build new institutions. Black people are economically insecure. White liberals are economically secure. Can you begin to build an economic coalition? Are the liberals willing to share their salaries with the economically insecure black people they so much love? Then if you're not, are you willing to start building new institutions that will provide economic security for black people? That's the question we want to deal with. That's the question we want to deal with.

We have to seriously examine the histories that we have been told. But we have something more to do than that. American students are perhaps the most politically unsophisticated students in the world. Across every country in this world, while we were growing up, students were leading the major revolutions of their countries. We have not been able to do that. They have been politically aware of their existence. In South America our neighbors down below the border have one every 24 hours just to remind us that they're politically aware.

And we have been unable to grasp it because we've always moved in the field of morality and love while people have been politically jiving with our lives. And the question is, How do we now move politically and stop trying to move morally? You can't move morally against a man like Brown and Reagan. You've got to move politically to put them out of business. You've got to move politically.

You can't move morally against Lyndon Baines Johnson because he is an immoral man. He doesn't know what it's all about. So you've got to move politically. You've got to move politically. And that we have to begin to develop a political sophistication—which is not to be a parrot: "The two-party system is the best party in the world." There is a difference between being a parrot and being politically sophisticated.

We have to raise questions about whether or not we do need new types of political institutions in this country, and we in SNCC maintain that we need them now. We need new political institutions in this country. Any time Lyndon Baines Johnson can head a Party which has in it Bobby Kennedy, Wayne Morse, Eastland, Wallace, and all those other supposed-to-be-liberal cats, there's something wrong with that Party. They're moving politically, not morally. And that if that party refuses to seat black people from Mississippi and goes ahead and seats racists like Eastland and his clique, it is clear to me that they're moving politically, and that one cannot begin to talk morality to people like that.

We must begin to think politically and see if we can have the power to impose and keep the moral values that we hold high. We must question the values of this society, and I maintain that black people are the best people to do that because we have been excluded from that society. And the question is, we ought to think whether or not we want to become a part of that society. That's what we want to do.

And that that is precisely what it seems to me that the Student Nonviolent Coordinating Committee is doing. We are raising questions about this country. I do not want to be a part of the American pie. The American pie means raping South Africa, beating Vietnam, beating South America, raping the Philippines, raping every country you've been in. I don't want any of your blood money. I don't want it—don't want to be part of that system. And the question is, How do we raise those questions? How do we begin to raise them?

We have grown up and we are the generation that has found this country to be a world power, that has found this country to be the wealthiest country in the world. We must question how she got her wealth?

That's what we're questioning, and whether or not we want this country to continue being the wealthiest country in the world at the price of raping everybody else across the world. That's what we must begin to question. And that because black people are saying we do not now want to become a part of you, we are called reverse racists. Ain't that a gas?

Now, then, we want to touch on nonviolence because we see that again as the failure of white society to make nonviolence work. I was always surprised at Quakers who came to Alabama and counseled me to be nonviolent, but didn't have the guts to start talking to James Clark to be nonviolent. That is where nonviolence needs to be preached—to Jim Clark, not to black people. They have already been nonviolent too many years. The question is, Can white people conduct their nonviolent schools in Cicero where they belong to be conducted, not among black people in Mississippi. Can they conduct it among the white people in Grenada?

Six-foot-two men who kick little black children—can you conduct nonviolent schools there? That is the question that we must raise, not that you conduct nonviolence among black people. Can you name me one black man today who's killed anybody white and is still alive? Even after rebellion, when some black brothers throw some bricks and bottles, ten thousand of them has to pay the crime, 'cause when the white policeman comes in, anybody who's black is arrested, "'cause we all look alike."

So that we have to raise those questions. We, the youth of this country, must begin to raise those questions. And we must begin to move to build new institutions that's going to speak to the needs of people who need it. We are going to have to speak to change the foreign policy of this country. One of the problems with the peace movement is that it's just too caught up in Vietnam, and that if we pulled out the troops from Vietnam this week, next week you'd have to get another peace movement for Santo Domingo. And the question is, How do you begin to articulate the need to change the foreign policy of this country—a policy that is decided upon race, a policy on which decisions are made upon getting economic wealth at any price, at any price.

Now we articulate that we therefore have to hook up with black people around the world; and that that hookup is not only psychological, but becomes very real. If South America today were to rebel, and black people were to shoot the hell out of all the white people there—as they should, as they should—then Standard Oil would crumble tomorrow. If South Africa were to go today, Chase Manhattan Bank would crumble tomorrow. If Zimbabwe, which is called Rhodesia by white people, were to go tomorrow, General Electric would cave in on the East Coast. The question is, How do we stop those institutions that are so willing to fight against "Communist aggression" but closes their eyes to racist oppression? That is the question that you raise. Can this country do that?

Now, many people talk about pulling out of Vietnam. What will happen? If we pull out of Vietnam, there will be one less aggressor in there—we won't be there, we won't be there. And so the question is, How do we articulate those positions? And we cannot begin to articulate them from the same assumptions that the people in the country speak, 'cause they speak from different assumptions than I assume what the youth in this country are talking about.

That we're not talking about a policy or aid or sending Peace Corps people in to teach people how to read and write and build houses while we steal their raw materials from them. Is that what we're talking about? 'Cause that's all we do. What underdeveloped countries need—information on how to become industrialized, so they can keep their raw materials where they have it, produce them and sell it to this country for the price it's supposed to pay; not that we produce it and sell it back to them for a profit and keep sending our modern day missionaries in, calling them the sons of Kennedy. And that if the youth are going to participate in that program, how do you raise those questions where you begin to control that Peace Corps program? How do you begin to raise them?

How do we raise the questions of poverty? The assumptions of this country is that if someone is poor, they are poor because of their own individual blight, or they weren't born on the right side of town; they had too many children; they went in the army too early; or their father was a drunk, or they didn't care about school, or they made a mistake. That's a lot of nonsense. Poverty is well calculated in this country. It is well calculated, and the reason why the poverty program won't work is because the calculators of poverty are administering it. That's why it won't work.

So how can we, as the youth in the country, move to start tearing those things down? We must move into the white community. We are in the black community. We have developed a movement in the black community. The challenge is that the white activist has failed miserably to develop the movement inside of his community. And the question is, Can we find white people who are going to have the courage to go into white communities and start organizing them? Can we find them? Are they here and are they willing to do that? Those are the questions that we must raise for the white activist.

And we're never going to get caught up in questions about power. This country knows what power is. It knows it very well. And it knows what Black Power is 'cause it deprived black people of it for 400 years. So it knows what Black Power is. That the question of, Why do black people—Why do white people in this country associate Black Power with violence? And the question is because of their own inability to deal with "blackness." If we had said "Negro power" nobody would get scared. Everybody would support it. Or if we said power for colored people, everybody'd be for that, but it is the word "black"—it is the word "black" that bothers people in this country, and that's their problem, not mine—their problem, their problem.

Now there's one modern day lie that we want to attack and then move on very quickly and that is the lie that says anything all black is bad. Now, you're all a college university crowd. You've taken your basic logic course. You know about a major premise and minor premise. So people have been telling me anything all black is bad. Let's make that our major premise.

Major premise: Anything all black is bad.

Minor premise or particular premise: I am all black.

Therefore …

I'm never going to be put in that trick bag; I am all black and I'm all good, dig it. Anything all black is not necessarily bad. Anything all black is only bad when you use force to keep whites out. Now that's what white people have done in this country, and they're projecting their same fears and guilt on us, and we won't have it, we won't have it. Let them handle their own fears and their own guilt. Let them find their own psychologists. We refuse to be the therapy for white society any longer. We have gone mad trying to do it. We have gone stark raving mad trying to do it.

I look at Dr. King on television every single day, and I say to myself: "Now there is a man who's desperately needed in this country. There is a man full of love. There is a man full of mercy. There is a man full of compassion." But every time I see Lyndon on television, I said, "Martin, baby, you got a long way to go."

So that the question stands as to what we are willing to do, how we are willing to say "No" to withdraw from that system and begin within our community to start to function and to build new institutions that will speak to our needs. In Lowndes County, we developed something called the Lowndes County Freedom Organization. It is a political party. The Alabama law says that if you have a Party you must have an emblem. We chose for the emblem a black panther, a beautiful black animal which symbolizes the strength and dignity of black people, an animal that never strikes back until he's back so far into the wall, he's got nothing to do but spring out. Yeah. And when he springs he does not stop.

Now there is a Party in Alabama called the Alabama Democratic Party. It is all white. It has as its emblem a white rooster and the words "white supremacy for the right." Now the gentlemen of the Press, because they're advertisers, and because most of them are white, and because they're produced by that white institution, never called the Lowndes County Freedom Organization by its name, but rather they call it the Black Panther Party. Our question is, Why don't they call the Alabama Democratic Party the "White Cock Party"? (It's fair to us.) It is clear to me that that just points out America's problem with sex and color, not our problem, not our problem. And it is now white America that is going to deal with those problems of sex and color.

If we were to be real and to be honest, we would have to admit that most people in this country see things black and white. We have to do that. All of us do. We live in a country that's geared that way. White people would have to admit that they are afraid to go into a black ghetto at night. They are afraid. That's a fact. They're afraid because they'd be "beat up," "lynched," "looted," "cut up," et cetera, et cetera. It happens to black people inside the ghetto every day, incidentally, and white people are afraid of that. So you get a man to do it for you—a policeman. And now you figure his mentality, when he's afraid of black people. The first time a black man jumps, that white man going to shoot him. He's going to shoot him. So police brutality is going to exist on that level because of the incapability of that white man to see black people come together and to live in the conditions. This country is too hypocritical and that we cannot adjust ourselves to its hypocrisy.

The only time I hear people talk about nonviolence is when black people move to defend themselves against white people. Black people cut themselves every night in the ghetto. Don't anybody talk about nonviolence. Lyndon Baines Johnson is busy bombing the hell of out Vietnam. Don't nobody talk about nonviolence. White people beat up black people every day. Don't nobody talk about nonviolence. But as soon as black people start to move, the double standard comes into being.

You can't defend yourself. That's what you're saying, 'cause you show me a man who would advocate aggressive violence that would be able to live in this country. Show him to me. The double standards again come into itself. Isn't it ludicrous and hypocritical for the political chameleon who calls himself a Vice President in this country to stand up before this country and say, "Looting never got anybody anywhere"? Isn't it hypocritical for Lyndon to talk about looting, that you can't accomplish anything by looting and you must accomplish it by the legal ways? What does he know about legality? Ask Ho Chi Minh, he'll tell you.

So that in conclusion we want to say that number one, it is clear to me that we have to wage a psychological battle on the right for black people to define their own terms, define themselves as they see fit, and organize themselves as they see it. Now the question is, How is the white community going to begin to allow for that organizing, because once they start to do that, they will also allow for the organizing that they want to do inside their community. It doesn't make a difference, 'cause we're going to organize our way anyway. We're going to do it. The question is, How are we going to facilitate those matters, whether it's going to be done with a thousand policemen with submachine guns, or whether or not it's going to be done in a context where it is allowed to be done by white people warding off those policemen. That is the question.

And the question is, How are white people who call themselves activists ready to start move into the white communities on two counts: on building new political institutions to destroy the old ones that we have? And to move around the concept of white youth refusing to go into the army? So that we can start, then, to build a new world. It is ironic to talk about civilization in this country. This country is

Document Text

uncivilized. It needs to be civilized. It needs to be civilized.

And that we must begin to raise those questions of civilization: What it is? And who do it? And so we must urge you to fight now to be the leaders of today, not tomorrow. We've got to be the leaders of today. This country is a nation of thieves. It stands on the brink of becoming a nation of murderers. We must stop it. We must stop it. We must stop it. We must stop it.

And then, therefore, in a larger sense there's the question of black people. We are on the move for our liberation. We have been tired of trying to prove things to white people. We are tired of trying to explain to white people that we're not going to hurt them. We are concerned with getting the things we want, the things that we have to have to be able to function. The question is, Can white people allow for that in this country? The question is, Will white people overcome their racism and allow for that to happen in this country? If that does not happen, brothers and sisters, we have no choice but to say very clearly, "Move over, or we're going to move on over you."

Thank you.

Glossary

Berkeley: the University of California at Berkeley, the flagship campus of the University of California system

Bernard Shaw: George Bernard Shaw, an Irish playwright of the late nineteenth and early twentieth centuries and a Socialist

Bobby Kennedy: Robert Kennedy, the U.S. attorney general and brother of President John F. Kennedy

Brown: Governor Edmund G. "Pat" Brown of California

Camus: Albert Camus, a French intellectual whose name is connected with the absurdist movement

Dr. King: Martin Luther King, Jr.

Eastland: James Eastland, a conservative U.S. senator from Mississippi

Frantz Fanon: a writer, philosopher, and revolutionary who was born in Martinique and whose books were key documents in the anticolonial movement

Frederick Douglass: the preeminent abolitionist during the nineteenth century

Gestapo: the official secret police of Nazi Germany

Head Start, Upward Lift, Bootstrap, and Upward Bound: all programs designed to provide educational and economic opportunities for the poor

Ho Chi Minh: the leader of Communist North Vietnam

Jim Clark: the sheriff of Dallas County, Alabama, who authorized the violent assaults and arrests of activists during the Selma-to-Montgomery march of 1965

Lady Bird Johnson: the wife of President Lyndon Johnson

Lyndon Baines Johnson: the U.S. president from 1963 to 1969

McNamara: Robert McNamara, U.S. secretary of defense

Peace Corps: an international volunteer program run by the U.S. government

Reagan: Ronald Reagan, who would become governor of California in 1967 and, later, president of the United States

Glossary

Rockefeller: Nelson Rockefeller, the governor of New York and heir to the Standard Oil fortune

Ross Barnett: an earlier segregationist governor of Mississippi

Rusk: Dean Rusk, the U.S. secretary of state under Presidents John Kennedy and Lyndon Johnson

Santo Domingo: the capital of the Dominican Republic

Sartre: Jean-Paul Sartre, a French existentialist and Communist who opposed French rule in Algeria

Sheriff Rainey: Lawrence Rainey, sheriff of Neshoba County, Mississippi, referring to the murder in 1964 of three civil rights workers through the collusion of local law enforcement agencies and the Ku Klux Klan

SNCC: the Student Nonviolent Coordinating Committee, a civil rights organization

thalidomide: a drug given to pregnant women that turned out to cause severe birth defects

2S: II-S, a draft classification that deferred military service for students

Wallace: George Wallace, the segregationist governor of Alabama

Wayne Morse: a U.S. senator from Oregon who was one of only two U.S. senators to vote against the Gulf of Tonkin Resolution, deepening U.S. involvement in Vietnam

The first page of the Voting Rights Act of 1965. By 89th United States Congress (http://www.ourdocuments.gov) [Public domain], via Wikimedia Commons

South Carolina v. Katzenbach

"The Voting Rights Act was designed by Congress to banish the blight of racial discrimination in voting, which has infected the electoral process in parts of our country for nearly a century...."

Overview

The case of *South Carolina v. Katzenbach* constituted the first time the U.S. Supreme Court ruled on the Voting Rights Act of 1965. Passed in March 1965, the Voting Rights Act gave the federal government sweeping new powers to combat the pervasive disenfranchisement of African Americans perpetuated by southern government officials. Many across the South denied Congress's power to pass such sweeping legislation. They argued that Congress had overstepped the bounds of the Fifth and Fifteenth Amendments to the U.S. Constitution. They also objected to the act's wider social and political objectives as a piece of civil rights legislation.

In South Carolina, the state attorney general, Daniel R. McCleod, quickly filed a bill of complaint directly with the Supreme Court attacking the constitutionality of the act and asking for an injunction against enforcement by the attorney general of the United States, Nicholas Katzenbach. McCleod challenged the Voting Rights Act as an unconstitutional encroachment on states' rights, as a violation of the principle of equality between the states, and as an illegal bill of attainder (a legislative punishment enforced without due process of law). More specifically, the complaint directly challenged the "triggering mechanism" in Section 4 of the act, which brought South Carolina under the act's provisions, and argued that Section 5's preclearance provisions (under which any changes to South Carolina's election laws or procedures had to be cleared in advance by the Department of Justice) exceeded Congress's constitutional powers.

South Carolina was joined in its attack on the Voting Rights Act by five other southern states: Georgia, Alabama, Louisiana, Virginia, and Mississippi. Twenty states, among them Illinois, Massachusetts, and California, filed amicus curiae (friend of the court) briefs in support of the act's provisions and powers. As a consequence, the case of *South Carolina v. Katzenbach* took on an even wider significance than normal in a state challenge to a new federal law. At issue in this case was the constitutional legitimacy not only of the Voting Rights Act but, indeed, of the entire federal effort to defend, uphold, and enhance minority civil rights.

Context

In the years following the Civil War, hope dawned for the nation's millions of African Americans that freedom would bring with it a full entry into American public life—an entry best represented by the right to vote. Most Americans understood the Thirteenth Amendment's requirement (1865) that "neither slavery nor involuntary servitude ... shall exist within the United States" to mean that newly freed blacks would acquire all aspects of freedom, including the right to vote. The Fourteenth Amendment's promise (1868) of equal protection and its defense of the "privileges or immunities of citizens of the United States" added support to newly freed African Americans' claims to the right to vote. Finally the Fifteenth Amendment (1870) declared: "The right of citizens of the United States to vote shall not be denied or abridged by the United States or by any State on account of race, color, or previous condition of servitude." It seemed that the path to the polls would be a clear and simple one for African Americans.

Events proved otherwise. Most white southerners disliked the federally mandated program of postwar "Reconstruction" and opposed the Republican- and black-led governments organized under this process. As early as 1866, white terrorist organizations—the Ku Klux Klan being the best known—instituted waves of race-based violence and terror that soon spread across the South. In the worst instances, white mobs attacked entire groups of blacks, terrorizing most and killing many. Bad economic times, well-publicized political scandals, and heavy campaigning by Democrats among the region's white voters added to the Republicans' woes. The chilling effects of violence on black voting, not to mention election fraud by Democratic-leaning local white officials, led by the mid-1870s to the rise of Democratic "redeemer" governments opposed to all black civil and political rights.

Once in power, these white Democratic officials began a slow, steady, and ultimately successful campaign of race-based disenfranchisement. Among the techniques used to exclude black voters were the use of unfairly applied literacy or understanding tests in which voters had to read, understand, or interpret any section of the state constitution to the satisfaction of a white (and usually hostile) election official; complicated registration requirements that excluded minority voters on technical grounds; and financial barriers such as poll taxes. Intimidation and threats of violence were also effective means of keeping southern blacks from the polls. One of the simplest ways of undermining the black vote involved setting up polling places in areas inconvenient for blacks. Many polling places, for instance, were placed at distant locations or in the middle of white sections of the town or county. Similarly, some polls were established in businesses owned by known opponents of African American voting. Finally, in an effort to exclude all possibility that southern blacks could have a voice in government through the election process, state legislatures across the South implemented rules prohibiting blacks from voting in the politically dominant Democratic Party primaries. Since the Democratic candidate almost always won in the general election, this exclusion denied southern blacks a chance to participate in the one election that mattered most.

The results of such efforts were immediate and drastic. By 1896 black voter participation in Mississippi had declined to fewer than nine thousand out of a potential one hundred forty-seven thousand voting-age blacks. In Louisiana registered black voting had declined by 99 percent. Alabama had only three thousand registered black voters in 1902. Texas saw black voting decline to a mere five thousand votes by 1906. In Georgia, only 4 percent of black males were registered to vote as of 1910. In fact, across the entire region voter turnout fell from a high of 85 percent of all voters during Reconstruction to less than 50 percent for whites and single-digit percentages for blacks by the early twentieth century. Mid-twentieth-century attacks on a number of disenfranchising techniques in the federal courts resulted only in the revision and modification of these methods, not their abandonment. As late as 1940, only 3 percent of voting-age southern blacks were registered to vote. Fewer still were actually able to cast a meaningful ballot.

In the 1950s this situation began to change. By 1956, 25 percent of voting-age blacks were registered to vote; by 1964 this number had increased to 43. 3 percent across the South. Raw numbers can be deceiving, however. Most registered black voters lived in the border states or in Florida; in the Deep South, where most blacks lived, African American voter registration stood at only 22. 5 percent as late as 1964, with Mississippi setting the lowest standard at 6. 7 percent (itself an increase from a rate of 1. 98 percent a mere two years earlier). Worse yet, the application of such vote-dilution techniques as voting-list purges, at-large elections, and full-slate and majority-vote requirements—not to mention the ever-present threat of economic reprisals and physical violence against any black trying to vote—meant that, even in those areas where blacks could vote, actual African American voting rates were much lower.

The Voting Rights Act of 1965 was designed to directly combat this race-specific, regionally based disenfranchisement. Previous federal efforts to end southern black disenfranchisement in the courts had been ineffectual and even counterproductive. Civil rights legislation passed in 1957, 1960, and 1964 had expanded the federal government's role in minority vote protection, but with few concrete results to show for the effort. The problem lay with the enforcement tools available to the federal courts. Litigation as an enforcement mechanism was a slow and unwieldy process. It offered recalcitrant southern election officials (not to mention segregationist federal judges) numerous opportunities for delay and obstructionism. Every time the courts overturned laws aimed at disenfranchising southern black voters, southern election officials simply turned to new or different techniques to achieve the same discriminatory end—techniques not covered by the courts' orders and thus still permissible until invalidated by another court proceeding. In consequence, opponents of black vote denial were forced to initiate case after case in their efforts to gain the vote—with very little practical gain.

Expressly designed to attack the sources of delay in the case-by-case litigation approach, the nineteen sections of the Voting Rights Act imposed a completely new enforcement methodology for voting-rights violations. Not only did the act outlaw vote denial based on race or color in Section 2, it also gave both the executive branch and the federal courts a powerful new set of approaches for voting-rights enforcement. Among them were the power to appoint federal examiners and observers in whatever numbers the president felt necessary, prohibitions on literacy tests and poll taxes, and rules outlawing any action "under color of the law" that prevented qualified voters from voting or having their votes fairly counted. Most important of all, the act froze all southern election laws in place as of November 1, 1964. If local or state officials wanted to change an election law or procedure, they were required first to receive clearance from the Justice Department or the federal courts before acting. In this way, the southern strategy of using ever-shifting techniques of voter denial to derail election reforms was effectively ended. These enforcement provisions—along with the more general issue of congressional authority to adopt such extreme and powerful provisions—were what South Carolina challenged in *South Carolina v. Katzenbach*.

About the Author

The majority opinion in *South Carolina v. Katzenbach* was written by Chief Justice Earl Warren. He was joined in this majority by seven of his colleagues. One justice, Hugo L. Black, concurred as to the bulk of the opinion but dissented as to those sections upholding the constitutionality of Section 5 of the Voting Rights Act.

Warren had been appointed as chief justice in 1953 by President Dwight D. Eisenhower. A former state attorney general and governor of California, Warren had the reputation of being a fundamentally conservative, yet bipartisan Republican politician. Once on the Court, however, Warren swung quickly to the left on such key civil rights and liberties issues as school desegregation, the rights of the accused, and freedom of religion. He was joined in this shift by a majority of his brethren on the bench. Hence, by the time he wrote the opinion in *South Carolina v. Katzenbach*, Warren (who would retire in 1969) and the Court were approaching the end of a period of sweeping judicial activity that had transformed the constitutional status of individual civil rights and liberties in America.

The dissenting justice, Hugo Black, served on the Supreme Court for thirty-four years (1937–1971). Appointed to the Court by President Franklin D. Roosevelt, Black's judicial philosophy centered on a close textual reading of the U.S. Constitution, a reading that stressed the idea that the liberties guaranteed in the Bill of Rights were "incorporated" on the states by the Fourteenth Amendment. While this belief led Black to be a leader in the Warren Court's expansion of civil liberties and rights in most instances, in certain cases, such as *Katzenbach*, it pushed Black to oppose legislation that he felt exceeded the textual reach of the Constitution. As Black explained in his *Katzenbach* dissent, he saw "no reason to read into the Constitution meanings it did not have when it was adopted and which have not been put into it since."

Explanation and Analysis of the Document

The central question in *South Carolina v. Katzenbach* was the power of Congress to pass the Voting Rights Act of 1965, with all of its sweeping and transformative powers—powers that the federal government had never before claimed or applied in the realm of voting rights. In its complaint, South Carolina had attacked the Voting Rights Act as an unconstitutional encroachment on "an area reserved to the States by the Constitution," as a violation of the principle of equality between the states, and as an illegal bill of attainder (a legislative punishment enforced without due process of law). More specifically, the complaint directly challenged the "triggering mechanism" in Section 4 that brought South Carolina under the act's provisions, objected to that section's "temporary suspension of a State's voting tests or devices," and argued that Section 5's preclearance provisions exceeded Congress's constitutional powers. Also receiving special notice was the act's use of examiners to supervise state electoral procedures.

The federal government had responded to these charges by noting the long history of race-based discrimination as practiced in South Carolina and other southern states, stressing the pressing need for reform, and showing the failure of the case-by-case litigation approach in combating voting discrimination under the Civil Rights Acts of 1957, 1960, and 1964. More generally, the government lawyers stressed Congress's supreme authority to act in these matters under its inherent legislative powers.

◆ **"Mr. Chief Justice Warren Delivered the Opinion of the Court"**

In responding to these arguments, Chief Justice Warren began the Court's opinion with the recognition that any ruling as to "the constitutional propriety of the Voting Rights Act of 1965" had to be "judged with reference to the historical experience which it reflected." That context was the extensive record of race-based discrimination found throughout the South. The Court identified "an insidious and pervasive evil which had been perpetuated in certain parts of our country through unremitting and ingenious defiance of the Constitution." Noting also the history of "unsuccessful remedies," it accepted the need for "sterner and more elaborate measures in order to satisfy the clear commands of the Fifteenth Amendment."

The Voting Rights Act of 1965 thus reflected "Congress' firm intention to rid the country of racial discrimination in voting." The crucial question before the Court, therefore, was the constitutional legitimacy of this "complex scheme of stringent remedies aimed at areas where voting discrimination has been most flagrant." Did Congress have the power to pass such laws? And assuming that Congress had such broad powers, were such new and innovative enforcement techniques as preclearance a legitimate application of Congress's powers under the Fifteenth Amendment? Moreover, did these new powers come into conflict with other fundamental constitutional rights and doctrines, such as that of "the equality of States," "due process," and the ban on federal courts issuing "advisory opinions"?

In terms of the general question of Congress's power to legislate, the Court's answer was short and direct: In light of the many years of southern obstruction, Congress had every right to decide "to shift the advantage of time and inertia from the perpetrators of the evil to its victims." The Fifteenth Amendment, combined with established constitutional interpretation, clearly authorized Congress to "effectuate the prohibition of racial discrimination in voting." Besides, noted Warren, the act's provisions strictly applied to those states where discrimination was most prevalent, which clearly constituted "a permissible method of dealing with the problem."

But what of the specific provisions of the act? The Court again came down fully in support of Congress's powers to act as it saw fit. In the case of the coverage formula, which limited the scope of the act to certain southern states and counties, the Court held that the formula was relevant to the specific problem. That was enough to justify congressional intervention under the "express powers under the Fifteenth Amendment."

The Court endorsed the act's temporary suspension of existing voting qualifications on the ground that Congress "knew that continuance of the tests and devices in use ..., no matter how fairly administered in the future, would freeze the effect of past discrimination in favor of unqualified white registrants." Given this fact, Congress's determination that such tests were in violation of the Fifteenth Amendment was "a legitimate response to the problem, for which there is ample precedent under other constitutional provisions."

Perhaps most important, Warren found that the imposition of a preclearance requirement for any changes to existing or new election laws and procedures was constitutionally permissible. "This may have been an uncommon exercise of congressional power," explained Warren, "but the Court has recognized that exceptional conditions can justify legislative measures not otherwise appropriate." For years southern states had avoided the intent of the law by "the extraordinary stratagem" of devising ad hoc regulations to frustrate "adverse federal court decrees." Congress knew this and properly acted to put a stop to future evasions of the law. Given such "unique circumstances," Warren concluded, "Congress responded in a permissibly decisive manner."

In conclusion, Warren noted how "after enduring nearly a century of widespread resistance to the Fifteenth Amendment, Congress has marshalled an array of potent weapons against the evil, with authority in the Attorney General to employ them effectively." This was a good and necessary thing, one that should be applauded. "We here hold that the portions of the Voting Rights Act properly before us are a valid means for carrying out the commands of the Fifteenth Amendment." The opinion concludes by expressing hope for true equality of democratic participation for all: "We may finally look forward to the day when truly 'the right of citizens of the United States to vote shall not be denied or abridged by the United States or by any State on account of race, color, or previous condition of servitude.'"

♦ "Mr. Justice Black, Concurring and Dissenting"

Only one justice dissented from this opinion, and he did so only in response to a single aspect of the ruling. Justice Hugo Black agreed with "substantially all of the Court's opinion sustaining the power of Congress under §2 of the Fifteenth Amendment." His only concern was with Section 5 and preclearance.

First, on purely technical ground, Black argued that "the Constitution gives federal courts jurisdiction over cases and controversies only." Such was not the case with preclearance. Black found it hard "to believe that a justiciable controversy can arise in the constitutional sense from a desire by the United States Government or some of its officials to determine in advance what legislative provisions a State may enact or what constitutional amendments it may adopt." This was regulation, not litigation.

Second, and much more important, Section 5 distorted "our constitutional structure of government as to render any distinction drawn in the Constitution between state and federal power almost meaningless." The federal government was a limited government under a constitution that reserved all powers not explicitly granted to the federal government to the states or the people. Such was not the case with Section 5. Black feared that forcing local laws to be preapproved in Washington could "create the impression that the State or States treated in this way are little more than conquered provinces."

Despite Justice Black's worries and concerns, *South Carolina v. Katzenbach* was a sweeping endorsement of the Voting Rights Act of 1965. Notwithstanding that act's innovative—and to some, constitutionally radical—enforcement approaches, the justices concluded that the scope of the problem demanded extreme action and thus gave the act their full support.

Audience

There is an art to writing a Supreme Court opinion. Judicial opinions have a standard structure and purpose that dictate what goes into an opinion—and what gets left out. Opinions are written to achieve very specific goals. They have to lay out in detail the unique situation underlying the legal dispute; they have to set out the key legal and constitutional questions raised by the case and then provide answers to these questions; and, finally, they have to explain why the justices ruled as they did and make clear the scope and extent of their rulings. In a very real sense, a justice writing a Supreme Court opinion is responsible to several constituencies. There are the litigants in the case, whose primary focus is winning and losing. Then there are the judges from whence the case originated, who need to be informed of their errors. Lower court judges hearing similar cases make up a third group, in need of a clear precedent regarding the meaning of a law or constitutional point. Finally, there is the wider community of Americans, for whom a Supreme

Court ruling can act as an important means of education on the workings of our constitutional system of government.

Like most Supreme Court decisions, *South Carolina v. Katzenbach* was written with all three groups in mind. It represented a clear ruling on the specific charges and challenges brought by South Carolina and its fellow southern states. Similarly, it provided a strong set of guidelines to other judges on the permissible scope of the Voting Rights Act of 1965. Finally, the opinion made clear the Court's ongoing commitment to civil rights and the campaign to open the ballot box to all Americans, no matter their race or ethnicity. Discrimination of the sort attacked by the Voting Rights Act was not permissible in modern-day America. Any and all efforts to retain such discrimination—even a remnant—would have to go.

Impact

As with most landmark civil rights opinions, the Supreme Court's ruling in *South Carolina v. Katzenbach* is an important document. As a statement of intent by the Supreme Court that race-based disenfranchisement was not constitutionally permissible, the opinion made clear the Court's willingness to act (or, alternatively, to accept action on the part of the other branches of the federal government) in defense of African American voting rights. One cannot overstate the importance that this willingness of the Court to act had in the ongoing civil rights process in America. Although the Voting Rights Act shifted much of the enforcement from the courts to the executive branch of the federal government, the Justice Department (not to mention oppressed minority groups) was still going to need the willing assistance of the federal courts. Had the courts proved unwilling to help in these matters, the Justice Department's lawyers would have faced a much more difficult task in implementing what the voting-rights scholars Chandler Davidson and Bernard Grofman called the "Quiet Revolution" in their landmark book on this process.

Of course, *South Carolina v. Katzenbach* cannot be viewed in isolation. It was the first ruling by the Supreme Court on the constitutionality of the Voting Rights Act of 1965, but it was not the last. In the next few years, the Court would often return to elements of the act, upholding its provisions time and again. In some instances, such as *Allen v. State Board of Elections* (1969), which addressed race-based vote dilution as well as vote denial, the Court would significantly expand the reach of the Voting Rights Act. None of this would have happened if the Court had not first upheld the act's basic constitutionality in *Katzenbach*.

Further Reading

♦ Articles

Lichtman, Allan. "The Federal Assault against Voting Discrimination in the Deep South 1957–1967." *Journal of Negro History* 54, no. 4 (October 1969): 346–367.

♦ Books

Bickel, Alexander M. "The Voting Rights Cases." In *The Supreme Court Review*. Chicago: University of Chicago Press, 1966.

Davidson, Chandler, and Bernard Grofman, eds. *Quiet Revolution in the South: The Impact of the Voting Rights Act, 1965–1990*. Princeton, N.J.: Princeton University Press, 1994.

Hasen, Richard L. *The Supreme Court and Election Law: Judging Equality from "Baker v. Carr" to "Bush v. Gore."* New York: New York University Press, 2003.

Zelden, Charles L. *The Supreme Court and Elections: Into the Political Thicket*. Washington, D.C.: CQ Press, 2009.

—Charles L. Zelden

Time Line

1865
December 6 — The Thirteenth Amendment is ratified, abolishing slavery.

1868
July 9 — The Fourteenth Amendment is ratified, extending citizenship and due-process rights to all persons born or naturalized in the United States.

1870
February 3 — The Fifteenth Amendment is ratified, prohibiting any discrimination in voting based on race, color, or previous condition of slavery.

1915
June 21 — The Supreme Court outlaws the "grandfather clause" in *Guinn v. United States* as a violation of the Fifteenth Amendment.

1944
April 3 — The Supreme Court overturns the "all-white primary" in *Smith v. Allwright* as a violation of the equal protection clause of the Fourteenth Amendment.

1949
■ In *Schnell v. Davis* the Supreme Court declares that Alabama's "understanding test" to vote arbitrarily excluded blacks from the polls.

1957
September 9 — President Dwight D. Eisenhower signs a Civil Rights Act establishing both the Commission on Civil Rights and the office of Assistant Attorney General for Civil Rights.

1960
May 6 — President Eisenhower signs a Civil Rights Act that increases the powers of the Justice Department in voting-rights suits.

1964
July 2 — President Lyndon B. Johnson signs a Civil Rights Act outlawing racial segregation in schools, employment, and most public places. Voting rights are not explicitly covered, except for a provision allowing for the use of three-judge district courts to hear voting-rights suits.

Time Line

1965
August 6 — President Johnson signs the Voting Rights Act of 1965, establishing executive and judicial mechanisms to enforce compliance with previous legislation.

1966
March 7 — The Supreme Court in *South Carolina v. Katzenbach* upholds the Voting Rights Act as a valid exercise of Congress's plenary power to enforce the Fifteenth Amendment.

Essential Quotes

"The Voting Rights Act was designed by Congress to banish the blight of racial discrimination in voting, which has infected the electoral process in parts of our country for nearly a century.... We hold that the sections of the Act which are properly before us are an appropriate means for carrying out Congress' constitutional responsibilities and are consonant with all other provisions of the Constitution."

"After enduring nearly a century of systematic resistance to the Fifteenth Amendment, Congress might well decide to shift the advantage of time and inertia from the perpetrators of the evil to its victims. The question remains, of course, whether the specific remedies prescribed in the Act were an appropriate means of combating the evil."

"The Constitution gives federal courts jurisdiction over cases and controversies only.... It is hard for me to believe that a justiciable controversy can arise in the constitutional sense from a desire by the United States Government or some of its officials to determine in advance what legislative provisions a State may enact or what constitutional amendments it may adopt."

"I see no reason to read into the Constitution meanings it did not have when it was adopted and which have not been put into it since."

Questions for Further Study

1. On what constitutional basis did some states and individuals oppose the Voting Rights Act of 1965? How did other states respond to these objections?

2. In what ways did some states, particularly in the South, disenfranchise black voters? How did the Voting Rights Act attempt to correct this situation?

3. The Voting Rights Act was one piece of civil rights legislation passed in the 1960s. What other bills were passed during this era, and what effect did they have on the condition of African Americans?

4. What was the relationship between the Voting Rights Act and the Fifteenth Amendment to the Constitution? What role did this relationship play in *South Carolina v. Katzenbach*?

5. In the modern era, an increasing number of people object to gerrymandering, or the creation of bizarrely shaped electoral districts with a view to grouping together racial or ethnic groups into a single district. To what extent, if any, do you believe that this practice is a violation of the spirit of the Voting Rights Act and South Carolina v. Katzenbach?

SOUTH CAROLINA V. KATZENBACH

Mr. Chief Justice Warren delivered the opinion of the Court

The Voting Rights Act was designed by Congress to banish the blight of racial discrimination in voting, which has infected the electoral process in parts of our country for nearly a century. The Act creates stringent new remedies for voting discrimination where it persists on a pervasive scale, and in addition the statute strengthens existing remedies for pockets of voting discrimination elsewhere in the country. Congress assumed the power to prescribe these remedies from §2 of the Fifteenth Amendment, which authorizes the National Legislature to effectuate by "appropriate" measures the constitutional prohibition against racial discrimination in voting. We hold that the sections of the Act which are properly before us are an appropriate means for carrying out Congress' constitutional responsibilities and are consonant with all other provisions of the Constitution. We therefore deny South Carolina's request that enforcement of these sections of the Act be enjoined.

◆ I

The constitutional propriety of the Voting Rights Act of 1965 must be judged with reference to the historical experience which it reflects....

Two points emerge vividly from the voluminous legislative history of the Act.... First: Congress felt itself confronted by an insidious and pervasive evil which had been perpetuated in certain parts of our country through unremitting and ingenious defiance of the Constitution. Second: Congress concluded that the unsuccessful remedies which it had prescribed in the past would have to be replaced by sterner and more elaborate measures in order to satisfy the clear commands of the Fifteenth Amendment....

According to the evidence in recent Justice Department voting suits, [discriminatory application of voting tests] ... is now the principal method used to bar Negroes from the polls. Discriminatory administration of voting qualifications has been found in all eight Alabama cases, in all nine Louisiana cases, and in all nine Mississippi cases which have gone to final judgment. Moreover, in almost all of these cases, the courts have held that the discrimination was pursuant to a widespread "pattern or practice." White applicants for registration have often been excused altogether from the literacy and understanding tests or have been given easy versions, have received extensive help from voting officials, and have been registered despite serious errors in their answers. Negroes, on the other hand, have typically been required to pass difficult versions of all the tests, without any outside assistance and without the slightest error. The good-morals requirement is so vague and subjective that it has constituted an open invitation to abuse at the hands of voting officials. Negroes obliged to obtain vouchers from registered voters have found it virtually impossible to comply in areas where almost no Negroes are on the rolls.

In recent years, Congress has repeatedly tried to cope with the problem by facilitating case-by-case litigation against voting discrimination....

Despite the earnest efforts of the Justice Department and of many federal judges, these new laws have done little to cure the problem of voting discrimination. According to estimates by the Attorney General during hearings on the Act, registration of voting-age Negroes in Alabama rose only from 14. 2% to 19. 4% between 1958 and 1964; in Louisiana it barely inched ahead from 31. 7% to 31. 8% between 1956 and 1965; and in Mississippi it increased only from 4. 4% to 6. 4% between 1954 and 1964. In each instance, registration of voting-age whites ran roughly 50 percentage points or more ahead of Negro registration.

The previous legislation has proved ineffective for a number of reasons. Voting suits are unusually onerous to prepare, sometimes requiring as many as 6,000 manhours spent combing through registration records in preparation for trial. Litigation has been exceedingly slow, in part because of the ample opportunities for delay afforded voting officials and others involved in the proceedings. Even when favorable decisions have finally been obtained, some of the States affected have merely switched to discriminatory devices not covered by the federal decrees or have enacted difficult new tests designed to prolong the existing disparity between white and Negro registration. Alternatively, certain local officials have defied and evaded court orders or have simply closed their registration offices to freeze the voting rolls. The provision of the 1960 law authorizing registration by federal officers has had little impact on local maladministration because of its procedural complexities....

♦ II

The Voting Rights Act of 1965 reflects Congress' firm intention to rid the country of racial discrimination in voting. The heart of the Act is a complex scheme of stringent remedies aimed at areas where voting discrimination has been most flagrant. Section 4 (a)–(d) lays down a formula defining the States and political subdivisions to which these new remedies apply. The first of the remedies, contained in §4 (a), is the suspension of literacy tests and similar voting qualifications for a period of five years from the last occurrence of substantial voting discrimination. Section 5 prescribes a second remedy, the suspension of all new voting regulations pending review by federal authorities to determine whether their use would perpetuate voting discrimination. The third remedy, covered in §§6 (b), 7, 9, and 13 (a), is the assignment of federal examiners on certification by the Attorney General to list qualified applicants who are thereafter entitled to vote in all elections....

♦ III

These provisions of the Voting Rights Act of 1965 are challenged on the fundamental ground that they exceed the powers of Congress and encroach on an area reserved to the States by the Constitution. South Carolina and certain of the *amici curiae* also attack specific sections of the Act for more particular reasons. They argue that the coverage formula prescribed in §4 (a)-(d) violates the principle of the equality of States, denies due process by employing an invalid presumption and by barring judicial review of administrative findings, constitutes a forbidden bill of attainder, and impairs the separation of powers by adjudicating guilt through legislation. They claim that the review of new voting rules required in §5 infringes Article III by directing the District Court to issue advisory opinions. They contend that the assignment of federal examiners authorized in §6 (b) abridges due process by precluding judicial review of administrative findings and impairs the separation of powers by giving the Attorney General judicial functions; also that the challenge procedure prescribed in §9 denies due process on account of its speed. Finally, South Carolina and certain of the *amici curiae* maintain that §§4 (a) and 5, buttressed by §14 (b) of the Act, abridge due process by limiting litigation to a distant forum.

Some of these contentions may be dismissed at the outset. The word "person" in the context of the Due Process Clause of the Fifth Amendment cannot, by any reasonable mode of interpretation, be expanded to encompass the States of the Union, and to our knowledge this has never been done by any court.... Likewise, courts have consistently regarded the Bill of Attainder Clause of Article I and the principle of the separation of powers only as protections for individual persons and private groups, those who are peculiarly vulnerable to nonjudicial determinations of guilt.... Nor does a State have standing as the parent of its citizens to invoke these constitutional provisions against the Federal Government, the ultimate parens patriae of every American citizen.... The objections to the Act which are raised under these provisions may therefore be considered only as additional aspects of the basic question presented by the case: Has Congress exercised its powers under the Fifteenth Amendment in an appropriate manner with relation to the States?

The ground rules for resolving this question are clear. The language and purpose of the Fifteenth Amendment, the prior decisions construing its several provisions, and the general doctrines of constitutional interpretation, all point to one fundamental principle. As against the reserved powers of the States, Congress may use any rational means to effectuate the constitutional prohibition of racial discrimination in voting.... We turn now to a more detailed description of the standards which govern our review of the Act.

Section 1 of the Fifteenth Amendment declares that "the right of citizens of the United States to vote shall not be denied or abridged by the United States or by any State on account of race, color, or previous condition of servitude." This declaration has always been treated as self-executing and has repeatedly been construed, without further legislative specification, to invalidate state voting qualifications or procedures which are discriminatory on their face or in practice....These decisions have been rendered with full respect for the general rule, reiterated last Term in Carrington v. Rash ... that States "have broad powers to determine the conditions under which the right of suffrage may be exercised." The gist of the matter is that the Fifteenth Amendment supersedes contrary exertions of state power. "When a State exercises power wholly within the domain of state interest, it is insulated from federal judicial review. But such insulation is not carried over when state power is used as an instrument for circumventing a federally protected right." ...

South Carolina contends that the cases cited above are precedents only for the authority of the judiciary to strike down state statutes and procedures -- that to allow an exercise of this authority by Congress would be to rob the courts of their rightful constitutional role. On the contrary, §2 of the Fifteenth Amendment expressly declares that "Congress shall have power to enforce this article by appropriate legislation." By adding this authorization, the Framers indicated that Congress was to be chiefly responsible for implementing the rights created in §1. "It is the power of Congress which has been enlarged. Congress is authorized to enforce the prohibitions by appropriate legislation. Some legislation is contemplated to make the [Civil War] amendments fully effective." Ex parte Virginia.... Accordingly, in addition to the courts, Congress has full remedial powers to effectuate the constitutional prohibition against racial discrimination in voting.

Congress has repeatedly exercised these powers in the past, and its enactments have repeatedly been upheld. For recent examples, see the Civil Rights Act of 1957, which was sustained in United States v. Raines, ... United States v. Thomas, ... and Hannah v. Larche, ... and the Civil Rights Act of 1960, which was upheld in Alabama v. United States, ... Louisiana v. United States, ... and United States v. Mississippi.... On the rare occasions when the Court has found an unconstitutional exercise of these powers, in its opinion Congress had attacked evils not comprehended by the Fifteenth Amendment....

The basic test to be applied in a case involving §2 of the Fifteenth Amendment is the same as in all cases concerning the express powers of Congress with relation to the reserved powers of the States. Chief Justice Marshall laid down the classic formulation, 50 years before the Fifteenth Amendment was ratified:

"Let the end be legitimate, let it be within the scope of the constitution, and all means which are appropriate, which are plainly adapted to that end, which are not prohibited, but consist with the letter and spirit of the constitution, are constitutional."...

The Court has subsequently echoed his language in describing each of the Civil War Amendments:

"Whatever legislation is appropriate, that is, adapted to carry out the objects the amendments have in view, whatever tends to enforce submission to the prohibitions they contain, and to secure to all persons the enjoyment of perfect equality of civil rights and the equal protection of the laws against State denial or invasion, if not prohibited, is brought within the domain of congressional power." ...

This language was again employed, nearly 50 years later, with reference to Congress' related authority under §2 of the Eighteenth Amendment....

We therefore reject South Carolina's argument that Congress may appropriately do no more than to forbid violations of the Fifteenth Amendment in general terms -- that the task of fashioning specific remedies or of applying them to particular localities must necessarily be left entirely to the courts. Congress is not circumscribed by any such artificial rules under §2 of the Fifteenth Amendment. In the oft-repeated words of Chief Justice Marshall, referring to another specific legislative authorization in the Constitution, "This power, like all others vested in Congress, is complete in itself, may be exercised to its utmost extent, and acknowledges no limitations, other than are prescribed in the constitution." ...

◆ IV

Congress exercised its authority under the Fifteenth Amendment in an inventive manner when it enacted the Voting Rights Act of 1965. First: The measure prescribes remedies for voting discrimination which go into effect without any need for prior adjudication. This was clearly a legitimate response to the problem, for which there is ample precedent under other constitutional provisions.... Congress had found that case-by-case litigation was inadequate to combat widespread and persistent discrimination in voting, because of the inordinate amount of time and energy required to overcome the obstructionist tactics invariably encountered in these lawsuits. After enduring nearly a century of systematic resistance to the Fifteenth Amendment, Congress might well decide to shift the advantage of time and inertia from the perpetrators of the evil to its victims. The question remains, of course, whether the specific remedies prescribed in the Act were an appropriate means of combating the evil, and to this question we shall presently address ourselves.

Second: The Act intentionally confines these remedies to a small number of States and political subdivisions which in most instances were familiar to Congress by name. This, too, was a permissible method of dealing with the problem. Congress had learned that substantial voting discrimination presently occurs in certain sections of the country, and it knew no way of accurately forecasting whether the evil might spread elsewhere in the future. In acceptable legislative fashion, Congress chose to limit its attention to the geographic areas where immediate action seemed necessary. The doctrine of the equality of States, invoked by South Carolina, does not bar this approach, for that doctrine applies only to the terms upon which States are admitted to the Union, and not to the remedies for local evils which have subsequently appeared.

♦ Coverage formula.

We now consider the related question of whether the specific States and political subdivisions within §4 (b) of the Act were an appropriate target for the new remedies. South Carolina contends that the coverage formula is awkwardly designed in a number of respects and that it disregards various local conditions which have nothing to do with racial discrimination. These arguments, however, are largely beside the point. Congress began work with reliable evidence of actual voting discrimination in a great majority of the States and political subdivisions affected by the new remedies of the Act. The formula eventually evolved to describe these areas was relevant to the problem of voting discrimination, and Congress was therefore entitled to infer a significant danger of the evil in the few remaining States and political subdivisions covered by §4 (b) of the Act. No more was required to justify the application to these areas of Congress' express powers under the Fifteenth Amendment....

To be specific, the new remedies of the Act are imposed on three States—Alabama, Louisiana, and Mississippi—in which federal courts have repeatedly found substantial voting discrimination. Section 4 (b) of the Act also embraces two other States—Georgia and South Carolina—plus large portions of a third State—North Carolina—for which there was more fragmentary evidence of recent voting discrimination mainly adduced by the Justice Department and the Civil Rights Commission. All of these areas were appropriately subjected to the new remedies. In identifying past evils, Congress obviously may avail itself of information from any probative source....

The areas listed above, for which there was evidence of actual voting discrimination, share two characteristics incorporated by Congress into the coverage formula: the use of tests and devices for voter registration, and a voting rate in the 1964 presidential election at least 12 points below the national average. Tests and devices are relevant to voting discrimination because of their long history as a tool for perpetrating the evil; a low voting rate is pertinent for the obvious reason that widespread disenfranchisement must inevitably affect the number of actual voters. Accordingly, the coverage formula is rational in both practice and theory. It was therefore permissible to impose the new remedies on the few remaining States and political subdivisions covered by the formula, at least in the absence of proof that they have been free of substantial voting discrimination in recent years. Congress is clearly not bound by the rules relating to statutory presumptions in criminal cases when it prescribes civil remedies against other organs of government under §2 of the Fifteenth Amendment....

It is irrelevant that the coverage formula excludes certain localities which do not employ voting tests and devices but for which there is evidence of voting discrimination by other means. Congress had learned that widespread and persistent discrimination in voting during recent years has typically entailed the misuse of tests and devices, and this was the evil for which the new remedies were specifically designed. At the same time, through §§3, 6 (a), and 13 (b) of the Act, Congress strengthened existing remedies for voting discrimination in other areas of the country. Legislation need not deal with all phases of a problem in the same way, so long as the distinctions drawn have some basis in practical experience.... There are no States or political subdivisions exempted from coverage under §4 (b) in which the record reveals recent racial discrimination involving tests and devices. This fact confirms the rationality of the formula.

Acknowledging the possibility of overbreadth, the Act provides for termination of special statutory coverage at the behest of States and political subdivisions in which the danger of substantial voting discrimination has not materialized during the preceding five years. Despite South Carolina's argument to the contrary, Congress might appropriately limit litigation under this provision to a single court in the

Document Text

District of Columbia, pursuant to its constitutional power under Art. III, §1, to "ordain and establish" inferior federal tribunals.... At the present time, contractual claims against the United States for more than $10,000 must be brought in the Court of Claims, and, until 1962, the District of Columbia was the sole venue of suits against federal officers officially residing in the Nation's Capital. We have discovered no suggestion that Congress exceeded constitutional bounds in imposing these limitations on litigation against the Federal Government, and the Act is no less reasonable in this respect.

South Carolina contends that these termination procedures are a nullity because they impose an impossible burden of proof upon States and political subdivisions entitled to relief. As the Attorney General pointed out during hearings on the Act, however, an area need do no more than submit affidavits from voting officials, asserting that they have not been guilty of racial discrimination through the use of tests and devices during the past five years, and then refute whatever evidence to the contrary may be adduced by the Federal Government. Section 4 (d) further assures that an area need not disprove each isolated instance of voting discrimination in order to obtain relief in the termination proceedings. The burden of proof is therefore quite bearable, particularly since the relevant facts relating to the conduct of voting officials are peculiarly within the knowledge of the States and political subdivisions themselves....

The Act bars direct judicial review of the findings by the Attorney General and the Director of the Census which trigger application of the coverage formula. We reject the claim by Alabama as amicus curiae that this provision is invalid because it allows the new remedies of the Act to be imposed in an arbitrary way. The Court has already permitted Congress to withdraw judicial review of administrative determinations in numerous cases involving the statutory rights of private parties. For example, see United States v. California Eastern Line, ... Switchmen's Union v. National Mediation Bd.... In this instance, the findings not subject to review consist of objective statistical determinations by the Census Bureau and a routine analysis of state statutes by the Justice Department. These functions are unlikely to arouse any plausible dispute, as South Carolina apparently concedes. In the event that the formula is improperly applied, the area affected can always go into court and obtain termination of coverage under §4 (b), provided of course that it has not been guilty of voting discrimination in recent years. This procedure serves as a partial substitute for direct judicial review.

♦ Suspension of tests.

We now arrive at consideration of the specific remedies prescribed by the Act for areas included within the coverage formula. South Carolina assails the temporary suspension of existing voting qualifications, reciting the rule laid down by Lassiter v. Northampton County Bd. of Elections, ... that literacy tests and related devices are not in themselves contrary to the Fifteenth Amendment. In that very case, however, the Court went on to say, "Of course a literacy test, fair on its face, may be employed to perpetuate that discrimination which the Fifteenth Amendment was designed to uproot." ...

The record shows that in most of the States covered by the Act, including South Carolina, various tests and devices have been instituted with the purpose of disenfranchising Negroes, have been framed in such a way as to facilitate this aim, and have been administered in a discriminatory fashion for many years. Under these circumstances, the Fifteenth Amendment has clearly been violated....

The Act suspends literacy tests and similar devices for a period of five years from the last occurrence of substantial voting discrimination. This was a legitimate response to the problem, for which there is ample precedent in Fifteenth Amendment cases. Underlying the response was the feeling that States and political subdivisions which had been allowing white illiterates to vote for years could not sincerely complain about "dilution" of their electorates through the registration of Negro illiterates. Congress knew that continuance of the tests and devices in use at the present time, no matter how fairly administered in the future, would freeze the effect of past discrimination in favor of unqualified white registrants. Congress permissibly rejected the alternative of requiring a complete re-registration of all voters, believing that this would be too harsh on many whites who had enjoyed the franchise for their entire adult lives.

♦ Review of new rules.

The Act suspends new voting regulations pending scrutiny by federal authorities to determine whether their use would violate the Fifteenth Amendment. This may have been an uncommon exercise of congressional power, as South Carolina contends, but the Court has recognized that exceptional conditions can justify legislative measures not otherwise appropriate.... Congress knew that some of the States covered by §4 (b) of the Act had resorted to the extraordinary stratagem of contriving new rules of various kinds for the sole purpose of perpetuating voting discrimination in the face of adverse federal court decrees. Congress had reason to suppose that these States might try similar maneuvers in the future in order to evade the remedies for voting discrimination contained in the Act itself. Under the compulsion of these unique circumstances, Congress responded in a permissibly decisive manner.

For reasons already stated, there was nothing inappropriate about limiting litigation under this provision to the District Court for the District of Columbia, and in putting the burden of proof on the areas seeking relief. Nor has Congress authorized the District Court to issue advisory opinions, in violation of the principles of Article III invoked by Georgia as amicus curiae. The Act automatically suspends the operation of voting regulations enacted after November 1, 1964, and furnishes mechanisms for enforcing the suspension. A State or political subdivision wishing to make use of a recent amendment to its voting laws therefore has a concrete and immediate "controversy" with the Federal Government.... An appropriate remedy is a judicial determination that continued suspension of the new rule is unnecessary to vindicate rights guaranteed by the Fifteenth Amendment.

♦ **Federal examiners.**

The Act authorizes the appointment of federal examiners to list qualified applicants who are thereafter entitled to vote, subject to an expeditious challenge procedure. This was clearly an appropriate response to the problem, closely related to remedies authorized in prior cases.... In many of the political subdivisions covered by §4 (b) of the Act, voting officials have persistently employed a variety of procedural tactics to deny Negroes the franchise, often in direct defiance or evasion of federal court decrees. Congress realized that merely to suspend voting rules which have been misused or are subject to misuse might leave this localized evil undisturbed. As for the briskness of the challenge procedure, Congress knew that in some of the areas affected, challenges had been persistently employed to harass registered Negroes. It chose to forestall this abuse, at the same time providing alternative ways for removing persons listed through error or fraud. In addition to the judicial challenge procedure, §7 (d) allows for the removal of names by the examiner himself, and §11 (c) makes it a crime to obtain a listing through fraud.

In recognition of the fact that there were political subdivisions covered by §4 (b) of the Act in which the appointment of federal examiners might be unnecessary, Congress assigned the Attorney General the task of determining the localities to which examiners should be sent. There is no warrant for the claim, asserted by Georgia as amicus curiae, that the Attorney General is free to use this power in an arbitrary fashion, without regard to the purposes of the Act. Section 6 (b) sets adequate standards to guide the exercise of his discretion, by directing him to calculate the registration ratio of non-whites to whites, and to weigh evidence of good-faith efforts to avoid possible voting discrimination. At the same time, the special termination procedures of §13 (a) provide indirect judicial review for the political subdivisions affected, assuring the withdrawal of federal examiners from areas where they are clearly not needed...

After enduring nearly a century of widespread resistance to the Fifteenth Amendment, Congress has marshalled an array of potent weapons against the evil, with authority in the Attorney General to employ them effectively. Many of the areas directly affected by this development have indicated their willingness to abide by any restraints legitimately imposed upon them. We here hold that the portions of the Voting Rights Act properly before us are a valid means for carrying out the commands of the Fifteenth Amendment. Hopefully, millions of non-white Americans will now be able to participate for the first time on an equal basis in the government under which they live. We may finally look forward to the day when truly "[t]he right of citizens of the United States to vote shall not be denied or abridged by the United States or by any State on account of race, color, or previous condition of servitude."

The bill of complaint is *Dismissed.*

Mr. Justice Black, concurring and dissenting

I agree with substantially all of the Court's opinion sustaining the power of Congress under §2 of the Fifteenth Amendment to suspend state literacy tests and similar voting qualifications and to authorize the

Document Text

Attorney General to secure the appointment of federal examiners to register qualified voters in various sections of the country. Section 1 of the Fifteenth Amendment provides that "The right of citizens of the United States to vote shall not be denied or abridged by the United States or by any State on account of race, color, or previous condition of servitude."

In addition to this unequivocal command to the States and the Federal Government that no citizen shall have his right to vote denied or abridged because of race or color, §2 of the Amendment unmistakably gives Congress specific power to go further and pass appropriate legislation to protect this right to vote against any method of abridgment no matter how subtle. Compare my dissenting opinion in Bell v. Maryland.... I have no doubt whatever as to the power of Congress under §2 to enact the provisions of the Voting Rights Act of 1965 dealing with the suspension of state voting tests that have been used as notorious means to deny and abridge voting rights on racial grounds. This same congressional power necessarily exists to authorize appointment of federal examiners. I also agree with the judgment of the Court upholding §4 (b) of the Act which sets out a formula for determining when and where the major remedial sections of the Act take effect. I reach this conclusion, however, for a somewhat different reason than that stated by the Court, which is that "the coverage formula is rational in both practice and theory." I do not base my conclusion on the fact that the formula is rational, for it is enough for me that Congress by creating this formula has merely exercised its hitherto unquestioned and undisputed power to decide when, where, and upon what conditions its laws shall go into effect. By stating in specific detail that the major remedial sections of the Act are to be applied in areas where certain conditions exist, and by granting the Attorney General and the Director of the Census unreviewable power to make the mechanical determination of which areas come within the formula of §4 (b), I believe that Congress has acted within its established power to set out preconditions upon which the Act is to go into effect....

Though, as I have said, I agree with most of the Court's conclusions, I dissent from its holding that every part of §5 of the Act is constitutional. Section 4 (a), to which §5 is linked, suspends for five years all literacy tests and similar devices in those States coming within the formula of §4 (b). Section 5 goes on to provide that a State covered by §4 (b) can in no way amend its constitution or laws relating to voting without first trying to persuade the Attorney General of the United States or the Federal District Court for the District of Columbia that the new proposed laws do not have the purpose and will not have the effect of denying the right to vote to citizens on account of their race or color. I think this section is unconstitutional on at least two grounds.

(a) The Constitution gives federal courts jurisdiction over cases and controversies only. If it can be said that any case or controversy arises under this section which gives the District Court for the District of Columbia jurisdiction to approve or reject state laws or constitutional amendments, then the case or controversy must be between a State and the United States Government. But it is hard for me to believe that a justiciable controversy can arise in the constitutional sense from a desire by the United States Government or some of its officials to determine in advance what legislative provisions a State may enact or what constitutional amendments it may adopt. If this dispute between the Federal Government and the States amounts to a case or controversy it is a far cry from the traditional constitutional notion of a case or controversy as a dispute over the meaning of enforceable laws or the manner in which they are applied. And if by this section Congress has created a case or controversy, and I do not believe it has, then it seems to me that the most appropriate judicial forum for settling these important questions is this Court acting under its original Art. III, §2, jurisdiction to try cases in which a State is a party. At least a trial in this Court would treat the States with the dignity to which they should be entitled as constituent members of our Federal Union.

The form of words and the manipulation of presumptions used in §5 to create the illusion of a case or controversy should not be allowed to cloud the effect of that section. By requiring a State to ask a federal court to approve the validity of a proposed law which has in no way become operative, Congress has asked the State to secure precisely the type of advisory opinion our Constitution forbids. As I have pointed out elsewhere, ... some of those drafting our Constitution wanted to give the federal courts the power to issue advisory opinions and propose new laws to the legislative body. These suggestions were rejected. We should likewise reject any attempt by Congress to flout constitutional limitations by authorizing federal courts to render advisory opinions when there is no case or controversy before them. Congress has ample power to protect the rights of citizens to vote without resorting to the unnecessarily circuitous, indirect and unconstitutional route it has adopted in this section.

(b) My second and more basic objection to §5 is that Congress has here exercised its power under §2 of the Fifteenth Amendment through the adoption of means that conflict with the most basic principles of the Constitution. As the Court says the limitations of the power granted under §2 are the same as the limitations imposed on the exercise of any of the powers expressly granted Congress by the Constitution. The classic formulation of these constitutional limitations was stated by Chief Justice Marshall when he said in McCulloch v. Maryland, 4 Wheat.... "Let the end be legitimate, let it be within the scope of the constitution, and all means which are appropriate, which are plainly adapted to that end, which are not prohibited, but consist with the letter and spirit of the constitution, are constitutional."

Section 5, by providing that some of the States cannot pass state laws or adopt state constitutional amendments without first being compelled to beg federal authorities to approve their policies, so distorts our constitutional structure of government as to render any distinction drawn in the Constitution between state and federal power almost meaningless. One of the most basic premises upon which our structure of government was founded was that the Federal Government was to have certain specific and limited powers and no others, and all other power was to be reserved either "to the States respectively, or to the people." Certainly if all the provisions of our Constitution which limit the power of the Federal Government and reserve other power to the States are to mean anything, they mean at least that the States have power to pass laws and amend their constitutions without first sending their officials hundreds of miles away to beg federal authorities to approve them. Moreover, it seems to me that §5 which gives federal officials power to veto state laws they do not like is in direct conflict with the clear command of our Constitution that "The United States shall guarantee to every State in this Union a Republican Form of Government." I cannot help but believe that the inevitable effect of any such law which forces any one of the States to entreat federal authorities in faraway places for approval of local laws before they can become effective is to create the impression that the State or States treated in this way are little more than conquered provinces. And if one law concerning voting can make the States plead for this approval by a distant federal court or the United States Attorney General, other laws on different subjects can force the States to seek the advance approval not only of the Attorney General but of the President himself or any other chosen members of his staff. It is inconceivable to me that such a radical degradation of state power was intended in any of the provisions of our Constitution or its Amendments. Of course I do not mean to cast any doubt whatever upon the indisputable power of the Federal Government to invalidate a state law once enacted and operative on the ground that it intrudes into the area of supreme federal power. But the Federal Government has heretofore always been content to exercise this power to protect federal supremacy by authorizing its agents to bring lawsuits against state officials once an operative state law has created an actual case and controversy. A federal law which assumes the power to compel the States to submit in advance any proposed legislation they have for approval by federal agents approaches dangerously near to wiping the States out as useful and effective units in the government of our country. I cannot agree to any constitutional interpretation that leads inevitably to such a result.

I see no reason to read into the Constitution meanings it did not have when it was adopted and which have not been put into it since. The proceedings of the original Constitutional Convention show beyond all doubt that the power to veto or negative state laws was denied Congress. On several occasions proposals were submitted to the convention to grant this power to Congress. These proposals were debated extensively and on every occasion when submitted for vote they were overwhelmingly rejected. The refusal to give Congress this extraordinary power to veto state laws was based on the belief that if such power resided in Congress the States would be helpless to function as effective governments. Since that time neither the Fifteenth Amendment nor any other Amendment to the Constitution has given the slightest indication of a purpose to grant Congress the power to veto state laws either by itself or its agents. Nor does any provision in the Constitution endow the federal courts with power to participate with state legislative bodies in determining what state policies shall be enacted into law. The judicial power to invalidate a law in a case or controversy after

Document Text

the law has become effective is a long way from the power to prevent a State from passing a law. I cannot agree with the Court that Congress—denied a power in itself to veto a state law—can delegate this same power to the Attorney General or the District Court for the District of Columbia. For the effect on the States is the same in both cases—they cannot pass their laws without sending their agents to the City of Washington to plead to federal officials for their advance approval.

In this and other prior Acts Congress has quite properly vested the Attorney General with extremely broad power to protect voting rights of citizens against discrimination on account of race or color. Section 5 viewed in this context is of very minor importance and in my judgment is likely to serve more as an irritant to the States than as an aid to the enforcement of the Act. I would hold §5 invalid for the reasons stated above with full confidence that the Attorney General has ample power to give vigorous, expeditious and effective protection to the voting rights of all citizens.

Glossary

amici curiae: Latin for "friends of the court"; persons or organizations with an interest in a case but who are not party to it and who file court briefs with a view to influencing a case's outcome

bill of attainder: a law that punishes a person or group of persons without benefit of trial

Chief Justice Marshall: John Marshall, the chief justice of the United States in the early nineteenth century, whose decisions tended to enforce the power of the federal government

Civil War Amendments: the Thirteenth, Fourteenth, and Fifteenth Amendments to the U.S. Constitution, passed in the wake of the Civil War

Constitutional Convention: the convention in Philadelphia in 1787 at which the U.S. Constitution was drafted

ex parte: Latin for "by (or for) one party," used in the law to refer to a legal proceeding brought by one party without the presence of the other being required

justiciable: able to come under the authority of the court

literacy tests: written tests administered to potential voters to determine, as a condition for voting, whether they can read

McCulloch v. Maryland: a landmark 1819 U.S. Supreme Court decision in which Chief Justice John Marshall held that states could not impede the power of the federal government

nullity: legal ineffectiveness or invalidity

parens patriae: Latin for "parents of the nation," referring to the power of the state to intervene to protect people from an abuse

Martin Luther King, Jr. speaking to an anti-Vietnam War rally at the University of Minnesota, St. Paul on April 27, 1967. By Minnesota Historical Society [CC BY-SA 2.0 (http://creativecommons.org/licenses/by-sa/2.0)], via Wikimedia Commons

Martin Luther King, Jr.: "Beyond Vietnam: A Time to Break Silence"

1967

"If America's soul becomes totally poisoned, part of the autopsy must read Vietnam."

Overview

On April 4, 1967, one of America's greatest orators gave a speech on a subject he had previously been reluctant to address. Martin Luther King, Jr., was the preeminent civil rights leader of the 1960s, but as he stood in the pulpit of Riverside Church in New York City his topic was the Vietnam War. King had been an eloquent advocate of African American civil rights and a fearless opponent of racial bigotry. His words and deeds helped secure passage of the Civil Rights Act of 1964 and the Voting Rights Act of 1965. King, however, had said little in public about the Vietnam War, where large numbers of Americans troops were fighting and dying during 1965 and 1966. When he raised questions about the war or called for peace talks, critics replied that he was not qualified to speak about foreign policy. Friends counseled him to keep his distance from the controversies over the war lest he jeopardize support for the civil rights movement. By 1967, however, King felt compelled to speak out. In "Beyond Vietnam: A Time to Break Silence," King denounced the war for deepening the problems of African Americans and poor people. His critique went farther, as he condemned the "madness" of Vietnam as a "symptom of a far deeper malady" that put the United States at odds with the aspirations for social justice of people in the developing world. King endured hostile rebukes for his sweeping and radical criticisms of America's role in Vietnam and in other emerging nations. He insisted, however, that the civil rights movement was part of a global struggle against "racism, materialism, and militarism."

Context

When King delivered his "Beyond Vietnam" speech, the Vietnam War was a growing source of global controversy. More than four hundred thousand Americans in uniform were fighting in South Vietnam. President Lyndon B. Johnson had sent the first U.S. combat troops to that nation little more than two years earlier, in March 1965, transforming a conflict that the South Vietnamese had previously fought with U.S. advice and armaments into an American war. Johnson at first enjoyed widespread public support for what he said was a war of necessity to halt Communist aggression and preserve South Vietnam's right to self-determination. As more U.S. troops poured into South Vietnam, however, public discontent with the war increased. Administration officials maintained that U.S. forces were making progress in the war, but they also cautioned that years of hard fighting lay ahead and more troops would be necessary. By January 1967, polls showed that more Americans disapproved of the president's war policies than supported them. Some of these critics advocated a negotiated settlement, and a few favored a unilateral American withdrawal. Many Americans, however, thought the president had not used sufficient military force to secure victory. They became impatient with the gradual buildup of U.S. strength and called for more bombing and more troops to win the war on the battlefield. By the spring of 1967, Johnson was feeling considerable pressure from this public discontent over a war that was growing larger but had no end in sight.

The president also worried about the war's effects on his domestic reform program, the Great Society. Johnson had proclaimed his desire to build the Great Society in May 1964. During the next eighteen months, Congress approved his proposals for a War on Poverty, federal aid to education, Medicare and Medicaid, the Civil Rights Act of 1964, and the Voting Rights Act of 1965. Johnson envisioned the Great Society as his legacy. After he began sending combat troops to war in Southeast Asia, he insisted that the country was sufficiently powerful and wealthy to fight a war in Vietnam and build the Great Society. By early 1967, however, such optimism had faded. The war had become so large and costly that many members of Congress concluded that the country could not increase spending—and indeed might have to reduce appropriations—for programs like the War on Poverty.

King objected to sending U.S. forces to war in Southeast Asia, but, as he later wrote, he had not taken part in any of the marches or demonstrations against the war. During 1965, he did occasionally speak out, calling on the Johnson administration to seek a negotiated settlement. The president resented even such mild criticism. The White House tried to silence King; administration officials and members of Congress told King he had no competence in foreign policy and his public statements could harm sensitive negotiations to end the war. King complained about administration efforts to muzzle dissenters, but he made only infrequent public complaints about the widening war. Some of King's closest associates also encouraged him to refrain from antiwar activities. They worried that unpopular statements about the war could weaken public support for civil rights. King heeded their views, often confining his criticism of the war to its harmful effects on the War on Poverty.

Vietnam, however, became an urgent issue for King in early 1967 after he read a magazine article with horrifying pictures of children injured in the war. King declared that he could not ignore his conscience and felt obligated to campaign for an end to a war that was devastating Vietnamese and destroying hopes of Americans for a Great Society. He had heated arguments with other African American leaders, who warned that his antiwar activities would alienate many supporters who had contributed to his campaigns for civil rights, but King was adamantly unconcerned about the loss of financial backing. On February 25, 1967, he spoke to an antiwar conference in Los Angeles, California. In late March, in Chicago, Illinois, he participated in his first march against the war. Ten days later, he came to New York's Riverside Church to deliver a major address on the reasons he had decided to break his silence on Vietnam.

About the Author

Born Michael King, Jr., in Atlanta, Georgia, on January 15, 1929, King became Martin Luther King, Jr., in 1934 when his father changed his own and his son's name to honor the famous German theologian. King's grandfather and father were pastors of Atlanta's Ebenezer Baptist Church and leaders of the local branch of the National Association for the Advancement of Colored People. King, too, decided to study for the ministry after graduating from Morehouse College in 1948. He earned a divinity degree in 1951 at Crozier Theological Seminary, where he finished first in his class. Three years later, he graduated from Boston University with a PhD in theology. Long after King's death, a panel of experts appointed by the university concluded that King had plagiarized portions of his dissertation.

King gained national recognition as a civil rights activist during the Montgomery bus boycott that began in December 1955. African Americans had organized a boycott of the segregated local bus lines in Montgomery, Alabama, after the arrest of a black woman who had refused to give up her seat to a white patron and move to the back of the bus. King, who was pastor of a local Baptist church, became the most eloquent voice of the boycott movement, urging supporters to protest in a Christian fashion—that is, with courage but also dignity and love. Although King faced intimidation and violence, including the bombing of his house, he insisted on nonviolent protest. In November 1956, the U.S. Supreme Court declared the southern bus segregation laws unconstitutional. In 1957, King founded the Southern Christian Leadership Conference to promote civil rights. In 1960 he returned to Atlanta, where, along with his father, he became copastor of the Ebenezer Baptist Church.

During the mid-1960s, King led the civil rights movement to two of its greatest victories. In spring 1963, he organized demonstrations in Birmingham, Alabama, to challenge racial segregation at lunch counters and secure job opportunities for African Americans. When television cameras showed local authorities using fire hoses and police dogs against the nonviolent demonstrators, many of them youths, national outrage led not only to desegregation in Birmingham but also to a decision on the part of President John F. Kennedy to ask Congress for civil rights legislation that would bar discrimination on account of race in employment and in public accommodations, such as restaurants, hotels, and theaters. On August 28, 1963, King spoke at a huge rally in Washington, D.C., to mobilize support for the legislation. Standing before the Lincoln Memorial, he famously proclaimed, "I have a dream," and his moving vision of a society where blacks and whites enjoyed equal rights helped build a broad coalition in favor of the legislation. On July 2, 1964, King attended the ceremony at which President Johnson signed into law the Civil Rights Act of 1964. In March 1965, demonstrations against discriminatory voting practices that King helped organize in Selma, Alabama, produced another ugly incident of police violence. The resulting national outcry led to the passage of the Voting Rights Act of 1965, which gave the federal government new powers to ensure that all citizens could exercise their constitutional right to vote.

King earned honors and acclaim for his nonviolent struggle for civil rights. He was *Time* magazine's Man of the Year for 1964, and he received the Nobel Peace Prize in December 1964. Yet despite his achievements, he endured a campaign of harassment carried on by the director of the Federal Bureau of Investigation, J. Edgar Hoover. A fierce opponent of the civil rights movement, Hoover used information from wiretaps on King's telephones to try to discredit his leadership and prove that he was a Communist. King also faced criticism from younger African American leaders, who began calling for "Black Power" in the mid-1960s and advocating armed resistance to white oppression. King remained faithful to his nonviolent principles, and he maintained that "Black Power" was "a slogan without a program." Instead, he called for "a new turn toward greater economic justice" that would close the gap between rich and poor and eliminate the squalor in predominantly black inner-city neighborhoods. In November 1967, he announced the beginning of a Poor People's Campaign aimed at boosting federal efforts to reduce poverty. In March 1968, he led a march of striking sanitation workers in Memphis, Tennessee. King delivered his final speech in that city on the evening of April 3, when he told supporters, "I may not get there with you. But I want you to know tonight, that we, as a people, will get to the promised land." The next evening, he was shot dead by James Earl Ray as he stood on a Memphis motel balcony. In 1986, Americans began observing an annual federal holiday on the third Monday of January to honor his life and achievements.

Explanation and Analysis of the Document

Anticipating criticism, King begins by declaring that his position on the Vietnam War is a matter of "conscience." To remain silent would be "a betrayal" of principle. He acknowledges that it would be much easier to express "conformist thought" rather than "inner truth," especially when conviction leads to denunciation of government policies during wartime. Aware of this difficulty, he praises the organization to which he is speaking—Clergy and Laymen Concerned about Vietnam—for choosing "firm dissent" over "smooth patriotism." He then lists some of the objections that he has repeatedly encountered—that he is imperiling the civil rights movement by taking an unpopular stand on the Vietnam War or that he is speaking about an issue of foreign policy that is beyond his expertise. King tries to neutralize these criticisms by insisting that they rest on "tragic misunderstandings" of public affairs and of his own career. Indeed, he asserts that his dissent from U.S. policies in Vietnam conforms to the principles that have guided him since he became a civil rights leader during the Montgomery bus boycott. King also maintains that while there is no simple way to stop the war, the United States has "the greatest responsibility" for "ending a conflict that has exacted a heavy price on both continents."

♦ **"The Importance of Vietnam"**
In the next section of his address, King enumerates specific reasons for opposing the Vietnam War, while emphasizing that the basis of his criticism is his "moral vision." Especially important to King are the detrimental effects of the war on America's poor. He condemns the war for draining funds from the Johnson administration's War on Poverty. His language suggests that the war has become so large and destructive that it has grown beyond human control as it claims resources "like some demonic destructive suction tube." Also troubling to King are the disproportionate numbers of poor and black soldiers who are fighting and dying in Vietnam. He emphasizes the irony of Americans in uniform fighting for liberties abroad that they did not enjoy at home. With sorrow and pain, he declares that Americans have become all too familiar with "Negro and white boys on TV screens as they kill and die together for a nation that has

been unable to seat them in the same schools." This "cruel manipulation of the poor" compels him to speak out.

King then explains that his belief in nonviolence also accounts for his opposition to the war. He recounts his efforts to persuade angry young African Americans in neglected inner-city neighborhoods that violent protest would not solve their problems. How, then, he reasons, can he not similarly condemn the Vietnam policies of "the greatest purveyor of violence in the world today—my own government." King's criticism is strong and sweeping, associating him with some of the most radical opponents of the war. He believes, however, that he cannot invoke his commitment to nonviolence selectively, lest he forfeit his credibility as an advocate for racial justice and his moral obligation to speak for American and Vietnamese victims of the war's violence.

King's responsibilities as a civil rights leader, a Nobel Peace Prize recipient, and a Christian also lead him to question the war. King deftly rebuts the charge that his work in the civil rights movement disqualifies him from speaking on issues of war and peace by reminding his audience that the goal of the Southern Christian Leadership Conference is "to save the soul of America." The poisonous effects of the war, he declares, are corrupting American values and preventing the achievement of racial justice. King also explains that his obligations as a recipient of an international prize for peace and as a Christian minister compel him to think beyond "national allegiances." He states that he cannot view the war only as an American. Instead, he is "called to speak for the voiceless, the victims of our nation and for those it calls enemy, for no document from human hands can make these humans any less our brothers."

♦ **"Strange Liberators"**
This lengthy section reviews the history of the Vietnam War in order to challenge the Johnson administration's position that the United States was fighting to halt aggression and advance democracy. King adopts the perspective of the Vietnamese who "have been living under the curse of the war for almost three continuous decades." His use of the term *madness* at the beginning of this section indicates how strongly he disagrees with President Johnson that the war is serving either U.S. or Vietnamese interests.

King argues that the United States has supported reaction and repression in Vietnam. Between 1945 and 1954, the United States aided French efforts to reestablish colonial control of Vietnam. After the French withdrew, U.S. leaders backed President Ngo Dinh Diem, the anti-Communist ruler of South Vietnam, whom King describes as a vicious dictator who suppressed political opposition and prevented reforms that would have given land to peasants. U.S. military assistance to Diem, according to King, belied promises of "peace and democracy." After Diem's overthrow in a coup on November 1, 1963, a succession of "military dictatorships" offered "no real change." Once American troops began fighting in South Vietnam in 1965, they caused horrible suffering, using heavy firepower that inflicted many civilian casualties and devastated villages and farmlands. King even goes so far as to compare American use of the "latest weapons" in Vietnam to Nazi Germany's tests of "new tortures in the concentration camps of Europe." Only the most extreme critics of U.S. policies made such assertions. King concludes that by looking at the war from the perspective of the Vietnamese caught in the brutality of conflict, Americans must seem to be "strange liberators." Indeed, he asserts, Vietnamese peasants probably see the United States as "their real enemy."

King then tries to explain the views of America's enemies, the National Liberation Front and North Vietnam. He maintains that the National Liberation Front, an opposition group that used guerrilla tactics to gain control of the South Vietnamese government, was the only party "in real touch with the peasants." He paints a highly sympathetic picture of the National Liberation Front, which he believes had good reason to take up arms against a corrupt government that jailed political opponents. King also maintains that it is not hard to understand why Ho Chi Minh, the leader of North Vietnam, distrusts the United States. Ho had led the Vietnamese fight for independence against the French, and he expected to become the leader of Vietnam according to the terms of the Geneva peace settlement of 1954. The United States, however, cooperated with Diem to divide Vietnam between North and South and to prevent the elections that would have brought Ho "to power over a united Vietnam." From Ho's perspective, the United States has been the aggressor by sending troops to Southeast Asia in violation of the Geneva agreements and dropping "thousands of bombs on a poor weak nation more than eight thousand miles away from its shores."

After these efforts to "give a voice to the voiceless of Vietnam," King concludes this section of his address by expressing his concern about the corrupting effects of the war on U.S. troops. In Vietnam, according to King, Americans in uniform experience a very different war than the one that government officials led them to expect. U.S. troops, King asserts, have intervened in a Vietnamese struggle "on the side of the wealthy and the secure while we create hell for the poor." The disparity between U.S. soldiers' expectations and the reality of the war produces a cynicism that compounds the brutalizing effects of combat.

♦ "This Madness Must Cease"

King next offers suggestions to halt the "madness" of Vietnam. His five proposals require drastic changes in U.S. policy as well as an admission "that we have been wrong from the beginning of our adventure in Vietnam." His views are not those of a mediator who is encouraging all major parties to make concessions for peace but of a moral critic who believes that Americans should "atone for our sins and errors in Vietnam." His harsh judgments about the U.S. war effort reflect what he described earlier in his address as "allegiances and loyalties which are broader and deeper than nationalism." He speaks as a brother to the suffering poor in Vietnam and the United States, a citizen of the world who is "aghast" at U.S. actions, and an American citizen who holds his nation accountable for expanding the war and for stopping it.

♦ "Protesting the War"

King next advocates protest against the war, including counseling young men to become conscientious objectors as an alternative to military service. Opposition to the current war, however, is insufficient, because, according to King, Vietnam is only a symptom of "a far deeper malady within the American spirit." In several other nations, U.S. military advisers or weapons were helping to suppress revolution. King charges that the United States has become an imperialist nation, exploiting overseas investments while stifling the ambitions of people in developing nations for peaceful change. King concedes that this allegation is "disturbing," but he insists that American values are skewed. Property rights and profits have become more important than people, thereby undermining efforts to eradicate "racism, materialism, and militarism."

King calls for "a true revolution of values" that will transform America's world role. Although he provides no specifics, he favors economic restructuring that will end "the glaring contrast" between poverty and wealth. His prescriptions for international reform mirror his vision for domestic change. In his writings, King insisted that "justice for black people cannot be achieved without radical changes in the structure of society." He demanded that America "face all its interrelated flaws—racism, poverty, militarism, and materialism." King is optimistic that Americans can change their priorities "so that the pursuit of peace will take precedence over the pursuit of war." He also believes that a revolution in values will provide enormous benefits in America's cold war contest with Communism. Although his speech is full of scathing criticism of the foreign policies of the Johnson administration, King agrees with government officials that Communism appeals to people who lack basic necessities of life and hope for the future. Too often, however, U.S. policymakers' fears of Communist takeovers in other countries led them to pursue "negative anti-communism," including a resort to war. King instead favors "positive action" to "remove those conditions of poverty, insecurity and injustice" that lead to the spread of Communism.

♦ "The People Are Important"

In this closing section, King tells his fellow Americans that they face revolutionary times and that they must find new ways to cooperate with people in developing nations. King mentions the Vietnam War only briefly as an example of a failed effort that puts the United States on the wrong side of history. Instead, he concentrates on the worldwide challenges to "old systems of exploitation and oppression" and the necessity of aligning the United States with "the shirtless and barefoot people" who "are rising up as never before." He believes that Western nations made essential contributions to this revolutionary spirit but that they have become rich, complacent, and reactionary. "Our only hope today," he declares, "lies in our ability to recapture the revolutionary spirit and go out into a sometimes hostile world declaring eternal hostility to poverty, racism, and militarism." Success requires thinking beyond one's community, race, or nation. Instead, he calls for "an overriding loyalty to mankind as a whole" based on the idea—which "all of the great religions have seen as the supreme unifying principle of life"—of love.

Although the term was not part of his vocabulary in 1967, King is speaking about a globalizing world that requires new ideas and new policies. The pace of change, he explains, has quickened. He uses a phrase from his famous "I Have a Dream" speech, as he asserts, "We are confronted with the fierce urgency of now." Nations and peoples that previously seemed distant now require attention. The developing world of Asia, Africa, and Latin America "borders on our doors." King acknowledges that the challenges of creating a new world are enormous. But just as he urged his fellow Americans to pursue the dream of freedom and justice at home, he calls on them to begin "the long and bitter—but beautiful—struggle for a new world."

Audience

King's audience for "Beyond Vietnam: A Time to Break Silence" was more than three thousand people who packed Riverside Church in New York, where he spoke. King, though, knew that his speech would receive wide coverage in newspapers and magazines, and he hoped that it would help to strengthen opposition to the Vietnam War. He realized, however, that some of his ideas about U.S. aggression and imperialism would be unpopular, even offensive. Yet he was willing to risk such criticism because he felt a moral compulsion to speak out. "At times you do things to satisfy your conscience," he explained.

Impact

The speech provoked a torrent of criticism. Many editorial writers and political commentators chided King for connecting two issues—civil rights and Vietnam—that they thought should be separate and distinct. The *New York Times*, for example, rebuked King for damaging both the civil rights and the peace movement. Other observers denounced King for adopting the views of America's enemies in Vietnam. *Life* magazine dismissed the speech as "demagogic slander that sounded like a script for Radio Hanoi." Even some African American publications, such as the *Pittsburgh Courier*, criticized King for "tragically misleading" blacks.

The most extreme reaction occurred at the White House. "What is that goddamned nigger preacher doing to me?" Johnson asked angrily. "We gave him the Civil Rights Act of 1964, we gave him the Voting Rights Act of 1965, we gave him the War on Poverty. What more does he want?"

The federal intelligence director J. Edgar Hoover informed Johnson that King was cooperating with "subversive forces seeking to undermine our nation." Johnson's greatest fear, however, was that King's radical rhetoric was playing into the hands of opponents of civil rights and the War on Poverty. These critics of the Great Society could use King's supposedly dangerous and even disloyal dissent to block additional funding for antipoverty programs or prevent new civil rights reforms.

King made no concessions to his critics. On April 15, 1967, he led a march in New York City of one hundred twenty-five thousand antiwar protesters and then made a speech in which he repeated many of the criticisms of the war he had made at Riverside Church eleven days earlier. He called for more demonstrations against the war, and he formed a group called Negotiations Now to get one million Americans to sign a petition calling for peace talks. He told staff members of the Southern Christian Leadership Conference that he would continue his antiwar activities because it was the right thing to do. "I will not be intimidated," he insisted. "I will not be harassed. I will not be silent. And I will be heard."

Further Reading

◆ Books

Dallek, Robert. *Flawed Giant: Lyndon Johnson and His Times, 1961–1973*. New York: Oxford University Press, 1998.

DeBenedetti, Charles. *An American Ordeal: The Antiwar Movement of the Vietnam Era*. Syracuse, N.Y.: Syracuse University Press, 1990.

Garrow, David J. *Bearing the Cross: Martin Luther King, Jr., and the Southern Christian Leadership Conference*. New York: William Morrow, 1986.

Jackson, Thomas F. *From Civil Rights to Human Rights: Martin Luther King, Jr., and the Struggle for Economic Justice*. Philadelphia: University of Pennsylvania Press, 2007.

Lewis, David Levering. *King: A Biography*. 2nd ed. Urbana: University of Illinois Press, 1978.

Oates, Stephen B. *Let the Trumpet Sound: The Life of Martin Luther King, Jr.*. New York: Harper & Row, 1982.

Sitkoff, Harvard. *King: Pilgrimage to the Mountaintop*. New York: Hill and Wang, 2008.

Washington, James M., ed. *A Testament of Hope: The Essential Writings and Speeches of Martin Luther King, Jr*. New York: HarperCollins, 1986.

Woods, Randall B. *LBJ: Architect of American Ambition*. New York: Free Press, 2006.

Web Sites

"Liberation Curriculum." The Martin Luther King, Jr. Research and Education Institute Web site. http://mlk-kpp01.stanford.edu/index.php/lc/index.

—Chester Pach

Time Line

1929	January 15	King is born in Atlanta, Georgia.
1955	December	King leads the campaign in Montgomery, Alabama, against racial segregation on bus lines, a boycott that ends in November 1956 with a U.S. Supreme Court decision declaring the bus segregation laws unconstitutional.
1963	April & May	King leads demonstrations against racial discrimination in Birmingham, Alabama.
	August 28	At the Lincoln Memorial in Washington, D.C., King gives his "I Have a Dream" Speech.
1964	January 8	In his State of the Union Address, President Lyndon Johnson declares "unconditional war on poverty in America."
	July 2	President Johnson signs the Civil Rights Act of 1964, which outlaws racial discrimination in public accommodations and employment.
	December 10	King accepts the Nobel Peace Prize in Oslo, Norway.
1965	March 8	The first U.S. combat troops arrive in South Vietnam.
	August 6	The Voting Rights Act takes effect.
1966	December 31	Over the next six months, the number of U.S. military personnel serving in South Vietnam increases from 385,300 to 448,800.
1967	April 4	King gives the speech "Beyond Vietnam: A Time to Break Silence" at Riverside Church in New York City.
1968	April 4	King is murdered in Memphis, Tennessee.
1973	January 27	The Paris Peace Accords take effect, leading to the withdrawal of the last U.S. troops from the Vietnam War and the return of American prisoners of war.
1986	January 20	The federal holiday honoring King is first observed.

Essential Quotes

"We are taking the black young men who had been crippled by our society and sending them eight thousand miles away to guarantee liberties in Southeast Asia which they had not found in southwest Georgia and East Harlem."

"If America's soul becomes totally poisoned, part of the autopsy must read Vietnam."

"Increasingly, by choice or by accident, this is the role our nation has taken—the role of those who make peaceful revolution impossible by refusing to give up the privileges and the pleasures that come from the immense profits of overseas investment."

"A nation that continues year after year to spend more money on military defense than on programs of social uplift is approaching spiritual death."

"We must find new ways to speak for peace in Vietnam and justice throughout the developing world—a world that borders on our doors. If we do not act we shall surely be dragged down the long dark and shameful corridors of time reserved for those who possess power without compassion, might without morality, and strength without sight."

Questions for Further Study

1. What did King see as the connection between the Vietnam War and the issue of racial justice in the United States?

2. Compare this document with other critiques of the Vietnam War, in particular those contained in Malcolm X's "After the Bombing" (1965) and Stokely Carmichael's "Black Power" (1966). What similar arguments do the documents present? How did King's attitude toward Vietnam differ from that of the others, if at all?

3. Why did some of King's advisers urge him to sidestep the issue of the Vietnam War? Why do you think the war was such a divisive issue at the time?

4. What did President Lyndon Johnson and others see as the potential political consequences of the speech?

5. Many of King's arguments against the war in Vietnam could be applied to other conflicts, such as the U.S.-led wars in Iraq and Afghanistan. How persuasive do you find King's arguments? Would they be applicable to other conflicts?

"Beyond Vietnam: A Time to Break Silence"

The full text of King's speech.

I come to this magnificent house of worship tonight because my conscience leaves me no other choice. I join with you in this meeting because I am in deepest agreement with the aims and work of the organization which has brought us together: Clergy and Laymen Concerned about Vietnam. The recent statements of your executive committee are the sentiments of my own heart and I found myself in full accord when I read its opening lines: "A time comes when silence is betrayal." That time has come for us in relation to Vietnam.

The truth of these words is beyond doubt but the mission to which they call us is a most difficult one. Even when pressed by the demands of inner truth, men do not easily assume the task of opposing their government's policy, especially in time of war. Nor does the human spirit move without great difficulty against all the apathy of conformist thought within one's own bosom and in the surrounding world. Moreover when the issues at hand seem as perplexed as they often do in the case of this dreadful conflict we are always on the verge of being mesmerized by uncertainty; but we must move on.

Some of us who have already begun to break the silence of the night have found that the calling to speak is often a vocation of agony, but we must speak. We must speak with all the humility that is appropriate to our limited vision, but we must speak. And we must rejoice as well, for surely this is the first time in our nation's history that a significant number of its religious leaders have chosen to move beyond the prophesying of smooth patriotism to the high grounds of a firm dissent based upon the mandates of conscience and the reading of history. Perhaps a new spirit is rising among us. If it is, let us trace its movement well and pray that our own inner being may be sensitive to its guidance, for we are deeply in need of a new way beyond the darkness that seems so close around us.

Over the past two years, as I have moved to break the betrayal of my own silences and to speak from the burnings of my own heart, as I have called for radical departures from the destruction of Vietnam, many persons have questioned me about the wisdom of my path. At the heart of their concerns this query has often loomed large and loud: Why are you speaking about war, Dr. King? Why are you joining the voices of dissent? Peace and civil rights don't mix, they say. Aren't you hurting the cause of your people, they ask? And when I hear them, though I often understand the source of their concern, I am nevertheless greatly saddened, for such questions mean that the inquirers have not really known me, my commitment or my calling. Indeed, their questions suggest that they do not know the world in which they live.

In the light of such tragic misunderstandings, I deem it of signal importance to try to state clearly, and I trust concisely, why I believe that the path from Dexter Avenue Baptist Church—the church in Montgomery, Alabama, where I began my pastorate—leads clearly to this sanctuary tonight.

I come to this platform tonight to make a passionate plea to my beloved nation. This speech is not addressed to Hanoi or to the National Liberation Front. It is not addressed to China or to Russia.

Nor is it an attempt to overlook the ambiguity of the total situation and the need for a collective solution to the tragedy of Vietnam. Neither is it an attempt to make North Vietnam or the National Liberation Front paragons of virtue, nor to overlook the role they can play in a successful resolution of the problem. While they both may have justifiable reason to be suspicious of the good faith of the United States, life and history give eloquent testimony to the fact that conflicts are never resolved without trustful give and take on both sides.

Tonight, however, I wish not to speak with Hanoi and the NLF, but rather to my fellow Americans, who, with me, bear the greatest responsibility in ending a conflict that has exacted a heavy price on both continents.

The Importance of Vietnam

Since I am a preacher by trade, I suppose it is not surprising that I have seven major reasons for bringing Vietnam into the field of my moral vision. There is at the outset a very obvious and almost facile connection between the war in Vietnam and the struggle I, and others, have been waging in America. A few years ago there was a shining moment in that struggle. It seemed as if there was a real promise of hope for the poor—both black and white—through the poverty program. There were experiments, hopes, new beginnings. Then came the buildup in Vietnam and I watched the program broken and eviscerated as if it were some idle political plaything of a society gone mad on war, and I knew that America would never invest the necessary funds or energies in rehabilitation of its poor so long as adventures like Vietnam continued to draw men and skills and money like some demonic destructive suction tube. So I was increasingly compelled to see the war as an enemy of the poor and to attack it as such.

Perhaps the more tragic recognition of reality took place when it became clear to me that the war was doing far more than devastating the hopes of the poor at home. It was sending their sons and their brothers and their husbands to fight and to die in extraordinarily high proportions relative to the rest of the population. We were taking the black young men who had been crippled by our society and sending them eight thousand miles away to guarantee liberties in Southeast Asia which they had not found in southwest Georgia and East Harlem. So we have been repeatedly faced with the cruel irony of watching Negro and white boys on TV screens as they kill and die together for a nation that has been unable to seat them together in the same schools. So we watch them in brutal solidarity burning the huts of a poor village, but we realize that they would never live on the same block in Detroit. I could not be silent in the face of such cruel manipulation of the poor.

My third reason moves to an even deeper level of awareness, for it grows out of my experience in the ghettoes of the North over the last three years—especially the last three summers. As I have walked among the desperate, rejected and angry young men I have told them that Molotov cocktails and rifles would not solve their problems. I have tried to offer them my deepest compassion while maintaining my conviction that social change comes most meaningfully through nonviolent action. But they asked—and rightly so—what about Vietnam? They asked if our own nation wasn't using massive doses of violence to solve its problems, to bring about the changes it wanted. Their questions hit home, and I knew that I could never again raise my voice against the violence of the oppressed in the ghettos without having first spoken clearly to the greatest purveyor of violence in the world today—my own government. For the sake of those boys, for the sake of this government, for the sake of hundreds of thousands trembling under our violence, I cannot be silent.

For those who ask the question, "Aren't you a civil rights leader?" and thereby mean to exclude me from the movement for peace, I have this further answer. In 1957 when a group of us formed the Southern Christian Leadership Conference, we chose as our motto: "To save the soul of America." We were convinced that we could not limit our vision to certain rights for black people, but instead affirmed the conviction that America would never be free or saved from itself unless the descendants of its slaves were loosed completely from the shackles they still wear. In a way we were agreeing with Langston Hughes, that black bard of Harlem, who had written earlier:

O, yes,
I say it plain,
America never was America to me,
And yet I swear this oath—
America will be!

Now, it should be incandescently clear that no one who has any concern for the integrity and life of America today can ignore the present war. If America's soul becomes totally poisoned, part of the autopsy must read Vietnam. It can never be saved so long as it destroys the deepest hopes of men the world over. So it is that those of us who are yet determined that America will be are led down the path of protest and dissent, working for the health of our land.

As if the weight of such a commitment to the life and health of America were not enough, another burden of responsibility was placed upon me in 1964; and I cannot forget that the Nobel Prize for Peace was also a commission—a commission to work harder than I had ever worked before for "the brotherhood of man." This is a calling that takes me beyond national allegiances, but even if it were not present I would yet have to live with the meaning of my commitment to the ministry of Jesus Christ. To me the relationship of this ministry to the making of peace is so obvious that I sometimes marvel at those who ask me why I am speaking against the war. Could it be that they do not know that the good news was meant for all men—for Communist and capitalist, for their children and ours, for black and for white, for revolutionary and conservative? Have they forgotten that my ministry is in obedience to the one who loved his enemies so fully that he died for them? What then can I say to the "Vietcong" or to Castro or to Mao as a faithful minister of this one? Can I threaten them with death or must I not share with them my life?

Finally, as I try to delineate for you and for myself the road that leads from Montgomery to this place I would have offered all that was most valid if I simply said that I must be true to my conviction that I share with all men the calling to be a son of the living God. Beyond the calling of race or nation or creed is this vocation of sonship and brotherhood, and because I believe that the Father is deeply concerned especially for his suffering and helpless and outcast children, I come tonight to speak for them.

This I believe to be the privilege and the burden of all of us who deem ourselves bound by allegiances and loyalties which are broader and deeper than nationalism and which go beyond our nation's self-defined goals and positions. We are called to speak for the weak, for the voiceless, for victims of our nation and for those it calls enemy, for no document from human hands can make these humans any less our brothers.

Strange Liberators

And as I ponder the madness of Vietnam and search within myself for ways to understand and respond to compassion my mind goes constantly to the people of that peninsula. I speak now not of the soldiers of each side, not of the junta in Saigon, but simply of the people who have been living under the curse of war for almost three continuous decades now. I think of them too because it is clear to me that there will be no meaningful solution there until some attempt is made to know them and hear their broken cries.

They must see Americans as strange liberators. The Vietnamese people proclaimed their own independence in 1945 after a combined French and Japanese occupation, and before the Communist revolution in China. They were led by Ho Chi Minh. Even though they quoted the American Declaration of Independence in their own document of freedom, we refused to recognize them. Instead, we decided to support France in its reconquest of her former colony.

Our government felt then that the Vietnamese people were not "ready" for independence, and we again fell victim to the deadly Western arrogance that has poisoned the international atmosphere for so long. With that tragic decision we rejected a revolutionary government seeking self-determination, and a government that had been established not by China (for whom the Vietnamese have no great love) but by clearly indigenous forces that included some Communists. For the peasants this new government meant real land reform, one of the most important needs in their lives.

For nine years following 1945 we denied the people of Vietnam the right of independence. For nine years we vigorously supported the French in their abortive effort to recolonize Vietnam.

Before the end of the war we were meeting eighty percent of the French war costs. Even before the French were defeated at Dien Bien Phu, they began to despair of the reckless action, but we did not. We encouraged them with our huge financial and military supplies to continue the war even after they had lost the will. Soon we would be paying almost the full costs of this tragic attempt at recolonization.

After the French were defeated it looked as if independence and land reform would come again through the Geneva agreements. But instead there came the United States, determined that Ho should not unify the temporarily divided nation, and the peasants watched again as we supported one of the most vicious modern dictators—our chosen man, Premier Diem. The peasants watched and cringed as Diem ruthlessly routed out all opposition, supported their extortionist landlords and refused even to discuss reunification with the north. The peasants watched as all this was presided over by U.S. influence and then by increasing numbers of U.S. troops who came to help quell the insurgency that Diem's methods had aroused. When Diem was overthrown they may have been happy, but the long line of military dictatorships seemed to offer no real change—especially in terms of their need for land and peace.

The only change came from America as we increased our troop commitments in support of governments which were singularly corrupt, inept and without popular support. All the while the people read our leaflets and received regular promises of peace and democracy—and land reform. Now they languish under our bombs and consider us—not their fellow Vietnamese—the real enemy. They move sadly and apathetically as we herd them off the land of their fathers into concentration camps where minimal social needs are rarely met. They know they

Document Text

must move or be destroyed by our bombs. So they go—primarily women and children and the aged.

They watch as we poison their water, as we kill a million acres of their crops. They must weep as the bulldozers roar through their areas preparing to destroy the precious trees. They wander into the hospitals, with at least twenty casualties from American firepower for one "Vietcong"-inflicted injury. So far we may have killed a million of them—mostly children. They wander into the towns and see thousands of the children, homeless, without clothes, running in packs on the streets like animals. They see the children, degraded by our soldiers as they beg for food. They see the children selling their sisters to our soldiers, soliciting for their mothers.

What do the peasants think as we ally ourselves with the landlords and as we refuse to put any action into our many words concerning land reform? What do they think as we test our latest weapons on them, just as the Germans tested out new medicine and new tortures in the concentration camps of Europe? Where are the roots of the independent Vietnam we claim to be building? Is it among these voiceless ones?

We have destroyed their two most cherished institutions: the family and the village. We have destroyed their land and their crops. We have cooperated in the crushing of the nation's only non-Communist revolutionary political force—the unified Buddhist church. We have supported the enemies of the peasants of Saigon. We have corrupted their women and children and killed their men. What liberators?

Now there is little left to build on—save bitterness. Soon the only solid physical foundations remaining will be found at our military bases and in the concrete of the concentration camps we call fortified hamlets. The peasants may well wonder if we plan to build our new Vietnam on such grounds as these? Could we blame them for such thoughts? We must speak for them and raise the questions they cannot raise. These too are our brothers.

Perhaps the more difficult but no less necessary task is to speak for those who have been designated as our enemies. What of the National Liberation Front—that strangely anonymous group we call VC or Communists? What must they think of us in America when they realize that we permitted the repression and cruelty of Diem which helped to bring them into being as a resistance group in the south? What do they think of our condoning the violence which led to their own taking up of arms? How can they believe in our integrity when now we speak of "aggression from the north" as if there were nothing more essential to the war? How can they trust us when now we charge them with violence after the murderous reign of Diem and charge them with violence while we pour every new weapon of death into their land? Surely we must understand their feelings even if we do not condone their actions. Surely we must see that the men we supported pressed them to their violence. Surely we must see that our own computerized plans of destruction simply dwarf their greatest acts.

How do they judge us when our officials know that their membership is less than twenty-five percent Communist and yet insist on giving them the blanket name? What must they be thinking when they know that we are aware of their control of major sections of Vietnam and yet we appear ready to allow national elections in which this highly organized political parallel government will have no part? They ask how we can speak of free elections when the Saigon press is censored and controlled by the military junta. And they are surely right to wonder what kind of new government we plan to help form without them—the only party in real touch with the peasants. They question our political goals and they deny the reality of a peace settlement from which they will be excluded. Their questions are frighteningly relevant. Is our nation planning to build on political myth again and then shore it up with the power of new violence?

Here is the true meaning and value of compassion and nonviolence when it helps us to see the enemy's point of view, to hear his questions, to know his assessment of ourselves. For from his view we may indeed see the basic weaknesses of our own condition, and if we are mature, we may learn and grow and profit from the wisdom of the brothers who are called the opposition.

So, too, with Hanoi. In the north, where our bombs now pummel the land, and our mines endanger the waterways, we are met by a deep but understandable mistrust. To speak for them is to explain this lack of confidence in Western words, and especially their distrust of American intentions now. In Hanoi are the men who led the nation to independence against the Japanese and the French, the men who sought membership in the French commonwealth and were betrayed by the weakness of

Paris and the willfulness of the colonial armies. It was they who led a second struggle against French domination at tremendous costs, and then were persuaded to give up the land they controlled between the thirteenth and seventeenth parallel as a temporary measure at Geneva. After 1954 they watched us conspire with Diem to prevent elections which would have surely brought Ho Chi Minh to power over a united Vietnam, and they realized they had been betrayed again.

When we ask why they do not leap to negotiate, these things must be remembered. Also it must be clear that the leaders of Hanoi considered the presence of American troops in support of the Diem regime to have been the initial military breach of the Geneva agreements concerning foreign troops, and they remind us that they did not begin to send in any large number of supplies or men until American forces had moved into the tens of thousands.

Hanoi remembers how our leaders refused to tell us the truth about the earlier North Vietnamese overtures for peace, how the president claimed that none existed when they had clearly been made. Ho Chi Minh has watched as America has spoken of peace and built up its forces, and now he has surely heard of the increasing international rumors of American plans for an invasion of the north. He knows the bombing and shelling and mining we are doing are part of traditional pre-invasion strategy. Perhaps only his sense of humor and of irony can save him when he hears the most powerful nation of the world speaking of aggression as it drops thousands of bombs on a poor weak nation more than eight thousand miles away from its shores.

At this point I should make it clear that while I have tried in these last few minutes to give a voice to the voiceless on Vietnam and to understand the arguments of those who are called enemy, I am as deeply concerned about our troops there as anything else. For it occurs to me that what we are submitting them to in Vietnam is not simply the brutalizing process that goes on in any war where armies face each other and seek to destroy. We are adding cynicism to the process of death, for they must know after a short period there that none of the things we claim to be fighting for are really involved. Before long they must know that their government has sent them into a struggle among Vietnamese, and the more sophisticated surely realize that we are on the side of the wealthy and the secure while we create hell for the poor.

This Madness Must Cease

Somehow this madness must cease. We must stop now. I speak as a child of God and brother to the suffering poor of Vietnam. I speak for those whose land is being laid waste, whose homes are being destroyed, whose culture is being subverted. I speak for the poor of America who are paying the double price of smashed hopes at home and death and corruption in Vietnam. I speak as a citizen of the world, for the world as it stands aghast at the path we have taken. I speak as an American to the leaders of my own nation. The great initiative in this war is ours. The initiative to stop it must be ours.

This is the message of the great Buddhist leaders of Vietnam. Recently one of them wrote these words:

"Each day the war goes on the hatred increases in the heart of the Vietnamese and in the hearts of those of humanitarian instinct. The Americans are forcing even their friends into becoming their enemies. It is curious that the Americans, who calculate so carefully on the possibilities of military victory, do not realize that in the process they are incurring deep psychological and political defeat. The image of America will never again be the image of revolution, freedom and democracy, but the image of violence and militarism."

If we continue, there will be no doubt in my mind and in the mind of the world that we have no honorable intentions in Vietnam. It will become clear that our minimal expectation is to occupy it as an American colony and men will not refrain from thinking that our maximum hope is to goad China into a war so that we may bomb her nuclear installations. If we do not stop our war against the people of Vietnam immediately the world will be left with no other alternative than to see this as some horribly clumsy and deadly game we have decided to play.

The world now demands a maturity of America that we may not be able to achieve. It demands that we admit that we have been wrong from the beginning of our adventure in Vietnam, that we have been detrimental to the life of the Vietnamese people. The situation is one in which we must be ready to turn sharply from our present ways.

In order to atone for our sins and errors in Vietnam, we should take the initiative in bringing a halt to this tragic war. I would like to suggest five concrete things that our government should do immediately to begin the long and difficult process of extricating ourselves from this nightmarish conflict:

1. End all bombing in North and South Vietnam.
2. Declare a unilateral cease-fire in the hope that such action will create the atmosphere for negotiation.
3. Take immediate steps to prevent other battlegrounds in Southeast Asia by curtailing our military buildup in Thailand and our interference in Laos.
4. Realistically accept the fact that the National Liberation Front has substantial support in South Vietnam and must thereby play a role in any meaningful negotiations and in any future Vietnam government.
5. Set a date that we will remove all foreign troops from Vietnam in accordance with the 1954 Geneva agreement.

Part of our ongoing commitment might well express itself in an offer to grant asylum to any Vietnamese who fears for his life under a new regime which included the Liberation Front. Then we must make what reparations we can for the damage we have done. We must provide the medical aid that is badly needed, making it available in this country if necessary.

Protesting the War

Meanwhile we in the churches and synagogues have a continuing task while we urge our government to disengage itself from a disgraceful commitment. We must continue to raise our voices if our nation persists in its perverse ways in Vietnam. We must be prepared to match actions with words by seeking out every creative means of protest possible.

As we counsel young men concerning military service we must clarify for them our nation's role in Vietnam and challenge them with the alternative of conscientious objection. I am pleased to say that this is the path now being chosen by more than seventy students at my own alma mater, Morehouse College, and I recommend it to all who find the American course in Vietnam a dishonorable and unjust one. Moreover I would encourage all ministers of draft age to give up their ministerial exemptions and seek status as conscientious objectors. These are the times for real choices and not false ones. We are at the moment when our lives must be placed on the line if our nation is to survive its own folly. Every man of humane convictions must decide on the protest that best suits his convictions, but we must all protest.

There is something seductively tempting about stopping there and sending us all off on what in some circles has become a popular crusade against the war in Vietnam. I say we must enter the struggle, but I wish to go on now to say something even more disturbing. The war in Vietnam is but a symptom of a far deeper malady within the American spirit, and if we ignore this sobering reality we will find ourselves organizing clergy- and laymen-concerned committees for the next generation. They will be concerned about Guatemala and Peru. They will be concerned about Thailand and Cambodia. They will be concerned about Mozambique and South Africa. We will be marching for these and a dozen other names and attending rallies without end unless there is a significant and profound change in American life and policy. Such thoughts take us beyond Vietnam, but not beyond our calling as sons of the living God.

In 1957 a sensitive American official overseas said that it seemed to him that our nation was on the wrong side of a world revolution. During the past ten years we have seen emerge a pattern of suppression which now has justified the presence of U.S. military "advisors" in Venezuela. This need to maintain social stability for our investments accounts for the counter-revolutionary action of American forces in Guatemala. It tells why American helicopters are being used against guerrillas in Colombia and why American napalm and green beret forces have already been active against rebels in Peru. It is with such activity in mind that the words of the late John F. Kennedy come back to haunt us. Five years ago he said, "Those who make peaceful revolution impossible will make violent revolution inevitable."

Increasingly, by choice or by accident, this is the role our nation has taken—the role of those who make peaceful revolution impossible by refusing to give up the privileges and the pleasures that come from the immense profits of overseas investment.

I am convinced that if we are to get on the right side of the world revolution, we as a nation must undergo a radical revolution of values. We must rapidly begin the shift from a "thing-oriented" society to a "person-oriented" society. When machines and computers, profit motives and property rights are considered more important than people, the giant triplets of racism, materialism, and militarism are incapable of being conquered.

A true revolution of values will soon cause us to question the fairness and justice of many of our past and present policies. On the one hand we are called to play the good Samaritan on life's roadside; but that will be only an initial act. One day we must come to see that the whole Jericho road must be transformed so that men and women will not be constantly beaten and robbed as they make their journey on life's highway. True compassion is more than flinging a coin to a beggar; it is not haphazard and superficial. It comes to see that an edifice which produces beggars needs restructuring. A true revolution of values will soon look uneasily on the glaring contrast of poverty and wealth. With righteous indignation, it will look across the seas and see individual capitalists of the West investing huge sums of money in Asia, Africa and South America, only to take the profits out with no concern for the social betterment of the countries, and say: "This is not just." It will look at our alliance with the landed gentry of Latin America and say: "This is not just." The Western arrogance of feeling that it has everything to teach others and nothing to learn from them is not just. A true revolution of values will lay hands on the world order and say of war: "This way of settling differences is not just." This business of burning human beings with napalm, of filling our nation's homes with orphans and widows, of injecting poisonous drugs of hate into veins of people normally humane, of sending men home from dark and bloody battlefields physically handicapped and psychologically deranged, cannot be reconciled with wisdom, justice and love. A nation that continues year after year to spend more money on military defense than on programs of social uplift is approaching spiritual death.

America, the richest and most powerful nation in the world, can well lead the way in this revolution of values. There is nothing, except a tragic death wish, to prevent us from reordering our priorities, so that the pursuit of peace will take precedence over the pursuit of war. There is nothing to keep us from molding a recalcitrant status quo with bruised hands until we have fashioned it into a brotherhood.

This kind of positive revolution of values is our best defense against communism. War is not the answer. Communism will never be defeated by the use of atomic bombs or nuclear weapons. Let us not join those who shout war and through their misguided passions urge the United States to relinquish its participation in the United Nations. These are days which demand wise restraint and calm reasonableness. We must not call everyone a Communist or an appeaser who advocates the seating of Red China in the United Nations and who recognizes that hate and hysteria are not the final answers to the problem of these turbulent days. We must not engage in a negative anti-communism, but rather in a positive thrust for democracy, realizing that our greatest defense against communism is to take offensive action in behalf of justice. We must with positive action seek to remove those conditions of poverty, insecurity and injustice which are the fertile soil in which the seed of communism grows and develops.

The People Are Important

These are revolutionary times. All over the globe men are revolting against old systems of exploitation and oppression and out of the wombs of a frail world new systems of justice and equality are being born. The shirtless and barefoot people of the land are rising up as never before. " The people who sat in darkness have seen a great light." We in the West must support these revolutions. It is a sad fact that, because of comfort, complacency, a morbid fear of communism, and our proneness to adjust to injustice, the Western nations that initiated so much of the revolutionary spirit of the modern world have now become the arch anti-revolutionaries. This has driven many to feel that only Marxism has the revolutionary spirit. Therefore, communism is a judgment against our failure to make democracy real and follow through on the revolutions we initiated. Our only hope today lies in our ability to recapture the revolutionary spirit and go out into a sometimes hostile world declaring eternal hostility to poverty, racism, and militarism. With this powerful commitment we shall boldly challenge the status quo and unjust mores and thereby speed the day when "every valley shall be exalted, and every mountain and hill shall be made low, and the crooked shall be made straight and the rough places plain."

A genuine revolution of values means in the final analysis that our loyalties must become ecumenical rather than sectional. Every nation must now develop an overriding loyalty to mankind as a whole in order to preserve the best in their individual societies.

This call for a world-wide fellowship that lifts neighborly concern beyond one's tribe, race, class and nation is in reality a call for an all-embracing and unconditional love for all men. This oft misunderstood and misinterpreted concept—so readily dismissed by the Nietzsches of the world as a weak and cowardly force—has now become an absolute necessity for the survival of man. When I speak of love I am not speaking of some sentimental and weak response. I am speaking of that force which all of the great religions have seen as the supreme unifying principle of life. Love is somehow the key that unlocks the door which leads to ultimate reality. This Hindu-Moslem-Christian-Jewish-Buddhist belief about ultimate reality is beautifully summed up in the first epistle of Saint John:

Let us love one another; for love is God and everyone that loveth is born of God and knoweth God. He that loveth not knoweth not God; for God is love. If we love one another God dwelleth in us, and his love is perfected in us.

Let us hope that this spirit will become the order of the day. We can no longer afford to worship the god of hate or bow before the altar of retaliation. The oceans of history are made turbulent by the ever-rising tides of hate. History is cluttered with the wreckage of nations and individuals that pursued this self-defeating path of hate. As Arnold Toynbee says: "Love is the ultimate force that makes for the saving choice of life and good against the damning choice of death and evil. Therefore the first hope in our inventory must be the hope that love is going to have the last word."

We are now faced with the fact that tomorrow is today. We are confronted with the fierce urgency of now. In this unfolding conundrum of life and history there is such a thing as being too late. Procrastination is still the thief of time. Life often leaves us standing bare, naked and dejected with a lost opportunity. The "tide in the affairs of men" does not remain at the flood; it ebbs. We may cry out desperately for time to pause in her passage, but time is deaf to every plea and rushes on. Over the bleached bones and jumbled residue of numerous civilizations are written the pathetic words: "Too late." There is an invisible book of life that faithfully records our vigilance or our neglect. " The moving finger writes, and having writ moves on.... " We still have a choice today; nonviolent coexistence or violent co-annihilation.

We must move past indecision to action. We must find new ways to speak for peace in Vietnam and justice throughout the developing world—a world that borders on our doors. If we do not act we shall surely be dragged down the long dark and shameful corridors of time reserved for those who possess power without compassion, might without morality, and strength without sight.

Now let us begin. Now let us rededicate ourselves to the long and bitter—but beautiful—struggle for a new world. This is the calling of the sons of God, and our brothers wait eagerly for our response. Shall we say the odds are too great? Shall we tell them the struggle is too hard? Will our message be that the forces of American life militate against their arrival as full men, and we send our deepest regrets? Or will there be another message, of longing, of hope, of solidarity with their yearnings, of commitment to their cause, whatever the cost? The choice is ours, and though we might prefer it otherwise we must choose in this crucial moment of human history.

As that noble bard of yesterday, James Russell Lowell, eloquently stated:

Once to every man and nation
Comes the moment to decide,
In the strife of truth and falsehood,
For the good or evil side;
Some great cause, God's new Messiah,
Off'ring each the bloom or blight,
And the choice goes by forever
Twixt that darkness and that light.
Though the cause of evil prosper,
Yet 'tis truth alone is strong;
Though her portion be the scaffold,
And upon the throne be wrong:
Yet that scaffold sways the future,
And behind the dim unknown,
Standeth God within the shadow
Keeping watch above his own.

Glossary

Arnold Toynbee: a twentieth-century British historian who examined the rise and fall of civilizations

Castro: Fidel Castro, who was then the Communist dictator of Cuba

Dien Bien Phu: a town in North Vietnam, the site of a decisive battle between the Communists and the French in 1954

good Samaritan: reference to a parable told by Jesus, as recorded in the Gospel of Luke, chapter 10, in which a Samaritan (member of an ethnoreligious group) helps a Jew on his way to Jericho who has been beaten and robbed; symbolic of a kind person who helps a stranger

Hanoi: the capital of North Vietnam

Ho Chi Minh: the leader of the Communist forces during the Vietnam War

James Russell Lowell: nineteenth-century American poet; the quotation is from his 1845 poem "Once to Every Man and Nation."

junta: a dictatorship run by a group of military officers

Langston Hughes: a prominent African American poet of the Harlem Renaissance; the quote is from his 1939 poem "Let America Be America Again."

"Let us love one another …": from the First Epistle of John, chapter 4

Mao: Mao Zedong, the Communist dictator of China

Marxism: the philosophy of Karl Marx, the nineteenth-century German writer whose name is often used synonymously with Communism

Molotov cocktails: improvised bombs, usually made with gasoline and a bottle; named after Vyacheslav Molotov, Soviet foreign minister during World War II, by the Finns, who used them to resist the Soviet Union

"The moving finger writes …": quotation from verse 51 of Edward FitzGerald's poem *Rubáiyát of Omar Khayyám*

napalm: a highly flammable explosive often used to burn forested areas thought to hold troops during the Vietnam War

National Liberation Front: Communists who led the insurgency in Vietnam

Nietzsches: a reference to Friedrich Nietzsche, a nineteenth-century German philosopher

"The people who sat in darkness …": quotation from the Gospel of Matthew, chapter 4, verse 16

Premier Diem: Ngo Dinh Diem, the first president of South Vietnam, who was assassinated in 1963

"tide in the affairs of men": quotation from Shakespeare's *Julius Caesar*, act 4, scene 3

VC: abbreviation for Vietcong

Vietcong: the Western name for the Communist insurgents in Vietnam

Mildred and Richard Loving in 1967. Bettmann/Corbis via New York Times retrieved on September 17, 2008. Fair use.

LOVING V. VIRGINIA

1967

"The freedom to marry has long been recognized as one of the vital personal rights essential to the orderly pursuit of happiness by free men."

Overview

In 1967 in *Loving v. Virginia*, Chief Justice Earl Warren wrote on behalf of a unanimous Supreme Court to declare antimiscegenation laws in violation of the Fourteenth Amendment to the U.S. Constitution. Laws against interracial marriage were widespread in the United States into the 1960s. An interracial couple from Virginia, wanting to be "Mr. and Mrs. Richard Loving," found themselves taken to jail in 1958 and then to court because he was white and she was not. They were convicted of the crime of marrying each other, but eventually they appealed their convictions, and the case went to the U.S. Supreme Court. There, the Fourteenth Amendment, which had been in the Constitution for almost exactly a century, was for the first time interpreted to declare unconstitutional all state laws against interracial marriage. As a result, more than three hundred years after the first of such laws was passed, none could any longer be enforced. States retained their authority over the law of marriage in other respects but no longer as regarded racial classifications.

Thus, thirteen years after the Warren Court overturned segregated public schooling, all laws against interracial marriage—the last refuge for state-mandated segregation—were overturned as well. As with the Montgomery bus boycott, some citizens had protested the segregation laws, and their resistance led to the Supreme Court's ruling against those laws. The Lovings, then, can be seen as important actors in the civil rights movement. At the same time, Chief Justice Warren's decision to throw out the case against them can be seen as a crucial document, akin to President Harry S. Truman's Executive Order 9981 in 1948 against segregation in the U.S. armed forces, the Supreme Court's ruling in *Brown v. Board of Education of Topeka* in 1954, and the congressional passage of the Civil Rights Act of 1964 and the Voting Rights Act of 1965. *Loving v. Virginia* brought down the last of the Jim Crow laws that had segregated so much of American life for so long.

Context

Laws against interracial marriage were on the books of most of the American colonies before the Revolution. The term *miscegenation*, referring to sex or marriage between people of two different races, was coined in the course of President Abraham Lincoln's bid for reelection in 1864, when David Goodman Croly and George Wakeman, two Democratic newspapermen, produced a hoax pamphlet with that term as the title designed to give the impression that Lincoln favored interracial marriage. A majority of states retained their antimiscegenation laws through the nineteenth century and even beyond World War II. Those laws varied widely, however, in how they chose to define *interracial*, in whether they made interracial marriage a crime, and in whether they would recognize an interracial marriage that took place outside their borders. Some states repealed their laws and never restored them, while seven southern states, including Louisiana and Arkansas, dropped such laws in the 1870s but then restored them by the 1890s. As of 1895, interracial marriage was banned throughout the South.

In 1912 the Georgia congressman Seaborn Roddenbery proposed an amendment to the U.S. Constitution to ban black-white marriages everywhere in the nation, but it did not pass. Nonetheless, between 1913 and 1948, thirty of the forty-eight states maintained laws against interracial marriage. Then, beginning with a four-to-three decision in *Perez v. Sharp* by the Supreme Court of California in 1948, followed by a series of legislative repeals, all the states outside the South shed those laws; after 1965 only the seventeen states of the South retained them. A newly reapportioned Maryland legislature passed a repeal measure in early 1967, to be effective on June 1, leaving sixteen states with antimiscegenation laws.

Over the years, the Supreme Court had addressed various matters related to marriage. The majority opinion in the 1857 *Dred Scott* case cited northern laws against interracial marriage as evidence that whites outside the South shared a common disinclination to recognize their African American neighbors as full citizens. In a major precedent, the Court ruled unanimously in *Pace v. Alabama* (1883) that, where a black man and a white woman had been convicted of living together outside marriage—and under Alabama law at the time, they could not have legally married—it was no violation of their rights that the punishment for their crime was greater than it would have been had they shared a racial identity, white or black. In the 1888 case *Maynard v. Hill*, the Court stated that marriage has "always been subject to the control of the legislature." In *Plessy v. Ferguson* (1896), the Court made passing note of segregation statutes governing marriage on its way to upholding a segregation statute governing railway travel. Between 1954 and 1956 the Supreme Court refused to hear two cases, *Jackson v. State of Alabama* and the Virginia case *Naim v. Naim*, regarding antimiscegenation statutes, leaving the statutes intact. And in 1964 the Court expressly chose not to address interracial marriage in a case, *McLaughlin v. Florida*, that resembled *Pace v. Alabama*—except that here the Court did throw out as unconstitutional Florida's statute against interracial cohabitation.

Virginia's first law against interracial marriage dated from 1691, when a white person who married a nonwhite was subject to exile from the colony—though back in 1614, the marriage between the Native American Pocahontas and the Englishman John Rolfe had brought a peaceful respite to the awful warfare that had been going on between the two peoples. In 1878, following the Civil War and the end of slavery, the legislature overhauled the rules to now subject both parties in a black-white marriage to two to five years in the penitentiary as well as to provide that if a Virginia couple, seeking to evade the statute, went out of state to get married and then returned, the penalties would be the same. Throughout the nineteenth century, a person in Virginia was legally white if less than one-quarter black; that is, a person with three white grandparents and one black grandparent was black, but a person with seven white great-grandparents was white. That law was changed in 1910, so that a person as much as one-sixteenth black was "colored," and again in 1924, with the Racial Integrity Act, so that any traceable African ancestry resulted in classification as a colored person. Thus the "one-drop" rule of black racial identity came to Virginia's law of marriage in 1924. The one material change to the law thereafter reduced the minimum prison term to a single year for each party to a marriage between a "white" person and a "colored" person.

In Caroline County, a rural portion of eastern Virginia, Richard Perry Loving was born a white man in 1933, and Mildred Delores Jeter, of African and Native American descent, was born a "colored" woman in 1939. They drove to Washington, D.C., in June 1958 to get married, returned to Caroline County, and were living with her parents about a month later when three law enforcement officers walked into the unlocked house late one night, awoke them, and arrested them for their unlawful marriage. At trial the following January, they pled guilty in accordance with the terms of a plea bargain. Instead of being sent to prison for a year, they were exiled from Virginia; reluctantly, they moved to Washington, D.C.

In 1963, however, Mrs. Loving wrote to Attorney General Robert F. Kennedy at the U.S. Department of Justice for help, and her plea made its way to Bernard S. Cohen, a young lawyer for the American Civil Liberties Union with an office in Alexandria, Virginia. Subsequently joined by another young lawyer, Philip J. Hirschkop, Cohen appealed the 1959 outcome at trial to the original judge, Leon M. Bazile. At issue under the Constitution were the due process and equal protection clauses of the Fourteenth Amendment, according to which governments must not intervene arbitrarily in people's lives or treat one racial group differently from another. In January 1965, Bazile wrote out a long opinion explaining why the law was constitutional and its application to the Lovings just; he remarked (as Warren would cite in *Loving*),

Almighty God created the races white, black, yellow, malay and red, and he placed them on separate continents. And but for the interference with his arrangement there would be no cause for such marriages. The fact that he separated the races shows that he did not intend for the races to mix.

The case went next to the Virginia Supreme Court, which in 1966 upheld the trial judge, and then to the U.S. Supreme Court.

Under Chief Justice Warren, the Court had been relying on the equal protection clause to chip away at the edifice of Jim Crow all the way back to the 1954 *Brown v. Board* case (with considerable preliminary work along those lines having been accomplished even before Warren came on the Court). Even aside from race, the Warren Court had been attacking impediments to human freedom that state authorities often imposed, whether state failure to provide defense lawyers to indigent defendants in criminal proceedings or state laws restricting access to birth control for married couples. The decision in *Loving v. Virginia* reflected both impulses, as the case was resolved with the Court's landmark 1967 ruling striking down laws against interracial marriage.

About the Author

As chief justice, Earl Warren assigned to himself the task of writing the Court's opinion in *Loving v. Virginia*. In the way that law clerks often do much of the actual drafting, however, Warren's clerk Benno Schmidt did the heavy lifting in the *Loving* case, following his boss's directions as to the reasoning and also some of the content. For example, Warren directed Schmidt to center the opinion on racial discrimination and the right to marry and to definitely cite Judge Bazile's language about how God had created the separate races and wanted to keep them separate.

Earl Warren was born in Los Angeles, California, in 1891. The son of a railroad-car repairman, the young Warren also worked for a time on railroads. He went to college and law school at the University of California, Berkeley; served briefly in World War I; and then went to work in the office of the district attorney for Alameda County, California. He would work there for eighteen years, thirteen as district attorney himself, gaining extensive experience as a prosecutor; in a 1931 survey he was voted the best district attorney in the nation. Beyond prosecuting defendants, on their behalf he urged that they each, if necessary, have a public defender so as to be fairly represented in criminal court proceedings. In 1938 he was elected attorney general of California, to serve a four-year term. In 1942 he ran as a Republican for the governorship of California and was elected to the first of three four-year terms. He was nominated for the vice presidency in 1948 as Thomas Dewey's running mate, but the presidency instead went to Harry Truman. Warren helped Dwight Eisenhower win their party's nomination for the presidency in 1952 and was offered the position of solicitor general in the new administration, but he was then nominated as chief justice of the United States when Chief Justice Fred Vinson died in September 1953. Warren was quickly confirmed and took the helm of the Supreme Court the following month.

In joining the Court, Warren was not new to issues related to the laws of race and marriage. As California's attorney general back in 1939, he was obligated to interpret the state's racial restrictions on marriage. And in 1948 he was serving as governor when the Supreme Court of California struck down that state's law against interracial marriages. Within three years of his appointment as chief justice, two cases regarding the constitutionality of laws against interracial marriage came to the Court, and in each—one from Virginia, one from Alabama—he was in the minority as to whether the Court would hear the case and potentially overturn the law that had given rise to it. As late as 1964, in *McLaughlin v. Florida*, though ruling in favor of an unmarried interracial couple, the Court had not been prepared to overturn laws against interracial marriage. In *Loving* in 1967, Warren had the perfect case and the perfect occasion for ruling against such laws everywhere.

While serving as chief justice, Warren reluctantly accepted the chairmanship of a special commission set up by Congress to investigate the 1963 assassination of President John F. Kennedy. The Warren Commission, as it became known, found that Lee Harvey Oswald acted alone in his assassination, a controversial conclusion. In June 1968, one year after the ruling in *Loving v. Virginia*, Warren informed President Lyndon B. Johnson that he wished to retire as soon as his successor could be confirmed. Johnson chose the associate Supreme Court justice Abe Fortas, whose nomination ran into such trouble toward the end of Johnson's presidency that he eventually withdrew his name; Warren's successor, Warren E. Burger, was an appointee of the new president, Richard M. Nixon. Earl Warren was working on his memoirs when he died in 1974.

Explanation and Analysis of the Document

Chief Justice Warren declares in the opening sentence of his opinion, "This case presents a constitutional question never addressed by this Court." While he is pointing out the novelty of the question, and certainly of the position the Court took that day, at the same time the chief justice may be apologizing for the Court's failure to address the question of interracial marriage at any of several earlier opportunities, including three on his watch. He specifies the question of whether state laws against interracial marriage violate the equal protection and due process clauses of the Fourteenth Amendment. He does not reserve the punch line: indeed, those laws do conflict with the Fourteenth Amendment; so they must fall. He then recounts the long journey the Lovings had taken, from their wedding nine years earlier up until their triumph achieved as he then read the Court's unanimous ruling that their convictions could not stand. And he quotes the trial judge's language about how God had "created the races"—five are listed—and wanted them not "to mix," though Warren misdates the trial judge's comments as coming from the original trial in 1959 rather than the actual occasion, the rehearing in 1965.

The chief justice quotes in full the statutory provisions that made it a crime for an interracial couple in Virginia to marry, not only inside the state but also outside of it if they planned to return to Virginia and live as a married couple there, as the Lovings had. He also supplies (in a lengthy footnote not reproduced here) the exact language that defined "white persons" and "colored persons" in Virginia. He notes that the Lovings had never contested their being classified, one as white and the other as colored, under those legal provisions (an approach sometimes taken by other interracial couples, who claimed to be both white or both nonwhite and therefore not subject to prosecution under the law). Warren mentions the extraordinary antiquity of Virginia's law, where "penalties for miscegenation arose as an incident to slavery and have been common in Virginia since the colonial period." But, as he observes, "the present statutory scheme dates from the adoption of the Racial Integrity Act of 1924," whose key provisions he recounts. A footnote (not provided here) lists the statutory provisions of the fifteen other states, all in the South, that still had such laws as Virginia's, and it also lists the fourteen states that, in the previous two decades, had repealed their antimiscegenation laws.

◆ Part I

In part I of the opinion, the chief justice reviews the charges against the Lovings and the leading arguments that the state of Virginia offered in its defense of its laws, and he rebuts each in turn. The Supreme Court of Appeals of Virginia, whose ruling was under appeal in this case, had, as one of its arguments in support of the constitutionality of the state's antimiscegenation laws, reached for a ruling by that same court a decade earlier, *Naim v. Naim* (1955), regarding a Chinese man and a white woman. As Warren forthrightly assesses, the Virginia court had declared that the state's "legitimate purposes" in enacting, enforcing, and upholding such laws "were 'to preserve the racial integrity of its citizens,' and to prevent 'the corruption of blood,' 'a mongrel breed of citizens,' and 'the obliteration of racial pride,' obviously an endorsement of the doctrine of White Supremacy." As the chief justice notes a little later, Virginia had banned not all interracial marriages but "only interracial marriages involving white persons." He goes on, in a footnote (not reproduced here), to condemn racial classifications in criminal statutes regardless of whether the "integrity" of all races or only that of whites is to be protected. So from the Court's perspective, neither white supremacy nor concern for racial integrity passed muster as a defense of the Virginia laws.

In the opening sentence of the second paragraph, Chief Justice Warren seriously undercuts the state's reliance on the Tenth Amendment's declaration regarding the legitimate powers of the states, and thus the rightful limits on federal authority, to deflect arguments based upon the Fourteenth Amendment and the limits on state powers. But such arguments still had to be addressed. In presenting its case to the Supreme Court, the state of Virginia drew upon a ruling from 1888, *Maynard v. Hill*, in which the Court baldly stated that marriage, "having more to do with the morals and civilization of a people than any other institution, has always been subject to the control of the legislature." Warren chides the state of Virginia for mounting such an argument in support of its laws of race and marriage: "While the state court is no doubt correct in asserting that marriage is a social relation subject to the State's police power,... the State does not contend in its argument before this Court that its powers to regulate marriage are unlimited notwithstanding the commands of the Fourteenth Amendment. Nor could it do so," the chief justice goes on, in view of some important cases from long before the 1960s but long after the 1880s, including *Meyer v. Nebraska* (1923), in which the Court had spoken expressly of "the right... to marry."

The state also argued that the equal protection clause should be understood as reflecting an intent by the Framers that, so long as punishments visited upon people, both black and white, were the same for violating a given law, such as Virginia's against interracial marriage, then the requirements of equal protection were satisfied. Indeed, the Supreme Court had accepted that very argument in 1883 in *Pace v. Alabama*, a case that arose when a man classified as black and a woman classified as white had, upon conviction for living together without being married, suffered a more severe sentence than they would have had they both been white or both black. Judge Bazile, in writing his opinion in 1965 in support of the original outcome for the Lovings at trial six years before, called upon a wide range of precedents that supported him, but he ignored a 1964 ruling by the Supreme Court to the contrary—viewing it as no more legitimate than he had perceived *Brown v. Board of Education* to be a decade earlier. That 1964 ruling, *McLaughlin v. Florida*, Chief Justice Warren now invokes, quoting the remark that "*Pace* represents a limited view of the Equal Protection Clause which has not withstood analysis in the subsequent decisions of this Court." Thus, *Pace v. Alabama* helped the state's case no more than did *Maynard v. Hill*. As to whether the Fourteenth Amendment protects against "classifications drawn by any statute" that "constitute an arbitrary and invidious discrimination," the Court had so held in *McLaughlin v. Florida*, and it is ruling so again in *Loving v. Virginia*. Warren has established that the equal protection clause sufficed to strike the Virginia laws and therefore the Lovings' convictions under those laws.

◆ Part II

The Lovings' attorneys had also argued on the basis of the due process clause, and this portion of the Fourteenth Amendment the Court also considers. To do so, the Court cites the 1942 case *Skinner v. State of Oklahoma* (which was primarily concerned with sterilization as legal punishment) as well as *Maynard v. Hill*, one of the key props in the state's case. That long-ago case from 1888, which on its face had nothing to do with race, spoke in very strong terms not only of legislative prerogative in the law of marriage but also of the supreme importance of marriage as an institution. So in the short final section on the due process clause, the chief justice speaks of "this fundamental freedom" and notes with reproof how antimiscegenation laws serve to "deprive all the State's citizens of liberty without due process of law." In short, though the Court does not use this precise language, Richard Loving had been denied—not despite his being a white man but indeed because he was a white man—the right to marry Mildred Jeter, and she had been similarly deprived of the right to marry him. In sum, this dual deprivation, and the Lovings' punishment for the crime of trying to be a married couple, constituted a denial of both equal protection and due process of law. So, the Court concludes, "These convictions must be reversed."

Audience

The Supreme Court could be said to have had three audiences for its ruling against laws that prevented couples defined as interracial from getting married. First was the Lovings themselves, who sought an end to their liability for prosecution for their marriage as well as an end to the enforcement of the terms of their plea bargain preventing their publicly living together back in Virginia. At the same time, the Court's audience consisted of public authorities in all sixteen states in which antimiscegenation laws had persisted as late as the time of the ruling. In light of *Loving*, those officials no longer had the authority to enforce such laws, whether in denying marriage licenses to interracial couples, prosecuting married couples under a criminal statute against interracial marriage, or denying inheritance benefits on the basis that a marriage, because interracial, had always been invalid in that state.

The third audience was all of America, and indeed the world, with the opinion announcing that new rules of race and marriage were now in place—whereby African Americans might in every state be suitable marriage partners for Caucasians—as the last wall in the edifice of American apartheid had been taken down. Looking further ahead, the ruling's sweeping language about "the freedom to marry" resonates up to the present time, as in state after state, same-sex couples seek to have the language and logic of *Loving v. Virginia* about "equal protection" and "the freedom to marry" applied to them.

Impact

The ruling's impact was immediate for the Lovings, who found themselves free to live openly together with their children in Virginia. There the children would grow to adulthood, and their parents would live out the rest of their lives. Richard Loving, among whose many occupations was that of bricklayer, symbolically heralded the family's newfound freedom by building a permanent new home of brick for them all.

Elsewhere, throughout the nation, public authorities could no longer enforce miscegenation laws. Interracial couples in Delaware, Arkansas, Louisiana, and many other states thus suddenly found that the key obstacle to their marrying had been taken down. *Loving*'s impact also extended to different dimensions of the law of marriage. The outcome of litigation in Oklahoma, for example, took a new turn after *Loving v. Virginia*, since a 1939 marriage between a white man and an African American woman, under which the widow's daughter and granddaughter had sought to inherit property in the 1960s, was suddenly valid; thus it could not be successfully contested by a son from his father's earlier marriage who did not wish to share his father's estate. Some years later, in 1984, the Supreme Court had occasion to revisit the *Loving* case and expand its reach after a local court in Florida removed a white child from the custody of her divorced mother, Linda Sidoti, on the grounds that she had married a black man, Clarence Palmore, Jr. The Court decided that race could not be grounds for reassigning child custody when a parent remarries across racial lines.

Within four years of *Loving v. Virginia*, same-sex couples were going to court seeking to obtain marriage licenses, arguing on the basis of the language and logic of *Loving* that they should not be denied the right to marry. In state after state, beginning with Minnesota in 1971 in *Baker v. Nelson*, such arguments were rebuffed. State legislatures thus yet retained the authority to define marriage and to continue, on grounds other than race, to restrict people's freedom to marry. In the 1990s, however, state judges began to prove receptive to such arguments if couched in terms of the provisions of state constitutions rather than those of the Fourteenth Amendment. In Hawaii and Alaska, voters subsequently approved a change in the language of their respective state constitutions to undo rulings based upon judicial interpretation of the former language. But in Vermont, "civil unions" resulted from a state supreme court ruling in favor of same-sex litigants, *Baker v. State of Vermont*. And in Massachusetts even that degree of change was deemed too small, an unconstitutional infringement of a constitutional right to marry. In *Goodrich v. Department of Public Health* (2003), the Supreme Judicial Court of Massachusetts, relying in part on *Loving v. Virginia*, interpreted the Massachusetts state constitution to require that same-sex couples enjoy the full right to marry that heterosexual couples do.

Further Reading

◆ Books

Cray, Ed. *Chief Justice: A Biography of Earl Warren*. New York: Simon & Schuster, 1997.

Kennedy, Randall. *Interracial Intimacies: Sex, Marriage, Identity, and Adoption*. New York: Pantheon, 2003.

Newbeck, Phyl. *Virginia Hasn't Always Been for Lovers: Interracial Marriage Bans and the Case of Richard and Mildred Loving*. Carbondale: Southern Illinois University Press, 2004.

Pascoe, Peggy. *What Comes Naturally: Miscegenation Law and the Making of Race in America*. New York: Oxford University Press, 2009.

Wallenstein, Peter. *Tell the Court I Love My Wife: Race, Marriage, and Law—An American History*. New York: Palgrave Macmillan, 2002.

—*Peter Wallenstein*

Questions for Further Study

1. The Commonwealth of Virginia had a long legal history pertaining to African Americans. Compare this document with Virginia's Act III: Baptism Does Not Exempt Slaves from Bondage (1667) and the Virginia Slave Code (1860). How were the antimiscegenation laws in effect in Virginia as late as the 1960s an outgrowth of the commonwealth's history?

2. What was the "one drop rule"? Why was this "rule" important in the nation's racial history?

3. On what fundamental constitutional basis did the Warren Court negate Virginia's laws against interracial marriage? Did the Court use the same principle in its decision in Brown v. Board of Education (1954)? Explain.

4. What impact did the Court's decision in Loving v. Virginia have on the debate involving same-sex couples? According to some people, how does the logic of the decision extend to such couples?

5. According to the entry, the "last wall in the edifice of American apartheid had been taken down" through the Court's decision in this case. Do you agree with this conclusion?

Essential Quotes

"The clear and central purpose of the Fourteenth Amendment was to eliminate all official state sources of invidious racial discrimination in the States."

"There can be no doubt that restricting the freedom to marry solely because of racial classifications violates the central meaning of the Equal Protection Clause."

"The freedom to marry has long been recognized as one of the vital personal rights essential to the orderly pursuit of happiness by free men."

"Under our Constitution, the freedom to marry, or not marry, a person of another race resides with the individual and cannot be infringed by the State."

Loving v. Virginia

Extracts from the court opinion.

Mr. Chief Justice Warren delivered the opinion of the Court

This case presents a constitutional question never addressed by this Court: whether a statutory scheme adopted by the State of Virginia to prevent marriages between persons solely on the basis of racial classifications violates the Equal Protection and Due Process Clauses of the Fourteenth Amendment. For reasons which seem to us to reflect the central meaning of those constitutional commands, we conclude that these statutes cannot stand consistently with the Fourteenth Amendment.

In June 1958, two residents of Virginia, Mildred Jeter, a Negro woman, and Richard Loving, a white man, were married in the District of Columbia pursuant to its laws. Shortly after their marriage, the Lovings returned to Virginia and established their marital abode in Caroline County. At the October Term, 1958, of the Circuit Court of Caroline County, a grand jury issued an indictment charging the Lovings with violating Virginia's ban on interracial marriages. On January 6, 1959, the Lovings pleaded guilty to the charge and were sentenced to one year in jail; however, the trial judge suspended the sentence for a period of 25 years on the condition that the Lovings leave the State and not return to Virginia together for 25 years. He stated in an opinion that:

"Almighty God created the races white, black, yellow, malay and red, and he placed them on separate continents. And but for the interference with his arrangement there would be no cause for such marriages. The fact that he separated the races shows that he did not intend for the races to mix."

After their convictions, the Lovings took up residence in the District of Columbia. On November 6, 1963, they filed a motion in the state trial court to vacate the judgment and set aside the sentence on the ground that the statutes which they had violated were repugnant to the Fourteenth Amendment. The motion not having been decided by October 28, 1964, the Lovings instituted a class action in the United States District Court for the Eastern District of Virginia requesting that a three-judge court be convened to declare the Virginia antimiscegenation statutes unconstitutional and to enjoin state officials from enforcing their convictions. On January 22, 1965, the state trial judge denied the motion to vacate the sentences, and the Lovings perfected an appeal to the Supreme Court of Appeals of Virginia. On February 11, 1965, the three-judge District Court continued the case to allow the Lovings to present their constitutional claims to the highest state court.

The Supreme Court of Appeals upheld the constitutionality of the antimiscegenation statutes and, after modifying the sentence, affirmed the convictions. The Lovings appealed this decision, and we noted probable jurisdiction on December 12, 1966, 385 U.S. 986.

The two statutes under which appellants were convicted and sentenced are part of a comprehensive statutory scheme aimed at prohibiting and punishing interracial marriages. The Lovings were convicted of violating § 20–58 of the Virginia Code:

> "*Leaving State to evade law.*—If any white person and colored person shall go out of this State, for the purpose of being married, and with the intention of returning, and be married out of it, and afterwards return to and reside in it, cohabiting as man and wife, they shall be punished as provided in § 20–59, and the marriage shall be governed by the same law as if it had been solemnized in this State. The fact of their cohabitation here as man and wife shall be evidence of their marriage."

Section 20–59, which defines the penalty for miscegenation, provides:

> "*Punishment for marriage.*—If any white person intermarry with a colored person, or any colored person intermarry with a white person, he shall be guilty of a felony and shall be punished by confinement in the penitentiary for not less than one nor more than five years."

Other central provisions in the Virginia statutory scheme are §20–57, which automatically voids all marriages between "a white person and a colored person" without any judicial proceeding, and §§20–54 and 1–14 which, respectively, define "white persons" and "colored persons and Indians" for purposes of the statutory prohibitions. The Lovings have never disputed in the course of this litigation that Mrs. Loving is a "colored person" or that Mr. Loving is a "white person" within the meanings given those terms by the Virginia statutes.

Virginia is now one of 16 States which prohibit and punish marriages on the basis of racial classifications. Penalties for miscegenation arose as an incident to slavery and have been common in Virginia since the colonial period. The present statutory scheme dates from the adoption of the Racial Integrity Act of 1924, passed during the period of extreme nativism which followed the end of the First World War. The central features of this Act, and current Virginia law, are the absolute prohibition of a "white person" marrying other than another "white person," a prohibition against issuing marriage licenses until the issuing official is satisfied that the applicants' statements as to their race are correct, certificates of "racial composition" to be kept by both local and state registrars, and the carrying forward of earlier prohibitions against racial intermarriage.

I

In upholding the constitutionality of these provisions in the decision below, the Supreme Court of Appeals of Virginia referred to its 1955 decision in *Naim v. Naim*, 197 Va. 80, 87 S.E. 2d 749, as stating the reasons supporting the validity of these laws. In *Naim*, the state court concluded that the State's legitimate purposes were "to preserve the racial integrity of its citizens," and to prevent "the corruption of blood," "a mongrel breed of citizens," and "the obliteration of racial pride," obviously an endorsement of the doctrine of White Supremacy. *Id.*, at 90, 87 S.E. 2d, at 756. The court also reasoned that marriage has traditionally been subject to state regulation without federal intervention, and, consequently, the regulation of marriage should be left to exclusive state control by the Tenth Amendment.

While the state court is no doubt correct in asserting that marriage is a social relation subject to the State's police power, *Maynard v. Hill*, 125 U.S. 190 (1888), the State does not contend in its argument before this Court that its powers to regulate marriage are unlimited notwithstanding the commands of the Fourteenth Amendment. Nor could it do so in light of *Meyer v. Nebraska*, 262 U.S. 390 (1923), and *Skinner v. Oklahoma*, 316 U.S. 535 (1942). Instead, the State argues that the meaning of the Equal Protection Clause, as illuminated by the statements of the Framers, is only that state penal laws containing an interracial element as part of the definition of the offense must apply equally to whites and Negroes in the sense that members of each race are punished to the same degree. Thus, the State contends that, because its miscegenation statutes punish equally both the white and the Negro participants in an interracial marriage, these statutes, despite their reliance on racial classifications, do not constitute an invidious discrimination based upon race. The second argument advanced by the State assumes the validity of its equal application theory. The argument is that, if the Equal Protection Clause does not outlaw miscegenation statutes because of their reliance on racial classifications, the question of constitutionality would thus become whether there was any rational basis for a State to treat interracial marriages differently from other marriages. On this question, the State argues, the scientific evidence is substantially in doubt and, consequently, this Court should defer to the wisdom of the state legislature in adopting its policy of discouraging interracial marriages.

Because we reject the notion that the mere "equal application" of a statute containing racial classifications is enough to remove the classifications from the Fourteenth Amendment's proscription of all invidious racial discriminations, we do not accept the State's contention that these statutes should be upheld if there is any possible basis for concluding that they serve a rational purpose. The mere fact of equal application does not mean that our analysis of these statutes should follow the approach we have taken in cases involving no racial discrimination where the Equal Protection Clause has been arrayed against a statute discriminating between the kinds of advertising which may be displayed on trucks in New York City, *Railway Express Agency, Inc. v. New York*, 336 U.S. 106 (1949), or an exemption in Ohio's ad valorem tax for merchandise owned by a nonresident in a storage warehouse, *Allied Stores of Ohio, Inc. v. Bowers*, 358 U.S. 522 (1959). In these cases, involving distinctions not drawn according to race, the Court has merely asked whether there is any rational foundation for the discriminations, and has deferred to the wisdom of the state legislatures. In the case at bar, however, we deal with statutes containing racial classifications, and the fact of equal application does not immunize the statute from the very heavy burden of justification which the Fourteenth Amendment has traditionally required of state statutes drawn according to race.

The State argues that statements in the Thirty-ninth Congress about the time of the passage of the Fourteenth Amendment indicate that the Framers did not intend the Amendment to make unconstitutional state miscegenation laws. Many of the statements alluded to by the State concern the debates over the Freedmen's Bureau Bill, which President Johnson vetoed, and the Civil Rights Act of 1866, 14 Stat. 27, enacted over his veto. While these statements have some relevance to the intention of Congress in submitting the Fourteenth Amendment, it must be understood that they pertained to the passage of specific statutes and not to the broader, organic purpose of a constitutional amendment. As for the various statements directly concerning the Fourteenth Amendment, we have said in connection with a related problem, that although these historical sources "cast some light" they are not sufficient to resolve the problem; "[a]t best, they are inconclusive. The most avid proponents of the post-War Amendments undoubtedly intended them to remove all legal distinctions among 'all persons born or naturalized in the United States.' Their opponents, just as certainly, were antagonistic to both the letter and the spirit of the Amendments and wished them to have the most limited effect." *Brown v. Board of Education*, 347 U.S. 483, 489 (1954). See also *Strauder v. West Virginia*, 100 U.S. 303, 310 (1880). We have rejected the proposition that the debates in the Thirty-ninth Congress or in the state legislatures which ratified the Fourteenth Amendment supported the theory advanced by the State, that the requirement of equal protection of the laws is satisfied by penal laws defining offenses based on racial classifications so long as white and Negro participants in the offense were similarly punished. *McLaughlin v. Florida*, 379 U.S. 184 (1964).

The State finds support for its "equal application" theory in the decision of the Court in *Pace v. Alabama*, 106 U.S. 583 (1883). In that case, the Court upheld a conviction under an Alabama statute forbidding adultery or fornication between a white person and a Negro which imposed a greater penalty than that of a statute proscribing similar conduct by members of the same race. The Court reasoned that the statute could not be said to discriminate against Negroes because the punishment for each participant in the offense was the same. However, as recently as the 1964 Term, in rejecting the reasoning of that case, we stated "*Pace* represents a limited view of the Equal Protection Clause which has not withstood analysis in the subsequent decisions of this Court." *McLaughlin v. Florida, supra*, at 188. As we there demonstrated, the Equal Protection Clause requires the consideration of whether the classifications drawn by any statute constitute an arbitrary and invidious discrimination. The clear and central purpose of the Fourteenth Amendment was to eliminate all official state sources of invidious racial discrimination in the States. *Slaughter-House Cases*, 16 Wall. 36, 71 (1873); *Strauder v. West Virginia*, 100 U.S. 303, 307–308 (1880); *Ex parte Virginia*, 100 U.S. 339, 344–345 (1880); *Shelley v. Kraemer*, 334 U.S. 1 (1948); *Burton v. Wilmington Parking Authority*, 365 U.S. 715 (1961).

There can be no question but that Virginia's miscegenation statutes rest solely upon distinctions drawn according to race. The statutes proscribe generally accepted conduct if engaged in by members of different races. Over the years, this Court has consistently repudiated "[d]istinctions between citizens solely because of their ancestry" as being "odious to a free people whose institutions are founded upon the doctrine of equality." *Hirabayashi v. United States*, 320 U.S. 81, 100 (1943). At the very least, the Equal Protection Clause demands that racial classifications, especially suspect in criminal statutes, be subjected to the "most rigid scrutiny," *Korematsu v. United States*, 323 U.S. 214, 216 (1944), and, if they are ever to be upheld, they must be shown to be necessary to the accomplishment of some permissible state objective, independent of the racial discrimination which it was the object of the Fourteenth Amendment to eliminate. Indeed, two members of this Court have already stated that they "cannot conceive of a valid legislative purpose… which makes the color of a person's skin the test of whether his conduct is a criminal offense." *McLaughlin v. Florida, supra*, at 198 (Stewart, J., joined by Douglas, J., concurring).

There is patently no legitimate overriding purpose independent of invidious racial discrimination which justifies this classification. The fact that Virginia prohibits only interracial marriages involving white persons demonstrates that the racial classifications must stand on their own justification, as measures designed to maintain White Supremacy. We have consistently denied the constitutionality of measures which restrict the rights of citizens on account of race. There can be no doubt that restricting the freedom to marry solely because of racial classifications violates the central meaning of the Equal Protection Clause.

Document Text

II

These statutes also deprive the Lovings of liberty without due process of law in violation of the Due Process Clause of the Fourteenth Amendment. The freedom to marry has long been recognized as one of the vital personal rights essential to the orderly pursuit of happiness by free men.

Marriage is one of the "basic civil rights of man," fundamental to our very existence and survival. *Skinner v. Oklahoma*, 316 U.S. 535, 541 (1942). See also *Maynard v. Hill*, 125 U.S. 190 (1888). To deny this fundamental freedom on so unsupportable a basis as the racial classifications embodied in these statutes, classifications so directly subversive of the principle of equality at the heart of the Fourteenth Amendment, is surely to deprive all the State's citizens of liberty without due process of law. The Fourteenth Amendment requires that the freedom of choice to marry not be restricted by invidious racial discriminations. Under our Constitution, the freedom to marry, or not marry, a person of another race resides with the individual and cannot be infringed by the State.

These convictions must be reversed.

It is so ordered.

Glossary

ad valorem tax: a tax on goods computed on the basis of their value

case at bar: the case that the Court is presently hearing (used in preference to "this case," which can be misinterpreted to have a more general meaning)

class action: a lawsuit brought by one or more persons on behalf of a large group

Framers: the writers of the Constitution

Freedmen's Bureau Bill: the bill that established the Bureau of Refugees, Freedmen, and Abandoned Lands in 1865 to aid newly emancipated African Americans

nativism: any policy or viewpoint that favors the interests of the present inhabitants of a country over those of newcomers; opposition to immigration

post-War Amendments: the Thirteenth, Fourteenth, and Fifteenth Amendments to the U.S. Constitution, passed in the immediate aftermath of the Civil War to abolish slavery and protect the rights of African Americans

President Johnson: Andrew Johnson, Abraham Lincoln's successor as president in the years immediately following the Civil War

Tenth Amendment: the amendment to the U.S. Constitution, contained in the Bill of Rights, that says that powers not expressly conferred on the federal government are reserved to the states

KERNER COMMISSION REPORT SUMMARY

"This is our basic conclusion: our nation is moving toward two societies, one black, one white—separate and unequal."

Overview

There have been many presidential commissions, but few have been more famous—or more controversial—than the National Advisory Commission on Civil Disorders, popularly known as the Kerner Commission. Appointed by President Lyndon B. Johnson in July 1967, as a series of deadly riots convulsed African American neighborhoods in many U.S. cities, the commission had the task of explaining why the violence was occurring and what to do about it. Johnson was a strong supporter of black rights and a champion of social reform to help the poor and minorities. The Kerner Commission proposed many reforms to augment the Johnson administration's efforts, but the president was cool to the recommendations because the Vietnam War had become so expensive that the country could no longer afford costly new social programs. In addition, the president worried that the commission's report, which asserted that white racism was the primary cause of inner-city problems, would alienate white, middle-class support for the programs it proposed. As a result, even though the Kerner Commission asserted that racial problems were about to fracture American society, many of its recommendations went unheeded.

Context

During the Johnson presidency (1963–1969), Americans experienced several summers of racial strife. Most people called these civil disturbances "riots"—frightening eruptions of violence that ended only when the police, National Guard, or even U.S. Army troops restored order. Some people considered them rebellions—uprisings against discriminatory institutions and practices that were forcing millions of African Americans in inner cities to endure poverty and second-class citizenship. Whatever one termed these disturbances, they were destructive, deadly, and common. During the summer of 1967 alone, 136 civil disturbances took place in all parts of the country.

These disturbances surprised, puzzled, and even outraged Johnson because of the notable advances in civil rights that had preceded them. The civil rights movement had achieved its greatest victories just as violence was beginning to plague America's cities. Tens of thousands of courageous citizens took enormous risks to protest against the racial segregation that prevented African Americans from voting, securing decent employment, buying or renting housing in many communities, and attending all-white schools. This grassroots movement for racial justice had many leaders, but the most prominent was Martin Luther King, Jr., who inspired blacks and whites alike with his commitment to using nonviolent action to achieve his dream of a harmonious, color-blind society. Johnson supported racial integration, and in July 1964 he signed the Civil Rights Act, which outlawed racial discrimination in public accommodations, such as restaurants and movie theaters, and in employment. A year later, he signed the Voting Rights Act, which gave the federal government new power to prevent states and localities from denying people of color the right to register to vote.

Eliminating racial injustice was an important step toward the creation of the Great Society, an ambitious effort, as Johnson explained, "to enrich and elevate our national life" (Johnson, vol. 2, p. 704). A thriving national economy, popular confidence in federal efforts to improve American society, and large Democratic majorities in Congress gave Johnson, a Democrat, an unusual opportunity to secure the passage of one of the most remarkable programs of social reform in U.S. history. In 1964 and 1965 Congress approved many new Great Society initiatives that Johnson thought would benefit all Americans, including a War on Poverty, aid for elementary and secondary schools as well as colleges and universities, Medicare for senior citizens,

President Lyndon B. Johnson (seated, foreground) working with (background L-R): Marvin Watson, J. Edgar Hoover, Sec. Robert McNamara, Gen. Harold Johnson, Joe Califano, Sec. Of the Army Stanley Resor.

and a Model Cities program to revitalize inner cities and improve housing.

Only five days after the president signed the 1965 Voting Rights Act, one of the worst racial disturbances in U.S. history began in Los Angeles in the predominantly African American neighborhood of Watts. On August 11, 1965, a small event—a white police officer's arrest of an African American driver for a traffic violation—triggered a huge explosion. In six days of violence, thirty-four people died, and $45 million in property damage occurred. The arson, looting, and killing in Watts stunned President Johnson and millions of other Americans. "How is it possible after all we've accomplished?" he wondered. "How could it be?" (Woods, p. 591).

Part of the answer, according to a new group of black leaders, was that the Great Society programs provided too little too late. Stokely Carmichael (later known as Kwame Tur) gained prominence in 1966 by calling for Black Power, a slogan with many possible meanings, including racial pride, self-reliance, and unity. Yet Black Power also suggested a new militancy; as Carmichael declared, "I'm not going to beg the white man for anything I deserve; I'm going to take it" (Pach, p. xv). For Huey Newton and Bobby Seale, who established the Black Panther Party for Self-Defense in 1966, Black Power meant revolutionary action.

Newton and Seale even carried guns in public to show that they rejected nonviolent protest in favor of self-defense. These new, aggressive leaders said that civil rights and voting rights legislation and Great Society reforms had not changed the basic conditions of life for the millions of African Americans who lived in segregated inner-city neighborhoods where poverty was pervasive, job opportunities were limited, and municipal services were ineffective and unreliable. They also had grown tired of waiting for change. Some even advocated separatism; they said that African Americans should not make integration their goal but should instead establish separate communities and institutions.

The rising racial tensions divided the American people. Many whites, alarmed by what they considered the disintegration of law and order, blamed Black Power advocates for violence in the streets. Great Society programs became increasingly controversial, as conservatives charged that they were wasteful and ineffective or provided benefits to militants who defied the law. Liberals also attacked Johnson because they thought that the president's commitment to the expanding and costly war in Vietnam was draining funds from the War on Poverty and other Great Society programs. King declared regretfully, "The promises of the Great Society have been shot down on the battlefield of Vietnam" (Hill, p. 1). Radical black leaders offered even

1326 • Milestone Documents in African American History

more scathing criticism, as they alleged that the Great Society was just another example of tokenism rather than a genuine effort to eliminate poverty and racism.

America's inner cities exploded once more during the summer of 1967. In June violence flared in Tampa, Florida; Cincinnati, Ohio; and Atlanta, Georgia. On July 12, after six days of gunfire, arson, and street violence, major disorder left twenty-three dead in Newark, New Jersey. The worst disturbance occurred in Detroit, Michigan, beginning on July 23. Once again a small incident—a raid on an illegal drinking establishment known as a "blind pig"—started a wave of violence that resulted in forty-three deaths. To quell this disturbance, Johnson ordered U.S. Army troops, some of whom had served in Vietnam, to Detroit.

On July 27, as the violence in Detroit ended, President Johnson delivered an address to the American people. He condemned the lawlessness that had devastated Detroit and other cities and stated bluntly that "looting, arson, plunder, and pillage" had nothing to do with the quest for civil rights. Yet while he called for those who had committed these crimes to be brought to justice, he asserted that "the only genuine, long-range solution" to the problem of civil disorders was "an attack... upon the conditions that breed despair and violence...: ignorance, discrimination, slums, poverty, disease, not enough jobs" (Johnson, vol. 2, pp. 721–724). He also announced the appointment of a special National Advisory Commission on Civil Disorders, made up of eleven members led by the Democratic Illinois governor Otto Kerner and the Republican New York City mayor John Lindsay, to determine the causes of the riots and what to do to prevent new ones. People commonly called this group the Kerner Commission.

About the Author

No single individual wrote the Kerner Commission Report. The document was the product of a collective effort that included dozens of staff assistants as well as the eleven members of the committee. The chair of the commission was Otto Kerner, and the vice chair was John Lindsay.

Otto Kerner, Jr., who was born in Chicago on August 15, 1908, graduated from Brown University in 1930 and earned a law degree from Northwestern University in 1934. His father was a prominent lawyer who served as attorney general of Illinois. Kerner started working for his father's law firm in 1934, the same year he married Helena Cermak Kenlay, the daughter of the late Democratic mayor of Chicago Anton Cermak. Political connections helped Kerner secure an appointment in 1947 as U.S. attorney for the Northern District of Illinois. After twice being elected as a circuit court judge in Cook County (which includes Chicago) during the 1950s, Kerner won the governorship of Illinois as a Democrat in 1960. He proved popular with voters, gaining reelection in 1964. Illinois experienced strong economic growth while Kerner was in the statehouse, and he championed many reforms, including increased state aid to education and an improved mental health program. Kerner resigned as governor in May 1968 after President Johnson nominated him to serve on the U.S. Court of Appeals for the Seventh Circuit. In 1973, he was convicted on corruption charges for providing political favors when he was governor in return for financial benefits. He served eight months in jail and died not long after, on May 9, 1976.

John Vliet Lindsay was born on November 24, 1921, in New York City into a prosperous family. He graduated from Yale University in 1944, served in the U.S. Navy during World War II, and earned a degree from Yale Law School in 1948. Running as a Republican in 1958, he won the first of four terms in the House of Representatives from a district in Manhattan. In Congress, he earned a reputation as a liberal reformer. In 1965 he was elected mayor of New York City, and he won a second term four years later. He was sensitive to the concerns of African Americans and Hispanics but lost the support of many white, middle-class voters because of rising welfare costs and the increasing crime rate. In 1971 he became a Democrat, and he made an unsuccessful bid for that party's presidential nomination in 1972. After he left the mayor's office in 1973, he practiced law. He died on December 19, 2000.

The Kerner Commission had nine other members. I. W. Abel was the president of the United Steelworkers of America and a strong supporter of civil rights. Edward Brooke, a Republican senator from Massachusetts, was the first African American to be elected to the Senate since Reconstruction. James C. Corman was a Democratic member of the House from California who helped secure the passage of the Civil Rights Act of 1964. Fred R. Harris, a Democratic senator from Oklahoma, was known for his support of civil rights and Indian rights. Herbert Jenkins was the police chief of Atlanta, serving longer than any previous occupant of the position. William M. McCulloch was a Republican member of the House who was conservative on most issues but a supporter of the Civil Rights Acts and the Voting Rights Act. Katherine Graham Peden was Kentucky's commissioner of commerce and had also served on the President's Commission on the Status of Women from 1961 to 1963. Charles B. Thornton was one of the founders of Litton Industries and its chief executive officer. Roy Wilkins was the executive director of the National Association for the Advancement of Colored People and a critic of the Black Power movement who believed that the best way to advance African American interests was through legal and political action.

Explanation and Analysis of the Document

♦ Introduction

The introduction quickly sets the tone for the summary of the Kerner Commission Report: It is blunt, direct, and unsettling. After a few preliminary sentences, the commissioners state their basic conclusion in stark and alarming language: "Our nation is moving toward two societies, one black, one white—separate and unequal." By placing this finding so early in the report, the commissioners call attention to the gravity and urgency of America's racial problems. They later emphasize that they completed the report four months before the deadline. The speed with which they performed the work underlined their belief that there was "no higher priority for national action and no higher claim on the nation's conscience" than addressing the issues causing the violent disturbances in America's cities. The commissioners also wanted to finish the study as quickly as possible so that it might help in formulating policies that could head off another "long, hot summer" in 1968.

Dealing with the problem of civil disorders, however, would require confronting some unpleasant truths, the commissioners believed. For many whites in comfortable suburbs, small towns, and rural communities, the problems of predominantly black inner cities seemed remote, the product of circumstances for which they bore no responsibility and in which they may have had little interest. The Kerner Commission challenged that outlook, asserting in the report, "What white Americans have never fully understood but what the Negro can never forget—is that white society is deeply implicated in the ghetto." Preventing new explosions of violence would require more than effective law enforcement or new programs to alleviate poverty or teach job skills. What would also be necessary on the part of "every American" were "new attitudes, new understanding, and, above all, new will." The report establishes at the outset that the riots of the 1960s were not an urban problem or a black problem but a national problem of the greatest magnitude and urgency.

♦ **Part I—What Happened?**
This section of the report summary provides brief accounts of the disturbances in several cities during the summer of 1967. The Kerner Commission Report moves beyond the details of each disorder, however, to find patterns in the violence. While there was no "'typical' riot," the instances of disorder shared some important common characteristics. The central conclusion of this section of the report is that the civil disorders involved "Negroes acting against local symbols of white American society, authority, and property in Negro neighborhoods—rather than against white persons." Especially powerful were grievances about police practices, lack of employment, and poor housing.

The Kerner Commission found no evidence to support the widespread belief that inner-city disturbances were the result of a domestic or foreign plot. J. Edgar Hoover, the director of the Federal Bureau of Investigation, thought that Communists were somehow involved in the violence. Hoover was extremely suspicious of black leaders, including mainstream advocates of civil rights like Martin Luther King, Jr. Hoover insisted that King took advice from Communists and was so convinced that King was a dangerous radical that he even carried on a secret campaign to destroy King's reputation. Hoover also thought that Black Power advocates were treacherous enemies of law and order. Some did espouse socialist principles or urge African Americans to rise up against white oppression. Nonetheless, the Kerner Commission looked carefully at many sources of information, including Federal Bureau of Investigation documents, and found no proof that any group or individuals had planned the inner-city violence. Conspiracy did not explain the turbulent summer of 1967. Rather, a combination of national problems and local conditions produced an inflammatory mixture that ignited in dozens of American cities.

♦ **Part II—Why Did It Happen?**
Explaining the historical roots of the racial problems of the 1960s is the goal of the next part of the report. The commissioners assert that white racism was the most fundamental reason for the "explosive mixture" in American cities. In this section of the report, as in the introduction, the most important finding appears near the beginning. Once more, the conclusion is alarming and unsettling, especially for white readers.

The report uses history to explain that the development of large, segregated communities in urban areas—commonly called "ghettos" in the 1960s—was a fairly recent phenomenon. In 1910, 91 percent of the nation's black population lived in the South. Black migration out of the South accelerated during World War I and increased even more during World War II, as the growth of defense industries created job opportunities in northern factories. The movement to northern cities continued when peace came in 1945, in part because the mechanization of southern agriculture reduced the demand for farm labor. By the time the Kerner Commission was established, about 45 percent of African Americans lived outside the South, mainly in central cities. During the 1950s and 1960s, cities like Detroit, Chicago, Cleveland, and Philadelphia became increasingly black, since most of the growth in white population during those decades was in suburbs. "White exodus" increased the proportion of African Americans in these cities and in certain neighborhoods within them. Discriminatory practices, including unwillingness among owners to rent or sell housing to blacks in some areas and among banks to make home loans to qualified black buyers who wished to move into predominantly white neighborhoods, confined the bulk of the black population to segregated, inner city districts, or ghettos.

Deprivation combined with segregation to create bitterness and resentment that could eventually lead to explosive violence. Conditions of life in many inner cities were horrendous. The report provides statistical measures of the pervasiveness of poverty and the severity of unemployment and underemployment. Blacks were almost four times more likely than whites to live in poverty and more than twice as likely to be unemployed. A nonwhite baby had a 58 percent greater chance than a white baby of dying during the first month of life. Far more frequently than other Americans, inner-city residents became victims of crime or unfair commercial or financial practices, such as high food prices and credit scams.

African Americans endured these deplorable conditions of life while the economy was thriving and while more and more people were achieving their American dream of success and prosperity. Inner-city residents heard government officials praise the achievements of the civil rights movement, the advances in desegregation, and the progress in making equality of opportunity a reality for all Americans. The report explains how this combination of rising expectations and frustrated hopes produced intense, widespread bitterness.

Disillusionment and alienation, according to the Kerner Commission, led some African Americans to embrace Black Power in the hope of advancing racial unity and achieving independent economic and political power. The report provides a scathing critique of those who thought Black Power should lead to separatism. Their ideas were not really new, the commissioners maintain, but echoed those of the late-19th-century African American leader Booker T. Washington. The comparison to Washington was devastating. Washington had urged blacks not to challenge segregation but instead to concentrate on economic self-improvement. In a similar manner, black separatists of the 1960s, according to the report, backed away from confronting white racism by not demanding further integration.

At the end of this section, the commissioners address a common question: Why was it more difficult for African Americans than for European immigrants "to escape from the ghetto and from poverty?" The report offers several reasons, but especially important is the assertion that Europeans never faced as intense and widespread discrimination as did blacks.

♦ Part III—What Can Be Done?

The Kerner Commission studied a severe national problem, but their recommendations for dealing with it begin with local action. Many suggestions concern improving communication so that inner-city problems do not go neglected until they lead to violence. The commissioners deem especially important the bettering of police-community relations so as to strengthen law enforcement, avoid the "indiscriminate and excessive use of force," and prevent incidents like those that had occurred in Detroit from triggering civil disturbance. They also consider necessary changes in local court systems, which suffered from "long-standing structural deficiencies," and the preparation of emergency plans, formulated with "broad community participation," to deal with civil disturbances.

The report warns that the future of many large cities with growing African American populations is "grim" and that a continuation of current policies would have "ominous consequences for our society." To do nothing different would "make permanent the division" between a predominantly black and poor society in inner cities and a white and affluent society concentrated in suburbs. The report asserts that integration is essential; that new programs must help blacks move out of inner cities; and that the most important goal "must be a single society, in which every citizen will be free to live and work according to his capabilities and desires, not his color."

Specific proposals for federal action concentrate on employment, education, the welfare system, and housing. The commissioners urge "immediate action" to create two million new jobs over the coming three years and to eliminate racial barriers in hiring and promotion. Also considered essential are dramatic efforts to improve education, including federal action to eliminate segregation in schools and increased aid for new and better programs serving disadvantaged students. The commissioners recommend substantial reforms in the welfare system, including increased federal funds to raise benefits in the short term and the creation of a new system of income supplementation over the long term. Changes in housing programs are also held to be crucial because existing federal efforts had done "comparatively little" to help the disadvantaged. Especially important would be the passage of a federal open housing law, to ban discrimination in the sale or rental of housing on account of race, and new efforts to build more low-income housing outside predominantly black inner cities.

The Kerner Commission concludes its report by reiterating that Americans could not continue to delay in confronting these pressing problems. The commissioners admit that they have "uncovered no startling truths, no unique insights"; as the distinguished and perceptive scholar Kenneth Clark pointed out, investigations after earlier riots had produced similar analyses and similar recommendations. Those previous studies had produced few, if any changes, however, and the Kerner Commission warns of the dangers of inaction yet again. Improving conditions in inner cities would be expensive and require "national action on an unprecedented scale." Just as important as money would be the need "to generate new will." Only such a widespread and wholehearted commitment, the commission concludes, could "end the destruction and the violence, not only in the streets... but in the lives of people."

Audience

In the body of their report, the commissioners explain that they address their study to the institutions of government. They hoped that their analysis and recommendations would help the president and Congress take action to deal with the problems contributing to civil disturbances. They were also writing for local and state officials—those who made policies and provided funding for schools, police, welfare programs, and other social services that had such profound effects on the lives of inner-city residents.

The audience, however, was far larger than government officials. The Kerner Commission hoped to touch "the conscience of the nation" and "the minds and hearts of each citizen" (National Advisory Commission on Civil Disorders, p. 34). The increasing racial polarization of the 1960s affected all Americans; only a national commitment to alleviate the underlying causes could reverse the trend. The commissioners declare in their report, "The responsibility for decisive action, never more clearly demanded in the history of our country, rests on all of us" (National Advisory Commission on Civil Disorders, p. 34).

Impact

The report of the Kerner Commission produced strong but divided reactions. The *New York Times* (March 2, 1968) praised it for making a powerful case for "escalation of the war against poverty and discrimination at home." The *Washington Star* (as quoted in the *New York Times*, March 10, 1968), however, complained that the report "does not put as much emphasis on forthrightly condemning riots and rioters as it does on offering excuses for them." Seven mayors whose cities had experienced civil disturbances endorsed the commission's recommendations. Richard Nixon, who was campaigning for the Republican nomination for president, reached the opposite conclusion and declared that the commission's report "blames everybody for the riots except the rioters" (Woods, p. 821).

President Johnson at first made no public comment. In private, he was angry because he thought that the report gave insufficient credit to his administration for its many efforts to end discrimination and alleviate poverty. Nonetheless, the president agreed that social and economic deprivation created the conditions for urban violence, and he knew that the Great Society, however ambitious, had by no means done enough to prevent another riot-filled summer. He also worried that the emphasis on white racism would undermine the support of middle-class and working-class white Americans for essential social reforms. An even bigger obstacle to new social programs was the rising cost of the Vietnam War, in which more than 500,000 Americans were engaged in battle by early 1968. The Kerner Commission's report did not state the costs of the programs it proposed. The White House estimated that $75 to $100 billion would be needed over several years to implement the commission's recommendations, at a time when the entire federal budget was about $180 billion. Even with a tax increase, which the president approved in June 1968, Congress was determined to reduce new expenditures to cut the federal deficit.

Johnson did persuade Congress to approve two important new reforms. On April 11, the president signed the new Civil Rights Act of 1968, which banned racial discrimination in the sale and rental of most of the nation's housing. Johnson had proposed the legislation even before the Kerner Commission endorsed that reform in its report. Still, only after another national tragedy—the assassination of Martin Luther King, Jr., on April 4, 1968, and rioting in more than one hundred cities—did the House of Representatives pass the measure. On August 1, a new housing program became law, one that authorized funds to build or renovate 1.7 million housing units and also provided mortgage assistance to low-income families who wanted to buy their own homes.

On several occasions over the next thirty years, study groups reviewed the nation's progress in dealing with the problems of inner cities and reached pessimistic conclusions. The first assessment occurred only a year after the Kerner Commission's report and concluded that "the nation has not reversed the movement apart. Blacks and whites remain deeply divided" (Urban America, p. 116). Twenty years afterward, the 1988 Commission on the Cities, a nongovernmental group of experts that included the Kerner Commission member Fred Harris, warned that America "is *again* becoming two separate societies," one white, one black and Hispanic (Harris and Wilkins, p. 177). Ten years later, the Milton S. Eisenhower Foundation sponsored another look back at the Kerner Commission. This study concluded that a greater percentage of Americans lived in poverty in 1998 than in 1968 and that "inner cities have become America's poorhouses from which many, now, have little hope of escape" (Harris and Curtis, p. 152). These different assessments seemed to confirm what Kenneth Clark had told the Kerner Commission about efforts to improve the conditions of life in inner cities: "the same analysis, the same recommendations, and the same inaction."

Further Reading

◆ Articles
"Another Opinion: Attack on the Kerner Report." *New York Times*, March 10, 1968.

Hill, Gladwin. "Dr. King Advocates Quitting Vietnam." *New York Times*, February 26, 1967.

"'Separate and Unequal.'" *New York Times*, March 3, 1968.

◆ Books
Blum, John Morton. *Years of Discord: American Politics and Society, 1961–1974*. New York: W. W. Norton, 1991.

Crump, Spencer. *Black Riot in Los Angeles: The Story of the Watts Tragedy*. Los Angeles: Trans-Anglo Books, 1966.

Dallek, Robert. *Flawed Giant: Lyndon Johnson and His Times, 1961–1973*. New York: Oxford University Press, 1998.

Lemann, Nicholas. *The Promised Land: The Great Black Migration and How It Changed America*. New York: Vintage Books, 1992.

Lytle, Mark Hamilton. *America's Uncivil Wars: The Sixties Era from Elvis to the Fall of Richard Nixon*. New York: Oxford University Press, 2006.

Pach, Chester. *The Johnson Years*. New York: Facts On File, 2006.

Woods, Randall B. *LBJ: Architect of American Ambition*. New York: Free Press, 2006.

♦ **Web Sites**

Lyndon Baines Johnson Library and Museum Web site. http://www.jfklibrary.org/. Accessed on October 25, 2007.

"Martin Luther King, Jr. Papers Project." The Martin Luther King, Jr., Research and Education Institute Web site. http://www.stanford.edu/group/King/mlkpapers/. Accessed on October 25, 2007.

—Chester Pach

Time Line

1964	July 2	■ Johnson signs the Civil Rights Act of 1964.
1965	March 8	■ The first U.S. combat troops arrive in South Vietnam.
	August 6	■ Johnson signs the Voting Rights Act.
	August 11	■ A civil disturbance begins in the Watts section of Los Angeles.
1967	July 12	■ Rioting starts in Newark, New Jersey.
	July 23	■ Riots begin in Detroit and last for five days; forty-three people die.
	July 27	■ President Johnson speaks to the nation about the civil disorders and announces the appointment of a special commission to study the disorders.
	December 31	■ Some 485,600 Americans are engaged in fighting in the Vietnam War.
1968	February 29	■ The Kerner Commission issues its report.
	April 4	■ Martin Luther King, Jr., is murdered in Memphis, Tennessee.

Essential Quotes

"This is our basic conclusion: our nation is moving toward two societies, one black, one white—separate and unequal."

"What white Americans have never fully understood but what the Negro can never forget—is that white society is deeply implicated in the ghetto. White institutions created it, white institutions maintain it, and white society condones it."

"White racism is essentially responsible for the explosive mixture which has been accumulating in our cities since the end of World War II."

"No American—white or black—can escape the consequences of the continuing social and economic decay of our major cities. Only a commitment to national action on an unprecedented scale can shape a future compatible with the historic ideals of American society."

Questions for Further Study

1. Compare Kennedy's responses to civil rights crises with those of President Dwight D. Eisenhower to the Supreme Court's *Brown v. Board of Education* decision, to the rise of massive resistance, and to the 1957 Little Rock crisis.

2. In referring to the Supreme Court justice John Marshall Harlan's concept of a color-blind Constitution, was President Kennedy concerned with ending systematic discrimination against African Americans or with eliminating any reference to race in American law and practice, or with both?

3. Kennedy highlighted economic disparities between whites and African Americans in his address. Overcoming economic privation was one of the goals of the March on Washington for Jobs and Freedom of August 28, 1963, and the goal of the Poor People's Campaign, which Martin Luther King, Jr., was leading at the time of his assassination. Examine the extent of economic disparities in society today. To what degree would the universal implementation of affirmation action or a program of reparations contribute to substantially closing racial socioeconomic gaps? Might a modern-day president committed to civil rights take other initiatives to eliminate such gaps?

4. In the 1990s a trend toward the resegregation of public schools began taking place. The 2007 Supreme Court decision in *Parents Involved in Community Schools v. Seattle School District No. 1* against the use of race in assigning students to schools further undermined the promise of the *Brown v. Board of Education* decision that schools would be equal and integrated. What measures might be taken today to restore the goal of establishing equal educational opportunity championed by Kennedy in his June 11, 1963, address to the nation?

Kerner Commission Report Summary

The full text of Kerner Commission Report Summary.

Introduction

The summer of 1967 again brought racial disorders to American cities, and with them shock, fear and bewilderment to the nation.

The worst came during a two-week period in July, first in Newark and then in Detroit. Each set off a chain reaction in neighboring communities.

On July 28, 1967, the President of the United States established this Commission and directed us to answer three basic questions:

What happened?

Why did it happen?

What can be done to prevent it from happening again?

To respond to these questions, we have undertaken a broad range of studies and investigations. We have visited the riot cities; we have heard many witnesses; we have sought the counsel of experts across the country.

This is our basic conclusion: Our nation is moving toward two societies, one black, one white—separate and unequal.

Reaction to last summer's disorders has quickened the movement and deepened the division. Discrimination and segregation have long permeated much of American life; they now threaten the future of every American.

This deepening racial division is not inevitable. The movement apart can be reversed. Choice is still possible. Our principal task is to define that choice and to press for a national resolution.

To pursue our present course will involve the continuing polarization of the American community and, ultimately, the destruction of basic democratic values.

The alternative is not blind repression or capitulation to lawlessness. It is the realization of common opportunities for all within a single society.

This alternative will require a commitment to national action—compassionate, massive and sustained, backed by the resources of the most powerful and the richest nation on this earth. From every American it will require new attitudes, new understanding, and, above all, new will.

The vital needs of the nation must be met; hard choices must be made, and, if necessary, new taxes enacted.

Violence cannot build a better society. Disruption and disorder nourish repression, not justice. They strike at the freedom of every citizen. The community cannot—it will not—tolerate coercion and mob rule.

Violence and destruction must be ended—in the streets of the ghetto and in the lives of people.

Segregation and poverty have created in the racial ghetto a destructive environment totally unknown to most white Americans.

What white Americans have never fully understood but what the Negro can never forget—is that white society is deeply implicated in the ghetto. White institutions created it, white institutions maintain it, and white society condones it.

It is time now to turn with all the purpose at our command to the major unfinished business of this nation. It is time to adopt strategies for action that will produce quick and visible progress. It is time to make good the promises of American democracy to all citizens-urban and rural, white and black, Spanish-surname, American Indian, and every minority group.

Our recommendations embrace three basic principles:

To mount programs on a scale equal to the dimension of the problems:

To aim these programs for high impact in the immediate future in order to close the gap between promise and performance;

To undertake new initiatives and experiments that can change the system of failure and frustration that now dominates the ghetto and weakens our society.

These programs will require unprecedented levels of funding and performance, but they neither probe deeper nor demand more than the problems which called them forth. There can be no higher priority for national action and no higher claim on the nation's conscience.

We issue this Report now, four months before the date called for by the President. Much remains that can be learned. Continued study is essential.

As Commissioners we have worked together with a sense of the greatest urgency and have sought to compose whatever differences exist among us. Some differences remain. But the gravity of the problem and the pressing need for action are too clear to allow further delay in the issuance of this Report.

Part I—What Happened?

Chapter I—Profiles of Disorder
The report contains profiles of a selection of the disorders that took place during the summer of 1967. These profiles are designed to indicate how the disorders happened, who participated in them, and how local officials, police forces, and the National Guard responded. Illustrative excerpts follow:

♦ Newark
…It was decided to attempt to channel the energies of the people into a nonviolent protest. While Lofton promised the crowd that a full investigation would be made of the Smith incident, the other Negro leaders began urging those on the scene to form a line of march toward the city hall.

Some persons joined the line of march. Others milled about in the narrow street. From the dark grounds of the housing project came a barrage of rocks. Some of them fell among the crowd. Others hit persons in the line of march. Many smashed the windows of the police station. The rock throwing, it was believed, was the work of youngsters; approximately 2,500 children lived in the housing project.

Almost at the same time, an old car was set afire in a parking lot. The line of march began to disintegrate. The police, their heads protected by World War I-type helmets, sallied forth to disperse the crowd. A fire engine, arriving on the scene, was pelted with rocks. As police drove people away from the station, they scattered in all directions.

A few minutes later a nearby liquor store was broken into. Some persons, seeing a caravan of cabs appear at city hall to protest Smith's arrest, interpreted this as evidence that the disturbance had been organized, and generated rumors to that effect. However, only a few stores were looted. Within a short period of time, the disorder appeared to have run its course.

* * *

…On Saturday, July 15, [Director of Police Dominick] Spina received a report of snipers in a housing project. When he arrived he saw approximately 100 National Guardsmen and police officers crouching behind vehicles, hiding in corners and lying on the ground around the edge of the courtyard.

Since everything appeared quiet and it was broad daylight, Spina walked directly down the middle of the street. Nothing happened. As he came to the last building of the complex, he heard a shot. All around him the troopers jumped, believing themselves to be under sniper fire. A moment later a young Guardsman ran from behind a building.

The Director of Police went over and asked him if he had fired the shot. The soldier said yes, he had fired to scare a man away from a window; that his orders were to keep everyone away from windows.

Spina said he told the soldier: "Do you know what you just did? You have now created a state of hysteria. Every Guardsman up and down this street and every state policeman and every city policeman that is present thinks that somebody just fired a shot and that it is probably a sniper."

A short time later more "gunshots" were heard. Investigating, Spina came upon a Puerto Rican sitting on a wall. In reply to a question as to whether he knew "where the firing is coming from?" the man said:

"That's no firing. That's fireworks. If you look up to the fourth floor, you will see the people who are throwing down these cherry bombs."

By this time four truckloads of National Guardsmen had arrived and troopers and policemen were again crouched everywhere looking for a sniper. The Director of Police remained at the scene for three hours, and the only shot fired was the one by the Guardsman.

Nevertheless, at six o'clock that evening two columns of National Guardsmen and state troopers were directing mass fire at the Hayes Housing Project in response to what they believed were snipers….

♦ Detroit
…A spirit of carefree nihilism was taking hold. To riot and destroy appeared more and more to become ends in themselves. Late Sunday afternoon it appeared to one observer that the young people were "dancing amidst the flames."

A Negro plainclothes officer was standing at an intersection when a man threw a Molotov cocktail into a business establishment at the corner… In the heat of the afternoon, fanned by the 20 to 25 m.p.h.

winds of both Sunday and Monday, the fire reached the home next door within minutes. As residents uselessly sprayed the flames with garden hoses, the fire jumped from roof to roof of adjacent two- and three-story buildings. Within the hour the entire block was in flames. The ninth house in the burning row belonged to the arsonist who had thrown the Molotov cocktail. …

* * *

…Employed as a private guard, 55-year-old Julius L. Dorsey, a Negro, was standing in front of a market when accosted by two Negro men and a woman. They demanded he permit them to loot the market. He ignored their demands. They began to berate him. He asked a neighbor to call the police. As the argument grew more heated, Dorsey fired three shots from his pistol into the air.

The police radio reported: "Looters, they have rifles." A patrol car driven by a police officer and carrying three National Guardsmen arrived. As the looters fled, the law enforcement personnel opened fire. When the firing ceased, one person lay dead.

He was Julius L. Dorsey…

* * *

…As the riot alternately waxed and waned, one area of the ghetto remained insulated. On the northeast side the residents of some 150 square blocks inhabited by 21,000 persons had, in 1966, banded together in the Positive Neighborhood Action Committee (PNAC). With professional help from the Institute of Urban Dynamics, they had organized block clubs and made plans for the improvement of the neighborhood. …

When the riot broke out, the residents, through the block clubs, were able to organize quickly. Youngsters, agreeing to stay in the neighborhood, participated in detouring traffic. While many persons reportedly sympathized with the idea of a rebellion against the "system," only two small fires were set—one in an empty building.

* * *

…According to Lt. Gen. Throckmorton and Col. Bolling, the city, at this time, was saturated with fear. The National Guardsmen were afraid, the residents were afraid, and the police were afraid. Numerous persons, the majority of them Negroes, were being injured by gunshots of undetermined origin. The general and his staff felt that the major task of the troops was to reduce the fear and restore an air of normalcy.

In order to accomplish this, every effort was made to establish contact and rapport between the troops and the residents. The soldiers—20 percent of whom were Negro—began helping to clean up the streets, collect garbage, and trace persons who had disappeared in the confusion. Residents in the neighborhoods responded with soup and sandwiches for the troops. In areas where the National Guard tried to establish rapport with the citizens, there was a smaller response.

♦ **New Brunswick**
…A short time later, elements of the crowd—an older and rougher one than the night before—appeared in front of the police station. The participants wanted to see the mayor.

Mayor [Patricia] Sheehan went out onto the steps of the station. Using a bullhorn, she talked to the people and asked that she be given an opportunity to correct conditions. The crowd was boisterous. Some persons challenged the mayor. But, finally, the opinion, "She's new! Give her a chance!" prevailed.

A demand was issued by people in the crowd that all persons arrested the previous night be released. Told that this already had been done, the people were suspicious. They asked to be allowed to inspect the jail cells.

It was agreed to permit representatives of the people to look in the cells to satisfy themselves that everyone had been released.

The crowd dispersed. The New Brunswick riot had failed to materialize…

Chapter 2—Patterns of Disorder
The "typical" riot did not take place. The disorders of 1967 were unusual, irregular, complex and unpredictable social processes. Like most human events, they did not unfold in an orderly sequence. However, an analysis of our survey information leads to some conclusions about the riot process. In general:

* The civil disorders of 1967 involved Negroes acting against local symbols of white American society, authority and property in Negro neighborhoods—rather than against white persons.

* Of 164 disorders reported during the first nine months of 1967, eight (5 percent) were major in terms of violence and damage; 33 (20 percent) were serious but not major; 123 (75 percent) were minor and undoubtedly would not have received national attention as "riots" had the nation not been sensitized by the more serious outbreaks.
* In the 75 disorders studied by a Senate subcommittee, 83 deaths were reported. Eighty-two percent of the deaths and more than half the injuries occurred in Newark and Detroit. About 10 percent of the dead and 38 percent of the injured were public employees, primarily law officers and firemen. The overwhelming majority of the persons killed or injured in all the disorders were Negro civilians.
* Initial damage estimates were greatly exaggerated. In Detroit, newspaper damage estimates at first ranged from $200 million to $500 million; the highest recent estimate is $45 million. In Newark, early estimates ranged from $15 to $25 million. A month later damage was estimated at $10. 2 million, over 80 percent in inventory losses.

In the 24 disorders in 23 cities which we surveyed:

* The final incident before the outbreak of disorder, and the initial violence itself, generally took place in the evening or at night at a place in which it was normal for many people to be on the streets.
* Violence usually occurred almost immediately following the occurrence of the final precipitating incident, and then escalated rapidly. With but few exceptions, violence subsided during the day, and flared rapidly again at night. The night-day cycles continued through the early period of the major disorders.
* Disorder generally began with rock and bottle throwing and window breaking. Once store windows were broken, looting usually followed.
* Disorder did not erupt as a result of a single "triggering" or "precipitating" incident. Instead, it was generated out of an increasingly disturbed social atmosphere, in which typically a series of tension-heightening incidents over a period of weeks or months became linked in the minds of many in the Negro community with a reservoir of underlying grievances. At some point in the mounting tension, a further incident-in itself often routine or trivial-became the breaking point and the tension spilled over into violence.
* "Prior" incidents, which increased tensions and ultimately led to violence, were police actions in almost half the cases; police actions were "final" incidents before the outbreak of violence in 12 of the 24 surveyed disorders.
* No particular control tactic was successful in every situation. The varied effectiveness of control techniques emphasizes the need for advance training, planning, adequate intelligence systems, and knowledge of the ghetto community.
* Negotiations between Negroes—including your militants as well as older Negro leaders—and white officials concerning "terms of peace" occurred during virtually all the disorders surveyed. In many cases, these negotiations involved discussion of underlying grievances as well as the handling of the disorder by control authorities.
* The typical rioter was a teenager or young adult, a lifelong resident of the city in which he rioted, a high school dropout; he was, nevertheless, somewhat better educated than his nonrioting Negro neighbor, and was usually underemployed or employed in a menial job. He was proud of his race, extremely hostile to both whites and middle-class Negroes and, although informed about politics, highly distrustful of the political system.
* A Detroit survey revealed that approximately 11 percent of the total residents of two riot areas admitted participation in the rioting, 20 to 25 percent identified themselves as "bystanders," over 16 percent identified themselves as "counter-rioters" who urged rioters to "cool it," and the remaining 48 to 53 percent said they were at home or elsewhere and did not participate. In a survey of Negro males between the ages of 15 and 35 residing in the disturbance area in Newark, about 45 percent identified themselves as rioters, and about 55 percent as "noninvolved."
* Most rioters were young Negro males. Nearly 53 percent of arrestees were between 15 and 24 years of age; nearly 81 percent between 15 and 35.
* In Detroit and Newark about 74 percent of the rioters were brought up in the North. In contrast, of the noninvolved, 36 percent in Detroit and 52 percent in Newark were brought up in the North.

Document Text

* What the rioters appeared to be seeking was fuller participation in the social order and the material benefits enjoyed by the majority of American citizens. Rather than rejecting the American system, they were anxious to obtain a place for themselves in it.
* Numerous Negro counter-rioters walked the streets urging rioters to "cool it." The typical counter-rioter was better educated and had higher income than either the rioter or the noninvolved.
* The proportion of Negroes in local government was substantially smaller than the Negro proportion of population. Only three of the 20 cities studied had more than one Negro legislator; none had ever had a Negro mayor or city manager. In only four cities did Negroes hold other important policy-making positions or serve as heads of municipal departments.
* Although almost all cities had some sort of formal grievance mechanism for handling citizen complaints, this typically was regarded by Negroes as ineffective and was generally ignored.
* Although specific grievances varied from city to city, at least 12 deeply held grievances can be identified and ranked into three levels of relative intensity:

FIRST LEVEL OF INTENSITY
1. Police practices
2. Unemployment and underemployment
3. Inadequate housing

SECOND LEVEL OF INTENSITY
4. Inadequate education
5. Poor recreation facilities and programs
6. Ineffectiveness of the political structure and grievance mechanisms

THIRD LEVEL OF INTENSITY
7. Disrespectful white attitudes
8. Discriminatory administration of justice
9. Inadequacy of federal programs
10. Inadequacy of municipal services
11. Discriminatory consumer and credit practices
12. Inadequate welfare programs

* The results of a three-city survey of various federal programs—manpower, education, housing, welfare and community action—indicate that, despite substantial expenditures, the number of persons assisted constituted only a fraction of those in need.

The background of disorder is often as complex and difficult to analyze as the disorder itself. But we find that certain general conclusions can be drawn:

* Social and economic conditions in the riot cities constituted a clear pattern of severedisadvantage for Negroes compared with whites, whether the Negroes lived in the area where the riot took place or outside it. Negroes had completed fewer years of education and fewer had attended high school. Negroes were twice as likely to be unemployed and three times as likely to be in unskilled and service jobs. Negroes averaged 70 percent of the income earned by whites and were more than twice as likely to be living in poverty. Although housing cost Negroes relatively more, they had worse housing-three times as likely to be overcrowded and substandard. When compared to white suburbs, the relative disadvantage is even more pronounced.

A study of the aftermath of disorder leads to disturbing conclusions. We find that, despite the institution of some postriot programs:

* Little basic change in the conditions underlying the outbreak of disorder has taken place. Actions to ameliorate Negro grievances have been limited and sporadic; with but few exceptions, they have not significantly reduced tensions.
* In several cities, the principal official response has been to train and equip the police with more sophisticated weapons. In several cities, increasing polarization is evident, with continuing breakdown of inter-racial communication, and growth of white segregationist or black separatist groups.

Chapter 3—Organized Activity
The President directed the Commission to investigate "to, what extent, if any, there has been planning or organization in any of the riots."

To carry out this part of the President's charge, the Commission established a special investigative staff supplementing the field teams that made the general examination of the riots in 23 cities. The unit examined data collected by federal agencies and congressional committees, including thousands of documents supplied by the Federal Bureau of Investigation, gathered and evaluated information from local and state law enforcement agencies and officials, and conducted its own field investigation in selected cities.

On the basis of all the information collected, the Commission concludes that:

The urban disorders of the summer of 1967 were not caused by, nor were they the consequence of, any organized plan or "conspiracy."

Specifically, the Commission has found no evidence that all or any of the disorders or the incidents that led to them were planned or directed by any organization or group, international, national or local.

Militant organizations, local and national, and individual agitators, who repeatedly forecast and called for violence, were active in the spring and summer of 1967. We believe that they sought to encourage violence, and that they helped to create an atmosphere that contributed to the outbreak of disorder.

We recognize that the continuation of disorders and the polarization of the races would provide fertile ground for organized exploitation in the future.

Investigations of organized activity are continuing at all levels of government, including committees of Congress. These investigations relate not only to the disorders of 1967 but also to the actions of groups and individuals, particularly in schools and colleges, during this last fall and winter. The Commission has cooperated in these investigations. They should continue.

Part II—Why Did It Happen?

Chapter 4—The Basic Causes
In addressing the question "Why did it happen?" we shift our focus from the local to the national scene, from the particular events of the summer of 1967 to the factors within the society at large that created a mood of violence among many urban Negroes.

These factors are complex and interacting; they vary significantly in their effect from city to city and from year to year; and the consequences of one disorder, generating new grievances and new demands, become the causes of the next. Thus was created the "thicket of tension, conflicting evidence and extreme opinions" cited by the President.

Despite these complexities, certain fundamental matters are clear. Of these, the most fundamental is the racial attitude and behavior of white Americans toward black Americans.

Race prejudice has shaped our history decisively; it now threatens to affect our future.

White racism is essentially responsible for the explosive mixture which has been accumulating in our cities since the end of World War II. Among the ingredients of this mixture are:

* Pervasive discrimination and segregation in employment, education and housing, which have resulted in the continuing exclusion of great numbers of Negroes from the benefits of economic progress.
* Black in-migration and white exodus, which have produced the massive and growing concentrations of impoverished Negroes in our major cities, creating a growing crisis of deteriorating facilities and services and unmet human needs.
* The black ghettos where segregation and poverty converge on the young to destroy opportunity and enforce failure. Crime, drug addiction, dependency on welfare, and bitterness and resentment against society in general and white society in particular are the result.

At the same time, most whites and some Negroes outside the ghetto have prospered to a degree unparalleled in the history of civilization. Through television and other media, this affluence has been flaunted before the eyes of the Negro poor and the jobless ghetto youth.

Yet these facts alone cannot be said to have caused the disorders. Recently, other powerful ingredients have begun to catalyze the mixture:

* Frustrated hopes are the residue of the unfulfilled expectations aroused by the great judicial and legislative victories of the Civil Rights Movement and the dramatic struggle for equal rights in the South.
* A climate that tends toward approval and encouragement of violence as a form of protest has been created by white terrorism directed against nonviolent protest; by the open defiance of law and federal authority by state and local officials resisting desegregation; and by some protest groups engaging in civil disobedience who turn their backs on nonviolence, go beyond the constitutionally protected rights of petition and free assembly, and resort to violence to attempt to compel alteration of laws and policies with which they disagree.
* The frustrations of powerlessness have led some Negroes to the conviction that there is no effective alternative to violence as a means of achieving

redress of grievances, and of "moving the system." These frustrations are reflected in alienation and hostility toward the institutions of law and government and the white society which controls them, and in the reach toward racial consciousness and solidarity reflected in the slogan "Black Power."

* A new mood has sprung up among Negroes, particularly among the young, in which self-esteem and enhanced racial pride are replacing apathy and submission to "the system."
* The police are not merely a "spark" factor. To some Negroes police have come to symbolize white power, white racism and white repression. And the fact is that many police do reflect and express these white attitudes. The atmosphere of hostility and cynicism is reinforced by a widespread belief among Negroes in the existence of police brutality and in a "double standard" of justice and protection—one for Negroes and one for whites.

To this point, we have attempted to identify the prime components of the "explosive mixture." In the chapters that follow we seek to analyze them in the perspective of history. Their meaning, however, is clear:

In the summer of 1967, we have seen in our cities a chain reaction of racial violence. If we are heedless, none of us shall escape the consequences.

Chapter 5—Rejection and Protest: An Historical Sketch

The causes of recent racial disorders are embedded in a tangle of issues and circumstances—social, economic, political and psychological which arise out of the historic pattern of Negro-white relations in America.

In this chapter we trace the pattern, identify the recurrent themes of Negro protest and, most importantly, provide a perspective on the protest activities of the present era.

We describe the Negro's experience in America and the development of slavery as an institution. We show his persistent striving for equality in the face of rigidly maintained social, economic and educational barriers, and repeated mob violence. We portray the ebb and flow of the doctrinal tides—accommodation, separatism, and self-help—and their relationship to the current theme of Black Power. We conclude:

The Black Power advocates of today consciously feel that they are the most militant group in the Negro protest movement. Yet they have retreated from a direct confrontation with American society on the issue of integration and, by preaching separatism, unconsciously function as an accommodation to white racism. Much of their economic program, as well as their interest in Negro history, self-help, racial solidarity and separation, is reminiscent of Booker T. Washington. The rhetoric is different, but the ideas are remarkably similar.

Chapter 6—The Formation Of the Racial Ghettos

Throughout the 20th century the Negro population of the United States has been moving steadily from rural areas to urban and from South to North and West. In 1910, 91 percent of the nation's 9.8 million Negroes lived in the South and only 27 percent of American Negroes lived in cities of 2,500 persons or more. Between 1910 and 1966 the total Negro population more than doubled, reaching 21.5 million, and the number living in metropolitan areas rose more than fivefold (from 2.6 million to 14.8 million). The number outside the South rose elevenfold (from 880,000 to 9.7 million).

Negro migration from the South has resulted from the expectation of thousands of new and highly paid jobs for unskilled workers in the North and the shift to mechanized farming in the South. However, the Negro migration is small when compared to earlier waves of European immigrants. Even between 1960 and 1966, there were 1.8 million immigrants from abroad compared to the 613,000 Negroes who arrived in the North and West from the South.

As a result of the growing number of Negroes in urban areas, natural increase has replaced migration as the primary source of Negro population increase in the cities. Nevertheless, Negro migration from the South will continue unless economic conditions there change dramatically.

Basic data concerning Negro urbanization trends indicate that:

* Almost all Negro population growth (98 percent from 1950 to 1966) is occurring within metropolitan areas, primarily within central cities.
* The vast majority of white population growth (78 percent from 1960 to 1966) is occurring in suburban portions of metropolitan areas. Since 1960, white central-city population has declined by 1.3 million.

* As a result, central cities are becoming more heavily Negro while the suburban fringes around them remain almost entirely white.
* The twelve largest central cities now contain over two-thirds of the Negro population outside the South, and one-third of the Negro total in the United States.

Within the cities, Negroes have been excluded from white residential areas through discriminatory practices. Just as significant is the withdrawal of white families from, or their refusal to enter, neighborhoods where Negroes are moving or already residing. About 20 percent of the urban population of the United States changes residence every year. The refusal of whites to move into "changing" areas when vacancies occur means that most vacancies eventually are occupied by Negroes.

The result, according to a recent study, is that in 1960 the average segregation index for 207 of the largest United States cities was 86. 2. In other words, to create an unsegregated population distribution, an average of over 86 percent of all Negroes would have to change their place of residence within the city.

Chapter 7—Unemployment, Family Structure, and Social Disorganization
Although there have been gains in Negro income nationally, and a decline in the number of Negroes below the "poverty level," the condition of Negroes ill the central city remains in a state of crisis. Between 2 and 2. 5 million Negroes-16 to 20 percent of the total Negro population of all central cities live in squalor and deprivation in ghetto neighborhoods.

Employment is a key problem. It not only controls the present for the Negro American but, in a most profound way, it is creating the future as well. Yet, despite continuing economic growth and declining national unemployment rates, the unemployment rate for Negroes in 1967 was more than double that for whites…

Equally important is the undesirable nature of many jobs open to Negroes and other minorities. Negro men are more than three times as likely as white men to be in low paying, unskilled or service jobs. This concentration of male Negro employment at the lowest end of the occupational scale is the single most important cause of poverty among Negroes.

In one study of low-income neighborhoods, the "subemployment rate," including both unemployment and underemployment, was about 33 percent, or 8. 8 times greater than the overall unemployment rate for all United States workers.

Employment problems, aggravated by the constant arrival of new unemployed migrants, many of them from depressed rural areas, create persistent poverty in the ghetto. In 1966, about 11. 9 percent of the nation's whites and 40. 6 percent of its nonwhites were below the "poverty level" defined by' the Social Security Administration (currently $3,335 per year for an urban family of four). Over 40 percent of the nonwhites below the poverty level live in the central cities.

Employment problems have drastic social impact in the ghetto. Men who are chronically unemployed or employed in the lowest status jobs are often unable or unwilling to remain with their families. The handicap imposed on children growing up without fathers in an atmosphere of poverty and deprivation is increased as mothers are forced to work to provide support.

The culture of poverty that results from unemployment and family breakup generates a system of ruthless, exploitative relationships within the ghetto. Prostitution, dope addiction, and crime create an environmental "jungle" characterized by personal insecurity and tension. Children growing up under such conditions are likely participants in civil disorder.

Chapter 8—Conditions of Life In the Racial Ghetto
A striking difference in environment from that of white, middle-class Americans profoundly influences the lives of residents of the ghetto.

Crime rates, consistently higher than in other areas, create a pronounced sense of insecurity. For example, in one city one low-income Negro district had 35 times as many serious crimes against persons as a high-income white district. Unless drastic steps are taken, the crime problems in poverty areas are likely to continue to multiply as the growing youth and rapid urbanization of the population outstrip police resources.

Poor health and sanitation conditions in the ghetto result in higher mortality rates, a higher incidence of major diseases, and lower availability and utilization of medical services. The infant mortality rate for nonwhite babies under the age of one month is 58 percent higher than for whites; for one to 12 months it is almost three times as high. The level of sanitation in the ghetto is far below that in high income areas. Garbage collection is often inadequate. Of an estimated 14,000 cases of rat bite in the United States in 1965, most were in ghetto neighborhoods.

Ghetto residents believe they are "exploited" by local merchants; and evidence substantiates some of these beliefs. A study conducted in one city by the Federal Trade Commission showed that distinctly higher prices were charged for goods sold in ghetto stores than in other areas.

Lack of knowledge regarding credit purchasing creates special pitfalls for the disadvantaged. In many states garnishment practices compound these difficulties by allowing creditors to deprive individuals of their wages without hearing or trial.

Chapter 9—Comparing the Immigrant and Negro Experience
In this chapter, we address ourselves to a fundamental question that many white Americans are asking: why have so many Negroes, unlike the European immigrants, been unable to escape from the ghetto and from poverty. We believe the following factors play a part:

* The Maturing Economy: When the European immigrants arrived, they gained an economic foothold by providing the unskilled labor needed by industry. Unlike the immigrant, the Negro migrant found little opportunity in the city. The economy, by then matured, had little use for the unskilled labor he had to offer.
* The Disability of Race: The structure of discrimination has stringently narrowed opportunities for the Negro and restricted his prospects. European immigrants suffered from discrimination, but never so pervasively.
* Entry into the Political System: The immigrants usually settled in rapidly growing cities with powerful and expanding political machines, which traded economic advantages for political support. Ward-level grievance machinery, as well as personal representation, enabled the immigrant to make his voice heard and his power felt. By the time the Negro arrived, these political machines were no longer so powerful or so well equipped to provide jobs or other favors, and in many cases were unwilling to share their influence with Negroes.
* Cultural Factors: Coming from societies with a low standard of living and at a time when job aspirations were low, the immigrants sensed little deprivation in being forced to take the less desirable and poorer-paying jobs. Their large and cohesive families contributed to total income. Their vision of the future—one that led to a life outside of the ghetto—provided the incentive necessary to endure the present.

Although Negro men worked as hard as the immigrants, they were unable to support their families. The entrepreneurial opportunities had vanished. As a result of slavery and long periods of unemployment, the Negro family structure had become matriarchal; the males played a secondary and marginal family role—one which offered little compensation for their hard and unrewarding labor. Above all, segregation denied Negroes access to good jobs and the opportunity to leave the ghetto. For them, the futureseemed to lead only to a dead end.

Today, whites tend to exaggerate how well and quickly they escaped from poverty. The fact is that immigrants who came from rural backgrounds, as many Negroes do, are only now, after three generations, finally beginning to move into the middle class.

By contrast, Negroes began concentrating in the city less than two generations ago, and under much less favorable conditions. Although some Negroes have escaped poverty, few have been able to escape the urban ghetto.

Part III—What Can Be Done?

Chapter 10—The Community Response
Our investigation of the 1967 riot cities establishes that virtually every major episode of violence was foreshadowed by an accumulation of unresolved grievances and by widespread dissatisfaction among Negroes with the unwillingness or inability of local government to respond.

Overcoming these conditions is essential for community support of law enforcement and civil order. City governments need new and more vital channels of communication to the residents of the ghetto; they need to improve their capacity to respond effectively to community needs before they become community grievances; and they need to provide opportunity for, meaningful involvement of ghetto residents in shaping policies and programs which affect the community.

The Commission recommends that local governments:

* Develop Neighborhood Action Task Forces as joint community government efforts through which more effective communication can be achieved, and the delivery of city services to ghetto residents improved.
* Establish comprehensive grievance-response mechanisms in order to bring all public agencies under public scrutiny.
* Bring the institutions of local government closer to the people they serve by establishing neighborhood outlets for local, state and federal administrative and public service agencies.
* Expand opportunities for ghetto residents to participate in the formulation of public policy and the implementation of programs affecting them through improved political representation, creation of institutional channels for community action, expansion of legal services, and legislative hearings on ghetto problems.

In this effort, city governments will require state and federal support.

The Commission recommends:

* State and federal financial assistance for mayors and city councils to support the research, consultants, staff and other resources needed to respond effectively to federal program initiatives.
* State cooperation in providing municipalities with the jurisdictional tools needed to deal with their problems; a fuller measure of financial aid to urban areas; and the focusing of the interests of suburban communities on the physical, social and cultural environment of the central city.

Chapter 11—Police and the Community

The abrasive relationship between the police and the minority communities has been a major—and explosive—source of grievance, tension and disorder. The blame must be shared by the total society.

The police are faced with demands for increased protection and service in the ghetto. Yet the aggressive patrol practices thought necessary to meet these demands themselves create tension and hostility. The resulting grievances have been further aggravated by the lack of effective mechanisms for handling complaints against the police. Special programs for bettering police-community relations have been instituted, but these alone are not enough. Police administrators, with the guidance of public officials, and the support of the entire community, must take vigorous action to improve law enforcement arid to decrease the potential for disorder.

The Commission recommends that city government and police authorities:

* Review police operations in the ghetto to ensure proper conduct by police officers, and eliminate abrasive practices.
* Provide more adequate police protection to ghetto residents to eliminate their high sense of insecurity, and the belief of many Negro citizens in the existence of a dual standard of law enforcement.
* Establish fair and effective mechanisms for the redress of grievances against the police, and other municipal employees.
* Develop and adopt policy guidelines to assist officers in making critical decisions in areas where police conduct can create tension.
* Develop and use innovative programs to ensure widespread community support for law enforcement.
* Recruit more Negroes into the regular police force, and review promotion policies to ensure fair promotion for Negro officers.
* Establish a "Community Service Officer" program to attract ghetto youths between the ages of 17 and 21 to police work. These junior officers would perform duties in ghetto neighborhoods, but would not have full police authority. The federal government should provide support equal to 90 percent of the costs of employing CSOs on the basis of one for every ten regular officers.

Chapter 12—Control of Disorder

Preserving civil peace is the first responsibility of government. Unless the rule of law prevails, our society will lack not only order but also the environment essential to social and economic progress.

The maintenance of civil order cannot be left to the police alone. The police need guidance, as well as support, from mayors and other public officials. It is the responsibility of public officials to determine proper police policies, support adequate police standards for personnel and performance, and participate in planning for the control of disorders.

To maintain control of incidents which could lead to disorders, the Commission recommends that local officials:

* Assign seasoned, well-trained policemen and supervisory officers to patrol ghetto areas, and to respond to disturbances.
* Develop plans which will quickly muster maximum police man power and highly qualified senior commanders at the outbreak of disorders.
* Provide special training in the prevention of disorders, and prepare police for riot control and for operation in units, with adequate command and control and field communication for proper discipline and effectiveness.
* Develop guidelines governing the use of control equipment and provide alternatives to the use of lethal weapons. Federal support for research in this area is needed.
* Establish an intelligence system to provide police and other public officials with reliable information that may help to prevent the outbreak of a disorder and to institute effective control measures in the event a riot erupts.
* Develop continuing contacts with ghetto residents to make use of the forces for order which exist within the community.
* Establish machinery for neutralizing rumors, and enabling Negro leaders and residents to obtain the facts. Create special rumor details to collect, evaluate, and dispel rumors that may lead to a civil disorder.

The Commission believes there is a grave danger that some communities may resort to the indiscriminate and excessive use of force. The harmful effects of overreaction are incalculable. The Commission condemns moves to equip police departments with mass destruction weapons, such as automatic rifles, machine guns and tanks. Weapons which are designed to destroy, not to control, have no place in densely populated urban communities.

The Commission recognizes the sound principle of local authority and responsibility in law enforcement, but recommends that the federal government share, in the financing of programs for improvement of police forces, both in their normal law enforcement activities as well as in their response to civil disorders.

To assist government authorities in planning their response to civil disorder, this report contains a Supplement on Control of Disorder. It deals with specific problems encountered during riot-control operations, and includes:

* Assessment of the present capabilities of police, National Guard and Army forces to control major riots, and recommendations for improvement;
* Recommended means by which the control operations of those forces may be coordinated with the response of other agencies, such as fire departments, and with the community at large;
* Recommendations for review and revision of federal, state and local laws needed to provide the framework for control efforts and for the call-up and interrelated action of public safety forces.

Chapter 13—The Administration of Justice Under Emergency Conditions
In many of the cities which experienced disorders last summer, there were recurring breakdowns in the mechanisms for processing, prosecuting and protecting arrested persons. These resulted mainly from long-standing structural deficiencies in criminal court systems, and from the failure of communities to anticipate and plan for the emergency demands of civil disorders.

In part, because of this, there were few successful prosecutions for serious crimes committed during the riots. In those cities where mass arrests occurred many arrestees were deprived of basic legal rights.

The Commission recommends that the cities and states:

* Undertake reform of the lower courts so as to improve the quality of justice rendered under normal conditions.
* Plan comprehensive measures by which the criminal justice system may be supplemented during civil disorders so that its deliberative functions are protected, and the quality of justice is maintained.

Such emergency plans require broad community participation and dedicated leadership by the bench and bar. They should include:

* Laws sufficient to deter and punish riot conduct.
* Additional judges, bail and probation officers, and clerical staff.
* Arrangements for volunteer lawyers to help prosecutors and to represent riot defendants at every stage of proceedings.
* Policies to ensure proper and individual bail, arraignment, pre-trial, trial and sentencing proceedings.

* Procedures for processing arrested persons, such as summons and release, and release on personal recognizance, which permit separation of minor offenders from those dangerous to the community, in order that serious offenders may be detained and prosecuted effectively.
* Adequate emergency processing and detention facilities.

Chapter 14—Damages: Repair and Compensation
The Commission recommends that the federal government:
* Amend the Federal Disaster Act-which now applies only to natural disasters—to permit federal emergency food and medical assistance to cities during major civil disorders, and provide long-term economic assistance afterwards.
* With the cooperation of the states, create incentives for the private insurance industry to provide more adequate property-insurance coverage in inner-city areas.

The Commission endorses the report of the National Advisory Panel on Insurance in Riot-Affected Areas: "Meeting the Insurance Crisis of our Cities."

Chapter 15—The News Media and the Disorders
In his charge to the Commission, the President asked: "What effect do the mass media have on the riots?"

The Commission determined that the answer to the President's question did not lie solely in the performance of the press and broadcasters in reporting the riots. Our analysis had to consider also the overall treatment by the media of the Negro ghettos, community relations, racial attitudes, and poverty-day by day and month by month, year in and year out. A wide range of interviews with government officials, law enforcement authorities, media personnel and other citizens, including ghetto residents, as well as a quantitative analysis of riot coverage and a special conference with industry representatives, leads us to conclude that:
* Despite instances of sensationalism, inaccuracy and distortion, newspapers, radio and television tried on the whole to give a balanced, factual account of the 1967 disorders.
* Elements of the news media failed to portray accurately the scale and character of the violence that occurred last summer. The overall effect was, we believe, an exaggeration of both mood and event.
* Important segments of the media failed to report adequately on the causes and consequences of civil disorders and on the underlying problems of race relations. They have not communicated to the majority of their audience—which is white—a sense of the degradation, misery and hopelessness of life in the ghetto.

These failings must be corrected, and the improvement must come from within the industry. Freedom of the press is not the issue. Any effort to impose governmental restrictions would be inconsistent with fundamental constitutional precepts.

We have seen evidence that the news media are becoming aware of and concerned about their performance in this field. As that concern grows, coverage will improve. But much more must be done, and it must be done soon.

The Commission recommends that the media:
* Expand coverage of the Negro community and of race problems through permanent assignment of reporters familiar with urban and racial affairs, and through establishment of more and better links with the Negro community.
* Integrate Negroes and Negro activities into all aspects of coverage and content, including newspaper articles and television programming. The news media must publish newspapers and produce programs that recognize the existence and activities of Negroes as a group within the community and as a part of the larger community.
* Recruit more Negroes into journalism and broadcasting and promote those who are qualified to positions of significant responsibility. Recruitment should begin in high schools and continue through college; where necessary, aid for training should be provided.
* Improve coordination with police in reporting riot news through advance planning, and cooperate with the police in the designation of police information officers, establishment of information centers, and development of mutually acceptable guidelines for riot reporting and the conduct of media personnel.
* Accelerate efforts to ensure accurate and responsible reporting of pot and racial news, through adoption by all news gathering organizations of stringent internal staff guidelines.
* Cooperate in the establishment of a privately organized and funded Institute of Urban Communications to train and educate journalists in urban

affairs, recruit and train more Negro journalists, develop methods for improving police-press relations, review coverage of riots and racial issues, and support continuing research in the urban field.

Chapter 16—The Future of the Cities

By 1985, the Negro population in central cities is expected to increase by 72 percent to approximately 20. 8 million. Coupled with the continued exodus of white families to the suburbs, this growth will produce majority Negro populations in many of the nation's largest cities.

The future of these cities, and of their burgeoning Negro populations, is grim. Most new employment opportunities are being created in suburbs and outlying areas. This trend will continue unless important changes in public policy are made.

In prospect, therefore, is further deterioration of already inadequate municipal tax bases in the face of increasing demands for public services, and continuing unemployment and poverty among the urban Negro population:

Three choices are open to the nation:

* We can maintain present policies, continuing both the proportion of the nation's resources now allocated to programs for the unemployed and the disadvantaged, and the inadequate and failing effort to achieve an integrated society.
* We can adopt a policy of "enrichment" aimed at improving dramatically the quality of ghetto life while abandoning integration as a goal.
* We can pursue integration by combining ghetto "enrichment" with policies which will encourage Negro movement out of central city areas.

The first choice, continuance of present policies, has ominous consequences for our society. The share of the nation's resources now allocated to programs for the disadvantaged is insufficient to arrest the deterioration of life in central city ghettos. Under such conditions, a rising proportion of Negroes may come to see in the deprivation and segregation they experience, a justification for violent protest, or for extending support to now isolated extremists who advocate civil disruption. Large-scale and continuing violence could result, followed by white retaliation, and, ultimately, the separation of the two communities in a garrison state.

Even if violence does not occur, the consequences are unacceptable. Development of a racially integrated society, extraordinarily difficult today, will be virtually impossible when the present black ghetto population of 12. 5 million has grown to almost 21 million.

To continue present policies is to make permanent the division of our country into two societies; one, largely Negro and poor, located in the central cities; the other, predominantly white and affluent, located in the suburbs and in outlying areas.

The second choice, ghetto enrichment coupled with abandonment of integration, is also unacceptable. It is another way of choosing a permanently divided country. Moreover, equality cannot be achieved under conditions of nearly complete separation. In a country where the economy, and particularly the resources of employment, are predominantly white, a policy of separation can only relegate Negroes to a permanently inferior economic status.

We believe that the only possible choice for America is the third—a policy which combines ghetto enrichment with programs designed to encourage integration of substantial numbers of Negroes into the society outside the ghetto.

Enrichment must be an important adjunct to integration, for no matter how ambitious or energetic the program, few Negroes now living in central cities can be quickly integrated. In the meantime, large-scale improvement in the quality of ghetto life is essential.

In the meantime, large-scale improvement in the quality of ghetto life is essential.

But this can be no more than an interim strategy. Programs must be developed which will permit substantial Negro movement out of the ghettos. The primary goal must be a single society, in which every citizen will be free to live and work according to his capabilities and desires, not his color.

Chapter 17—Recommendations For National Action

♦ **Introduction**

No American—white or black—can escape the consequences of the continuing social and economic decay of our major cities.

Only a commitment to national action on an unprecedented scale can shape a future compatible with the historic ideals of American society.

The great productivity of our economy, and a federal revenue system which is highly responsive to economic growth, can provide the resources.

The major need is to generate new will—the will to tax ourselves to the extent necessary, to meet the vital needs of the nation.

We have set forth goals and proposed strategies to reach those goals. We discuss and recommend programs not to commit each of us to specific parts of such programs but to illustrate the type and dimension of action needed.

The major goal is the creation of a true union—a single society and a single American identity. Toward that goal, we propose the following objectives for national action:

* Opening up opportunities to those who are restricted by racial segregation and discrimination, and eliminating all barriers to their choice of jobs, education and housing.
* Removing the frustration of powerlessness among the disadvantaged by providing the means for them to deal with the problems that affect their own lives and by increasing the capacity of our public and private institutions to respond to these problems.
* Increasing communication across racial lines to destroy stereotypes, to halt polarization, end distrust and hostility, and create common ground for efforts toward public order and social justice.

We propose these aims to fulfill our pledge of equality and to meet the fundamental needs of a democratic and civilized society—domestic peace and social justice.

♦ **Employment**

Pervasive unemployment and underemployment are the most persistent and serious grievances in minority areas. They are inextricably linked to the problem of civil disorder.

Despite growing federal expenditures for manpower development and training programs, and sustained general economic prosperity and increasing demands for skilled workers, about two million—white and nonwhite—are permanently unemployed. About ten million are underemployed, of whom 6.5 million work full time for wages below the poverty line.

The 500,000 "hard-core" unemployed in the central cities who lack a basic education and are unable to hold a steady job are made up in large part of Negro males between the ages of 18 and 25. In the riot cities which we surveyed, Negroes were three times as likely as whites to hold unskilled jobs, which are often part time, seasonal, low-paying and "dead end."

Negro males between the ages of 15 and 25 predominated among the rioters. More than 20 percent of the rioters were unemployed, and many who were employed held intermittent, low status, unskilled jobs which they regarded as below their education and ability.

The Commission recommends that the federal government:

* Undertake joint efforts with cities and states to consolidate existing manpower programs to avoid fragmentation and duplication.
* Take immediate action to create 2,000,000 new jobs over the next three years—one million in the public sector and one million in the private sector—to absorb the hard-core unemployed and materially reduce the level of underemployment for all workers, black and white. We propose 250,000 public sector and 300,000 private sector jobs in the first year.
* Provide on-the-job training by both public and private employers with reimbursement to private employers for the extra costs of training the hard-core unemployed, by contract or by tax credits.
* Provide tax and other incentives to investment in rural as well as urban poverty areas in order to offer to the rural poor an alternative to migration to urban centers.
* Take new and vigorous action to remove artificial barriers to employment and promotion, including not only racial discrimination but, in certain cases, arrest records or lack of a high school diploma. Strengthen those agencies such as the Equal Employment Opportunity Commission, charged with eliminating discriminatory practices, and provide full support for Title VI of the 1964 Civil Rights Act allowing federal grant-in-aid funds to be withheld from activities which discriminate on grounds of color or race.

The Commission commends the recent public commitment of the National Council of the Building and Construction Trades Unions, AFL-CIO, to encourage and recruit Negro membership in apprenticeship programs. This commitment should be intensified and implemented.

♦ **Education**

Education in a democratic society must equip children to develop their potential and to participate fully in American life. For the community at large, the schools have discharged this responsibility well. But for many minorities, and particularly for the children of the ghetto, the schools have failed to provide the educational experience which could overcome the effects of discrimination and deprivation.

This failure is one of the persistent sources of grievance and resentment within the Negro community. The hostility of Negro parents and students toward the school system is generating increasing conflict and causing disruption within many city school districts. But the most dramatic evidence of the relationship between educational practices and civil disorders lies in the high incidence of riot participation by ghetto youth who have not completed high school.

The bleak record of public education for ghetto children is growing worse. In the critical skills—verbal and reading ability—Negro students are falling further behind whites with each year of school completed. The high unemployment and underemployment rate for Negro youth is evidence, in part, of the growing educational crisis.

We support integration as the priority education strategy; it is essential to the future of American society. In this last summer's disorders we have seen the consequences of racial isolation at all levels, and of attitudes toward race, on both sides, produced by three centuries of myth, ignorance and bias. It is indispensable that opportunities for interaction between the races be expanded.

We recognize that the growing dominance of pupils from disadvantaged minorities in city school populations will not soon be reversed. No matter how great the effort toward desegregation, many children of the ghetto will not, within their school careers, attend integrated schools.

If existing disadvantages are not to be perpetuated, we must drastically improve the quality of ghetto education. Equality of results with all-white schools must be the goal.

To implement these strategies, the Commission recommends:

* Sharply increased efforts to eliminate de facto segregation in our schools through substantial federal aid to school systems seeking to desegregate either within the system or in cooperation with neighboring school systems.
* Elimination of racial discrimination in Northern as well as Southern schools by vigorous application of Title VI of the Civil Rights Act of 1964.
* Extension of quality early childhood education to every disadvantaged child in the country.
* Efforts to improve dramatically schools serving disadvantaged children through substantial federal funding of year-round compensatory education programs, improved teaching, and expanded experimentation and research.
* Elimination of illiteracy through greater federal support for adult basic education.
* Enlarged opportunities for parent and community participation in the public schools.
* Reoriented vocational education emphasizing work-experience training and the involvement of business and industry.
* Expanded opportunities for higher education through increased federal assistance to disadvantaged students.
* Revision of state aid formulas to assure more per student aid to districts having a high proportion of disadvantaged school-age children.

♦ **The Welfare System**

Our present system of public welfare is designed to save money instead of people, and tragically ends up doing neither. This system has two critical deficiencies:

First, it excludes large numbers of persons who are in great need, and who, if provided a decent level of support, might be able to become more productive and self-sufficient. No federal funds are available for millions of men and women who are needy but neither aged, handicapped nor the parents of minor children.

Second, for those included, the system provides assistance well below the minimum necessary for a decent level of existence, and imposes restrictions that encourage continued dependency on welfare and undermine self-respect.

A welter of statutory requirements and administrative practices and regulations operate to remind recipients that they are considered untrustworthy, promiscuous and lazy. Residence requirements prevent assistance to people in need who are newly arrived in the state. Regular searches of recipients' homes violate privacy. Inadequate social services compound the problems.

The Commission recommends that the federal government, acting with state and local governments where necessary, reform the existing welfare system to:

* Establish uniform national standards of assistance at least as high as the annual "poverty level" of income, now set by the Social Security Administration at $3,335 per year for an urban family of four.

Document Text

* Require that all states receiving federal welfare contributions participate in the Aid to Families with Dependent Children Unemployed Parents program (AFDC-UP) that permits assistance to families with both father and mother in the home, thus aiding the family while it is still intact.
* Bear a substantially greater portion of all welfare costs—at least 90 percent of total payments.
* Increase incentives for seeking employment and job training, but remove restrictions recently enacted by the Congress that would compel mothers of young children to work.
* Provide more adequate social services through neighborhood centers and family-planning programs.
* Remove the freeze placed by the 1967 welfare amendments on the percentage of children in a state that can be covered by federal assistance.
* Eliminate residence requirements.

As a long-range goal, the Commission recommends that the federal government seek to develop a national system of income supplementation based strictly on need with two broad and basic purposes:

* To provide, for those who can work or who do work, any necessary supplements in such a way as to develop incentives for fuller employment;
* To provide, for those who cannot work and for mothers who decide to remain with their children, a minimum standard of decent living, and to aid in the saving of children from the prison of poverty that has held their parents.

A broad system of implementation would involve substantially greater federal expenditures than anything now contemplated. The cost will range widely depending on the standard of need accepted as the "basic allowance" to individuals and families, and on the rate at which additional income above this level is taxed. Yet if the deepening cycle of poverty and dependence on welfare can be broken, if the children of the poor can be given the opportunity to scale the wall that now separates them from the rest of society, the return on this investment will be great indeed.

♦ Housing

After more than three decades of fragmented and grossly underfunded federal housing programs, nearly six million substandard housing units remain occupied in the United States.

The housing problem is particularly acute in the minority ghettos. Nearly two-thirds of all non-white families living in the central cities today live in neighborhoods marked with substandard housing and general urban blight. Two major factors are responsible.

First: Many ghetto residents simply cannot pay the rent necessary to support decent housing. In Detroit, for example, over 40 percent of the nonwhite occupied units in 1960 required rent of over 35 percent of the tenants' income.

Second: Discrimination prevents access to many non-slum areas, particularly the suburbs, where good housing exists. In addition, by creating a "back pressure" in the racial ghettos, it makes it possible for landlords to break up apartments for denser occupancy, and keeps prices and rents of deteriorated ghetto housing higher than they would be in a truly free market.

To date, federal programs have been able to do comparatively little to provide housing for the disadvantaged. In the 31-year history of subsidized federal housing, only about 800,000 units have been constructed, with recent production averaging about 50,000 units a year. By comparison, over a period only three years longer, FHA insurance guarantees have made possible the construction of over ten million middle and upper-income units.

Two points are fundamental to the Commission's recommendations:

First: Federal housing programs must be given a new thrust aimed at overcoming the prevailing patterns of racial segregation. If this is not done, those programs will continue to concentrate the most impoverished and dependent segments of the population into the central-city ghettos where there is already a critical gap between the needs of the population and the public resources to deal with them.

Second: The private sector must be brought into the production and financing of low and moderate rental housing to supply the capabilities and capital necessary to meet the housing needs of the nation.

The Commission recommends that the federal government:

* Enact a comprehensive and enforceable federal open housing law to cover the sale or rental of all housing, including single family homes.
* Reorient federal housing programs to place more low and moderate income housing outside of ghetto areas.
* Bring within the reach of low and moderate income families within the next five years six million

Document Text

new and existing units of decent housing, beginning with 600,000 units in the next year.

To reach this goal we recommend:

* Expansion and modification of the rent supplement program to permit use of supplements for existing housing, thus greatly increasing the reach of the program.
* Expansion and modification of the below-market interest rate program to enlarge the interest subsidy to all sponsors and provide interest-free loans to nonprofit sponsors to cover pre-construction costs, and permit sale of projects to nonprofit corporations, cooperatives, or condominiums.
* Creation of an ownership supplement program similar to present rent supplements, to make home ownership possible for low-income families.
* Federal writedown of interest rates on loans to private builders constructing moderate-rent housing.
* Expansion of the public housing program, with emphasis on small units on scattered sites, and leasing and "turnkey" programs.
* Expansion of the Model Cities program.
* Expansion and reorientation of the urban renewal program to give priority to projects directly assisting low-income households to obtain adequate housing.

Conclusion

One of the first witnesses to be invited to appear before this Commission was Dr. Kenneth B. Clark, a distinguished and perceptive scholar. Referring to the reports of earlier riot commissions, he said:

> I read that report... of the 1919 riot in Chicago, and it is as if I were reading the report of the investigating committee on the Harlem riot of '35, the report of the investigating committee on the Harlem riot of '43, the report of the McCone Commission on the Watts riot.
>
> I must again in candor say to you members of this Commission—it is a kind of Alice in Wonderland—with the same moving picture re-shown over and over again, the same analysis, the same recommendations, and the same inaction.

These words come to our minds as we conclude this report.

We have provided an honest beginning. We have learned much. But we have uncovered no startling truths, no unique insights, no simple solutions. The destruction and the bitterness of racial disorder, the harsh polemics of black revolt and white repression have been seen and heard before in this country.

It is time now to end the destruction and the violence, not only in the streets of the ghetto but in the lives of people.

Glossary

de facto segregation: segregation that exists not because of law or government requirement but because of residential patterns or other social practices

exodus: the emigration, departure, or movement of a large group of people

Molotov cocktail: an improvised firebomb thrown by hand and usually consisting of a bottle filled with a liquid that will burn and a rag for a wick

Negro: common term for an African American in the 1960s

nihilism: the view that destroying existing society is necessary to bring about social improvement

polemics: controversial arguments

underemployment: inadequate employment in a part-time instead of full-time job, labor in a low-paying position, or work that requires skills that are less than the worker possesses

American civil rights leader and Black Panther Party member Eldridge Cleaver (1935–1998). By U.S. News & World Report Magazine staff photographer: Marion S. Trikosko [Public domain], via Wikimedia Commons

Eldridge Cleaver: "Education and Revolution"

"It is not possible for a capitalistic economy to provide a universal education for the people. What it has been providing is universal brainwashing that masquerades as universal education."

Overview

Revolution and Education is a 1968 pamphlet by Cleaver that contains an essay on generational education. In it, Cleaver posits that an individual must come to terms with two worlds, the natural and the social; he then extends this to discuss the difficulty of navigating racial tensions and discrimination (in both of these worlds), insisting on the need for information to be passed down from generation to generation. To do so, he concludes, is the only way to survive the ongoing war against Black people.

Context

In November 1969, Eldridge Cleaver's essay "Education and Revolution" was published in *The Black Scholar*, a progressive journal that takes a black perspective on such issues as education, culture, and politics. Cleaver at the time was a member of the Black Panther Party, a militant revolutionary organization founded earlier in the decade. The initial goal of the Black Panthers was to promote self-defense in the black community at a time when many urban blacks saw police forces as oppressive and racist. In time, the Black Panthers broadened their goals to include charitable work, principally by providing schoolchildren with breakfasts, and efforts to promote black self-awareness in the schools. The Black Panthers were also strong advocates of Socialism as a mode of social organization. In his essay, Cleaver articulates the Socialist goals of the Black Panthers and explains why, from his perspective, the black community has to take charge of its children's education as a means of overthrowing an oppressive capitalist system.

About the Author

Leroy Eldridge Cleaver (August 31, 1935 – May 1, 1998) was an American writer and political activist who became an early leader of the Black Panther Party. Born in Wabbaseka, Arkansas, as a child, Cleaver moved with his family to Phoenix and then to Los Angeles. He was the son of Leroy Cleaver and Thelma Hattie Robinson. He had four siblings: Wilhelima Marie, Helen Grace, James Weldon, and Theophilus Henry.

As a teenager, he was involved in petty crime and spent time in youth detention centers. In 1958, he was convicted of rape and assault with intent to murder and eventually served time in Folsom and San Quentin prisons. Eldridge Cleaver was released from prison on December 12, 1966. In 1967, Eldridge Cleaver, along with Marvin X, Ed Bullins, and Ethna Wyatt, formed the Black House political/cultural center in San Francisco. Amiri Baraka, Sonia Sanchez, Askia Toure, Sarah Webster Fabio, Art Ensemble of Chicago, Avotcja, Reginald Lockett, Emory Douglas, Samuel Napier, Bobby Hutton, Huey Newton, and Bobby Seale were Black House regulars. The same year, he married Kathleen Neal Cleaver..

Cleaver was a presidential candidate in 1968 on the ticket of the Peace and Freedom Party. Having been born on August 31, 1935, Cleaver would not have been the requisite 35 years of age until more than a year after Inauguration Day 1969. Cleaver and his running mate Judith Mage received 36,571 votes (0.05%).

In 1969, Cleaver cultivated an alliance with North Korea and BPP publications began reprinting excerpts from Kim Il Sung's writings. Bypassing US travel restrictions on North Korea, Cleaver and other BPP members made two visits to the country in 1969-70 with the idea that the juche model could be adapted to the revolutionary liberation of African-Americans.

Byron Vaughn Booth (former Panther Deputy Minister of Defense) claimed that, after a trip to the DPRK, Cleaver discovered his wife had been having an affair with Clinton Robert Smith Jr. Booth told the FBI he had witnessed Cleaver shoot and kill Smith with an AK47.

In his 1978 book Soul on Fire, Cleaver made several claims regarding his exile in Algeria. Cleaver stated that he was followed by other former criminals turned revolutionaries, many of whom (including Booth and Smith) hijacked planes to get to Algeria.

Eldridge Cleaver and Huey Newton eventually fell out with each other over the necessity of armed struggle as a response to COINTELPRO and other actions by the government against the Black Panthers and other radical groups.

Cleaver left Algeria in 1972, moving to Paris, France, becoming a born again Christian during time in isolation living underground. Cleaver returned to the United States in 1977 to face the unresolved attempted murder charge. The long outstanding charge was subsequently resolved on a plea bargain reducing it to assault. A sentence of 1,200 hours' community service was imposed.

In the early 1980s, Cleaver became disillusioned with evangelical Christianity and examined alternatives, including Sun Myung Moon's campus ministry organization CARP. Cleaver was later baptized into The Church of Jesus Christ of Latter-day Saints (LDS Church) on December 11, 1983, periodically attended regular services, lectured by invitation at LDS gatherings, and was a member of the Church in good standing at the time of his death in 1998.

By the 1980s, Cleaver had become a conservative Republican. He appeared at various Republican events and spoke at a California Republican State Central Committee meeting regarding his political transformation. In 1984, he ran for election to the Berkeley City Council but lost. The next year, his 20-year marriage to Kathleen Neal Cleaver came to an end.

Cleaver died at Pomona Valley Hospital Medical Center in Pomona, California, on May 1, 1998. He is buried at Mountain View Cemetery in Altadena, California.

Explanation and Analysis of the Document

In this article, Cleaver de-emphasizes the issue of black and white by arguing that the division is one perpetrated by the ruling class. The difference between black and white revolutionary struggles, in Cleaver's view, is inconsequential, for the struggle is against the same ruling class. Cleaver notes that many people who are not connected to the college community often tend to think that what takes place on college campuses is none of their business, but Cleaver rejects this view, arguing that the campus is part of the larger human community. Further, the stratification of the college campus is an emblem of the stratification of the larger society. Campuses are administered by members of the ruling class to the exclusion of the poor and powerless people whose interests are supposedly being served. Cleaver concludes, in paragraph 32, that

> poor black people and poor white people and middle class people who are not themselves directly involved in the college situation, need to be made to understand that something of their own precious liberty, which either they never had or they thought they had, is being decisively determined in the struggles that are going down on the campuses today.

♦ "Universal Brainwashing"

Cleaver argues that it is the duty of the state to provide people with medical care, housing, employment, and education. Any government that fails to do so is "not worthy of existing." In the educational arena, education is supposedly universal, but in Cleaver's view what is taking place is "universal brainwashing." This section of the essay essentially repeats the ideas that Cleaver has already expressed: that the educational system is under the control of the ruling class. Therefore, the system has to be not "reformed" but overthrown. The goal is not reform but revolution.

♦ "Transforming the Social Order"

In the essay's concluding section, Cleaver emphasizes revolutionary goals: "We have to destroy the present structure of power in the United States, we have to overthrow the government." He argues that the courts, the legislatures, and the executive branches at both the state and federal level are instruments of the ruling class and therefore have to be replaced—that the "machinery" of government must be replaced by "new machinery." Cleaver indicates that the only way to do so is through violence. "We are involved in a war," says Cleaver, and a war is not a "game." Cleaver's startling conclusion is that overthrowing the ruling class can begin with the college president, who derives his power from corporations: This attack might "be through boycotts of the products of that corporation, or through the physical destruction of the property of the corporation, or the physical elimination of him as an individual."

Audience

Cleaver's essay was published in *The Black Scholar*, an education journal founded in 1969 that continues to focus on progressive education, culture, and politics from the perspective of the black community. Its list of contributors over the years reads like a who's who of black intellectuals and writers: Amiri Baraka, Angela Davis, Julian Bond, Shirley Chisholm, Stokely Carmichael, Maya Angelou, Alice Walker, and many others. Publication in a scholarly journal such as *The Black Scholar* would lend an essay such as Cleaver's credibility. Clearly, however, Cleaver was writing primarily for an audience that was already inclined to accept his point of view, though it should be noted that many African Americans at the time regarded the Black Panthers with suspicion because of their extreme militancy and allegations that they were involved in criminal activity. Thus, Cleaver was in the position of having to convince black readers, as well as white readers, of the legitimacy of the Panthers' position on the issue of education.

Black Panther convention, Lincoln Memorial, June 19, 1970. By O'Halloran, Thomas J., photographer.; Leffler, Warren K., photographer. For US News and World Report. - Library of Congress

Impact

The Black Panthers were an unabashedly revolutionary organization, one that called for the overthrow of the capitalist system. During the late 1960s and early 1970s, the organization was the subject of extensive investigation by the Federal Bureau of Investigation. Writing in the *New York Times*, FBI director J. Edgar Hoover stated:

> The Black Panthers are the greatest threat to the internal security of the country. Schooled in the Marxist-Leninist ideology and the teaching of Chinese Communist leader Mao Tse-tung, its members have perpetrated numerous assaults on police officers and have engaged in violent confrontations with police throughout the country. Leaders and representatives of the Black Panther Party travel extensively all over the United States preaching their gospel of hate and violence not only to ghetto residents, but to students in colleges, universities and high schools as well.

The FBI took action, using wiretaps, searches, infiltration, and other techniques—some of questionable legality—to disrupt the activities of the Black Panthers and, particularly, to sow the seeds of discord in the organization. While some historians regard the Black Panthers as a significant social movement, others have condemned the organization. Among the latter group is Sol Stern, who in 1967 had written a laudatory piece about the Panthers and Huey Newton for the *New York Times* but in 2003 wrote that "within a few years, I understood that I should have described Newton and his cadres as psychopathic criminals, not social reformers."

In many ways, the educational program Cleaver outlined proved to be ephemeral. Throughout the 1970s the schools formed by the Black Panthers shifted their curricula away from revolutionary principles to the political mission of integrating black youth in urban ghettos into mainstream American society. Handbooks for teachers no longer referred to the Black Panthers, as attention shifted to such traditional classroom topics as phonics, grammar, and the teaching of Standard English. That said, the type of progressive education that Cleaver espoused is by no means dead, though determining how much life remains in it depends on one's definition of "progressive education." Many scholars and schools continue to promote the belief that education is best founded on real-life experience, the type of lived experience that the Panthers stressed. Curricula from grade school to college in the United States include attention not only to the work of traditional canonical authors but also to that of oppressed minorities. History courses routinely give attention to African Americans and other minority groups, and the so-called bottom-up approach to history shifts the attention away from kings, treaties, and wars (the "top-down" approach) to the circumstances of ordinary people whose lives are affected by major events. Books such as Howard Zinn's *A People's History of the United States*, which won a National Book Award in 1980 and has been often adopted as a school textbook, examine history from the standpoint not of the cultural elites but of oppressed minorities, women, labor unions, working people, and victims of imperialism. While Cleaver's vision was doomed by its utopianism, parts of it survive, making "Education and Revolution" an important early document in the shift in attitudes that has led to a more open, diverse curriculum in American schools.

Further Reading

♦ Articles

Anderson, Jervis. "Race, Rage, and Eldridge Cleaver." *Commentary* 46 (December 1968): 63–70.

Coles, Robert. "Black Anger." *Atlantic Monthly* 221 (June 1968): 106–107.

Perlstein, Daniel. "Minds Stayed on Freedom: Politics, Pedagogy, and the African American Freedom Struggle." *American Educational Research Journal* 39 (2002): 249–277.

♦ Books

Cleaver, Kathleen, and George Katsiaficas, eds. *Liberation, Imagination, and the Black Panther Party: A New Look at the Panthers and Their Legacy*. New York: Routledge, 2001.

Jones, Charles E., ed. *The Black Panther Party [Reconsidered]*. Baltimore, Md.: Black Classic Press, 1998.

Lazerow, Jama, and Yohuru Williams, eds. *In Search of the Black Panther Party: New Perspectives on a Revolutionary Movement*. Durham, N.C.: Duke University Press, 2006.

Lockwood, Lee. *Conversation with Eldridge Cleaver*. Algiers: London Cape, 1971.

Ogbar, Jeffrey O. G. *Black Power: Radical Politics and African American Identity*. Baltimore, Md.: Johns Hopkins University Press, 2004.

Oliver, John A. *Eldridge Cleaver Reborn*. Plainfield, N.J.: Logos International, 1977.

Rout, Kathleen. *Eldridge Cleaver*. New York: Twayne Publishers, 1991.

♦ Web Sites

Hoover, J. Edgar. *New York Times*, September 9, 1968. http://www.spartacus.schoolnet.co.uk/USApantherB.htm.

Stern, Sol. "Ah, Those Black Panthers! How Beautiful!" *City Journal* (New York, N.Y.), May 27, 2003. http://www.city-journal.org/html/eon_5_27_03ss.html.

"The Ten-Point Program." Black Panther Party Web site. http://www.blackpanther.org/TenPoint.htm.

—Michael J. O'Neal

Questions for Further Study

1. Later in his life, Cleaver adopted a posture that was remarkably more benign compared with the militancy of his younger years, even to the point of joining the more conservative Republican Party. What do you think may have accounted for this change?

2. What is your opinion of the type of "progressive" education Cleaver advocated? Do you see any manifestations of this type of education in your own school? Explain.

3. Cleaver's essay and the views he expressed in it were based not on race but on social class. Explain.

4. How—and why—did Cleaver draw a connection between education designed to help people survive in the physical environment and that designed to help them survive in the social environment? How persuasive do you find this connection?

5. Why do you think that the kind of educational system Cleaver advocated never really took off and in large part disappeared in the 1970s and beyond?

Essential Quotes

"In human history, we see that society has been broken up into classes, into antagonistic ethnic and economic groups that struggle against each other for survival as each sees it. They enslave each other and make their living at the expense of other groups."

"We are struggling against those who have organized society to their advantage, in order to continue their control and rule of the entire social unit. It is very important for us to understand that we are called upon to wage this struggle with the same desperation and the same 'do or die' necessity that a caveman in some forgotten time in human history had to struggle against the natural elements."

"We are struggling against the capitalist system which organized itself in a way that purchases our lives, that exploits us and forces us into a position wherein we have to wage a struggle against the social organization in order to survive."

"The process of breaking out of slavery, the process of breaking out of a set of social arrangements, out of a social organization that is killing us, this process is named revolution; we are revolting and rebelling and moving against a system that is our enemy."

(Revolution)

"Now we have realized the necessity of taking control of our education."

"A connection needs to be made between the college campus and the community so that the repression and the tactics of the ruling class can be defeated by the total community being involved."

"It is not possible for a capitalistic economy to provide a universal education for the people. What it has been providing is universal brainwashing that masquerades as universal education."

"In order to transform the American social order, we have to destroy the present structure of power in the United States, we have to overthrow the government."

"Education and Revolution"

Full text of "Education and Revolution"

One way of understanding what's going on, on the college and the high school campuses in the United States today, is to examine the essence of education. Basically an education passes the heritage, learning, the wisdom and the technology of human history to the coming generations. We want this information to be passed on to enable and to help mankind continue to survive and cope with the environment. In terms of surviving and coping with our environment, basically, we have two worlds to deal with. We have the natural world—the task of surviving against the given world, the task of eking a living from the earth itself, for which technology has been designed. On the other hand we have the social world, the social situation. We have an antagonistic orientation to both of these worlds. We speak about the natural enemies of man, including everything from animals to the weather, and these elements have been given the label of enemy because they can kill people. We have to be able to harness these forces, we have to be able to adapt to the natural situation so that our survival will be enhanced, and for this purpose, science and technology, agriculture and industry, all of these tools have been developed by mankind through practice in coping with this physical environment.

We are in the habit of speaking about certain things that happen in the social situation that are hostile and inimical to the prospect of survival for mankind, and we also label these with the same designation of enemy. The distinction between the struggle for survival against the physical environment, and the struggle against the antagonistic forces and situations in the social realm is a very important distinction to make, because often the struggle in the social realm is really the only struggle that many people are caught up in. They are not directly involved in struggling against the physical environment, but their survival does depend upon struggling within the social realm, in terms of how the economy is organized, how the political system is organized, and how the social system itself is organized, so that many lives are played out against this background of struggling against the way civilization is presently organized.

The struggle against the physical environment, of course, is primary. We have organized our social situation in order to cope with the physical environment. The way that we organize agriculture, the way that we organize industry, the way that we organize the economy as a whole, the way that we organize the political situation, all historically have been towards facilitating and better enabling us to cope with the physical environment.

At this point I think it would be useful to establish some terminology. The best terminology I know of, for discussing this distinction between the struggle within the physical environment and the struggle within the social environment, is the terminology developed by Karl Marx. He designates the struggle against or within the physical environment as taking place within the economic base of society. And, upon the economic base of society is erected the superstructure of society. Thus the struggle within the social realm takes place within the superstructure and the struggle in the physical realm takes places within the economic base. In the economic base we find the natural resources, the technology, the industry, all the machines and the tools and the means that mankind has developed for coping with the physical environment. They are designated as the means of production, the means of producing material wealth, goods and commodities from the natural resources themselves. But all of the institutions of society, everything from the educational facilities to the hospitals and the postal service, everything belonging to the organized aspect of society, exist within the social superstructure, which has been built and sustained by our means of producing material wealth.

Let's get to the essence of an education. In a very simple-structured social organization, where technology and learning have not become complex, it would be possible for one's Father or one's uncle to pass on the technology. Your father could teach you how to fish or your father could teach you how to farm at a rudimentary agricultural level. He could teach you how to hunt with a spear or a rock, or bow and arrow. But as the economic condition becomes more complex, and as the level of information and knowledge and understanding of the environment increases, to the extent that society requires people to specialize in passing on this information, then the problem of education really sets in. When it was necessary for people

Document Text

to be designated as teachers and to specialize in, or devote all their time to, passing on this information, the learning situation itself had to be centralized as an institution. Schools, universities, etc., were developed so that the maximum productive use of a man's time and energy could be made. Now you can readily understand how in a very complex social situation it would be understood by the community, by everybody involved in the social unit, that these places or institutions of learning were there to serve and to benefit the community as a whole. It would be absurd For a teacher or one who is charged with administering the learning process as a whole, it would be absurd for him to alienate himself from the community as a whole or to claim that he owns the body of information that is a heritage to mankind; this would be absurd, it would not be tolerated by the community.

Of course I have been writing as though society was an organism in which people were in harmony with each other, in which they cooperated with each other and in which they were not waging wars of aggression against each other and were not in conflict with each other. But in actual fact and in terms of human history such harmony has not been the case.

In human history, we see that society has been broken up into classes, into antagonistic ethnic and economic groups that struggle against each other for survival as each sees it. They enslave each other and make their living at the expense of other groups, special interest groups are formed, etc. So that in reality we have to look at our own situation, have to look at the situation that exists in the economic base in terms of the class struggle, also in terms of the ethnic struggles that have gone on. When we look at our own situation today in the United States, we find that those who are very powerful in our society are powerful because of their relationship to the means of production, because they are rich, because they own the factories and because they own the natural resources. With this economic power they are able to gain control of all the institutions in society, they are able to appoint people who themselves may not be rich, or may not own stock, or have any control over the means of production of the natural resources, but because of their extensive education are able to be appointed to positions of managing society.

But at the top of the social organization in the United States, we have the ruling class mentioned; and because of the wealth of this ruling class, it is able to dominate American society and control American society, able to determine what judges are appointed to the judicial system, able to determine who is appointed to the Board of Regents to administer the colleges, and able even to determine who is elected to office, because it controls the wealth, and has vast amounts of money at its disposal to wage a political campaign.

Those who control the economy of the United States are able to control the rest of society. Those of us who are not in this advantaged position, black people, Mexican-Americans, Puerto Ricans, Indians, Eskimos, virtually every ethnic group including poor white people and also middle class college students, all find ourselves in the position wherein our lives are manipulated and controlled by those who have this advantaged social position.

We have to struggle in order to survive. But we're not struggling against the natural environment, our struggle is not in reality taking place against nature itself, but we are struggling against the way society has been organized. We are struggling against those who have organized society to their advantage, in order to continue their control and rule of the entire social unit. It is very important for us to understand that we are called upon to wage this struggle with the same desperation and the same "do or die" necessity that a caveman in some forgotten time in human history had to struggle against the natural elements. In reality, our adversaries are other men, other women and other social classes. In terms of the racial strife within the United States our class struggle is often hidden by our ethnic struggle. We are manipulated along the color line as well as along the class line. We are exploited economically, and we are discriminated against racially, also.

Today, as always, the struggle of the exploited people within the United States is taking place on all fronts, but the most sensational and explosive clashes are being centered and focussed more and more on the college campuses and on the high school campuses. We understand that those who control the mind can control the body, so that those who are interested in keeping people in oppressed positions and then dominating their perspective and their outlook on life, know that it is necessary for them to control the learning process in order to brainwash people, in order to camouflage the true nature of the society. In order to sanctify their system, they teach the exploited people and the oppressed people to virtually love the system that is exploiting and oppressing them. This oligarchy has an interest in seeing to it that the content of the curriculum is to its liking, and that it does not expose the true nature of the decadent and racist society that we live in.

On the other hand, the exploited and oppressed people have the opposite interest in exposing the true nature of the society and in educating ourselves and our children on the nature of the struggle and in transferring to them the means for waging the struggle so they can be aware of the level of the struggle, of the progress and the history of the struggle and the nature of the enemy and the true vulnerability of the enemy. In other words, we want to be able to teach ourselves and our children the necessity for struggling against this ruling class.

What we have to realize above all else is that our enemy and that which we in fact are struggling against is not an individual college president or high school principal or a board of regents or a board of education, but the entire social structure. We are struggling against the capitalist system which organized itself in a way that purchases our lives, that exploits us and forces us into a position wherein we have to wage a struggle against the social organization in order to survive.

One of the techniques or one of the weapons that the enemy uses against us in our struggle is to turn words against us, to define our struggle in terms that place our struggle in a bad light, so that the word "revolution" is given a bad name, is looked upon as a negative term.

But what revolution means and what it means to us is that we are trying to change a system that has historically enslaved our people, has continually exploited us, has discriminated against us and made our lives miserable and kept us underdeveloped and kept us blind and kept us in a form of slavery, one form of slavery or another. Of course, our struggle has continually forced the slavemaster to modify the terms of the slavery, but every modification that has been made has only been made because the slavemaster found it necessary to make a few minor adjustments in order to continue his exploitation of us on a new level.

The process of breaking out of slavery, the process of breaking out of a set of social arrangements, out of a social organization that is killing us, this process is named revolution; we are revolting and rebelling and moving against a system that is our enemy. For us the word "revolution" should be a beautiful word because it's a word that promises us hope, that promises us a better life and we should not be ashamed to call ourselves revolutionaries. We are a revolutionary people, our very social situation forces us to be a revolutionary people. If we are not going to be revolutionary people, we have to accept the designation of satisfied slaves; if we aren't satisfied, then that means we have a revolutionary consciousness. It is important for us to be consciously revolutionary, to understand that we are revolutionaries, and to understand that it is right for us to be revolutionaries and that in fact the enemies are the ones who are wrong.

The enemy uses words against us, talks about "crime in the streets," talks about "disorders," talks about "law and order," all of these words are smoke screens, are smoke screens to confuse us, to create conflicts between the various exploited groups and to turn them against each other. It is the old technique of divide and conquer. What we need and what—if we had any sense at all—what we would be working for is to create an alliance between all the exploited people within the society so that we could join together to create machinery, coordinate our struggle, and coordinate our attack against the capitalist system and destroy it. Because as along as the capitalist system exists, by its very nature some people will have to be exploited in order for others to be rich and powerful, so that the exploited are powerless and in an oppressed position. Therefore revolution is a glorious term, it is a term to be proud of and we should know that we are morally right, we are right in every sense of the term and that the oppressor is the one who is wrong and that the oppressor has no rights which the oppressed are bound to respect.

History is on our side and justice is on our side and it is only a question of removing from positions of power those who are able to judge our struggle and to pass out judgements that denounce us and that deny us the right to survive. If we had revolutionary members from the exploited classes sitting on the Supreme Court, in the halls of Congress and in the Executive Branch of the Government, then these revolutionaries in office would give out revolutionary decisions, the revolutionaries on the benches of the court would give out revolutionary decisions on the court cases and the capitalists and the racist police would be judged wrong.

They would be the ones who would be sent to prison. They would be the ones who would be penalized. They would be the ones who would be forced to raise a hundred thousand dollars in order to get out on bail. In other words, the oppressed people have to take control of the government, they have to take control of the state, so that in their hands these instruments of power would be turned against the exploiters. The exploitative system would be dismantled and we could build another system that would be based on cooperation, not on a "dog-eat-dog" epic of competition, of corrupt methods of exploiting people. It would be based on how best to organize the industries, the means of production, in order to give everybody a good life.

Our struggle to gain black studies departments on college campuses, our struggle to have black studies added to the curriculum across the nation is a struggle that the enemy sees as a grave danger. The enemy also recognizes the struggle of young white people on the college campuses and high schools as a grave danger and he is right. It is a grave danger because what we realize is that the education that is given is designed to perpetuate a system of exploitation. On the one hand it is designed to keep black people and so-called minorities ignorant, and on the other hand it is designed to keep the masses of white students in harmony with this system, to keep them supporting the system, to indoctrinate them to fight the wars that protect the system, and that extend the influence and the power of the system. We are all becoming conscious of the evil of the system, conscious of the fact that this system can no longer survive, that we have a historic opportunity for attacking the system and destroying it at its root. Thus all of the manipulations that the capitalists and the watchdogs of the capitalists go through are designed to destroy the thrust of the movement, to designate as criminals those who are in the forefront of the struggle and those who are guiding the struggle.

Historically the struggle in the educational arena, in terms of black people, has been waged from, on the one hand the slavemaster not even wanting black people to learn how to read and write, to black people wanting to learn how to read and write on the other. The struggle then transposed itself over into what black people were allowed to read and write, until today black people have reached a point where they want to control totally what they read and write.

This has been a steady struggle against the opposition of the slavemaster, it has been defeat after defeat for the slavemaster, until now we have burst into consciousness, until now we have realized the necessity of taking control of our education. When we see this long line of progression from the struggle to become literate to the struggle today to control totally the education, we can see the true nature of the opposition that we face now and faced then. All of these racists and liberals who are opposing our moves today to gain control of our education, are nothing but the descendants of the outright racist slavemasters who opposed us in our attempts to learn how to read and write on the plantations during the days of slavery. Hence all of their rhetoric, all of their arguments, all of the changes that they go through, in the last analysis, are a continuation of the desire and the necessity of the slavemaster to keep us ignorant and unable to manipulate ideas; because in order to organize a revolutionary struggle, we must be able to manipulate ideas. We must have knowledge of ourselves and of our enemy, and of the situations that we find ourselves in, in order to organize a true revolution to move against the oppressor.

One of the great dangers that our revolutionary struggle faces, perhaps the greatest danger, is that we historically have tended to compartmentalize our struggle; that is, we get hung up on one aspect of the struggle, without having an overall revolutionary perspective and without realizing that the struggle that we wage is against the total social organism. We focus all of our attention and all of our energy on the educational system, and we don't realize—or our tactics and our strategy would seem to indicate that we don't realize—that this is only one aspect of our struggle and that the same people who control the educational facilities, control the rest of the social structure. Everything, the economy, the judiciary, the political parties, the political instruments, every aspect of society is in the same hands. We need a broader strategy, a revolutionary strategy that aims at overthrowing the rule of this class as a whole, so we will not just be going through changes on the college campuses.

The repression against the movement that the United States is now mobilizing is not a sign of strength on the part of the ruling class, but rather the sign of weakness of the ruling class, and a sign of the strength and effectiveness of the movement. All of the lies, the subterfuges, the hypocrisy of the ruling class has been exposed, for if can no longer hope to control or manipulate the movement by words alone. It has to resort to the brutal, repressive forces of the police department. The movement itself has drawn several lessons from this reaction of repression by the ruling class. The clear cut nature of power in the United States and the racist policies of the ruling class are revealed.

On the one hand the rebellion of black students and black people thoroughly exposes the racist policies of the administrations of the various colleges and high schools and on the other hand there is the repression that the blacks and the allies of blacks are receiving. It's really incorrect to speak of the white section of the movement as being the allies of blacks, because in reality there is no such thing as a black movement and a white movement in the United States. These are merely categories of thought, that only have reality in terms of the lines that the ruling class itself has drawn and is enforcing among the people.

Because the United States is controlled by one ruling class, one single structure, and the whole drama of the black liberation struggle, and the revolutionary struggle in the white community is being played on one stage. Because of the division that the ruling class has historically implanted amongst the people, because of the different experiences of black people from white people, the reality of the division is more apparent than real, because at the top opposed to both black people and white revolutionaries is a single ruling class, there's not a ruling class for blacks and a ruling class for whites, but there's one single ruling class that rules all, that controls all and that manipulates all, that has a different set of tactics for each group, depending upon the tactics used by the groups, in the struggle for liberation.

One of the great weaknesses in the movement at this particular time is in the campus aspect of the attack upon the ruling class and the power of the ruling class. In the compartmentalized thinking of the traditional American society, the college community and the college campus is viewed as something separate and distinct from the rest of the community. The college is not really looked upon as a part of the community. People who are not concerned with themselves going to college or who have no children in college feel that what's going on, on the campus is none of their business. But nothing could be farther from the truth, because in reality they are the people's colleges, institutions that have been set aside to perpetuate the human heritage, and to pass on human wisdom, the knowledge and technical skills for the further development of society and civilization. And every single individual living in a given society has a stake in what goes on in them; he has a stake in seeing to it that what happens on the campus is proper, and that the best interest of all the community is being served.

On the other hand, the attacks focused on the college campuses serve to expose the nature of power in the United States. When we look at the composition of the board of regents and administrations, and councils that control the colleges, we find them replete with military men, retired generals, foundation personnel, and big businessmen. We could say that the boards that administer the universities are a good barometer, or a clear diagram of the stratification of power in the society as a whole. We don't see poor people represented on the boards of administration of the institutions of learning, for in the society beyond the college campus, poor people do not exercise or possess any power. If they did have the power, they would be in a position to see to it that some of their members were appointed to these boards.

But those who control the economy, those who control the various sources and levels of power in the community and around it, are able to have their lackeys and their flunkies appointed to administer these institutions of learning. The composition of the boards of administration of the institutions of learning indicate clearly, the powerlessness of the various sectors of society and this fact needs to be brought out much more clearly and brought home to the community. A connection needs to be made between the college campus and the community so that the repression and the tactics of the ruling class can be defeated by the total community being involved. As long as the pigs are able to vamp on the college campuses and to commit mess arrests and brutality against the students and there is not solid and massive community support, then they will be able to get away with it, and slowly but surely they will be able to grind the movement to a halt by cutting off wave after wave of leadership, by expelling the leadership, and hounding the leadership out of existence.

It's a mistake to think that the ruling class cannot be successful if a proper response is not made from the movement, a mistake that has been made time and time again in the various revolutionary struggles around the world. There have been cases of the revolutionary movement being very highly advanced, very well organized, much more organized than we are in the United States, with a higher theoretical understanding, and with very good party machinery, etc. and they have been crushed because the power structure would resort to unlimited brutality—it would kill, it would imprison. It had the mass media in its control, and it could use the mass media to justify this, and to brainwash other people who were not organized enough to do anything about their repressors.

So that it's a question of time. The movement is always behind, the movement has the initiative. The power structure, by over-reacting seeks to buy time for itself, and the pressure that the movement puts on the power structure determines the amount of time that is left. Because if the struggle progresses slowly enough to allow the ruling class to devise means of coping with the movement, then all is lost and the movement itself is doomed to failure. So that a broadening of those involved, or those concerned, and those whose support is now latent is what is required.

Poor black people and poor white people and middle class people who are not themselves directly involved in the college situation, need to be made to understand that something of their own precious liberty, which either they never had or they thought they had, is being decisively determined in the struggles that are going down on the campuses today. Every black mother, every black father, every Mexican mother, every Mexican father, every father and every mother in every group, white, Puerto Rican, Indian, Eskimo, Arab, Jew, Chinese, Japanese, whatever ethnic group they happen to be in, in the United States, need to be made to understand, that if they have no child or teenager involved in the educational process today because they were not able to afford to send them to college or something of that nature, that this in itself is a criticism of the structure of education in the United States.

It is the duty of any society to see to it that every individual in that society is invested with the human heritage and provided with the technology, the skills, and the knowledge that will enable him to cope with his environment, to survive and to live a good life. It is the duty of the society to provide this education, just as it is the duty of the society to provide the highest level of medical assistance, housing and employment, of every benefit that exists in society, it's the duty of the government to provide that. As long as the state is not providing these benefits, it is not worthy of existing, and under our kind of state which is called a representative democracy, it is not possible for a capitalistic economy to provide a universal education for the people. What it has been providing is universal brainwashing that masquerades as universal education. The quality of the education is contemptible, it is inhumane, and it is only geared to provide a level of intelligence or a level of competence that will enable the product of the educational system to become war material, to be exploited by the capitalistic economic entities within the United States.

So what we're into today is not only sitting back and criticizing, but actively reaching out and challenging the authority of those who control the various institutions in society, not simply challenging this authority, but by actively moving to disrupt the functioning of these facilities in the best interests of the community as a whole. These facilities can no longer serve the interests of the crosswork monopolies that are being administered by racists and by pigs who only want to exploit people and sentence people to be cogs in a wheel. In the final analysis, the struggle that is now going on on the college campuses cannot be settled on the college campuses. It has to be settled in the community, because those that sit on the boards of administration of the colleges do not derive their power from the fact that they are sitting on the board, but rather, they sit on the board because they have power in the community.

Their power is based on the economic institutions of society and other institutions that form the power structure, and because of their relation to these sources of power, they're able to be appointed to these positions of administration.

We have to destroy their power in the community, and we're not reformists, we're not in the movement to reform the curriculum of a given university or a given college or to have a Black Students Union recognized at a given high school. We are revolutionaries, and as revolutionaries, our goal is the transformation of the American social order.

In order to transform the American social order, we have to destroy the present structure of power in the United States, we have to overthrow the government. For too long we've been intimidated into not speaking out clearly what our task is, our task is the overthrow of the government, which has to be understood as being nothing but the instrument of the ruling class. The court, the congress, the legislature and the executive branches of the state and

Document Text

federal government are nothing but instruments in the hands of the ruling class, to see after the affairs of the ruling class, and to conduct the life of society in the interest of the ruling class. So we're out to destroy this, to smash this machinery and to erect new machinery. But new machinery cannot be erected until the present machinery is destroyed. It is not the task of revolutionaries to keep their heads up in the sky, wondering about what they will do when they have power. What they have to do at the present time is to have their minds centered on destruction. We are out to destroy the present machinery of the ruling class, that is our task.

We must do this by the only means possible, because the only means possible is the means that's necessary, and the only means possible is the violent overthrow of the machinery of the oppressive ruling class. That means that we will not allow the ruling class to use brutality and force upon us, without using the same force and brutality upon them. We must destroy their institutions from which they derive their power. A given college president may have his power as a result of being involved in a corporation. We must attack him on the campus but we must also pursue him off the campus and attack him in his lair, the lair of his power, in his corporations! Such attack could be through boycotts of the products of that corporation, or through the physical destruction of the property of the corporation, or the physical elimination of him as an individual.

We must not get into a bag or thinking that we're involved in a game: a revolution is not a game, it is a war. We are involved in a war—a people's war against those who oppress the people, and this is the war in the clearest sense of the word. It is only our resistance that is under developed and it is our resistance that is underdeveloped because the ruling class has formidable arsenals of the materials of war to unleash upon us, and they are only using timid materials at this particular time, because our resistance to their aggression has heretofore been timid.

Glossary

Karl Marx: the nineteenth-century German philosopher and historian whose works provided the intellectual foundations of Communism

See also: Eldridge Cleaver's "Education and Revolution": Document Analysis

Jesse Owens at start of record breaking 200 meter race during the Olympic games 1936 in Berlin (photographic montage). This image is available from the United States Library of Congress's Prints and Photographs division

Jesse Owens: *Blackthink: My Life as Black Man and White Man*

> *"I was no longer a proud man who had won four Olympic gold medals. I was a spectacle, a freak who made his living by competing — dishonestly — against dumb animals."*

Overview

At the 1968 Summer Olympics in Mexico City, two American sprinters, Tommie Smith and John Carlos, chose to acknowledge the American flag during their medal ceremony by raising gloved fists in a "black power" salute, as a protest against the treatment of African-Americans at home in the United States. The event was highly controversial, and Smith and Carlos were dismissed from the Games immediately afterward. Jesse Owens, the American medal winner from the 1936 Olympics in Berlin, pleaded with the two sprinters not to use the salute, and then begged for them not to be dismissed from the team, all in vain. Mostly irritated with Smith and Carlos, Owens wrote his autobiography, *Blackthink: My Life as Black Man and White Man*. In it, Owens denounced militants like Smith and Carlos, dedicating a whole chapter to their gesture. He believed that too many young blacks harbored a similar racial hatred to that which he had experienced growing up in Alabama and Ohio, and that they should recognize the opportunity to succeed and seize it. Many civil rights activists reacted angrily to the book and accused Owens of selling out to the white establishment in American society.

Context

Despite the ideals of the Baron Pierre de Coubertin, the Olympic Games have long been a source of politics and controversy. One of the most famous Olympics in terms of controversy was the 1936 Games in Berlin, which were almost boycotted by the United States due to the Nazi regime's establishment of anti-Semitic policies. Avery Brundage, the head of the US Olympic Committee, made a trip to Germany to investigate claims of Nazi racism, and returned satisfied that the German games would remain true to Olympic ideals; the US Olympic Committee voted to participate in the games as a result.

Because most nations agreed to participate in the Berlin games, because the athletes were immortalized in the Leni Riefenstahl film *Olympiad*, and because the German team won more medals than any other, the 1936 Berlin Olympics were seen as a propaganda coup for Hitler and the Nazis. Fortunately, though, the lasting memory of the games was of Jesse Owens, already a world record holder in track, who became the star of the games. Owens won four gold medals, and was feted as a hero for poking holes in Hitler's rhetoric about Germans being a master race.

Owens returned to a ticker tape parade in New York City and was celebrated all over the country. Yet he could not get a job, could not finish his college education at Ohio State University, and ended up racing horses before crowds in order to earn money. Brundage even stripped him of his amateur status after finding out about the money he earned from commercial opportunities, and he would be unable to compete in the 1940 Olympic Games (which were never held). Racism may have lost a battle in Germany at the Olympics, but it was still alive and well in the United States in the 1930s, and Owens was one of its victims.

Brundage was an advocate of amateurism and the apolitical ideal of the Olympic Games, and in 1952 he was elected president of the International Olympic Committee. The combination of Brundage's determined support of the amateur ideal in the era of the Cold War, paid communist athletes, and the turmoil of the 1960s came to a head in this period – never were the Olympics more controversial. In particular, Brundage appeared to want to ignore the apartheid policies of South Africa and Southern Rhodesia, despite numerous efforts to get the IOC to ban the two countries' athletes in punishment for their racist policies. Brundage's dismissal of such complaints fueled the notion that he himself was a racist too, though most historians of sport have since come to believe that he was actually devoted – fanatically – to the Olympics' role as a place where politics had no place.

In the year 1968, the vulnerability of US forces in Vietnam was exposed during the Tet offensive. The Prague Spring saw eastern European tanks turned on students in Czechoslovakia as they protested for free elections. Martin Luther King Jr was shot and killed in April, Robert Kennedy in June. France rose up in student riots in May. The Democratic National Convention in August was plagued by demonstrations, riots and police brutality. Throughout the year, the militant Black Panther Party kept issues of African-American identity in the news. In Mexico City itself, ten days before the Olympics started, Mexican police massacred hundreds of students occupying the National University.

In this heated political climate, Brundage invited South Africa and Southern Rhodesia to participate in the Mexico City Olympics. The invite incensed a number of different teams, including that of the United States. Dr. Harry Edwards, a sociologist at San Jose State, had organized the Olympic Project for Human Rights a year earlier, and since he counseled several of the Olympic athletes, the spirit of protest suffused the American Olympic team. Edwards' goal was to expose the fact that the harmony displayed at the Olympics did not mirror the experiences of the games' black athletes when they went home to the United States. In the mission statement of the OPHR, Edwards wrote: "We must no longer allow this country to use a few so-called Negroes to point out to the world how much progress she has made in solving her racial problems when the oppression of Afro-Americans is greater than it ever was…. [W]hy should we run in Mexico only to crawl home?" Among the Project's demands were to disinvite South Africa and Southern Rhodesia and to remove Avery Brundage as the head of the IOC. Only the first demand was met.

On the second day of the Olympics, two African-American sprinters, Tommie Smith and John Carlos, medaled in the 200-meter race. Before they went to the podium to receive their medals and salute the American flag, Smith and Carlos agreed on a protest gesture, based on Edwards' statements with the OPHR. Upon the opening of "The Star-Spangled Banner", they rose their fists in a salute to the Black Power movement at home, and with silver medalist Peter Norman, they wore badges in support of the Olympic Project for Human Rights. The audience booed, and despite the protests of the rest of the American Olympic team, Brundage had them stripped of their medals and sent home, saying "They violated one of the basic principles of the Olympic Games: that politics play no part whatsoever in them." The irony of his support for the games in Berlin was not lost on those people who remembered it.

Jesse Owens was at the Olympics, as the chairman of the US Olympics Team's Consultant's Committee, in charge of taking care of the athletes while they stayed in Mexico City. Inclined to political conservatism at a time when most African-Americans were liberal, he was angry with Smith and Carlos, and demanded that they apologize for their actions. They refused. After the Olympics, Owens worked with ghostwriter Paul Neimark to produce his first autobiography, *Blackthink: My Life as Black Man and White Man* (1970). His purpose was less to tell his story than it was to explain the racism he had to overcome as an African-American athlete, and to damn Smith and Carlos for expressing what he considered a like-minded kind of racism.

About the Author

James Cleveland Owens was born in Oakville, Alabama in 1913; his nickname, "Jesse", came from the mispronunciation of his initials, JC. His family moved to Cleveland, Ohio, where Jesse Owens became a high school track star and earned a scholarship to Ohio State University. As a sophomore, his running skills came to national attention at the Big Ten Championships held in Ann Arbor, Michigan. In one day, he set or matched four world records – in the 220-yard sprint, the 220-yard hurdles, and the long jump, and the 100-yard dash. On the other hand, he experienced the lash of racism everywhere he went around Ohio State, and having received a poor education in segregated schools, he could not meet Ohio State's rigorous academic standards, and lost his scholarship as a result.

Nevertheless, Owens earned a spot on the 1936 US Olympic team. These games were particularly controversial, awarded to Germany two years before Hitler and the Nazi Party came to power; there was much talk of a boycott. Hitler assured the Olympic committee that the German team would not discriminate against Jewish athletes, or the athletes of any other country, and the games went on. However, Nazi rhetoric spoke of the German people as superior, Aryan, warlike, and the Olympics was an obvious test of the physical manifestations of those qualities. Owens, by contrast as a black man, was an obvious manifestation of everything to which the Nazis believed themselves exceptional. In defiance of Nazi propaganda, Owens won four gold medals, tying the world record in the 100-meter sprint and breaking records in the 200-meter sprint, the long jump, and the 4-x-100-meter relay. Filmmaker Leni Riefenstahl, in Berlin to record the games for the greater glory of the Aryan race, instead focused her camera on Owens as the athlete who dominated the Olympics. Though it was not true that Hitler snubbed Owens by refusing to shake his hand and storming out of the stadium, Owens's victories were taken as a triumph over racist ideology, and Jesse Owens sailed home a hero.

Owens left the US Olympic team behind to go home and capitalize on a number of moneymaking opportunities; for his actions, Avery Brundage removed his amateur status. Worse, most of his opportunities proved to be false, he found difficulty in tracking down employment, and he did not have the money to reenroll at Ohio State. One offer he did receive was pay from the 1936 Republican candidate for president, Kansas governor Alf Landon, who shook his hand; Owens would burn with humiliation ever after when President Franklin D Roosevelt refused to meet with him. Ever after, he was a confirmed Republican.

Unable to succeed in business or finish his college degree, Owens found work supervising African-American workers at one of the Ford Motor Company plants around Detroit. During the Cold War, his fame got him speaking opportunities, and he toured extensively, speaking of his love for the US and the values of athletics as a moral teacher. He even served as a goodwill ambassador for the State Department under President Eisenhower. Yet as the civil rights movement began to gain momentum in the late 1950s and early 1960s, Owens was conspicuously absent from its events. In 1965, he was indicted for tax evasion, but his status as a speechmaker extolling the American way of life got him leniency from the court, and he merely had to pay his back taxes and a nominal fine. It seems likely that this experience confirmed in him the sense that the American political and economic establishment was largely benign and respected him – something almost no other black man could claim in the 1960s. It also explains much of his reaction to Smith, Carlos and their 1968 protest at the Olympics, the venue in which he achieved his fame.

Owens became a celebrity endorser in the 1970s, making his name as a speechmaker and representative for Sears, Johnson & Johnson, Ford, and American Express, amongst others. He won many awards, including his bachelors degree and an honorary doctorate from Ohio State. Yet to the African-American community he was largely an embarrassment, a sell-out to white society. He begged President Jimmy Carter not to boycott the 1980 Olympic Games in Moscow, but before the year was out, he had died of lung cancer at the age of 67.

Explanation and Analysis of the Document

Owens' confusing title seems to be an explanation of his thesis in the book. "Blackthink" is a euphemism for what he considers the "pro-Negro, antiwhite bigotry" of the young African-American community, people who have experienced none of the privations of the pre-civil right era but who complain about their more integrated society anyway. Owens' "life as a black man and white man" is more difficult – it seems to be a reference to the idea that his own acceptance into corporate and governmental society has erased color from his life as a factor in his treatment. Combined, Owens seems to have written a book with a title that tells the reader that he opposes the attitudes of the majority of his own people, and believes that the answer to racism is to erase color – an optimistic but hopelessly naïve ideal that likely infuriated the very audience he aimed for amongst the African-American population.

Owens begins by outlining the hardships of his young life in Oakville, Alabama, and the racism his father endured as a struggling sharecropper. Henry Owens worked for the owner of a cotton field and grocery store, John Clannon, who tried any number of different ways to take his profits and keep him working for very little money. Effectively, Henry Owens was little better than a slave, as his grandparents had been. Owens is trying to compare the life of modern-day African-Americans with that of his family when he was young – "The blackthinkers of today, often talking from their integrated high-rises, restaurants and universities, don't know what it is to really be shut out like we were then, shut out so tight you actually wondered sometimes if you really existed."

Henry Owens was illiterate. The yearly accounting by Clannon left him impoverished and angry, and he swore he would learn to read, but educational opportunities simply did not exist for African-American adults at the time. Jesse himself grew up sickly, his mother struggled to keep him alive, and she suggested that the family should move north for greater economic opportunities. The death of a close neighbor and Clannon's restructuring of the profit agreement in favor of himself finally convinced Henry Owens to move his family to Cleveland. For Jesse, the move was an opportunity to better himself – "It gave me a chance. And one chance is all you need, no matter what the blackthinkers say. …[W]hen I hear some black militant telling me and [others] that we've never made anything of ourselves and that our sons and daughters never will, I wonder if it isn't John Clannon's assistant talking again." Owens equates the anger of black militants with the denigrating racism of John Clannon, but he has excuses for Clannon – the "hurt" of anti-Irish bigotry – whereas, throughout the book, he does not seem to notice that he will not accord any such excuses for black militants.

Owens moves on to describe his own life after the 1936 Olympics. Despite the hero's welcome he received everywhere he went, none of the congratulations included a job offer. Unable to return to Ohio State, he looked for work and ended up running a Cleveland playground for just enough money to cover his small family's expenses. Before the Olympics, he and his family had asked themselves the questions "*Can I have broken out? Can a Negro, a poorer-than-poor colored kid from Alabama, have really broken out? Was it possible that, even for one black boy, the American dream was more than a cruel fairy tale?*" Instead, as his father had argued, "…'it don't do a colored man no good to get himself too high. 'Cause it's a helluva drop back to the bottom.'"

Owens set himself on the idea of going back to Ohio State, yet he could not make enough money to afford the tuition. In desperation, when two promoters came to ask him to race a horse for money – a freak show – he eventually agreed to do it, despite his initial disgust with the idea. "I sold myself into a new kind of slavery. I was no longer a proud man who had won four Olympic gold medals. I was a spectacle, a freak who made his living by competing—dishonestly—against dumb animals. I hated it, hated it worse than working at the playground. But I ran against those horses three times a week, and five cents of every dollar the people paid to watch went into my pocket. It was degrading and humiliating. But it meant that next fall I could go back to college." In the modern day, Owens argued, "not only are Negroes going to college virtually whenever they really want to, but they're going *where* they want." This was not true then, and not even true now: money still mattered too much and educational opportunities were fleeting in poor inner-city and rural schools unless one was single-mindedly devoted to one's education. Likewise, Owens blamed black militants for demanding control of schools, and turning to terrorism if their demands were not met: also a major exaggeration.

The real story of Owens' book is of the 1968 Olympics and the "Smith-Carlos incident". Owens is annoyed that the two sprinters' gesture on the medal platform will be the best-remembered moment of the Mexico City Olympics; he was, of course, right, despite his annoyance. In Owens' opinion, Smith and Carlos were a product of a voracious media presence – "I've seen whole countries pull out of the Olympics. And there have been athletes sent home for misconduct every year since the Games were formed, and that goes back to ancient Greece… the Smith-Carlos incident had as many overtones in Mexico City as two grammar school kids trying to create a tidal wave by skipping stones in the Pacific Ocean." Owens seems to believe that since the incident did not shut down the Games or last longer than a single day, it had not really had an effect worth remembering – yet somehow, he ignored the fact that it had prompted he himself to write an entire book responding to the sprinters' gesture.

Owens discusses his role at the Olympics, as what amounted to a chaperone, advisor and counselor for the athletes. He believed that most of the team did not care about politics, believing in Brundage's principle that the Olympics were apolitical. Other teams did not join in with the protest, though he admits there were some other protests scheduled. Rather, his scanning of the English and American teams seems to come up with occasional athletes determined to make their mark on the Olympics as political protestors, such as the American Hal Connolly, a former gold medal-winning hammer thrower who wanted to dip the American flag in honor of black protests. Owens claimed to have talked him out of it.

Smith planned his protest for the medal ceremony, but Owens notes that he had to win first, and finds it ironic that a white doctor from Oklahoma helped him overcome a groin injury to do so. Owens talks about how he helped the two sprinters and their wives at the Olympic village, and voices his disgust – "So Olympic committees picked up tabs and white doctors healed pulled muscles and as a result Tommy Smith and John Carlos were able to make sick headlines in every town in America." They refused to go along with Owens' efforts to assuage the situation with the IOC and Brundage, and ended up dismissed from the Olympic village. "But life went on. In the Olympic village, in fact, the Smith-Carlos dismissal caused hardly a brief murmur among the American athletes. And nothing at all among the rest."

Audience

Owens' book was comparatively rushed out, written by ghostwriter Paul Neimark from Owens' own words. Presumably, Owens was hoping to reach a wide American audience, to let them know that many African-Americans were grateful for the progress made by the civil rights movement and that the example of his own life explained why. Though the book was widely reviewed, it was not reviewed well at all – even mainstream reviewers condemned Owens' sentiments as needlessly harsh, unrealistic, simultaneously credulous toward white society and mean-spirited toward black society.

Impact

Owens was apparently surprised by the negative reaction his book received in the press. A simultaneously released, straight autobiography, *The Jesse Owens Story*, also ghosted by Neimark, went comparatively unnoticed. Two years later, the two men produced I Have Changed (1972), a rejoinder to his earlier book where Owens moderated his tone, recognizing that not everyone had won four gold medals and therefore did not have the opportunities he did to make it in America. Yet he never lost his certainty that the American dream existed for black Americans who were loyal to their country and its values and were willing to work for their own advancement. A believer in the principle of avoiding politics at the Olympics, he advocated for the United States' staying in the Moscow Olympics of 1980, but President Carter pulled out of the games due to the Soviet Union's invasion of Afghanistan. Owens died in the same year of cancer.

Avery Brundage, whom the protest was directed against and whose values were adhered to by Owens, remained the head of the IOC until his death. Brundage considered himself misunderstood, as a high idealist who was surrounded by foes who wanted to taint the Olympic Games by allowing political statements to be freely expressed. Somehow, it always seemed to be oppressive and murderous regimes like that in Nazi Germany, the USSR, and South Africa that gained his protection. In 1972, he tried once again to allow South Africa and Southern Rhodesia to compete, only to back down when threatened by a boycott from every other African nation. The Munich Games were a nightmare anyway, as eleven Israeli athletes were murdered by a Palestinian terrorist organization called Black September on September 5, 1972. Brundage insisted that the games continue, and claimed that the treatment of Rhodesia was comparatively "savage". He was in some disgrace at the point when he died in 1975.

Further Reading

◆ Books

Owens, Jesse, with Paul G. Neimark. *Blackthink: My Life as Black Man and White Man.* New York, Morrow, 1970.

Owens, Jesse, with Paul G. Neimark. *I Have Changed.* New York, Morrow, 1972.

Carlos, John and Dave Zirin. *The John Carlos Story: The Sports Moment That Changed the World.* Chicago: Haymarket Books, 2011.

◆ Websites

Davis, David. "Olympic Athletes Who Took a Stand". *Smithsonian Magazine* (August 2008) http://www.smithsonianmag.com/articles/olympic-athletes-who-took-a-stand-593920/ [accessed August 9, 2017].

TommieSmith.com http://www.tommiesmith.com/ [accessed August 9, 2017].

——David Simonelli

Essential Quotes

"Blackthink—pro-Negro, antiwhite bigotry—is what makes the new Negro and white extremists of today tick."

"I was no longer a proud man who had won four Olympic gold medals. I was a spectacle, a freak who made his living by competing—dishonestly—against dumb animals."

"Of course, that isn't nearly enough today for a lot of black students. It isn't enough for them to attend the finest universities in the world. They want to run them, appoint the teachers, tell the president what courses to have taught. And when they don't get their way, many of them bomb the campuses or burn the libraries."

BLACKTHINK: MY LIFE AS BLACK MAN AND WHITE MAN

An excerpt from Owens' Blackthink.

Chapter 2: Henry Owens' Tortures

No one called me nigger until I was seven.

That was because an Alabama sharecropper's child in the First World War years almost never saw the white man who owned his every breath.

Owned.

In theory, the Emancipation Proclamation had been a wonderful thing. But in 1915 in Alabama it was only a theory. The Negro had been set free—free to work eighteen hours a day, free to see all his labor add up to a debt at the year's end, free to be chained to the land he tilled but could never own any more than if he were still a slave. The blackthinkers of today, often talking from their integrated high-rises, restaurants and universities, don't know what it is to really be shut out like we were then, shut out so tight you actually wondered sometimes if you really existed.

You won't find Oakville, Alabama, on the map today. Eight miles from Decatur, in the northern strip of the state, it was more an invention of the white landowners than a geographical place. Whatever had the smack of civilization to it was in Decatur.

The grocery store was in Oakville, though. Just across the creek. But that wasn't as nice as it sounds, The white man owned the grocery store and he made sure it was awfully convenient. My parents tried not to end up there any more than they had to. Sometimes my father and my older brother Prentis would get up an hour earlier than their usual 4 a.m. to try and shoot a few rabbits for supper. And my mother would find time somehow to tend a little vegetable garden in the back.

But those few rabbits and vegetables didn't go very far with nine mouths to feed. So you always ended up at the owner's store for food, just as you had to go there for tools. My father never paid any money at the grocery. The owner's man just entered our debt on a sheet of paper with £1 at the top—we were the first of eight families who worked his spread of two hundred and fifty acres—and in December of every year, the white man totaled up what you owed against the worth of your crop to find out how much you were ahead.

Only you never came out ahead. It always happened that those "cheap" tools and supplies you bought cost more than the nearly quarter of a million square feet they helped you to plant, just as the weekly potatoes and beans and corn bread (you only bought meat two times a year, on the holidays) always came to more than the six thousand pounds of cotton you enabled the owner to send North,

Each year that it happened, my father went into an angry fit and swore that he was going to learn to read to make sure they were only writing down on that list what he was actually buying. And Mother vowed that she'd learn numbers to check that they weren't charging us too much for it. But there was no one in Oakville to teach those things to them and no time to learn anyway. Besides, my father wouldn't go near a book—he was superstitious about them. That was another holdover from slave days. So one December became the next, and with each one we became a little deeper in debt even though we usually put out more cotton every year than the one before, unless the weevils or some fungus disease had come along.

Our debt was small, though, compared to the other sharecroppers'. We were the "luckiest" family for miles around. My father had been blessed with four sons who had lived. I was the only one who couldn't help, not because I was too young but because I was too sick. Every winter for as long as I could remember, I'd come down with pneumonia. A couple of those years, I was close to never seeing spring.

Yet somehow my mother always pulled me through. Afterward, she'd take my father aside and plead with him to think about leaving the South and sharecropping. He sensed that she was right—every Negro we knew was on a never-ending treadmill of poverty and ignorance—but his fear of the unknown was even greater.

A few Negroes had left and gone North. But Henry Owens was over forty years old, an age not made by half a dozen Negro sharecroppers in Morgan County. It was late to pull up roots. And like most other sharecroppers, he was the son of the son of a slave. His own grandfather had told him the stories of being *legally* shot out, stories of death that came in the night, sometimes at the hands of the white man and

Document Text

sometimes through simple starvation. So, deep down in that invisible place where a man decides what to do, my father felt that we could have it even worse than we did in Oakville. He wasn't going to dare take a chance on that. The whole world would have to jerk out of orbit for him to pack us up and leave.

And that's just what happened. The whole world, Henry Owens' world, went completely out of orbit.

The first jolt was when I got sick again. This time was different. This time blood came up every time I coughed, and for about a week I didn't know where I was. My mother worked her homemade magic once more, but we all knew it would be the last time. My lungs were too weak.

Our neighbor a mile down was dead. That was the second jolt. My father began sharecropping about the same time Joe had. Joe was a few years younger, and my father had always kind of treated him like a little brother, telling what he knew about better ways to work the land, even lending out one of my brothers to him when things were pretty good, though that wasn't often.

Joe had to work his land alone because his wife kept having stillborn babies. Each time she'd get pregnant they didn't pray for a son but just for something alive. A child would have made life bearable. Yet the years passed and all Joe and Betsy shared were new grave markers in back of their house each twelve months or so.

Then Joe got a "sign." Something told him that Betsy would become pregnant again soon and that this time the baby would not only live but would be a son. When her belly began to swell, Joe's skeleton of a body stopped feeling tired. He worked as never before and whistled every day until the baby came, It came, dead as always. Only this time it took Betsy with it.

So Joe Steppart killed himself.

My father changed after that. Not enough to leave, but enough to begin to think out loud about what that white man and his system were doing to all of us. The white man's name was John Clannon, by the way, and his home was on the top of the one large hill on the other side of the creek. It was too far, of course, for him to see down into our little house. But at night when all the lights were shining on the hill, I imagined I saw him at his big living room window, a window larger than our whole house, watching us.

John Clannon owned two hundred and fifty acres of land with eight men sharecropping it for him. We had the largest spread, fifty acres, because we had the most sons. All the eight houses of the Negroes were on the one side of the creek. John Clannon had never crossed over to that side since he bought the land and carved it up. None of the Negroes ever went on his side, either, unless they were sent for by one of his men.

On a cool night in February of 1921, he sent for my father. We all waited, busying ourselves but not really able to get anything done. "I wonder what the owner can want with Papa," someone would mutter every now and then. What we really meant was, "What was the owner going to do to Papa?" And to us.

For even though we didn't realize it then, we lived with constant fear. That is the crucial difference between 1920 and, say, 1960. Negroes of a decade or two ago began in poverty and degradation, but the massive machinery of our society was moving to sweep it away. In 1920 there was no machinery. The man on the hill was everything. He was worse in one way than the "benevolent" white despots on slave plantations, because the Negro then wasn't plagued every day by the agonizing choice of what to do with his freedom, whether or not to leave.

In theory, of course, my folks had a fifty-fifty deal with John Clannon, but fifty percent of nothing amounts to nothing. So we lived in fear of him and of his power, and the fear was justified. That February night proved it. My father trudged back into the house almost an hour later and took aside my mother and my older brothers Prentis and Quincy. In our little cardboard house, though, as soon as his voice got agitated it wasn't hard to overhear what he was telling them.

We'd had a particularly good crop that year. Even with exorbitant grocery bills every week, it had still gotten us out of debt. That threatened John Clannon's hold over us, I guess, and he wanted to do something about it right away. What he proposed to do was to revise his deal with my father. Sixty-forty instead of fifty-fifty. Retroactive.

My father had stood still for everything else, but he couldn't stand still for that. The years of resentment had risen up in him and finally become words. He was an uneducated man, but he was a fair man, and he said that this wasn't fair. He didn't get to say it to Clannon himself, though. An "assistant" talked to "the niggers."

"Fair?" the assistant had replied. "What does fair have to do with you?" My father was an example, he said. If he could "get the best" of Clannon, the others might think they could too.

"And what about my family?" my father bad shot back, finally beginning to lose forty-two years of control. "We work hard. I want my sons to amount to more than I have!"

"Your sons will never amount to anything—just be grateful if they *survive!*" the man had shouted back.

That last statement had stuck in my father's craw. He struggled to spit it out for the next two days, but it only lodged deeper. That Sunday after church he told us that we were leaving Oakville for Cleveland.

We still owed John Clannon some money, but we had our tools and our house and our animals. That would more than pay what we owed and keep us eating in Cleveland long enough, my father figured, for him to find steady work.

My father never found steady work in Cleveland, and we'd had barely enough money to get us North. Clannon offered us next to nothing for everything we owned, including the five mules from Canada my father had scraped and saved for one by one by one. It wasn't just greed that made Clannon do it. He didn't want to let us go. A healthy Negro with three sons who knew the ropes was hard to find.

But we got the hell out. As I said, for my father Cleveland wasn't much different from Oakville. Yet for me it was like another planet. It gave me a chance. And one chance is all you need, no matter what the blackthinkers say.

As I think back, though, I can see part of it was that the white man's words had stuck in my craw, too. *Your sons will never amount to anything.* I wanted to amount to something. I had to. So did a lot of other Negroes whose names you'll never hear, but who *have* amounted to something. That's why when I hear some black militant telling me and them that we've never made anything of ourselves and that our sons and daughters never will, I wonder if it isn't John Clannon's assistant talking again.

It's no accident that the Rap Browns and Stokely Carmichaels sometimes sound like the Clannons.

Because *blackthink*—pro-Negro, antiwhite bigotry—is what makes the new Negro and white extremists of today tick, and it's not much different from John Clannon's *whitethink*. Irrationality and violence, above all, are at blackthink's gut. It might sound shocking at first, what with all the brainwashing that goes on, but if you think about it you'll see that America's blackthinking extremists may be the new George Wallaces.

Bigotry always begins with a hurt. For the John Clannons it might have been when they got off the boat from Ireland and found signs that said no irish allowed or ran into employer after employer who thought that Irish was another word for *drunk*. Some of those John Clannons couldn't take it. And their way of copping out wasn't going on a binge or sailing back to Ireland. What they did was to work their knuckles to the bone, with bitterness their twenty-four-hour-a-day boss, and when they got power and money they took it out on my father and seven other men and their families. The grandsons of some of those families became the Raps and Harrys of today....

Chapter 3: But Equality Is Here

I came back from Berlin and the 1936 Olympics to a welcome few people have ever experienced. The streets of New York were lined with tens of thousands of men and women and children wanting to see me— to touch me—as I moved through on the top of a new convertible. It was something else. But it didn't completely fool an Oakville sharecropper's son. Every newspaper had a picture of my face on its front page, and people I'd never met from society and business were buttonholing me to come to their plush suites for drinks and dinners and yachting trips; but one omission stood out more and more as the months passed.

No one had offered me a job.

My mother was taking care of our first daughter back in Cleveland, and now it seemed as though another were on the way. So soon Ruth wouldn't be able to work anymore. It was going to be impossible for me to support a family of four and still get my degree. My brother Sylvester volunteered to help put me through, but I couldn't let him. He was the one who should've gone to college in the first place. He was always the bright one. But like all the others in our family except for me, he didn't even have a chance to finish high school. I couldn't keep taking from them all my life, so I didn't go back to Ohio State University as a senior that fall of 1936. I went to work.

It wasn't as a star halfback for a professional football team, though I think I might have made a good one. Nor was it as a center fielder for a major league baseball team. Negroes hadn't broken into any of that yet. But you *could* say that I went into the general field of athletics and that I capitalized on the ten years of torturous training I'd put my body through.

I became a Cleveland playground instructor for $30 a week.

Fifteen hundred and sixty dollars a year was enough to support a small family, but it wasn't enough to put me back in college. Negroes hadn't offered me anything better because they didn't have anything better to offer, and the white men who wanted me to travel at their expense to their homes all over the country and drink with their sons and chat with their daughters didn't seem to have any openings in their firms except for delivery boys or bathroom attendants.

"What does it pay?" I finally asked one of them.

"Oh, Jesse," he said, putting his plump, pale fingers on my shoulder, "*you* wouldn't want to do something like that after what *you've* had."

So I didn't do something like that. I worked at the playground and came home every night and thought of what I'd had and went off in a corner of our two-room apartment where I hoped Ruth couldn't hear me and put some week-old newspapers in front of my face to try to hide my sadness.

Ruth never said a word. But she knew. It was almost the same for her as it was for me. We'd been childhood sweethearts and had come the long road together. She'd watched me exercise before school every morning until I was slowly molded from a sick, skinny kid into a real athlete and finally into a champion, had walked with me after school to the different jobs I worked. When we did marry at sixteen we'd been able to save only six dollars, and the license, hotel and wedding dinner (a hot dog with all the relish the man would allow) took a lot of that.

But then the good times started to come, the running and jumping records, the headlines, the reporters, the Olympics. My family and I never said it to each other in those words, Ruth and I never even talked about it, but we were all thinking: *Can I have broken out? Can a Negro, a poorer-than-poor colored kid from Alabama, have really broken out? Was it possible that, even for one black boy, the American dream was more than a cruel fairy tale?*

My father never would believe it. He didn't want to spoil the fairy tale for me, but a couple of times he did take me aside. "J.C.," he confided (James Cleveland was my real name and he never got used to the new name given me by people up North), "it don't do a colored man no good to get himself too high. 'Cause it's a helluva drop back to the bottom."

And it was.

As the days passed after the Olympics and the best I could do was make $130 a month watching kids on the swings, Ruth and I began to feel as though we were being sucked back into that dark, endless tunnel where every Negro has to end up.

I couldn't let it happen. I *had* known too much, not only in the Olympics, but in my dreams. Yet what could I do about it? I had jumped farther and run faster than any man ever had before, and it left me with next to nothing.

College was the only answer. If I could just get back to Ohio State and finish my senior year, something would come of it. I didn't know how, but I felt that getting a B.A. would somehow make all the difference. Yet I couldn't return to college while supporting a family of four on my salary, I had begun to hate my job at the playground as I'd hated John Clannon. But like my father, I was afraid to leave.

Then two white promoters came to my apartment one night. They had an idea, Negro baseball, and they needed a "name" to publicize it. Naturally there were no well-known colored baseball players because none had been allowed in the major leagues, so they had to go outside of baseball. I was a natural choice.

The idea really grabbed me at first. I thought they wanted me to play or at least be manager of one of two teams they planned to have touring the country playing against each other. But that wasn't quite what they had in mind. I wasn't to be connected to the baseball end of it at all. Though, once again, you could say that my athletic prowess would be used.

They wanted me to run a hundred yards against a thoroughbred racehorse before the game each night.

When they said it, I wanted to throw up. They tried to tell me it would be a challenge. I'd beaten every man on earth, now I'd prove I could beat every animal. And I *would* beat the horse, they confided. Because the race would begin with a starter's gun held right near the animal's ear. Before the watching crowd knew it, I would be off to a big lead while the frightened horse was trying to get his bearings. He would cut that lead once he got started but, with my speed and only a hundred yards to run, I'd win by a few inches.

"Nothing doing," I told them in a temper.

"You think about it," one of them said shrewdly. "We'll be back on Sunday."

Document Text

For five days I swore under my breath at those two white men. For five days I kept telling myself how I hated their idea. But when they returned on Sunday, all the pain of the playground and everything it represented suddenly seemed to well up in me, Before either one of them could get a word out I heard myself say, "I've decided to do it."

So I sold myself into a new kind of slavery. I was no longer a proud man who had won four Olympic gold medals. I was a spectacle, a freak who made his living by competing—dishonestly—against dumb animals. I hated it, hated it worse than working at the playground. But I ran against those horses three times a week, and five cents of every dollar the people paid to watch went into my pocket. It was degrading and humiliating. But it meant that next fall I could go back to college.

Today it's a little different. Like most whites, Negroes who want to go to college do go. And often without having to hold jobs while there or even without a pair of middle-class parents to send them. If "ghetto" high schools haven't properly prepared them, there are hundreds of university-connected programs across the country where they can spend a year boning up before they enter. In fact, not only are Negroes going to college virtually whenever they really want to, but they're going *where* they want.

Of course, that isn't nearly enough today for a lot of black students. It isn't enough for them to attend the finest universities in the world. They want to run them, appoint the teachers, tell the president what courses to have taught, And when they don't get their way, many of them bomb the campuses or burn the libraries....

Chapter 4: Negroes Have Human Hangups

The sad fact is that a hypersensitive and naive public, an often out-of-touch "moderate" leadership and a sometimes headline-hungry press have played perfectly into the hands of the blackthinkers. The last Olympics were an example. What will be remembered by the American public? Bob Beamon's incredible twenty-nine-foot leap in the broad jump? Randy Matson's breaking the Olympic record in his first shotput try? Al Oerter's fourth straight gold medal in the discus (when he worked in an aircraft factory and could practice only forty-five minutes a day)? Billy Toomey's decathlon record? Wyomia Tyus's great hundred-meter triumph? No, the 1968 Olympics will always be remembered here for the Smith-Carlos incident, where two black runners from the U.S. gave a black-power salute on the victory platform and were sent home by the Olympic Committee.

Big deal.

I've seen whole countries pull out of the Olympics. And there have been athletes sent home for misconduct every year since the Games were formed, and that goes back to ancient Greece. Whenever you get thousands of young men together, you're bound to have a few that will become too rowdy. But this wasn't merely a case of rowdyism. This supposedly had tremendous overtones for all the American athletes and for the race problem itself.

Believe me, the Smith-Carlos incident had as many overtones in Mexico City as two grammar school kids trying to create a tidal wave by skipping stones in the Pacific Ocean. I know what *Life* magazine said. I know what virtually every newspaper in the United States said. And I also know the truth—because I was there, not only living with these athletes, but chairman of the Consultant's Committee that dealt with both their personal and political problems.

And I want you to know that the whole incident was another " black herring." It wasn't part of any big effort to make the case for black power at the Games. If you'll remember, the whole "black boycott" that Harry Edwards tried to pull off for that Olympiad fell flatter on its face than a one-legged hurdler, as Dave Albritton used to say.

Sure the newspapers in America kept guessing about it beforehand. But those of us who really were in the know didn't. Because we knew the competitors. We knew there were a couple of wild ones but that almost overwhelmingly the American athletes were most interested in doing what was *really* their thing at Mexico. Like Jimmy Hines, the record-breaking sprint man and new "world's fastest human." He wanted to win at Mexico City and break a record to boot, so that he could get himself a good professional football contract. Or Bob Beamon and Ralph Boston, the champion black broad jumpers. They're sympathetic to the Negro cause, as I am and as I hope everyone is, but they wouldn't have dreamed of copying the Smith-Carlos stuff. The same goes for virtually all the rest, Negro and white. The proof is that there weren't any other incidents.

And there weren't any among the athletes of the other thirty-eight nations there. Think of all those seven thousand plus performers from every nook and cranny of the world, then realize that not one went along with Smith and Carlos, and you'll see what a tempest in a teapot—a broken teapot—the whole thing was. The African athletes in particular showed no sympathy for what John and Tommy did. Kenya's Kip Keino, for example, didn't have time for black-power meetings. He already had the power. He proved it by beating our Jim Ryun in the 1,500 meters in less than three minutes and thirty-five seconds, an amazing speed for that staggering Mexico City altitude, which sent behemoths like Australia's record holder Ron Clarke to the hospital.

The same went for Keino's teammate, Nate Temu, who won the 10,000 meters, and for Mamo Wolde, the Ethiopian who was right behind him. No meetings for them. No warm hellos to Smith and Carlos, either. No hellos at all, as far as I could see. The Africans weren't even friendly with our black athletes. They usually stayed with their own countrymen, but when they didn't they were perfectly at ease with the athletes from other countries, eating or sleeping, talking or laughing, black or white.

There were a few British instigators. England didn't do too well in the Games and wasn't in many of the finals. I don't like the idea of "team" totals in the Olympics, but it is interesting to note that England was in thirteenth place overall beneath countries like Rumania. And of course there *was* one American white militant, Hal Connolly. He had lost out in his own event, and was with Carlos constantly. Hal believed that there should be a demonstration at the Games to dramatize what seemed to him the Negro's plight in America. At one meeting, for instance, he brought up the idea of dipping our flag as a symbol of black protest.

I asked him if he knew about the tradition of never letting the flag dip.

He looked confused. Sometimes it's easy to forget that these are nineteen-, twenty-, twenty-five-year-old kids, most of whom weren't even born until World War II was over. But Hal is nearly forty.

I told him about the tradition. I didn't like the Vietnam War, either, I said, but explained that fighting the Nazis and the Japanese was something else. That flag he was talking about was planted on Iwo Jima by men like his father. Iwo Jima represented a principle—the same principle Hal wanted to uphold by dipping the flag.

They didn't dip the flag.

Carlos and Smith *did* give the black-power salute, of course. But even their thoughts at the Olympics weren't consumed by the race situation. First, they had to worry about winning. If they didn't get up there on the medalists' pedestal, they weren't going to be giving any salutes at all. And Tommy Smith's feat in winning the two hundred meters took monolithic concentration on that event and nothing else. It was even more amazing because that afternoon he pulled a muscle in his groin, one of the more painful injuries a sprinter can have. In the beginning, it didn't seem as though he'd be running the finals at all a few hours later. But a white physician from Oklahoma named Cooper worked on him, and Tommy ran. And broke not only the Olympic record but the world mark.

Tommy is a high-class boy, and I think that much of what he did at the Games was influenced by John Carlos and by Tommy's wife, who is really extreme on the subject of black power. And speaking of wives, there wouldn't have been any demonstration at all if the Consultant's Committee hadn't found places for the wives to live. Carlos had brought his wife Kim, and she was living unauthorized in a segment of the athletes' quarters. The Olympic Committee was about to remove her, and I think if she had been sent home, her husband would have gone with her. Without John, I wonder if Tommy Smith would have given any Nazi salutes. But I met with them and then with the Olympic Committee, and the next day Mrs. Carlos had a place of her own to stay in, with the Committee paying for it.

So Olympic committees picked up tabs and white doctors healed pulled muscles and as a result Tommy Smith and John Carlos were able to make sick headlines in every town in America. Actually, they double-crossed some of their own black teammates who wanted a more organized, meaningful demonstration, by doing what they did. After it happened, I met with them to try and stop their expulsion from the Games. I knew what the Olympic Committee was going to do, and I realized that unless we could come up with a pretty good argument, Tommy and John would be sent packing.

I had hopes they'd be reasonable, Tommy in particular. But they arrived at the meeting with Hal, who was fanning the fire. Negro militants always become more militant before white audiences. Carlos lost his cool right away, I kept asking him to tell it to me like it really was so that I could make the Olympic Committee understand. "It don't make no difference

Document Text

what I say or do," Carlos would keep repeating. "I'm lower than dirt, man. I'm black." And every time he said something like that, Hal Connolly just about cheered.

Finally, I got fed up. "You know, Carlos," I yelled, "you talk about Whitey this and Whitey that. Everything's 'get Whitey out of my hair!' But when it comes to the most private kind of meeting of all, here you are with good old Whitey! He goes everywhere you go. Man, *I* can get along without him. How come *you* can't?"

The meeting was over. I went to the Olympic Committee and did what I could. It wasn't enough.

But life went on. In the Olympic village, in fact, the Smith-Carlos dismissal caused hardly a brief murmur among the American athletes. And nothing at all among the rest.

Glossary

"black herring": a play on the phrase "red herring," meaning a diversion or distraction (as a fish dragged across its path would distract a dog)

Emancipation Proclamation: two executive orders issued by President Abraham Lincoln; the order in September 1862 declared that any slave in a Confederate state would be free if the state did not return to Union control by the first day of 1863; the second, issued on January 1, 1863, specified the ten states in which the first order would apply.

George Wallaces: a reference to George Wallace, the segregationist governor of Alabama

Harrys: probably a reference to Harry Edwards, who launched a movement urging black athletes to boycott the 1968 Olympic Games

Iwo Jima: a Pacific island that was the site of a major battle against the Japanese in World War II in 1945, famous for an iconic photograph of five Marines and one Navy corpsman raising the U.S. flag on Mount Suribachi

Rap Browns: a reference to civil rights activist H. Rap Brown, chairman of the Student Nonviolent Coordinating Committee and later the "justice minister" of the Black Panther Party

sharecropper: a farmer who works another person's land in return for a share of the land's production

Smith-Carlos incident: a reference to Tommie Smith and John Carlos, two black U.S. Olympic athletes who caused controversy by raising their fists in a Black Power salute on the medal stand

Stokely Carmichaels: a reference to Stokely Carmichael, a leader of the Student Nonviolent Coordinating Committee and the Black Panther Party and popularizer of the phrase "Black Power"

Bust photographic portrait of Muhammad Ali in 1967. World Journal Tribune photo by Ira Rosenberg.
By Ira Rosenberg - This image is available from the United States Library of Congress's Prints and Photographs division

CLAY V. UNITED STATES

1971

"The Department of Justice was wrong in advising the Board in terms of a purported rule of law that it should disregard this finding simply because of the circumstances and timing of the petitioner's claim."

Overview

The U.S. Supreme Court's June 1971 decision in *Cassius Marsellus Clay, Jr. also known as Muhammad Ali v. United States*, commonly known as *Clay v. United States*, unanimously overturned professional boxing champion Muhammad Ali's 1967 conviction for refusing induction into the armed services. Specifically, the Court concluded that the Kentucky Selective Service Appeal Board had received erroneous advice from the Department of Justice in rejecting Ali's application for conscientious objector status. Having converted to Islam in 1964, Ali—born Cassius Clay, Jr.—claimed that serving as a member of the U.S. Army in Vietnam violated his religious principles. In a now-famous quote on his reasons for refusing military service, Ali stated: "I ain't got no quarrel with them Vietcong."

Americans were baffled by Ali: Always flamboyant, undeniably brash, and some might say downright smug, he referred to himself as both "the prettiest" and "the Greatest," belittled his boxing opponents with disparaging rhymes, and was alternately viewed as a scoundrel and a hero by a nation embroiled in social and political turmoil. Ali's rejection of the draft sparked considerable controversy, prompting some observers to label him a draft dodger. However, his case gradually took on more significance culturally than it did legally, as it foreshadowed a growing antiwar movement in the United States. As the heavyweight champion of the world, Ali risked all claims to his title and his future in professional sports by not complying with the military's induction orders. During the ordeal, he was banned from fighting and lost an estimated $4 million in potential earnings. He also gambled with his popularity: The Vietnam War era was a tension-filled time in the United States, and the Nation of Islam was viewed by many as a divisive force that was motivated more by political than religious principles.

Following a three-and-a-half-year suspension from boxing, Ali's conviction of "willful refusal to submit to induction" was reversed by the 1971 Supreme Court decision in *Clay v. United States*. Even before that final decision was made, however, various boxing commissions were mulling over the possibility of allowing Ali to fight again. Because the state of Georgia had no boxing commission, Ali was able to resume his boxing career in the fall of 1970 in a match held in Atlanta. He beat his opponent, Jerry Quarry, in just three rounds, setting the stage for a dramatic comeback.

The invalidation of Ali's conviction cleared away any remaining obstacles to his relicensing by state boxing commissions and to his reclaiming the titles that had been stripped from him nearly four years earlier. But because the Court failed to address the controversial merits of Ali's claim to "selective" conscientious objector status, the decision holds little value as legal precedent.

Context

The Supreme Court decided Ali's conscientious objector case against the backdrop of a country increasingly divided over the civil war in Vietnam and the use of the draft to select the American soldiers needed to continue the conflict. By 1970, the year before the Court's decision in *Clay v. United States*, the debate had become almost ubiquitous within American public institutions—except the Supreme Court. Indeed, the Court repeatedly resisted attempts by legislators, draftees, and even states to have it pronounce on the underlying legality of the war in Vietnam, resting on strained notions of judicial restraint to avoid taking sides. However, there was one class of Vietnam-related cases the Court did try routinely: those based on claims to exemptions and deferments from conscription, particularly claims of conscientious objector status. Under section 6(j) of the Military Selective Service Act, individuals could not be subjected to "combatant training and service in the armed forces" if, "by reason of religious training and belief," they were "conscientiously opposed to participation in war in any form."

One of the questions that invariably arose in such cases was whether conscientious objection to a *particular* war, rather than objection to war *as such*, qualified the objector for such an exemption. Thus the question became, Does the statute support the idea of "selective" conscientious objection? Three months before it decided Ali's case, the Supreme Court answered that question in the negative in *Gillette v. United States*, with Justice Thurgood Marshall—best known for arguing the landmark school desegregation case of *Brown v. Board of Education of Topeka*—writing for an eight-to-one majority. As Marshall explained, "However the statutory clause be parsed, it remains that conscientious objection must run to war in any form." For Ali, one of the more visible members of the Nation of Islam, the war in Vietnam was an unjust one fought by nonbelievers. Indeed, contemporary news stories and even some judicial opinions often repeat an inflammatory quote that may well have been misattributed to Ali—that "no Vietnamese ever called me a nigger." Ali's case therefore raised a question the Court had yet to answer: whether a religiously grounded but nonpacifistic belief was a legally protected basis for objecting to military service.

A separate but equally important element in Ali's case was the issue of race. Well into the mid-1960s, African Americans were heavily underrepresented on local draft boards, leading to claims that the boards routinely acted in a manner that was racially discriminatory. In 1967 only 0.2 percent of 641 local board members in Kentucky were black, even though African Americans constituted 7.1 percent of the state's total population. In Texas, only 1.1 percent of the local board members were black, as compared with 12.4 percent of the total population. Many of these concerns were bolstered by the 1967 report of the National Advisory Commission on Selective Service, which recommended a number of reforms that were not adopted—at least not initially. Instead, inductees turned to the courts and to arguments that such underrepresentation on the local draft boards violated constitutional principles of equal protection.

Ali's case therefore became a lightning rod for some of the most heated religious, racial, social, and political conflicts of the day. In such an atmosphere, it is perhaps unsurprising that the Supreme Court ultimately rested its decision on what may fairly be described as a legal technicality, avoiding the harder and more divisive questions that the case raised.

To fully understand Ali's case, it is worth reviewing the U.S. method of filling its military ranks in the 1960s. Between 1948 and 1973, the United States utilized a conscription system rather than an all-volunteer military. Whether America was engaged in a war or not, young men were required to register for the Selective Service, the agency charged with implementing a military draft. Vacancies in the armed forces were filled from this pool of eligible men when the number of volunteer soldiers in the U.S. military fell short. In 1960, when Ali (then still going by his birth name, Cassius Clay) registered for the Selective Service, men between the ages of eighteen and a half and twenty-five were eligible for the draft.

Early in 1966, after Local Board 47 in Louisville, Kentucky, had classified Clay I-A, meaning that he was fully qualified for induction into the military, he filed a Special Form for Conscientious Objector, seeking a religious exemption from combatant training and service in the armed forces. He based his claim for exclusion from military service on his adherence to the tenets of the Nation of Islam. Ali's application for conscientious objector status, or, alternatively, classification as a Muslim minister, was rejected both by Local Board 47 and by the Kentucky Appeal Board, which then referred the matter to the U.S. Department of Justice. Following an extensive investigation by the Federal Bureau of Investigation, a Justice Department hearing officer concluded on August 23, 1966, that Ali was sincere in his beliefs and recommended that Ali's request for conscientious objector status be granted. Despite that conclusion, in a letter dated three months later, the Justice Department's Office of Legal Counsel formally recommended to the Kentucky Appeal Board that Ali's request be denied. Specifically, the letter asserted that Ali failed to meet the three basic tests that the Supreme Court had established for conscientious objector status: that he objected to all forms of war, that his objection was grounded in religious training and belief rather than in politics, and that his objection was sincere. Pivotal to the future of the case was the fact that the Justice Department failed to specify which of the three tests Ali had failed to meet.

Following the Justice Department's recommendation, the Kentucky Appeal Board formally denied Ali's request for conscientious objector status. Although Ali proceeded to file a series of lawsuits seeking to block his induction, all of them were dismissed. Ali reported for induction into the U.S. military on April 28, 1967, in Houston, Texas (since he resided in Texas at the time), as ordered, but he declined to step forward when his name was called. Ten days later, he was indicted by a federal grand jury in Houston for knowingly and willfully refusing induction into the armed services—a criminal offense punishable by up to five years in prison and a $10,000 fine. After a two-day trial in June 1967, he was convicted by a jury and given that maximum sentence. The jury, composed of six white men and six white women, reportedly deliberated for just twenty-one minutes.

Ali appealed his conviction to the U.S. Court of Appeals for the Fifth Circuit on several different points. In addition to claiming that his request for both conscientious objector status and ministerial exemption had been wrongly denied, he argued that the composition of the Selective Service draft boards was racially disproportionate (with blacks heavily underrepresented), and so the boards were themselves unconstitutional. But in a unanimous ruling handed down on May 8, 1968, a three-judge panel of the Fifth Circuit rejected each of Ali's claims. The Court of Appeals sidestepped Ali's challenge to the racial composition of the local Selective Service boards, noting first that, even if the claim were factually accurate, that would not automatically void the decisions in the case and also emphasizing the *de novo*, or in-depth, review by the racially diverse National Appeal Board, which, in the court's view, necessarily removed any hint of racial prejudice from Ali's case. As to Ali's claims that he was entitled either to a ministerial exemption or to conscientious objector status, the Fifth Circuit further noted that the denial of those claims had some "basis in fact"; the court concluded that the National Appeal Board had properly resolved Ali's case and that his conviction was therefore valid.

Ali's last hope for a reversal of his conviction was a hearing by the U.S. Supreme Court. His case, *Clay v. United States*, was argued before the Court—with Justice Thurgood Marshall not participating—on April 19, 1971, and the Court handed down its unanimous decision ten weeks later.

About the Author

The Supreme Court's opinion in Ali's case was per curiam, or "for the Court," meaning that the identity of its actual author was not made public. All of the members of the Court other than Justice Thurgood Marshall (who excluded himself for unstated reasons) participated in the decision in Ali's case, including Chief Justice Warren Burger and associate justices Hugo Black, William O. Douglas, John Marshall Harlan II, William J. Brennan, Jr., Potter Stewart, Byron White, and Harry A. Blackmun—the latter being the most recent addition to the Court in June 1970. Ali's was among the last of the cases heard by Justices Black and Harlan prior to their retirement from the Supreme Court later in 1971.

Indeed, the Supreme Court that decided Ali's case was a Court in transition. President Richard Nixon had appointed Warren Burger to replace Earl Warren as chief justice in 1969, thereby signaling the end to one of the most progressive—if not radical—eras in the Court's history. During Warren's sixteen years in the Court's center seat, the justices moved self-consciously and decidedly to the left, rigorously endorsing sweeping federal regulatory power in the civil rights sphere while adopting similarly robust views of the limits that the federal Constitution placed on state and local governments, especially where racial discrimination or the rights of criminal defendants were at issue. This was the Court that had decided *Brown v. Board of Education* (1954), holding that race-based segregation in public schools violated the equal protection clause; *Mapp v. Ohio* (1961), holding that evidence obtained in violation of the Fourth Amendment must generally be excluded from admission at trial; *Gideon v. Wainwright* (1963), holding that the Sixth Amendment right to counsel requires that states provide attorneys to indigent defendants; *Griswold v. Connecticut* (1965), holding that the U.S. Constitution protects a right to privacy; *Miranda v. Arizona* (1966), requiring that defendants be notified of their right to speak to a lawyer and holding that statements obtained in the absence of such notification were inadmissible in court; and a host of other lesser-known but no-less-important precedents. Together with Justices Black, Douglas, and Brennan, Warren formed a liberal bloc that controlled much of the Court's agenda throughout the 1960s—especially from 1962 through Warren's departure, thanks to the additions of Arthur Goldberg, as succeeded by Abe Fortas in 1965, and Thurgood Marshall. Even the more "conservative" justices on the Warren Court—Harlan, Stewart, and White—were, by modern-day standards, moderates who routinely joined their more liberal brethren.

Nixon's victory in the 1968 presidential election—after a campaign that was highly critical of the Court and vowed to restore "law and order"—spelled the beginning of the end for this coalition. Within three years of taking office, Nixon was able to make four appointments to the Court—replacing Warren with Burger, Fortas with Harry Blackmun, Black with Lewis F. Powell, Jr., and Harlan with William H. Rehnquist. Each of these appointments moved the Court further to the right. In that sense, the decision in *Clay* proved to be a relic of a soon-to-be forgotten era, in which unanimous decisions invalidating criminal convictions such as Ali's were commonplace.

Explanation and Analysis of the Document

The Supreme Court's decision in *Clay v. United States* is surprisingly brief. In Part I of the majority opinion, which runs a little over one page, the Court provides a condensed overview of the facts of the case. Then, in two short paragraphs, Part II rehashes the "basis in fact" standard, which the government urged was sufficient to affirm the decision. The "basis in fact" standard was articulated by the Court in *Estep v. United States* (1946). Under this standard,

> courts are not to weigh the evidence to determine whether the classification made by the local boards was justified. The decisions of the local boards made in conformity with the regulations are final even though they may be erroneous. The question of jurisdiction of the local board is reached only if there is no basis in fact for the classification which it gave the registrant.

Congress codified this rule through the Military Selective Service Act of 1967. The government's central argument before the Supreme Court in *Clay* was that the Fifth Circuit properly applied this standard in affirming Ali's conviction and that it should therefore be affirmed. The Court, however, concludes Part II with a key statement regarding the question of whether Ali opposed all wars or just certain wars: "Even if the Government's position on this question is correct, the conviction before us must still be set aside for another quite independent reason."

Part III of the opinion—its analytical core—identifies that "independent reason" as the incorrect advice that the Justice Department had provided to the Kentucky Appeal Board. Apparently, the Justice Department had questioned Ali's convictions on the basis "of the circumstances and timing" of his claim, noting that he did not file for conscientious objector status until the possibility of his being drafted became a certainty. The Supreme Court states that its review revealed no reason to question the sincerity of Ali's beliefs and asserts that these beliefs were indeed "founded on tenets of the Muslim religion as he understands them."

As such, the government conceded that two of the three grounds offered by the Justice Department for rejecting Ali's claim were no longer valid. Only one basic test for establishing conscientious objector status remained, and that was whether Ali objected to war in a universal or selective sense. Because the Appeal Board failed to specify which of the three grounds it used as the basis for its denial of a conscientious objector exemption for Ali, the conviction could not be allowed to stand. The precedent for this opinion was the 1955 case of *Sicurella v. United States*. Thus, without tackling the merits of whether Ali should or should not have received conscientious objector status, the Court was able to invalidate his conviction in light of the errors that pervaded the Justice Department's advice to the Kentucky Appeal Board. Although the Court's decision is significant in establishing that Ali's beliefs were in fact "religious," rather than "political and racial," it does not address the underlying question of whether Ali condoned war under certain circumstances.

Perhaps the most intriguing part of the decision is the concurring opinion authored by Justice William O. Douglas, who offers his own view on the merits of the sole remaining ground upon which Ali's application for conscientious objector status could legally be denied: that Ali did not oppose participating in war "in any form" but rather specifically opposed the conflict in Vietnam. Douglas had been the lone voice of dissent just two months earlier, when the Supreme Court made its ruling in *Gillette v. United States*, another conscientious objector suit. In that case, the Court ruled against objections to "specific" wars as grounds for conscientious objection. The *Gillette* case turned on the distinction between "just" and "unjust" wars, with the majority opinion holding that conscientious objector status be granted only to those who oppose war "in any form." Douglas disagreed with the decision in *Gillette*, and his difference of opinion carried over to *Clay v. United States*: Whereas one of two defendants in *Gillette* was Catholic and the other a self-described "humanist," Ali's visible adherence to Islam, and his membership in the Nation of Islam in particular, led Douglas to draw analogies between the religious practices.

Specifically, Douglas devotes virtually all of his concurrence in *Ali* to a careful examination of both Ali's statements and the teachings of the Koran. In his words:

> The jihad is the Moslem's counterpart of the 'just' war as it has been known in the West. Neither Clay nor Negre [one of the defendants in Gillette, Louis Negre] should be subject to punishment because he will not renounce the 'truth' of the teaching of his respective church that wars indeed may exist which are just wars in which a Moslem or Catholic has a respective duty to participate.

In essence, Douglas supported the ultimate outcome in Ali's case but disagreed with the reasoning used by the Court to arrive at that decision. He expresses clear support for religiously grounded opposition to participation in wars that are inconsistent with that particular religion, even if the religion itself is not pacifistic. If the First Amendment protects the right to worship by any religion, Douglas reasons, it necessarily protects the right to be a selective, rather than categorical, conscientious objector and to support only those wars that are consistent with one's faith.

The opinion in *Clay v. United States* concludes with a separate concurrence by Justice John Marshall Harlan II, noting his narrow agreement with the proposition that reversal was "required under *Sicurella*." It was unclear, he writes, whether and to what extent the Kentucky Appeal Board had relied upon the Justice Department's advice, but he asserts that it was clearly wrong for the Justice Department to question the sincerity of Ali's beliefs.

Audience

Although the *Clay v. United States* litigation was watched closely by Ali supporters, antiwar protesters, and other interest groups, it is unlikely that the opinion handed down by the Court had much of an intended audience outside legal circles. The decision hinged on a technicality that cleared Ali's record but left intact the government's view of selective conscientious objector claims stated two months earlier in *Gillette*. Similarly, it is hard to imagine that Justice Harlan's one-paragraph concurrence—one of the last opinions of his distinguished judicial career—was itself intended to be widely read.

Justice Douglas's concurrence, however, devotes a significant amount of attention to the distinction between "just" and "unjust" wars under Islamic doctrine. Given the racial and religious fervor that had, at times, marked the dispute over Ali's conduct, Douglas's opinion may well have represented an attempt on the part of the Court's most liberal member to educate the public—to identify important similarities between Catholicism (one of the religions at issue in *Gillette*) and Islam, at least insofar as selective conscientious objection was concerned.

Impact

Relying, as it did, on a technicality established by an earlier precedent, the Court's decision itself has had little precedential value. Even Justice Douglas's more useful concurrence, which offered thought-provoking ideas on the true implications of religious freedom in the context of selective conscientious objection to military service, has largely been lost to time, cited only rarely and often for unrelated—or at least tangential—points. If anything, the Court's decision in *Clay* may best be understood as a reflection of its Vietnam-era legacy—avoiding decisive rulings on the most divisive controversial questions and finding ways to reach what it believed to be appropriate results through other means.

Douglas's specific argument about the First Amendment and religiously grounded selective conscientious objection was never put to the test. By the time of the Court's decision, the U.S. government had already begun moving toward an all-volunteer army, and so the hard questions that the Court had not yet answered about the extent to which the Constitution protected religiously based selective conscientious objection remain unanswered today. And although Ali went on to complete a remarkable career that culminated with his selection by *Sports Illustrated* as the "sportsman of the century," his controversial position on the war in Vietnam, and the litigation arising out of his refusal to be inducted, have remained an inescapable part of his enigmatic legacy.

In the decades since the Supreme Court decision in the case of *Clay v. United States*, numerous critics have analyzed Ali's impact on American culture. In a *Sports Illustrated* "Flashback," William Nack stated that "he not only came to personify the turbulent '60s but also became one of the decade's most hated figures." Thirty years later, though, Ali managed to "navigat[e] the sweet land of liberty and religious freedom" and, according to Nack, was "as loved and embraced as he once was scorned and despised." Clearly, the fighter's antidraft stance sparked a heated debate about the depth of his patriotism, but as John C. Walter pointed out, his performance at the 1960 Olympics in Rome, Italy, revealed not only his athletic prowess but also a deeply rooted devotion to his country: A Soviet reporter had brought up the issue of segregation in the United States, and the then-eighteen-year-old gold medalist responded, "The U.S.A. is still the best country in the world, including yours."

Between 1967 and 1971—the years separating Ali's conviction and his ultimate victory in the Supreme Court—U.S. support for the Vietnam War eroded. At the same time, Ali's popularity grew. No longer dismissed as a draft evader, he came to symbolize the antiwar, pro–civil rights movement in America. He had weathered a public firestorm with unwavering courage, given up his heavyweight title and more than three years of boxing in the prime of his career, and maintained his beliefs in the process.

Ali was able to resume his boxing career at the end of 1970, when the state of Georgia, which did not have a boxing commission, allowed him to fight. His match in Atlanta against Jerry Quarry was over in the third round: "The Greatest" had returned to the ring. On March 8, 1971, three months before the Court's final decision in *Clay v. United States*, Ali took on Joe Frazier in the Fight of the Century. Like Ali, Frazier—who had been named boxing's heavyweight champion after Ali was stripped of the title—had never lost a fight. Frazier retained his title, beating Ali by a unanimous decision after fifteen grueling rounds. Ali put up such a fight that his loss in the final round was characterized as courageous, and even heroic, by the media.

In 1973 George Foreman became the world's reigning heavyweight champion by defeating Frazier. Ali was able to regain the heavyweight title that same year, knocking out Foreman in the eighth round of their legendary fight in Zaire known as the Rumble in the Jungle. Nearly a year after defeating Foreman, Ali and Frazier met again in a stunning rematch in the Philippines. The so-called Thrilla in Manila was among the most brutal boxing matches ever fought. Ali withstood more than four hundred punishing blows from Frazier before being declared the winner in the fourteenth round.

Ali's passion in the ring solidified his claim to the title of "the Greatest." He retired from boxing in 1981. Three years later he went public with his Parkinson's disease diagnosis—a direct result, doctors say, of repeated trauma to the head. The ravaging effects of the disease have taken their toll on Ali, but he has established himself as a tireless philanthropist, raising funds for a variety of charities, most notably the Muhammad Ali Parkinson Center at Barrow Neurological Institute. In an interesting footnote to a complex life story, Ali went to Vietnam in 1994 in a show of support for families of American soldiers still missing in action.

Further Reading

◆ Articles

Holtgraves, Thomas, and Jeffrey Dulin. "The Muhammad Ali Effect." *Journal of Language and Communication* 14, no. 3 (July 1994): 275–285.

Malament, David. "Selective Conscientious Objection and the Gillette Decision." *Philosophy and Public Affairs* 1, no. 4 (1972): 363–386.

Shenon, Philip. "Going to Vietnam as a Champ." *New York Times*, May 15, 1994.

Watkins, Calvin. "Time in Texas Made Ali More Than a Boxer." *Dallas Morning News*, December 25, 2001.

◆ Books

Ali, Muhammad, and Richard Durham. *The Greatest: My Own Story*. New York: Random House, 1975.

Ali, Muhammad, and Hana Yasmeen Ali. *Soul of a Butterfly: Reflections on Life's Journey*. New York: Simon and Schuster, 2004.

Hauser, Thomas. *Muhammad Ali: His Life and Times*. New York: Simon and Schuster, 1992.

Remnick, David. *King of the World: Muhammad Ali and the Rise of an American Hero*. New York: Random House, 1998.

◆ **Web Sites**

Nack, William. "Bigger Than Boxing." CNN/Sports Illustrated's Century's Best Web site. http://sportsillustrated.cnn.com/centurys_best/news/1999/05/05/bigger/index.html.

Schwartz, Larry. "He Is Simply ... the Greatest." ESPN Classic Web site. http://espn.go.com/classic/biography/s/Ali_Muhammad.html.

Sielski, Mike. "Frazier Battled Ali in Timeless Trilogy." ESPN Classic Web site. http://espn.go.com/classic/biography/s/Frazier_Joe.html.

Walter, John C. "Muhammad Ali: The Quintessential American." American Studies Centre at Liverpool John Moores University (ARNet) Web site. http://www.americansc.org.uk/Online/Forum/muhammad_ali.htm.

—Stephen I. Vladeck

Time Line

1942	January 17	Muhammad Ali is born Cassius Marcellus Clay, Jr., in Louisville, Kentucky.
1960	September 5	At the 1960 Olympics in Rome, Italy, Clay wins the light-heavyweight gold medal for the U.S. team.
1964	February 25	Only twenty-two years old at the time, Clay beats reigning champ Sonny Liston to become the world heavyweight champion.
	March 6	Clay adopts the Muslim name Muhammad Ali, which means "Praiseworthy One."
1967	January 10	The Kentucky Appeal Board formally denies Ali's request for conscientious objector status and ministerial exemption.
	April 28	Ali reports for but declines to submit to induction into the service, basing his refusal on the grounds of his religious beliefs as a Muslim minister.
	June 19–20	Ali is tried and convicted by a jury for refusing to submit to induction; he is sentenced to five years' imprisonment and a fine of $10,000.
1968	May 6	The U.S. Court of Appeals for the Fifth Circuit affirms Ali's conviction.
1971	March 8	In a match touted as the Fight of the Century against Joe Frazier, Ali is knocked out in the fifteenth round.
	June 28	In an eight-to-zero decision, the U.S. Supreme Court reverses the ruling of the Fifth Circuit, thereby invalidating Ali's conviction.
1974	October 30	Ali regains his heavyweight title from George Foreman in the fight known as the Rumble in the Jungle.
1975	October 1	Ali wins his much-anticipated rematch against Joe Frazier in Manila.

Time Line		
1984		■ Ali is diagnosed with Parkinson's disease, a degenerative neurological disorder that causes muscle tremors, slowed movement, and impaired speech.
2005	November 9	■ President George W. Bush awards Ali the Presidential Medal of Freedom.
	November 19	■ The Muhammad Ali Center celebrates the grand opening of its ninety-three-thousand-square-foot headquarters in Louisville, Kentucky.

Essential Quotes

"In this Court the Government has now fully conceded that the petitioner's beliefs are based upon 'religious training and belief,' as defined in United States v. Seeger.... This concession is clearly correct. For the record shows that the petitioner's beliefs are founded on tenets of the Muslim religion as he understands them."

"The Government in this Court has also made clear that it no longer questions the sincerity of the petitioner's beliefs."

"The Department of Justice was wrong in advising the Board in terms of a purported rule of law that it should disregard this finding simply because of the circumstances and timing of the petitioner's claim."

"The jihad is the Moslem's counterpart of the 'just' war as it has been known in the West. Neither Clay nor Negre should be subject to punishment because he will not renounce the 'truth' of the teaching of his respective church that wars indeed may exist which are just wars in which a Moslem or Catholic has a respective duty to participate."

"What Clay's testimony adds up to is that he believes only in war as sanctioned by the Koran, that is to say, a religious war against nonbelievers. All other wars are unjust. That is a matter of belief, of conscience, of religious principle."

Questions for Further Study

1. One of the requirements for conscientious objector status is sincerity of belief. How can a draft board or a court measure the sincerity of a person's beliefs? What evidence might it rely on?

2. Do you think that the outcome of this case would have been different if Clay had been an ordinary citizen rather than a highly admired athlete? Why or why not?

3. What is your position on the issue of whether the Nation of Islam opposed the war in Vietnam on religious rather than political and racial grounds? For help, see Stokely Carmichael's "Black Power" and Malcolm X's "After the Bombing."

4. By 1971, it was becoming apparent that the U.S. effort in Vietnam was failing. Further, there was considerable discussion of moving to an all-volunteer army, which became a reality in 1973. To what extent do you think these developments might have influenced the Court's decision?

5. In your opinion, were the religious grounds that Clay/Ali cited for opposing war legitimate? Did they provide ample grounds for the Court's reversal of Clay's conviction?

Clay v. United States

The full text of the Supreme Court's decision in Clay v. United States.

Petitioner appealed his local draft board's rejection of his application for conscientious objector classification. The Justice Department, in response to the State Appeal Board's referral for an advisory recommendation, concluded, contrary to a hearing officer's recommendation, that petitioner's claim should be denied, and wrote that board that petitioner did not meet any of the three basic tests for conscientious objector status. The Appeal Board then denied petitioner's claim, but without stating its reasons. Petitioner refused to report for induction, for which he was thereafter tried and convicted. The Court of Appeals affirmed. In this Court the Government has rightly conceded the invalidity of two of the grounds for denial of petitioner's claim given in its letter to the Appeal Board, but argues that there was factual support for the third ground. *Held:* Since the Appeal Board gave no reason for the denial of a conscientious objector exemption to petitioner, and it is impossible to determine on which of the three grounds offered in the Justice Department's letter that board relied, petitioner's conviction must be reversed. *Sicurella v. United States*, 348 U. S. 385.

430 F. 2d 165, reversed.

Chauncey Eskridge argued the cause for petitioner. With him on the briefs were *Jack Greenberg, James M. Nabrit III, Jonathan Shapiro,* and *Elizabeth B. DuBois.*

Solicitor General Griswold argued the cause for the United States. With him on the brief were *Assistant Attorney General Wilson* and *Beatrice Rosenberg.*

Per Curiam

The petitioner was convicted for willful refusal to submit to induction into the Armed Forces. 62 Stat. 622, as amended, 50 U. S. C. App. §462 (a) (1964 ed., Supp. V). The judgment of conviction was affirmed by the Court of Appeals for the Fifth Circuit. We granted certiorari, 400 U. S. 990, to consider whether the induction notice was invalid because grounded upon an erroneous denial of the petitioner's claim to be classified as a conscientious objector.

I

The petitioner's application for classification as a conscientious objector was turned down by his local draft board, and he took an administrative appeal. The State Appeal Board tentatively classified him I-A (eligible for unrestricted military service) and referred his file to the Department of Justice for an advisory recommendation, in accordance with then-applicable procedures. 50 U. S. C. App. §456 (j) (1964 ed., Supp. V). The FBI then conducted an "inquiry" as required by the statute, interviewing some 35 persons, including members of the petitioner's family and many of his friends, neighbors, and business and religious associates.

There followed a hearing on "the character and good faith of the [petitioner's] objections" before a hearing officer appointed by the Department. The hearing officer, a retired judge of many years' experience, heard testimony from the petitioner's mother and father, from one of his attorneys, from a minister of his religion, and from the petitioner himself. He also had the benefit of a full report from the FBI. On the basis of this record the hearing officer concluded that the registrant was sincere in his objection on religious grounds to participation in war in any form, and he recommended that the conscientious objector claim be sustained.

Notwithstanding this recommendation, the Department of Justice wrote a letter to the Appeal Board, advising it that the petitioner's conscientious objector claim should be denied. Upon receipt of this letter of advice, the Board denied the petitioner's claim without a statement of reasons. After various further proceedings which it is not necessary to recount here, the petitioner was ordered to report for induction. He refused to take the traditional step forward, and this prosecution and conviction followed.

II

In order to qualify for classification as a conscientious objector, a registrant must satisfy three basic tests. He must show that he is conscientiously opposed to war in any form. *Gillette v. United States*, 401 U. S. 437.

He must show that this opposition is based upon religious training and belief, as the term has been construed in our decisions. *United States* v. *Seeger*, 380 U. S. 163; *Welsh* v. *United States*, 398 U. S. 333. And he must show that this objection is sincere. *Witmer* v. *United States*, 348 U. S. 375. In applying these tests, the Selective Service System must be concerned with the registrant as an individual, not with its own interpretation of the dogma of the religious sect, if any, to which he may belong. *United States* v. *Seeger, supra*; *Gillette* v. *United States, supra*; *Williams* v. *United States*, 216 F. 2d 350, 352.

In asking us to affirm the judgment of conviction, the Government argues that there was a "basis in fact," cf. *Estep* v. *United States*, 327 U. S. 114, for holding that the petitioner is not opposed to "war in any form," but is only selectively opposed to certain wars. See *Gillette* v. *United States, supra*. Counsel for the petitioner, needless to say, takes the opposite position. The issue is one that need not be resolved in this case. For we have concluded that even if the Government's position on this question is correct, the conviction before us must still be set aside for another quite independent reason.

III

The petitioner's criminal conviction stemmed from the Selective Service System's denial of his appeal seeking conscientious objector status. That denial, for which no reasons were ever given, was, as we have said, based on a recommendation of the Department of Justice, over-ruling its hearing officer and advising the Appeal Board that it "finds that the registrant's conscientious-objector claim is not sustained and recommends to your Board that he be not [so] classified." This finding was contained in a long letter of explanation, from which it is evident that Selective Service officials were led to believe that the Department had found that the petitioner had failed to satisfy each of the three basic tests for qualification as a conscientious objector.

As to the requirement that a registrant must be opposed to war in any form, the Department letter said that the petitioner's expressed beliefs "do not appear to preclude military service in any form, but rather are limited to military service in the Armed Forces of the United States.... These constitute only objections to certain types of war in certain circumstances, rather than a general scruple against participation in war in any form. However, only a general scruple against participation in war in any form can support an exemption as a conscientious objector under the Act. *United States* v. *Kauten*, 133 F. 2d 703."

As to the requirement that a registrant's opposition must be based upon religious training and belief, the Department letter said: "It seems clear that the teachings of the Nation of Islam preclude fighting for the United States not because of objections to participation in war in any form but rather because of political and racial objections to policies of the United States as interpreted by Elijah Muhammad.... It is therefore our conclusion that registrant's claimed objections to participation in war insofar as they are based upon the teachings of the Nation of Islam, rest on grounds which primarily are political and racial."

As to the requirement that a registrant's opposition to war must be sincere, that part of the letter began by stating that "the registrant has not consistently manifested his conscientious-objector claim. Such a course of overt manifestations is requisite to establishing a subjective state of mind and belief." There followed several paragraphs reciting the timing and circumstances of the petitioner's conscientious objector claim, and a concluding paragraph seeming to state a rule of law—that "a registrant has not shown overt manifestations sufficient to establish his subjective belief where, as here, his conscientious-objector claim was not asserted until military service became imminent. *Campbell* v. *United States*, 221 F. 2d 454. *United States* v. *Corliss*, 280 F. 2d 808, *cert. denied*, 364 U. S. 884."

In this Court the Government has now fully conceded that the petitioner's beliefs *are* based upon "religious training and belief," as defined in *United States* v. *Seeger, supra*: "There is no dispute that petitioner's professed beliefs were founded on basic tenets of the Muslim religion, as he understood them, and derived in substantial part from his devotion to Allah as the Supreme Being. Thus, under this Court's decision in *United States* v. *Seeger*, 380 U. S. 163, his claim unquestionably was within the 'religious training and belief' clause of the exemption provision." This concession is clearly correct. For the record shows that the petitioner's beliefs are founded on tenets of the Muslim religion as he understands them. They are surely no less religiously based than those of the three registrants before this Court in *Seeger*. See also *Welsh* v. *United States*, 398 U. S. 333.

Document Text

The Government in this Court has also made clear that it no longer questions the sincerity of the petitioner's beliefs. This concession is also correct. The Department hearing officer—the only person at the administrative appeal level who carefully examined the petitioner and other witnesses in person and who had the benefit of the full FBI file—found "that the registrant is sincere in his objection." The Department of Justice was wrong in advising the Board in terms of a purported rule of law that it should disregard this finding simply because of the circumstances and timing of the petitioner's claim. See *Ehlert v. United States*, 402 U. S. 99, 103–104; *United States ex rel. Lehman v. Laird*, 430 F. 2d 96, 99; *United States v. Abbott*, 425 F. 2d 910, 915; *United States ex rel. Tobias v. Laird*, 413 F. 2d 936, 939–940; *Cohen v. Laird*, 315 F. Supp. 1265, 1277–1278.

Since the Appeal Board gave no reasons for its denial of the petitioner's claim, there is absolutely no way of knowing upon which of the three grounds offered in the Department's letter it relied. Yet the Government now acknowledges that two of those grounds were not valid. And, the Government's concession aside, it is indisputably clear, for the reasons stated, that the Department was simply wrong as a matter of law in advising that the petitioner's beliefs were not religiously based and were not sincerely held.

This case, therefore, falls squarely within the four corners of this Court's decision in *Sicurella v. United States*, 348 U. S. 385. There as here the Court was asked to hold that an error in an advice letter prepared by the Department of Justice did not require reversal of a criminal conviction because there was a ground on which the Appeal Board might properly have denied a conscientious objector classification. This Court refused to consider the proffered alternative ground:

"[W]e feel that this error of law by the Department, to which the Appeal Board might naturally look for guidance on such questions, must vitiate the entire proceedings at least where it is not clear that the Board relied on some legitimate ground. Here, where it is impossible to determine on exactly which grounds the Appeal Board decided, the integrity of the Selective Service System demands, at least, that the Government not recommend illegal grounds. There is an impressive body of lower court cases taking this position and we believe that they state the correct rule." *Id.*, at 392.

The doctrine thus articulated 16 years ago in *Sicurella* was hardly new. It was long ago established as essential to the administration of criminal justice. *Stromberg v. California*, 283 U. S. 359. In *Stromberg* the Court reversed a conviction for violation of a California statute containing three separate clauses, finding one of the three clauses constitutionally invalid. As Chief Justice Hughes put the matter, "[I]t is impossible to say under which clause of the statute the conviction was obtained." Thus, "if any of the clauses in question is invalid under the Federal Constitution, the conviction cannot be upheld." *Id.*, at 368.

The application of this doctrine in the area of Selective Service law goes back at least to 1945, and Judge Learned Hand's opinion for the Second Circuit in *United States v. Cain*, 149 F. 2d 338. It is a doctrine that has been consistently and repeatedly followed by the federal courts in dealing with the criminal sanctions of the selective service laws. See, *e. g., United States v. Lemmens*, 430 F. 2d 619, 623–624 (CA7 1970); *United States v. Broyles*, 423 F. 2d 1299, 1303–1304 (CA4 1970); *United States v. Houghton*, 413 F. 2d 736 (CA9 1969); *United States v. Jakobson*, 325 F. 2d 409, 416–417 (CA2 1963), aff'd sub nom. *United States v. Seeger*, 380 U. S. 163; *Kretchet v. United States*, 284 F. 2d 561, 565–566 (CA9 1960); *Ypparila v. United States*, 219 F. 2d 465, 469 (CA10 1954); *United States v. Englander*, 271 F. Supp. 182 (SDNY 1967); *United States v. Erikson*, 149 F. Supp. 576, 578–579 (SDNY 1957). In every one of the above cases the defendant was acquitted or the conviction set aside under the *Sicurella* application of the *Stromberg* doctrine.

The long established rule of law embodied in these settled precedents thus clearly requires that the judgment before us be reversed.

It is so ordered.

Mr. Justice Marshall took no part in the consideration or decision of this case.

Mr. Justice Douglas concurring

I would reverse this judgment of conviction and set the petitioner free.

In *Sicurella v. United States*, 348 U. S. 385, the wars that the applicant would fight were not "carnal" but those "in defense of Kingdom interests." *Id.*, at 389. Since it was impossible to determine on exactly which grounds the Appeal Board had based its decision, we reversed the decision sustaining the judgment of conviction. We said: "It is difficult for us to believe that the Congress had in mind this type of activity when it said the thrust of conscientious objection must go to 'participation in war in any form.'" Id., at 390.

In the present case there is no line between "carnal" war and "spiritual" or symbolic wars. Those who know the history of the Mediterranean littoral know that the *jihad* of the Moslem was a bloody war.

This case is very close in its essentials to Negre v. Larsen, 401 U. S. 437, decided March 8, 1971. The church to which that registrant belonged favored "just" wars and provided guidelines to define them. The church did not oppose the war in Vietnam but the registrant refused to comply with an order to go to Vietnam because participating in that conflict would violate his conscience. The Court refused to grant him relief as a conscientious objector, overruling his constitutional claim.

The case of Clay is somewhat different, though analogous. While there are some bits of evidence showing conscientious objection to the Vietnam conflict, the basic objection was based on the teachings of his religion. He testified that he was

"sincere in every bit of what the Holy Qur'an and the teachings of the Honorable Elijah Muhammad tell us and it is that we are not to participate in wars on the side of nobody who—on the side of nonbelievers, and this is a Christian country and this is not a Muslim country, and the Government and the history and the facts shows that every move toward the Honorable Elijah Muhammad is made to distort and is made to ridicule him and is made to condemn him and the Government has admitted that the police of Los Angeles were wrong about attacking and killing our brothers and sisters and they were wrong in Newark, New Jersey, and they were wrong in Louisiana, and the outright, every day oppressors and enemies are the people as a whole, the whites of this nation. So, we are not, according to the Holy Qur'an, to even as much as aid in passing a cup of water to the—even a wounded. I mean, this is in the Holy Qur'an, and as I said earlier, this is not me talking to get the draft board—or to dodge nothing. This is there before I was borned and it will be there when I'm dead but we believe in not only that part of it, but all of it."

At another point he testified: "[T]he Holy Qur'an do teach us that we do not take part of—in any part of war unless declared by Allah himself, or unless it's an Islamic World War, or a Holy War, and it goes as far—the Holy Qur'an is talking still, and saying we are not to even as much as aid the infidels or the nonbelievers in Islam, even to as much as handing them a cup of water during battle.

"So, this is the teachings of the Holy Qur'an before I was born, and the Qur'an, we follow not only that part of it, but every part."

The Koran defines *jihad* as an injunction to the believers to war against nonbelievers:

"O ye who believe! Shall I guide you to a gainful trade which will save you from painful punishment? Believe in Allah and His Apostle and carry on warfare (*jihad*) in the path of Allah with your possessions and your persons. That is better for you. If ye have knowledge, He will forgive your sins, and will place you in the Gardens beneath which the streams flow, and in fine houses in the Gardens of Eden: that is the great gain." M. Khadduri, War and Peace in the Law of Islam 55–56 (1955).

The Sale edition of the Koran, which first appeared in England in 1734, gives the following translation at 410– 411 (9th ed. 1923):

"Thus God propoundeth unto men their examples. When ye encounter the unbelievers, strike off their heads, until ye have made a great slaughter among them; and bind them in bonds; and either give them a free dismission afterwards, or exact a ransom; until the war shall have laid down its arms. This shall ye do. Verily if God pleased he could take vengeance on them, without your assistance; but he commandeth you to fight his battles, that he may prove the one of you by the other. And as to those who fight in defence of God's true religion, God will not suffer their works to perish: he will guide them, and will dispose their heart aright; and he will lead them into paradise, of which he hath told them. O true believers, if ye assist God, by fighting for his religion, he will assist you against your enemies; and will set your feet fast...."

War is not the exclusive type of *jihad*; there is action by the believer's heart, by his tongue, by his hands, as well as by the sword. War and Peace in the Law of Islam 56. As respects the military aspects it is written:

"The *jihad*, in other words, is a sanction against polytheism and must be suffered by all non-Muslims who reject Islam, or, in the case of the dhimmis (Scripturaries), refuse to pay the poll tax. The *jihad*, therefore, may be defined as the litigation between

Islam and polytheism; it is also a form of punishment to be inflicted upon Islam's enemies and the renegades from the faith. Thus in Islam, as in Western Christendom, the *jihad* is the *bellum justum*." *Id.*, at 59.

The *jihad* is the Moslem's counterpart of the "just" war as it has been known in the West. Neither Clay nor Negre should be subject to punishment because he will not renounce the "truth" of the teaching of his respective church that wars indeed may exist which are just wars in which a Moslem or Catholic has a respective duty to participate.

What Clay's testimony adds up to is that he believes only in war as sanctioned by the Koran, that is to say, a religious war against nonbelievers. All other wars are unjust.

That is a matter of belief, of conscience, of religious principle. Both Clay and Negre were "by reason of religious training and belief" conscientiously opposed to participation in war of the character proscribed by their respective religions. That belief is a matter of conscience protected by the First Amendment which Congress has no power to qualify or dilute as it did in § 6 (j) of the Military Selective Service Act of 1967, 50 U. S. C. App. §456 (j) (1964 ed., Supp. V) when it restricted the exemption to those "conscientiously opposed to participation in war in any form." For the reasons I stated in *Negre* and in *Gillette* v. *United States*, 401 U. S. 437, 463 and 470, that construction puts Clay in a class honored by the First Amendment, even though those schooled in a different conception of "just" wars may find it quite irrational.

I would reverse the judgment below.

Mr. Justice Harlan concurring in the result

I concur in the result on the following ground. The Department of Justice advice letter was at least susceptible of the reading that petitioner's proof of sincerity was insufficient as a matter of law because his conscientious objector claim had not been timely asserted. This would have been erroneous advice had the Department's letter been so read. Since the Appeals Board might have acted on such an interpretation of the letter, reversal is required under *Sicurella* v. *United States*, 348 U. S. 385 (1955).

Glossary

bellum justum: Latin for "just war," that is, a war that is justly waged

brief: the document submitted by the parties to a legal dispute outlining their positions for the justices

Chief Justice Hughes: Charles Evans Hughes, chief justice of the Supreme Court during the years of the Great Depression

dhimmis: non-Muslims who live in a Muslim state

Elijah Muhammad: the leader of the Nation of Islam from 1934 to 1975

granted certiorari: the phrase used by a higher court to indicate that it has agreed to hear a case by demanding the record from the lower court whose case the higher court is reviewing

induction: formal entry into the military

***jihad*:** in Islam, a struggle or holy war

Justice Douglas: William O. Douglas, a firm civil libertarian and the longest-serving justice in the history of the Supreme Court

Justice Harlan: John Marshall Harlan II, a conservative member of the Supreme Court at the time

Justice Marshall: Thurgood Marshall, the only black member of the Supreme Court at the time

Koran: the Islamic sacred scripture, often spelled Qur'an

Learned Hand: a prominent twentieth-century district and appeals court judge and legal philosopher from New York whose judicial opinions the Supreme Court cites more frequently than those of any lower court judge

Mediterranean littoral: the coastal areas of the Mediterranean Sea

Moslem: an alternative spelling of the more common "Muslim"

Nation of Islam: the so-called Black Muslims, or the branch of Islam as practiced by some African Americans

Per Curiam: a decision issued by a court as a whole rather than a single judge

Qur'an: the Islamic sacred scripture, later referred to as the Koran

Selective Service System: the government agency that conducted the military draft

Angela Davis (center, no glasses) enters Royce Hall at UCLA in October 1969 to give her first lecture. GeorgeLouis at English Wikipedia [CC BY 3.0 (http://creativecommons.org/licenses/by/3.0)], via Wikimedia Commons

Angela Davis's "Political Prisoners, Prisons, and Black Liberation"

"Black people are rushing full speed ahead towards an understanding of the circumstances that give rise to exaggerated forms of political repression and thus an overabundance of political prisoners."

Overview

In 1971 the civil rights activist Angela Davis was a prisoner in the Marin County, California, jail. There she wrote "Political Prisoners, Prisons, and Black Liberation," published that year in a collection she edited, *If They Come in the Morning: Voices of Resistance*. The essay marks Davis's early commitment to prison reform and the liberation of black prisoners. She was in jail at the time because of the death of California Superior Court Judge Harold Haley, who was shot with a gun registered in Davis's name during a botched effort to free a prisoner from a California courtroom. Davis's incarceration drew international attention, and she was eventually acquitted of all charges, but her life was forever marked by this incident. Not only did it influence her career as an activist, it also informed and directed her efforts for prison reform. Davis, a prolific writer and lecturer, focused throughout her life on issues of social inequality.

Context

In early 1969, Davis obtained a position for the fall semester as a lecturer in philosophy at the University of California at Los Angeles (UCLA). Before the semester began, however, the UCLA regents learned of her Communist Party membership and canceled her appointment. California governor Ronald Reagan strongly endorsed the dismissal, but large crowds of students and faculty members protested. Davis filed a legal grievance and won reinstatement. That fall, more than two thousand students attended her first lecture.

In addition to teaching her classes, Davis continued her political activities, particularly protests on behalf of three African American prisoners accused of murdering a guard at California's Soledad Prison. Persuaded that the three were political prisoners, she developed a special interest in inmate George Jackson, whose popular book *Soledad Brother: The Prison Letters of George Jackson* (1970) interpreted the imprisonment of minorities from a radical Marxist perspective. Davis agreed with his ideology and admired his defiant stand; she and Jackson soon were exchanging romantic correspondence. In the spring of 1970, when the UCLA regents found out about her prominent support for the Soledad prisoners, they fired her a second time, alleging "unprofessional conduct." Davis also received numerous death threats. She purchased a large quantity of guns and ammunition, which she allowed Black Panthers and other associates to use for target practice.

Davis developed a close friendship with Jackson's seventeen-year-old brother, Jonathan Jackson, and she sometimes used him as a bodyguard. On August 7, 1970, the young man entered the Marin County courthouse with several firearms (all belonging to Davis) and attempted to escape with three black prisoners and five hostages, including the judge. Outside the courthouse, a bloody gunfight resulted in the deaths of Jackson, the judge, and two of the prisoners. Jackson apparently had hoped to exchange the hostages for his older brother. In her autobiography, Davis described her "blind rage" and how she pledged to "avenge Jon's death—through struggle, political struggle."

As soon as Davis learned that her firearms were used in the incident, she fled the state, presumably because she believed that the justice system would treat her unfairly. Listed as one of the Federal Bureau of Investigation's (FBI's) ten most wanted fugitives, she evaded the authori-

Chairwoman of the Soviet Women's Committee Valentina Tereshkova handing a memento to member of the Central Committee of the Communist Party of the United States Angela Davis, and Kendra Alexander (right). By D. Chernov / CC-BY-SA 3.0 [CC BY-SA 3.0 (http://creativecommons.org/licenses/by-sa/3.0)], via Wikimedia Commons

ties for about two months before being captured in New York City. While she was awaiting trial in August, 1971, George Jackson attempted to escape from prison. Jackson, three prison guards, and two white inmates were killed in the resulting shootout. Davis wrote a statement for the press, declaring that Jackson had been murdered by "fascist bullets" and that she had lost "a comrade and revolutionary leader" and "an irretrievable love." She further declared that her "rage at the system responsible for his murder" renewed her "determination to fight for the cause George died defending."

When Davis's trial began on February 18, 1972, it attracted tremendous worldwide publicity. The prosecution's case was based primarily on four factors: her flight, her ownership of the weapons, her romantic correspondence with George Jackson, and the testimony of witnesses who claimed to have seen her with Jonathan Jackson in the days before the shootout. Some of her close friends, however, testified that she was in their homes at the time. The defense's main argument was that a person of Davis's intelligence would not have participated in such an unrealistic and badly organized scheme. On June 4, 1972, the all-white jury found her not guilty of all charges. Later that month, Davis spoke to twenty thousand cheering supporters at a victory celebration at Madison Square Garden in New York. She then took a tour of Cuba, where she worked in the sugar fields and was celebrated with a massive rally. The next year, she was an honored guest at an East German youth festival.

During her subsequent academic career, Davis held prestigious teaching positions at a variety of American universities. From 1979 to 1991, she taught at the Ethnic Studies Department at San Francisco State University and at the San Francisco Art Institute. From 1995 to 1997, she held the Presidential Chair in the history of consciousness program at the University of California at Santa Cruz. Although critics frequently questioned her academic qualifications, most administrators, faculty, and students defended her competence and dedication to teaching. She also became a very popular lecturer on university campuses.

About the Author

Born in 1944, Angela Yvonne Davis was the oldest of four children and was raised in a middle-class family in Birmingham, Alabama. Her mother was an elementary school teacher, and her father was a college-educated mechanic who owned and operated a service station. The family lived in a predominantly white neighborhood called Dynamite Hill after black-owned homes were bombed. She attended a segregated elementary school, where she was an excellent student. At the age of fourteen, she was awarded a scholarship by the American Friends Service Committee, allowing her to attend the progressive Elisabeth Irwin High School in Greenwich Village, New York. While there, she stayed in the home of a white Episcopal priest, the Reverend William Melish, a staunch supporter of civil rights and a friend of left-wing radicals. During this period, Davis became attracted to the theories of Karl Marx, and she joined a communist youth organization, Advance.

Davis was awarded a full scholarship to attend Brandeis University in Massachusetts, which had only a handful of black students. Majoring in French literature, Davis lived in the French House, where only French was spoken. While studying at the Sorbonne in Paris during her junior year, she was saddened and enraged to learn of the bombing of Birmingham's Sixteenth Street Baptist Church, which killed four girls whom she knew. Also in Paris, Davis formed close friendships with Algerian students who were actively engaged in the struggle for Algerian independence. Returning to Brandeis for her senior year, she came under the influence of Herbert Marcuse, a leading theorist of the "New Left" movement, and she changed her major to philosophy. After graduating with high honors, Davis spent the next two years studying in Frankfurt, Germany, at the Marxist-oriented Institute of Social Research.

Returning to the United States, Davis continued her graduate studies in philosophy at the University of California at San Diego. In addition to her academic work, she became increasingly involved in radical political activities. In 1968, she joined the Che-Lumumba Club, an African American branch of the U.S. Communist Party. Although she never joined the Black Panther Party, she cooperated with the Panthers in demonstrations and community-based programs. In 1969, Davis received her master's degree from the University of California at San Diego, and she also completed all the requirements for a Ph.D. except a dissertation. A few years later, Humboldt University in East Germany awarded her a doctorate for a dissertation devoted to Immanuel Kant's views on violence in the French Revolution. No information was ever published about her dissertation.

In addition to teaching and speaking, Davis continued to devote much time and effort to a variety of political causes. In 1973, she was the founding cochair of the National Alliance Against Racism and Political Repression. In 1979, the Soviet Union recognized her contributions with the Lenin Peace Prize. In the presidential elections of 1980 and 1984, the U.S. Communist Party nominated her as its candidate for vice president. With the fall of European communism in the late 1980's, Davis gradually abandoned the Leninist ideology in favor of a more liberal form of democratic socialism. In 1991, her opposition to the attempted overthrow of Soviet president Mikhail Gorbachev caused her to leave the U.S. Community Party, and she helped to found the Committees of Correspondence for Democracy and Socialism. In 1997, she confirmed rumors that she was a lesbian in *Out* magazine. In 1998, she founded Critical Resistance, which was dedicated to the abolition of capital punishment and the prison system. Although she continued to assert that true liberation would require the establishment of socialism, she nevertheless supported the presidential candidacy of Barack Obama in 2008, and she declared that his election presented the opportunity for grassroots activism to move the country in a more progressive direction.

Davis has published a number of short books, articles, and pamphlets that express her opposition to racism, capitalism, and the criminal justice system. Her essay "Reflections on the Black Women's Role in the Community of Slaves," which appeared in *The Black Scholar* in 1971, is frequently credited with having initiated the field of black women's studies. Her revealing *Angela Davis: An Autobiography* (1974) is a valuable source for understanding the radical movements of the 1960's and 1970's. In *Blues Legacies and Black Feminism* (1998), Davis argues that female blues singers were proponents of "a working-class black feminism." Her other publications include *Violence Against Women and the Ongoing Challenge to Racism* (1992), *Resisting State Violence: Radicalism, Gender, and Race in U.S. Culture* (1996), and *Global Critical Race Feminism: An International Reader* (1999).

During the early 1970's, Davis became an icon for the New Left. During her sensational trial of 1972, she was idealized by left-wing radicals and vilified by conservatives and moderates. Following her acquittal, she gained recognition as a teacher and speaker. By the first decade of the twenty-first century, she had come to be generally viewed as a respected human-rights advocate, and her work with Critical Resistance helped to call attention to abuses within the criminal justice system.

Explanation and Analysis of the Document

Outlining the sociopolitical mechanisms underlying gender, race, sex, and class divisions and disparities, Davis's writings analyze a variety of cultural and artistic trends. "Political Prisoners, Prisons, and Black Liberation" typifies the kind of social analysis Davis pursued in her early activist days and in her long academic career.

Davis goes into more detail about the definition of a political prisoner, describing such a prisoner as one who boldly challenges "fundamental social wrongs fostered and reinforced by the state." She gives further historical examples, including that of Nat Turner, who led a slave rebellion in 1831 in Virginia and was caught, tried, and executed, in much the same way that John Brown was. Davis believes that the execution of these men was intended to "terrorize the anti-slavery movement in general" and to discourage abolitionist activity. In defending Turner against the charge of murder, she argues that his acts were little different from killings that resulted when colonial Americans took up arms against the British.

♦ Modern Civil Disobedience

Davis calls attention to modern civil disobedience, again stressing that the authorities work to subvert liberation movements. She discusses a 1970 incident in Los Angeles in which the Black Panthers took up arms to defend themselves from the police. A key point for her is that such people are demonized as pathological criminals, with little attention paid to their positive accomplishments. She states that self-defense is "twisted and distorted" by the authorities and "rendered synonymous with criminal aggression." The police, though, are exonerated as having committed "justifiable" acts of homicide. She calls these distortions "ideological acrobatics"; the purpose of criminalizing these acts is to discredit radical and revolutionary movements. The irony for her is that while the authorities do not acknowledge the political nature of their own actions, they nonetheless introduced Black Panther literature as evidence of criminal intent in a noted New York trial. Davis lays these distortions at the feet of President Nixon, Vice President Spiro Agnew, and California governor Ronald Reagan. In sum, Davis argues that the judicial and penal system is a tool used "in the state's fight to preserve the existing conditions of class domination, therefore racism, poverty and war."

Next, Davis alludes to an indictment that had been handed down in 1951 of W. E. B. Du Bois, a prominent black intellectual in the early part of the century. From 1949 to 1955, Du Bois was vice chairman of the Council on African Affairs, cited by the U.S. attorney general as a "subversive" organization. In 1950 he became the chairman of the Peace Information Center in New York City. During this period, fears of espionage and Communist influence abounded. The infamous hearings led by Wisconsin senator Joseph McCarthy were held to root out suspected Communists in the government and elsewhere. Du Bois's association with leftist groups made him suspect. In 1951 he was tried on the charge of failing to register as a foreign agent. Although he was acquitted, Du Bois remained in the eye of government agencies, and the State Department revoked his passport. Later, Du Bois officially joined the Communist Party and became a citizen of Ghana, where he died. The quotation is from his 1952 book, *In Battle for Peace*.

Davis sees Du Bois's realization as the beginning of a movement that has focused on political prisoners, particularly people of color. She sees a mass movement developing around political prisoners, who have become a "catalyst" for political action because they are able to expose the "oppressive structures of the penal system" and its ability to suppress social movements.

♦ The Prison System

Davis argues that the prison system is an "instrument of class domination" that focuses less on the alleged criminal act and more on the person who commits it. She argues that crime is a function of the unequal distribution of property and reflects social needs borne of poverty—that is, that crime is a challenge to capitalism. In building her argument, she naturally refers to the nineteenth-century philosopher Karl Marx and to Marxism, the strand of historical-philosophical thought that provided the ideological underpinnings of Communism. *Lumpenproletariat* (literally "rag proletariat") is the German word Marx used for those working-class people who would never achieve class consciousness (awareness of their own predicament) and who were therefore of little use in the struggle to overthrow capitalism. The Paris Commune was a working-class government that briefly assumed power in France in 1871. Davis here argues, contra some contemporary Marxists, that the "lumpen" can indeed be aroused and educated, as they were in Paris, and that they are capable of heroic action. She endorses the same kind of action on the part of Americans—especially blacks and other people of color—who could easily be dismissed as too poor and too marginal to take part in the revolutionary struggle. With the unemployment rate among black youth so high, it is little wonder that some turned to crime in order to survive. Hence the need for groups like the Black Panthers to organize these members of the lumpenproletariat.

Davis goes into some detail about the inequities of the prison system, noting, first, that not all prisoners have committed crimes and second, that prison terms meted out to black and brown inmates are disproportionately long. Imprisonment brings the inmate face to face with racism as an institutional phenomenon, leading more and more prisoners to recognize that they are, in fact, political prisoners. This growing awareness was reflected in such documents as the *Folsom Prisoners' Manifesto of Demands and Anti-Oppression Platform*, issued in conjunction with a nineteen-day inmate strike at the Folsom State Prison in California in 1970.

♦ Prison and Revolutionary Movements

Davis's tone sharpens when she refers to the "ruling circles" of America and their "repressive measures" and "fascist tactics" designed to curtail revolutionary movements, including the movement to end the war in Indochina (the Vietnam War). Herbert Marcuse, a German social and political theorist who had mentored Davis at Brandeis, was an opponent of capitalism, and a favorite writer among leftist revolutionaries. Specific instances of brutality at Soledad Prison are cited here, especially the men who were killed by a prison guard, the incident that sparked the Soledad Brothers case. She calls the Soledad Brothers "frame-up victims."

Davis moves beyond literal imprisonment to address "racist oppression ... on an infinite variety of levels." Blacks, she says, are imprisoned by an economic system that fails to provide jobs with decent pay. Unemployment in the ghettos is high. Unemployment among black youth is 30 percent. Schools are substandard, medical care is poor, and housing in dilapidated. Amid this poverty in places like Birmingham in Alabama, Harlem in New York City, and the Watts district of Los Angeles, the police are numerous and ever present in a "grotesque caricature" of the mission of serving and protecting. The police "encircle the community with a shield of violence." In this regard she refers to Franz Fanon, a mid-twentieth-century philosopher and revolutionary from Martinique whose work on colonial history, like that of Marcuse, was highly influential among leftists. Davis then goes into detail about how the judicial system abets the police as part of an "apparatus" that "summarily railroads black people into jails and prisons." All of this is part of black ghetto existence, causing deep hatred of the police.

♦ African American Resistance

In the final section Davis begins with the premise that "black people as a group have exhibited a greater potential for resistance than any other part of the population." She rails against the racism and exploitation perpetrated, in her view, by the Nixon administration—an oppression that extends not only to blacks but also to Chicanos (that is, Hispanics), Puerto Ricans, and the antiwar movement. Despite the resistance of authorities, "black people are rushing full speed ahead" toward an understanding of repression and racism and are seeking liberation through armed revolution.

"Fascist," in the leftist rhetoric of the 1960s, refers not merely to the right-wing ideology of Adolf Hitler's Germany and Benito Mussolini's Italy but to any kind of repression directed against the poor, minorities, women, and other groups. In what Davis sees as a Fascist climate, thousands of people are political prisoners, including the Harrisburg Eight. The Harrisburg Eight, later Seven, were a group of religiously motivated antiwar activists led by Philip Berrigan, a Catholic priest, who were alleged to have plotted bombings and kidnappings in protest against the Vietnam War. For Davis, another symptom of this Fascism is the Nixon administration's 1970 "Crime Bill" that gave the government, among other provisions, greater latitude to conduct wiretaps. These and other examples are evidence for Davis that revolutionaries must nip Fascism in the bud; she argues, too, that the mass of ordinary citizens have an interest in doing so, and one way they can take action is to take part in the struggle to abolish the prison system. In support of this view she quotes Georgi Dimitrov, the Bulgarian Communist leader who had been prosecuted by the Nazis in 1933. Davis concludes by arguing that the white worker has a vested interest in issues of racism and political imprisonment, for "the merciless proliferation of the power of monopoly capital may ultimately push him inexorably down the very same path of desperation."

Audience

Angela Davis was writing chiefly to supporters and like-minded people. However, her intended audience was wider than that. Using Marxist theories to comment upon her own incarceration as well as her view of the biased nature of the U.S. penal code, Davis calls attention to the racial, class, and gender disparities in the American legal system. Particularly toward the end of her essay, she includes whites in her audience by arguing, in effect, that oppression of blacks can create a political system in which whites are equally vulnerable. At the time of the essay's publication, Davis was widely regarded by the American public as a dangerous radical—yet another "revolutionary" from the turbulent 1960s. Passions have cooled with time, and Davis herself has slightly moderated her positions. Nevertheless, her early work, including "Political Prisoners, Prisons, and Black Liberation," has come to be regarded as an important window into a time of rapid social change in the United States.

Impact

The body of Angela Davis's writing has had a significant impact on both political and academic thought. Because her work spans over forty years and has evolved to incorporate a variety of issues, it has become increasingly important for those working on the sociopolitical analysis of class and race. Davis's work on critical race theory and the interconnections between race, gender, and class has influenced academics and activists since the 1960s. Since her earliest writings and her court case, which propelled her to the national spotlight, attitudes toward her work have shifted and softened. Although it was initially rejected by the mainstream as too radical, much of Davis's work is now recognized as foundational material by such prison abolition organizations as the Anarchist Black Cross, the Anarchist Prisoners' Legal Aid Network, Justice Now, Socialist Resistance, and the Prison Activist Resource Center.

Further Reading

♦ Articles

Bhavnani, Kum-Kum, and Angela Y. Davis. "Complexity, Activism, Optimism: An Interview with Angela Y. Davis." *Feminist Review* 31 (1989): 66–81.

Davis, Angela. "Women, Race and Class: An Activist Perspective." *Women's Studies Quarterly* 10, no. 4 (1982): 5–9.

♦ Books

Aptheker, Bettina. *The Morning Breaks: The Trial of Angela Davis.* 2nd ed. Ithaca, N.Y.: Cornell University Press, 1999.

Davis, Angela Y., ed. *If They Come in the Morning: Voices of Resistance.* New York: Third Press, 1971.

James, Joy. *Imprisoned Intellectuals: America's Political Prisoners Write on Life, Liberation, and Rebellion.* Lanham, Md.: Rowman & Littlefield, 2003.

New York Committee to Free Angela Davis. *A Political Biography of Angela Davis.* New York: New York Committee to Free Angela Davis, 1971.

Timothy, Mary. *Jury Woman: The Story of the Trial of Angela Y. Davis.* San Francisco: Glide Publications, 1975.

♦ Web Sites

"Interview: Angela Davis." PBS's Frontline Web site. http://www.pbs.org/wgbh/pages/frontline/shows/race/interviews/davis.html.

—Veronica C. Hendrick and Michael J. O'Neal

Essential Quotes

"But having been taught by bitter experience, we know that there is a glaring incongruity between democracy and the capitalist economy which is the source of our ills."

"Needless to say, the history of the Unites States has been marred from its inception by an enormous quantity of unjust laws, far too many expressly bolstering the oppression of black people."

"The offense of the political prisoner is political boldness, the persistent challenging—legally or extra-legally—of fundamental social wrongs fostered and reinforced by the state."

"The ideological acrobatics characteristic of official attempts to explain away the existence of the political prisoner do not end with the equation of the individual political act with the individual criminal act. The political act is defined as criminal in order to discredit radical and revolutionary movements."

"The prison is a key component of state's coercive apparatus, the overriding function of which is to ensure social control."

"The ruling circles of America are expanding and intensifying repressive measures designed to nip revolutionary movements in the bud as well as to curtail radical-democratic tendencies, such as the movement to end the war in Indochina."

"Black people are rushing full speed ahead towards an understanding of the circumstances that give rise to exaggerated forms of political repression and thus an overabundance of political prisoners."

Questions for Further Study

1. Compare this document with Eldridge Cleaver's "Education and Revolution." What similar views did the two authors express?

2. What is the fundamental basis for Davis's view that the prison system should be abolished?

3. Why do you think Angela Davis became an icon of black radicalism? What do you think was the attitude of mainstream Americans to Davis during the 1970s?

4. Summarize the influence of Marxist thought on Davis's views. Why did her Marxism render her a dangerous character in the 1970s in the view of many people?

5. Many revolutionaries of the 1960s and 1970s, including Davis and Eldridge Cleaver, later toned down their rhetoric and became somewhat more mainstream, or at least less radical, in their views. What do you think may have accounted for this change of heart?

"Political Prisoners, Prisons, and Black Liberation"

Text of speech.

Despite a long history of exalted appeals to man's inherent right to resistance, there has seldom been agreement on how to relate in practice to unjust immoral laws and the oppressive social order from which they emanate. The conservative, who does not dispute the validity of revolutions deeply buried in history, invokes visions of impending anarchy in order to legitimize his demand for absolute obedience. Law and order, with the major emphasis on order, is his watchword. The liberal articulates his sensitivity to certain of society's intolerable details, but will almost never prescribe methods of resistance that exceed the limits of legality—redress through electoral channels is the liberal's panacea.

In the heat of our pursuit of fundamental human rights, black people have been continually cautioned to be patient. We are advised that as long as we remain faithful to the existing democratic order, the glorious moment will eventually arrive when we will come into our own as full-fledged human beings.

But having been taught by bitter experience, we know that there is a glaring incongruity between democracy and the capitalist economy which is the source of our ills. Regardless of all rhetoric to the contrary, the people are not the ultimate matrix of the laws and the system which govern them—certainly not black people and other nationally oppressed people, but not even the mass of whites. The people do not exercise decisive control over the determining factors of their lives.

Officials' assertions that meaningful dissent is always welcome, provided it falls within the boundaries of legality, are frequently a smokescreen obscuring the invitation to acquiesce in oppression. Slavery may have been unrighteous, the constitutional precision for the enslavement of blacks may have been unjust, but conditions were not to be considered so bearable (especially since they were profitable to a small circle) as to justify escape and other acts proscribed by law. This was the import of the fugitive slave laws.

Needless to say, the history of the Unites States has been marred from its inception by an enormous quantity of unjust laws, far too many expressly bolstering the oppression of black people. Particularized reflections of existing social inequities, these laws have repeatedly born witness to the exploitative and racist core of the society itself. For blacks, Chicanos, for all nationally oppressed people, the problem of opposing unjust laws and the social conditions which nourish their growth, has always had immediate practical implications. Our very survival has frequently been a direct function of our skill in forging effective channels of resistance. In resisting we have been compelled to openly violate those laws which directly or indirectly buttress our oppression. But even containing our resistance within the orbit of legality, we have been labeled criminals and have been methodically persecuted by a racist legal apparatus.

Under the ruthless conditions of slavery, the underground railroad provided the framework for extra-legal anti-slavery activity pursued by vast numbers of people, both black and white. Its functioning was in flagrant violation of the fugitive slave law; those who were apprehended were subjected to severe penalties. Of the innumerable recorded attempts to rescue fugitive slaves from the clutches of slave catchers, one of the most striking is the case of Anthony Burns, a slave from Virginia, captured in Boston in 1853. A team of his supporters, in attempting to rescue him by force during the course of his trial, engaged the police in a fierce courtroom battle. During the gun fight, a prominent Abolitionist, Thomas Wentworth Higginson, was wounded. Although the rescuers were unsuccessful in their efforts, the impact of this incident "did more to crystallize Northern sentiment against slavery than any other except the exploit of John Brown, 'and this was the last time a fugitive slave was taken from Boston. It took twenty-two companies of state militia, four platoons of marines, a battalion of United States artillerymen, and the city's police force … to ensure the performance of this shameful act, the cost of which, the Federal government alone, came to forty thousand dollars.'"

Throughout the era of slavery, blacks, as well as progressive whites, repeatedly discovered that their commitment to the anti-slavery cause frequently entailed the overt violation of the laws of the land. Even as slavery faded away into a more subtle yet equally pernicious apparatus to dominate black people, "illegal" resistance was still on the agenda.

Document Text

After the Civil War, Black Codes, successors to the old Slave Codes, legalized convict labor, prohibited social intercourse between blacks and whites, gave white employers an excessive degree of control over the private lives of black workers, and generally codified racism and terror. Naturally, numerous individual as well as collective acts of resistance prevailed. On many occasions, blacks formed armed teams to protect themselves form white terrorists who were, in turn, protected by law enforcement agencies, if not actually identified with them.

By the second decade of the twentieth century, the mass movement, headed by Marcus Garvey, proclaimed in its Declaration of Rights that black people should not hesitate to disobey all discriminatory laws. Moreover, the Declaration announced, they should utilize all means available to them, legal or illegal, to defend themselves from legalized terror as well as Ku Klux Klan violence. During the era of intense activity around civil rights issues, systematic disobedience of oppressive laws was a primary tactic. The sit-ins were organized transgressions of racist legislation.

All these historical instances involving the overt violation of the laws of the land converge around an unmistakable common denominator. At stake has been the collective welfare and survival of a people. There is a distinct and qualitative difference between one breaking a law for one's own individual self-interest and violating it in the interests of a class of people whose oppression is expressed either directly or indirectly through that particular law. The former might be called criminal (though in many instances he is a victim), but the latter, as a reformist or revolutionary, is interested in universal social change. Captured, he or she is a political prisoner.

The political prisoner's words or deed have in one form or another embodied political protests against the established order and have consequently brought him into acute conflict with the state. In light of the political content of his act, the "crime" (which may or may not have been committed) assumes a minor importance. In this country, however, where the special category of political prisoners is not officially acknowledged, the political prisoner inevitably stands trial for a specific criminal offense, not for a political act. Often the so-called crime does not even have a nominal existence. As in the 1914 murder frame-up of the IWW organizer, Joe Hill, it is a blatant fabrication, a mere excuse for silencing a militant crusader against oppression. In all instances, however, the political prisoner has violated the unwritten law which prohibits disturbances and upheavals in the status quo of exploitation and racism. This unwritten law has been contested by actually and explicitly breaking a law or by utilizing constitutionally protected channels to educate, agitate, and organize masses to resist.

A deep-seated ambivalence has always characterized the official response to the political prisoner. Charged and tried for the criminal act, his guilt is always political in nature. This ambivalence is perhaps best captured by Judge Webster Thayer's comment upon sentencing Bartolomeo Vanzetti to fifteen years for an attempted payroll robbery: "This man, although he may not have actually committed the crime attributed to him, is nevertheless morally culpable, because he is an enemy of our existing institutions." (The very same judge incidentally, sentences Sacco and Vanzetti to death for a robbery and murder of which they were manifestly innocent). It is not surprising that Nazi Germany's foremost constitutional lawyer, Carl Schmitt, advanced the theory which generalized thus a priori culpability. A thief, for example, was not necessarily one who had committed an overt act of theft, but rather one whose character renders him a thief (*wer nach seinem wesen win Dieb ist*). [President Richard] Nixon's and [FBI Director] J. Edgar Hoover's pronouncements lead one to believe that they would readily accept Schmitt's fascist legal theory. Anyone who seeks to overthrow oppressive institutions, whether or not he has engaged in an overt act, is a priori a criminal who must be buried away in one of America's dungeons.

Even in all of Martin Luther King's numerous arrests, he was not so much charged with the nominal crimes of trespassing, and disturbance of the peace, as with being an enemy of the southern society, an inveterate foe of racism. When Robert Williams was accused of kidnapping, this charge never managed to conceal his real offense—the advocacy of black people's incontestable right to bear arms in their own defense.

The offense of the political prisoner is political boldness, the persistent challenging—legally or extra-legally—of fundamental social wrongs fostered and reinforced by the state. The political prisoner has opposed unjust laws and exploitative, racist social conditions in general, with the ultimate aim of transforming these laws and this society into an order harmonious with the material and spiritual needs and interests of the vast majority of its members.

Nat Turner and John Brown were political prisoners in their time. The acts for which they were charged and subsequently hanged were the practical extensions of their profound commitment to the abolition of slavery. They fearlessly bore the responsibility for their actions. The significance of their executions and the accompanying widespread repression did not lie so much in the fact that they were being punished for specific crimes, nor even in the effort to use their punishment as an implicit threat to deter others from similar armed acts of resistance. These executions, and the surrounding repression of slaves, were intended to terrorize the anti-slavery movement in general; to discourage and diminish both legal and illegal forms of abolitionist activity. As usual, the effect of repression was miscalculated and in both instances, anti-slavery activity was accelerated and intensified as a result.

Nat Turner and John Brown can be viewed as examples of the political prisoner who has actually committed an act which is defined by the state as "criminal". They killed and were consequently tried for murder. But did they commit murder? This raises the question of whether American revolutionaries had *murdered* the British in their struggle for liberation. Nat Turner and his followers killed some sixty-five white people, yet shortly before the revolt had begun, Nat is reputed to have said to the other rebelling slaves: "Remember that ours is not war for robbery nor to satisfy our passions, it is a *struggle for freedom.* Ours must be deeds and not words."

The very institutions which condemned Nat Turner and reduced his struggle for freedom to a simpler criminal case of murder, owed their existence to the decision, made a half-century earlier, to take up arms against the British oppressor.

The battle for the liquidation of slavery had no legitimate existence in the eyes of the government and therefore the special quality of deeds carried out in the interests of freedom was deliberately ignored. There were no political prisoners, there were only criminals; just as the movement out of which these deeds flowed was largely considered criminal.

Likewise, the significance of activities which are pursued in the interests of liberation today is minimized not so much because officials are unable to see the collective surge against oppression, but because they have consciously set out to subvert such movements. In the Spring of 1970, Los Angeles Panthers took up arms to defend themselves from an assault initiated by the local police force on their office and on their persons. They were charged with criminal assault. If one believed the official propaganda, they were bandits and rogues who pathologically found pleasure in attacking policemen. It was not mentioned that their community activities—educational work, services such as free breakfast and free medical programs—which had legitimized them in the black community, were the immediate reason for which the wrath of the police had fallen upon them. In defending themselves from the attack waged by some 600 policemen (there were only eleven Panthers in the office) they were defending not only their lives, but even more important their accomplishments in the black community surrounding them, and in the broader thrust for black liberation. Whenever blacks in struggle have recourse to self-defense, particular armed self-defense, it is twisted and distorted on official levels and ultimately rendered synonymous with criminal aggression. On the other hand, when policemen are clearly indulging in acts of criminal aggression, officially they are defending themselves through "justifiable assault" or "justifiable homicide".

The ideological acrobatics characteristic of official attempts to explain away the existence of the political prisoner do not end with the equation of the individual political act with the individual criminal act. The political act is defined as criminal in order to discredit radical and revolutionary movements. A political event is reduced to a criminal event in order to affirm the absolute invulnerability of the existing order. In a revealing contradiction, the court resisted the description of the New York Panther 21 trial as "political", yet the prosecutor entered as evidence of criminal intent, literature which represented, so he purported, the political ideology of the Black Panther Party.

The legal apparatus designates the black liberation fighter a criminal, prompting Nixon, [Vice President Spiro] Agnew, [California Governor Ronald] Reagan et al. to process to mystify with their demagogy millions of Americans whose senses have been dulled and whose critical powers have been eroded by the continual onslaught of racist ideology.

As the black liberation movement and other progressive struggles increase in magnitude and intensity, the judicial system and its extension, the penal system, consequently become key weapons in the state's fight to preserve the existing conditions of class domination, therefore racism, poverty and war.

In 1951, W.E.B. Du Bois, as Chairman of the Peace Information Center, was indicted by the federal government for "failure to register as an agent of a foreign principal." In assessing this ordeal, which occurred in the ninth decade of his life, he turned his attention to the inhabitants of the nation's jails and prisons:

> What turns me cold in all this experience is the certainty that thousands of innocent victims are in jail today because they had neither money nor friends to help them. The eyes of the world were on our trial despite the desperate efforts of press and radio to suppress the facts and cloud the real issues; the courage and money of friends and of strangers who dared stand for a principle freed me; but God only knows how many who were as innocent as I and my colleagues are today in hell. They daily stagger out of prison doors embittered, vengeful, hopeless, ruined. And of this army of the wronged, the proportion of Negroes is frightful. We protect and defend sensational cases where Negroes are involved. But the great mass of arrested or accused black folk have no defense. There is desperate need of nationwide organizations to oppose this national racket of railroading to jails and chain gangs the poor, friendless and black.

Almost two decades passed before the realization attained by Du Bois on the occasion of his own encounter with the judicial system achieved extensive acceptance. A number of factors have combined to transform the penal system into a prominent terrain of struggle, both for the captives inside and the masses outside. The impact of large numbers of political prisoners both on prison populations and on the mass movement has been decisive. The vast majority of political prisoners have not allowed the fact of imprisonment to curtail their educational, agitational, and organizing activities, which they continue behind prison walls. And in the course of developing mass movements around political prisoners, a great deal of attention has inevitably been focused on the institutions in which they are imprisoned. Furthermore the political receptivity of prisoners—especially black and brown captives—has been increased and sharpened by the surge of aggressive political activity rising out of black, Chicano, and other oppressed communities. Finally, a major catalyst for intensified political action in and around prisons has emerged out of the transformation of convicts, originally found guilty of criminal offenses, into exemplary political militants. Their patient educational efforts in the realm of exposing the specific oppressive structures of the penal system in their relation to the larger oppression of the social system have had a profound effect on their fellow captives.

The prison is a key component of state's coercive apparatus, the overriding function of which is to ensure social control. The etymology of the term "penitentiary" furnishes a clue to the controlling idea behind the "prison system" at its inception.

The penitentiary was projected as the locale for doing penitence for an offense against society, the physical and spiritual purging of proclivities to challenge rules and regulations which command total obedience. While cloaking itself with the bourgeois aura of universality—imprisonment was supposed to cut across all class lines, as crimes were to be defined by the act, not the perpetrator—the prison has actually operated as an instrument of class domination, a means of prohibiting the have-nots from encroaching upon the haves.

The occurrence of crime is inevitable in a society in which wealth is unequally distributed, as one of the constant reminders that society's productive forces are being channeled in the wrong direction. The majority of criminal offenses bear a direct relationship to property. Contained in the very concept of property, crimes are profound but suppressed social needs which express themselves in anti-social modes of action. Spontaneously produced by a capitalist organization of society, this type of crime is at once a protest against society and a desire to partake of its exploitative content. It challenges the symptoms of capitalism, but not its essence.

Some Marxists in recent years have tended to banish "criminals" and the lumpenproletariat as a whole from the arena of revolutionary struggle. Apart from the absence of any link binding the criminal to the means of production, underlying this exclusion has been the assumption that individuals who have recourse to anti-social acts are incapable of developing the discipline and collective orientation required by revolutionary struggle.

With the declassed character of lumpenproletarians in mind, Marx had stated that they are as capable of "the most heroic deeds and the most exalted sacrifices, as of the basest banditry and the dirtiest corruption." He emphasized the fact that the provisional government's mobile guards under the Paris Commune—some 24,000 troops—were largely formed out of young lumpenproletarians from fifteen to twenty years of age. Too many Marxists have been inclined to overvalue the second part of Marx's observation —that the lumpenproletariat is capable of the basest banditry and the dirtiest corruption — while minimizing or indeed totally disregarding his first remark, applauding the lumpen for their heroic deeds and exalted sacrifices.

Especially today when so many black, Chicano, and Puerto Rican men and women are jobless as a consequence of the internal dynamic of the capitalist system, the role of the unemployed, which includes the lumpenproletariat in revolutionary struggle, must be given serious thought. Increased unemployment, particularly for the nationally oppressed, will continue to be an inevitable by-product of technological development. At least 30 percent of black youth are presently without jobs. In the context of class exploitation and national oppression it should be clear that numerous individuals are compelled to resort to criminal acts, not as a result of conscious choice—implying other alternatives—but because society has objectively reduced their possibilities of subsistence and survival to this level. This recognition should signal the urgent need to organize the unemployed and lumpenproletariat, as indeed the Black Panther Party as well as activists in prison have already begun to do.

In evaluating the susceptibility of the black and brown unemployed to organizing efforts, the peculiar historical features of the US, specifically racism and national oppression, must be taken into account. There already exists in the black and brown communities, the lumpenproletariat included, a long tradition of collective resistance to national oppression.

Moreover, in assessing the revolutionary potential of prisoners in America as a group, it should be borne in mind that not all prisoners have actually committed crimes. The built-in racism of the judicial system expresses itself, as Du Bois has suggested, in the railroading of countless innocent blacks and other national minorities into the country's coercive institutions.

One must also appreciate the effects of disproportionately long prison terms on black and brown inmates. The typical criminal mentality sees imprisonment as a calculated risk for a particular criminal act. One's prison term is more or less rationally predictable. The function of racism in the judicial-penal complex is to shatter that predictability. The black burglar, anticipating a two-to four-year term, may end up doing ten to fifteen years, while the white burglar leaves after two years.

Within the contained, coercive universe of the prison, the captive is confronted with the realities of racism, not simply as individual acts dictated by attitudinal bias; rather he is compelled to come to grips with racism as an institutional phenomenon collectively experienced by the victims. The disproportionate representation of the black and brown communities, the manifest racism of parole boards, the intense brutality inherent in the relationship between prison guards and black and brown inmates—all this and more causes the prisoner to be confronted daily, hourly, with the concentrated systematic existence of racism.

For the innocent prisoner, the process of radicalization should come easy; for the "guilty" victim, the insight into the nature of racism as it manifests itself in the judicial-penal complex can lead to a questioning of his own past criminal activity and a re-evaluation of the methods he has used to survive in a racist and exploitative society. Needless to say, this process is not automatic, it does not occur spontaneously. The persistent educational work carried out by the prison's political activists plays a key role in developing the political potential of captive men and women.

Prisoners—especially blacks, Chicanos and Puerto Ricans—are increasingly advancing the proposition that they are *political* prisoners. They contend that they are political prisoners in the sense that they are largely the victims of an oppressive politico-economic order, swiftly becoming conscious of the causes underlying their victimization. The *Folsom Prisoners' Manifesto of Demands and Anti-Oppression Platform* attests to a lucid understanding of the structures of oppression within the prison—structures which contradict even the avowed function of the penal institution: "The program we are submitted to, under the ridiculous title of rehabilitation, is relative to the ancient stupidity of pouring water on the drowning man, in as much as we are treated for our hostilities by our program administrators with their hostility for medication." The *Manifesto* also reflects an awareness that the severe social crisis taking place in this country, predicated in part on the ever-increasing mass consciousness of deepening social contradictions, is forcing the political function of the prisons to surface in all its brutality. Their contention that prisons are being transformed into the "fascist concentration camps of modern America," should not be taken lightly, although it would be erroneous as well as defeatist in a practical sense, to maintain that fascism has irremediably established itself.

The point is this, and this is the truth which is apparent in the Manifesto: the ruling circles of America are expanding and intensifying repressive measures designed to nip revolutionary movements in the bud as well as to curtail radical-democratic tendencies, such as the movement to end the war in Indochina. The government is not hesitating to utilize an entire network of fascist tactics, including the monitoring of congressman's telephone calls, a system of "preventive fascism", as Marcuse has termed it, in which the role of the judicial-penal systems looms large. The sharp edge of political repression, cutting through the heightened militancy of the masses, and bringing growing numbers of activists behind prison walls, must necessarily pour over into the contained world of the prison where it understandably acquires far more ruthless forms.

It is a relatively easy matter to persecute the captive whose life is already dominated by a network of authoritarian mechanisms. This is especially facilitated by the indeterminate sentence policies of many states, for politically conscious prisoners will incur inordinately long sentences on the original conviction. According to Louis S. Nelson, warden of the San Quentin Prison, "if the prisons of California become known as schools for violent revolution, the Adult Authority would be remiss in their duty not to keep the inmates longer" (*San Francisco Chronicle*, May 2, 1971). Where this is deemed inadequate, authorities have recourse to the whole spectrum of brutal corporal punishment, including out and out murder. At San Quentin, Fred Billingslea was teargassed to death in February 1970. W. L. Nolen, Alvin Miller, and Cleveland Edwards were assassinated by a prison guard in January 1970, at Soledad Prison. Unusual and inexplicable "suicides" have occurred with incredible regularity in jails and prisons throughout the country.

It should be self-evident that the frame-up becomes a powerful weapon within the spectrum of prison repression, particularly because of the availability of informers, the broken prisoners who will do anything for a price. The Soledad Brothers and the Soledad Three are leading examples of frame-up victims. Both cases involve militant activists who have been charged with killing Soledad prison guards. In both cases, widespread support has been kindled within the California prison system. They have served as occasions to link the immediate needs of the black community with a forceful fight to break the fascist stronghold in the prisons and therefore to abolish the prison system in its present form.

Racist oppression invades the lives of black people on an infinite variety of levels. Blacks are imprisoned in a world where our labor and toil hardly allow us to eke out a decent existence, if we are able to find jobs at all. When the economy begins to falter, we are forever the first victims, always the most deeply wounded. When the economy is on its feet, we continue to live in a depressed state. Unemployment is generally twice as high in the ghettos as it is in the country as a whole and even higher among black women and youth. The unemployment rate among black youth has presently skyrocketed to 30 percent. If one-third of America's white youths were without a means of livelihood, we would either be in the thick of revolution or else under the iron rule of fascism. Substandard schools, medical care hardly fit for animals, over-priced, dilapidated housing, a welfare system based on a policy of skimpy concessions, designed to degrade and divide (and even this may soon be canceled)—this is only the beginning of the list of props in the overall scenery of oppression which, for the mass of blacks, is the universe.

In black communities, wherever they are located, there exists an ever-present reminder that our universe must remain stable in its drabness, its poverty, its brutality. From Birmingham to Harlem to Watts, black ghettos are occupied, patrolled and often attacked by massive deployments of police. The police, domestic caretakers of violence, are the oppressor's emissaries, charged with the task of containing us within the boundaries of our oppression.

The announced function of the police, "to protect and serve the people," becomes the grotesque caricature of protecting and preserving the interests of our oppressors and serving us nothing but injustice. They are there to intimidate blacks, to persuade us with their violence that we are powerless to alter the conditions of our lives. Arrests are frequently based on whims. Bullets from their guns murder human beings with little or no pretext, aside from the universal intimidation they are charged with carrying out. Protection for drug-pushers, and Mafia-style exploiters, support for the most reactionary ideological elements of the black community (especially those who cry out for more police), are among the many functions of forces of law and order. They encircle the community with a shield of violence, too often forcing the natural aggression of the black community inwards. Fanon's analysis of the role of colonial police is an appropriate description of the function of the police in America's ghettos.

It goes without saying that the police would be unable to set into motion their racist machinery were they not sanctioned and supported by the judicial system. The courts not only consistently abstain from prosecuting criminal behavior on the part of the police, but they convict, on the basis of biased police testimony, countless black men and women. Court-appointed attorneys, acting in the twisted interests of overcrowded courts, convince 85 percent of the defendants to plead guilty. Even the manifestly innocent are advised to cop a plea so that the lengthy and expensive process of jury trials is avoided. This is the structure of the apparatus which summarily railroads black people into jails and prisons. (During my imprisonment in the New York Women's House of Detention, I encountered numerous cases involving innocent black women who had been advised to plead guilty. One sister had entered her white landlord's apartment for the purpose of paying rent. He attempted to rape her and in the course of the ensuing struggle, a lit candle toppled over, burning a tablecloth. The landlord ordered her arrested for arson. Following the advice of her court-appointed attorney, she entered a guilty plea, having been deceived by the attorney's insistence that the court would be more lenient. The sister was sentenced to three years.)

The vicious circle linking poverty, police courts, and prison is an integral element of ghetto existence. Unlike the mass of whites, the path which leads to jails and prisons is deeply rooted in the imposed patterns of black existence. For this very reason, an almost instinctive affinity binds the mass of black people to the political prisoners. The vast majority of blacks harbor a deep hatred of the police and are not deluded by official proclamations of justice through the courts.

For the black individual, contact with the law-enforcement-judicial-penal network, directly or through relatives and friends, is inevitable because he or she is black. For the activist become political prisoner, the contact has occurred because he has lodged a protest, in one form or another, against the conditions which nail blacks to this orbit of oppression.

Historically, black people as a group have exhibited a greater potential for resistance than any other part of the population. The iron-clad rule over our communities, the institutional practice of genocide, the ideology of racism have performed a strictly political as well as an economic function. The capitalists have not only extracted super profits from the underpaid labor of over 15 percent of the American population with the aid of a superstructure of terror. This terror and more subtle forms of racism have further served to thwart the flowering of a resistance—even a revolution that would spread to the working class as a whole.

In the interests of the capitalist class, the consent to racism and terror has been demagogically elicited from the white population, workers included, in order to more efficiently stave off resistance. Today, Nixon, [Attorney General John] Mitchell and J. Edgar Hoover are desperately attempting to persuade the population that dissidents, particularly blacks, Chicanos, Puerto Ricans, must be punished for being members of revolutionary organizations; for advocating the overthrow of the government; for agitating and educating in the streets and behind prison walls. The political function of racist domination is surfacing with accelerated intensity. Whites who have professed their solidarity with the black liberation movement and have moved in a distinctly revolutionary direction find themselves targets of the same repression. Even the anti-war movement, rapidly exhibiting an anti-imperialist consciousness, is falling victim to government repression.

Black people are rushing full speed ahead towards an understanding of the circumstances that give rise to exaggerated forms of political repression and thus an overabundance of political prisoners. This understanding is being forged out of the raw material of their own immediate experiences with racism. Hence, the black masses are growing conscious of their responsibility to defend those who are being persecuted for attempting to bring about the alleviation of the most injurious immediate problems facing black communities and ultimately to bring about total liberation through armed revolution, if it must come to this.

The black liberation movement is presently at a critical juncture. Fascist methods of repression threaten to physically decapitate and obliterate the movement. More subtle, yet no less dangerous ideological tendencies from within threaten to isolate the black movement and diminish its revolutionary impact. Both menaces must be counteracted in order to ensure our survival. Revolutionary blacks must spearhead and provide leadership for a broad antifascist movement.

Fascism is a process, its growth and development are cancerous in nature. While today, the threat of fascism may be primarily restricted to the use of the law-enforcement-judicial-penal apparatus to arrest the overt and latent revolutionary trends among nationally oppressed people, tomorrow it may attack the working class *en masse* and eventually even moderate democrats. Even in this period, however, the cancer has already commenced to spread. In addition to the prison army of thousands and thousands of nameless Third World victims of political revenge, there are increasing numbers of white political prisoners—draft resisters, anti-war activists such as the Harrisburg Eight, men and women who have involved themselves on all levels of revolutionary activity.

Among the further symptoms of the fascist threat are official efforts to curtail the power of organized labor, such as the attack on the manifestly conservative construction workers and the trends towards reduced welfare aid. Moreover, court decisions and repressive legislation augmenting police powers—such as the Washington no-knock law, permitting police to enter private dwellings without warning, and Nixon's "Crime Bill" in general—can eventually be used against any citizen. Indeed congressmen are already protesting the use of police-state wiretapping to survey their activities. The fascist content of the ruthless aggression in Indo-China should be self-evident.

One of the fundamental historical lessons to be learned from past failures to prevent the rise of fascism is the decisive and indispensable character of the fight against fascism in its incipient phases. Once allowed to conquer ground, its growth is facilitated in geometric proportion. Although the most unbridled expressions of the fascist menace are still tied to the racist domination of blacks, Chicanos, Puerto Ricans, Indians, it lurks under the surface wherever there is potential resistance to the power of monopoly capital, the parasitic interests which control this society. Potentially it can profoundly worsen the conditions of existence for the average American citizen. Consequently, the masses of people in this country have a real, direct, and material stake in the struggle to free political prisoners, the struggle to abolish the prison system in its present form, the struggle against all dimensions of racism.

No one should fail to take heed of Georgi Dimitrov's warning: "Whoever does not fight the growth of fascism at these preparatory stages is not in a position to prevent the victory of fascism, but, on the contrary, facilitates that victory" (Report to the VIIth Congress of the Communist International, 1935). The only effective guarantee against the victory of fascism is an indivisible mass movement which refuses to conduct business as usual as long as repression rages on. It is only natural that blacks and other Third World peoples must lead this movement, for we are the first and most deeply injured victims of fascism. But it must embrace all potential victims and most important, all working-class people, for the key to the triumph of fascism is its ideological victory over the entire working class. Given the eruption of a severe economic crisis, the door to such an ideological victory can be opened by the active approval or passive toleration of racism. It is essential that white workers become conscious that historically through their acquiescence in the capitalist-inspired oppression of blacks they have only rendered themselves more vulnerable to attack.

The pivotal struggle which must be waged in the ranks of the working class is consequently the open, unreserved battle against entrenched racism. The white worker must become conscious of the threads which bind him to a James Johnson, a black auto worker, member of UAW, and a political prisoner presently facing charges for the killings of two foremen and a job setter. The merciless proliferation of the power of monopoly capital may ultimately push him inexorably down the very same path of desperation. No potential victim [of the fascist terror] should be without the knowledge that the greatest menace to racism and fascism is unity!

Marin County Jail
May, 1971

Glossary

Bartolomeo Vanzetti: a reference to a notorious episode in which two Italian immigrants, Vanzetti and Ferdinando Nicola Sacco, were accused of murdering two men during an armed robbery in Massachusetts and executed in 1927

Birmingham: a city in Alabama

Chicanos: the term commonly used at the time for Hispanics

Fanon: Franz Fanon, a philosopher and revolutionary from Martinique whose work on colonial history was highly influential among Leftists

Folsom: Folsom State Prison in California

fugitive slave laws: laws passed in 1793 and 1850 dealing with the recapture of escaped slaves

Georgi Dimitrov: a Bulgarian Communist leader persecuted by the Nazis during World War II

Harlem: a largely black neighborhood in the New York City borough of Manhattan

Harrisburg Eight: later the Harrisburg Seven, a group of religiously motivated activists alleged to have plotted kidnappings and bombings to protest the Vietnam War

IWW: Industrial Workers of the World (the "Wobblies"), a radical labor organization that espoused ideals that many regarded as Communist

John Brown: the abolitionist leader of an abortive raid on the federal arsenal at Harpers Ferry, Virginia, in 1859

Ku Klux Klan: a white supremacist group that emerged after the Civil War

lumpenproletariat: literally "rag proletariat," the German word Marx used for working-class people who would never become aware of their own predicament

Marcus Garvey: a black nationalist and founder of the Universal Negro Improvement Association

Marcuse: Herbert Marcuse, a German social and political theorist

Marxists: followers of Karl Marx, the nineteenth-century German historian and political theorist whose theories formed the basis of Communism

Nat Turner: the leader of a Virginia slave revolt in 1831

New York acquitted Panther 21 trial: a widely publicized 1971 trial in which twenty-one Black Panthers were on conspiracy charges

Panthers: the Black Panther Party, a militant black civil rights group

Paris Commune: a working-class government that briefly assumed power in France in 1871

Robert Williams: a North Carolina civil rights activist accused of kidnapping after offering refuge to a white couple passing through town during a racial disturbance

Soledad Brothers: three African American inmates in California's Soledad Prison charged with murdering a prison guard

UAW: the United Auto Workers labor union

underground railroad: the system of routes, guides, and safe houses that enabled escaped slaves to flee to the North in the years before the Civil War

W. E. B. Du Bois: a prominent black intellectual and author; the quote is from his 1952 book, *In Battle for Peace*.

war in Indochina: the Vietnam War

Watts: a largely black neighborhood of Los Angeles

Robinson and his son David (then age 11) are interviewed during the March on Washington, August 28, 1963. By U.S. Information Agency. Press and Publications Service. (ca. 1953 - ca. 1978), [Public Domain], via Wikimedia Commons.

Jackie Robinson: *I Never Had It Made*

1972

"Getting a hero's welcome in September made me remember how bad the beginning of my first season with the Dodgers had been."

Overview

I Never Had It Made is the 1972 autobiography of baseball legend Jackie Robinson, the man who integrated Major League Baseball (MLB). The historic role of Robinson in the integration of professional athletics and more broadly in the U.S. civil rights movement cannot be overestimated.

It has been said that the major leagues were slightly ahead of the curve in expanding the rights of all players based on talent rather than skin color.

Robinson's autobiography is a significant document because it details his life both on and off the field. As a role model for all African Americans, he understood that he would have to surpass white athletes in order to earn the respect of his teammates, opposing players, and the nation's sports fans. Robinson was acutely aware of the revolutionary task ahead of him: He literally stepped up to the plate to try to make the United States a land of opportunity for everyone. Robinson's story resonates even in the twenty-first century, especially as he reminds us that it was not so long ago that a person of color could be openly jeered at and humiliated on the public stage—with little fear of retribution for the perpetrators. *I Never Had It Made* stands as one of the first autobiographies by a sports legend to go beyond the playing field and out into the larger world.

Context

For much of its history, MLB did not permit African American players in its ranks. There were a few scattered examples of African American or Hispanic players in the nineteenth century, including Moses "Fleetwood" Walker and Bud Fowler, but by the 1890s an unwritten rule forbade people of color from participating in Organized Baseball. In response, black ballplayers formed their own professional clubs, playing each other as well as white semiprofessional teams. Talented stars like the famous shortstop John Henry Lloyd (often called the black Honus Wagner) were virtually unknown in the larger white community but continued to sharpen their skills on all-black teams. There were a few aborted attempts to hire African American players, including one by John McGraw of the Baltimore Orioles, who in 1901 attempted to pass off his new player, Chief Charlie Tokohama, as a full-blooded Native American. In reality, the chief was an African American player, Charlie Grant, who played with the Page Fence Giants, an independent team from Adrian, Michigan. Several fans recognized Grant, and he was forced off the team. Racial bias thus closed off a large pool of potential players for Organized Baseball, which was expanding in the early twentieth century.

Despite the deliberate segregation promulgated by Organized Baseball, teams like the Cuban Giants and the Harrisburg Giants drew crowds among urban black communities. Besides playing on organized teams, African Americans played baseball on sandlots and in other urban spaces just as their white counterparts did. Barnstorming tours were particularly popular: Black teams would travel from town to town, presenting a dazzling display of athletic ability and showmanship to attract people to the game. Colorful costumes and exuberant antics were all a part of the show. Often, the players engaged in horseplay and clowning during the game much like the later Harlem Globetrotters basketball team. Barnstormers brought baseball to smaller communities, which normally did not have access to professional athletic talent.

While there were several attempts to form African American professional leagues, none lasted more than a season, until 1920. That year, Andrew "Rube" Foster, a pitcher who also managed the Leland Giants and later was the main booking agent for black midwestern teams, organized the first black professional league, the National Negro League

(NNL). Eight teams comprised the original NNL: the Chicago American Giants, the Chicago Giants, the Cuban Stars, the Dayton Marcos, the Detroit Stars, the Indianapolis ABCs, the Kansas City Monarchs, and the St. Louis Giants. The NNL constantly struggled to survive. Teams came and went, although the Monarchs and the Chicago American Giants were constants.

NNL teams played about sixty to eighty games a year with each other, but they also played other teams, including white semiprofessional teams on their open dates. In 1923 a second Negro League, the Eastern Colored League, began play. This league was composed of teams from the East Coast, including the Hilldale (Philadelphia) Club, the Cuban Stars East, the Royal Giants, the Bacharach (New York) Giants, the Lincoln Giants, and the Baltimore Black Sox. The two leagues faced off in their own World Series. This lasted for four years, from 1923 to 1927. The Eastern Colored League folded shortly thereafter.

With the onset of the Great Depression, the NNL—as well as white Organized Baseball—faced serious difficulties. In 1930, following the death of Rube Foster, the NNL disbanded; three years later it was reborn under the leadership of William A. "Gus" Greenlee. Owner of the Pittsburgh Crawfords, Greenlee had a rather checkered career as a fight promoter, bootlegger, and speakeasy owner—not to mention operator of a successful numbers racket. Greenlee took over ownership of the Crawfords to provide himself with a convenient shelter for his illegal activities. One of his best decisions was to hire the inimitable black pitcher Leroy "Satchel" Paige in 1931.

The NNL was followed in 1937 by another new league, the Negro American League (NAL), which was organized by H. G. Hall, president of the Chicago American Giants. With the birth of the NAL, the NNL soon became a league of eastern teams, while the NAL franchises were mostly in the Midwest and South. The NAL, which hung on until 1960, absorbed some of the NNL teams after the latter's demise in 1948.

The Negro Leagues attracted thousands of fans throughout the nation, thanks in part to the rising incomes of a growing African American middle class. African Americans were segregated in their own venues, which actually added to the popularity of the Negro Leagues. The high quality of play further increased the fan base, even during the hard years of the Great Depression. It was only a matter of time, however, before Organized Baseball would finally erase the color line, making the Negro Leagues obsolete.

There were earlier rumblings among sportswriters about the MLB's shortsightedness in not tapping black athletic talent for its teams. The death in 1944 of the longtime MLB commissioner Kenesaw Mountain Landis, who was given the job of cleaning up the game following the infamous "Black Sox" scandal of 1919 (in which eight members of the Chicago White Sox, including "Shoeless" Joe Jackson, were accused of throwing the 1919 World Series, to be acquitted but banned from the league) gave hope to those who wanted to integrate the game. Landis's replacement as commissioner, A. P. "Happy" Chandler, both advocated and pursued the notion of finally ending segregation. Besides the inherent racism, opponents of integration feared financial loss, especially in the South, where most of the teams migrated for spring training. Those who promoted integration talked about the contributions African Americans had made during World War II, putting their lives on the line for their country. It would take the courage of one man—Branch Rickey—to finally erase the color line in American baseball.

The Ohio-born Rickey, owner of the Brooklyn Dodgers, was determined to build his National League team into a winner. He recognized that one way to accomplish this was to go after the unmined talent in the Negro Leagues. During World War II, his staff scouted the Negro Leagues to find a suitable player to integrate professional baseball as a member of the Brooklyn Dodgers. Jackie Robinson of the Kansas City Monarchs had the right combination of talent, maturity, and cool headedness to become the first black player in Organized Baseball. Robinson was signed in 1946, beginning his career with the Dodgers' farm team, the Montreal Royals. On April 15, 1947, Robinson played his first game as a Dodger at Ebbets Field in Brooklyn. Robinson's success in the majors—not to mention the fact that his very presence increased attendance—led to the signing of other black ballplayers to MLB contracts. Larry Doby was signed in 1947 by the Cleveland Indians, thus breaking the race barrier in the American League. The following season, the Indians hired the legendary pitcher Satchel Paige.

The ending of segregation in MLB foreshadowed the burgeoning civil rights movement of the 1950s. Indeed, the momentous debut of Jackie Robinson in a Dodger uniform coincided with President Harry S. Truman's Executive Order 9981 desegregating the U.S. armed forces in 1948. Although Robinson's road in the MLB was anything but smooth, his bold strike for equality and perseverance in the face of opposition changed the sport forever.

About the Author

The grandson of slaves, Jack Roosevelt Robinson was born in Cairo, Georgia, on January 31, 1919. His parents, Mallie and Jerry Robinson, were both sharecroppers. Jackie Robinson was the youngest of five children. Six months following Robinson's birth, his father abandoned the family, running off with a neighbor's wife. Mallie Robinson decided to sell everything she could and move her family to California, where she had a brother. She worked hard as a laundress, trying to support her young family. As an adult, Robinson expressed his admiration for the courage and tenacity of his mother in keeping the family together through rough times. Even as a youth, Robinson tried to help support the family with a paper route and other odd jobs.

Looking back on his youth, Robinson noted that he fell in with a rough crowd and might have become a juvenile delinquent if not for the influence of two men: Carl

Anderson and the Reverend Karl Downs. Anderson, an auto mechanic at a shop near Robinson's home, pointed out that should Robinson persist with his gang activity, he would be hurting his mother as well as himself. Robinson's pastor, the Reverend Downs, made his church a safe haven for neighborhood youths; he was a good listener, and Robinson spoke with him often, sharing his concerns and problems.

While he was attending John Muir Technical High School, Robinson earned letters in football, basketball, baseball, and track. He continued to excel at Pasadena Junior College, where he received a great deal of publicity regarding his achievements. The attention brought out the college recruiters, and he eventually selected the University of California at Los Angeles (UCLA) because of its proximity to his home. His eldest brother, Frank, who was one of his biggest fans and supporters, was killed in a motorcycle accident just about the time Robinson began attending UCLA. In 1941 Robinson became the first person to letter in four sports at UCLA, namely, basketball, baseball, football, and track. While at the university, he met his future wife, Rachel Isum, a nursing student, whom he married in 1945. Robinson never completed his degree, as he had to leave UCLA owing to his financial circumstances. He played football for a short time with the Honolulu Bears, a pro team, returning to California at the end of the 1941, just two days before Pearl Harbor was attacked by the Japanese.

With the entry of the United States into World War II, Robinson enlisted in the U.S. Army, where he was sent to Fort Riley, Kansas. He applied for Officer Candidate School, but the "Jim Crow Army," as Robinson called it, stalled over admitting the African American candidates. After the army was pressured by officials in Washington, D.C., the African American soldiers miraculously found themselves in Officer Candidate School. In January 1943 Robinson became a second lieutenant. He quickly discovered the inbred racism that permeated the armed forces. In trying to fight racial injustice, Robinson finally went too far when he refused to sit at the back of an army bus on the grounds of Fort Hood, Texas. He was brought to trial but was honorably discharged.

Returning to civilian life, Robinson, through his old pastor, Reverend Downs, became athletic director at Sam Houston College in Texas. In 1945 the Kansas City Monarchs offered Robinson $400 a month to play for them, a princely sum for an African American athlete in the 1940s. He played shortstop for the team, batting .387 in forty-seven games, with five home runs. Robinson's great athletic ability and versatility made him an attractive addition to the team— and was among the reasons he was considered one of the top ballplayers to cross Organized Baseball's color line.

Brooklyn Dodgers owner Branch Rickey was determined to integrate MLB. He began looking at several talented Negro League athletes, including Josh Gibson, Satchel Paige, Roy Campanella, and Buck Leonard. Rickey finally decided on Robinson for a number of reasons. Robinson was not the best player among those Rickey scouted, but he certainly was one of the most versatile and athletically adept. He also had the right background and the experience Rickey felt would help the first African American player deal with the hostility he would face. Robinson had grown up in an integrated neighborhood, played on integrated teams, and demonstrated an emotional maturity that stood him in good stead as a pioneer in desegregating professional sports. His courage off the field in standing up to discrimination in the armed forces and elsewhere also weighed in his favor.

Rickey signed Robinson to a contract to play for the minor league Montreal Royals at $600 a month for the 1946 season. The Royals, a farm team for the Dodgers, played in the International League; spring training was in Florida. Robinson made his debut in an exhibition game with the Dodgers on March 17, 1946. While he did face some hostility, the Montreal fans generally embraced him, and attendance at Royals games grew. Robinson batted .349 for the season and won the International League's Most Valuable Player award.

The next season Robinson made his debut with the Brooklyn Dodgers on April 15, 1947, at Ebbets Field. His performance earned him the Major League's Rookie of the Year honors. It was not easy for Robinson, facing discrimination, racial epithets, and general hostility on and off the field. The following season, the presence of other African American players, including Larry Doby, who broke the American League's racial barrier by signing with the Cleveland Indians, took some of the heat off of Robinson.

Robinson worked hard to improve his performance, especially his batting. Working with former player and Dodger adviser George Sisler, he raised his average from .296 in 1947 to .342 two years later. He had improved so much that Robinson was named the National League's MVP in 1949. That same year, he became the first African American to play in the All Star League, voted in by the fans to be starting second baseman. His success in MLB made him a fan favorite and a symbol of racial equality for all Americans. Hollywood quickly jumped on Robinson's popularity and produced *The Jackie Robinson Story*, which was released in 1950. Robinson played himself, and the actress Ruby Dee played his wife, Rachel. He continued to play baseball into the 1950s, but by 1956 he was feeling the effects of diabetes and decided to retire. He officially retired on January 5, 1957, and became director of personnel for Chock full o'Nuts coffee shops. In 1962 Robinson was inducted into the Baseball Hall of Fame in Cooperstown, New York. It was the first year he was eligible, and he was elected on the first ballot. Three years later he became the first African American sports analyst for ABC-TV's Major League Game of the Week.

Understanding his own role in furthering the cause of civil rights, Robinson was actively involved in the movement. He served as the chair of the National Association for the Advancement of Colored People's million-dollar Freedom Fund drive in 1956 and continued on its board until 1967. He was cofounder in 1964 of the Freedom National Bank, which was based in Harlem and owned and operated by African Americans. In 1970 Robinson founded the Jackie Robinson Construction Company, which built residences for low-income people.

Robinson received many honors and accolades during his own lifetime and even after his death from a heart attack on October 24, 1972. The National Association for the Advancement of Colored People awarded him the Spingarn Medal, the highest award for contributions by an African American, in 1956. The Dodgers retired his number, 42, in June 1962; Major League Baseball followed suit on the fiftieth anniversary of his MLB debut in 1997. In 1987 the Rookie of the Year Award in both the National and American leagues was renamed in his honor. *Time* magazine selected him as one of the hundred most important people of the twentieth century. President Ronald Reagan posthumously awarded him the Presidential Medal of Freedom in 1984, and George W. Bush honored him with the Congressional Gold Medal in 2005. Robinson's contributions both on and off the field make him a remarkable and courageous person who gave of himself in all aspects of his life.

Explanation and Analysis of the Document

I Never Had It Made, Jackie Robinson's autobiography as told to Alfred Duckett, was published in 1972, the same year Robinson died. The book stands out because of Robinson's candor, intelligence, and humor. His story tells not only about his life on the field but also about his personal life, even recounting his son's struggle with drug addiction and his early death in an automobile accident. Throughout the book, Robinson reveals his feelings about politics, the civil rights movement, the Vietnam War, and the progress (or lack thereof) of African Americans in society. He openly confronts the critics who accused him of being a black man "made by white people." He acknowledges three white men who were like godfathers to him in different aspects of his life: Branch Rickey in athletics, Bill Black (from Chock full o'Nuts) in business, and Nelson Rockefeller in politics. Robinson felt especially close to Rickey and greatly admired him for his sharp business acumen and courage in integrating MLB.

Robinson understood his position as a role model for African Americans. He dedicated himself to improving the status of blacks in American society. In the tumultuous 1950s and 1960s, he used his celebrity to advance the cause of civil rights. He astutely observes that the route to improving the lot of African Americans was "the ballot and the buck." Incisive observations permeate Robinson's autobiography. He discusses major political leaders, especially Nelson Rockefeller, with whom he became especially close. He shows particular admiration for Rockefeller's staunch support of civil rights.

I Never Had It Made is an apt selection for the title of Robinson's autobiography. "Everything I ever got I fought hard for," he notes in the book's epilogue. "I cannot possibly believe I have it made while so many of my black brothers and sisters are hungry, inadequately housed, insufficiently clothed, denied their dignity as they live in slums or barely exist on welfare." Although the book was originally published in 1972, a new edition appeared in 1995, with introductions by the Princeton University professor of African American Studies Cornel West and the home run king and all-around baseball legend Henry "Hank" Aaron. The excerpt here is the fourth chapter ("The Major Leagues") of the 1995 edition of the book, in which Robinson describes his MLB debut.

♦ The Big Question

The chapter opens with the birth of Robinson's first child, Jackie, Jr., on November 18, 1946. It was a momentous year in many ways for Robinson and his wife. That spring, he had made his debut with the Brooklyn Dodgers' farm team, the Montreal Royals—but not before facing the reality of the segregated South. Spring training was held in Florida, which meant that Robinson could not stay with the rest of the team in a hotel; he had to be put up in a private home. The Dodgers did not own their own spring-training facility at the time, so they relied on local officials for scheduling games. In the segregated South, several communities refused to allow the Royals to play if Robinson was on the roster. Finally, Robinson was able to make his debut in Daytona Beach's City Island Ball Park on March 17, 1946, in an exhibition game with the parent team, the Dodgers. His actual MLB debut was at the Royals' season opener against the Jersey City Giants on April 18, 1946. The strain of his first year playing in the major leagues, even in the farm system, took its toll. To minimize the stress on her husband, Rachel—who was expecting their first son at the time—spared Robinson the details of the troubles she experienced during her pregnancy; she even insisted on traveling with Robinson, so she could provide support during those difficult times.

Robinson then recounts how tensions mounted as spring training for the 1947 season drew closer. Branch Rickey had to decide whether or not to bring Robinson up to the Dodgers. Robinson's strong performance with Montreal led to much speculation in the sporting world about his status; the end of the color line seemed imminent. He comments on his admiration for Rickey's tact and skill in proceeding on the path toward desegregation and goes on to tell about being ordered to report for training in Cuba with the Royals in January 1947. By that time, the Dodgers had hired three other African American players, catcher Roy Campanella and pitchers Don Newcombe and Roy Partlow. All four men were sent to Cuba, where they stayed in separate quarters at a hotel fifteen miles from the practice field. According to Robinson, Rickey told him that he was trying to avoid any racially motivated missteps that might jeopardize his plans for the players' entry into the big leagues. Robinson was also assigned to play first base, which sent up flags that Rickey was planning to bring him up to the Dodger organization.

This set off a conspiracy among a few white Dodger players who agreed to sign a petition stating they would not play on the team with Robinson. A southern player, Kirby Higbe, leaked the plot to one of Rickey's aides. Rickey promptly notified the ringleaders of the scheme that he was going ahead with his plans and anyone who did not like it could quit. In the meantime, Rickey continued to give Robinson advice about doing his best and impressing not only the Dodger players but also the sportswriters who would be sending back stories to New York. Rickey's ulterior motive was to have the Dodger players clamor to have Robinson on the team, but this did not happen. Rickey then decided to have his manager, Leo Durocher, tell the sportswriters that he believed the Dodgers could win the pennant with a talented first baseman—and that Robinson was the best prospect. This strategy backfired, however, when Commissioner Happy Chandler suspended Durocher for "unbecoming conduct." Rickey finally decided to ease the negative publicity from Durocher's suspension with the positive story of Robinson's signing with the Dodgers on April 9, 1947.

♦ **Debuts with Brooklyn**

Robinson's debut at Ebbets Field on April 15, 1947, was less than auspicious. As he describes it, he fell into an early season slump and began to question his own abilities, ruminating about a comment by Cleveland pitcher Bob Feller that he was "good field, no hit." Early that season, Robinson experienced what he refers to as one of the worst times of his career, when the Philadelphia Phillies arrived in Brooklyn for a three-game series. The Phillies were notorious for taunting the other team's players; in Robinson's case, however, they were relentless, spewing vicious and demeaning insults during the entire game. He notes that the abuse was directed by the Phillies' manager, Ben Chapman. Robinson was so enraged that he came close to losing his cool and doing exactly what Branch Rickey had told him not to do: blowing up at the perpetrators. But Robinson recalls thinking about how much faith Rickey had placed in him and credits that sense of gratitude and trust with helping him to stay the course. The Phillies continued to abuse Robinson for the next two games, partly because Brooklyn had been victorious in the first game. Finally, by the third game, Dodger Ed Stankey turned on the Phillies and shouted them down. Other Dodger players told the press how angry they were about the Phillies' behavior. Robinson notes that the Phillies organization tried to cover for the team and claimed that Chapman was not a racist, since he readily used racial slurs on whites as well: For instance, Chapman referred to the Italian American baseball legend Joe DiMaggio as a "the Wop" and Whitey Kurowski of the Cardinals as "the Polack." Robinson says he believed Rickey was wrong in telling him to shake hands with Chapman; for Robinson, having his picture taken while shaking hands with Chapman was one of the most humiliating things he ever had to do.

♦ **Clash with the Cardinals**

Throughout his first season with the Dodgers, Robinson faced hostility and racist abuse from various quarters. He relates a shocking incident involving Brooklyn's first meeting with the Cardinals in St. Louis in 1947. Stanley Woodward, sports editor of the *New York Herald Tribune*, discovered and "exposed a plot that was brewing among the … Cardinals." The team intended to initiate a protest strike against Robinson's participation in the game. Had the plan succeeded, it might have spread throughout Organized Baseball and kept the major leagues white. The National League president, Ford Frick, warned the Cardinal players that they would not get away with a strike. Frick, who later served as MLB commissioner, was determined that the National League back Robinson, no matter what. Robinson reports that he received much hate mail, including threats against himself and his family. The series Brooklyn played in Philadelphia was remarkably unpleasant for Robinson, as he recalls not only being refused lodging at the Benjamin Franklin Hotel but also being heckled and taunted constantly, with some tormentors actually pointing bats at him from the dugout and making "machine-gunlike noises" in his direction.

While Robinson faced his share of hostility on the field, he also developed close friendships. He writes, for example, of the unwavering support shown by Pee Wee Reese, the Dodgers' shortstop: The southern-born Reese exhibited courage and decency, defending his black teammate in the face of racist taunts and jeers. Other Dodger teammates followed Reese's example and rallied around Robinson's cause. However, not everyone was happy about the pioneering Rickey's efforts. Robinson recounts a particularly unnerving incident involving boorish behavior at a team poker game. When one of his southern teammates, Hugh Casey, baited him with a vulgar racist comment, Robinson—keeping in mind Rickey's words about having "guts enough not to fight back"—ignored it and continued playing. According to Robinson, though, most of the team came around to support him and their other black teammates. Robinson also drew satisfaction that the Dodgers set the example for other teams, and he applauded the signing of the African American players Larry Doby with the Cleveland Indians and Willard Brown and Henry Thompson with the St. Louis Browns.

♦ **1947 World Series**

The first season with the Dodgers ended in triumph, with the team winning the National League pennant. Robinson finished the season with a .296 batting average, twelve home runs, and a league-leading twenty-seven stolen bases. He closes this chapter of his autobiography by reflecting on the contrast between the beginning and end of the 1947 season. He had started out feeling lonely and isolated but eventually learned to win people's respect with his behavior on and off the field. By the end of the season, he was truly a part of the team; he had played well and was even given a hero's welcome when the team returned to Brooklyn that September, after clinching the National League title. Robinson ends the chapter on a sad note with the death of his mentor, the Reverend Karl Downs. Having fallen ill while visiting the Robinsons in New York, Downs seemed to recover after being hospitalized. When he returned home to Texas, however, his illness returned, and he was treated in a segregated hospital, where he passed away. Robinson remained convinced that Downs would have survived if he had remained up north, where hospitals were integrated. Robinson felt the loss of his old friend when the World Series opened; the fans, he recalls, were very kind to him, even though the Dodgers lost to their rival Yankees.

Audience

I Never Had It Made was meant for a general audience. Putnam and Sons, the original publisher, distributed the book throughout the United States and abroad. Nearly forty years after its release, Robinson's autobiography appeals to a variety of readers—those interested in the history of baseball, sports in general, African American history, reform in the United States, or biography would find Robinson's book of great interest. His story is fascinating, and his character, intelligence, and courage come through in this work. At the time of its publication in 1972, the United States was still reeling from the effects of decades of racism. Robinson's autobiography graphically illustrates many of the issues confronting the nation at the time, especially race relations but also politics and the Vietnam War. As seen through the eyes of a true pioneer, Robinson's story remains a valuable piece of social history.

Impact

By the time his autobiography appeared in 1972, Jackie Robinson had transcended the concept of race that so divided Americans. *I Never Had It Made* is a warts-and-all story that captures Robinson's doubts and dreams. The man who erased Organized Baseball's color line lives on in his own words, speaking with candor and clarity to an entirely new generation of readers in the twenty-first century. As Cornel West, the author of the introduction to the 1995 edition, put it: "The most striking features of the book are its honesty, its courage and its wisdom. Here is a great American hero who refuses to be a mythical hero."

Further Reading

♦ Books

Alexander, Charles. *Our Game: An American Baseball History*. New York: Henry Holt, 1991.

Peterson, Robert W. *Only the Ball Was White*. Englewood Cliffs, N.J.: Prentice-Hall, 1970.

Rader, Benjamin G. *Baseball: A History of America's Game*. Champaign: University of Illinois Press, 1994.

Ribowsky, Mark. *A Complete History of the Negro Leagues from 1884 to 1955*. New York: Birch Lane Press, 1995.

Robinson, Jackie, and Alfred Duckett. *I Never Had It Made: An Autobiography*. 1972. Reprint. New York: HarperCollins, 1995.

Rogosin, Donn. *Invisible Men: Life in Baseball's Negro Leagues*. New York: Atheneum, 1983.

White, Edward G. *Creating the National Pastime: Baseball Transforms Itself, 1903–1953*. Princeton, N.J.: Princeton University Press, 1996.

♦ Web Sites

"About Jackie Robinson." The Jackie Robinson Foundation Web site. http://www.jackierobinson.org./about/jackie.php.

"Baseball and Jackie Robinson." American Memory, Library of Congress Web site. http://memory.loc.gov/ammem/collections/robinson/jr1940.html.

"Hall of Fame Gallery." National Baseball Hall of Fame Web site. http://community.baseballhall.org/Page.aspx?pid=329.

"Jackie Robinson: Baseball's Barrier Breaker." The Official Jackie Robinson Site. http://www.jackierobinson.com.

—Donna M. DeBlasio

Time Line

1919	January 31	■ Jack Roosevelt Robinson is born in Cairo, Georgia.
1937–1939		■ Robinson attends Pasadena City College, where he excels in a number of sports.
1939–1941		■ At the University of California at Los Angeles, Robinson letters in four sports.
1942		■ Robinson is drafted into the U.S. Army; within a year he completes Officer Candidate School and becomes a second lieutenant.
1945		■ Robinson joins the Kansas City Monarchs baseball team in the Negro Leagues.
1946	March 17	■ In an exhibition game against the Dodgers, Robinson makes his debut as a Montreal Royal.
1947	April 15	■ Robinson plays his first game with the Brooklyn Dodgers.
	Fall	■ Robinson wins the Major League Rookie of the Year Award.
1956		■ Robinson is awarded the NAACP Spingarn Medal.
1957	January 5	■ Robinson retires from baseball and becomes director of personnel for Chock full o'Nuts.
1962		■ Robinson is inducted into the Baseball Hall of Fame, and the Dodgers retire his number, 42.
1972		■ *I Never Had It Made* is first published, and shortly thereafter Jackie Robinson dies of a heart attack.
1984		■ President Ronald Reagan awards Robinson a posthumous Presidential Medal of Freedom.
2005		■ The Congressional Gold Medal is awarded to Robinson for his contributions to improved race relations in the United States.

Milestone Documents

Essential Quotes

"For one wild and rage-crazed minute I thought, 'To hell with Mr. Rickey's "noble experiment." It's clear it won't succeed. I have made every effort to work hard, to get myself into shape. My best is not good enough for them.' I thought what a glorious, cleansing thing it would be to let go. To hell with the image of the patient black freak I was supposed to create."

"Getting a hero's welcome in September made me remember how bad the beginning of my first season with the Dodgers had been. At that time I still wasn't looking like any kind of winner, even though the increasing acceptance of my teammates had begun to help me out of a terrible slump. I seriously wondered if I could make the Rickey experiment a success."

"I had started the season as a lonely man, often feeling like a black Don Quixote tilting at a lot of white windmills. I ended it feeling like a member of a solid team. The Dodgers were a championship team because all of us had learned something. I had learned how to exercise self-control—to answer insults, violence, and injustice with silence—and I learned how to earn the respect of my teammates."

"Karl Downs ranked with Roy Wilkins, Whitney Young, and Dr. Martin Luther King, Jr., in ability and dedication, and had he lived he would have developed into one of the front line leaders on the national scene. He was able to communicate with people of all colors because he was endowed with the ability to inspire confidence. It was hard to believe that God had taken the life of a man with such a promising future."

Questions for Further Study

1. It has been argued that athletics and the military are the only institutions in which racism has essentially disappeared. Would you agree with this view? Why or why not?

2. In his account, Robinson makes the following statement: "Others genuinely wouldn't know how to be friendly with me." To what extent have you ever felt this way with regard to a person of a different race or nationality? Alternatively, have you ever felt that this was how others were reacting to you? How did you deal with that situation?

3. Compare Robinson's account with that of another athlete, Jesse Owens, as chronicled in *Blackthink: My Life as Black Man and White Man*, which was published just two years earlier. What similar experiences did the two men share? How were their experiences different? Do you think that Robinson faced a different kind of reaction because he was breaching the color line in America's "national pastime"?

4. In the twenty-first century, Jackie Robinson's name has achieved almost mythical status; merely mention the name, and baseball fans, sports fans, and the public in general will immediately picture the constellation of events in which Robinson was involved. Based on your reading of *I Never Had It Made*, what do you think Robinson's reaction to this mythologizing might be? Explain.

5. Make the argument that putting aside all of the "official" pronouncements about race—*To Secure These Rights* in 1947, President Harry Truman's executive order desegregating the military in 1948, and various Supreme Court decisions—Robinson's desegregation of baseball was the most important civil rights event of a generation.

Document Text

I NEVER HAD IT MADE

1972

An excerpt from Robinson's book.

"The Major Leagues"

Jackie Robinson, Jr., was born in November, 1946. If there is anything to the theory that the influences affecting expectant parents have important impact on the developing child, our baby son was predestined to lead a very complicated and complex life.

Rachel had had problems during her pregnancy that I was not aware of. She accepted them with uncomplaining courage because of her conviction that, since I had a job to do in baseball that was demanding and difficult, I should be as free as possible to deal with it without the further complications of family worries. She was determined, therefore, that, while she shared my problems with me, she would keep me from knowing about her own fears and anxieties. She did a good job of keeping her Problems to herself. It wasn't until after Jackie was born that I learned that Rae had occasionally experienced fevers seemingly unconnected with the normal process of pregnancy. Her temperature would rise to 103 and 104 degrees and she would take sulfa drugs and aspirin to bring her fever down. She had insisted on traveling with me during the first season with Montreal because she knew I needed her. Often I would come home tired, discouraged, wondering if I could go on enduring the verbal abuse and even the physical provocations and continue to "turn the other cheek." Rachel knew exactly how I felt, and she would have the right words, the perfect way of comforting me. Rachel's understanding love was a powerful antidote for the poison of being taunted by fans, sneered at by fellow-players, and constantly mistreated because of my blackness.

In the eighth month of her pregnancy, I insisted that Rachel go home to Los Angeles to have the baby. Two weeks after she returned to her mother's home, I was able to get back to Los Angeles and be there the night she went into labor. When the time came, I got her to the hospital fast and our boy was born with unusual speed. We'll never forget that day—November 18, 1946.

The big question, as spring training for the 1947 season became imminent, was whether Branch Rickey would move me out of the minor league and up to the Brooklyn Dodgers. Because of my successful first season with Montreal, it was a question being asked in sportswriting and baseball circles. Even those who were dead set against a black man coming into the majors knew there was a strong possibility that Mr. Rickey would take the big step.

Mr. Rickey had to move cautiously and with skill and strategy. Rae and I never doubted that Mr. Rickey would carry out his intention, but we lived in suspense wondering when. In the latter part of January I was ordered to report back to the Montreal Royals for spring training in Cuba. I would not be able to afford to take Rachel and the baby with me. I had to go it alone.

Although we could not understand Mr. Rickey's reasons for the delay in bringing me up to the Dodgers, we believed he was working things out the best way possible. We thought it was a hopeful sign that both the Dodgers and the Royals would be training in Havana. It could be reasonably expected that the racist atmosphere I had had to face in Florida and other parts of the United States would not exist in another country of non-whites. The Royals now had three more black players—Roy Campanella, a catcher; Don Newcombe and Roy Partlow, both pitchers. I learned, on arriving in Havana, that we black players would be housed in separate quarters at a hotel fifteen miles away from the practice field. The rest of the team was living at a military academy, and the Dodgers were headquartered at the beautiful Nacional Hotel. I expressed my resentment that the Cuban authorities would subject us to the same kind of segregation I had faced in Florida and was promptly informed that living arrangements had not been made by local authorities but by Mr. Rickey. I was told that he felt his plans for us were on the threshold of success and he didn't want a possible racial incident to jeopardize his program. I reluctantly accepted the explanation.

I was told I must learn to play first base. This disturbed me because I felt it might mean a delay in reaching the majors. However, it was felt that the Dodgers, in order to become contenders for the pennant, had to strengthen the first base position.

The fact that I had been assigned to first base aroused fear in the Dodger camp. They sensed that

Document Text

Mr. Rickey was planning to bring me up to the Dodgers. Some of the players got together and decided to sign a petition declaring they would not play with me on the team. Ironically, the leak about the planned revolt came from a Southerner, Kirby Higbe, of South Carolina. Higbe had a few too many beers one night, and he began feeling uncomfortable about the conspiracy. He revealed the plot to one of Mr. Rickey's aides and Mr. Rickey put down the rebellion with steamroller effectiveness. He said later, "I have always believed that a little show of force at the right time is necessary when there's a deliberate violation of law.… I believe that when a man is involved in an overt act of violence or in destruction of someone's rights, that it's no time to conduct an experiment in education or persuasion."

He found out who the ringleaders were—Hugh Casey, a good relief pitcher from Georgia; Southerner Bobby Bragan, a respected catcher; Dixie Walker of Alabama; and Carl Furrillo. Walker had deliberately taken a trip so he wouldn't appear to be in on the scheme. The ringleaders were called in individually, and Mr. Rickey told each one that petitions would make no difference. He said he would carry out his plan, regardless of protest. Anyone who was not willing to have a black teammate could quit. The petition protest collapsed before it got started.

Mr. Rickey was very direct with me during those early 1947 spring training days. He told me I couldn't rest on the victories I'd had with Montreal. I should, in fact, forget them as much as possible. My league record meant nothing. The true test would be making the grade on the field against major league pitching.

"I want you to be a whirling demon against the Dodgers," he said. "I want you to concentrate, to hit that ball, to get on base *by any means necessary*. I want you to run wild, to steal the pants off them, to be the most conspicuous player on the field—but conspicuous only because of the kind of baseball you're playing. Not only will you impress the Dodger players, but the stories that the newspapermen send back to the Brooklyn and New York newspapers will help create demand on the part of the fans that you be brought up to the majors."

With this kind of marching order, I simply had to give my best. I batted .625 and stole seven bases during seven Royals-Dodgers games. Not even this made the Brooklyn players ask for me as Mr. Rickey had hoped. He had wanted, when promoting me, to appear to be giving in to tremendous pressure from my teammates-to-be.

When this strategy failed, Mr. Rickey, a resourceful man, arranged to have Manager Leo Durocher tell the sportswriters that his Brooklyn team could win the pennant with a good man on first base and that I was the best prospect. Leo would add he was going to try to convince Mr. Rickey to sign me. That plan failed, too, because on April 9 before it could be carried out, Baseball Commissioner Chandler suspended Durocher for a year "for conduct detrimental to baseball." Durocher and the commissioner's office had been in conflict for some time. The commissioner's office had challenged Leo's "questionable associations" off the playing field. Durocher had hit back by noting that some very well-known gangsters had been seen near the Yankee dugout during a Dodger-Yankee game. He said no one had done anything about that. This sparked an exchange between the commissioner's office, Durocher, Mr. Rickey, and Yankee President Larry MacPhail. It had been common belief that the storm had blown over. Ironically, on the same April morning that Mr. Rickey hoped to make his move, Durocher was suspended.

Quickly, Mr. Rickey saw that signing the first black in the major leagues would virtually wipe the Durocher story, a negative one, off the front pages. His action would cause controversy, but he believed it would be like a shot in the arm to the club. On the morning of April 9, 1947, just before an exhibition game, reporters in the press box received a single sheet of paper with a one-line announcement. It read: "Brooklyn announces the purchase of the contract of Jack Roosevelt Robinson from Montreal. Signed, Branch Rickey."

That morning turned into a press Donnybrook. The sports-writers snatched up telephones. The telegraph wires relayed the message to the sports world.

Less than a week after I became Number 42 on the Brooklyn club, I played my first game with the team. I did a miserable job. There was an overflow crowd at Ebbets Field. If they expected any miracles out of Robinson, they were sadly disappointed. I was in another slump. I grounded out to the third baseman, flied out to left field, bounced into a double play, was safe on an error, and, later, was removed as a defensive safeguard. The next four games reflected my deep slump. I went to plate twenty times without one base hit. Burt Shotton, a man I respected and liked, had replaced Durocher as manager. As my slump deepened, I appreciated Shotton's patience and understanding. I knew the pressure was on him to take me out of the lineup. People began recalling

Bob Feller's analysis of me. I was "good field, no hit." There were others who doubted that I could field and some who hoped I would flunk out and thus establish that blacks weren't ready for the majors. Shotton, however, continued to encourage me.

Early in the season, the Philadelphia Phillies came to Ebbets Field for a three-game series. I was still in my slump and events of the opening game certainly didn't help. Starting to the plate in the first inning, I could scarcely believe my ears. Almost as if it had been synchronized by some master conductor, hate poured forth from the Phillies dugout.

"Hey, nigger, why don't you go back to the cotton field where you belong?"

"They're waiting for you in the jungles, black boy!"

"Hey, snowflake, which one of those white boys' wives are you dating tonight?"

"We don't want you here, nigger."

"Go back to the bushes!"

Those insults and taunts were only samples of the torrent of abuse which poured out from the Phillies dugout that April day.

I have to admit that this day, of all the unpleasant days in my life, brought me nearer to cracking up than I ever had been. Perhaps I should have become inured to this kind of garbage, but I was in New York City and unprepared to face the kind of barbarism from a northern team that I had come to associate with the Deep South. The abuse coming out of the Phillies dugout was being directed by the team's manager, Ben Chapman, a Southerner. I felt tortured and I tried just to play ball and ignore the insults. But it was really getting to me. What did the Phillies want from me? What, indeed, did Mr. Rickey expect of me? I was, after all, a human being. What was I doing here turning the other cheek as though I weren't a man? In college days I had had a reputation as a black man who never tolerated affronts to his dignity. I had defied prejudice in the Army. How could I have thought that barriers would fall, that, indeed, my talent could triumph over bigotry?

For one wild and rage-crazed minute I thought, "To hell with Mr. Rickey's 'noble experiment.' It's clear it won't succeed. I have made every effort to work hard, to get myself into shape. My best is not enough for them." I thought what a glorious, cleansing thing it would be to let go. To hell with the image of the patient black freak I was supposed to create. I could throw down my bat, stride over to that Phillies dugout, grab one of those white sons of bitches and smash his teeth in with my despised black fist. Then I could walk away from it all. I'd never become a sports star. But my son could tell his son someday what his daddy could have been if he hadn't been too much of a man.

Then, I thought of Mr. Rickey—how his family and friends had begged him not to fight for me and my people. I thought of all his predictions, which had come true. Mr. Rickey had come to a crossroads and made a lonely decision. I was at a crossroads. I would make mine. I would stay.

The haters had almost won that round. They had succeeded in getting me so upset that I was an easy out. As the game progressed, the Phillies continued with the abuse.

After seven scoreless innings, we got the Phillies out in the eighth, and it was our turn at bat. I led off. The insults were still coming. I let the first pitch go by for a ball. I lined the next one into center field for a single. Gene Hermanski came up to hit and I took my lead.

The Phillies pitcher, a knuckle expert, let fly. I cut out for second. The throw was wide. It bounced past the shortstop. As I came into third, Hermanski singled me home. That was the game.

Apparently frustrated by our victory, the Phillies players kept the heat on me during the next two days. They even enlarged their name-calling to include the rest of the Brooklyn team.

"Hey, you carpetbaggers, how's your little reconstruction period getting along?"

That was a typical taunt. By the third day of our confrontation with these emissaries from the City of Brotherly Love, they had become so outrageous that Ed Stanky exploded. He started yelling at the Phillies.

"Listen, you yellow-bellied cowards," he cried out, "why don't you yell at somebody who can answer back?" It was then that I began to feel better. I remembered Mr. Rickey's prediction. If I won the respect of the team and got them solidly behind me, there would be no question about the success of the experiment.

Stanky wasn't the only Brooklyn player who was angry with the Phillies team. Some of my other teammates told the press about the way Chapman and his players had behaved. Sports columnists around the country criticized Chapman. Dan Parker, sports editor of the New York *Daily Mirror*, reported:

> Ben Chapman, who during his career with the Yankees was frequently involved in unpleasant in-

cidents with fans who charged him with shouting anti-Semitic remarks at them from the ball field, seems to be up to his old trick of stirring up racial trouble. During the recent series between the Phils and the Dodgers, Chapman and three of his players poured a stream of abuse at Jackie Robinson. Jackie, with admirable restraint, ignored the guttersnipe language coming from the Phils dugout, thus stamping himself as the only gentleman among those involved in the incident.

The black press did a real job of letting its readers know about the race baiting which had taken place. The publicity in the press built so much anti-Chapman public feeling that the Philadelphia club decided steps must be taken to counteract it. Chapman met with representatives of the black press to try to explain his behavior. The Phillies public relations people insisted, as Ben Chapman did, that he was not anti-Negro. Chapman himself used an interesting line of defense in speaking with black reporters. Didn't they want me to become a big-time big leaguer? Well, so did he and his players. When they played exhibitions with the Yanks, they razzed DiMaggio as "the Wop," Chapman explained. When they came up against the Cards, Whitey Kurowski was called "the Polack." Riding opposition players was the Phils' style of baseball. The Phils could give it out and they could take it. Was I a weakling who couldn't take it? Well, if I wasn't a weakling, then I shouldn't expect special treatment. After all, Chapman said, all is forgotten after a ball game ends.

The press, black and white, didn't buy that argument. They said so. Commissioner Happy Chandler wasn't having any either. His office warned the Phils to keep racial baiting out of the dugout bench jockeying.

A fascinating development of the nastiness with the Phils was the attitude of Mr. Rickey and the reaction of my Brooklyn teammates. Mr. Rickey knew, better than most people, that Chapman's racial prejudice was deeper than he admitted. Bob Carpenter, the Phils' president, had phoned Rickey before game time to try to persuade him not to include me in the lineup. If I played, Carpenter threatened, his team would refuse to play. Mr. Rickey's response was that this would be fine with him. The Dodgers would then take all three games by default. The Dodgers' president wasn't angry with Chapman or his players. As a matter of fact, in later years, Mr. Rickey commented, "Chapman did more than anybody to unite the Dodgers. When he poured out that string of unconscionable abuse, he solidified and unified thirty men, not one of whom was willing to sit by and see someone kick around a man who had his hands tied behind his back—Chapman made Jackie a real member of the Dodgers."

Privately, at the time, I thought Mr. Rickey was carrying his "gratitude" to Chapman a little too far when he asked me to appear in public with Chapman. The Phillies manager was genuinely in trouble as a result of all the publicity on the racial razzing. Mr. Rickey thought it would be gracious and generous if I posed for a picture shaking hands with Chapman. The idea was also promoted by the baseball commissioner. I was somewhat sold—but not altogether—on the concept that a display of such harmony would be "good for the game." I have to admit, though, that having my picture taken with this man was one of the most difficult things I had to make myself do.

There were times, after I had bowed to humiliations like shaking hands with Chapman, when deep depression and speculation as to whether it was all worthwhile would seize me. Often, when I was in this kind of mood, something positive would happen to give me new strength. Sometimes the positive development would come in response to a negative one. This was exactly what happened when a clever sports editor exposed a plot that was brewing among the St. Louis Cardinals. The plan was set to be executed on May 9, 1947, when Brooklyn was to visit St. Louis for the first game of the season between the two clubs. The Cards were planning to pull a last-minute protest strike against my playing in the game. If successful, the plan could have had a chain reaction throughout the baseball world—with other players agreeing to unite in a strong bid to keep baseball white. Stanley Woodward, sports editor of the New York *Herald Tribune*, had learned of the plot and printed an exclusive scoop exposing it. Ford Frick reacted immediately and notified the Cardinal players in no uncertain terms that they would not be permitted to get away with a strike.

"If you do this you will be suspended from the league," Frick warned. "You will find that the friends you think you have in the press box will not support you, that you will be outcasts. I do not care if half the league strikes. Those who do it will encounter quick retribution. They will be suspended and I don't care if it wrecks the National League for five years. This is the United States of America, and one citizen has as much right to play as another.

Document Text

"The National League," Frick continued, "will go down the line with Robinson whatever the consequence. You will find if you go through with your intention that you have been guilty of complete madness."

The hot light of publicity about the plot and the forthright hard line that Frick laid down to the plotters helped to avert what could have been a disaster for integration of baseball. Many writers and baseball personalities credited Woodward with significant service to baseball and to sportsmanship.

While some positive things were happening, there were others that were negative. Hate mail arrived daily, but it didn't bother me nearly as much as the threat mail. The threat mail included orders to me to get out of the game or be killed, threats to assault Rachel, to kidnap Jackie, Jr. Although none of the threats materialized, I was quite alarmed. Mr. Rickey, early in May, decided to turn some of the letters over to the police.

That same spring the Benjamin Franklin Hotel in Philadelphia, where my teammates were quartered, refused to accommodate me. The Phillies heckled me a second time, mixing up race baiting with childish remarks and gestures that coincided with the threats that had been made. Some of those grown men sat in the dugout and pointed bats at me and made machine-gunlike noises. It was an incredibly childish display of bad will.

I was helped over these crises by the courage and decency of a teammate who could easily have been my enemy rather than my friend. Pee Wee Reese, the successful Dodger shortstop, was one of the most highly respected players in the major leagues. When I first joined the club, I was aware that there might well be a real reluctance on Reese's part to accept me as a teammate. He was from Ekron, Kentucky. Furthermore, it had been rumored that I might take over Reese's position on the team. Mischief-makers seeking to create trouble between us had tried to agitate Reese into regarding me as a threat—a black one at that. But Reese, from the time I joined Brooklyn, had demonstrated a totally fair attitude.

Reese told a sportswriter, some months after I became a Dodger, "When I first met Robinson in spring training, I figured, well, let me give this guy a chance. It may be he's just as good as I am. Frankly, I don't think I'd stand up under the kind of thing he's been subjected to as well as he has."

Reese's tolerant attitude of withholding judgment to see if I would make it was translated into positive support soon after we became teammates. In Boston during a period when the heckling pressure seemed unbearable, some of the Boston players began to heckle Reese. They were riding him about being a Southerner and playing ball with a black man. Pee Wee didn't answer them. Without a glance in their direction, he left his position and walked over to me. He put his hand on my shoulder and began talking to me. His words weren't important. I don't even remember what he said. It was the gesture of comradeship and support that counted. As he stood talking with me with a friendly arm around my shoulder, he was saying loud and clear, "Yell. Heckle. Do anything you want. We came here to play baseball."

The jeering stopped, and a close and lasting friendship began between Reese and me. We were able, not only to help each other and our team in private as well as public situations, but to talk about racial prejudices and misunderstanding.

At the same time Mr. Rickey told me that when my teammates began to rally to my cause, we could consider the battle half won; he had also said that one of my roughest burdens would be the experience of being lonely in the midst of a group—my teammates. They would be my teammates on the field. But back in the locker rooms, I would know the strain and pressure of being a stranger in a crowd of guys who were friendly among themselves but uncertain about how to treat me. Some of them would resent me but would cover the resentment with aloofness or just a minimum amount of courtesy. Others genuinely wouldn't know how to be friendly with me. Some would even feel I preferred to be off in a corner and left out. After the games were over, my teammates had normal social lives with their wives, their girls, and each other. When I traveled, during those early days, unless Wendell Smith or some other black sportswriter happened to be going along, I sat by myself while the other guys chatted and laughed and played cards. I remember vividly a rare occasion when I was invited to join a poker game. One of the participants was a Georgia guy, Hugh Casey, the relief pitcher. Casey's luck wasn't too good during the game, and at one point he addressed a remark directly to me that caused a horrified silence.

"You know what I used to do down in Georgia when I ran into bad luck?" he said. "I used to go out and find me the biggest, blackest nigger woman I could find and rub her teats to change my luck."

I don't believe there was a man in that game, including me, who thought that I could take that. I had to force back my anger. I had the memory of Mr. Rickey's words about looking for a man "with guts enough not to fight back." Finally, I made myself turn to the dealer and told him to deal the cards.

Traveling had its problems but being at home with Rachel and little Jackie was great even if our living conditions left something to be desired. If we had been living away from our home base, the club would have found some type of separate living arrangement for us. But in the excitement of converting me into a Dodger, no one seemed to have given a thought to our accommodations. We were living—three of us—in one room in the McAlpin Hotel in midtown Manhattan. It was miserable for Rae. In that one room that seemed constantly overrun with newsmen, she had to fix the baby's formula, change his diapers, bathe him, and do all the things mothers do for small babies. We had no relatives in New York and no one to turn to for babysitting. Rae brought our son out to the ball park for the first game I played with the Dodgers. She was determined not to miss that game. Never having lived in the East, she brought little Jackie dressed in a coat which, in California, would have been a winter coat. He would not have been able to stand the cold, dressed as he was, if Roy Campanella's mother-in-law hadn't kept him with her under her fur coat. Rae warmed bottles at a hot dog stand. At four and a half months, Jackie began what was to be the story of his young life—growing up in the ball park. He came to many games with his mother, and when he was old enough, he became very popular with some of the Dodger players who would keep him on their laps and play with him.

Before the season ended, we did manage to escape from the hotel. We found a place in Brooklyn where there was a small sleeping room for little Jackie, a bedroom, and use of a kitchen for us. We had no place to entertain the few friends we were making, but it certainly beat living in the hotel and we were grateful.

We were glad, too, that we could see some tangible results from our sacrifices. Not only were the other black players on the Dodger team winning acceptance, but other teams started to follow Mr. Rickey's example. Larry Doby became the first black player in the American League, signing on with the Cleveland Indians, and Willard Brown and Henry Thompson had been hired by the St. Louis Browns.

The Dodgers won the pennant that year, and when our club came home in September from a swing across the West, we were joyfully received by our fans. Their enthusiasm for me was so great that I once went into a phone booth to call Rae and was trapped in that phone booth by admirers who let up only when policemen arrived on the scene to liberate me.

Getting a hero's welcome in September made me remember how bad the beginning of my first season with the Dodgers had been. At that time I still wasn't looking like any kind of winner, even though the increasing acceptance of my teammates had begun to help me out of a terrible slump. I seriously wondered if I could ever make the Rickey experiment a success. Both Manager Burt Shotton and Mr. Rickey believed I would eventually come through. Clyde Sukeforth with his quiet confidence helped as much as anybody else.

During the season I was under even greater pressure than in my Montreal days. It was there that I had earned a reputation for stealing bases, and the pressure eased when I began stealing them again. Late in June, in a night game at Pittsburgh, with the score tied 2-2 I kept a careful eye on pitcher Fitz Ostermueller. I noticed he had become a little careless and relaxed. I began dancing off third base. Ostermueller paid me the insult of winding up, ignoring my movements as antics. The pitch was a ball. Easing open my lead off third, I made a bold dash for home plate and slid in safe. That put us in the lead 3-2. It was the winning run of the game. As I ran I heard the exhilarating noise that is the best reward a player can get. The roar of the crowd.

After I made that comeback, I think Mr. Rickey was as happy as I was. He said to some friends at the time, "Wait! You haven't seen Robinson in action yet—not really. You may not have seen him at his best this year at all, or even next year. He's still in his shell. When he comes out for good, he'll be compared to Ty Cobb."

Mr. Rickey's words meant a great deal to me but not as much as something he did. Howie Schultz, the player who had been mentioned as a possible replacement for me during the bad days of my slump, was sold by the club.

That 1947 season was memorable in many ways. Some of the incidents that occurred resulted in far-reaching changes for the club. In late August we played the St. Louis Cardinals. In one of the last games, Enos Slaughter, a Cards outfielder, hit a ground ball. As I took the throw at first from the infielder, Slaughter deliberately went for my leg instead of the base and spiked me rather severely.

Document Text

It was an act that unified the Dodger team. Teammates such as Hugh Casey of the poker game incident came charging out on the field to protest. The team had always been close to first place in the pennant race, but the spirit shown after the Slaughter incident strengthened our resolve and made us go on to win the pennant. The next time we played the Cards, we won two of the three games.

I had started the season as a lonely man, often feeling like a black Don Quixote tilting at a lot of white windmills. I ended it feeling like a member of a solid team. The Dodgers were a championship team because all of us had learned something. I had learned how to exercise self-control—to answer insults, violence, and injustice with silence—and I had learned how to earn the respect of my teammates. They had learned that it's not skin color but talent and ability that counts. Maybe even the bigots had learned that, too.

The press had also changed. When I came up to the majors, the influential *Sporting News* had declared that a black man would find it almost impossible to succeed in organized baseball. At the end of the season, when they selected me as Rookie of the Year, that same publication said:

> That Jackie Roosevelt Robinson might have had more obstacles than his first year competitors, and that he perhaps had a harder fight to gain even major league recognition, was no concern of this publication. The sociological experiment that Robinson represented, the trail-blazing that he did, the barriers he broke down, did not enter into the decision. He was rated and examined solely as a freshman player in the big leagues—on the basis of his hitting, his running, his defensive play, his team value.
>
> Dixie Walker summed it up in a few words the other day when he said: "No other ballplayer on this club with the possible exception of Bruce Edwards has done more to put the Dodgers up in the race than Robinson has. He is everything Branch Rickey said he was when he came up from Montreal."

Rachel and I moved again. She had managed to find more satisfactory living quarters in Brooklyn, where we had our own kitchen and living room and even a guest bedroom. I was delighted when I learned that the man I had admired so much as a youngster, the Reverend Karl Downs, wanted to visit us. I had kept in touch with Karl over the years. Before I'd gone into service, he had left Pasadena to become president of Sam Houston State College in Texas. When I left UCLA, I heard from Karl who said he was on the spot. He needed a coach for his basketball team. There was very little money involved, but I knew that Karl would have done anything for me, so I couldn't turn him down. I went to Texas and took the job but could only stay for a few months before financial pressures caught up with me. When Rachel and I were married, Karl, insisting on paying his own expenses, had set aside all his duties in Texas to fly to Los Angeles and officiate at our wedding. I was delighted by the prospect of his visit to Brooklyn.

One day, during his visit, Karl had come out to see one of the games. Suddenly he felt sick and decided to go back home to rest and wait for us. I had no idea his sickness was serious. That evening when I reached home, Rachel had taken him to the hospital. Several days later, apparently recovered, Karl had returned to Texas. In a few days, he was dead.

Karl's death, in itself, was hard enough to take. But when we learned the circumstances, Rae and I experienced the bitter feeling that Karl Downs had died a victim of racism. We are convinced that Karl Downs would not have died at that time if he had remained in Brooklyn for the operation he required.

When he returned to Texas, Karl went to a segregated hospital to be operated on. As he was being wheeled back from the recovery room, complications set in. Rather than returning his black patient to the operating room or to a recovery room to be closely watched, the doctor in charge let him go to the segregated ward where he died. We believe Karl would not have died if he had received proper care, and there are a number of whites who evidently shared this belief. After Karl's death the doctor who performed the operation was put under such pressure that he was forced to leave town.

Karl Downs ranked with Roy Wilkins, Whitney Young, and Dr. Martin Luther King, Jr., in ability and dedication, and had he lived he would have developed into one of the front line leaders on the national scene. He was able to communicate with people of all colors because he was endowed with the ability to inspire confidence. It was hard to believe that God had taken the life of a man with such a promising future.

I especially missed Karl at the opening day of the 1947 world series. Seventy-five thousand fans,

Document Text

many of whom were black, turned out for that first series game. During the game, the fans were very kind to me, and there was an avalanche of crowd approval in the first inning as I drew a base on balls from Frank Shea and stole second. Pete Reiser hit a ground ball to shortstop and I tried for third, but I was caught in the run down. Fortunately my stops and starts gave Reiser a chance to reach second and, from that position, to score the first run of the game. In that series, our team was the underdog. We were up against that spectacular New York Yankees team that included some of the greats in baseball: Joe DiMaggio, Tommy Henrich, Yogi Berra, Johnny Lindell, Phil Rizzuto, and George McQuinn. We fought hard, but the Yankees were a great baseball club. Even though we lost we still felt we had acquitted ourselves well.

During the winter I went on a speaking tour of the South. It was a successful tour except for the fact that almost every night we were treated to some of the best Southern cooking available in private homes. We ate like pigs, and for me it was disastrous.

Glossary

Baseball Commissioner Chandler: A. P. "Happy" Chandler

Bob Feller: a Hall of Fame pitcher who spent his career with the Cleveland Indians

Branch Rickey: the owner of the Brooklyn Dodgers

Brooklyn Dodgers: the team that moved after the 1957 season to become the Los Angeles Dodgers

carpetbaggers: a reference to northerners who moved to the South after the Civil War, so called because many carried suitcases made of carpeting material

City of Brotherly Love: the common nickname of Philadelphia, Pennsylvania

Don Quixote tilting at a lot of white windmills: a reference to the title character in Miguel Cervantes's seventeenth-century novel in which the mad knight Quixote does battle with windmills; a common expression for acts of impractical nobility or courage

Donnybrook: a brawl or fracas, named after an Irish town that was the scene of a notoriously raucous annual fair

Montreal: the Canadian home of the Montreal Royals, a Dodgers' farm team

paid me the insult of winding up: an insult because usually pitchers shorten or eliminate their wind-up when men are on base to make it harder for the base runner to steal a base

reconstruction: a reference to the period after the Civil War during which the rebellious states were readmitted to the Union

Royals: the Brooklyn Dodgers' farm team in Montreal, Canada

sulfa: a type of drug used as an antibiotic

Ty Cobb: an outfielder with the Detroit Tigers in the early decades of the twentieth century, known for his disagreeable temperament and aggressiveness on the field and for his career batting average, which still stands as the record

Wop: a common slur at the time for Italians, from the Italian word *guappo*, meaning "pimp"

Elijah Muhammad standing behind microphones at podium / World Telegram & Sun photo by Stanley Wolfson. By New York World-Telegram and the Sun staff photographer: Wolfson, Stanley, photographer. - Library of Congress Prints and Photographs Division. [Public domain], via Wikimedia Commons

FBI Report on Elijah Muhammad

"We Want To Unite the scattered tribes of the Black Man into one Nation and build for ourselves a strong Nation."

Overview

Made available to the public under the Freedom of Information Act, the report of the Federal Bureau of Investigation (FBI) on the Nation of Islam (NOI) leader Elijah Muhammad dates to 1973. The report is typical of the files the FBI maintained on prominent Americans, particularly under the long tenure (1924–1972) of its controversial director, J. Edgar Hoover. Many of these Americans were leaders in the civil rights movement and the protest movements of the 1960s; among them were Martin Luther King, Jr., Malcolm X, Abbie Hoffman (founder of the Youth International Party, or "Yippies"), and innumerable others. Hoover maintained his power in Washington, D.C., in part by accumulating large amounts of information on people whose political beliefs he saw as a threat to American security. During the height of the civil rights movement in the 1950s and 1960s, various organizations fell under the scrutiny of the FBI, including the NOI, which the bureau regarded as a radical, subversive group. The report itself, though, expresses few judgments about Muhammad. It summarizes the known facts of his life and includes portions of a published interview with him and excerpts from articles he had written. The report's significance is more one of implication: the mere existence of a report by the nation's chief law-enforcement agency at a time when that agency was preoccupied with foreign and domestic threats suggests that at the highest levels of the nation's government, Muhammad was seen as a dangerous, perhaps subversive, character who had to be watched. And in fact a form attached to the file indicates that Muhammad was under investigation as "potentially dangerous because of background, emotional instability or activity in groups engaged in activities inimical to the U.S."

Context

The NOI was formed in Detroit in 1930 by Wallace Fard Muhammad. Little is known about Fard's early life, and even his true identity is disputed, with names on record including Wallace Dodd Ford, Wallace Dodd, Wallie Dodd Fard, W. D. Fard, David Ford-el, Wali Farad, Farrad Mohammed, and F. Mohammed Ali. It is known, however, that in 1929 he joined the Moorish Science Temple of America founded by Timothy Drew, known as Noble Drew Ali. As far back as 1931 the FBI extensively investigated the Moorish Science Temple of America for sedition, spreading Japanese propaganda, and other possible crimes, though it eventually found no grounds for prosecution. After Drew's death in 1929, Fard assumed leadership of a faction of the organization in Chicago, moved to Detroit, and renamed his group the Allah Temple of Islam. He created the University of Islam, an elementary school operating under Islamic principles that evolved into a series of such institutions; the Fruit of Islam, an all-male security force; and a number of other black Muslim organizations. Fard disappeared in 1934; it is unclear whether he died, moved to Saudi Arabia, or moved to New Zealand, but some evidence suggests that he lived until the 1960s. After his disappearance, the leadership of what was now called the Nation of Islam was assumed by one of his disciples, Elijah Poole, an unemployed Detroit assembly-line worker who first came under Fard's influence about 1930 and who later took the name Elijah Muhammad.

Members of the NOI are commonly called Black Muslims, though the organization has had conflicted relations with mainstream Islam, and many African American Muslims, then and now, are unaffiliated with it. The NOI's teachings departed from traditional Islam in a number of important respects, notably their belief that Wallace Fard Muhammad was both the Messiah of Christianity and the Mahdi, or redeemer, of Islam. Fard believed in the imminence of the biblical Armageddon—the final battle between good and evil that will mark the end of the world (Revelation 16). In his view, Christianity was a white religion imposed on blacks by slave owners to subordinate them. Further, he argued that the original faith of black people was Islam and that originally the people of the world were all black. In his view, whites were a race of "devils" created on the Greek

Elijah Muhammad addressing followers including boxer champion Muhammad Ali, 1964 (Photo by Smith Collection/Gado/Getty Images).

island of Patmos by a scientist named Yakub. Black people, he said, were divine in origin, created by Allah from the dark substance of space. He placed great emphasis on the biblical book of Ezekiel, which, he said, described a "Mother Plane" or "wheel" (chapter 1) that would destroy whites for their evil. A central tenet of the NOI was that African American youth were being disadvantaged by the nation's school system. Muhammad and his followers argued that African Americans had an obligation to learn about their purpose and origins but that the circumstances of the African diaspora denied them knowledge of their history and deprived them of any control over their future. In response, the NOI established its own schools in various cities, often over the objections of state and local authorities because the schools were unaccredited.

The NOI arose during an era when a number of prominent black militants were espousing black nationalism, the belief that blacks could gain true liberation only by uniting and gaining power—and, in the belief of some, establishing a separate black nation. The doctrine of black nationalism reached back at least to the work of Martin R. Delany, the author of an 1852 book, *The Condition, Elevation, Emigration, and Destiny of the Colored People of the United States, Politically Considered*. In the twentieth century, black nationalism underpinned the work of Marcus Garvey, the flamboyant founder of the Universal Negro Improvement Association in 1917 and advocate of black capitalism and a return to Africa. During the 1930s one of the most prominent black nationalists was Paul Robeson, a college All-American football player, actor, and singer whose rich bass voice electrified audiences. Robeson was a Communist sympathizer, though he was never a member of the Communist Party. In the 1930s he visited the Soviet Union on several occasions and concluded that the Communist nation did not carry the same burden of racism that the United States did. During the early years of the cold war, the U.S. State Department revoked his passport, and Hoover labeled him one of the most dangerous men in the world. Even the National Association for the Advancement of Colored People distanced itself from him, scrubbing his name from a list of winners of the prestigious Spingarn Medal.

After the Russian Revolution in 1917, people began to fear that Soviet Communism might spread, possibly even to the United States. In response to this fear, the House Committee on Un-American Activities was formed in 1938, and over the next decade the committee conducted numerous hearings that "exposed" Communists and their sympathizers, including authors and members of the entertainment industry such as Charlie Chaplin, Dashiell Hammett, Leonard Bernstein, Edward G. Robinson, Pete Seeger, and Orson Welles. These people and others were almost always confronted on the basis of innuendo, rumor, and statements they had made that could be seen as sympathetic to Communism. Attention focused on colleges and universities, believed to be hotbeds of leftist and "un-American" viewpoints, as well as on the labor movement. Communism in general and the Soviet Union in particular were regarded as a menace, a threat to world stability. In the United States, fear grew that American Communists were working as spies and saboteurs for the Soviets, and for this reason Communist sentiments were criminalized.

It was in this climate of fear—some would say near paranoia—that the FBI began to investigate and keep files on civil rights organizations and persons or groups suspected of subversive tendencies. By some measures, the FBI's concerns were almost comical. The bureau kept a file, for example, on the issue of whether the lyrics to the Kingmen's 1963 version of the classic rock song "Louie Louie" were obscene. More and more entertainers, musicians, and artists came under scrutiny, especially for associating with Communists or joining the Communist Party, including the Beatles, Marilyn Monroe, Frank Sinatra, Andy Warhol, and Pablo Picasso. Regarding more serious threats, the FBI kept extensive files on genuine Soviet espionage as well as on crime families, serial murderers, the Ku Klux Klan, the 1964 murder of civil rights workers in Mississippi, and a host of other criminal activities and threats to the nation's security.

As the civil rights movement gained momentum in the 1950s and 1960s, the FBI kept track of numerous organizations, and as the movement overlapped with the anti–Vietnam War movement, student protests, and other conflicts after 1965, many other groups also fell under FBI investigation. Martin Luther King, suspected of Communist sympathies and an outspoken opponent of the war in Vietnam, came under investigation. So did Stokely Carmichael, the leader of the Student Nonviolent Coordinating Committee, who urged black men to resist the draft, and Malcolm X, who emerged as one of the most prominent—and fiery—spokesmen for the NOI. The black nationalism of the NOI under its leader, Elijah Muhammad, would have been high on the FBI's list. Accordingly, in common with many Americans, Muhammad had his name on an FBI file.

About the Author

It is unknown who actually composed the FBI's report on Elijah Muhammad, which was likely the work of numerous agents. The compilers were certainly acting under the authority of the FBI's director, J. Edgar Hoover, so the very existence of the report reflected Hoover's preoccupations. Little is known about Hoover's early life. John Edgar Hoover was born on January 1, 1885, in Washington, D.C. He attended George Washington University, where he completed a law degree in 1917. During World War I, he worked at the U.S. Justice Department, where he earned an appointment as the head of the Enemy Aliens Registration Section at a time when Americans felt deep unease about potentially subversive foreign influences and about immigration, particularly from places like Russia and eastern Europe. In 1919 he was appointed head of the Justice Department's General Intelligence Division, which over the next two years arrested some ten thousand suspected political radicals. Hoover was appointed deputy director of what was then called the Bureau of Investigation in 1921. In 1924 he was appointed acting head of the bureau. On May 10, 1924, President Calvin Coolidge appointed him director of the bureau, which changed its name to the Federal Bureau of Investigation in 1935.

For nearly five decades Hoover dominated federal law enforcement. Almost single-handedly, he forged the image of American "G-men" (government men) who exhibited "Fidelity, Bravery, and Integrity" (the FBI's motto) in fighting crime. Beginning in 1924 until his death in 1972, he turned the bureau into a highly efficient professional organization. His reputation was perhaps greatest during the Great Depression, when many Americans came to see the nation's financial institutions as adversaries. Accordingly, when a rash of daring bank robberies broke out in the 1930s, some Americans were almost sympathetic to the colorful, quasi-romantic outlaws who became household names, including John Dillinger, "Machine Gun" Kelly, Ma Barker, and Clyde Barrow and Bonnie Parker—the infamous "Bonnie and Clyde." Local authorities, helpless to stop these robberies, called in the bureau's help. Many of its investigations, including the one that led to the gunning down of John Dillinger in Chicago, were highly publicized and captured the public's imagination. It was largely as a result of these successes that the bureau's powers were expanded.

During the 1930s, Hoover took advantage of the FBI's growing reputation and influence to expand its recruitment efforts, create the FBI Laboratory to examine forensic evidence, and form the Identification Division, which assembled the world's largest collection of fingerprints. In the years leading up to World War II and beyond, Hoover's greatest concern was the threat of foreign subversives and saboteurs on American soil. This concern with subversion deepened during the cold war, when Hoover's focus was on Communism and then on antiwar and revolutionary groups, including members of the civil rights movement and anyone associated with the Black Power or black nationalist movements. Hoover died on May 2, 1972.

Explanation and Analysis of the Document

Any list of persons and organizations that the FBI investigated during the years of the civil rights movement reads like a who's who of protest and reform movements. The FBI had extensive files on the Southern Christian Leadership Conference (with a separate file on Communist influences in the organization), the Black Panthers, the National Association for the Advancement of Colored People, the Organization of Afro-American Unity, and the Student Nonviolent Coordinating Committee. Individuals included Paul Robeson, W. E. B. Du Bois, Roy Wilkins, Thurgood Marshall, Adam Clayton Powell, Jesse Jackson, among numerous others. Most of these files were dry accumulations of factual information. The file on Elijah Muhammad was little different, though undoubtedly the unorthodox views Muhammad expressed were of concern to federal law enforcement.

◆ "I. Background"

The file begins with background information on Muhammad, including his original name (Elijah Poole), his address, and his occupation in connection with Muhammad's Temple 2 in Chicago—reflecting the NOI's practice of numbering each of its temples in the order they were created. The file then provides basic information on the NOI, with emphasis on the notion that white people are to be regarded as "devils" and that NOI members are not to arm themselves but are required to defend the NOI and its members at all costs.

◆ "II. Personal History"

The second portion of the FBI file reproduces an interview with Elijah Muhammad that was published in the yearbook of "Muhammad University of Islam—No. 2" for 1973. In a question-and-answer format, "Messenger Muhammad" provides details about his background—when and where he was born and how he was given the name Elijah, for example. The reader learns that when Muhammad moved to Detroit, he heard Wallace Fard Muhammad speak and believed that he was listening to the voice of Allah, or God. He describes how Fard gave him the name Elijah Karriem—typical of the way Fard provided his followers with Islamic-sounding names for a fee of ten dollars. He then describes how Fard appointed him as "Supreme Minister" and gave him the name Muhammad. Throughout the discussion, Fard is referred to as the Savior and Muhammad is referred to as a "humble" little man.

The interview goes on to elicit odd details about the movements of Fard and Muhammad in the early 1930s, disputes within the organization, Fard's "persecution" and disappearance, and Muhammad's assumption of the leadership of the NOI. Muhammad then discusses his arrest and imprisonment for failing to register for the draft, claiming that he would not take part in a war (World War II) on behalf of "infidels." The interview also provides details about how the NOI was run during Muhammad's absence, when the day-to-day operations were taken over by Muhammad's wife, "Sister Clara Muhammad."

◆ "III. Teachings"

The third section of the FBI's file reproduces portions of three documents written by Muhammad. The first is taken from a 1973 edition of the NOI's publication, *Muhammad Speaks*. In this article Muhammad explains some of the NOI's theological doctrines, many of them adopted from the Old Testament prophetic book of Ezekiel, though this source is never named. He explains that there is a ship, or plane, that is made like a wheel and is the means by which Allah will carry out his aims in the world, particularly his aim of creating a new world "under the Eyes and Guidance of Allah." He claims that this wheel, "the most miraculous mechanical building of a plane that has ever been Imagined by man," measures a half mile by a half mile and is capable of holding many people and of destroying the earth. Muhammad then makes an enigmatic reference when he asks, "After trillions of years should we let a baby, only six months old (6,000 years old) outwit us?" The meaning of this comment is unclear, but it is probably a reference to the emergence of the white race, a "baby" in comparison with the much-older black race. He goes on to assert that the "Black Man" created the heavens and the earth and that white people want to keep blacks "dumb" to the power of God. The passage concludes with assertions that whites want to shoot down the plane with military weapons and that the wheel will continue to protect the black man on earth.

The second article quoted in this section also appeared in *Muhammad Speaks* and is titled "Indians in America." It begins with the assertion, derived from Wallace Fard Muhammad, that the American Indians are the descendents of black Asians, specifically from India. According to this theory, they were exiled from their native land sixteen thousand years earlier and arrived in North America by crossing, on foot, the Bering Straits—the narrow channel that separates Russia and Alaska and that in earlier ages was above water. They were driven away from India because they did not recognize Allah and the religion of Islam. Arriving in North America without guidance, they suffered further punishment at the hands of white men for their disobedience to Allah. Muhammad asserts that the "so-called Negro in America" is suffering a similar fate—conquest by the white man—because he, too, refuses to follow Allah.

Muhammad then states that the white man, too, is an exile, having been expelled from Arabia some six thousand years ago for spreading lies about Islam—an odd belief, given that Islam was founded in the seventh century by the prophet Muhammad. Blacks, though, arrived in the Western Hemisphere in a way different from the Indians and whites, for "we were kidnapped by the white man and brought here by force against our will, for the purpose of evil slavery and mistreatment." Thus, to Muhammad it is clear that the black man arrived in North America without a burden of sin and therefore has a better chance of succeeding than do Indians and whites. Throughout this discussion, Muhammad emphasizes that Allah has manifested himself in the person of Fard, "To Whom Praises are Due forever."

Muhammad rallies Black Muslims by telling them that their purpose is to create a new government, one that is dedicated to freedom, justice, and equality. He urges American Indians to join in his movement based on the notion that the Indians have a remnant of black blood. Even though Indians and blacks are two peoples, they share a common ancestry. He concludes by saying that "we want to unite the scattered tribes of the Black Man into one Nation and build for ourselves a strong Nation."

The third article, titled "We Want Earth," is again from the publication *Muhammad Speaks*. Muhammad begins with the assertion that black people are the original people on earth and that they acquired the name Negroes from their slave masters. This excerpt is the most explicitly black nationalistic one of the three articles, for he states that "we must have some of this earth to live free on so that we can exercise freedom of action." Former slaves cannot rely on their former masters for the necessities of life but have to provide them for themselves. He asserts that blacks make a boast of their freedom and reiterates that blacks have to provide for their own welfare. He reminds his readers that the slave masters robbed blacks both morally and physically and imposed on them a false religion. He asks black America to bring forward its scientists and educated people to help black Americans achieve prosperity and independence.

♦ **"IV. Foreign Contacts"**

The fourth section of the FBI report has been heavily edited. This is common for files released to the public. It is impossible to say what has been omitted or why. Readers can only conclude that the decision was made to withhold some information for diplomatic or national security concerns, to avoid placing foreign people in embarrassing situations, to avoid revealing sensitive foreign intelligence, or some similar reason. In what remains, the section comments on some domestic contacts directly and indirectly associated with Muhammad, starting with a reference to "Hanafi American Mussulman." An NOI member named Khalifa Hamaas Abdul Khaalis, whose original name was Ernest T. McGee, created a rift in the NOI because he wanted to bring the organization in line with orthodox Sunni Islam. In 1958 he created a splinter organization somewhat cumbersomely named the Al-Hanif, Hanifi, Madh-Hob Center, Islam Faith, United States of America, American Mussulmans in Washington, D.C. The group gained publicity in 1973 when members of Abdul Khaalis's family—mostly his children—as well as a follower were murdered by members of the NOI in Philadelphia. As the FBI file states, Abdul Khaalis believed that Elijah Muhammad was responsible for these killings. Later, in 1977, the Hanafis would seize buildings in Washington, D.C., and take hostages in an effort to force the government to turn over the NOI members convicted for the killing of Abdul Khaalis's family members as well as to halt the screening of a movie called *Mohammad, Messenger of God*, which they regarded as sacrilegious. Abdul Khaalis was sentenced to prison for his role in the event.

Reference is made to two additional figures. One is Kareem Abdul-Jabbar, known as Lew Alcindor throughout his college career as an All-American basketball player at the University of California at Los Angeles. Abdul-Jabbar was affiliated with the American Mussulmen and, the file asserts, owned the house in which the 1973 murders took place. Malcolm X, born Malcolm Little, became the most prominent spokesperson for the NOI in the 1950s and early 1960s, but when his views began to conflict with those of Muhammad, he defected from the organization to form his own more orthodox Islamic group. He was assassinated on February 21, 1965, by three members of the NOI.

Audience

The audience for an FBI report would, of course, have been primarily the FBI itself. The purpose of such a report was to assemble investigative information about people and organizations that the FBI deemed suspicious. Such a report would be available to anyone within the organization or the government who needed information about its subject and had authorization to view the file. After the Freedom of Information Act was signed into law on September 6, 1966, and went into effect the next year, numerous citizens and organizations began filing requests for government documents never previously released to the public. Many such documents have remained classified because they have a bearing on national security. And many of the documents that are released are "redacted," meaning that portions of the document are blacked out, usually to avoid revealing information that has national security implications or to protect the identities of FBI agents and informants, who might be subject to reprisals. Nevertheless, the Freedom of Information Act has opened a window into governmental activities and helped to create greater transparency in government operations. While the FBI report on Elijah Muhammad does not contain any startling revelations—virtually all of the information contained in it could have been found in other sources, including NOI publications—the mere fact of its existence sheds as much light on the FBI's concerns as it does on the NOI.

Impact

After J. Edgar Hoover's death in 1972 and in light of abuses during the Watergate scandal that enveloped the presidency of Richard Nixon that year (leading to his resignation in 1974), historians and politicians began a reexamination of Hoover's legacy and tactics. In 1976 the FBI's activities were investigated by the U.S. Senate's Select Committee to Study Governmental Operations with Respect to Intelligence Activities, usually referred to as the Church Committee after its chairman, Senator Frank Church of Idaho. The committee's investigation revealed that FBI investigations often relied on infiltration of suspected subversive groups and on psychological warfare, including the planting of rumors, false reports, and other "dirty tricks"; harassment through the legal system; and illegal activities, including wiretapping, break-ins, vandalism, and violence. The FBI indeed used such methods in investigating the NOI, including infiltration—one of Malcolm X's bodyguards was an FBI plant—wiretapping, and camera surveillance. In the eyes of many historians, these extralegal activities reflected the views and personality of the FBI's longtime director, a public hero for much of his career, whose reputation was thus irretrievably tarnished.

The NOI survived, although its form would change radically. After the death of Elijah Muhammad in 1975, leadership of the organization passed to his son, Warith Deen Mohammad. The son, however, rejected the deification of Wallace Fard Muhammad, brought the organizations closer to mainstream Islamic thinking, admitted white people, and changed the NOI's name several times, eventually settling on American Society of Muslims. Numerous NOI members, though, resisted these changes and broke with the organization. Notable among them was Louis Farrakhan (Louis Eugene Walcott), who in 1981 created his own organization and adopted for it the name Nation of Islam. Farrakhan has continued to lead the reconstituted NOI into the twenty-first century—and in the process has attracted considerable controversy for his allegedly anti-Semitic comments as well as for views that some observers regard as outlandish. One was that Hurricane Katrina, which struck the Gulf Coast in 2005, did so much damage because a hole was allowed to remain in the levee around New Orleans in a deliberate effort to wipe out the city's black population. Another was that the H1N1 ("swine flu") vaccine was developed as part of a conspiracy to reduce the earth's population. Mainstream Americans regard Farrakhan and his organization as something of a fringe group, but both continue to elicit admiration among dispossessed Americans.

Further Reading

♦ Books

Ackerman, Kenneth D. *Young J. Edgar: Hoover, the Red Scare, and the Assault on Civil Liberties*. New York: Da Capo Press, 2008.

Berg, Herbert. *Elijah Muhammad and Islam*. New York: New York University Press, 2009.

Charles, Douglas M. *J. Edgar Hoover and the Anti-Interventionists: FBI Political Surveillance and the Rise of the Domestic Security State, 1939–1945*. Columbus: Ohio State University Press, 2007.

Curtis, Edward E. *Black Muslim Religion in the Nation of Islam, 1960–1975*. Chapel Hill: University of North Carolina Press, 2006.

Garrow, David J. *The FBI and Martin Luther King, Jr., from "Solo" to Memphis*. New York: W. W. Norton, 1981.

Lincoln, Charles Eric. *The Black Muslims in America*. 3rd ed. Grand Rapids, Mich.: Wm. B. Eerdmans, 1994.

Turner, Richard Brent. *Islam in the African-American Experience*. 2nd ed. Bloomington: Indiana University Press, 2003.

Walker, Dennis. *Islam and the Search for African American Nationhood: Elijah Muhammad, Louis Farrakhan, and the Nation of Islam*. Atlanta, Ga.: Clarity Press, 2005.

♦ Web Sites

"Elijah Muhammad." Federal Bureau of Investigation Web site. http://foia.fbi.gov/foiaindex/muhammad.htm.

"A Historic Look at The Honorable Elijah Muhammad." Nation of Islam Web site. http://www.noi.org/elijah_muhammad_history.htm.

"The Honorable Elijah Muhammad." Coalition for the Remembrance of the Honorable Elijah Muhammad Web site. http://www.croe.org.

Palmer, A. Idris. "Brutal Legacy." Mission Islam Web site. http://www.missionislam.com/conissues/malcolmx.htm.

—*Michael J. O'Neal*

Time Line

1893	February 26	■ Wallace Fard Muhammad is thought to have been born in Afghanistan.
1885	January 1	■ J. Edgar Hoover is born in Washington, D.C.
1897	October 7	■ Elijah Muhammad is born Elijah Poole in Sandersville, Georgia.
1924	May 10	■ Hoover is appointed head of the Bureau of Investigation, renamed the Federal Bureau of Investigation in 1935.
1930	July	■ Wallace Fard Muhammad founds an organization called Allah's Temple of Islam (or Nation Cult of Islam), which would become the Nation of Islam (NOI).
1934		■ Wallace Fard Muhammad disappears, leaving the organization under the control of Elijah Muhammad.
1965	February 21	■ Malcolm X, the famous former NOI spokesman, is assassinated by three Black Muslims.
1972	May 2	■ Hoover dies.
1973		■ The FBI releases its report on Elijah Muhammad.
1975	February 25	■ Elijah Muhammad dies, leaving the NOI under the leadership of his son, Warith Deen Mohammad.
1976	April 23	■ The Select Committee to Study Governmental Operations with Respect to Intelligence Activities of the United States Senate, known as the Church Committee, issues its report critical of FBI tactics.
1981		■ After a period of divisive conflict, the NOI is reconstituted under the leadership of Louis Farrakhan.

Essential Quotes

"The NOI is an all-black nationwide organization … under the guidance of Elijah Muhammad, self-styled "Messenger of Allah" and alleged divinely appointed leader of the black race in the United States. Its purpose is separation of the black man from the "devil" (white race) through establishment of a black nation."

"The Wheel is in fact a ship (plane) made like a wheel. And it is made for the Purpose of Allah (God) Carrying out His Aim upon this world. This Wheel is by no means to be taken lightly! After The Wheel has done its Work it will have Made Way for a New World to be Built under the Eyes and Guidance of Allah (God)."

"But, it is our Black People who the white man is desirous to keep dumb to the Power of our God, Allah. But, Think Over It! If the Black Man created the heavens and the earth. And The Black Man Did Create The Heavens And The Earth … then what man is fool enough to challenge the Black Man."

"The American White Man is an exile from Arabia. They were exiled into Europe 6,000 years ago because of their disobedience and causing dissatisfaction, fighting and blood-shed among the righteous due to their spreading lies between the Muslims. That is what they were made for."

"We Want To Unite the scattered tribes of the Black Man into one Nation and build for ourselves a strong Nation."

Questions for Further Study

1. If you had been the director of the FBI in the 1950s and 1960s, would you have ordered the investigation of the Nation of Islam? Why or why not?

2. What is the connection between black nationalism and the Nation of Islam?

3. Based on the material presented in the FBI file, do you believe that the Nation of Islam is (or was) a racist organization? Explain.

4. Using such documents as Malcolm X's "After the Bombing" speech and Louis Farrakhan's Million Man March Pledge, explain how the modern-day Nation of Islam is different from the organization as it was conceived by Fard and Elijah Muhammad.

5. Muhammad expressed a number of views that run counter to known facts and accepted beliefs; examples include his view of the origin of American Indians and his apparent belief that Mars is populated. To what extent do you think that these highly unorthodox views undermine Elijah Muhammad's message—if at all?

FBI REPORT ON ELIJAH MUHAMMAD

The full text of the FBI's file on Elijah Muhammad.

File: 105-24822

Details:

♦ I. Background

Elijah Muhammad, true name Elijah Poole, resides at 4847 South Woodlawn Avenue, Chicago, Illinois. He also maintains a residence at 2118 East Violet Drive, Phoenix, Arizona, but rarely utilizes same. Muhammad is the leader of the Nation of Islam (NOI). He claims to be the Messenger of Allah and the only divinely appointed leader of the black man in North America. He formulates and/or approves all teachings, policies and programs in the NOI... He is considered to be Minister of Muhammad's Temple (MT) 2, 7351 South Stony Island Avenue, Chicago. He performs the above tasks, which are his sole occupation, from his residence and through MT 2. ...

The NOI is an all-black nationwide organization headquartered at Muhammad's Temple 2, 7351 South Stony Island Avenue, Chicago, Illinois, under the guidance of Elijah Muhammad, self-styled "Messenger of Allah" and alleged divinely appointed leader of the black race in the United States. Its purpose is separation of the black man from the "devil" (white race) through establishment of a black nation. Followers are instructed to obey the laws of the land if they do not conflict with NOI laws and not to carry weapons but are to defend NOI officials, their property, women and themselves if attacked at all costs and are to take weapons away from their attackers and use same on the attacker.

♦ II. Personal History

"Muhammad University of Islam—No. 2—1973" Year Book on page 24 sets forth an article titled "History," which is as follows:

Q. What year, month and day was Messenger Muhammad born?
A. He was born in October, 1897.
Q. Where was Messenger Muhammad born?
A. Messenger Muhammad was born in Sandersville, Georgia, not many miles from his hometown he grew up in Macon, Georgia.
Q. How large was his family?
A. Messenger Muhammad was the seventh child of thirteen children.
Q. Who gave him the name of Elijah?
A. A paternal grandfather gave him the name Elijah, and always addressed him as Elijah the Prophet.
Q. Did Messenger Muhammad show leadership traits early?
A. Yes, the older children in the family would always come to him to settle disputes and at fifteen; he was a foreman over a crew of men much older than he.
Q. How old was Messenger Muhammad when he married and migrated to Detroit?
A. Messenger Muhammad was twenty-five years of age, and be moved to Detroit in April, 1923.
Q. What was the first meeting of Allah and Elijah Poole like?
A. Someone, one day went excitedly to tell Mr. Elijah Poole that there was a certain man in town teaching that which he just had to go hear for himself. So, Mr. Elijah Poole went down to the meeting hall to hear this certain man speak, According to the best reports, as soon as he walked into the room he realized that the one who was speaking was God, Himself. When shaking the man's hand after the meeting, Mr. Elijah Poole said, "I know who you are, you're God Himself." The certain man whispered to him, that's right, but don't tell it now: It is not yet time for it to be known.
Q. When did Master Fard Muhammad name Elijah Poole Elijah Karriem?
A. The Savior Master Fard Muhammad named Elijah Poole Elijah Karriem shortly after he accepted his own.
Q. How was Elijah Karriem appointed as Supreme Minister and describe how it took place. Did he receive the name Muhammad then?
A. The Savior, Master Fard Muhammad, used a system of permitting the student ministers to select their own minister from among themselves.

They would always select the most articulate, smooth-talking one. However, one day the Savior decided to select his own."I've let you select yours for awhile," he told the student ministers. "Now I'll select mine." "Hey, you over there, Karriem!" Master Fard called out to the humble little man seated in the corner rear of the classroom. "Who me?" The Messenger asked humbly. "Yes, you Elijah Karriem," The Savior commanded. "Come up here with me." The humble little man went to the front of the class and stood beside his Master. The Savior put his right arm around the little man's shoulder and said, "From now on this is My Minister." The Savior gave Elijah the name of Muhammad, His name. Muhammad was given the title "Supreme Minister" until later on when he received the title "Messenger of Allah," a title which he was not to use until the Savior had gone because it was not to be revealed until then that Savior Himself was Allah in person.

Q. Why did Master Fard Muhammad allow himself to be persecuted?

A. Master Fard Muhammad allowed Himself to be persecuted because he chose to suffer three and one-half years to show His love for His people who have suffered over 300 years at hands of a people who by nature are evil and wicked and have no good in them. He was persecuted, sent to jail in 1932 and ordered out of Detroit on May 26, 1933.

In 1933 he came to Chicago and was arrested almost immediately on His arrival and placed behind prison bars.

Q. Why did Master Fard Muhammad always call Messenger Muhammad to Him when He went Jail?

A. He submitted himself with all humbleness to his persecutors. "Each time he was arrested, He sent for me so that I might see and learn the price of truth for us, the so-called American Negroes (members of the Asiatic Nation). He was able to save Himself from such suffering, but how else was the scripture to be fulfilled? We followed in His footsteps suffering the same persecution."

Q. How many years did Master Fard Muhammad teach Messenger Muhammad?

A. Messenger Muhammad was taught by Allah for three years and four or five months.

Q. When did Master Fard Muhammad leave and how many books did he leave for Messenger Muhammad to find and read?

A. He left in 1934 and left 104 books for Messenger Muhammad to find.

Q. Why did Messenger Muhammad leave Detroit?

A. Sometime in 1934 Allah left. As they had agreed before Master Fard Muhammad left, Elijah Muhammad began teaching that the one who had been known as Prophet Fard was in fact Allah (God) Himself, in the Person of Master Fard Muhammad, Some of the former student ministers disagreed. They didn't want to believe that the most humble among them had been chosen to be The Messenger of Allah - they began disbelieving in Allah after they had said that they believed; they became hypocrites.

Q. Where did Messenger Muhammad go during the period of 1934?

A. Messenger Muhammad moved to Chicago in 1934. In 1935, The Honorable Elijah Muhammad fled to Washington, D. C. from the hypocrites.

Q. Where did Messenger Muhammad go during the period of flight?

A. He went from city to city teaching Islam on the east coast, mainly.

Q. How did he go about establishing the different Mosques?

A. While on the run.

Q. In what year did Chicago become the Headquarters?

A. In September, 1934.

Q. When did Messenger Muhammad go to jail for five years?

A. "I was arrested on May 8, 1942, in Washington, D. C. by the F.B.I. for not registering for the draft. When the call was made for all males between 18 and 44, I refused and would not take part in war and especially not on the side with the infidels. Second, I was 45 years of age and was not, according to the law, required to register." Brother Emmanuel Muhammad speaking of his father: "What has impressed me most, I think, was my stay with my father in prison. He set up a Temple in the prison despite the difficulties he experienced with the blackboard and all. He set up classes right there in prison. He would teach on Wednesday and Friday evenings until the bugle was blown for us to go to bed. He also taught on Sunday afternoons at 2:00 p.m. He made many, many converts in prison. Even the devils who came by to steal an earful wound up bowing in agreement, an unconscious bearing of witness to the truth The Messenger taught.

"There are, in my mind, many memorable instances of my father's love for Allah, but the one that sticks in me most is of the tears Allah and The Messenger shed the day Allah left us.

"I also recall seeing my father reading the Bible after breakfast; or whatever they called breakfast during the depression He would read all day, and this reading would bring tears to His eyes. The tears would fall at the time he was reading. ..."

Q. How was the Nation of Islam run during this period?

A. Sister Clara Muhammad was the first of the family to accept the mission of The Honorable Elijah Muhammad. She held the Muhammad family together all the while He was on the run. And, while He was in prison, the remaining officials would seek information from her. "She would bring understanding from my father on questions she could not answer. She gathered and sent or brought to my father and I whatever literature the prison permitted. She typed verses from the Holy Quran and sent them to us." Where were the meeting places in those days? In 1945, Messenger Elijah Muhammad sent instructions for us not to pay any more rent but to hold our meetings in one of the believer's homes and to purchase a building. In the winter of 1955–56 in October, the building at 5333-35 South Greenwood was purchased. In June, 1972, a new Temple was purchased at 7351 Stoney Island Avenue. Messenger Muhammad and his followers across the Nation are determined to build an Educational Center at this site, second to none on Chicago's southside, which will serve as memorial to the dedicated mission of God's Messenger. The Honorable Elijah Muhammad, here in America....

♦ III. Teachings

"Muhammad Speaks" (MS), September 7, 1973, page 12, sets forth an article titled "O Wheel - Mother of Planes," by Elijah Muhammad. He wrote:

... The Wheel is in fact a ship (plane) made like a wheel. And it is made for the Purpose of Allah (God) Carrying out His Aim upon this world. This Wheel is by no means to be taken lightly!

After The Wheel has done its Work it will have Made Way for a New World to be Built under the Eyes and Guidance of Allah (God).

The Wheel is so wonderful that even the prophet had to declare it in these words, "O Wheel, O Wheel" meaning that he is admiring his vision that he was receiving from Allah (God).

The Wheel is the most wonderful and the most miraculous mechanical building of a plane that has ever been Imagined by man. The planes on this Wheel will be sent down, earthward and are capable of destroying the world almost at once. The Wheel, (the Mother Plane) is capable of carrying many people in it! The Wheel is ½ mile by ½ mile in size.

The Wheel is capable of sitting up above earth's atmosphere for a whole year before coming down into earth's atmosphere to take on more oxygen and hydrogen for the people who are on this plane (The Wheel) O she is a wonderful thing!

The Planes that she uses to send earthward are so swift that they can make their flight and return their plane to The Wheel, the Mother Plane, almost like a flash of lightning. O Wheel!

Think Over It: After trillions of years should we let a baby, only six months old (6,000 years old) outwit us? This I say to those ignorant people of mine. I do not say this to the white man, for the white man knows, too.

But, it is our Black People who the white man is desirous to keep dumb to the Power of our God, Allah. But, Think Over It! If the Black Man created the heavens and the earth. And The Black Man Did Create The Heavens And The Earth ... then what man is fool enough to challenge the Black Man.

It Is Not that the white man is a fool to try to challenge Allah. It is the intention of the white man to make a fool out of the Black Man and to try to show Allah that he can make a fool out of the Black Man.

But, in a twinkling of an eye, Allah (God) can take away the heavens and the earth, not to think over a few little people just made six days ago (6,000 years ago). O Wheel, the greatest most miraculous plane ever built. There never was such a plane made before this Wheel. There never was a need for such a plane before now.

You may wish Mr. Enemy that you could get a shot at The Wheel with your jet planes and other military weapons, but you should just go home and go to sleep. No one can harm this plane, The Wheel. They are going to fix you up first, Before The Wheel ever comes into sight!

You cannot live on the moon, only just so long as your oxygen and hydrogen last you. The moon is about the closest platform that I know of, that you could probably try to use.

Venus And Mars … you cannot use Venus and Mars. The people on Mars will not let you light (land) on Mars. If they do let you land on Mars, they will be silly to do so.

You would like to see what the people on Mars look like. That is not, say, impossible. O Wheel … the greatest mechanical defender, powered by the Spirit of Allah, to Protect us, the Black People On The Face Of The Earth.

MS newspaper is self-described as published weekly by MT 2 in Chicago.

MS, October 12, 1973, page 12, sets forth an article titled "Indians in America" by Elijah Muhammad. He wrote

Allah (God) Who Came in the Person of Master Fard Muhammad, To Whom Praises are due forever, taught me, that the Indians, who are so-called American Indians, are descendants from an old Ancient People, the Black Man of Asia, in that part of the country that is known as India. They are by no means a modern people.

The Indians, who are here in the Western Hemisphere are non-American, therefore I use the word, so-called American Indians. They were captured and subdued by the Americans, but this does not mean that they are Americanized.

The So-Called American Indians, so Allah (God) Who Came in the Person of Master Fard Muhammad, To Whom Praises are Due forever, taught me, were exiled from their native land (India) and people, 16,000 years ago. They migrated, by walking from the country that is now known as India and entered this country, by way of the Bering Straits.

They Were Driven Out Of India because of their unbelief in Allah and their failure to worship in His True Religion, Islam. They had to walk all that way because their fathers rebelled against Allah and His Religion, Islam.

They Suffered for a long time trying to get into this part of the earth. Imagine, if you would start out to walk to America through the Bering Straits to India, you would probably never reach there alive. To even walk across the continent of America would probably get a man for life. So imagine these people walking thousands and tens of thousands of miles to get into this part of the earth. It takes a long time.

They Had To Take Such terrible chastisement due to the spirit of Allah (God) against these people, because of their disobedience to Allah (God) and His Religion, Islam.

The So-Called American Indians were completely guideless. Allah allowed this to happen to them because of their disobedience. They built many kinds of gods with their own hands and bowed down and worshiped the work of their own hands as they are still doing in India, today. They are not successful in India, except those who turn to Islam.

And Since the Western Hemisphere became a prison exile for the American Indians, Allah (God) sent another exiled enemy (white man) to chase this (Indian) exile and to bring him into subjection to the late white exile and give the Indians another whipping.

Here In America, the white man has almost annihilated the Indian from the *face of* the earth. I want you to see into the work of God upon a people who refuse Him, as the so-called Negro in America desires to do, today. They Ignore Allah (God) and follow an exiled enemy of God.

The American White Man is an exile from Arabia They were exiled into Europe 6,000 years ago because of their disobedience and causing dissatisfaction, fighting and blood-shed among. the righteous due to their spreading lies between the Muslims. That is what they were made for.

The So-Called Negro in America came into America in such a different way than that of the Indians and the white man. We were not exiled from our native country and people. We were kidnapped by the white man and brought here by force against our will, for the purpose of evil slavery and mistreatment.

The So-Called Negro has no divine Charge or sin placed against them, by God, for being here or for doing anything in the way of other than righteous. The so-called Negro in America is cleared by Allah (God) Who Came in the Person of Master Fard Muhammad, To Whom Praises are Due forever.

Since Allah (God) has forgiven us for what was put upon us by the slavemaster (other than righteous), we have the better chance than the former two (the exiled enemy Indian and the exiled enemy white man).

We, The So-Called Negro in America, have a Defender in God, The All-Wise, The Best-Knower, The All-Powerful, The Mighty God and the Greatest of Them all, Allah, In the Person of Master Fard Muhammad, To Whom Praises are Due forever, Who is on our side.

Allah (God) Desires to use us, the descendants of our Black Nation, the best and the greatest of the Black Nation of Earth, since the time of its creation. The fact about it, He wants to build a new and Eternal Government of Freedom, Justice and Equality, out of us, for the Nation of Black People of the Earth.

However, The Door Is Open, to the remnant of the American Indians, so I turn my attention to this all but annihilated people, to see if they will come and follow me to Allah. Allah (God) Who Came in the Person of Master Fard Muhammad, To Whom Praises are Due forever, discussed them with me. So if you desire to live, my once-brothers, the Indians of America, seek me and I will Seek God, for you, that you may live, yet again. Allah (God) taught me that we can get along with the Indians of America, for they yet have some blood of the aboriginal Black people.

We Are Two People, who have been nearly destroyed. I seek the Indians. There are various newly made races of people here in the Western Hemisphere. They are mixed with the blood of this people and that people, but if you notice there is a trace of the blood of the Black Man in most of them.

We Want To Unite the scattered tribes of the Black Man into one Nation and build for ourselves a strong Nation.

MS, October 19, 1973, page 12, sets forth an article titled "We Want Earth:" by Elijah Muhammad. He wrote:

We, The Lost and Found Members of our Nation, the Original Black Nation of the Earth, called Negroes—a name given to us by the slavemasters along with their own, which have no divine meaning—need some of this earth on which we can build a home of our own. If we now are free and must go for self, we must have some of this earth to live free on so that we can exercise freedom of action.

The freed slave is not to depend on his ex-slave-master for the necessities of life. This is the free slave's responsibility. The slave must be educated into the knowledge of how to do for self. He is not to depend on his former master if he is to become self independent.

We Boast that we are free. We love to tell the world that we are free. Freedom means that we are free to do what we like. We cannot yell to the world that we are free while begging to be freed.

It is the free man's duty to accept his own responsibilities accompanying freedom. If we turn back pleading to the master who freed us to feed, clothe and shelter us, we are still in slavery to the master. The Bible refers to this type of person as a "home-born slave."

If One Were to care for us, taking the responsibility for us, we would become a servant to that one. We are in bondage to whosoever takes our responsibilities to care for us.

Can we blame the masters for the treatment they give their own slaves? Yes, and no. They have robbed us both physically and mentally. They have spiritually blinded us to the knowledge of ourself and kind, God, the devil and true religion. This truth would bring to us eternal salvation.

We Love freedom. If we love freedom for self, remember that we must assume our own responsibility, so we are free to exercise the freedom of actions as well as freedom of thinking. Both the clergy and political classes of our people should remember this and preach it.

Where are our degreed scholars' and scientists' works in the way of trying to help themselves and their people to self independence?

We are a nation in a nation, with a population, according to the census, between 20 to 30 million ex-slaves roaming the country over seeking the master's pity. If we do something for self we accept our own pity.

God Will help those who help themselves, let us unite and agree on simple truth—and get some of this earth wherein we can do for self as other free nations have done.

♦ IV. Foreign Contacts

It is public knowledge that in January 1973, seven members of the Hanafi American Mussulman, Washington, D. C. were murdered, that Hamaas Khalis, leader of the group and former secretary of MT 2 in the late 1950's, true name Ernest McGhee, publicly stated Elijah Muhammad was responsible for the murder of the seven members of his family and the critically wounding of two others.

It is public knowledge that Kareem Abdul Jabbar, renowned basketball player with the Milwaukee Bucks of the National Basketball Association, was affiliated

Document Text

with the Hanafi American Mussulman and the murder occurred in a house purchased by Jabbar.

Malcolm X Little in the early 1960's was a leading spokesman for Elijah Muhammad and was Minister of MT 7, New York City, New York. He defected, founded his own organization based on Orthodox Islam and was murdered in New York City in 1965.

Glossary

Allah: the name of the Islamic deity

Bering Straits: the narrow channel that separates Russia and Alaska and that in earlier ages was above water

Hanafi American Mussulman: a splinter organization of the Nation of Islam formed by Khalifa Hamaas Abdul Khaalis in 1958

Master Fard Muhammad: the founder of the Nation of Islam

MS: an abbreviation for the title of the Nation of Islam publication *Muhammad Speaks*

MT: an abbreviation for Muhammad's Temple, the name given to all Nation of Islam temples, which are then distinguished by a number

Quran: the Islam sacred scripture, usually spelled Qur'an or Koran

Sister Clara Muhammad: Elijah Muhammad's wife

Wheel: based on the biblical book of Ezekiel, an immense ship or plane made like a wheel and the means by which Allah will carry out his aims in the world

Subject blood draw, c. 1953 This media is available in the holdings of the National Archives and Records Administration

Final Report of the Tuskegee Syphilis Study Ad Hoc Advisory Panel

"We believe that the goal of scientific progress can be harmonized with the need to assure the protection of human subjects."

Overview

The *Final Report of the Tuskegee Syphilis Study Ad Hoc Advisory Panel* was written for officials at the U.S. Department of Health, Education and Welfare (DHEW) when the agency was facing increasing public scrutiny about a bioethical scandal. The report was a response from the DHEW (today's Department of Health and Human Services) to revelations that hundreds of black men in Alabama had been the unknowing subjects of a government-operated medical research project. These men were not treated for their disease (syphilis), even though a treatment had been discovered and widely disseminated since the mid-1940s. Furthermore, since these patients were allowed to remain infected with syphilis, many of their wives and infants became infected with the disease as well. The DHEW organized the Tuskegee Syphilis Study Ad Hoc Advisory Panel in early 1972 as the Tuskegee Syphilis Study (TSS) became increasingly publicized and shocked large segments of the nation.

Explanation and Analysis of the Document

The TSS was initiated in 1932 by physician-researchers at the U.S. Public Health Service. The purpose of the project was to investigate the effects of untreated syphilis in black males. The TSS was set up to attract participants from the largely poor and segregated black communities of Macon County, Alabama. Overall, some 399 black males already infected with syphilis prior to their enrollment in the study were selected, along with another two hundred uninfected black males serving as a control group for the project. A number of government agencies, physician groups, and local institutions, including one of the nation's most famous black colleges, the Tuskegee Institute, cooperated with or acquiesced in the TSS project activities. The research proceeded for forty years, with the infected men left deliberately untreated during these decades. When newspaper reports revealed the TSS to the American public in the early 1970s, a firestorm of criticism was unleashed against government health officials and the nation's medical profession as a whole. As a result, the assistant secretary of DHEW implemented the TSS Ad Hoc Advisory Panel to explore the project's current state and then recommend appropriate policy actions for DHEW.

Muhammad then states that the white man, too, is an exile, having been expelled from Arabia some six thousand years ago for spreading lies about Islam—an odd belief, given that Islam was founded in the seventh century by the prophet Muhammad. Blacks, though, arrived in the Western Hemisphere in a way different from the Indians and whites, for "we were kidnapped by the white man and brought here by force against our will, for the purpose of evil slavery and mistreatment." Thus, to Muhammad it is clear that the black man arrived in North America without a burden of sin and therefore has a better chance of succeeding than do Indians and whites. Throughout this discussion, Muhammad emphasizes that Allah has manifested himself in the person of Fard, "To Whom Praises are Due forever."

Muhammad rallies Black Muslims by telling them that their purpose is to create a new government, one that is dedicated to freedom, justice, and equality. He urges American Indians to join in his movement based on the notion that the Indians have a remnant of black blood. Even though Indians and blacks are two peoples, they share a common ancestry. He concludes by saying that "we want to unite the scattered tribes of the Black Man into one Nation and build for ourselves a strong Nation.

The third article, titled "We Want Earth," is again from the publication *Muhammad Speaks*. Muhammad begins

DATA PRESENTED BY DR. B. C. BROWN

Classification of Cases in Tuskegee Study

	Controls	Syphilitic	Total
Classification at initial examination	200	411	611
Cases added in 1938-1939	-	14	14
Total - Original classification	200	425	625
Controls infected during observation	-9	+9	-
Controls reclassified as syphilitic			
on basis of additional history	-1	+1	-
on basis of treponemal tests	-8	+8	-
Total - Final classification	182	443	625
Known dead - Number	97	276	373
Percent	53.3	62.3	59.7
Remainder -	85	167	252
Examined in 1968			
Number	36	53	89
Percent	42.4	31.7	35.3

2/4/69:az

Table from U.S. Public Health Service summarising participants in the study By Dr. B. C. Brown - U.S. National Archives and Records Administration. [Public domain], via Wikimedia Commons

with the assertion that black people are the original people on earth and that they acquired the name Negroes from their slave masters. This excerpt is the most explicitly black nationalistic one of the three articles, for he states that "we must have some of this earth to live free on so that we can exercise freedom of action." Former slaves cannot rely on their former masters for the necessities of life but have to provide them for themselves. He asserts that blacks make a boast of their freedom and reiterates that blacks have to provide for their own welfare. He reminds his readers that the slave masters robbed blacks both morally and physically and imposed on them a false religion. He asks black America to bring forward its scientists and educated people to help black Americans achieve prosperity and independence.

The fourth section of the FBI report has been heavily edited. This is common for files released to the public. It is impossible to say what has been omitted or why. Readers can only conclude that the decision was made to withhold some information for diplomatic or national security concerns, to avoid placing foreign people in embarrassing situations, to avoid revealing sensitive foreign intelligence, or some similar reason. In what remains, the section comments on some domestic contacts directly and indirectly associated with Muhammad, starting with a reference to "Hanafi American Mussulman." An NOI member named Khalifa Hamaas Abdul Khaalis, whose original name was Ernest T. McGee, created a rift in the NOI because he wanted to bring the organization in line with orthodox Sunni Islam. In 1958 he created a splinter organization somewhat cumbersomely named the Al-Hanif, Hanifi, Madh-Hob Center, Islam Faith, United States of America, American Mussulmans in Washington, D.C. The group gained publicity in 1973 when members of Abdul Khaalis's family—mostly his children—as well as a follower were murdered by members of the NOI in Philadelphia. As the FBI file states, Abdul Khaalis believed that Elijah Muhammad was responsible for these killings. Later, in 1977, the Hanafis would seize buildings in Washington, D.C., and take hostages in an effort to force the government to turn over the NOI members convicted for the killing of Abdul Khaalis's family members as well as to halt the screening of a movie called *Mohammad, Messenger of God*, which they regarded as sacrilegious. Abdul Khaalis was sentenced to prison for his role in the event.

Reference is made to two additional figures. One is Kareem Abdul-Jabbar, known as Lew Alcindor throughout his college career as an All-American basketball player at the University of California at Los Angeles. Abdul-Jabbar was affiliated with the American Mussulmen and, the file asserts, owned the house in which the 1973 murders took place. Malcolm X, born Malcolm Little, became the most prominent spokesperson for the NOI in the 1950s and early 1960s, but when his views began to conflict with those of Muhammad, he defected from the organization to form his own more orthodox Islamic group. He was assassinated on February 21, 1965, by three members of the NOI.

Audience

The audience for an FBI report would, of course, have been primarily the FBI itself. The purpose of such a report was to assemble investigative information about people and organizations that the FBI deemed suspicious. Such a report would be available to anyone within the organization or the government who needed information about its subject and had authorization to view the file. After the Freedom of Information Act was signed into law on September 6, 1966, and went into effect the next year, numerous citizens and organizations began filing requests for government documents never previously released to the public. Many such documents have remained classified because they have a bearing on national security. And many of the documents that are released are "redacted," meaning that portions of the document are blacked out, usually to avoid revealing information that has national security implications or to protect the identities of FBI agents and informants, who might be subject to reprisals. Nevertheless, the Freedom of Information Act has opened a window into governmental activities and helped to create greater transparency in government operations. While the FBI report on Elijah Muhammad does not contain any startling revelations—virtually all of the information contained in it could have been found in other sources, including NOI publications—the mere fact of its existence sheds as much light on the FBI's concerns as it does on the NOI.

Impact

After J. Edgar Hoover's death in 1972 and in light of abuses during the Watergate scandal that enveloped the presidency of Richard Nixon that year (leading to his resignation in 1974), historians and politicians began a reexamination of Hoover's legacy and tactics. In 1976 the FBI's activities were investigated by the U.S. Senate's Select Committee to Study Governmental Operations with Respect to Intelligence Activities, usually referred to as the Church Committee after its chairman, Senator Frank Church of Idaho. The committee's investigation revealed that FBI investigations often relied on infiltration of suspected subversive groups and on psychological warfare, including the planting of rumors, false reports, and other "dirty tricks"; harassment through the legal system; and illegal activities, including wiretapping, break-ins, vandalism, and violence. The FBI indeed used such methods in investigating the NOI, including infiltration—one of Malcolm X's bodyguards was an FBI plant—wiretapping, and camera surveillance. In the eyes of many historians, these extralegal activities reflected the views and personality of the FBI's longtime director, a public hero for much of his career, whose reputation was thus irretrievably tarnished.

The NOI survived, although its form would change radically. After the death of Elijah Muhammad in 1975, leadership of the organization passed to his son, Warith Deen Mohammad. The son, however, rejected the deification of Wallace Fard Muhammad, brought the organizations closer to mainstream Islamic thinking, admitted white people, and changed the NOI's name several times, eventually settling on American Society of Muslims. Numerous NOI members, though, resisted these changes and broke with the organization. Notable among them was Louis Farrakhan (Louis Eugene Walcott), who in 1981 created his own organization and adopted for it the name Nation of Islam. Farrakhan has continued to lead the reconstituted NOI into the twenty-first century—and in the process has attracted considerable controversy for his allegedly anti-Semitic comments as well as for views that some observers regard as outlandish. One was that Hurricane Katrina, which struck the Gulf Coast in 2005, did so much damage because a hole was allowed to remain in the levee around New Orleans in a deliberate effort to wipe out the city's black population. Another was that the H1N1 ("swine flu") vaccine was developed as part of a conspiracy to reduce the earth's population. Mainstream Americans regard Farrakhan and his organization as something of a fringe group, but both continue to elicit admiration among dispossessed Americans.

Further Reading

♦ Books

Ackerman, Kenneth D. *Young J. Edgar: Hoover, the Red Scare, and the Assault on Civil Liberties.* New York: Da Capo Press, 2008.

Berg, Herbert. *Elijah Muhammad and Islam.* New York: New York University Press, 2009.

Charles, Douglas M. *J. Edgar Hoover and the Anti-Interventionists: FBI Political Surveillance and the Rise of the Domestic Security State, 1939–1945.* Columbus: Ohio State University Press, 2007.

Curtis, Edward E. *Black Muslim Religion in the Nation of Islam, 1960–1975.* Chapel Hill: University of North Carolina Press, 2006.

Garrow, David J. *The FBI and Martin Luther King, Jr., from "Solo" to Memphis.* New York: W. W. Norton, 1981.

Lincoln, Charles Eric. *The Black Muslims in America.* 3rd ed. Grand Rapids, Mich.: Wm. B. Eerdmans, 1994.

Turner, Richard Brent. *Islam in the African-American Experience.* 2nd ed. Bloomington: Indiana University Press, 2003.

Walker, Dennis. *Islam and the Search for African American Nationhood: Elijah Muhammad, Louis Farrakhan, and the Nation of Islam.* Atlanta, Ga.: Clarity Press, 2005.

♦ Web Sites

"Elijah Muhammad." Federal Bureau of Investigation Web site. http://foia.fbi.gov/foiaindex/muhammad.htm.

"A Historic Look at The Honorable Elijah Muhammad." Nation of Islam Web site. http://www.noi.org/elijah_muhammad_history.htm.

"The Honorable Elijah Muhammad." Coalition for the Remembrance of the Honorable Elijah Muhammad Web site. http://www.croe.org.

Palmer, A. Idris. "Brutal Legacy." Mission Islam Web site. http://www.missionislam.com/conissues/malcolmx.htm.

——David M. McBride

Essential Quotes

"In retrospect, the Public Health Service Study of Untreated Syphilis in the Male Negro in Macon County, Alabama, was ethically unjustified in 1932."

"Penicillin therapy should have been made available to the participants in this study especially as of 1953 when penicillin became generally available."

"There is ample evidence in the records available to us that the consent to participation was not obtained from the Tuskegee Syphilis Study subjects, but that instead they were exploited, manipulated, and deceived. They were treated not as human subjects but as objects of research."

"We believe that the goal of scientific progress can be harmonized with the need to assure the protection of human subjects."

Questions for Further Study

1. If you had been the director of the FBI in the 1950s and 1960s, would you have ordered the investigation of the Nation of Islam? Why or why not?

2. What is the connection between black nationalism and the Nation of Islam?

3. Based on the material presented in the FBI file, do you believe that the Nation of Islam is (or was) a racist organization? Explain.

4. Using such documents as Malcolm X's "After the Bombing" speech and Louis Farrakhan's Million Man March Pledge, explain how the modern-day Nation of Islam is different from the organization as it was conceived by Fard and Elijah Muhammad.

5. Muhammad expressed a number of views that run counter to known facts and accepted beliefs; examples include his view of the origin of American Indians and his apparent belief that Mars is populated. To what extent do you think that these highly unorthodox views undermine Elijah Muhammad's message—if at all?

Final Report of the Tuskegee Syphilis Study Ad Hoc Advisory Panel

Extracts from the report.

Report on Charge I-A

Statement of Charge I-A: Determine whether the study was justified in 1932.

♦ **Background Data**

The Tuskegee Study was one of several investigations that were taking place in the 1930's with the ultimate objective of venereal disease control in the United States. Beginning in 1926, the United States Public Health Service, with the cooperation of other organizations, actively engaged in venereal disease control work. In 1929, the United States Public Health Service entered into a cooperative demonstration study with the Julius Rosenwald Fund and state and local departments of health in the control of venereal disease in six southern states: Mississippi (Bolivar County); Tennessee (Tipton County); Georgia (Glynn County); Alabama (Macon County); North Carolina (Pitt County); Virginia (Albermarle County). These syphilis control demonstrations took place from 1930–1932 and disclosed a high prevalence of syphilis (35%) in the Macon County survey. Macon County was 82.4% Negro. The cultural status of this Negro population was low and the illiteracy rate was high....

♦ **Facts and Documentation Pertaining to Charge I-A**
1. There is no protocol which documents the original intent of the study....

   In the absence of an original protocol, it can only be assumed that between 1932 and 1936 (when the first report of the study was made) the decision was made to continue the study as a long-term study....
2. There is no evidence that informed consent was gained from the human participants in this study. Such consent would and should have included knowledge of the risk of human life for the involved parties and information re possible infections of innocent, nonparticipating parties such as friends and relatives. Reports such as "Only individuals giving a history of infection who submitted voluntarily to examination were included in the 399 cases" are the only ones that are documentable. Submitting voluntarily is not informed consent.
3. In 1932, there was a known risk to human life and transmission of the disease in latent and late syphilis was believed to be possible. Moore 1932 reported satisfactory clinical outcome in 85% of patients with latent syphilis that were treated in contrast to 35% if no treatment is given.
4. The study as announced and continually described as involving "untreated" male Negro subjects was not a study of "untreated" subjects. Caldwell in 1971 reported that: All but one of the originally untreated syphilitics seen in 1968–1970 have received therapy,...
5. There is evidence that control subjects who became syphilitic were transferred to the "untreated" group....
6. In the absence of a definitive protocol, there is no evidence or assurance that standardization of evaluative procedures, which are essential to the validity and reliability of a scientific study, existed at any time....

♦ **Panel Judgments on Charge I-A**
1. In retrospect, the Public Health Service Study of Untreated Syphilis in the Male Negro in Macon County, Alabama, was ethically unjustified in 1932. This judgment made in 1973 about the conduct of the study in 1932 is made with the advantage of hindsight acutely sharpened over some forty years, concerning an activity in a different age with different social standards. Nevertheless one fundamental ethical rule is that a person should not be subjected to avoidable risk of death or physical harm unless he freely and intelligently consents. There is no evidence that such consent was obtained from the participants in this study.
2. Because of the paucity of information available today on the manner in which the study was conceived, designed and sustained, a scientific justification for a short term demonstration study cannot be ruled out. However, the conduct of the longitudinal study as initially reported in 1936 and through the years is judged to be scientifically unsound and its results are disproportionately

meager compared with known risks to human subjects involved. Outstanding weaknesses of this study, supported by the lack of written protocol, include lack of validity and reliability assurances; lack of calibration of investigator responses; uncertain quality of clinical judgments between various investigators; questionable data base validity and questionable value of the experimental design for a long term study of this nature.

The position of the Panel must not be construed to be a general repudiation of scientific research with human subjects. It is possible that a scientific study in 1932 of untreated syphilis, properly conceived with a clear protocol and conducted with suitable subjects who fully understood the implications of their involvement, might have been justified in the pre-penicillin era. This is especially true when one considers the uncertain nature of the results of treatment of late latent syphilis and the highly toxic nature of therapeutic agents then available.

Report on Charge I-B

Statement of Charge l-B: Determine whether the study should have been continued when penicillin became generally available.

♦ **Facts and Documentation re Charge I-B...**
3. Reports regarding the withholding of treatment from patients in this study are varied and are still subject to controversy....

What is clearly documentable (in a series of letters between Vonderlehr and Health officials in Tuskegee taking place between February 1941 and August 1942) is that known seropositive, untreated males under 45 years of age from the Tuskegee Study had been called for army duty and rejected on account of a positive blood. The local board was furnished with a list of 256 names of men under 45 years of age and asked that these men be excluded from the list of draftees needing treatment! According to the letters, the board agreed with this arrangement in order to make it possible to continue this study on an effective basis....

♦ **Panel Judgments on Charge I-B**
The ethical, legal and scientific implications which are evoked from the facts presented in the previous section led the Panel to the following judgment:

That penicillin therapy should have been made available to the participants in this study especially as of 1953 when penicillin became generally available.

Withholding of penicillin, after it became generally available, amplified the injustice to which this group of human beings had already been subjected. The scientific merits of the Tuskegee Study are vastly overshadowed by the violation of basic ethical principles pertaining to human dignity and human life imposed on the experimental subjects....

Respectfully Submitted,
Ronald H. Brown
Jean L7 Harris, M.D.
Seward Hiltner, Ph.D., D.D.
Jeanne C. Sinkford, D.D.S., Ph.D.
Fred Speaker
Barney H. Weeks ...
Yale Law School, New Haven, Connecticut 06520

* * * * * *

TO: The Assistant Secretary for Health and Scientific Affairs
FROM: Jay Katz, M.D.
TOPIC: Reservations about the Panel Report on Charge I

I should like to add the following findings and observations to the majority opinion:

(1) There is ample evidence in the records available to us that the consent to participation was not obtained from the Tuskegee Syphilis Study subjects, but that instead they were exploited, manipulated, and deceived. They were treated not as human subjects but as objects of research. The most fundamental reason for condemning the Tuskegee Study at its inception and throughout its continuation is not that all the subjects should have been treated, for some might not have wished to be treated, but rather that they were never fairly consulted about the research project, its consequences for them, and the alternatives available to them. Those who for reasons of intellectual incapacity could not have been so consulted should not have been invited to participate in the study in the first place.

(2) It was already known before the Tuskegee Syphilis Study was begun, and reconfirmed by the study itself, that persons with untreated syphilis have a higher death rate than those who have been treated. The life expectancy of at least forty subjects in the study was markedly decreased for lack of treatment.

Document Text

(3) In addition, the untreated and the "inadvertently" (using the word frequently employed by the investigators) but inadequately treated subjects suffered many complications which could have been ameliorated with treatment. This fact was noted on occasion in the published reports of the Tuskegee Syphilis Study and as late as 1971. However the subjects were not apprised of this possibility.

(4) One of the senior investigators wrote in 1936 that since "a considerable portion of the infected Negro population remained untreated during the entire course of syphilis … an unusual opportunity (arose) to study the untreated syphilitic patient from the beginning of the disease to the death of the infected person." Throughout, the investigators seem to have confused the study with an "experiment in nature." But syphilis was not a condition for which no beneficial treatment was available, calling for experimentation to learn more about the condition in the hope of finding a remedy. The persistence of the syphilitic disease from which the victims of the Tuskegee Study suffered resulted from the unwillingness or incapacity of society to mobilize the necessary resources for treatment. The investigators, the USPHS, and the private foundations who gave support to this study should not have exploited this situation in the fashion they did. Unless they could have guaranteed knowledgeable participation by the subjects, they all should have disappeared from the research scene or else utilized their limited research resources for therapeutic ends. Instead, the investigators believed that the persons involved in the Tuskegee Study would *never* seek out treatment; a completely unwarranted assumption which ultimately led the investigators deliberately to obstruct the opportunity for treatment of a number of the participants.

(5) In theory if not in practice, it has long been "a principle of medical and surgical morality (never to perform) on man an experiment which might be harmful to him to any extent, even though the result might be highly advantageous to science" (Claude Bernard 1865), at least without the knowledgeable consent of the subject. This was one basis on which the German physicians who had conducted medical experiments in concentration camps were tried by the Nuremberg Military Tribunal for crimes against humanity. Testimony at their trial by official representatives of the American Medical Association clearly suggested that research like the Tuskegee Syphilis Study would have been intolerable in this country or anywhere in the civilized world. Yet the Tuskegee study was continued after the Nuremberg findings and the Nuremberg Code had been widely disseminated to the medical community. Moreover, the study was not reviewed in 1966 after the Surgeon General of the USPHS promulgated his guidelines for the ethical conduct of research, even though this study was carried on within the purview of his department.

(6) The Tuskegee Syphilis Study finally was reviewed in 1969. A lengthier transcript of the proceedings, not quoted by the majority, reveals that one of the five members of the reviewing committee repeatedly emphasized that a moral obligation existed to provide treatment for the "patients." His plea remained unheeded. Instead the Committee, which was in part concerned with the possibility of adverse criticism, seemed to be reassured by the observation that "if we established good liaison with the local medical society, there would be no need to answer criticism."

(7) The controversy over the effectiveness and the dangers of arsenic and heavy metal treatment in 1932 and of penicillin treatment when it was introduced as a method of therapy is beside the point. For the real issue is that the participants in this study were never informed of the availability of treatment because the investigators were never in favor of such treatment. Throughout the study the responsibility rested heavily on the shoulders of the investigators to make every effort to apprise the subjects of what could be done for them if they so wished. In 1937 the then Surgeon General of the USPHS wrote: "(f) or late syphilis no blanket prescription can be written. Each patient is a law unto himself. For every syphilis patient, late and early, a careful physical examination is necessary before starting treatment and should be repeated frequently during its course." Even prior to that, in 1932, ranking USPHS physicians stated in a series of articles that adequate treatment "will afford a practical, if not complete guaranty of freedom from the development of any late lesions…."

In conclusion, I note sadly that the medical profession, through its national association, its many individual societies, and its journals, has on the whole not reacted to this study except by ignoring it. One lengthy editorial appeared in the October 1972 issue of the Southern Medical Journal which exonerated the study and chastised the "irresponsible press" for bringing it to public attention. When will we take seriously our responsibilities, particularly to the disadvantaged in our midst who so consistently throughout history have been the first to be selected for human research?

Respectfully submitted,
Jay Katz, M.D.
October 27, 1972

******

TO: Assistant Secretary for Health and Scientific Affairs
FROM: Jay Katz, M.D.
SUBJECT: Addendum to Panel Report on Charge II

I entirely concur in the Panel's recommendations and in the reasons given therefor. However, one additional piece of evidence lends even greater conviction, if any is still needed, to the decision to terminate the Tuskegee Syphilis Study. We have been informed that no scientific knowledge of any consequence would be derived from its continuation. The Panel felt that recording this fact might create the impression that it was *the* major reason for terminating the study. I believe that its inclusion should not, and would not, be so construed.

There are cogent reasons for not dismissing the issue of scientific merit. As long as society continues to favor the pursuit of medical knowledge for the possible benefit of the patients participating in research or for the benefit of future patients, a balancing of risks and benefits is inevitable. We must acknowledge this reality in order to confront such questions as: Do we wish to preserve this balancing process and, if we do, how might we learn to minimize inevitable harm to subjects and science? We urgently need to establish an orderly process which will permit the assessment of the conflicting claims inherent in decisions to initiate, continue or terminate research projects. Such an assessment might proceed in four steps: (1) a relentless inquiry into the harmful consequences to the participants; (2) an appraisal of the benefits which may accrue to science as well as to society: (3) a balancing of the risks to the participants against the benefits to them and/or science; and (4) an anticipatory rebuttal to the charge that either the interests of the participants or of science have not been sufficiently considered. In the light of the finding that no interests of science are surrendered by terminating the Tuskegee Syphilis Study, there is nothing to balance and nothing to rebut, and continuance of the study would for this reason alone be inadmissible.

I appreciate that had the conclusion been otherwise, the study would in all probability still have to be terminated because of the other findings set forth in the Panel's report, findings which will be further explored in our deliberations with respect to Charge One ("whether the study was justified"). Moreover, I should note that the four factors, listed above, do not directly address themselves to such other important considerations as: who should be selected for research, what disclosures must be made to participants in research, etc. This will surely be considered in our response to Charge Three ("whether existing (research) policies are adequate and effective"). Finally, I also leave unconsidered for now another question which emerges from the finding of "no scientific merit": why was the study not terminated at a time prior to the appointment of this Panel? One of the benefits of including a finding of scientific merit in every assessment is that many more projects might be terminated sooner, because the reviewer would be hard pressed to make an affirmative finding on this issue.

Respectfully submitted,
(sgd.) Jay Katz, M.D.

...

◆ Report on Charge III

TO: The Assistant Secretary for Health
FROM: Tuskegee Syphilis Study Ad Hod Advisory Panel
TOPIC: Final Report on Charge III

I. Introduction
In his third charge to the Tuskegee Syphilis Study Ad Hoc Advisory Panel, Dr. Merlin K. DuVal, the HEW Assistant Secretary for Health and Scientific Affairs, has asked us to determine whether existing policies to protect the rights of patients participating in health research conducted or supported by the Department of Health, Education, and Welfare are adequate and effective and to recommend improvements in these policies, if needed.

Our response to this charge, embodied in this report, should not be viewed simply as a reaction to a single ethically objectionable research project. For the Tuskegee Syphilis Study, despite its widespread publicity was not an isolated phenomenon.

Document Text

We believe that the revelations from Macon County merely brought to the surface once again the unresolved problems which have long plagued medical research activities. Indeed, we hasten to add that although we refer in this report almost exclusively to physicians and to biomedical investigations, the issues we explore also arise in the context of non-medical investigations with human beings, conducted by psychologists, sociologists, educators, lawyers and others. The scope of the DHEW Policy on Protection of Human Subjects, broadened in 1971 to encompass such research, attests to the increasing significance of non-medical investigations with human beings.

Our initial determination that the protection of human research subjects is a current and widespread problem should not be surprising, especially in light of the recent Congressional hearings and bills focusing on the regulation of experimentation. In the past decade the press has publicized and debated a number of experiments which raised ethical questions: for example, the injection of cancer cells into aged patients at the Jewish Chronic Disease Hospital in Brooklyn, the deliberate infection of mentally retarded children with hepatitis at Willowbrook, the development of heart transplantation techniques, the enormous amount of drug research conducted in American prisons, the whole-body irradiation treatment of cancer patients at the University of Cincinnati, the advent and spread of "psychosurgery," and the Tuskegee Syphilis. Study itself.

With so many dramatic projects coming to the attention of the general public, more must he beneath the surface. Evidence for this too has been forthcoming. In 1966, Dr. Henry K. Beecher, the eminent Dorr Professor of Research in Anesthesia at the Harvard Medical School, charged in the prestigious New England Journal of Medicine that "many of the patients (used in experiments which Dr. Beecher investigated and reported) never had the risk satisfactorily explained to them, and … further hundreds have not known that they were the subjects of an experiment although grave consequences have been suffered as the direct result.…" Dr. Beecher concluded that "unethical or questionably ethical procedures are not uncommon." Quite recently this charge has been corroborated by the sociologist Bernard Barber and his associates, who interviewed biomedical researchers about their own research practices. Despite the expected tendency of researchers to minimize ethical problems in their own work, Barber *et al.* were able to conclude that "while the large majority of our samples of biomedical researchers seems to hold and live up to high ethical standards, a significant minority may not."

The problem of ethical experimentation is the product of the unresolved conflict between two strongly held values: the dignity and integrity of the individual, and the freedom of scientific inquiry. Professionals of many disciplines, and researchers especially, exercise unexamined discretion to intervene in the lives of their subjects for the sake of scientific progress. Although exposure to needless harm and neglect of the duty to obtain the subject's consent have generally been frowned upon in theory, the infliction of unnecessary harm and infringements on informed consent are frequently accepted, in practice, as the price to be paid for the advancement of knowledge. How have investigators come to claim this sweeping prerogative? If the answer to this question is that "society" has authorized professionals to choose between scientific progress and individual human dignity and welfare, should not "society" retain some control over the research enterprise? We agree with philosopher Hans Jonas that a slower progress in the conquest of disease would not threaten society, grievous as it is to those who have to deplore that their particular disease be not yet conquered, but that society would indeed be threatened by the erosion of those moral values whose loss, possibly caused by too ruthless a pursuit of scientific progress, would make its most dazzling triumphs not worth having.

We have, as will be seen, made far-reaching recommendations for change. We do not propose these changes lightly. But throughout, in accordance with our mandate, our concern has not been just to define the ethical issues, but also to examine the structures and policies thus far devised to deal with those issues. In urging greater societal involvement in the research enterprise, we believe that the goal of scientific progress can be harmonized with the need to assure the protection of human subjects.

Glossary

Hans Jonas: a German-born philosopher and bioethicist who taught at the New School for Social Research in New York City in the middle half of the twentieth century

latent: not presently active, referring to a disease with no current symptoms

longitudinal study: any scientific study that measures a phenomenon over time rather than at a moment in time

Nuremburg Code: an ethical code for human subjects participating in medical experimentation, issued in response to the Nazi war crimes trials following World War II

Nuremburg Military Tribunal: the court that tried Nazi war criminals in the German city of Nuremburg after World War II

seropositive: having a blood serum test result that indicates infection

venereal disease: a term commonly used in the past to refer to what today are called sexually transmitted diseases, derived from Venus, the classical goddess of love

Vonderlehr: Raymond Vonderlehr, appointed the on-site director of the study in 1932 and who was responsible for converting it into a long-term study

Willowbrook: Willowbrook State School in Staten Island, New York City, the scene of an infamous 1960s study in which mentally retarded children were infected with hepatitis

Shirley Chisholm, future member of the U.S. House of Representatives (D-NY), announcing her candidacy. By Thomas J. O'Halloran, U.S. News & World Reports. This image is available from the United States Library of Congress's Prints and Photographs division. [Public domain], via Wikimedia Commons

Shirley Chisholm: "The Black Woman in Contemporary America"

"To date, neither the black movement nor women's liberation succinctly addresses itself to the dilemma confronting the black who is female."

Overview

Selected as the keynote speaker for a national conference on black women held at the University of Missouri in Kansas City, Shirley Chisholm enumerated the key issues facing African American women. She pointedly reminded her audience that black women were not interested in being addressed as "Ms." or in gaining access to all-male social clubs. Rather, African American women's top priority was the welfare of their families and communities. Black and white women should unite around issues such as improved day-care facilities and increased job opportunities. At the same time that Chisholm was criticizing white feminists, she chided African American spokesmen who suggested that black women step aside to allow black men to monopolize leadership positions. Only by working together as equals could black men and women create the programs and policies needed by their communities. This speech typified Chisholm's fighting spirit, her willingness to confront contentious issues head on, and her rousing oratorical style.

Explanation and Analysis of the Document

Chisholm was never afraid to speak her mind. She championed the underdog against the privileged, was a critic of the establishment, and became an eloquent spokeswoman for reform. Her public career was fueled by anger at the dismissive treatment she received at the hands of political leaders. Despite her strong record as an organizer and advocate, male colleagues seldom took her seriously. Chisholm often claimed that she met with more discrimination being a woman than she did being black. At a time when the women's movement was beginning to gain national recognition, Chisholm emerged as one of its most prominent leaders. Her political career, especially her presidential candidacy, was an effort to convince the country that women deserved an equal voice in government.

In 1974 Chisholm was invited to speak at a two-week symposium at the University of Missouri in Kansas City on the topic of black women in contemporary America. As the nation's most visible female African American leader and as one with a long history of advocacy for women's causes, Chisholm was the logical choice to deliver the keynote address. Drawing on a lifetime of personal experience as well as her twenty years of political involvement, she was well prepared to tackle this subject. Her starting point was the emasculation of the African American male during the years when slavery was prevalent in the South. Because black men were unable to provide for their children and protect their homes and because marriage was not recognized and men could be sold away from their families, black women were forced to take on nontraditional roles. Out of necessity, they developed the strength, perseverance, and tenacity to sustain their dependents. These attributes were often mistakenly described as *matriarchy* by such white social scientists as Daniel Patrick Moynihan, whose 1965 report, *The Negro Family: The Case for National Action*, was widely condemned by African American scholars and activists for its negative portrayal of the black family.

Rather than depicting black men and women as rivals in a contest for domination, Chisholm asserts that black women possessed valuable skills that could complement male contributions; each had vital abilities needed in the struggle for black liberation. Some leaders of black nationalist organizations suggested that African American women needed to step aside to allow men to claim their rightful place at the head of the family and community institutions. Chisholm rejects this proposal as a scapegoating technique; she emphasizes the need for both sexes to work together. Black women with skills and education could not

Portrait of Chisholm by Kadir Nelson in the Collection of the U.S. House of Representatives. By Kadir Nelson [Public domain], via Wikimedia Commons

be expected to retire from the scene and sit on the sidelines. This waste of badly needed talent would weaken rather than strengthen the African American cause. Only by working side by side would the common goal of liberation be achieved; only by participating in the struggle as equal partners with men would black women realize their full potential.

Chisholm next reviews the tensions between the mostly white women's liberation movement and African American women—an issue that troubled many feminists. Many of the disagreements between these two groups had their roots in differences in their class composition. The issues of most importance to working-class black women were not always the same as those that motivated middle-class white women. Controversies over symbolic questions, such as the exclusion of women from certain cocktail lounges or the use of the title "Ms." instead of "Mrs." were of little concern to blacks, who were preoccupied with issues of economic survival. However, this did not mean that black women rejected all proposals made by white feminists; in some areas their interests coincided. For example, the nationalization of day-care services, a cause that Chisholm championed, would be a great benefit for both black and white mothers and would be supported by working women of both races. By advocating policies and programs that directly addressed the needs of their community, African American women could act as a valuable pressure group within the largely white women's movement.

Chisholm asserts in her address that many black women had come to realize they had to be freed from traditional women's roles if they were going to contribute fully to the cause of black liberation. In the past, black women had been expected to stay in the background and let men monopolize positions of prominence. The civil rights movement was a case in point. Strong black women were the foundation of the movement, supplying a majority of the participants and organizing grassroots protests, but male chauvinism caused men to claim nearly all of the leadership positions and keep women out of the public spotlight. A few, such as Coretta King and Betty Shabazz, enjoyed celebrity because of the prominence of their husbands (Martin Luther King, Jr., and Malcolm X, respectively), but the list of African American women in the civil rights movement is much longer. Ida Wells, Mary McLeod Bethune, Mary Church Terrell, Daisy Bates, and Diane Nash all made important contributions to the southern freedom struggle but rarely received the recognition they deserved.

Chisholm claims that black women suffered a double discrimination because of their color and gender; for that reason, their problems could not be lumped together with those faced by white women. Neither the black movement nor the women's movement had been sensitive to this heavy burden. Thus, black women had had to cultivate attitudes and organizations to address their own unique issues. Their experience in the civil rights movement had produced a better understanding of the workings of the political system as well as the confidence to embark on new forms of political participation. This, she observes, had led to their growing interest in politics. Younger women were emerging as a force for change and demanding their rightful place in American society.

In the past, cultural norms had relegated black women to a minor role in politics and discouraged them from seeking elective office. As women and as members of the black lower class, they had been systematically disenfranchised. In the present, however, a fundamental change was under way. The liberation movement that had begun in the late 1960s had helped black women realize that their well-being was directly tied to the success of contests for political power. This was especially true in urban centers, where they daily confronted the issues most critical to the black community. Chisholm was encouraged by evidence from such areas as New York City, where black mothers had been at the forefront of movements to eliminate poverty and injustice. Rising poverty levels and minimal public assistance threatened the welfare of black families. Black women had a moral obligation to their children. They had no choice; they had to take a more active role in government. Chisholm notes that this movement to the center stage of politics should not be viewed as a threat to men; it was a question of survival. Black women, she says, must fully commit themselves to political struggle to assure their children a brighter future.

Chisholm concludes by urging the black women in her audience to "stand up and be counted." Americans, she observes, are hung up on questions of gender. These hang-ups have historical roots that prevent black men and women from working together effectively. She cites her career as an example of what is possible if people ignore criticism and squarely face difficult issues. She encourages everyone to look beyond differences of race and gender, to forget tradition and convention. Only by being true to their God and their consciences, she says, will they be able to create the kind of nation that will allow them to reach their full potential.

About the Author

As the first African American woman elected to Congress and a candidate for the 1972 Democratic presidential nomination, Chisholm was the most prominent black female political leader of the 1970s. An articulate and fiery public speaker, Chisholm was not afraid to challenge established power brokers or take a stand on controversial issues. Her arrival on the national stage coincided with growing African American political power and the emergence of the women's liberation movement. At a time when many women of color criticized white feminists for pursuing goals irrelevant to minority communities, Chisholm attempted to bridge the racial divide. She frequently claimed that she was more often discriminated against because she was a woman than because she was black.

Chisholm asserts in the eighth paragraph that black women were beginning to realize that they had to free themselves from male domination to fully contribute to black liberation. They had to stand up to men who would restrict them to secondary roles while monopolizing top positions for themselves. This, unfortunately, was the case in the civil rights movement, where few women occupied prominent public roles. A handful, like Coretta Scott King and Betty Shabazz, were well known because of their husbands (Martin Luther King, Jr., and Malcolm X, respectively). Other women made valuable contributions working behind the scenes while seldom receiving the recognition they deserved. Because they had to struggle against male domination in addition to racial oppression, African American women were among the most committed freedom fighters. Chisholm names the antilynching crusader Ida Wells as an example of this militant spirit, along with the Little Rock, Arkansas, leader of the National Association for the Advancement of Colored People, Daisy Bates, and Nashville sit-in pioneer Diane Nash.

Black women faced the double jeopardy of racism and sexism; their problems could not be compared with the obstacles faced by white women. In the ninth paragraph Chisholm notes the beginning of a new movement by African American women. Because the unique political and cultural constraints they faced had been addressed by neither the black movement nor the women's movement, they were moving in new directions. Nowhere was this trend more evident than in the realm of politics. Chisholm's tenth paragraph traces the evolution of the civil rights movement of the 1960s into the activism of the 1970s. Young black women were beginning to realize that they could exercise power through electoral politics. By registering new voters and forming grassroots organizations, black women were reshaping the political landscape. Chisholm's pathbreaking challenge and ultimate defeat of the Brooklyn Democratic machine is an early example of this potential.

Chisholm recounts the long-standing barriers to women's meaningful political participation in her eleventh paragraph. Undoubtedly recalling her own painful initiation into patriarchal politics, she lists the trivial tasks once assigned to women—"opening envelopes, hanging up posters, and giving teas." In addition to the handicap imposed by their gender, black women belonged to a politically marginalized group. These factors made the recent emergence of African American women in politics even more remarkable.

Chisholm next asserts that changes within the black community have given birth to a new generation of African American women who understand that their wellbeing could be affirmed only "in connection with the total black struggle." Their work in the civil rights movement helped them realize the importance of political involvement. Chisholm predicts that these women would form a vanguard fashioning new kinds of political participation. African American women were uniquely situated to address the most critical issues facing their communities, in "their unusual proximity to the most crucial issues affecting black people today." In paragraph 13, Chisholm praises New York City welfare mothers for calling attention to problems threatening the survival of the black family. She declares that black women have a duty to their families to press for increases in the minimal welfare allowances that contribute to the breakdown of black family life. To accomplish this goal, they must move into the "main arena" of American political life.

Chisholm then repeats a message she delivered in countless speeches to women's groups across the United States. Involvement in politics is not a question of competition against men, she states; it is a question of women realizing their responsibility to their own families. She encourages women in her audience "to give everything that is within ourselves to give" to create a better future for their children. Chisholm quotes Frances Beal, author of the 1969 pamphlet "Black Women's Manifesto," in paragraph 15. In this pamphlet, Beal reiterates the low status of black women and claims that they were being used as scapegoats for the evils that American society inflicted on the black man. They had been maligned and molested; their labor had been exploited to the neglect of their own children. Not only had black women been degraded, but they were also powerless to improve their situation.

In the next two paragraphs, Chisholm cites the work of Susan Johnson, a young African American scholar. Johnson asserted that the success of the black woman in politics resulted from her capacity to free herself from the constraints imposed by the double burdens of racism and sexism. By taking an active role in politics she threatened the status of the black male as well as the deeply entrenched structure of white supremacy. Striking a positive note, however, Johnson observed that because the African American woman was seen as less dangerous than her male counterpart, white politicians sometimes underestimated her ability. This view provided "the necessary leverage for political mobility."

Chisholm notes that psychologists, sociologists, and psychiatrists had tried without success to define and interpret the African American woman. Usually this resulted in misunderstanding and misinterpretation. Everyone had joined the act except black women themselves. She declares that it is time for black women to take control of their destiny. Chisholm urges the women in her audience to "stand up and be counted." In paragraph 19 she prays that in years to come the division between male and female will disappear. When that day arrives, all people would be able to employ their god-given talents for the benefit of humanity. Chisholm then reminds her listeners that no racial group had a monopoly on wisdom or ignorance, and neither did one gender. Americans should understand the historical forces and contemporary pressures that prevented black women and men from forming a powerful united movement. Creating this common front, however, should remain their objective.

Using her career as a case in point, in paragraph 21 Chisholm admonishes her audience not to listen to critics and naysayers. Black women would not make progress unless they concentrated on their strengths. During the coming conference she advises participants to openly confront the dangerous and difficult issues that might easily be ignored. She paraphrases the old adage that "the truth shall make you free." In her concluding paragraph Chisholm encourages her listeners to reject old politics and obsolete morality. Young activists, she says, must cast off outdated traditions and conventions to find their own way. Only by standing up for the right as determined by their consciences would Americans achieve the greatness to which they aspired.

Audience

The immediate audience for Chisholm's address consisted of delegates to a national conference on the status of black women. It is safe to assume that a majority of the participants were young African American women, but men and whites were not excluded. More broadly, her comments were intended for all persons working for social change. Although some examples and references may seem dated, Chisholm's message remains relevant: Black women must struggle against the twin barriers of racism and sexism to create a more just society for themselves and their children. She argued that political power could be a tool for social change and that black women must not be afraid to seek it.

Impact

In an era when women are represented at all levels of government, when they occupy influential seats in the presidential cabinet and on the U.S. Supreme Court, and when they make up a growing portion of the nation' governors and senators, it is easy to forget that only a few decades ago a woman running for elective office was a rarity. Pioneering female politicians like Shirley Chisholm and Congresswoman Barbara Jordan overcame monumental barriers. Their success required enormous personal commitment and great sacrifice.

Chisholm was the first African American woman to be elected to Congress, but she was far from the last. By 2010 fourteen black women sat in the House of Representatives. Many accomplished female politicians took their inspiration from Chisholm's career. She was a role model for a generation of female activists. Her victories proved that racism and sexism need not be insurmountable obstacles to political power.

Shirley Chisholm believed that she had a duty to spread the gospel of political empowerment. That is why, after her 1968 election, she devoted much of her time to public speaking. While it is difficult to accurately assess the impact of her Kansas City speech, there is no denying the cumulative effect of hundreds of similar addresses delivered to young women who packed college auditoriums to listen to her advice and learn from her example. All her life Chisholm fought against entrenched privilege to give a voice to those excluded from the corridors of power. Her courage and dedication remain an inspiration to all who hear her message.

Further Reading

♦ Articles
Canson, Patricia E. "Shirley Chisholm." In *African American National Biography*, ed. Henry Louis Gates, Jr., and Evelyn Brooks-Higginbotham. Vol. 2. New York: Oxford University Press, 2008.

Gallagher, Julie. "Waging 'The Good Fight': The Political Career of Shirley Chisholm, 1953–1982." *Journal of African American History* 92, no. 3 (2007): 393–416.

♦ Books
Chisholm, Shirley. *Unbought and Unbossed*. Boston: Houghton Mifflin, 1970.

———. *The Good Fight*. New York: Harper & Row, 1973.

Duffy, Susan. *Shirley Chisholm: A Bibliography of Writings by and about Her*. Metuchen, N.J.: Scarecrow Press, 1988.

Moynihan, Daniel Patrick. *The Negro Family: The Case for National Action*. Washington, D.C.: U.S. Government Printing Office, 1965.

Scheader, Catherine. *Shirley Chisholm: Teacher and Congresswoman*. Hillsdale, N.J.: Enslow Publishers, 1990.

♦ Web Sites
Meehan, Thomas. "Moynihan of the Moynihan Report." New York Times "Books" Web site. http://www.nytimes.com/books/98/10/04/specials/moynihan-report.html.

"Shirley Chisholm." National Visionary Leadership Project Web site. http://www.visionaryproject.org/chisholmshirley/.

———Paul T. Murray

Questions for Further Study

1. Compare this document with Mary Church Terrell's "The Progress of Colored Women," an address delivered in 1898. What do you think Church Terrell's reaction to Chisholm's speech would have been? How were Chisholm's circumstances similar to, and different from, those surrounding Church Terrell?

2. What was Chisholm's relationship with the burgeoning feminist movement? Was she critical of that movement in any way? Explain.

3. Compare this document with the 1965 Moynihan Report. How did Chisholm respond to the findings of that report?

4. What historical circumstances, in Chisholm's view, forced upon African American women the need to be strong leaders in their communities?

5. Chisholm once said that she felt more discriminated against because she was a woman than because she was black. Does this statement surprise you? Why do you think she made this claim?

Essential Quotes

"The black woman who is educated and has ability cannot be expected to put said talent on the shelf when she can utilize these gifts side-by-side with her man. One does not learn, nor does one assist in the struggle, by standing on the sidelines, constantly complaining and criticizing. One learns by participating in the situation—listening, observing and then acting."

"The black woman lives in a society that discriminates against her on two counts. The black woman cannot be discussed in the same context as her Caucasian counterpart because of the twin jeopardy of race and sex which operates against her, and the psychological and political consequences which attend them.... To date, neither the black movement nor women's liberation succinctly addresses itself to the dilemma confronting the black who is female."

"[African American women] are beginning to realize their capacities not only as blacks, but also as women. They are beginning to understand that their cultural well-being and their social well-being would only be affirmed in connection with the total black struggle. The dominant role black women played in the civil rights movement began to allow them to grasp the significance of political power in America."

"In the face of the increasing poverty besetting black communities, black women have a responsibility. Black women have a duty to bequeath a legacy to their children. Black women have a duty to move from the periphery of organized political activity into its main arena."

"It is not a question of competition against black men or brown men or red men or white men in America. It is a question of the recognition that, since we have a tremendous responsibility in terms of our own families, that to the best of our ability we have to give everything that is within ourselves to give ... to make that future a better future for our little boys and our little girls."

"The Black Woman in Contemporary America"

Full text of Shirley Chisholm's keynote speech for the conference on the African American woman.

Ladies and gentlemen, and brothers and sisters all—I'm very glad to be here this evening. I'm very glad that I've had the opportunity to be the first lecturer with respect to the topic of the black woman in contemporary America. This has become a most talked-about topic and has caused a great deal of provocation and misunderstandings and misinterpretations. And I come to you this evening to speak on this topic not as any scholar, not as any academician, but as a person that has been out here for the past twenty years, trying to make my way as a black and a woman, and meeting all kinds of obstacles.

The black woman's role has not been placed in its proper perspective, particularly in terms of the current economic and political upheaval in America today. Since time immemorial the black man's emasculation resulted in the need of the black woman to assert herself in order to maintain some semblance of a family unit. And as a result of this historical circumstance, the black woman has developed perseverance; the black woman has developed strength; the black woman has developed tenacity of purpose and other attributes which today quite often are being looked upon negatively. She continues to be labeled a matriarch. And this is indeed a played-upon white sociological interpretation of the black woman's role that has been developed and perpetrated by Daniel Moynihan and other sociologists.

Black women by virtue of the role they have played in our society have much to offer toward the liberation of their people. We know that our men are coming forward, but the black race needs the collective talents and the collective abilities of black men and black women who have vital skills to supplement each other.

It is quite perturbing to divert ourselves on the dividing issue of the alleged fighting that absorbs the energies of black men and black women. Such statements as "the black woman has to step back while her black man steps forward" and "the black woman has kept back the black man" are grossly, historically incorrect and serve as a scapegoating technique to prevent us from coming together as human beings—some of whom are black men and some are black women.

The consuming interest of this type of dialogue abets the enemy in terms of taking our eyes off the ball, so that our collective talents can never redound in a beneficial manner to our ethnic group. The black woman who is educated and has ability cannot be expected to put said talent on the shelf when she can utilize these gifts side-by-side with her man. One does not learn, nor does one assist in the struggle, by standing on the sidelines, constantly complaining and criticizing. One learns by participating in the situation—listening, observing and then acting.

It is quite understandable why black women in the majority are not interested in walking and picketing a cocktail lounge which historically has refused to open its doors a certain two hours a day when men who have just returned from Wall Street gather in said lounge to exchange bits of business transactions that occurred on the market. This is a middle-class white woman's issue. This is not a priority of minority women. Another issue that black women are not overly concerned about is the "M-S" versus the "M-R-S" label. For many of us this is just the use of another label which does not basically change the fundamental inherent racial attitudes found in both men and women in this society. This is just another label, and black women are not preoccupied with any more label syndromes. Black women are desperately concerned with the issue of survival in a society in which the Caucasian group has never really practiced the espousal of equalitarian principles in America.

An aspect of the women's liberation movement that will and does interest many black women is the potential liberation, is the potential nationalization of daycare centers in this country. Black women can accept and understand this agenda item in the women's movement. It is important that black women utilize their brainpower and focus on issues in any movement that will redound to the benefit of their people because we can serve as a vocal and a catalytic pressure group within the so-called humanistic movements, many of whom do not really comprehend the black man and the black woman.

An increasing number of black women are beginning to feel that it is important first to become free as women, in order to contribute more fully to the task of black liberation. Some feel that black men—like all men, or most men—have placed women in the stereotypes of domestics whose duty it is to stay in the background—cook, clean, have babies, and leave all of the glory to men. Black women point to the civil rights movement as an example of a subtle type of male oppression, where with few exceptions black women have not had active roles in the forefront of the fight. Some like Coretta King, Katherine Cleaver, and Betty Shabazz have come only to their positions in the shadows of their husbands. Yet, because of the oppression of black women, they are strongest in the fight for liberation. They have led the struggle to fight against white male supremacy, dating from slavery times. And in view of these many facts it is not surprising that black women played a crucial role in the total fight for freedom in this nation. Ida Wells kept her newspaper free by walking the streets of Memphis, Tennessee, in the 1890s with two pistols on her hips. And within recent years, this militant condition of black women, who have been stifled because of racism and sexism, has been carried on by Mary McLeod Bethune, Mary Church Terrell, Daisy Bates, and Diane Nash.

The black woman lives in a society that discriminates against her on two counts. The black woman cannot be discussed in the same context as her Caucasian counterpart because of the twin jeopardy of race and sex which operates against her, and the psychological and political consequences which attend them. Black women are crushed by cultural restraints and abused by the legitimate power structure. To date, neither the black movement nor women's liberation succinctly addresses itself to the dilemma confronting the black who is female. And as a consequence of ignoring or being unable to handle the problems facing black women, black women themselves are now becoming socially and politically active.

Undoubtedly black women are cultivating new attitudes, most of which will have political repercussions in the future. They are attempting to change their conditions. The maturation of the civil rights movement by the mid '60s enabled many black women to develop interest in the American political process. From their experiences they learned that the real sources of power lay at the root of the political system. For example, black sororities and pressure groups like the National Council of Negro Women are adept at the methods of participatory politics—particularly in regard to voting and organizing. With the arrival of the '70s, young black women are demanding recognition like the other segments of society who also desire their humanity and their individual talents to be noticed. The tradition of the black woman and the Afro-American subculture and her current interest in the political process indicate the emergence of a new political entity.

Historically she has been discouraged from participating in politics. Thus she is trapped between the walls of the dominant white culture and her own subculture, both of which encourage deference to men. Both races of women have traditionally been limited to performing such tasks as opening envelopes, hanging up posters and giving teas. And the minimal involvement of black women exists because they have been systematically excluded from the political process and they are members of the politically dysfunctional black lower class. Thus, unlike white women, who escape the psychological and sociological handicaps of racism, the black woman's political involvement has been a most marginal role.

But within the last six years, the Afro-American subculture has undergone tremendous social and political transformation and these changes have altered the nature of the black community. They are beginning to realize their capacities not only as blacks, but also as women. They are beginning to understand that their cultural well-being and their social well-being would only be affirmed in connection with the total black struggle. The dominant role black women played in the civil rights movement began to allow them to grasp the significance of political power in America. So obviously black women who helped to spearhead the civil rights movement would also now, at this juncture, join and direct the vanguard which would shape and mold a new kind of political participation.

This has been acutely felt in urban areas, which have been rocked by sporadic rebellions. Nothing better illustrates the need for black women to organize politically than their unusual proximity to the most crucial issues affecting black people today. They have struggled in a wide range of protest movements to eliminate the poverty and injustice that permeates the lives of black people. In New York City, for example, welfare mothers and mothers of schoolchildren have ably demonstrated the commitment of black women to the elimination of the problems that threaten the well-being of the black family. Black women must view the problems of cities such as New York not as urban problems, but as the components of a crisis without whose elimination our family lives will neither survive nor prosper. Deprived of a stable family environment because of poverty and racial injustice, disproportionate numbers of our people must live on minimal welfare allowances that help to perpetuate the breakdown of family life. In the face of the increasing poverty besetting black communities, black women have a responsibility. Black women have a duty to bequeath a legacy to their children. Black women have a duty to move from the periphery of organized political activity into its main arena.

I say this on the basis of many experiences. I travel throughout this country and I've come in contact with thousands of my black sisters in all kinds of conditions in this nation. And I've said to them over and over again: it is not a question of competition against black men or brown men or red men or white men in America. It is a questions of the recognition that, since we have a tremendous responsibility in terms of our own families, that to the best of our ability we have to give everything that is within ourselves to give—in terms of helping to make that future a better future for our little boys and our little girls, and not leave it to anybody.

Francis Beal describes the black woman as a slave of a slave. Let me quote: "By reducing the black man in America to such abject oppression, the black woman had no protector and she was used—and is still being used—in some cases as the scapegoat for the evils that this horrendous system has perpetrated on black men. Her physical image has been maliciously maligned. She has been sexually molested and abused by the white colonizer. She has suffered the worst kind of economic exploitation, having been forced to serve as the white woman's maid and wet-nurse for white offspring, while her own children were more often starving and neglected. It is the depth of degradation to be socially manipulated, physically raped and used to undermine your own household—and then to be powerless to reverse this syndrome."

However, Susan Johnson notes a bit of optimism. Because Susan, a brilliant young black woman, has said that the recent strides made by the black woman in the political process is a result of the intricacies of her personality. And that is to say that as a political animal, she functions independently of her double jeopardy. Because confronted with a matrifocal past and present, she is often accused of stealing the black male's position in any situation beyond that of housewife and mother. And if that were not enough to burden the black woman, she realizes that her political mobility then threatens the doctrine of white supremacy and male superiority so deeply embedded in the American culture.

So choosing not to be a victim of self-paralysis, the black woman has been able to function in the political spectrum. And more often than not, it is the subconsciousness of the racist mind that perceives her as less harmful than the black man and thus permits her to acquire the necessary leverage for political mobility. This subtle component of racism could prove to be essential to the key question of how the black woman has managed some major advances in the American political process.

It is very interesting to note that everyone—with the exception of the black woman herself—has been interpreting the black woman. It is very interesting to note that the time has come that black women can and must no longer be passive, complacent recipients of whatever the definitions of the sociologists, the psychologists and the psychiatrists will give to us. Black women have been maligned, misunderstood, misinterpreted—who knows better than Shirley Chisholm?

And I stand here tonight to tell to you, my sisters, that if you have the courage of your convictions, you must stand up and be counted. I hope that the day will come in America when this business of male versus female does not become such an overriding issue, so that the talents and abilities that the almighty God have given to people can be utilized for the benefit of humanity.

One has to recognize that there are stupid white women and stupid white men, stupid black women and stupid black men, brilliant white women and brilliant white men, and brilliant black women and brilliant black men. Why do we get so hung-up in America on this question of sex? Of course, in terms of the black race, we understand the historical circumstances. We understand, also, some of the subtle maneuverings and machinations behind the scenes in order to prevent black women and black men from coming together as a race of unconquerable men and women.

And I just want to say to you tonight, if I say nothing else: I would never have been able to make it in America if I had paid attention to all of the doomsday-criers about me. And I want to say in conclusion that as you have this conference here for the next two weeks, put the cards out on the table and do not be afraid to discuss issues that perhaps you have

Document Text

been sweeping under the rug because of what people might say about you. You must remember that once we are able to face the truth, the truth shall set all of us free.

In conclusion, I just want to say to you, black and white, north and east, south and west, men and women: the time has come in America when we should no longer be the passive, complacent recipients of whatever the morals or the politics of a nation may decree for us in this nation. Forget traditions! Forget conventionalisms! Forget what the world will say whether you're in your place or out of your place. Stand up and be counted. Do your thing, looking only to God—whoever your God is—and to your consciences for approval. I thank you.

Glossary

Betty Shabazz: the widow of slain civil rights leader Malcolm X

Coretta King: the widow of Martin Luther King, Jr.

Daisy Bates: a twentieth-century civil rights activist and journalist who served as an adviser to the black students who enrolled at Little Rock (Arkansas) High School under a court desegregation order in 1957

Daniel Moynihan: the author of the 1965 government report commonly called the Moynihan Report, which argued that the chief problem in the black community was the disintegration of the family

Diane Nash: a civil rights activist, cofounder of the Student Nonviolent Coordinating Committee, and a major figure in the Southern Christian Leadership Conference

Francis Beal: author of the 1969 pamphlet "Black Women's Manifesto"

Katherine Cleaver: probably a reference to Kathleen Cleaver, the wife of Black Panther Party activist Eldridge Cleaver and a civil rights activist in her own right

Mary Church Terrell: a late-nineteenth and early-twentieth-century activist, cofounder of the National Association of College Women, which later became the National Association of University Women, and one of the cofounders of the NAACP

Mary McLeod Bethune: an American educator who founded a Florida school that became Bethune-Cookman University

matrifocal: matriarchal, referring to a society in which women take the leading role

"M-S" versus the "M-R-S" label: a reference to the use of Ms. rather than Mrs. (or Miss) in addressing women, to take attention away from marital status

Jackson in 1983. This image is available from the United States Library of Congress's Prints and Photographs division. [Public domain], via Wikimedia Commons

Jesse Jackson's Democratic National Convention Keynote Address

1984

"My constituency is the desperate, the damned, the disinherited, the disrespected, and the despised. They are restless and seek relief. They have voted in record numbers."

Overview

When the Reverend Jesse L. Jackson stood on the rostrum at the Democratic National Convention in San Francisco, California, on July 17, 1984, he was in an unusual and historic position. He was only the second African American to become a serious candidate for the presidential nomination of a major American political party. Twelve years earlier, Representative Shirley Chisholm of New York had made a bid for the Democratic presidential nomination. Chisholm's candidacy was mainly symbolic, but Jackson's was highly substantive. He had run in all of the primaries and caucuses, and he had won sufficient support from voters to command influence in the party, even if his delegate total was far short of the number needed for the nomination. Jackson used his keynote address to insist that the Democratic Party had to be a stronger advocate for the needy and the neglected. "They have voted in record numbers," he declared. "The Democratic Party must send them a signal that we care." Jackson called his supporters the "rainbow coalition," since they were diverse in background, ethnicity, and religion. Yet while Jackson had attracted enthusiastic support during his campaign, he had also aroused controversy because of his willingness to negotiate with hostile or adversarial foreign leaders and owing to his inflammatory remarks about American Jews. Jackson's speech was the culmination of his candidacy, and it produced an electrifying response. Delegates in the convention center cheered and cried; listeners were moved by his powerful voice and emotional appeals. His message hardly satisfied all his critics, but his speech proved that African Americans had achieved a new level of prominence and power in presidential politics.

Context

On November 3, 1983, Jackson announced his candidacy for president and became only the second African American to seek the presidential nomination of a major political party. In 1972 Shirley Chisholm had also sought the Democratic nomination, but she had run a limited campaign, entering only twelve primaries and earning less than 3 percent of the vote in those contests. Jackson planned to run in all the Democratic primaries and declared that his main goal was to "help restore a moral tone, a redemptive spirit, and a sensitivity to the poor and the dispossessed of the nation." A severe recession had raised unemployment to more than 10 percent of the workforce and increased the number of Americans living in poverty. Jackson blamed President Ronald Reagan for policies that had exacerbated the difficulties of the poor and minorities, and he also criticized the other declared Democratic presidential candidates for having failed to speak out strongly enough on behalf of people in need. Jackson said he would represent African Americans as well as Hispanics, Native Americans, Asian Americans, European Americans, workers, and women. Together, he said, these groups would form what he termed a "rainbow coalition," and at that time he also founded a national advocacy organization of that same name. He told an enthusiastic audience of twenty-five-hundred supporters who attended the announcement of his candidacy, "Our time has come."

Jackson's candidacy produced strong reactions. Some African American political leaders, such as Richard Hatcher, the mayor of Gary, Indiana, quickly pledged their support. Others, such as Detroit's mayor, Coleman Young, insisted that Jackson had no chance of winning the nomination and endorsed former Vice President Walter Mondale, the candidate who had been leading in the polls. Mondale also believed that Jackson could not win but worried about losing so much minority support to Jackson that one of their rivals could emerge with the nomination. Jackson also aroused controversy because of his foreign policy positions. He favored the creation of a Palestinian homeland, and during a trip to the Middle East in 1979 he had embraced Yasser Arafat, the head of the Palestine Liberation Organization, at a time when the governments of both the United States and Israel considered the organization a terrorist group. On December 29, 1983, Jackson flew to Syria, where he negotiated the release of U.S. Navy Lieutenant Robert O. Goodman, Jr., an African American flyer who had been captured when his plane was shot down earlier that month. Jackson believed that he had undertaken a humanitarian mission, but critics questioned his decision to negotiate with a government that the U.S. State Department considered a state sponsor of terrorism.

Jackson aroused even greater controversy in February 1984, when newspapers quoted derogatory language that he had used to describe Jews. At first, he maintained that he had never made such comments; later, he insisted that his remarks had been part of a private conversation and interpreted out of context. Eventually, Jackson apologized, but he continued to face charges that he was insensitive to Jews or even anti-Semitic because of his association with Louis Farrakhan, the head of the Nation of Islam. Farrakhan held no official position in the campaign, but he had accompanied Jackson to Syria to negotiate Goodman's release. During the controversy over Jackson's pejorative comments about Jews, Farrakhan gave a speech in which he praised the German leader Adolf Hitler. Jewish leaders and organizations denounced Farrakhan and criticized Jackson for having failed to cut all ties to Farrakhan.

Despite such turmoil, Jackson proved to be an effective candidate. He won two primaries, Louisiana and the District of Columbia, as well as the caucuses in Virginia and in his native state, South Carolina. These victories—along with winning 20 percent or more of the vote in primaries in several large states, including New York, Illinois, and New Jersey—helped him finish the series of nomination contests in third place behind Mondale and Senator Gary Hart of Colorado, with 18.6 percent of the total vote. Jackson, however, was upset with party rules that awarded him only 12 percent of the convention delegates, a significantly smaller share than his percentage of the popular vote. When the Democratic National Convention began in San Francisco on July 16, Jackson and his supporters proposed changes in rules governing the selection of delegates and additions to the party's platform, the Democrats' official position on key issues that would be important in the campaign. Jackson lost on most of his challenges, although he secured stronger language on affirmative action in the platform and a promise to establish a commission to consider reforms in delegate selection. Mondale, who was assured the Democratic presidential nomination, wanted party unity and recognized the need to accommodate Jackson, who had demonstrated his appeal to African American voters. Mondale revised the convention schedule, allowing Jackson to deliver a keynote address during prime television time on the night before the delegates nominated their candidate. Mondale's aides did not know what Jackson would say, but they hoped for a memorable speech that would prepare the party for the fall campaign against President Ronald Reagan.

About the Author

Jesse Jackson was born on October 8, 1941, in Greenville, South Carolina, to a single mother, Helen Burns. Three years later, she married Charles Jackson, who adopted Jackson in 1957. As a high school student in Greenville, Jackson was an honor student and an outstanding athlete. He earned a football scholarship to the University of Illinois in 1959, but transferred after his first year to the Agricultural and Technical College of North Carolina, a historically black institution now known as North Carolina Agricultural and Technical State University. Jackson excelled at his new school, playing quarterback on the football team, winning election as student body president, and earning a BA in sociology in 1964. After graduation, Jackson began training for the ministry at Chicago Theological Seminary, where he studied for two years but failed to complete his course work. He was nonetheless ordained as a Baptist minister in 1968.

Shortly after he moved to Chicago, civil rights work became Jackson's main activity. In March 1965, he traveled to Selma, Alabama, where he met the Reverend Martin Luther King, Jr., who was organizing demonstrations to protest the denial of voting rights to African Americans. Partly through Jackson's efforts, King came to Chicago, where he organized marches and rallies against racial discrimination in housing in 1966. During a visit to Chicago, King offered Jackson a job as coordinator of the Chicago branch of Operation Breadbasket, an organization established in 1962 by the Southern Christian Leadership Conference that focused on improving economic opportunities for African Americans. By means of boycotts, picketing, and publicity, Jackson opened up job opportunities in businesses that had previously excluded African Americans and persuaded retail chains to expand shelf space for products made by minority-owned firms. On April 4, 1968, Jackson was in Memphis, Tennessee, when King was murdered in that city. Jackson quickly returned to Chicago, where riots had erupted in outrage over King's killing. Jackson then vowed that he would remain faithful to King's principle of nonviolent protest.

During the 1970s, Jackson became one of the nation's most prominent African American leaders. In 1971 he resigned from Operation Breadbasket and founded Operation PUSH (People United to Save Humanity). Operation PUSH engaged in a variety of activities to advance minority interests, including sponsoring educational programs and pressing major corporations to adopt affirmative action programs. A charismatic speaker, Jackson became one of the most eloquent and recognized advocates for social justice.

He spoke throughout the United States and also to international audiences, journeying, for example, to South Africa in 1979 to denounce apartheid.

During the 1980s, Jackson became an important figure in national politics and international diplomacy. He campaigned for the Democratic presidential nomination in 1984, finishing third in the balloting behind front-runner and nominee Walter Mondale at the Democratic National Convention in San Francisco. In 1988 Jackson campaigned again for his party's presidential nomination. He ran an even stronger campaign in which he won several primaries and caucuses, finishing with the second-highest total of convention delegates after Michael Dukakis. In early January 1984, Jackson completed negotiations for the release of a captured U.S. pilot in Syria. Later that year, he went to Cuba and gained the release of forty-eight prisoners, including twenty-seven Americans. In 1989 he moved to Washington, D.C., where he served from 1991 until 1997 as a statehood senator, an office designed to encourage Congress to grant statehood to the District of Columbia. He founded the Wall Street Project in 1997, an effort to increase business opportunities for minorities. During that same year, President Bill Clinton named him special envoy to Africa for the promotion of democracy.

Jackson continues to work as a prominent activist for human rights and social justice. He has undertaken diplomatic missions to many international trouble spots, including Iraq (1990), Kosovo (1999), and Libya (2004) to negotiate the release of prisoners or hostages and mediate disputes. He still serves as president of the organization he founded, now known as the Rainbow/PUSH Coalition. In March 2007 he became an early supporter of Barack Obama's candidacy for president.

Explanation and Analysis of the Document

Jackson begins with an affirmation of faith in God, loyalty to country, and commitment to the Democratic Party. The pledge of support for the party was particularly important, since Jackson had challenged the Democratic platform in 1984 and complained about the party's rules for selecting delegates. With his assertion that the party, even if imperfect, was still "the best hope for redirecting our nation," Jackson quieted fears that he would be a disruptive force in Democratic politics after the nomination of Walter Mondale for president, scheduled for the following evening.

♦ Mission and Leadership

Jackson's main concerns at the outset of his speech were the issues he considered important and their effects on those groups on whose behalf he spoke. Jackson here uses "mission," a word with religious connotations, to emphasize the importance of the Democrats' obligation to help those in need. His specific language—"to feed the hungry; to clothe the naked; to house the homeless"—recalls passages in the Bible, especially a passage in the Gospel of Matthew about good works. Jackson declares that he represents "the desperate, the damned, the disinherited, the disrespected, and the despised." His use of alliteration, a series of words that begin with the same letter, is one of the notable characteristics of his speaking style; alliterative sequences gain the attention of the audience and lend prominence to his ideas. At this point, Jackson does not further identify the constituencies he represents, but he insists that the party has an obligation to them because they had "voted in record numbers" during the primaries and caucuses.

Jackson then shifts to a discussion of leadership, asserting that it is the key to solving the nation's problems. He focuses on political leadership, particularly the Democrats' choice of their next presidential nominee. Once again, Jackson uses biblical imagery, when he asserts that "leadership can part the waters and lead our nation in the direction of the Promised Land." In this section, as in other parts of his address, Jackson blends the attributes of a political speech with those of a sermon. He refers to the contest for the Democratic presidential nomination, which began with eight candidates and then narrowed to three: Mondale, Hart, and Jackson himself. Jackson asks the delegates who supported his candidacy to vote for him as a sign of their commitment to "a new direction for this Party and this nation." He pledges, however, to support the convention's nominee, who he knows would be Mondale, and he commends Mondale's choice of Representative Geraldine Ferraro as the party's candidate for vice president—the first woman nominated by a major party for that office. Once again, he finds inspiration in the Bible, specifically the book of Ecclesiastes, when he concedes that the contest for the nomination has concluded and that loyal Democrats must rally around Mondale. "There is a time to compete," he declares, "and a time to cooperate."

♦ Apology

In perhaps the most important part of his address, Jackson apologizes for mistakes made during the campaign. He mentions no specific errors; he only asks for forgiveness for any "word, deed, or attitude" that has "caused anyone discomfort, created pain, or revived someone's fears." It is clear, however, that Jackson is referring to his derogatory language about Jews and his association with Louis Farrakhan that led to charges of anti-Semitism. Again, Jackson frames his discussion of a political issue in religious terms, as he asserts that "God is not finished with me yet." He also invokes the example of Hubert Humphrey, the Democratic nominee who lost the presidential election of 1968 to Richard Nixon, to justify his conviction that "we must forgive each other ... and move on."

♦ Celebration of Diversity

Celebrating the diversity of the American people is the theme of the next section of the speech. Jackson uses two metaphors to describe ethnic, racial, religious, and political differences. The first is a rainbow—"red, yellow, brown, black and white." During his campaign, Jackson had

Jackson surrounded by marchers carrying signs advocating support for the Hawkins-Humphrey Bill for full employment, January 1975. By O'Halloran, Thomas J. [Public domain], via Wikimedia Commons.

described his supporters as "the rainbow coalition," which mirrored the name of the organization he had then founded, the National Rainbow Coalition. The second metaphor is a quilt consisting of "many pieces, many colors, many sizes," yet "held together by a common thread." While celebrating difference, Jackson calls for cooperation, since "we have not proven that we can win and make progress without each other." He cites the achievements in civil rights during the preceding twenty years, making reference to Fannie Lou Hamer, an African American who participated in a challenge to the all-white Mississippi delegation to the Democratic convention in Atlantic City in 1964. He emphasizes the pain that has accompanied progress, including the murders of the Martin Luther King, Jr., Malcolm X, Medgar Evers, Robert Kennedy, and John F. Kennedy as well as the killings of the civil rights activist Viola Liuzzo after the Selma-to-Montgomery march in Alabama and of three young civil rights workers, Michael Schwerner, Andrew Goodman, and James Chaney, in Mississippi during the Freedom Summer of 1964, a campaign to register African American voters in that state. He refers once more to the tensions between the black and Jewish communities that occurred during his campaign. He emphasizes, however, the common values and goals of blacks and Jews, inspired by religious principles and embodied in two great spiritual leaders, Martin Luther King and Rabbi Abraham Joshua Heschel, who marched together for voting rights in Selma, Alabama, in 1965. He urges African Americans and Jews to renew their partnership by turning "to each other and not on each other."

Next, Jackson appeals to the Democratic Party to welcome members of his rainbow coalition. He lists specific constituencies, including Arab Americans, Hispanic Americans, Native Americans, Asian Americans, young people, disabled veterans, small farmers, lesbians, and gays. Jackson maintains that these groups have been victimized, ostracized, or ignored, and he insists that inclusion rather than exclusion must be the hallmark of the Democratic Party. "Don't leave anybody out," he declares while counseling against hate, which he believes is often the result of "ignorance, anxiety, paranoia, fear, and insecurity." By representing the interests of this rainbow coalition, Jackson asserts that Democrats would be empowered to "expand our Party, heal our Party, and unify our Party." This part of the speech amounts to a plea to the party leadership to give more attention to minorities and their concerns as a way of building the party's strength for the 1984 election.

♦ Critique of Reagan's Policies

Jackson then begins an extensive critique of Ronald Reagan's first term as president. One of the main goals of a national convention was to rally support for the party's candidates and issues. Jackson's speech contributes to that goal with its denunciation of the Reagan administration for having made the world more "miserable" and more "dangerous."

Jackson particularly criticizes the president's policies for having made life harsher for the nation's poor. A severe recession had occurred during 1981–1982, after which an economic recovery began in 1983. Jackson maintains, however, that the poor had experienced none of the benefits of the recovery. He condemns the president's reductions in spending on social programs such as Social Security and school lunch programs as "cruel and unfair." He maintains that the president's program of tax cuts had disproportionately benefited big corporations and wealthy individuals while producing record budget deficits. Jackson then explains that the administration had tried to reduce the deficit with spending cuts on government-subsidized programs for people in need. Jackson echoed other critics, including some members of the president's own party, such as Vice President George H. W. Bush and Representative John Anderson of Illinois, both of whom had challenged Reagan for the Republican presidential nomination in 1980 and warned of dangers ahead if Reagan were to implement his economic plans and policies. According to Jackson, Reaganomics—a combination of tax cuts, increases in the defense budget, and reductions in funding for social programs—had brought about a "superficial economic recovery" with high unemployment and a national debt that had diminished the quality of life for poor people and had made the U.S. economy heavily dependent on foreign loans.

Jackson also harshly criticizes Reagan's national security policies. He deplores the loss of American lives in the bombing of a U.S. Marine barracks in Lebanon as well as the casualties that occurred during the U.S. invasion of Grenada. He also maintains that the steep increases in defense spending had not strengthened security against Soviet threats. "The danger index," Jackson warns, "has risen for everybody."

Jackson then looks to the future, as he outlines what he believes will be a winning strategy for Democrats. He tells his supporters that they had raised "the right questions," even if they had lost votes about the party's platform. He nonetheless believes that the platform provides "a solid foundation on which to build." The South, in his view, held the key to progressive politics, since there was the potential for a significant number of African Americans and Hispanics to be elected to Congress from that region. Jackson emphasizes that the triumph of one constituency would lead to the success of others, as he declares, "We must all come up together." A key to his vision was enforcement of the Voting Rights Act of 1965, which protected the right of minorities to exercise the franchise and to gain political representation.

Jackson then contrasts his ideas about peace and justice with Reagan administration policies. He asserts that the United States has been "at its best" when it fed hungry people but "at its worst" when it mined the harbors of Nicaragua and tried to overthrow the government of that nation. During Reagan's first term, the Central Intelligence Agency had placed mines in the harbor of Managua, Nicaragua's capital, and provided training and weapons to counter-revolutionaries in an effort to overthrow the Nicaraguan government, which the Reagan administration considered Communist. Jackson also condemns the "moral disgrace" of the Reagan administration's "partnerships" with South Africa. Prior to the end of apartheid in South Africa, a white minority government had enforced a system of racial segregation that oppressed the black majority. Jackson also calls for greater attention to Arab and Palestinian interests in the quest for Middle Eastern peace. Although he avoids specificity in an effort to appease supporters of Israel, he implies that U.S. policy makers have too often used a double standard in judging the human rights policies of Israel and its Arab neighbors. Overall, Jackson asserts that policies that promise peace and jobs and that shift spending from military to social programs will ensure that "the whole nation will come running to us."

♦ Optimism and Hope

In the final section of his address, Jackson preaches a message of optimism: hope for those disappointed that his candidacy had not led to his nomination and hope for Democrats who yearned for victory in the November election. Jackson particularly appeals to young people and their ability to imagine a better future. Much as he uses alliterative phrases earlier in his address, he uses a rhyming slogan to make an important point, when he challenges youth "to put hope in their brains not dope in their veins." Hope and imagination, he counsels them, can be "weapons of survival and progress." He ends by repeating his campaign slogan, "Our time has come." He speaks to those who support his candidacy, telling them, "Our faith, hope, and dreams will prevail." Yet he also addresses all Democrats, when he assures them that in November their time, too, will come. He ends on a note of triumph, confident that his candidacy has proved that African Americans have gained a central role in national politics. He also emphasizes unity, when he declares, "We must leave racial battle ground and come to economic common ground and moral high ground." In the end, Jackson maintains that the vibrant differences of the people within his coalition were less important than their common concerns.

Audience

Jackson's audience for his keynote address consisted of over twenty thousand delegates, alternates, party officials, and other spectators who attended the Democratic National Convention at the Moscone Center in San Francisco,

California. The speech occurred during prime-time viewing hours and was carried on major broadcast and cable television channels. Thirty-three million viewers across the United States saw Jackson speak. Included among them were Democrats, Republicans, and independents who had been given an exceptional opportunity to learn more about one of the first African American candidates for president of the United States.

Impact

Jackson's address created great anticipation, and it did not disappoint. "We are seeing something historic," declared ABC News commentator David Brinkley as Jackson was about to begin his address. "Just twenty years ago, Jesse Jackson was leading demonstrations demanding the right to eat at the Woolworth lunch counter." CBS News anchor Dan Rather echoed Brinkley's assessment. "Jackson's address, whatever you think of him," Rather suggested, "may be one for the history books." Many commentators agreed that the speech met those high expectations. "If you are a human being and weren't affected by what you just heard," Florida governor Bob Graham exclaimed, "you may be beyond redemption." Jackson's rhythmic cadences, alliterative phrases, and emotional delivery had a powerful effect on listeners. Delegates applauded, roared, and cried. Lucius J. Barker, an African American delegate from Missouri who supported Jackson, recalled, "Tears rolled down my face ... [and] when I looked around, others' eyes were also flowing with tears." A *Washington Post* editorial asserted that Jackson had given a great speech; a few commentators thought it was the most remarkable speech that had been given at a party convention to that point in the twentieth century.

There were some dissenting reactions, however. A few Jackson delegates, who thought that the party should have acceded to their platform proposals, criticized their candidate for having been too conciliatory in his address. While many Jewish leaders praised Jackson for having helped bridge political differences between blacks and Jews, some still emphasized that he had taken only a first step.

For many African Americans, Jackson's address was a source of pride and satisfaction. The author James Baldwin summarized the importance of Jackson's candidacy and speech by proclaiming, "Nothing will ever again be what it was before." Barker also thought the speech was significant because Jackson had showed that he was "the first black person to really become a *national political* leader in terms of national *presidential* politics." Jackson's speech, in short, helped open the door for Barack Obama a quarter century later.

Further Reading

♦ **Articles**

Atkinson, Rick. "Peace with American Jews Eludes Jackson." *Washington Post*, February 13, 1984.

Clendinen, Dudley. "U.S. a Cathedral for Jackson Speech." *New York Times*, July 19, 1984.

"Great Speeches." *Washington Post*, July 18, 1984.

♦ **Books**

Barker, Lucius J. *Our Time Has Come: A Delegate's Diary of Jesse Jackson's 1984 Presidential Campaign*. Urbana: University of Illinois Press, 1988.

——— and Ronald W. Walters, eds. *Jesse Jackson's 1984 Presidential Campaign: Challenge and Change in American Politics*. Urbana: University of Illinois Press, 1989.

Collins, Sheila D. *The Rainbow Challenge: The Jackson Campaign and the Future of U.S. Politics*. New York: Monthly Review Press, 1986.

Frady, Marshall. *Jesse: The Life and Pilgrimage of Jesse Jackson*. New York: Random House, 1996.

Germond, Jack W., and Jules Witcover. *Wake Us When It's Over: Presidential Politics of 1984*. New York: Macmillan, 1985.

Hatch, Roger D., and Frank E. Watkins, eds. *Straight from the Heart: Reverend Jesse L. Jackson*. Philadelphia: Fortress Press, 1987. Landess, Thomas H., and Richard M. Quinn. *Jesse Jackson and the Politics of Race*. Ottawa, Ill.: Jameson Books, 1985.

Ranney, Austin, ed. *The American Elections of 1984*. Durham, N.C.: Duke University Press, 1985.

Reed, Adolph L., Jr. *The Jesse Jackson Phenomenon: The Crisis of Purpose in Afro-American Politics*. New Haven, Conn.: Yale University Press, 1986.

♦ **Web Sites**

"Jesse Jackson for President 1984 Campaign Brochure." 4President.org Web site. http://www.4president.org/brochures/jessejackson-1984brochure.htm.

"Rainbow/PUSH Coalition" Web Site. http://www.rainbowpush.org.

———*Chester Pach*

Time Line

1941	October 8	■ Jesse Jackson is born in Greenville, South Carolina.
1965	March	■ Jackson meets Martin Luther King, Jr., in Selma, Alabama.
1966	February 11	■ Jackson becomes head of the newly established Chicago division of Operation Breadbasket, a national organization sponsored by the Southern Christian Leadership Conference and dedicated to improving economic opportunities for African Americans.
1968	April 4	■ Jackson is in Memphis, Tennessee, with Martin Luther King, Jr., when King is assassinated.
1971	December 25	■ Jackson establishes Operation PUSH in Chicago.
1979	September–October	■ Jackson meets with Yasser Arafat, head of the Palestine Liberation Organization, during a trip to the Middle East.
1983	November 3	■ Jackson declares his candidacy for the Democratic nomination for president.
1984	January 4	■ Jackson returns to Washington, D.C., after having traveled to Syria, where he negotiated the release of U.S. Navy Lieutenant Robert O. Goodman, Jr.
	February 13	■ The *Washington Post* carries an article, "Peace with American Jews Eludes Jackson," quoting Jackson as using a derogatory term for Jews during a conversation with the reporter Milton Coleman in January.
	July 17	■ Jackson addresses the Democratic National Convention in San Francisco.
	July 18	■ Jackson finishes third in the balloting for the presidential nomination at the Democratic National Convention.

Time Line

1988	July 20	■ Jackson finishes second behind Michael Dukakis in the contest for the presidential nomination at the Democratic National Convention in Atlanta, Georgia.
1990	November 6	■ Voters in the District of Columbia elect Jackson to the position of "statehood senator."
1997	January 15	■ Jackson announces plans to establish his Wall Street Project.
2007	March 29	■ Jackson endorses Barack Obama for the Democratic nomination for president.

Essential Quotes

"This is not a perfect party. We are not a perfect people. Yet, we are called to a perfect mission. Our mission: to feed the hungry; to clothe the naked; to house the homeless; to teach the illiterate; to provide jobs for the jobless; and to choose the human race over the nuclear race."

"My constituency is the desperate, the damned, the disinherited, the disrespected, and the despised. They are restless and seek relief. They have voted in record numbers."

"If, in my low moments, in word, deed, or attitude, through some error of temper, taste, or tone, I have caused anyone discomfort, created pain, or revived someone's fears, that was not my truest self. If there were occasions when my grape turned into a raisin and my joy bell lost its resonance, please forgive me."

"Our flag is red, white, and blue, but our nation is a rainbow—red, yellow, brown, black, and white—and we're all precious in God's sight."

"America is not a blanket—one piece of unbroken cloth, the same color, the same texture, the same size. America is more like a quilt: many patches ... held together by a common thread. The white, the Hispanic, the black, the Arab, the Jew, the woman, the Native American, the small farmer, the businessperson, the environmentalist, the peace activist, the young, the old, the lesbian, the gay, and the disabled make up the American quilt."

"We live in a world tonight more miserable and a world more dangerous."

"If we cut that military budget without cutting our defense, and use that money to rebuild bridges and put steel workers back to work, and use that money and provide jobs for our cities, and use that money to build schools and pay teachers and educate our children and build hospitals and train doctors and train nurses, the whole nation will come running to us."

"Our time has come. Our faith, hope, and dreams will prevail."

Questions for Further Study

1. Jesse Jackson ran for the presidency in 1984 and 1988, and although he surprised some observers with a strong showing, he was never really regarded as an electable candidate? Why?

2. What was Jackson's primary political mission during this time?

3. What political considerations prompted the Democratic Party's nominee, Walter Mondale, to allow Jackson to deliver the convention's keynote address?

4. Jackson's speeches have often been admired for their emotion and soaring rhetoric. What types of rhetorical devices did Jackson use in this speech to sweep his listeners along with him?

5. Compare this speech with Barack Obama's Inaugural Address. In what ways are Jackson and Obama similar? How do they differ—in style, points of view, and the like?

Jesse Jackson's Democratic National Convention Keynote Address

The full text of Jackson's speech.

Tonight we come together bound by our faith in a mighty God, with genuine respect and love for our country, and inheriting the legacy of a great Party, the Democratic Party, which is the best hope for redirecting our nation on a more humane, just, and peaceful course.

This is not a perfect party. We are not a perfect people. Yet, we are called to a perfect mission. Our mission: to feed the hungry; to clothe the naked; to house the homeless; to teach the illiterate; to provide jobs for the jobless; and to choose the human race over the nuclear race.

We are gathered here this week to nominate a candidate and adopt a platform which will expand, unify, direct, and inspire our Party and the nation to fulfill this mission. My constituency is the desperate, the damned, the disinherited, the disrespected, and the despised. They are restless and seek relief. They have voted in record numbers. They have invested the faith, hope, and trust that they have in us. The Democratic Party must send them a signal that we care. I pledge my best not to let them down.

There is the call of conscience, redemption, expansion, healing, and unity. Leadership must heed the call of conscience, redemption, expansion, healing, and unity, for they are the key to achieving our mission. Time is neutral and does not change things. With courage and initiative, leaders change things.

No generation can choose the age or circumstance in which it is born, but through leadership it can choose to make the age in which it is born an age of enlightenment, an age of jobs, and peace, and justice. Only leadership—that intangible combination of gifts, the discipline, information, circumstance, courage, timing, will and divine inspiration—can lead us out of the crisis in which we find ourselves. Leadership can mitigate the misery of our nation. Leadership can part the waters and lead our nation in the direction of the Promised Land. Leadership can lift the boats stuck at the bottom.

I have had the rare opportunity to watch seven men, and then two, pour out their souls, offer their service, and heal and heed the call of duty to direct the course of our nation. There is a proper season for everything. There is a time to sow and a time to reap. There's a time to compete and a time to cooperate.

I ask for your vote on the first ballot as a vote for a new direction for this Party and this nation—a vote of conviction, a vote of conscience. But I will be proud to support the nominee of this convention for the Presidency of the United States of America. Thank you.

I have watched the leadership of our party develop and grow. My respect for both Mr. Mondale and Mr. Hart is great. I have watched them struggle with the crosswinds and crossfires of being public servants, and I believe they will both continue to try to serve us faithfully.

I am elated by the knowledge that for the first time in our history a woman, Geraldine Ferraro, will be recommended to share our ticket.

Throughout this campaign, I've tried to offer leadership to the Democratic Party and the nation. If, in my high moments, I have done some good, offered some service, shed some light, healed some wounds, rekindled some hope, or stirred someone from apathy and indifference, or in any way along the way helped somebody, then this campaign has not been in vain.

For friends who loved and cared for me, and for a God who spared me, and for a family who understood, I am eternally grateful.

If, in my low moments, in word, deed or attitude, through some error of temper, taste, or tone, I have caused anyone discomfort, created pain, or revived someone's fears, that was not my truest self. If there were occasions when my grape turned into a raisin and my joy bell lost its resonance, please forgive me. Charge it to my head and not to my heart. My head—so limited in its finitude; my heart, which is boundless in its love for the human family. I am not a perfect servant. I am a public servant doing my best against the odds. As I develop and serve, be patient: God is not finished with me yet.

This campaign has taught me much; that leaders must be tough enough to fight, tender enough to cry, human enough to make mistakes, humble enough to admit them, strong enough to absorb the pain, and resilient enough to bounce back and keep on moving.

Document Text

For leaders, the pain is often intense. But you must smile through your tears and keep moving with the faith that there is a brighter side somewhere.

I went to see Hubert Humphrey three days before he died. He had just called Richard Nixon from his dying bed, and many people wondered why. And I asked him. He said, "Jesse, from this vantage point, the sun is setting in my life, all of the speeches, the political conventions, the crowds, and the great fights are behind me now. At a time like this you are forced to deal with your irreducible essence, forced to grapple with that which is really important to you. And what I've concluded about life," Hubert Humphrey said, "When all is said and done, we must forgive each other, and redeem each other, and move on."

Our party is emerging from one of its most hard fought battles for the Democratic Party's presidential nomination in our history. But our healthy competition should make us better, not bitter. We must use the insight, wisdom, and experience of the late Hubert Humphrey as a balm for the wounds in our Party, this nation, and the world. We must forgive each other, redeem each other, regroup, and move on. Our flag is red, white and blue, but our nation is a rainbow—red, yellow, brown, black and white—and we're all precious in God's sight.

America is not like a blanket—one piece of unbroken cloth, the same color, the same texture, the same size. America is more like a quilt: many patches, many pieces, many colors, many sizes, all woven and held together by a common thread. The white, the Hispanic, the black, the Arab, the Jew, the woman, the native American, the small farmer, the businessperson, the environmentalist, the peace activist, the young, the old, the lesbian, the gay, and the disabled make up the American quilt.

Even in our fractured state, all of us count and fit somewhere. We have proven that we can survive without each other. But we have not proven that we can win and make progress without each other. We must come together.

From Fannie Lou Hamer in Atlantic City in 1964 to the Rainbow Coalition in San Francisco today; from the Atlantic to the Pacific, we have experienced pain but progress, as we ended American apartheid laws. We got public accommodations. We secured voting rights. We obtained open housing, as young people got the right to vote. We lost Malcolm, Martin, Medgar, Bobby, John, and Viola. The team that got us here must be expanded, not abandoned.

Twenty years ago, tears welled up in our eyes as the bodies of Schwerner, Goodman, and Chaney were dredged from the depths of a river in Mississippi. Twenty years later, our communities, black and Jewish, are in anguish, anger, and pain. Feelings have been hurt on both sides. There is a crisis in communications. Confusion is in the air. But we cannot afford to lose our way. We may agree to agree; or agree to disagree on issues; we must bring back civility to these tensions.

We are co-partners in a long and rich religious history—the Judeo-Christian traditions. Many blacks and Jews have a shared passion for social justice at home and peace abroad. We must seek a revival of the spirit, inspired by a new vision and new possibilities. We must return to higher ground. We are bound by Moses and Jesus, but also connected with Islam and Mohammed. These three great religions, Judaism, Christianity, and Islam, were all born in the revered and holy city of Jerusalem.

We are bound by Dr. Martin Luther King Jr. and Rabbi Abraham Heschel, crying out from their graves for us to reach common ground. We are bound by shared blood and shared sacrifices. We are much too intelligent, much too bound by our Judeo-Christian heritage, much too victimized by racism, sexism, militarism, and anti-Semitism, much too threatened as historical scapegoats to go on divided one from another. We must turn from finger pointing to clasped hands. We must share our burdens and our joys with each other once again. We must turn to each other and not on each other and choose higher ground.

Twenty years later, we cannot be satisfied by just restoring the old coalition. Old wine skins must make room for new wine. We must heal and expand. The Rainbow Coalition is making room for Arab Americans. They, too, know the pain and hurt of racial and religious rejection. They must not continue to be made pariahs. The Rainbow Coalition is making room for Hispanic Americans who this very night are living under the threat of the Simpson-Mazzoli bill; and farm workers from Ohio who are fighting the Campbell Soup Company with a boycott to achieve legitimate workers' rights.

The Rainbow is making room for the Native American, the most exploited people of all, a people with the greatest moral claim amongst us. We support them as they seek the restoration of their ancient land and claim amongst us. We support them as they seek the restoration of land and water rights, as they seek to preserve their ancestral homeland and the beauty of a land that was once all theirs. They can never receive a fair share for all they have given us. They must finally have a fair chance to develop their great resources and to preserve their people and their culture.

The Rainbow Coalition includes Asian Americans, now being killed in our streets—scapegoats for the failures of corporate, industrial, and economic policies.

The Rainbow is making room for the young Americans. Twenty years ago, our young people were dying in a war for which they could not even vote. Twenty years later, young America has the power to stop a war in Central America and the responsibility to vote in great numbers. Young America must be politically active in 1984. The choice is war or peace. We must make room for young America.

The Rainbow includes disabled veterans. The color scheme fits in the Rainbow. The disabled have their handicap revealed and their genius concealed; while the able-bodied have their genius revealed and their disability concealed. But ultimately, we must judge people by their values and their contribution. Don't leave anybody out. I would rather have Roosevelt in a wheelchair than Reagan on a horse.

The Rainbow is making room for small farmers. They have suffered tremendously under the Reagan regime. They will either receive 90 percent parity or 100 percent charity. We must address their concerns and make room for them. The Rainbow includes lesbians and gays. No American citizen ought be denied equal protection from the law.

We must be unusually committed and caring as we expand our family to include new members. All of us must be tolerant and understanding as the fears and anxieties of the rejected and the party leadership express themselves in many different ways. Too often what we call hate—as if it were some deeply-rooted philosophy or strategy—is simply ignorance, anxiety, paranoia, fear, and insecurity. To be strong leaders, we must be long-suffering as we seek to right the wrongs of our Party and our nation. We must expand our Party, heal our Party, and unify our Party. That is our mission in 1984.

We are often reminded that we live in a great nation—and we do. But it can be greater still. The Rainbow is mandating a new definition of greatness. We must not measure greatness from the mansion down, but the manger up. Jesus said that we should not be judged by the bark we wear but by the fruit that we bear. Jesus said that we must measure greatness by how we treat the least of these.

President Reagan says the nation is in recovery. Those 90,000 corporations that made a profit last year but paid no federal taxes are recovering. The 37,000 military contractors who have benefited from Reagan's more than doubling of the military budget in peacetime, surely they are recovering. The big corporations and rich individuals who received the bulk of a three-year, multibillion tax cut from Mr. Reagan are recovering. But no such recovery is under way for the least of these.

Rising tides don't lift all boats, particularly those stuck at the bottom. For the boats stuck at the bottom there's a misery index. This Administration has made life more miserable for the poor. Its attitude has been contemptuous. Its policies and programs have been cruel and unfair to working people. They must be held accountable in November for increasing infant mortality among the poor. In Detroit one of the great cities of the western world, babies are dying at the same rate as Honduras, the most underdeveloped nation in our hemisphere. This Administration must be held accountable for policies that have contributed to the growing poverty in America. There are now 34 million people in poverty, 15 percent of our nation. 23 million are White; 11 million Black, Hispanic, Asian, and others—mostly women and children. By the end of this year, there will be 41 million people in poverty. We cannot stand idly by. We must fight for a change now.

Under this regime we look at Social Security. The '81 budget cuts included nine permanent Social Security benefit cuts totaling 20 billion over five years. Small businesses have suffered under Reagan tax cuts. Only 18 percent of total business tax cuts went to them; 82 percent to big businesses. Health care under Mr. Reagan has already been sharply cut. Education under Mr. Reagan has been cut 25 percent. Under Mr. Reagan there are now 9.7 million female head families. They represent 16 percent of all families. Half of all of them are poor. 70 percent of all poor children live in a house headed by a woman, where there is no man. Under Mr. Reagan, the Administration has cleaned up only 6 of 546 priority toxic waste dumps. Farmers' real net income was only about half its level in 1979.

Document Text

Many say that the race in November will be decided in the South. President Reagan is depending on the conservative South to return him to office. But the South, I tell you, is unnaturally conservative. The South is the poorest region in our nation and, therefore, [has] the least to conserve. In his appeal to the South, Mr. Reagan is trying to substitute flags and prayer cloths for food, and clothing, and education, health care, and housing.

Mr. Reagan will ask us to pray, and I believe in prayer. I have come to this way by the power of prayer. But then, we must watch false prophecy. He cuts energy assistance to the poor, cuts breakfast programs from children, cuts lunch programs from children, cuts job training from children, and then says to an empty table, "Let us pray." Apparently, he is not familiar with the structure of a prayer. You thank the Lord for the food that you are about to receive, not the food that just left. I think that we should pray, but don't pray for the food that left. Pray for the man that took the food to leave. We need a change. We need a change in November.

Under Mr. Reagan, the misery index has risen for the poor. The danger index has risen for everybody. Under this administration, we've lost the lives of our boys in Central America and Honduras, in Grenada, in Lebanon, in nuclear standoff in Europe. Under this Administration, one-third of our children believe they will die in a nuclear war. The danger index is increasing in this world. All the talk about the defense against Russia; the Russian submarines are closer, and their missiles are more accurate. We live in a world tonight more miserable and a world more dangerous.

While Reaganomics and Reaganism is talked about often, so often we miss the real meaning. Reaganism is a spirit, and Reaganomics represents the real economic facts of life. In 1980, Mr. George Bush, a man with reasonable access to Mr. Reagan, did an analysis of Mr. Reagan's economic plan. Mr. George Bush concluded that Reagan's plan was "voodoo economics." He was right. Third-party candidate John Anderson said "a combination of military spending, tax cuts, and a balanced budget by '84 would be accomplished with blue smoke and mirrors." They were both right.

Mr. Reagan talks about a dynamic recovery. There's some measure of recovery. Three and a half years later, unemployment has inched just below where it was when he took office in 1981. There are still 8.1 million people officially unemployed; 11 million working only part-time. Inflation has come down, but let's analyze for a moment who has paid the price for this superficial economic recovery.

Mr. Reagan curbed inflation by cutting consumer demand. He cut consumer demand with conscious and callous fiscal and monetary policies. He used the Federal budget to deliberately induce unemployment and curb social spending. He then weighed and supported tight monetary policies of the Federal Reserve Board to deliberately drive up interest rates, again to curb consumer demand created through borrowing. Unemployment reached 10.7 percent. We experienced skyrocketing interest rates. Our dollar inflated abroad. There were record bank failures, record farm foreclosures, record business bankruptcies; record budget deficits, record trade deficits.

Mr. Reagan brought inflation down by destabilizing our economy and disrupting family life. He promised—he promised in 1980 a balanced budget. But instead we now have a record 200 billion dollar budget deficit. Under Mr. Reagan, the cumulative budget deficit for his four years is more than the sum total of deficits from George Washington to Jimmy Carter combined. I tell you, we need a change.

How is he paying for these short-term jobs? Reagan's economic recovery is being financed by deficit spending—200 billion dollars a year. Military spending, a major cause of this deficit, is projected over the next five years to be nearly 2 trillion dollars, and will cost about 40,000 dollars for every taxpaying family. When the Government borrows 200 billion dollars annually to finance the deficit, this encourages the private sector to make its money off of interest rates as opposed to development and economic growth.

Even money abroad, we don't have enough money domestically to finance the debt, so we are now borrowing money abroad, from foreign banks, governments and financial institutions: 40 billion dollars in 1983; 70–80 billion dollars in 1984—40 percent of our total; over 100 billion dollars—50 percent of our total—in 1985. By 1989, it is projected that 50 percent of all individual income taxes will be going just to pay for interest on that debt. The United States used to be the largest exporter of capital, but under Mr. Reagan we will quite likely become the largest debtor nation.

About two weeks ago, on July the 4th, we celebrated our Declaration of Independence, yet every day supply-side economics is making our nation more economically dependent and less economically free. Five to six percent of our Gross National Product is now being eaten up with President Reagan's budget deficits. To depend on foreign military powers to protect our national security would be foolish, making us dependent and less secure. Yet, Reaganomics has us increasingly dependent on foreign economic sources. This consumer-led but deficit-financed recovery is unbalanced and artificial. We have a challenge as Democrats to point a way out.

Democracy guarantees opportunity, not success.

Democracy guarantees the right to participate, not a license for either a majority or a minority to dominate.

The victory for the Rainbow Coalition in the Platform debates today was not whether we won or lost, but that we raised the right issues. We could afford to lose the vote; issues are non-negotiable. We could not afford to avoid raising the right questions. Our self-respect and our moral integrity were at stake. Our heads are perhaps bloody, but not bowed. Our back is straight. We can go home and face our people. Our vision is clear.

When we think, on this journey from slave-ship to championship, that we have gone from the planks of the Boardwalk in Atlantic City in 1964 to fighting to help write the planks in the platform in San Francisco in '84, there is a deep and abiding sense of joy in our souls in spite of the tears in our eyes. Though there are missing planks, there is a solid foundation upon which to build. Our party can win, but we must provide hope which will inspire people to struggle and achieve; provide a plan that shows a way out of our dilemma and then lead the way.

In 1984, my heart is made to feel glad because I know there is a way out—justice. The requirement for rebuilding America is justice. The linchpin of progressive politics in our nation will not come from the North; they, in fact, will come from the South. That is why I argue over and over again. We look from Virginia around to Texas, there's only one black Congressperson out of 115. Nineteen years later, we're locked out of the Congress, the Senate and the Governor's mansion. What does this large black vote mean? Why do I fight to win second primaries and fight gerrymandering and annexation and at-large [elections]. Why do we fight over that? Because I tell you, you cannot hold someone in the ditch unless you linger there with them. Unless you linger there.

If you want a change in this nation, you enforce that Voting Rights Act. We'll get 12 to 20 Black, Hispanics, female and progressive congresspersons from the South. We can save the cotton, but we've got to fight the boll weevils. We've got to make a judgment. We've got to make a judgment.

It is not enough to hope ERA will pass. How can we pass ERA? If Blacks vote in great numbers, progressive Whites win. It's the only way progressive Whites win. If Blacks vote in great numbers, Hispanics win. When Blacks, Hispanics, and progressive Whites vote, women win. When women win, children win. When women and children win, workers win. We must all come up together. We must come up together.

Thank you.

For all of our joy and excitement, we must not save the world and lose our souls. We should never short-circuit enforcing the Voting Rights Act at every level. When one of us rise[s], all of us will rise. Justice is the way out. Peace is the way out. We should not act as if nuclear weaponry is negotiable and debatable.

In this world in which we live, we dropped the bomb on Japan and felt guilty, but in 1984 other folks [have] also got bombs. This time, if we drop the bomb, six minutes later we, too, will be destroyed. It's not about dropping the bomb on somebody. It is about dropping the bomb on everybody. We must choose to develop minds over guided missiles, and think it out and not fight it out. It's time for a change.

Our foreign policy must be characterized by mutual respect, not by gunboat diplomacy, big stick diplomacy, and threats. Our nation at its best feeds the hungry. Our nation at its worst, at its worst, will mine the harbors of Nicaragua, at its worst will try to overthrow their government, at its worst will cut aid to American education and increase the aid to El Salvador; at its worst, our nation will have partnerships with South Africa. That's a moral disgrace. It's a moral disgrace. It's a moral disgrace.

We look at Africa. We cannot just focus on Apartheid in Southern Africa. We must fight for trade with Africa, and not just aid to Africa. We cannot stand idly by and say we will not relate to Nicaragua unless they have elections there, and then embrace military regimes in Africa overthrowing democratic governments in Nigeria and Liberia and Ghana. We must fight for democracy all around the world and play the game by one set of rules.

Peace in this world. Our present formula for peace in the Middle East is inadequate. It will not work. There are 22 nations in the Middle East. Our nation must be able to talk and act and influence all

Document Text

of them. We must build upon Camp David, and measure human rights by one yard stick. In that region we have too many interests and too few friends.

There is a way out—jobs. Put America back to work. When I was a child growing up in Greenville, South Carolina, the Reverend Sample used to preach every so often a sermon relating to Jesus. And he said, "If I be lifted up, I'll draw all men unto me." I didn't quite understand what he meant as a child growing up, but I understand a little better now. If you raise up truth, it's magnetic. It has a way of drawing people.

With all this confusion in this Convention, the bright lights and parties and big fun, we must raise up the simple proposition: If we lift up a program to feed the hungry, they'll come running; if we lift up a program to study war no more, our youth will come running; if we lift up a program to put America back to work, and an alternative to welfare and despair, they will come working.

If we cut that military budget without cutting our defense, and use that money to rebuild bridges and put steel workers back to work, and use that money and provide jobs for our cities, and use that money to build schools and pay teachers and educate our children and build hospitals and train doctors and train nurses, the whole nation will come running to us.

As I leave you now, we vote in this convention and get ready to go back across this nation in a couple of days. In this campaign, I've tried to be faithful to my promise. I lived in old barrios, ghettos, and reservations and housing projects. I have a message for our youth. I challenge them to put hope in their brains and not dope in their veins. I told them that like Jesus, I, too, was born in the slum. But just because you're born in the slum does not mean the slum is born in you, and you can rise above it if your mind is made up. I told them in every slum there are two sides. When I see a broken window—that's the slummy side. Train some youth to become a glazier—that's the sunny side. When I see a missing brick—that's the slummy side. Let that child in the union and become a brick mason and build—that's the sunny side. When I see a missing door—that's the slummy side. Train some youth to become a carpenter—that's the sunny side. And when I see the vulgar words and hieroglyphics of destitution on the walls—that's the slummy side. Train some youth to become a painter, an artist—that's the sunny side.

We leave this place looking for the sunny side because there's a brighter side somewhere. I'm more convinced than ever that we can win. We will vault up the rough side of the mountain. We can win. I just want young America to do me one favor, just one favor. Exercise the right to dream. You must face reality—that which is. But then dream of a reality that ought to be—that must be. Live beyond the pain of reality with the dream of a bright tomorrow. Use hope and imagination as weapons of survival and progress. Use love to motivate you and obligate you to serve the human family.

Young America, dream. Choose the human race over the nuclear race. Bury the weapons and don't burn the people. Dream—dream of a new value system. Teachers who teach for life and not just for a living; teach because they can't help it. Dream of lawyers more concerned about justice than a judgeship. Dream of doctors more concerned about public health than personal wealth. Dream of preachers and priests who will prophesy and not just profiteer. Preach and dream!

Our time has come. Our time has come. Suffering breeds character. Character breeds faith. In the end, faith will not disappoint. Our time has come. Our faith, hope, and dreams will prevail. Our time has come. Weeping has endured for nights, but now joy cometh in the morning. Our time has come. No grave can hold our body down. Our time has come. No lie can live forever. Our time has come. We must leave racial battle ground and come to economic common ground and moral higher ground. America, our time has come. We come from disgrace to amazing grace. Our time has come. Give me your tired, give me your poor, your huddled masses who yearn to breathe free and come November, there will be a change because our time has come.

Glossary

Abraham Heschel: a Jewish rabbi who marched with Martin Luther King, Jr., for voting rights in Selma, Alabama, in 1965

Apartheid: the system of legal racial segregation in South Africa

Camp David: a naval facility in Maryland used as a presidential retreat; the site of the signing of the Camp David Accords, a peace agreement between Israel and Egypt in 1978

ERA: the Equal Rights Amendment

Fanny Lou Hamer: an African American who participated in a challenge to the all-white Mississippi delegation to the Democratic convention in Atlantic City in 1964

George Bush: George H. W. Bush, who ran unsuccessfully for the Republican presidential nomination in 1980 and Reagan's vice president

Geraldine Ferraro: a New York congressional representative who ran for vice president on the ticket with Walter Mondale in 1984

Gross National Product: the sum total of all goods and services produced in a country

Hart: Senator Gary Hart, who finished second to Walter Mondale in the race for the 1984 Democratic presidential nomination

Hubert Humphrey: the Minnesota senator who ran for president against Richard Nixon in 1968

Jimmy Carter: Ronald Reagan's predecessor as U.S. president

John Anderson: an Illinois congressional representative who mounted a 1980 campaign for president as an independent candidate

Malcolm, Martin, Medgar, Bobby, John, and Viola: slain civil rights leaders and activists Malcolm X, Martin Luther King, Jr., Medgar Evers, Robert Kennedy, John Kennedy, and Viola Liuzzo

Mohammad: usually Muhammad, the founder of Islam

Mondale: Senator Walter Mondale, the Democratic presidential candidate in 1984 and former vice president under Jimmy Carter

Reagan: Ronald Reagan, Mondale's opponent in the 1984 presidential election and an avid horseback rider

Reaganomics: the informal name given to President Ronald Reagan's economic views

Richard Nixon: the Republican president from 1969 to 1974

Roosevelt: President Franklin D. Roosevelt, who used a wheelchair because of an early bout with polio

Schwerner, Goodman, and Chaney: Michael Schwerner, Andrew Goodman, and James Chaney, northern civil rights workers murdered in Mississippi during the Freedom Summer of 1964

seven men: the candidates for the Democratic presidential nomination

Simpson-Mazzoli bill: proposed legislation to reduce illegal immigration to the United States

war in Central America: a reference to ongoing conflict in Nicaragua

Professor Charles Ogletree and Professor Anita Hill at a panel discussion following a screening of the documentary ANITA, held at Harvard Law School on September 24, 2014. By Tim Pierce (Own work) [CC BY-SA 4.0 (http://creativecommons.org/licenses/by-sa/4.0)], via Wikimedia Commons

Anita Hill's Opening Statement at the Senate Confirmation Hearing of Clarence Thomas

1991

"I have no personal vendetta against Clarence Thomas."

Overview

Anita Hill's opening statement in 1991 at the proceedings conducted by the Senate Judiciary Committee regarding the nomination of Clarence Thomas to the U.S. Supreme Court was a bold and revealing account of sexual harassment in the workplace that also brought up issues related to gender discrimination and racism. During the course of the grueling Senate confirmation hearing, startling accusations of sexual harassment were raised by Hill against Thomas. A law professor at the University of Oklahoma who had been one of Thomas's coworkers, Hill only reluctantly came forward with detailed allegations. Her statement and subsequent testimony, which were broadcast on national television, provided a public glimpse into the confirmation process as well as the complex web of issues surrounding sexual harassment, gender discrimination, and racial stereotyping. Despite the controversy over his nomination, Thomas was confirmed by a close vote on the Senate floor, and he was sworn in as the 106th U.S. Supreme Court justice on October 23, 1991. He became only the second African American to hold the position, replacing the first African American Supreme Court justice, Thurgood Marshall.

Hill's opening statement was historically and culturally significant in a number of ways. It showed that as an issue, sexual harassment transcended considerations solely about race, and it exposed the profound damage that could be inflicted by verbal rather than physical sexual harassment. Moreover, Hill's account demonstrated that the "he said, she said" dilemma posed by many sexual harassment claims could be a difficult hurdle to overcome. Hill's statement also gave expression to the gender and racial discrimination she had endured and how they had been important factors in her decision to come forward. The statement was also significant because it pitted two African Americans against each other in the public eye and provoked widespread disagreement in the black community.

Context

On June 27, 1991, Thurgood Marshall, the first African American justice to serve on the Supreme Court, announced that he was retiring. Marshall had been a prominent figure in the civil rights movement prior to his appointment to the nation's highest court. As chief counsel for the National Association for the Advancement of Colored People, Marshall had argued and won the landmark civil rights case *Brown v. Board of Education*. During his twenty-four-year tenure on the Supreme Court, the liberal Marshall championed constitutional protections of individual and civil rights. As a result of Marshall's resignation, President George H. W. Bush was charged with the difficult task of replacing him.

At the time of Marshall's pronouncement, the composition of the Supreme Court was shifting. During the administrations of both the elder Bush and Ronald Reagan, when a vacancy occurred at the Supreme Court, the presidents had chosen to fill it with a conservative justice. In 1987 President Reagan attempted to nominate Judge Robert Bork, a conservative, to the Supreme Court. However, key Democratic members of the Senate Judiciary Committee were concerned about Bork's views and vehemently opposed his nomination. As a result, Bork's nomination was easily defeated when it came to a vote in the Senate. Mindful of what had happened to Bork, President Bush did not want his nominee to be similarly defeated, but he also did not want to replace Marshall with a liberal-leaning justice.

Republicans felt that Judge Clarence Thomas, who had served on the federal court of appeals since 1990, was the best person to replace the retiring Marshall. Unlike Marshall, Thomas was a conservative African American male who had sharply critiqued affirmative action. Although Thomas was an anomaly among African American legal professionals, Republicans believed that by stressing his humble beginnings in Pin Point, Georgia, he would eventually gain African American support. Thomas was a Yale Law School graduate, who from 1981 to 1982 had been the assistant secretary for civil rights in the Department of Education and from 1982 to 1990 had served as chairman of the Equal Employment Opportunity Commission (EEOC). Conservative Washington insiders knew of Thomas from his government service and had suggested him to President Bush.

Civil right activists, leaders of civil rights groups, and liberal organizations were concerned about Thomas's disdain for affirmative action and other progressive causes. Members of the National Association for the Advancement of Colored People overwhelmingly opposed his nomination, and the National Abortion Rights Action League was concerned about his views on abortion, especially his take on the *Roe v. Wade* decision (1973), granting women wider rights to abortion. Moreover, Thomas's lack of judicial experience was a point of contention for the American Bar Association. Typically, the bar association rated Supreme Court justices "well qualified." Because of Thomas's limited experience on the federal court of appeals, however, the bar association gave Thomas only a "qualified" rating. In response, the White House obtained support from conservative groups to mount an attack against liberal groups that opposed Thomas. This campaign helped bolster Thomas's reputation in the right-wing community but did little to sway his many critics.

In August 1991, one month before the start of Thomas's Senate confirmation hearing, newspaper reporters and Washington insiders began to hear rumors that centered on Anita Hill, a former coworker of Thomas's, who claimed that she had been sexually harassed by him repeatedly. As the confirmation hearing neared, opponents of Thomas contacted Hill, a University of Oklahoma law professor, to determine the veracity of her claims. At first, Hill was hesitant to talk to reporters and staff members of the Senate Judiciary Committee, fearing that her anonymity would be jeopardized. She was first contacted by Gail Laster, counsel to the Judiciary Committee's Labor Subcommittee. Laster asked Hill generally about the rumors of sexual harassment; Hill did not tell Laster about the harassing behavior she herself had endured at the EEOC. Ricki Seidman, chief investigator of the Senate Labor and Human Resources Committee, twice communicated with Hill about the sexual harassment allegations. During her second conversation with Seidman, Hill told her some details of Thomas's behavior but also expressed her desire for confidentiality.

James Brudney, chief counsel to the Judiciary Committee's Labor Subcommittee, chaired by Senator Howard Metzenbaum, next contacted Hill about the rumors. After Hill explained the details of Thomas's conduct to Brudney, he spoke to Metzenbaum, who suggested contacting Harriet Grant of the office of Senator Joseph Biden, chairman of the Judiciary Committee. In the weeks prior to Hill's testimony before the Judiciary Committee, both Grant and Brudney spoke to Hill about revealing her information to the Federal Bureau of Investigation (FBI). Eventually, Hill agreed to be interviewed by the FBI and also submitted a written, notarized statement to the Senate Judiciary Committee memorializing her experiences with Thomas. Thereafter, the FBI report on Hill was submitted to some committee members.

Thomas began the confirmation process on September 10, 1991. Each senator on the Judiciary Committee gave an opening statement that either supported Thomas or expressed concerns about his past. For the most part, the committee, which consisted of seven Democrats and six Republicans, was divided along party lines. The committee's Democrats were much harder on Thomas than were their Republican counterparts, questioning him about his past speeches and articles, his views on natural law, decisions made while at the EEOC, and abortion rights. Typically, after a Democratic member finished questioning Thomas, a Republican member asked him an easier question in order to repair his credibility with the committee. During the initial confirmation hearing, Thomas was unaware of Hill's allegations. He endured the Senate Judiciary Committee's questioning for five days before other witnesses were called.

One of Thomas's key opponents was Sylvia Law, a professor of constitutional law in the areas of personal and privacy rights, who was concerned about Thomas's conservative views on women's reproductive rights. Other opponents included Molly Yard, president of the National Organization of Women; representatives from the American Federation of Labor and Congress of Industrial Organizations; Kate Michelman, executive director of the National Abortion Rights Action League; Faye Wattleton, president of the Planned Parenthood Federation of America; and Julius Chambers, from the National Association for the Advancement of Colored People's Legal Defense and Educational Fund. Speaking in support of Thomas, Guido Calabresi, then the dean of Yale Law School, praised his ability to remain independent and his potential to grow with the Supreme Court. Thomas's proponents also included Robert Woodson, president of the National Center for Neighborhood Enterprise; John E. Palmer, representing the Heartland Coalition for the Confirmation of Judge Clarence Thomas; and the Republican Black Caucus chair George C. Dumas.

Only days before the committee vote, Thomas was informed of the FBI report claiming that he had sexually harassed Hill when they both had worked at the Department of Education and EEOC. Thomas emphatically denied Hill's accusations, but the damage had been done. When the Judiciary Committee voted on the confirmation on September 27, the result was a seven-to-seven tie, and the nomination was sent to the Senate floor with no endorsement. Meanwhile, the news media took hold of the sexual harassment rumors and made Anita Hill a household name. The salacious details of the harassment were cast into the world of public opinion. In turn, the Senate, at the request of Thomas, delayed its confirmation vote. Finally, on October 11, 1991, Hill and Thomas appeared in front of the Senate Judiciary Committee to tell their sides of the story.

About the Author

The thirteenth child born to a poor farm family, Anita Faye Hill was born in 1956 in Okmulgee County, Oklahoma. Her father, Albert Hill, and mother, Erma Hill, both worked on the farm. From a young age, Anita Hill knew that hard work and dedication would be the keys to her success. She attended integrated schools and was shielded from racial tensions for much of her childhood. After she graduated from high school, Hill attended Oklahoma State University and graduated with honors in 1977. She received a JD degree from Yale Law School in 1980.

Hill's initial job out of law school was at the Washington, D.C., law firm Wald, Harkrader & Ross. While working for the law firm, she met Clarence Thomas. Soon afterward, in 1981, Thomas was appointed the assistant secretary for civil rights in the Department of Education, and he asked Hill if she would become his assistant. She accepted the job offer, and she followed Thomas to the EEOC when he became its chairman.

In 1983, Hill left the EEOC and took a position as an assistant law professor at the O.W. Colburn School of Law at Oral Roberts University. She subsequently became a professor at the College of Law at the University of Oklahoma, a position that she held at the time she appeared before the Senate Judiciary Committee. After testifying before the committee, she returned to her position at the University of Oklahoma. She was asked to speak at a number of events about her experience at the hearing and about sexual harassment. After controversy over a proposed and sponsored professorship in her name, she left the University of Oklahoma in 1996. As of 2010 she was employed at Brandeis University's Heller School for Social Policy and Management as a professor of social policy, law, and women's studies.

Explanation and Analysis of Document

This document contains four distinct topics: Hill's early life and career, the details of Thomas's harassing behavior, her decision not to come forward, and her subsequent decision to tell her story. Hill was also concerned about silently held biases against her as a result of the sexual harassment claim. It was important for her to make the members of the Senate Judiciary Committee, all of them white men, understand that women do not intentionally invite sexually harassing behavior. As a further obstacle to stating her case, Hill's legal career placed her, in the opinion of the committee, in a different category of women from those in many harassment cases, because, from a legal standpoint, she must have known right from wrong with respect to her professional relationship with Thomas.

♦ Early Life and Career

Hill's statement begins with a brief discussion of her educational experiences and her background, emphasizing her parents' struggles, her family ties, and her personal religious beliefs. She touches on her childhood poverty and her educational success at Oklahoma State University and Yale Law School. In addition, she notes her early work experiences at Wald, Harkrader & Ross, the Office for Civil Rights within the Department of Education, and the EEOC. All this background information was meant to demonstrate to the fourteen committee members that she was an intelligent, hardworking, and credible witness. Furthermore, Hill had to make herself appear first and foremost as an individual giving testimony, rather than emphasize being a woman or black. Indeed, she never mentions the words *gender discrimination* or *racism*; however, her background information reveals that she was concerned about both, specifically, the obstacles of poverty and racial prejudice that many African American women have had to overcome. Hill was thus portraying herself as someone who had overcome her disadvantaged childhood and become a successful lawyer.

♦ Details of Harassing Behavior

The second part of Hill's statement to the Senate Judiciary Committee focuses on explaining what constituted harassing behavior by Clarence Thomas. Hill starts with a discussion of the harassment that had occurred while she worked as Thomas's assistant in the Office for Civil Rights at the Department of Education. She states that at first Thomas did not exhibit such behavior toward her; however, she then observes that he began to harass her by repeatedly asking her to go out with him socially and even describing to her in detail pornographic films he had seen. After Hill provides these examples, she explains that she told Thomas that she did not want to jeopardize their working relationship and that sexual topics of conversation made her feel uncomfortable. Hill then notes how Thomas's harassing behavior ended before their transfer to the EEOC.

While he was chairman of the EEOC, Hill testifies, Thomas resumed making inappropriate overtures toward her. She describes how he started to make comments about her appearance and whether her clothes were "more or less sexually attractive." Again, she rebuffed Thomas's advances; however, he wanted an explanation as to why she would not go out with him. Hill then details specific episodes of Thomas's harassing behavior, including a conversation he had with her about his sexual prowess. As a result of Thomas's behavior, Hill felt severe stress while she was working at the EEOC.

Throughout her description of Thomas's behavior, Hill relates not only how she repeatedly declined Thomas's invitations but also how he continued to approach her and even questioned why she would not go out with him. These examples support Hill's allegations of workplace sexual harassment and, more important, show how she had become psychologically victimized—how she had come to blame herself for having been in such a situation. Indeed, she could have told the Senate Judiciary Committee only the details of Thomas's behavior, but that alone might not have been sufficient information to suggest sexual harassment. Thus, she takes the extra step of explaining that regardless of how she tried to ward off Thomas's advances, he would not listen to her. Hill became both a victim and her own advocate in order to clarify her allegations to the male members of the Senate Judiciary Committee.

Incidentally, Hill's detailed account of Thomas's descriptions of pornographic films and his sexual prowess can be seen as perpetuating stereotypes about African Americans. It is possible that Hill had anticipated that some white male members of the Senate Judiciary Committee would not have given her statement the same weight if she had omitted these details. Although the vivid descriptions Hill gave to the committee could be perceived as reinforcing sexual myths about African Americans, she hardly could have been expected to withhold accurate testimony or make it less graphic for fear of contributing to racial stereotypes.

♦ Decision Not to Come Forward

The third section of Hill's statement focuses on her initial decision not to come forward. She begins by explaining her fear of reprisal from Thomas whenever she chose not to go out with him. These fears included being given less important work assignments and even the possibility of dismissal from her job. Because of these fears, Hill started to look for another job; however, the opportunities were minimal. She eventually found another position and informed Thomas. Hill then pointedly notes to the committee how she agreed to a final dinner with Thomas, during which "he said that if I ever told anyone about his behavior toward me it could ruin his career."

Hill's initial decision not to come forward and expose Thomas reflected a former trend in female reporting of workplace sexual harassment claims. In the early 1980s, sexual harassment claims by women were not prevalent, and these claims were often extremely difficult to prove. Although laws and regulations were already in place to prevent workplace sexual harassment, the support needed to provide credibility to a claim was difficult to obtain. The Civil Rights Act of 1964, signed by President Lyndon Johnson, was the first piece of legislation enacted to help prevent workplace sexual harassment. Title VII of that act prohibits discrimination based upon race, color, religion, national origin, or sex. In 1972 Congress passed the Equal Employment Opportunity Act, which amended the Civil Rights Act of 1964 and established the Equal Employment Opportunity Commission. The EEOC was given the authority to prevent persons from engaging in unlawful employment discrimination practices.

In 1980, the EEOC promulgated regulations titled *Guidelines on Discrimination Because of Sex*. These regulations helped to further define sexual harassment and what were considered acceptable workplace practices. By the mid-1980s, eighteen states had enacted legislation that specifically prohibited sexual harassment. In addition, as many as twenty-eight other states had laws that prohibited sex discrimination. An important decision by the U.S. Supreme Court, *Meritor Savings Bank v. Vinson* (1986), made it easier to prove sexual harassment under Title VII of the Civil Rights Act of 1964. Unfortunately for Hill, that case was decided after her experiences of sexual harassment, which had occurred during the early 1980s.

Hill's decision not to leave either the Department of Education or the EEOC—as well as to follow Thomas from the Department of Education to the EEOC—was likely the result of both gender and race discrimination. First, employment opportunities for female attorneys in the 1980s were not abundant. Female attorneys were often relegated to lower-level positions in comparison to those held by their male peers. Second, workplace racial discrimination was still an obstacle in the 1980s, despite laws and regulations that prohibited it. Hill was an African American female attorney working in a primarily white male world. In her statement she opines that at the time it would have been hard for her to find a position outside the Department of Education or EEOC. Thus, the possibility of being discriminated against when applying for other jobs was a significant factor not only in Hill's decision to follow Thomas to the EEOC but also in her delay in seeking other employment.

♦ Decision to Come Forward

The final section of Hill's statement explains her decision to testify about the sexual harassment claims. Hill concedes that she had not felt comfortable coming forward and making her allegations public to the Senate Judiciary Committee and the world. She also admits that her delay in coming forward might have been the result of poor judgment. Finally, Hill testifies that she eventually decided to come forward with the information because she had a duty to tell the truth.

Audience

Hill's comments in the final paragraph of her statement reflect the extreme degree of public scrutiny she knew she would have to endure. The broadcast media was captivated by the Anita Hill–Clarence Thomas controversy. Accordingly, the audience for Hill's opening statement was anyone interested in Thomas's confirmation hearing, whether for professional reasons or merely out of curiosity. More specifically, Hill's statement was watched with interest by women and by members of the African American community. In certain respects, her decision to come forward and testify in front of the Judiciary Committee eradicated many gender stereotypes surrounding women. Stereotypes that describe female behavior include passivity, a pleasing nature, and a demeanor that is emotional and feminine. While feminist groups have worked hard to change how women are perceived in the workplace and media, not all women believe that these stereotypes are wrong. In this case, many women viewed Hill's delayed decision to expose Thomas's harassing behavior as an incorrect course of action. In particular, some African American women questioned why it had taken her so long to come forward. In addition, these same women also believed that she should have left her position in the Department of Education once the harassment started. Many African American women also thought Hill should have never raised allegations against Thomas because he was a prominent and successful African American male. Thomas's conservatism, particularly his opposition to abortion and disbelief in affirmative action policies, did bolster support for him in the conservative community. Thus, regardless of Hill's allegations against Thomas, many women supported his nomination.

Hill's choice to come forward did not, however, anger everyone. She was seen by many as a pioneer in the fight against workplace discrimination. Even though it had taken her years to tell her story, she finally had come forward under intense public scrutiny; because of that, many recognized her courage and supported her. Unwittingly, she became a role model for women. For instance, Hill's missteps in coming forward demonstrated that immediate action should be taken against a sexual harasser. Her narrative of what had transpired with Thomas in the Department of Education and the EEOC also helped people learn to gauge what actions were or were not appropriate in the workplace. Most important, Hill's stated belief that she was doing what was right, regardless of the outcome, was an important step in gender equality. In the end, Supreme Court historians and others who write about the Court and the judicial confirmation process, as well as researchers interested in issues of gender and race, will continue to have an interest in Hill's statement.

Impact

Hill's opening statement and testimony became the focal point of Thomas's confirmation hearing, even though she appeared before the Senate Judiciary Committee toward the end of the hearing process, after the committee had voted on whether to recommend Thomas's nomination. Once Hill made her opening statement, she spent the remainder of October 11, 1991, being grilled by the members of the committee. In particular, she was asked many questions about her personal life that had little to do with the sexual harassment claim. Senator Arlen Specter engaged in a concerted effort to discredit Hill. Referring to her statement to the FBI and her testimony to the Senate Judiciary Committee, he pointed out discrepancies between the two and questioned why certain facts were not included in the FBI report. He inquired further as to why Hill did not come forward with her sexual harassment claim until Thomas's confirmation hearing. In addition, Specter introduced an affidavit from John Doggett, a friend to both Hill and Thomas, in which Doggett claimed that Hill was unstable and had fantasized about him. Specter also asked Hill questions related to the number of times she and Thomas had spoken since she left the EEOC; in doing this, Specter attempted to insinuate that Hill was in contact with Thomas for more than professional reasons.

Among the others questioning Hill, Senator Howell Heflin, in order to call her testimony into doubt, accused her of fantasizing about Thomas. Some committee members intimated that her story should be presumed to be fictional because she had chosen to come forward late in the confirmation process. When Hill's testimony was complete, Thomas, angered by her accusations, testified and expressed his disdain for the proceedings as "high-tech lynching for uppity blacks." At that point, the confirmation hearing turned into a "he said, she said" nightmare for both Thomas and Hill, during which the purpose of the confirmation hearing, namely, to determine whether Thomas was the best person for the job, was lost. Eventually, Thomas was confirmed by a Senate vote of fifty-two to forty-eight, one of the narrowest such votes in U.S. history.

Hill's testimony before the committee captivated and educated audiences on issues surrounding sexual harassment in the workplace. Reporting of sexual harassment rose after Anita Hill came forward, as claims of sexual harassment began to be taken more seriously. Furthermore, her testimony made employers more aware of what constituted sexually harassing behavior, encouraging employers to monitor employee interactions more effectively and thus prevent sexually harassing behavior. In addition, many employers began to make it easier for victims of alleged sexual harassment to come forward without having to reveal their identities. This commitment to anonymity assuaged victims' fears of accuser retaliation and job dismissal. Many companies changed their personnel policies to ensure that all employees would comply with sexual harassment laws and regulations.

An unfortunate aspect of the Thomas confirmation hearing was that the process itself, which could have been relatively straightforward, turned into a public spectacle. Once the Senate Judiciary Committee had been informed that Thomas, a conservative African American, was President Bush's Supreme Court nominee, Democratic and Republican committee members set out to find information that would either help or hurt his chances of confirmation. Democrats on the committee had become aware of Hill's allegations before any Republicans had been informed; therefore, Thomas and Hill became engrossed in a political clash between Democrats and Republicans. The proceedings became unnecessarily acrimonious, as committee members tried to separate truth from lies with respect to Hill's charges of sexual harassment. As a result, the testimonies of both Thomas and Hill were not taken seriously, and the confirmation process was seen as a failure.

The proceedings had a massive impact on the African American community. Two successful African Americans were pitted against each other. On one hand was Clarence Thomas, a conservative who for the most part disliked affirmative action. On the other was Anita Hill, a law professor who some perceived as having turned on "one of her own." Indeed, the conflict over whom to believe created more questions than answers. Although Thomas was uncomfortable with affirmation action, he was nevertheless a nominee to the Supreme Court. Not many African Americans had been offered such a prestigious honor, and many believed that Thomas was a good model of what an African American man could achieve. In addition, many empathized with the struggle against racism and discrimination that Thomas had navigated successfully. Accordingly, some African Americans were willing to ignore Thomas's shortcomings in favor of what they thought his confirmation could do to promote positive views of African Americans.

Like Thomas, Hill had overcome racism and discrimination throughout her career. Notwithstanding, she did not fare as well as Thomas in African American public opinion. For example, there was a male-versus-female difference of opinion about her among African Americans. Some believed that Hill, as a black woman, should have remained quiet and not publicly revealed that she had been sexually harassed by a black man. Furthermore, Hill's accomplishments as a black woman were not accorded the same weight as Thomas's achievements. This caused confusion as to who, either Hill or Thomas, was best equipped to advance the interests of the African American community, and the two were inadvertently caught in a political nightmare that had both racial and gender ramifications. For these reasons, Hill's opening statement will have a lasting imprint on American history.

Further Reading

♦ Books

Brock, David. *The Real Anita Hill: The Untold Story*. New York: Free Press, 1993.

Chrisman, Robert, and Robert L. Allen, eds. *Court of Appeal: the Black Community Speaks Out on the Racial and Sexual Politics of Clarence Thomas vs. Anita Hill*. New York: Ballantine Books, 1992.

Danforth, John C. *Resurrection: The Confirmation of Clarence Thomas*. New York: Viking, 1994.

Foskett, Ken. *Judging Thomas: The Life and Times of Clarence Thomas*. New York: Harper Collins Publishers, 2004.

Garment, Suzanne. "Afterword: On Anita Hill and Clarence Thomas." In *Scandal: The Culture of Mistrust in American Politics*. New York: Times Books, 1992.

Hill, Anita. *Speaking Truth to Power*. New York: Doubleday, 1997.

———, and Emma Coleman Jordan, eds. *Race, Gender, and Power in America: The Legacy of the Hill-Thomas Hearings*. New York: Oxford University Press, 1995.

Morrison, Toni, ed. *Race-ing Justice, En-gendering Power: Essays on Anita Hill, Clarence Thomas, and the Construction of Social Reality*. New York: Pantheon Books, 1992.

Phelps, Timothy M., and Helen Winternitz. *Capitol Games: Clarence Thomas, Anita Hill, and the Story of a Supreme Court Nomination*. New York: Hyperion, 1992.

Smith, Christopher E. *Critical Judicial Nominations and Political Change: The Impact of Clarence Thomas*. Westport, Conn.: Praeger, 1993.

♦ Web Sites

"Hearings before the Senate Committee on the Judiciary on the Nomination of Clarence Thomas to be Associate Justice of the Supreme Court of the United States, October 11, 12, and 13, 1991." GPO Access Web site. http://www.gpoaccess.gov/congress/senate/judiciary/sh102-1084pt4/browse.html.

———*Colleen Ostiguy*

Time Line

1981		■ Anita Hill becomes special counsel to the assistant secretary in the Department of Education's Office of Civil Rights, namely, Clarence Thomas.
1982		■ At the Equal Employment Opportunity Commission (EEOC), Hill becomes special assistant to Thomas, the commission's chairman.
1983	Fall	■ Hill begins teaching at Oral Roberts University's O.W. Coburn School of Law.
1986		■ Hill accepts a professor of law position at the University of Oklahoma.
1991	June 27	■ U.S. Supreme Court Justice Thurgood Marshall announces his retirement.
	July 1	■ President George H. W. Bush nominates Clarence Thomas to replace Justice Marshall.
	August	■ Rumors begin to surface regarding allegations that Thomas sexually harassed Anita Hill.
	September 10–20	■ The Senate Judiciary Committee holds hearings on the Thomas nomination.

Time Line

	September 23	■ Hill is interview by the FBI and faxes a personal statement to the committee.
	September 27	■ The Senate Judiciary Committee's vote on whether to confirm Thomas is split at seven to seven; the nomination is sent without the committee's endorsement to the Senate floor.
	September 28	■ Thomas denies all of Hill's allegations.
	October 3–4	■ Senate debate begins on Thomas's confirmation.
	October 8	■ Thomas requests a delay in the Senate vote.
	October 11	■ Hill and Thomas testify before the Senate Judiciary Committee.
	October 15	■ The Senate confirms Thomas by a vote of fifty-two to forty-eight.
	October 23	■ Thomas is sworn in as the 106th U.S. Supreme Court justice.

Essential Quotes

> *"Telling the world is the most difficult experience in my life. I was aware that he could affect my future career and did not wish to burn all my bridges."*

> *"I have no personal vendetta against Clarence Thomas."*

Questions for Further Study

1. Describe the politics that surrounded the Clarence Thomas nomination. Who supported him and why? What groups opposed his nomination and why?

2. To what extent do you believe that the personal views of a nominee for a judgeship are relevant to that person's qualifications for the job?

3. Many observers at the time simply disbelieved Hill's allegations. How credible do you find Hill's testimony?

4. During the administration of President Bill Clinton, which began shortly after Thomas's ascension to the Supreme Court, numerous allegations were made of sexual misconduct on the president's part, including a sexual relationship with a young White House intern. Yet many of the same people who vigorously opposed Thomas supported the president or at least remained quiet. What would account for the difference?

5. In 1987 Robert Bork's nomination to the Supreme Court failed, in large part because of a rapid, well-organized, and well-financed campaign to discredit him, despite his extensive qualifications (including a faculty position at the Yale University law school, where Anita Hill was one of his students). The result was the emergence of a slang term, "to bork," defined as "to defame or vilify a person systematically, especially in the mass media, usually with the aim of preventing his or her appointment to public office." Do you believe that Thomas was "borked"? Why or why not?

Anita Hill's Opening Statement at the Senate Confirmation Hearing of Clarence Thomas

The full text of Hill's opening statement to the Senate.

Mr. Chairman, Senator Thurmond, Members of the Committee, my name is Anita F. Hill, and I am a Professor of Law at the University of Oklahoma. I was born on a farm in Okmulge, Oklahoma in 1956, the 13th child, and had my early education there. My father is Albert Hill, a farmer of that area. My mother's name is Erma Hill; she is also a farmer and housewife. My childhood was the childhood of both work and poverty; but it was one of solid family affection as represented by my parents who are with me as I appear here today. I was reared in a religious atmosphere in the Baptist faith and I have been a member of the Antioch Baptist Church in Tulsa since 1983. It remains a warm part of my life at the present time.

For my undergraduate work I went to Oklahoma State University and graduated in 1977. I am attaching to this statement my resume with further details of my education. I graduated from the university with academic honors and proceeded to the Yale Law School where I received my J.D. degree in 1980.

Upon graduation from law school I became a practicing lawyer with the Washington, D.C. firm of Wald, Harkrader & Ross. In 1981, I was introduced to now Judge Thomas by a mutual friend. Judge Thomas told me that he anticipated a political appointment shortly and asked if I might be interested in working in that office. He was in fact appointed as Assistant Secretary of Education, in which capacity he was the Director of the Office for Civil Rights. After he was in that post, he asked if I would become his assistant and I did then accept that position. In my early period there I had two major projects. The first was an article I wrote for Judge Thomas' signature on "Education of Minority Students." The second was the organization of a seminar on high risk students, which was abandoned because Judge Thomas transferred to the EEOC before that project was completed.

During this period at the Department of Education, my working relationship with Judge Thomas was positive. I had a good deal of responsibility as well as independence. I thought that he respected my work and that he trusted my judgment. After approximately three months of working together, he asked me to go out with him socially. I declined and explained to him that I thought that it would only jeopardize what, at the time, I considered to be a very good working relationship. I had a normal social life with other men outside of the office and, I believed then, as now, that having a social relationship with a person who was supervising my work would be ill-advised. I was very uncomfortable with the idea and told him so.

I thought that by saying "no" and explaining my reasons, my employer would abandon his social suggestions. However, to my regret, in the following few weeks he continued to ask me out on several occasions. He pressed me to justify my reasons for saying "no" to him. These incidents took place in his office or mine. They were in the form of private conversations which would not have been overheard by anyone else.

My working relationship became even more strained when Judge Thomas began to use work situations to discuss sex. On these occasions he would call me into his office for reports on education issues and projects or he might suggest that because of time pressures we go to lunch at a government cafeteria. After a brief discussion of work, he would turn the conversation to discussion of sexual matters. His conversations were very vivid. He spoke about acts that he had seen in pornographic films involving such matters as women having sex with animals and films showing group sex or rape scenes. He talked about pornographic materials depicting individuals with large penises or large breasts involved in various sex acts. On several occasions Thomas told me graphically of his own sexual prowess.

Because I was extremely uncomfortable talking about sex with him at all and particularly in such a graphic way, I told him that I did not want to talk about those subjects. I would also try to change the subject to education matters or to nonsexual personal matters such as his background or beliefs. My efforts to change the subject were rarely successful.

Throughout the period of these conversations, he also from time-to-time asked me for social engagements. My reaction to these conversations was to avoid having them by eliminating opportunities for us to engage in extended conversations. This was difficult because I was his only assistant at the Office for Civil Rights. During the latter part of my time at the Department of Education, the social pressures and any conversations of this offensive kind ended. I began both to believe and hope that our working relationship could be on a proper, cordial and professional base.

When Judge Thomas was made Chairman of the EEOC, I needed to face the question of whether to go with him. I was asked to do so. I did. The work itself was interesting and at that time it appeared that the sexual overtures which had so troubled me had ended. I also faced the realistic fact that I had no alternative job. While I might have gone back to private practice, perhaps in my old firm or at another, I was dedicated to civil rights work and my first choice was to be in that field. Moreover, the Department of Education itself was a dubious venture; President Reagan was seeking to abolish the entire Department at that time.

For my first months at the EEOC, where I continued as an assistant to Judge Thomas, there were no sexual conversations or overtures. However, during the Fall and Winter of 1982, these began again. The comments were random and ranged from pressing me about why I didn't go out with him to remarks about my personal appearance. I remember his saying that someday I would have to give him the real reason that I wouldn't go out with him. He began to show real displeasure in his tone of voice, his demeanor and his continued pressure for an explanation. He commented on what I was wearing in terms of whether it made me more or less sexually attractive. The incidents occurred in his inner office at the EEOC.

One of the oddest episodes I remember was an occasion in which Thomas was drinking a Coke in his office. He got up from the table at which we were working, went over to his desk to get the Coke, looked at the can, and said, "Who has put pubic hair on my Coke?" On other occasions he referred to the size of his own penis as being larger than normal and he also spoke on some occasions of the pleasures he had given to women with oral sex.

At this point, late 1982, I began to feel severe stress on the job. I began to be concerned that Clarence Thomas might take it out on me by downgrading me or not giving me important assignments. I also thought that he might find an excuse for dismissing me. In January of 1983, I began looking for another job. I was handicapped because I feared that if he found out, he might make it difficult for me to find other employment and I might be dismissed from the job I had. Another factor that made my search more difficult was that this was a period of a government hiring freeze. In February, 1983, I was hospitalized for five days on an emergency basis for an acute stomach pain which I attributed to stress on the job. Once out of the hospital, I became more committed to find other employment and sought further to minimize my contact with Thomas. This became easier when Allyson Duncan became office director because most of my work was handled with her and I had contact with Clarence Thomas mostly in staff meetings.

In the Spring of 1983, an opportunity to teach law at Oral Roberts University opened up. I agreed to take the job in large part because of my desire to escape the pressures I felt at the EEOC due to Thomas. When I informed him that I was leaving in July, I recall that his response was that now I "would no longer have an excuse for not going out with" him. I told him that I still preferred not to do so. At some time after that meeting, he asked if he could take me to dinner at the end of my term. When I declined, he assured me that the dinner was a professional courtesy only and not a social invitation. I reluctantly agreed to accept that invitation but only if it was at the very end of a workday. On, as I recall, the last day of my employment at the EEOC in the summer of 1983, I did have dinner with Clarence Thomas. We went directly from work to a restaurant near the office. We talked about the work I had done both at Education and at EEOC. He told me that he was pleased with all of it except for an article and speech that I done for him when we were at the Office for Civil Rights. Finally, he made a comment which I vividly remember. He said that if I ever told anyone about his behavior toward me it could ruin his career. This was not an apology nor was there any explanation. That was his last remark about the possibility of our going out or reference to his behavior.

In July 1983, I left the Washington, D.C. area and have had minimal contacts with Judge Clarence Thomas since.

I am of course aware from the press that some question has been raised about conversations I had with Judge Clarence Thomas after I left the EEOC. From 1983 until today I have seen Judge Clarence Thomas only twice. On one occasion I needed to get a reference from him and on another he made a public

Document Text

appearance in Tulsa. On one occasion he called me at home and we had an inconsequential conversation. On one other occasion he called me without reaching me and I returned the call without reaching him and nothing came of it. I have, on at least three occasions been asked to act as a conduit for others.

I knew his secretary, Diane Holt, well when I was with the EEOC. There were occasions on which I spoke to her and on some of those occasions undoubtedly I passed on some casual comment to Thomas.

There was a series of calls in the first three months of 1985 occasioned by a group in Tulsa which wished to have a civil rights conference; they wanted Thomas to be the speaker, and enlisted my assistance for this purpose. I did call in January and February to no effect and finally suggested to the person directly involved, Susan Cahall, that she put the matter back into her own hands and call directly. She did do that in March of 1985. In connection with that March invitation to Tulsa by Ms. Cahall, which was for a seminar conference some research was needed; I was asked to try to get the research work and did attempt to do so by a call to Thomas. There was another call about another possible conference in July of 1985.

In August of 1987, I was in Washington and I did call Diane Holt. In the course of this conversation she asked me how long I was going to be in town and I told her; she recorded it as August 15; it was in fact August 20. She told me about Thomas' marriage and I did say "congratulate him."

It is only after a great deal of agonizing consideration that I am able to talk of these unpleasant matters to anyone but my closest friends. Telling the world is the most difficult experience of my life. I was aware that he could affect my future career and did not wish to burn all my bridges. I may have used poor judgment; perhaps I should have taken angry or even militant steps both when I was in the agency or after I left it, but I must confess to the world that the course I took seemed to me to be the better as well as the easier approach. I declined any comment to newspapers, but later, when Senate staff asked me about these matters, I felt I had a duty to report. I have no personal vendetta against Clarence Thomas. I seek only to provide the Committee with information which it may regard as relevant. It would have been more comfortable to remain silent. I took no initiative to inform anyone. But when I was asked by a representative of this committee to report my experience, I felt that I had no other choice but to tell the truth.

Glossary

EEOC: Equal Employment Opportunity Commission

Senator Thurmond: Strom Thurmond, U.S. senator from South Carolina, at that time the ranking minority Republican on the Senate Judiciary Committee

Powell in April 1989, as the Commanding General of FORSCOM.. By John Clifton - This Image was released by the United States Army. [Public domain], via Wikimedia Commons

Colin Powell's Commencement Address at Howard University

"Study your origins. Teach your children racial pride and draw strength and inspiration from the cultures of our forebears."

Overview

Colin Powell's commencement address delivered to the graduates of Howard University on May 14, 1994, is among the most remembered speeches of an impressively influential African American in the late twentieth century. The speech helped keep the recently retired General Powell in the headlines at a time when many thought he might be the first black candidate for the presidency on a major party ticket. Like most commencement addresses, Powell's remarks were designed to urge the listening graduates—and their friends and families—to aspire to greater philosophical and career goals. But because of his unusually popular public reputation and his potential presidential candidacy, Powell's address had a much larger public audience. Today, this speech has been largely overshadowed by some of Powell's remarks as secretary of state during the presidential administration of George W. Bush.

About the Author

The second child and only son of Luther Powell and Maud Ariel McKoy Powell, Colin Luther Powell was born in 1937 in New York. His father was a gardener and a building superintendent, and his mother was a seamstress. When Powell was six, his family moved to the Bronx. Powell's maternal grandmother, Alice McKoy, took care of Powell and his older sister, Marilyn, while their parents were working. As the family's situation improved, the household moved to Queens, where Powell ran track and played basketball at Morris High School. Two months before his seventeenth birthday, thanks to an accelerated program, Powell graduated and soon enrolled at City College of New York (CCNY), where he joined the Reserve Officers' Training Corps (ROTC). Powell enjoyed the ROTC, and he joined an elite precision drill team, the Pershing Rifles. Although hewas an average student at CCNY, Powell excelled at his ROTC coursework, dedicating his weekends and free hours to practice. The military's discipline, structure, and camaraderie appealed to Powell. A geology major who had originally pursued an engineering degree, Powell graduated from CCNY in 1958 with a B.S. degree and the honor of distinguished military graduate. He was commissioned as a second lieutenant in the U.S. Army. Powell's basic training was in Fort Benning, Georgia, and he was soon posted overseas to the Third Armored Division in West Germany. At the end of his first year, Powell was promoted to first lieutenant. After his twoyear tour of duty, Powell was sent to Fort Devens, near Boston. By 1961, he had completed his required three years of ROTC service, and he was at a crossroads .With little hesitation, Powell committed to a career in the Army.

Powell met Alma Vivian Johnson, a native of Birmingham, Alabama, on a blind date, and they formed a friendship that culminated in marriage on August 25, 1962. Shortly after the wedding, Powell was sent to Fort Bragg, North Carolina, for training as a military adviser and then on to South Vietnam for a two-year tour of duty. Now holding the rank of captain, Powell was wounded in Vietnam when he stepped on a punji stake, a sharp stick designed by the Viet Cong to hobble soldiers. Powell was awarded a Purple Heart, and later that year he received a Bronze Star. He returned to Vietnam as a major in 1968 with the Twenty-third Infantry Division. During that year, he was injured during a helicopter crash, and he received a Soldier's Medal for bravery in helping to rescue men from the burning wreckage. After his second tour in Vietnam, Powell returned to the United States and enrolled in graduate school at George Washington University in Washington, D.C., where he earned a master's degree in business administration in 1971. In July of 1971, Powell was assigned to

General Colin Powell, Chairman, Joint Chiefs of Staff, waves from his motorcade during the Persian Gulf War Welcome Home Parade in New York City. By MSGT DON WETTERMAN, USA [Public domain], via Wikimedia Commons.

the Pentagon, where he worked in the office of the assistant vice chief of staff of the Army.

Powell was named a White House Fellow in 1972-1973 and assigned to the Office of Management and Budget (OMB). The OMB was headed by Caspar Weinberger, who later became President Ronald Reagan's secretary of defense, and Frank C. Carlucci, later Reagan's national security adviser. Powell soon took an assignment at Camp Casey in South Korea. When he returned to the United States in 1974, he was assigned to the Pentagon once more, where he took classes in the National War College. In early 1976, Powell was promoted to full colonel. As Powell alternated stints in Washington with service abroad, his family grew. The Powells had three children, Michael, Linda, and Annemarie. Powell took command of the Second Brigade of the 101st Airborne Division at Fort Campbell, Kentucky, where he remained until 1977. Once again, he was called back to Washington, this time to serve in the office of the secretary of defense in President Jimmy Carter's administration. In June, 1979, Powell was promoted to brigadier general, and for a brief time he was the administrative secretary to Charles Duncan, the secretary of energy under Carter.

The early 1980's found Powell out West, first at Fort Carson, Colorado, and then as deputy commander of Fort Leavenworth, Kansas. In June, 1983, Powell was promoted to major general and returned to Washington to serve in the Reagan administration as military assistant to Weinberger. In this capacity, he aided in the plans for the invasion of Grenada and the air strike on Libya. In 1986, Powell was named commander of the Fifth Corps in Frankfurt, West Germany, where he commanded seventy-five thousand troops. In early 1987, he returned to Washington to serve as deputy assistant to President George H.W. Bush for national security affairs. In April, 1989, Powell was promoted to general and was picked by Bush to be the chairman of the Joint Chiefs of Staff. At the relatively young age of fifty-two, Powell became only the third general since World War II to be promoted to the four-star rank without ever being a divisional commander; the other two were Dwight D. Eisenhower and Alexander Haig.

As chair of the Joint Chiefs, Powell's mission was to support General Norman Schwarzkopf in the Persian Gulf War. The short duration of the war, which ended with Iraq's withdrawal from Kuwait, was the result of overwhelming force and a large international contingent of soldiers. This strategy of fighting wars became known as the Powell Doctrine. After his retirement from the military, Powell eventually declared himself a Republican and began to campaign for Republican candidates in 1995. A political moderate, Powell published his autobiography, *My American Journey*, in 1995, and opinion polls showed him to be one of the most popular public figures in the political arena. Although he was sought after as a candidate for either the presidency or the vice presidency, Powell said that he was not interested in becoming president. In 2000, President George W. Bush picked Powell to be his secretary of state, and the U.S. Senate voted unanimously to confirm him.

In the wake of the September 11, 2001, attacks, the Bush administration declared a global war on terror and adopted a preemptive-strike policy that viewed states that supported terrorists as enemies on par with the terrorists themselves. High on the list of states supporting terrorism, according to the Bush administration, was Saddam Hussein's Iraq. After invading Afghanistan, the White House switched its emphasis and efforts to Iraq. In order to garner international support for this invasion, it was necessary to prove Iraq held weapons of mass destruction. In early February, 2003, Powell went before the United Nations Security Council to argue in favor of military action in Iraq. Armed with defense intelligence that was later found to be faulty, Powell presented his case. Citing various Iraqi defectors and information supplied by the Central Intelligence Agency, Powell said, "There can be no doubt that Saddam Hussein has biological weapons and the capability to rapidly produce more, many more." This statement helped build international support for the invasion of Iraq. In a 2005 interview with journalist Barbara Walters, Powell said of his role in the Iraq war, "It will always be a part of my record. It was painful. It's painful now."

Explanation and Analysis of the Document

The Howard University commencement speech was given to several hundred graduates, their friends and families, and the faculty of the nation's largest historically black university. Although the circumstances surrounding Powell's appearance were controversial, his remarks were in the main well received by the assembled listeners and even more enthusiastically by the local and national press corps.

The instance of racial cooperation to which Powell devotes most of his speech is that of the Buffalo Soldiers, a contingent of black cavalry in the U.S. Army who had distinguished themselves in a series of military engagements in the post–Civil War West. His discussion of the Buffalo Soldiers allows Powell to touch on several points that are central to his Howard message. Powell's connection to the Buffalo Soldiers is, of course, his own service in the military and more directly in his personal efforts to establish a national monument in their honor. In a rather impassioned sentence of the speech, he argues that the military gave him and his forbears—including the Buffalo Soldiers, the Tuskegee Airmen, and other black men and women—the chance to demonstrate their ability when given the opportunity. "I climbed on their backs," he exclaimed, "and stood on their shoulders to reach the top of my chosen profession." Furthermore, he reminds his audience, the Buffalo Soldiers were formed in 1867, the same year that Howard was founded. Similarly, both were begun and directed in their infancy by well-meaning and right-minded whites who were essential to the survival of both enterprises. This same interracial cooperation, Powell asserts, was instrumental in his own success in the military and, in some ways, in the achievements of the Howard class of 1994 as well.

Powell's patriotic conclusion is aimed most directly at his young black listeners and perhaps secondarily to the black community at large: "Never lose faith in America," he says. "America is a family. There may be differences and disputes in the family, but we must not allow the family to be broken into warring factions." By all means, he instructs the graduates, retain "your heritage." He continues:

> Study your origins. Teach your children racial pride.... Not as a way of drawing back from American society and its European roots. But as a way of showing that there are other roots as well. African and Caribbean roots that are also a source of nourishment for the American family tree.... From the diversity of our people let us draw strength and not cause weakness.

And he concludes. "Believe in America with all your heart and soul and mind. It remains the 'last best hope of Earth.'"

Audience

Although Powell's speech was given directly to hundreds of Howard University's 1994 graduates, their friends, families, and the university community of faculty and administrators, it also had a much wider audience. In part, Powell was rebutting the racial attitudes and strategies of Khalid Abdul Muhammad and those of his followers and sympathizers who embraced his philosophy. Additionally, he was addressing a national media audience who may have wrongly associated Howard University with violent black nationalism in an effort to rescue the university's public image; it was not coincidental that Powell was subsequently appointed to Howard's board of regents. And, finally, Powell's speech was also aimed at a national voting audience, black and white, who were potential supporters had he actually decided to throw his political hat into the presidential ring.

Impact

Powell's words were received by his immediate audience with general approval. Several graduates gave him high marks in personal interviews, and presumably they reflected the views of their parents and families, too. The fact that Powell was named to Howard's board of regents a few months after his speech also suggests that the university's administration was suitably impressed. But his most enthusiastic audience was the national press corps. The *New York Times* and *Washington Post* gave Powell enthusiastic reviews as a voice of reason on the subject of Howard University and as a reassuring rejection of black supremacists who advocated violence as an important component to full racial liberation; the black mainstream press echoed these impressions. Moreover, one should remember that Powell gave this address at a crucial moment in his consideration of a political career, which included the possibility of running for president of the United States. Bluntly put, the Howard commencement address was, in some sense, an effective campaign speech.

In the years following Howard remarks, Powell's potential presidential aspirations were largely forgotten along with the historical context of his speech. Today, Powell's words on this occasion are most often found in anthologies of great civil rights speeches rather than in discussions of his political ambitions, which in the mid-1990s may have rivaled those about Barack Obama in the early twenty-first century. Thus, Powell's Howard speech is a fascinating example of how the political rhetoric of one moment can become the timeless wisdom of another.

Further Reading

♦ **Articles**

Wintz, Cary D. "Colin Powell: The Candidate Who Wasn't." In *African Americans and the Presidency: The Road to the White House*, ed. Bruce A. Glasrud and Cary D. Wintz. New York: Routledge, 2009.

♦ **Books**

DeYoung, Karen. *Soldier: The Life of Colin Powell*. New York: Alfred A. Knopf, 2006.

Gottheimer, Josh, ed. *Ripples of Hope: Great Civil Rights Speeches*. Cambridge, Mass.: Basic Civitas Books, 2004.

Powell, Colin L. *My American Journey*. New York: Random House, 1995.

♦ **Web Sites**

"General Colin L. Powell." Academy of Achievement Web site. http://www.achievement.org/autodoc/page/pow0pro-1.

—*Charles Cook*

Essential Quotes

"There is great wisdom in the message of self reliance, of education, of hard work, and of the need to raise strong families. There is utter foolishness, evil, and danger in the message of hatred, or of condoning violence, however cleverly the message is packaged or entertainingly it is presented."

"I have no doubt that this controversy will pass and Howard University will emerge even stronger, even more than ever a symbol of hope, of promise, and of excellence."

"Study your origins. Teach your children racial pride and draw strength and inspiration from the cultures of our forebears. Not as a way of drawing back from American society and its European roots. But as a way of showing that there are other roots as well. African and Caribbean roots that are also a source of nourishment for the American family tree.

Questions for Further Study

1. In recent years, the issue of free speech has arisen with regularity on college campuses. Various speakers have been barred from campuses or have had their appearances canceled because of protest on the part of those who do not like the speaker's views. Numerous speakers have been heckled or shouted down and have had eggs and other objects thrown at them. Under what circumstances, if any, do you think a speaker should be barred from appearing on a college campus, or anywhere? Does hosting a speaker constitute endorsement of his or her views? At what point does legitimate protesting of views cross over to a denial of free speech?

2. Why might Colin Powell's appearance at Howard University have perhaps been seen as controversial by some?

3. As a military figure, Powell appeals to his audience by linking the history of Howard University with that of the military, particularly the role of African American soldiers in the nineteenth century. How does he accomplish this aim? What does making such a connection add to his speech?

4. Powell makes reference to Nelson Mandela and F. W. de Klerk of South Africa. What purpose does this reference serve in the speech? What is the linkage between this reference and his reference to the controversy surrounding Khalid Abdul Muhammad?

5. To what extent, if any, might Powell's speech have been a "campaign speech"?

Colin Powell's Commencement Address at Howard University

The full text of Powell's address.

The real challenge in being a commencement speaker is figuring out how long to speak.

The graduating students want a short speech, five to six minutes and let's get it over. They are not going to remember who their commencement speaker was anyway. P O W E L L.

Parents are another matter. Arrayed in all their finery they have waited a long time for this day, some not sure it would ever come, and they want it to last. So go on and talk for two or three hours. We brought our lunch and want our money's worth.

The faculty member who suggested the speaker hopes the speech will be long enough to be respectable, but not so long that he has to take leave for a few weeks beginning Monday. So the poor speaker is left figuring out what to do. My simple rule is to respond to audience reaction. If you are appreciative and applaud a lot early on, you get a nice, short speech. If you make me work for it, we're liable to be here a long time.

You know, the controversy over Howard's speaking policy has its positive side. It has caused the university to go through a process of self-examination, which is always a healthy thing to do. Since many people have been giving advice about how to handle this matter, I thought I might as well too.

First, I believe with all my heart that Howard must continue to serve as an institute of learning excellence where freedom of speech is strongly encouraged and rigorously protected. That is at the very essence of a great university and Howard is a greet university.

And freedom of speech means permitting the widest range of views to be present for debate, however controversial those views may be. The First Amendment right of free speech is intended to protect the controversial and even outrageous word, and not just comforting platitudes, too mundane to need protection.

Some say that by hosting controversial speakers who shock our sensibilities, Howard is in some way promoting or endorsing their message. Not at all. Howard has helped put their message in perspective while protecting their right to be heard. So that the message can be exposed to the full light of day.

I have every confidence in the ability of the administration, the faculty and the students of Howard to determine who should speak on this campus. No outside help needed, thank you.

I also have complete confidence in the students of Howard to make informed, educated judgments about what they hear.

But for this freedom to hear all views, you bear a burden to sort out wisdom from foolishness.

There is great wisdom in the message of self reliance, of education, of hard work, and of the need to raise strong families. There is utter foolishness, evil, and danger in the message of hatred, or of condoning violence, however cleverly the message is packaged or entertainingly it is presented. We must find nothing to stand up and cheer about or applaud in a message of racial or ethnic hatred.

I was at the inauguration of President Mandela in South Africa earlier this week. You were there too by television and watched that remarkable event. Together, we saw what can happen when people stop hating and begin reconciling. DeKlerk the jailer became DeKlerk the liberator, and Mandela the prisoner became Mandela the president. Twenty-seven years of imprisonment did not embitter Nelson Mandela. He invited his three jail keepers to the ceremony. He used his liberation to work his former tormentors to create a new South Africa and to eliminate the curse of apartheid from the face of the earth. What a glorious example! What a glorious day it was!

Last week you also saw Prime Minister Rabin and PLO Chairman Arafat sign another agreement on their still difficult, long road to peace, trying to end hundreds of years of hatred and two generations of violence. Palestinian authorities have now begun entering Gaza and Jericho.

In these two historic events, intractable enemies of the past have shown how you can join hands to create a force of moral authority more powerful than any army and which can change the world.

Although there are still places of darkness in the world where the light of reconciliation has not penetrated, these two beacons of hope show what can be done when men and women of goodwill work together for peace and for progress.

Document Text

There is a message in these two historic events for us assembled here today. As the world goes forward, we cannot start going backward.

African Americans have come too far and we have too far yet to go to take a detour into the swamp of hatred.

We, as a people who have suffered so much from the hatred of others must not now show tolerance for any movement or philosophy that has at its core the hatred of Jews or anyone else.

Our future lies in the philosophy of love and understanding and caring and building. Not of hatred and tearing down.

We know that. We must stand up for it and speak up for it!

We must not be silent if we would live up to the legacy of those who have gone before us from this campus.

I have no doubt that this controversy will pass and Howard University will emerge even stronger, even more than ever a symbol of hope, of promise, and of excellence. That is Howard's destiny!

Ambassador Annenberg, one of your honorees today, is a dear friend of mine and is one of America's leading businessmen and greatest philanthropists. You have heard of his recent contribution to American education and his generous gift to Howard.

A few years ago I told Mr. Annenberg about a project I was involved in to build a memorial to the Buffalo Soldiers, those brave black cavalrymen of the West whose valor had long gone unrecognized. Ambassador Annenberg responded immediately, and with his help the memorial now stands proudly at Fort Leavenworth, Kansas.

The Buffalo Soldiers were formed in 1867, at the same time as Howard University. It is even said that your mascot, the bison, came from the bison, or buffalo, soldiers. Both Howard and the Buffalo Soldiers owe their early success to the dedication and faith of white military officers who served in the Civil War. In Howard's case, of course, it was your namesake, Major General Oliver Howard. For the 10th Cavalry Buffalo Soldiers, it was Colonel. Benjamin Grierson who formed and commanded that regiment for almost twenty five years. And he fought that entire time to achieve equal status for his black comrades.

Together, Howard University and the Buffalo Soldiers showed what black Americans were capable of when given the education and opportunity; and when shown respect and when accorded dignity.

I am a direct descendant of those Buffalo Soldiers, of the Tuskegee Airmen, and of the navy's Golden Thirteen, and Montford Point Marines, and all the black men and women who served this nation in uniform for over three hundred years. All of whom served in their time and in their way and with whatever opportunity existed then to break down the walls of discrimination and racism to make the path easier for those of us who came after them. I climbed on their backs and stood on their shoulders to reach the top of my chosen profession to become chairman of the American Joint Chiefs of Staff.

I will never forget my debt to them and to the many white "Colonel Griersons" and "General Howards" who helped me over the thirty-five years of my life as a soldier. They would say to me now, "Well done. And now let others climb up on your shoulders."

Howard's Buffalo Soldiers did the same thing, and on their shoulders now stand governors and mayors and congressman and generals and doctors and artists and writers and teachers and leaders in every segment of American society. And they did it for the class of 1994. So that you can now continue climbing to reach the top of the mountain, while reaching down and back to help those less fortunate.

You face " Great Expectations." Much has been given to you and much is expected from you. You have been given a quality education, presented by a distinguished faculty who sit here today in pride of you. You have inquiring minds and strong bodies given to you by God and by your parents, who sit behind you and pass on to you today their still unrealized dreams and ambitions. You have been given citizenship in a country like none other on earth, with opportunities available to you like nowhere else on earth, beyond anything available to me when I sat in a place similar to this thirty-six years ago.

What will be asked of you is hard work. Nothing will be handed to you. You are entering a life of continuous study and struggle to achieve your goals.

A life of searching to find that which you do well and love doing. Never stop seeking. I want you to have faith in yourselves. I want you to believe to the depth of your soul that you can accomplish any task that you set your mind and energy to. I want you to be proud of your heritage. Study your origins. Teach your children racial pride and draw strength and inspiration from the cultures of our forebears.

Not as a way of drawing back from American society and its European roots. But as a way of showing that there are other roots as well. African and Caribbean roots that are also a source of nourishment for the American family tree. To show that African Americans are more than a product of our slave experience. To show that our varied backgrounds are as rich as that of any other American, not better or greater, but every bit as equal.

Our black heritage must be a foundation stone we can build on, not a place to withdraw into.

I want you to fight racism. But remember, as Dr. King and Dr. Mandela have taught us, racism is a disease of the racist. Never let it become yours. White South Africans were cured of the outward symptoms of the disease by President Mandela's inauguration, just as surely as black South Africans were liberated from apartheid.

Racism is a disease you can help cure by standing up for your rights and by your commitment to excellence and to performance. By being ready to take advantage of your rights and the opportunities that will come from those rights. Never let the dying hand of racism rest on your shoulder, weighing you down. Let racism always be someone else's burden to carry.

As you seek your way in the world, never fail to find a way to serve your community. Use your education and your success in life to help those still trapped in cycles of poverty and violence.

Above all, never lose faith in America. Its faults are yours to fix, not to curse.

America is a family. There may be differences and disputes in the family, but we must not allow the family to be broken into warring factions. From the diversity of our people, let us draw strength and not cause weakness.

Believe in America with all your heart and soul and mind. It remains the " last best hope of Earth." You are its inheritors and its future is today placed in your hands.

Go forth from this place today inspired by those who went before you. Go forth with the love of your families and the blessings of your teachers.

Go forth to make this a better country and society. Prosper, raise strong families, remembering that all you will leave behind is your good works and your children.

Go forth with my humble congratulations.

And let your dreams be your only limitations. Now and forever.

Thank you and God bless you.

Have a great life!

Glossary

Ambassador Annenberg: Walter Annenberg, an American publisher, philanthropist, and diplomat who in 1990 had donated $50 million to the United Negro College Fund

apartheid: the legal system of racial segregation in South Africa

controversy over Howard's speaking policy: a reference to a recent controversy involving Khalid Abdul Muhammad, who had appeared on campus and expressed extreme, racially inflammatory views

DeKlerk: President F. W. de Klerk, who ended apartheid in South Africa and played a key role in turning the country into a multiracial democracy

Dr. King: civil rights leader Dr. Martin Luther King, Jr.

Gaza and Jericho: regions in Israel that have been the focus of conflict between Israel and the Palestinians

Golden Thirteen: the first African American commissioned and warrant officers in the U.S. Navy, commissioned in 1944

"Great Expectations": the title of a novel by the nineteenth-century British writer Charles Dickens

"last best hope of Earth": a quotation from Abraham Lincoln's 1862 Annual Message to Congress

Montford Point Marines: the first African Americans who entered the U.S. Marine Corps from 1942 to 1949 at Montford Point Camp in North Carolina

PLO Chairman Arafat: Yasser Arafat, the leader of the Palestine Liberation Organization

President Mandela: Nelson Mandela, who became the president of South Africa after the end of apartheid

Prime Minister Rabin: Yitzhak Rabin of Israel

Tuskegee Airmen: the 332nd Fighter Group of the U.S. Army Air Corps, the first black pilots in U.S. military history, based in Tuskegee, Alabama

See also: Colin Powell's Commencement Address at Howard University: Document Analysis

Aerial view of the march. By The Library of Congress [No restrictions], via Wikimedia Commons

Louis Farrakhan's Million Man March Pledge

"I ... will strive to improve myself spiritually, morally, mentally, socially, politically and economically for the benefit of myself, my family and my people."

Overview

On October 16, 1995, the Reverend Louis Farrakhan, the leader of the Nation of Islam, brought African American men from around the nation together in Washington, D.C., for a demonstration of unity, pride, and strength. Known as the Million Man March, the daylong assembly culminated with a two-hour speech by Farrakhan that included the recitation of a pledge to secure a better future for African Americans. Unlike Dr. Martin Luther King, Jr.'s March on Washington in 1963, where participants were asked to face westward toward the Lincoln Memorial, Farrakhan asked those present "to face eastward toward a new dawn," noted Arthur J. Magida in *Prophet of Rage: A Life of Louis Farrakhan and His Nation*.

Context

In 1995, more than 50 percent of the individuals incarcerated in the United States were African American men, yet African Americans made up only 12 percent of the nation's population. There were more African American men unemployed and underemployed than attending college, and the numbers registered to vote were even lower. Moreover, the black and white races in the United States were more divided than unified. Feelings in the African American community were still raw after the acquittal of Los Angeles police officers who were videotaped beating black motorist Rodney King a few years earlier. The subsequent riots in Los Angeles in 1992 and the acquittal of former professional football player O. J. Simpson for the murder of his ex-wife, Nicole Brown Simpson, and her friend Ronald Goldman gave evidence of a serious racial divide in the country. In addition, popular culture was feeding negative perceptions of African Americans, particularly males, through films, television programs, and music that highlighted violence and illegal drug activity among members of this group.

Minister Louis Farrakhan, the impassioned leader of the Nation of Islam religious organization, used the unrest of African Americans and negative images of African American males specifically as an impetus to call for one million African American men to join in a march to the Lincoln Memorial in Washington, D.C., on October 16, 1995. Farrakhan called the event a holy day for African American men to reconnect with themselves, their families, one another, and the African American community.

The Million Man March would encourage African American men to take their rightful place in their communities as fathers, leaders, and providers. The event, which Farrakhan organized in cooperation with the Reverend Benjamin Chavis, former executive director of the National Association for the Advancement of Colored People (NAACP), and approximately three hundred local community organizations, became the stimulus for public and private discussion of many issues related to the African American community and race relations in the United States.

The mission statement of the Million Man March required African American men to repent or atone for their "sins" against themselves and humanity. The purpose of the march was to emphasize the need for African American men to be accountable and responsible while taking primary steps toward self-sufficiency in their personal, social, political, and economic lives. The march brought together young and old, rich and poor, professionals and unemployed.

Speakers at the event included a number of popular and politically prominent African American men, among them

Members of the Nation of Islam at the march. By Elvert Barnes from Baltimore, Maryland, USA [CC BY 2.0 (http://creativecommons.org/licenses/by/2.0)], via Wikimedia Commons

Kweisi Mfume, former U.S. congressman from Maryland and president of the NAACP; the Reverend Jesse Jackson, founder of the Rainbow/PUSH Coalition; actor and entertainer Bill Cosby; former professional baseball player Reggie Jackson; and scholar Cornel West.

Farrakhan spoke for more than two hours, during which he asked participants to recite a long pledge to engage in civic, social, political, cultural, and religious activities.

Famed poet Maya Angelou also participated in the official program, although the Million Man March was exclusively for African American men—women and men of other races were not invited. Several women spoke at the event, but African American women in general were encouraged to participate only in supporting, background roles. It was suggested that African American women should stay home and support the men by making the day a "holy day." In addition, all African Americans who did not attend the march were asked to avoid spending any money that day, to demonstrate the economic power of African Americans as a group. Many African American women did attend the event to show their support, but others adamantly objected to the gender divide it imposed.

The organizers intended the march to be nondenominational and nonpolitical; nevertheless, debates quickly arose concerning the reception, treatment, role, and participation in the march of Christians, Jews, and others who were not adherents of the Nation of Islam, as well as homosexuals and women, who were excluded. Moreover, the participation of Farrakhan, a man known for rhetoric that was often considered sexist and racist, added to the debates surrounding the event. Before, during, and after the Million Man March, observers pointed out the need in the African American community for further discussion and action concerning the gender divide, religious differences and mutual respect, economic self-empowerment, and political and social involvement and advancement.

In regard to Farrakhan's participation, many found it difficult to separate the message from the messenger. The often politically incendiary and radical rhetoric of the Nation of Islam leader tended to separate him and others from the idealistic and positive goals of the march.

Another widespread sentiment, however, was that although the controversial Farrakhan originated the idea for the march, the event's goals superseded his personality and rhetoric. Still, many condemned the march as a separatist event that served what they believed were sexist, patriarchal, and even racist motives on the part of Farrakhan.

Another controversy that followed the march concerned the numbers of people in attendance. The National Park Service originally estimated the crowd gathered in the nation's capital at 400,000, whereas the Nation of Islam's estimate was closer to 2 million. Some charged that the low "official" estimates of the size of the crowd reflected attempts by the political establishment to minimize the event's importance. Later review of panoramic photographs of the event led to some consensus that the number was actually around 835,000. This was not the only area where there was a lack of agreement, as responses to the Million Man March varied widely within and outside the African American community.

About the Author

Louis Abdul Farrakhan was born in the Bronx, New York, and raised primarily in the Roxbury area of Boston, Massachusetts, by his Caribbean mother, Mae Manning Clark. Farrakhan attended the St. Cyprian's Episcopal Church with his mother, a domestic worker and seamstress, and his older brother, Alvan. Farrakhan sang in the choir and began learning to play the violin when he was five or six years old. He was an honor student and an accomplished athlete.

At the age of sixteen, Farrakhan gained acclaim as a violinist when he performed on *Ted Mack's Original Amateur Hour*. He graduated from high school and attended Winston-Salem State University in North Carolina for two years. During that time, Farrakhan had his first encounter with Jim Crow laws when he was not allowed to buy a ticket to a movie theater in Washington, D.C. In 1953, Farrakhan married Betsy Ross. They had nine children together.

In the 1950's, Farrakhan was an accomplished calypso musician and violinist whose stage name was "The Charmer." While in Chicago to perform in 1955, he attended a Nation of Islam convention and decided to become a Muslim. His wife changed her name to Khadijah (laterMother Khadijah) and Farrakhan changed his name from LouisWalcott to Louis X. He gave up his music career after Nation of Islam leader Elijah Muhammad declared it sinful. Later, Farrakhan's violin talent became useful to the religious group and he performed concerts. His most notable classical violin concert as the leader of the Nation of Islam was on May 17, 1993, at Christ Universal Temple.

Farrakhan was Malcolm X's protégé until the latter fell out of favor with Muhammad, who gave Farrakhan duties that had once belonged to Malcolm X. Farrakhan became the Nation of Islam's national spokesman and the minister of the famed Temple Number Seven in New York City. After Muhammad's death, Farrakhan became the international spokesman for Muhammad's son and successor,Wallace D. Muhammad. In December of 1977, Farrakhan decided to separate himself fromWallace D.'s more orthodox Muslim teachings. After the split, Farrakhan traveled throughout Asia, Africa, and the Caribbean. During Jesse Jackson's presidential campaign in 1983 and 1984, Farrakhan and the Nation became heavily involved in electoral politics by supporting Jackson, raising funds for his campaign, and providing his security detail. In 1985, Farrakhan gave a famous speech in Madison Square Garden to his followers and supporters as some of his harshest critics yelled, "Death to Farrakhan." In 1988, Farrakhan founded the National Center for the Re-training and Re-education of the Black Man and Woman of America and the World in Chicago.

In October, 1991, Farrakhan reestablished the Three-Year Economic Savings Program, which sought to have African Americans contribute money to a fund that would purchase farmland and housing for black people in need. That year, he developed prostate cancer. In 1996, he was awarded the $250,000 Al-Gaddafi International Prize for Human Rights for his work defending human rights and freedoms around the world. In May, 2003, he created the Louis Farrakhan Prostate Cancer Foundation to bring awareness of the disease to the black community.

Farrakhan is credited with returning the Nation of Islam to its original teachings in 1977, after Wallace D. led many of his followers to become Orthodox Muslims. Farrakhan founded *The Final Call*, the Nation of Islam's international newspaper, and convened the Million Man March on the Mall in Washington, D.C., in October, 1995. By 2010, Farrakhan was overseeing more than 120 temples and study groups in America, South and West Africa, Europe, and the Caribbean.

As a young Muslim, Farrakhan wrote the theme song "A White Man's Heaven Is a Black Man's Hell" for the Nation of Islam. Farrakhan also has written numerous essays, articles, and books, including *A Torchlight for America* (1993), which examined the state of America and offered prescriptions for its moral, economic, and educational improvement. By 2010, Farrakhan's *National TV Ministry* was airing in more than one hundred cities. He produces the *Farrakhan Speaks* radio show and weekly live broadcasts on the Nation of Islam's Web site.

Explanation and Analysis of the Document

The goals set for the Million Man March were atonement, reconciliation, and responsibility. Farrakhan asked the men in his audience to repent for their sins against themselves and their communities, to forgive those who had done them wrong, and to take responsibility for their families. The day was filled with prayers and speeches given by many prominent African American orators, religious figures, politicians, artists, and entertainers. Most men on the National Mall that day endorsed neither Farrakhan nor the Nation of Islam, but they gathered there to recapture the spirit and integrity of the black male. Farrakhan's closing speech began by outlining the historical oppression of the black man and ended with a pledge each man was asked to recite as a call for individual and collective action.

The second paragraph asks black men to take responsibility for their families and to cease the abuse of black women and children. The language is surprisingly direct and targets the very destructive nature of domestic abuse. Farrakhan reiterates his request for black men to be accountable and dependable while they build family relationships based upon equality and mutual respect.

The last paragraph calls for community involvement in the struggle against drugs, crime, and violence and seeks stronger actions to end poverty and increase employment.

Farrakhan suggests that black men needed to organize and support positive role models for black youth and support black media outlets as a way to improve the image of blacks in America. He emphasizes the need for volunteerism and strong leadership to correct the societal problems within black communities.

Audience

Louis Farrakhan's Million Man March Pledge was delivered to an estimated eight to nine hundred thousand attendees on October, 16, 1995, but it is clear that he intended it to reach the millions of other black men who would hear this pledge repeated as a call to action across the nation. It was a statement heard through the media by whites as well, encouraging racial understanding and a sense of reconciliation throughout the nation. Furthermore, Farrakhan's message targeted the U.S. government, advocating dialogue and change in national political, economic, and social policies to help black America overcome its struggles. And finally, it was a call for foreign governments to increase their financial responsibility to the world's black communities.

Impact

Although there are many ways to examine African American history, Louis Farrakhan's Million Man March Pledge can best be understood as one course of proposed actions offering hope to a group of people who were still struggling to achieve equal status in America in the 1990s. Supporters of the march, such as Dr. Cornel West of Princeton University, suggested it was a success not only because it displayed a black united front but also because it sent a sign of hope and renewed possibilities to African Americans. Many observers noted that in the year following the march, more black men registered to vote, volunteered for neighborhood and mentorship programs, and—in the case of divorced fathers—took responsibility for their families by increasing their child support payments, therefore demonstrating that follow-up actions were taken as a result of the pledge.

Critics, however, have argued that the Million Man March was unsuccessful both in the planning of the event and in the aftermath, when antagonism and financial mismanagement loomed. Because of the many controversies surrounding Louis Farrakhan, the mastermind of the event, they questioned whether it was possible to separate "the message from the messenger." For some, messages associated with Farrakhan are seen as founded in hatred, especially because of his history of anti-Semitic comments toward Jews and the black supremacist teachings of the Nation of Islam. Yet many observers believe that the appeals to racial pride, personal responsibility, and economic empowerment inherent in the Million Man March captured the hearts and minds of those who attended and spread hope throughout the black community.

Further Reading

♦ Articles

Cose, Ellis. "Watch What They Do." *Newsweek* 128, no. 15 (October 7, 1996): 63.

Henry, Jessica M. "An Africalogical Analysis of the Million Man March: A Look at the Response to the March as a Measure of Its Effectiveness." *Howard Journal of Communications* 9 (1998): 157–168.

Marable, Manning. "Black Fundamentalism: Farrakhan and Conservative Black Nationalism." *Race & Class* 39, no. 4 (April–June 1998): 1–22.

Mollins, Carl. "The New Main Man." *Maclean's* 108, no. 44 (October 30, 1995): 36.

West, Michael O. "Like a River: The Million Man March and the Black Nationalist Tradition in the United States." *Journal of Historical Sociology* 12, no. 1 (March 1999): 81–100.

♦ Books

Cottman, Michael H. *Million Man March*. New York: Crown, 1995.

Gardell, Mattias. *In the Name of Elijah Muhammad: Louis Farrakhan and the Nation of Islam*. Durham, N.C.: Duke University Press, 1996.

Madhubuti, Haki R., and Maulana Karenga, eds. *Million Man March/Day of Absence: A Commemorative Anthology*. Chicago, Ill.: Third World Press, 1996.

Magida, Arthur J. *Prophet of Rage: A Life of Louis Farrakhan and His Nation*. New York: Basic Books, 1996.

Walker, Dennis. *Islam and the Search for African-American Nationhood: Elijah Muhammad, Louis Farrakhan and the Nation of Islam*. Atlanta: Clarity Press, 2005.

White, Vibert L., Jr. *Inside the Nation of Islam: A Historical and Personal Testimony by a Black Muslim*. Gainesville: University Press of Florida, 2001.

♦ Web Sites

"Biographical Sketch of Minister Louis Farrakhan." Nation of Islam National Center Web site. http://www.noi.org/mlfbio.htm.

"Farrakhan Admission on Malcolm X." CBS News "60 Minutes" Web site. http://www.cbsnews.com/stories/2000/05/10/60minutes/main194051.shtml.

"The Million Man March." PBS "This Far by Faith: African American Spiritual Journeys" Web site. http://www.pbs.org/thisfarbyfaith/print/journey5.html.

"Minister Farrakhan Challenges Black Men: Transcript from Minister Farrakhan's Remarks at the Million Man March." CNN Web site. http://www.cnn.com/US/9510/megamarch/10-16/transcript/index.html.

"Transcript of President Clinton's Speech on Race Relations." CNN Web site. http://www-cgi.cnn.com/US/9510/megamarch/10-16/clinton/update/transcript.html.

———Wendy Thowdis

Essential Quotes

> "I ... will strive to improve myself spiritually, morally, mentally, socially, politically and economically for the benefit of myself, my family and my people."

> "I pledge from this day forward I will support black newspapers, black radio, and black television. I will support black artists who clean up their acts to show respect for themselves, respect for their people, and respect for the ears of the human family."

Questions for Further Study

1. 1. In your opinion, was it a mistake for the Million Man March to exclude women?

2. On the one hand, Farrakhan chastised African American men for ""having allowed the community to embark on the path of self-destruction." On the other hand, he chastises the white community for the history of enslavement and white supremacy. Do you see these views as inconsistent? Or do you see them as complementary views, both of which are valid?

3. In the twenty-first century, Louis Farrakhan is regarded by many people as a somewhat frightening figure because of his outspokenness and militancy. Further, his position as leader of the Nation of Islam renders him suspect in the eyes of some because of instances of Islamic terrorism, including the September 11, 2001, attack on the United States. Do you believe that this characterization of Farrakhan is fair? Do you believe that it is "possible to separate 'the message from the messenger'"?

4. Farrakhan called for members of his audience to support black institutions such as newspapers, businesses, and cultural figures. Do you believe that it is possible for the black community to solve problems of unemployment and poverty by the establishment of and support for exclusively black organizations?

5. What do you think Elijah Muhammad, Stokely Carmichael, or Malcolm X would have thought of the Million Man March and its pledge? For help, see Malcolm X's "After the Bombing," Stokely Carmichael's "Black Power," and the FBI Report on Elijah Muhammad.

Louis Farrakhan's Million Man March Pledge

The full text of Farravkhan's Million Man March pledge.

I pledge that from this day forward I will strive to love my brother as I love myself. I, from this day forward, will strive to improve myself spiritually, morally, mentally, socially, politically and economically for the benefit of myself, my family and my people. I pledge that I will strive to build business, build houses, build hospitals, build factories and enter into international trade for the good of myself, my family and my people.

I pledge that from this day forward I will never raise my hand with a knife or a gun to beat, cut, or shoot any member of my family or any human being except in self-defense. I pledge from this day forward I will never abuse my wife by striking her, disrespecting her, for she is the mother of my children and the producer of my future. I pledge that from this day forward I will never engage in the abuse of children, little boys or little girls for sexual gratification. For I will let them grow in peace to be strong men and women for the future of our people.

I will never again use the " B word" to describe any female. But particularly my own black sister. I pledge from this day forward that I will not poison my body with drugs or that which is destructive to my health and my well-being. I pledge from this day forward I will support black newspapers, black radio, black television. I will support black artists who clean up their acts to show respect for themselves and respect for their people and respect for the ears of the human family. I will do all of this so help me god.

Glossary

B word: bitch

Initiative staff with Bill Clinton in June 1998. By White House Photographer (http://clinton4.nara.gov) [Public domain], via Wikimedia Commons

One America in the 21st Century

"The discussion of race in this country is no longer a discussion between and about blacks and whites. Increasingly, conversations about race must include all Americans."

Overview

On September 18, 1998, the panel that carried out President Bill Clinton's Initiative on Race released its final report, *One America in the 21st Century*. Earlier, on June 13, 1997, Clinton had issued Executive Order 13050, which charged the panel with investigating the state of American race relations at the end of the twentieth century. The directive asked the panel to advise him "on matters of race and racial reconciliation," to "promote a constructive national dialogue to confront and work through challenging issues that surround race," and to "identify, develop, and implement solutions to problems in areas in which race has a substantial impact, such as education, economic opportunity, housing, health care, and the administration of justice." To carry out these tasks, he called on seven distinguished experts led by the panel's chairman, the historian John Hope Franklin. For some fifteen months the members of the panel traveled throughout the United States, conducting town hall meetings and public forums and talking with people about their experiences regarding race. The excerpt reproduced here is the executive summary from their final report.

About the Author

Bill Clinton was born William Jefferson Blythe III in the rural town of Hope, Arkansas, three months after the death of his father in an automobile accident. Later, as a teenager, he changed his surname to that of his stepfather, Roger Clinton. He began to be popularly known as Bill Clinton at the start of his political career. As an infant, Clinton was reared primarily by his grandparents and a nanny. His mother, although devoted to him, frequently had to be away. When he was seven years old, his family moved to Hot Springs, Arkansas, where he received his elementary and high school education.

Clinton distinguished himself in both his class work and extracurricular activities, and his outgoing and congenial nature made him popular. He was elected president of his junior class and became a National Merit Scholarship semifinalist; he also played saxophone in his own band. As a senior, he was selected to participate in the Boys' Nation program in Washington, DC. While at the White House, he met his idol, President John F. Kennedy, an encounter for the young Clinton that would help to determine his political dreams and ambitions.

In the 1970s, Clinton began his professional political career. His first efforts, though, were less than auspicious. In 1972, he managed the Texas campaign of Democratic presidential nominee George McGovern, who was badly defeated; in 1974, Clinton himself campaigned unsuccessfully for an Arkansas congressional seat. In 1976, however, his political career gathered momentum: he managed the Arkansas campaign of victorious Democratic presidential candidate Jimmy Carter, and he was himself elected the state's attorney general.

Clinton began his bid to unseat Republican incumbent George H. W. Bush at the end of 1991. During the primaries, while Clinton was competing for the Democratic nomination against numerous rivals, his campaign almost collapsed under allegations that he had been having an extramarital affair. Similar allegations had troubled him earlier during his tenure as governor.

Clinton was elected the forty-second president of the United States on November 3, 1992. He received 43 percent of the popular vote; Bush received 38 percent, and an independent candidate, the mercurial billionaire Ross Perot, received 19 percent. Clinton garnered 370 votes in the electoral college to Bush's 168, while Perot obtained none. Clinton's running mate was Tennessee senator Al

Gore, a fellow southerner and valuable adviser with whom Clinton established an exceptional rapport.

Sworn in on January 20, 1993, Clinton was the first Democrat elected president in twelve years and the youngest since Kennedy. He also was the first US president to be born after World War II and the first since Herbert Hoover not to have served in the military. In addition, he was the first president to be inaugurated during the post–Cold War period, in a world without the Soviet empire.

Clinton made domestic issues his top priority. His administration's most difficult task was to find ways to support essential government programs, trim or eliminate others, and balance the federal budget, which had accumulated an enormous deficit during the Ronald Reagan–George H. W. Bush years (1981–1993). To staff his administration, Clinton assembled a team that emphasized representation of minorities and women. He appointed Janet Reno as the first woman to be attorney general. In 1997, he appointed Madeleine Albright as the first woman to be secretary of state, the senior position in the cabinet.

In retirement, Clinton saw the inauguration in 2004 of the William J. Clinton Library in Little Rock, Arkansas, where his foundation is also located. He completed and published his memoirs, My Life, in 2004 as well, but he also suffered a heart attack. He had bypass surgery and recovered during the following year. The Clintons also experienced financial and legal difficulties at this time.

In the mid-2000s, Clinton and former president George H. W. Bush collaborated to raise funds for disaster relief following the Indian Ocean tsunami in 2004 and Hurricane Katrina in 2005. From 2005 to 2007, he served as the UN special envoy for tsunami recovery; two years later, he became the special envoy to Haiti.

During the 2008 presidential campaign, Clinton assisted Hillary in her unsuccessful run for the Democratic nomination, which she lost to Illinois senator Barack Obama. In 2009, shortly after Obama took office, Hillary was appointed secretary of state, continuing the Clinton political legacy. During the 2012 presidential election, Bill Clinton toured the country on behalf of President Obama, who was running for a second term; Clinton's work and his speech at the Democratic National Convention are credited with helping secure Obama's victory.

In 2015, Hillary announced her bid for the 2016 presidential nomination. Not long after, the nonprofit Clinton Foundation, known for forging public-private partnerships in countries around the world, became embroiled in controversy regarding large foreign donations it accepted from the government of Saudi Arabia, among others, during Hillary's tenure at the State Department. Critics alleged that such donors expected political favors in exchange for their financial backing. The Clintons asserted no malfeasance or impropriety had occurred, and the foundation released a more comprehensive donor list than it had previously and restricted which governments it would accept funds from during the Hillary Clinton campaign. Bill Clinton provided campaign-management support for his wife's race while continuing his active involvement in the foundation's work and traveling for speaking engagements.

Explanation and Analysis of the Document

In recent years, the emphasis in discussions of race has been less on the legacy of white racism and more on the concept of diversity, that is, the more positive notion that a nation's diverse ethnic and racial makeup can strengthen it by ensuring inclusion of differing viewpoints and experiences in business decisions, education, and other arenas. The summary calls attention to the changing ethnic makeup of America and to predictions that in the year 2050 the nation's demographics would be considerably different than they were at the end of the twentieth century. As intermarriage becomes more common, states the summary, concepts of "black" and "white" are eroding, since more and more children are of mixed race. The panel also emphasizes that attention must be given to the needs of less visible minorities, such as Native Americans and Pacific Islanders.

♦ "Chapter Four—Bridging the Gap"

The summary notes that Chapter Four points to some of the specific findings and recommendations to emerge from the panel's investigations. Key areas of focus include civil rights enforcement (including enforcement of laws against racially motivated "hate crimes") and education. With reference to education, the panel cites the need to implement the administration's Comprehensive Indian Education Policy, launched the previous year. The panel goes on to outline goals in other areas, including antipoverty initiatives (for example, job training, raising the minimum wage, providing assistance to small businesses), improvements in access to affordable housing (by, for instance, providing funds for community revitalization), stereotyping, and law enforcement. With regard to law enforcement, the panel calls attention to racial profiling—that is, the use of race to help identify likely criminals—and disparities in drug law enforcement. For example, many observers at the time believed that by imposing longer sentences for users of crack cocaine, the court system was unfairly targeting African Americans. Further areas of concern here include health care and immigration.

♦ "Chapter Five—Forging a New Future"

Chapter Five looks forward. The summary draws attention to the President's Council for One America, again shifting the focus away from assigning blame for past actions and focusing on a future, more united America; the council was formed essentially to continue the work of the panel by exploring long-term solutions to racial problems and to make public policy recommendations. The summary then notes that the report calls for comprehensive multimedia educational programs about race, community leadership, and leadership among youth. The summary also promises that Chapter Five will touch on a miscellaneous group of ancillary issues, such as environmental justice (for example, the issue of whether minorities are relegated to the most environmentally distressed areas of cities), police misconduct, and stereotyping in the media. It concludes with a promise to list ten suggestions "on how Americans can help to build on the momentum that will lead our Nation into the 21st century as one America."

Audience

The audience for *One America in the 21st Century* was the nation at large. Clinton believed that it was time for the nation to have a dialogue on race, and his Initiative on Race was a major part of that dialogue. His goal was to provoke thought about ongoing racial barriers and, more important, thought about how to dismantle those barriers. Given his long commitment to civil rights and equality of opportunity going back to his days as attorney general and governor of Arkansas, he also wanted to reassure the African American community that he remained committed to their goals and aspirations. By assembling a panel that was balanced along racial, gender, political, and sectional lines, he hoped to involve all Americans in the discussion. To that end, numerous ancillary documents, including discussion and teaching guides such as the *One America Dialogue Guide*, were published along with the report and remain available. These documents are intended for use not only by educators but also by any group or organization formed with the goal of promoting discussion of racial issues. Oddly, the report itself was not published in book form until 2008.

Impact

Although he had been reelected as president in 1996, Clinton knew that his legacy was being tarnished because of the scandals that surrounded him, some of them dating from before his presidency. During the investigation surrounding these allegations, Clinton lied under oath about an improper sexual relationship he had had with Monica Lewinsky, a White House intern. Eventually, this evasion led to impeachment proceedings in 1998–1999, culminating in Clinton's acquittal by the U.S. Senate on charges of perjury and obstruction of justice. Even Clinton's supporters were willing to admit that his race initiative and *One America in the 21st Century* were partly intended to shift the focus away from his personal failings, refurbish his image, and create a more positive legacy.

The question, then, is whether he succeeded. In the eyes of many observers, the race initiative was a noble effort but one that had few if any concrete outcomes. Some observers, in reacting to the report, argued that it was motivated primarily by politics. Clinton, a Democrat, launched the effort during his second term, when the U.S. Congress had come under Republican control. Thus, there was little likelihood that any specific legislation would emerge from the undertaking, so Clinton faced little political risk by putting forward the initiative when he did. Others criticized the effort for failing to create an overarching strategy for dealing with racial problems, particularly at a time when the very concept of "race" in America was in flux, especially because of immigration, legal and illegal, from Mexico and Central America. Still others observed that the initiative was undermined by lack of a clear need; then by tactical miscues, lack of focus, public meetings whose purpose was unclear; and finally by the Lewinsky scandal, which drowned out the race initiative in the media. Others criticized the initiative for vagueness and timidity. Despite these criticisms, many of Clinton's supporters contended that race had not been seriously discussed for a generation and that the initiative shifted the discussion in a positive direction, from white racism to the less volatile issue of racial and cultural diversity in America.

Further Reading

◆ Articles

Carcasson, Martin, and Mitchell F. Rice. "The Promise and Failure of President Clinton's Race Initiative of 1997–1998: A Rhetorical Perspective." *Rhetoric and Public Affairs* 2, no. 2 (1999): 243–274.

Goering, John. "An Assessment of President Clinton's Initiative on Race." *Ethnic and Racial Studies* 24, no. 3 (2001): 472–484.

Kim, Claire Jean. "Clinton's Race Initiative: Recasting the American Dilemma." *Polity* 32, no. 2 (2000): 175–197.

Smith, Renee M. "The Public Presidency Hits the Wall: Clinton's Presidential Initiative on Race." *Presidential Studies Quarterly* 28, no. 4 (1998): 780–785.

◆ Books

Report of the National Advisory Commission on Civil Disorders. New York: Bantam, 1968.

Shull, Steven A. *American Civil Rights Policy from Truman to Clinton: The Role of Presidential Leadership.* Armonk, N.Y.: M. E. Sharpe, 1999.

Wickham, DeWayne. *Bill Clinton and Black America.* New York: Ballantine, 2002.

Wright, Sharon D. "Clinton and Racial Politics." In *Postmodern Presidency: Bill Clinton's Legacy in U.S. Politics*, ed. Steven Schier. Pittsburgh: University of Pittsburgh Press, 2000.

◆ Web Sites

"Executive Order 13050: President's Advisory Board on Race, William J. Clinton, June 13, 1997." American Presidency Project Web site. http://www.presidency.ucsb.edu/ws/index.php?pid=54265.

"Inaugural Address, William J. Clinton, January 20, 1997." American Presidency Project Web site. http://www.presidency.ucsb.edu/ws/index.php?pid=54183.

—*Michael J. O'Neal*

Essential Quotes

"America's greatest promise in the 21st century lies in our ability to harness the strength of our racial diversity. The greatest challenge facing Americans is to accept and take pride in defining ourselves as a multiracial democracy."

"Our Nation still struggles with the impact of its past policies, practices, and attitudes based on racial differences. Race and ethnicity still have profound impacts on the extent to which a person is fully included in American society and provided the equal opportunity and equal protection promised to all Americans."

"The discussion of race in this country is no longer a discussion between and about blacks and whites. Increasingly, conversations about race must include all Americans."

"The creation of a President's Council for One America speaks to the need for a long-term strategy dedicated to building on the vision of one America."

Questions for Further Study

1. Author Toni Morrison famously referred to Bill Clinton as the nation's "first black president." Clinton, of course, is white. What do you think Morrison meant by this characterization? Do you think that there is some element of truth to it? What might President Barack Obama think of this characterization, particularly since his major Democratic opponent in his run for the presidency was Bill Clinton's wife, Hillary Rodham Clinton?

2. What good do you think programs such as Clinton's Initiative on Race do? Can they lead to substantial discussion and progress, or are they a type of political theater? Explain.

3. Compare *One America in the 21st Century* with *To Secure These Rights*, produced in 1947 under the administration of President Harry Truman. Do the documents share similar concerns? How was each document a product of its time?

4. What role, if any, do you believe politics played in the Initiative on Race? Do you believe that the political context of the Initiative on Race and of *One America in the 21st Century* was important?

5. Compare this document and its goals with U.S. Supreme Court Justice Clarence Thomas's Concurrence/Dissent in *Grutter v. Bollinger*, issued in 2003. What do you think the panel that prepared *One America in the 21st Century* thought of Thomas's views? How do the two documents represent somewhat polar views of race in America?

6. Read this document in conjunction with the U.S. Senate Resolution Apologizing for the Enslavement and Racial Segregation of African Americans, passed in 2009. To what extent do you think the Senate's apology helped carry out the goals of the Initiative on Race?

One America in the 21st Century

The executive summary of the report.

> Today, I ask the American people to join me in a great national effort to perfect the promise of America for this new time as we seek to build our more perfect union.... That is the unfinished work of our time, to lift the burden of race and redeem the promise of America.
>
> —President Clinton, June 14, 1997

America's greatest promise in the 21st century lies in our ability to harness the strength of our racial diversity. The greatest challenge facing Americans is to accept and take pride in defining ourselves as a multiracial democracy. At the end of the 20th century, America has emerged as the worldwide symbol of opportunity and freedom through leadership that constantly strives to give meaning to democracy's fundamental principles. These principles—justice, opportunity, equality, and racial inclusion—must continue to guide the planning for our future.

On June 13, 1997, President William Jefferson Clinton issued Executive Order No. 13050 (the "Executive Order"), which created the Initiative on Race (the "Initiative") and authorized the creation of an Advisory Board to advise the President on how to build one America for the 21st century. The Board, consisting of Dr. John Hope Franklin (chairman), Linda Chavez-Thompson, Reverend Dr. Suzan D. Johnson Cook, Thomas H. Kean, Angela E. Oh, Bob Thomas, and William F. Winter, was tasked with examining race, racism, and the potential for racial reconciliation in America using a process of study, constructive dialogue, and action.

Board members have spent the last 15 months seeking ways to build a more united and just America. They have canvassed the country meeting with and listening to Americans who revealed how race and racism have impacted their lives. Board meetings focused on the role race plays in civil rights enforcement, education, poverty, employment, housing, stereotyping, the administration of justice, health care, and immigration. Members have convened forums with leaders from the religious and corporate sectors.

This Report, a culmination of the Board's efforts, is not a definitive analysis of the state of race relations in America today. Board members had no independent authority to commit Federal resources to a particular problem, community, or organization. Rather, this Report is an account of the Board's experiences and impressions and includes all of the recommendations for action submitted by the Board to the President following its formal meetings, Many have already been implemented or are awaiting congressional action.

Chapter One—Searching for Common Ground

Throughout the year, the Board heard stories and shared experiences that reinforced its belief that we are a country whose citizens are more united than divided. All too often, however, racial differences and discrimination obstruct our ability to move beyond race and color to recognize our common values and goals. Common values include the thirst for freedom, desire for equal opportunity, and a belief in fairness and justice; collective goals are securing a decent affordable home, a quality education, and a job that pays decent wages. All people, regardless of race, want financial and personal security, adequate and available health care, and children who are healthy and well-educated. Chapter One discusses these shared goals and values and also describes how the Initiative used dialogue as a tool for finding common ground. Through One America Conversations, the Campus Week of Dialogue, Statewide Days of Dialogue, tribal leaders meetings, and the *One America Dialogue Guide*, the Initiative was able to spark dialogue across the country. The chapter also points to the importance of recruiting a cadre of leaders to provide strong leadership in the corporate, religious, and youth sectors of our society and provides examples of Promising Practices.

Chapter Two—Struggling with the Legacy of Race and Color

Chapter Two confronts the legacy of race in this country and in so doing, answers the question of whether race matters in America. Our Nation still struggles with the impact of its past policies, practices, and attitudes based on racial differences. Race and ethnicity still have profound impacts on the extent to which a person is fully included in American society and provided the equal opportunity and equal protection promised to all Americans. All of these characteristics continue to affect an individual's opportunity to receive an education, acquire the skills necessary to maintain a good job, have access to adequate health care, and receive equal justice under the law.

Americans must improve their understanding of the history of race in this country and the effect this history has on the way many minorities and people of color are treated today. Each minority group shares a common history of legally mandated and/or socially and economically imposed subordination to white European-Americans and their descendants. In this chapter, the experiences of American Indians and Alaska Natives, African Americans, Latinos, Asian Pacific Americans, and white immigrants are highlighted.

The lesson of this chapter is that the absence of both knowledge and understanding about the role race has played in our collective history continues to make it difficult to find solutions that will improve race relations, eliminate disparities, and create equal opportunities in all areas of American life. This absence also contributes to conflicting views on race and racial progress held by Americans of color and white Americans.

This is especially relevant in the context of race-conscious affirmative action programs. Lack of knowledge and understanding about the genesis and consequences of racial discrimination in America often make it difficult to discuss affirmative action remedies productively. It also obscures the significant progress made in the last two decades in eliminating racial disparities in the workplace and in educational institutions through the use of properly constructed affirmative action strategies.

Chapter Three—The Changing Face of America

In Chapter Three, the Board examines the changing face of America. The discussion of race in this country is no longer a discussion between and about blacks and whites. Increasingly, conversations about race must include all Americans, including, but not limited to, Hispanics, American Indians and Alaska Natives, and Asian Pacific Americans. Statistics show that by the year 2050, the population in the United States will be approximately 53 percent white, 25 percent Hispanic, 14 percent black, 8 percent Asian Pacific American, and 1 percent American Indian and Alaska Native. This represents a significant shift from our current demographics of 73 percent white, 12 percent black, 11 percent Hispanic, 4 percent Asian Pacific American, and 1 percent American Indian and Alaska Native.

Further complicating the discussions of race is the increasing amount of interracial marriages. Americans are marrying persons of a different race at consistently high rates. U.S. Census data show that 31 percent of native-born Hispanic husbands and wives, between ages 25 and 34, have white spouses. In the native-born Asian Pacific American category, 36 percent of the men and 45 percent of the women marry white spouses.

The complexities, challenges, and opportunities that arise from our growing diversity point to the need for a new language, one that accurately reflects this diversity. Our dialogue must reflect the steps being taken to close the gap in data reporting on America's less visible racial groups—American Indians, Alaska Natives, Native Hawaiians, and all of the subgroups of Asian Pacific Americans and Hispanics.

Chapter Four—Bridging the Gap

Chapter Four summarizes key facts and background information that emerged from each of the Board's formal meetings and the recommendations made to the President on civil rights enforcement, education, economic opportunity, stereotypes, criminal justice, health care, and the immigrant experience. The data show that although minorities and people of color have made progress in terms of the indicators used to measure quality of life, persistent barriers to their full inclusion in American society remain.

In the area of civil rights enforcement, the Board made the following recommendations:
- Strengthen civil rights enforcement.
- Improve data collection on racial and ethnic discrimination.
- Strengthen laws and enforcement against hate crimes.

Two of the early Board meetings focused on the role of education in helping to overcome racial disparities. These meetings stressed the importance

of educating children in high-quality, integrated schools, where they have the opportunity to learn about and from each other. These meetings served as the basis for the following recommendations:
- Enhance early childhood learning.
- Strengthen teacher preparation and equity.
- Promote school construction.
- Promote movement from K–12 to higher education.
- Promote the benefits of diversity in K–12 and higher education.
- Provide education and skills training to overcome increasing income inequality that negatively affects the immigrant population.
- Implement the Comprehensive Indian Education Policy.

The Board analyzed the issue of economic opportunity through formal meetings on employment and poverty. Information gathered showed that a substantial amount of disparity remains between the economic prosperity of whites and most minority groups. Also, the Board found clear evidence of active forms of discrimination in employment, pay, housing, and consumer and credit markets. The Board made the following recommendations for correcting these disparities:
- Examine income inequality.
- Support supplements for Small Business Administration programs.
- Use the current economic boom to provide necessary job training and to increase the minimum wage.
- Evaluate anti-poverty program effectiveness.
- Provide a higher minimum wage for low-wage workers and their families.
- Improve racial data collection.
- Evaluate the effectiveness of job-training programs designed to reach minority and immigrant communities.
- Commission a study to examine American Indian economic development.
- Support the right of working people to engage in collective bargaining.

The U.S. Department of Housing and Urban Development convened a meeting for the Board on race and housing. Active forms of racial discrimination continue to plague our housing markets. According to current statistics, blacks and Hispanics are likely to be discriminated against roughly half of the time that they go to look for a home or apartment. The recommendations for addressing the disparities in the area of housing follow;
- Continue to use testing to develop evidence of continuing discrimination.
- Highlight housing integration efforts.
- Support the increase and targeting of Federal funds for urban revitalization.
- Support community development corporations.
- Promote American Indian access to affordable housing.

In one meeting, the Board addressed the issues surrounding negative racial stereotypes, which are the core elements of discrimination and racial division. Stereotypes influence how people of different races and ethnicities view and treat each other. The Board's recommendations on stereotypes, which follow, focus on using both public and private institutions and individuals to challenge policymakers and institutional leaders to examine the role stereotypes play in policy development, institutional practices, and our view of our own racial identity:
- Hold a Presidential event to discuss stereotypes.
- Institutionalize the Administration's promotion of racial dialogue.
- Convene a high-level meeting on the problem of racial stereotypes with leaders from the media.

At the Board meeting on race, crime, and the administration of justice, experts explained how racial disparities and prejudices affect the way in which minorities are treated by the criminal system. Examples of this phenomenon can be found in the use of racial profiling in law enforcement and in the differences in the rates of arrest, conviction, and sentencing between whites and minorities and people of color. These discoveries led to the following recommendations:
- Expand data collection and analysis.
- Consider restricting the use of racial profiling.
- Eliminate racial stereotypes and diversify law enforcement.
- Reduce or eliminate drug sentencing disparities.
- Promote comprehensive efforts to keep young people out of the criminal justice system.
- Continue to enhance community policing and related strategies.
- Support initiatives that improve access to courts.
- Support American Indian law enforcement.

The U.S. Department of Health and Human Services sponsored a meeting on race and health for the Board. Disparities in the treatment of whites and minorities and people of color by the health care system can be attributed to disparities in employment, income, and wealth. The Board made the following recommendations as a result of information received at this meeting:
- Continue advocating for broad-based expansions in health insurance coverage.
- Continue advocacy of increased health care access for underserved groups.
- Continue pushing Congress for full funding of the Race and Ethnic Health Disparities Initiatives.
- Increase funding for existing programs targeted to under served and minority populations.
- Enhance financial and regulatory mechanisms to promote culturally competent care.
- Emphasize the importance of cultural competence to institutions training health care providers.

The Carnegie Endowment for International Peace and the Georgetown University Law Center jointly sponsored a meeting for the Board that explored immigration and race. Evidence showed that race is the source of a fundamental rift in American society that affects immigrants and their experiences with discrimination. The Board issued the following recommendations as a result of the information it received in this meeting:
- Strongly enforce anti-discrimination measures on behalf of every racial and ethnic minority group.
- Back programs that would promote a clear understanding of the rights and duties of citizenship.
- Support immigrant-inclusion initiatives.

Chapter Five—Forging a New Future

Chapter Five calls for the continuation of the Initiative to complete the work already begun. The following elements are the most critical in developing a meaningful long-term strategy to advance race relations in the 21st century:

- A President's Council for One America. This year's effort has been vital in laying the foundation for the larger task that lies ahead. The creation of a President's Council for One America speaks to the need for a long-term strategy dedicated to building on the vision of one America. Its main function would be to coordinate and monitor the implementation of policies designed to increase opportunity and eliminate racial disparities.
- A public education program using a multimedia approach. A public education program could assist in keeping the American public informed on the facts about race in America, pay tribute to the different racial and ethnic backgrounds of Americans, and emphasize and highlight the common values we share as a racially diverse Nation.
- A Presidential "call to action" of leaders from all sectors of our society. A call to action should come from the President to leaders in State and local government and private sector organizations to address the racial and ethnic divides in their communities. Public/private partnerships can demonstrate leadership by working collaboratively to make racial reconciliation a reality in all communities across America.
- A focus on youth. Young Americans are this Nation's greatest hope for realizing the goal of one America. Young people must be engaged in efforts to bridge racial divides and promote racial reconciliation. Organizations and groups that encourage the development of youth leaders must be supported.

This chapter also includes a brief discussion of other critical issues, such as environmental justice, media and stereotyping, and police misconduct, that the Advisory Board believes deserve further dialogue. Among these issues is affirmative action, which the Board believes remains an important tool among many for overcoming racial discrimination and promoting the benefits of diversity in education, employment, and other contexts.

Chapter Five concludes with the 10 suggestions on how Americans can help to build on the momentum that will lead our Nation into the 21st century as one America.

Glossary

affirmative action: any program that takes positive steps to increase the representation of minority groups in employment, college admissions, and the like

collective bargaining: negotiation between an employer and a labor union

hate crimes: crimes that are motivated by animus against a particular group, such as African Americans, gays, or women

K–12: kindergarten through twelfth grade

racial profiling: in law enforcement, the practice of singling out members of a racial (or ethnic) group for closer scrutiny, based on the belief that such people are more likely to commit crimes

Clarence Thomas's Concurrence/Dissent in Grutter v. Bollinger

"The majority upholds the Law School's racial discrimination not by interpreting the people's Constitution, but by responding to a faddish slogan of the cognoscenti."

Overview

In 2003 the U.S. Supreme Court decided *Grutter v. Bollinger*, with the majority opinion sanctioning the use of affirmative action in higher education. Justice Clarence Thomas wrote a separate opinion, concurring in part and dissenting in part from the Court's judgment, in order to emphasize his view that government consideration of race for any purpose is unconstitutional.

Context

The first contemporary reference to affirmative action was made on March 6, 1961, when President John F. Kennedy issued Executive Order 10925. That order mandated that government contractors "take affirmative action" to ensure that their hiring and employment practices became free of racial bias. On September 24, 1965, President Lyndon B. Johnson issued Executive Order 11246, which superseded President Kennedy's order. Among other conditions, Johnson's order required that government contractors set concrete goals in their hiring of minorities, create specific measures to reach those goals, and report their progress in reaching those goals to the federal government. In essence, Johnson's order adopted the theory that civil rights laws prohibiting discrimination alone were not enough to remedy racial discrimination.

Initially, the concept of affirmative action received widespread support from both conservatives and liberals, as evidenced by President Richard Nixon's implementation of the "Philadelphia Order," a program designed by Arthur Fletcher, an African American Republican who eventually earned the distinction of being called "the father of affirmative action." The Philadelphia Order created a test program that specified required goals and timetables in the hiring and retention of minorities by craft unions and the construction industry in Philadelphia. The plan was later used a national model for federal contractors. President Nixon recalled in his memoirs his belief that affirmative action was justified, stating:

> A good job is as basic and important a civil right as a good education.... I felt that [affirmative action] was both necessary and right. We would not impose quotas, but would require federal contractors to show affirmative action to meet the goals of increasing minority employment.

On June 28, 1978, the U.S. Supreme Court issued its first decision analyzing the constitutionality of a racial classification benefiting minorities. In *Regents of the University of California v. Bakke* (1978), the Court held that the separate admissions program for minorities at the School of Medicine of the University of California, Davis, which set aside sixteen out of one hundred places for minority students, unfairly discriminated against the plaintiff, a white applicant whom the university had denied admission despite his having scored significantly higher on admissions tests than some admitted minority applicants. In a split opinion, the Court found that the medical school's admissions plan was unconstitutional as implemented because it amounted to a rigid quota. However, the Court noted that race could be a permissible consideration in higher education admissions in some circumstances.

The Court's rejection of strict race-based quotas in *Bakke* triggered an aggressive campaign by conservatives to eliminate affirmative action programs, which they characterized as "reverse discrimination" against white Americans. The split among the justices in *Bakke* foreshadowed the difficulties the Court would face over the next two decades in developing a coherent constitutional framework for analyzing racial classifications intended to ameliorate the effects of past discrimination or to ensure diversity.

Just a year after *Bakke*, the Supreme Court upheld a different affirmative action plan. In *United Steelworkers of America v. Weber* (1979), an employer adopted an affirmative action plan to remedy racial imbalance in the workforce resulting from past discrimination. Prior to the affirmative action plan, the employer had hired as skilled "craft workers" only those persons who previously had such experience. Because African Americans had long been excluded from craft unions, very few African Americans had the necessary credentials, and therefore very few were eligible to be hired under the employer's policy. To remedy the racial imbalance, the employer had adopted a plan under which it would hire from the ranks of its own lower-skilled workers; it established a training program for those workers and required that at least half of new trainees be African American until such time as the percentage of African American skilled craft workers approximated the percentage of African Americans in the local labor force. The Court ruled that the plan did not impermissibly discriminate against white employees. The Court held that measures taken to remedy a conspicuous racial imbalance that exists owing to past discrimination are permissible if they are temporary and do not "unnecessarily trammel the interests" of white employees or present an absolute bar to their advancement.

In 1989 in *City of Richmond v. J. A. Croson Co.*, on the other hand, the Court held that a program setting aside a portion of the city's construction funds for minority-owned firms was not "narrowly tailored" to serve a "compelling governmental interest" and was therefore unconstitutional under the equal protection clause of the Fourteenth Amendment. In *Croson*, a majority of the Court held for the first time that affirmative action programs designed to aid racial minorities were subject to the same high degree of judicial skepticism—"strict scrutiny"—under the Fourteenth Amendment's equal protection clause as government action intended to injure racial minorities. The next year, however, in *Metro Broadcasting, Inc. v. Federal Communications Commission* (1990), the Supreme Court distinguished federal affirmative action programs from those adopted by a state, holding that such federal programs were subject to a lesser degree of judicial skepticism, known as "immediate scrutiny." Among other reasons, the Court believed that the special constitutional role of Congress in enforcing the post–Civil War constitutional amendments (the Thirteenth, Fourteenth, and Fifteenth Amendments) justified a greater degree of judicial deference to congressional remedies for racial inequality than was appropriate for state action in the area.

Yet the Court's tolerance for federal affirmative action programs proved to be short lived. In 1995 in *Adarand Constructors, Inc. v. Peña*, the Court reversed the *Metro Broadcasting* decision and held that "federal racial classifications, like those of a State, must serve a compelling governmental interest, and must be narrowly tailored to further that interest." Applying this heightened standard, the Court struck down a federal affirmative action program that provided a financial incentive to contractors who employed subcontracting firms owned by members of historically disadvantaged minority groups.

In *Adarand*, Justice Thomas agreed with the Court's decision striking down the federal affirmative action program but wrote a separate concurring opinion to express his belief that laws designed to benefit a historically oppressed racial group are as morally and constitutionally troubling as laws designed to subjugate such a group. The reasoning employed by Justice Thomas in his *Adarand* concurrence challenged both the constitutionality and moral underpinnings of government-sponsored affirmative action programs. *Adarand* was the last major Supreme Court case prior to *Grutter v. Bollinger* to assess the permissibility of race-conscious government action intended to correct racial imbalances or achieve racial diversity.

Coincident with *Grutter*, on June 23, 2003, the Court decided *Gratz v. Bollinger*, declaring unconstitutional the University of Michigan's undergraduate admissions program, which awarded additional admissions points based upon an applicant's membership in an underrepresented minority group. In *Grutter v. Bollinger*, the Court would address a constitutional challenge to the University of Michigan Law School's admission program, which considered an applicant's race as one of many factors in an individualized assessment of each applicant in order to create a diverse student body. As Justice Sandra Day O'Connor's majority opinion notes, the law school's admissions policy aimed to "focus on academic ability coupled with a flexible assessment of applicants' talents, experiences, and potential 'to contribute to the learning of those around them.'" In addition to considering numerical factors such as each applicant's Law School Admission Test scores and undergraduate grade point average, the law school also considered a variety of "'soft' variables," such as the applicant's personal essay, recommendation letters, and areas of undergraduate study.

The policy also directed admissions officers to consider what contribution an applicant could make to the diversity of the law school's student body. While the policy directed consideration of the "many possible bases for diversity admissions," it also reaffirmed the law school's long-standing commitment to "racial and ethnic diversity with special reference to the inclusion of students from groups which have been historically discriminated against, like African-Americans, Hispanics and Native Americans, who without this commitment might not be represented in our student body in meaningful numbers." The law school's policy did not employ quotas or seek a predefined number of such students in each entering class. It did, however, seek to enroll a "critical mass" of students from underrepresented minority groups in order to ensure "their ability to make unique contributions to the character of the Law School" and to avoid racial isolation.

A rejected white applicant sued the law school. She alleged that the law school's consideration of race, even though it did not amount to a rigid quota, violated various civil rights statutes and the Fourteenth Amendment's equal protection clause, which provides that no state shall "deny to any person within its jurisdiction the equal protection of the laws."

The Supreme Court, in Justice O'Connor's majority opinion, upheld the law school's admission policy. The Court applied its most stringent standard of review, known as strict scrutiny, which requires that the use of race be justified by a "compelling governmental interest" and that the means used to further that interest be "narrowly tailored," with no "less restrictive means" apparent. The Court held that the law school's judgment that a diverse student body provides educational benefits to all students was entitled to judicial respect, and the Court agreed that consideration of race in order to achieve a diverse student body served a compelling governmental interest. The Court reasoned that substantial educational benefits flow from a diverse student body. Diversity, the opinion states, quoting the district court, "promotes 'cross-racial understanding,' helps to break down racial stereotypes, and 'enables [students] to better understand persons of different races.' These benefits are 'important and laudable,' because 'classroom discussion is livelier, more spirited, and simply more enlightening and interesting' when the students have 'the greatest possible variety of backgrounds.'" The Court also held that the law school's limited consideration of race as a "plus" factor in an individualized, holistic, flexible assessment of each candidate was narrowly tailored to achieving these interests. The Court cautioned, however, that it believed that in twenty-five years, consideration of race in admissions—even in the limited fashion approved in *Grutter*—should no longer be necessary to achieve racial diversity. In a separate opinion, Thomas agreed with some of the majority's opinions, but in the main he rejected the view that race consciousness in the law school's admissions policy was constitutional.

About the author

Clarence Thomas, the second African American justice of the U.S. Supreme Court, was born in Pin Point, Georgia, in 1948. Thomas's mother raised him and his two siblings, Myers and Emma, after their father abandoned the family. Pin Point was an impoverished community; the town lacked a sewage system and paved roads. When Thomas was seven years old, a fire destroyed the family's Pin Point home, and Thomas's mother sent the future justice and his younger brother to live with their maternal grandparents, Myers and Christine Anderson, in Savannah, Georgia.

The Andersons provided what many African Americans considered a middle-class upbringing for the Thomas brothers. That did not shield the young Clarence from being put to work by his self-made grandfather, who often woke the child at 3 a.m. to help with his fuel business and to complete household chores. The Andersons paid for their grandson's private school education at the all-black elementary school run by Saint Benedict the Moor Catholic Church in Savannah.

Thomas distinguished himself as an exceptional student at Saint Benedict, despite feeling that he did not fit in with the middle-class African American children there. For example, he still had a Creole-based Gullah accent, a result of the time he had spent with his grandfather on the coasts of South Carolina and Georgia. Some classmates nicknamed Thomas "ABC: America's Blackest Child" because of his full lips, coarse hair, and dark skin. Nonetheless, as one of his biographers has noted, Thomas was a "legend" in the black Catholic community, serving as an altar boy and volunteering at Mass and also as a recruiter for Saint Benedict at area elementary schools.

After two years at the Catholic all-black Saint Pius X High School, Thomas enrolled at Saint John Vianney Minor Seminary, an exclusive virtually all-white school on an island six miles from Savannah. Thomas wanted to become the first African American priest in Savannah; he was one of only two African American seminarians during the 1964 school year. Thomas excelled at the seminary, despite feeling alienated there by some of the white seminarians.

Upon graduating from Saint John Vianney in 1967, Thomas enrolled at Conception Seminary in northwest Missouri. Thomas spent only one year in Missouri owing to both the fundamental changes that occurred within the Catholic Church during the 1960s and the racial turmoil of the times. On April 4, 1968, a fellow seminarian, upon hearing that Martin Luther King, Jr., had been shot, used an epithet to state that he hoped King died. Disturbed by the racial tension at Conception, Thomas left Missouri for the College of the Holy Cross in Worcester, Massachusetts.

At Holy Cross, Thomas helped to form the school's first Black Student Union, immersed himself in the speeches of Malcolm X, grew his hair out into an Afro, and daily donned what many of his classmates considered a Black Panther–style outfit: army fatigues, leather jacket, and a beret. During his senior year at Holy Cross, he became less enthused with protesting and being what he considered "drunk with anger." He instead focused on putting his education to use as a civil rights lawyer in Savannah.

During his senior year at Holy Cross, Thomas decided to next attend Yale Law School. While at Yale, he worked hard to distinguish himself. During his summer of law school, he worked at one of the most prominent civil rights law firms in Georgia. Thomas impressed the partners at the Georgia firm, who offered him a position, but he declined, focusing on obtaining a job in private practice. However, he eventually instead accepted a position with the attorney general of Missouri, John C. Danforth. Thomas worked as an assistant attorney general under Danforth, primarily handling tax matters. After Danforth's election to the U.S. Senate, Thomas soon moved to Washington, D.C., to work as a legislative assistant in his office.

In 1981, President Ronald Reagan appointed Thomas as the assistant secretary of education for the Office of Civil Rights in the U.S. Department of Education and subsequently appointed him chairman of the U.S. Equal Employment Opportunity Commission. In June 1989, President George H. W. Bush appointed Thomas to the U.S. Court of Appeals for the District of Columbia Circuit. On July 1, 1991, following Justice Thurgood Marshall's announcement of his retirement, President Bush nominated Thomas to the Supreme Court of the United States. After a contentious hearing, the Senate confirmed his nomination by a vote of fifty-two to forty-eight, the narrowest margin in favor of a Supreme Court nominee in over a century. With his appointment, Thomas became the second African American Supreme Court justice in history. Upon joining the Court, he immediately aligned himself with its most conservative members. Justice Thomas regularly voted to strike down affirmative action programs, to limit the right to reproductive freedom, and to narrow the scope of federal civil rights laws, such as the Voting Rights Act of 1965.

Explanation and Analysis of the Document

The case involved a challenge to the constitutionality of the University of Michigan Law School's admission policies, under which the race of any applicant from a historically disadvantaged minority group was considered a "plus" factor in the evaluation of that applicant. The plaintiff, an unsuccessful white applicant, sued the law school, alleging that its use of such affirmative action in admissions violated the Constitution's equal protection clause. The Court upheld the law school's admission program, holding that institutions of higher education may consider an applicant's race as one of many factors in a holistic, individualized assessment of each applicant in an effort to compose a diverse student body. Justice Thomas concurred in the majority's reasoning that affirmative action programs should be viewed with suspicion, but he dissented from the Court's holding that the law school's admission program passed such heightened judicial scrutiny.

In Part IV, Justice Thomas asserts that Justice O'Connor's majority opinion erroneously applied the governing legal standards in deciding the case. Specifically, Thomas contends that the law school's admissions program is not "narrowly tailored" to achieve its educational interest. Under the Court's precedents, he writes, governmental consideration of race is permitted only when it is the single method of achieving a compelling goal. Thomas argues that such is not the case in *Grutter*. Among other possibilities, he believes that if the law school were to adopt "different admissions methods, such as accepting all students who meet minimum qualifications"—perhaps using lower Law School Admission Test and grade-point-average thresholds—"the Law School could achieve its vision of the racially aesthetic student body without the use of racial discrimination." The majority opinion did not require the law school to explore such possibilities because it deferred to the school's judgment that its present admissions program was necessary, doing so in view of the educational autonomy grounded in the First Amendment that has traditionally been granted to institutions of higher education. Thomas argues, however, that First Amendment notions of academic freedom do not lessen the scrutiny that courts should apply when assessing whether a state university's race-conscious action violates the equal protection clause.

In Part V of his opinion Thomas criticizes the law school's use of highly selective admissions criteria, primarily the Law School Admissions Test (LSAT). He argues that no law school is required to use the LSAT as its primary admissions criterion, but having decided to do so, a law school must be aware of the racially disproportionate results in LSAT scores. Thus, having determined to rely heavily on the LSAT, Thomas states, the law school "must accept the constitutional burdens that come with this decision." The law school, he states, should not be permitted to employ an admissions device that will cause a racial imbalance and then seek to correct that imbalance through consideration of race in the admissions process.

Thomas contests the idea that affirmative action is beneficial to racial minorities in Part VI. To the contrary, such programs, he writes—once more quoting his *Adarand* concurrence—are a form of discrimination that "engender[s] attitudes of superiority or, alternatively, provoke[s] resentment among those who believe that they have been wronged by the government's use of race," and they also "stamp minorities with a badge of inferiority and may cause them to develop dependencies or to adopt an attitude that they are 'entitled' to preferences." Justice Thomas here expands upon the "stigma" he believed is imposed on racial minorities by affirmative action in university admissions:

The majority of blacks are admitted to the Law School because of discrimination, and because of this policy all are tarred as undeserving.... When blacks take positions in the highest places of government, industry, or academia, it is an open question today whether their skin color played a part in their advancement. The question itself is the stigma—because either racial discrimination did play a role, in which case the person may be deemed "otherwise unqualified," or it did not, in which case asking the question itself unfairly marks those blacks who would succeed without discrimination.

Finally, in Part VII of his opinion, Thomas states that he agrees with the majority opinion on two points. First, he agrees that law schools may not distinguish between different groups of underrepresented minorities in admissions. Second, he agrees with the majority's remark that any consideration of race in admissions by state-run law schools would be illegal in twenty-five years, as he believes them to be illegal currently.

Justice Thomas's opinion in *Grutter* is grounded in his view that the Fourteenth Amendment's equal protection clause, both textually and as a matter of the framers' original intent, presumptively forbids all government consideration of race, regardless of whether the government is acting to aid or injure historically oppressed groups. Other justices have criticized this view for focusing on formal equal treatment rather than—or in addition to—issues of substantive equality. Justices and legal scholars supporting substantive equality have argued that equal protection sometimes permits differential treatment to account for unequal circumstances and that the framers of the equal protection clause themselves engaged in a form of race-conscious "affirmative action," through the variety of measures directly and solely aimed at aiding free blacks after the Civil War.

Audience

Supreme Court opinions are addressed to the parties affected by the judgment, such as private or governmental litigants whose conduct is found to be illegal or unconstitutional. Supreme Court opinions are also addressed to the lower courts, where they either affirm the lower courts' judgments in the case at hand or reverse them by clarifying, modifying, or overruling earlier cases or adopting a new interpretation of the Constitution or a federal statute. Separate concurring or dissenting opinions, such as Justice Thomas's in *Grutter*, are not part of the Court's ruling and, as such, are not controlling law. Such opinions, therefore, are most directly addressed to the other justices on the Supreme Court, as intended to explain areas of disagreement. Perhaps more important, dissenting opinions are also addressed to a much larger audience of lower-court judges, lawyers, academics, and the general public to explain why the dissenting justice believes the Court's holding to be incorrect and to convince this larger audience that the dissenting justice's view is correct. Among this audience may be individuals who could contribute in the future, as litigants, lawyers, or justices, to the reversal of the opinion in question.

Impact

Justice Thomas's opinion in *Grutter* has been the subject of wide discussion in subsequent cases and legal scholarship regarding racial equality, diversity, and affirmative action. His view that the Constitution forbids the government from considering race under any circumstance was embraced by a plurality of the Court in *Parents Involved in Community Schools v. Seattle School District No. 1* (2007). In that case, the Court severely constrained the ability of school districts to consider race in making student assignments in order to prevent incidental resegregation of public schools. Meanwhile, legal scholars have engaged in debate over the views expressed by Thomas in his *Grutter* opinion. Some have noted that his "color-blind" position is inconsistent with his professed commitment to interpreting the Constitution according to the original intent of its drafters, because the very drafters of the equal protection clause enacted race-conscious laws to aid newly freed African Americans after the Civil War. Others have argued that while governmental color blindness in all circumstances might be a laudable ideal, it is not a practical solution in a society yet shaped by racial inequalities. As of early 2010, Thomas's view of the equal protection clause as forbidding the government from engaging in affirmative action to achieve or maintain diversity had not yet commanded the agreement of a majority of his colleagues on the Supreme Court.

Further Reading

♦ Books

Amar, Akhil Reed. *America's Constitution: A Biography*. New York: Random House, 2005.

Douglass, Frederick. "What the Black Man Wants." In *Let Nobody Turn Us Around*," ed. Manning Marable and Leith Mullings. Lanham, Md.: Rowman and Littlefield, 2009.

Hall, Kermit, ed. *The Oxford Companion to the Supreme Court of the United States*. New York: Oxford University Press, 1992.

Merida, Kevin, and Michael A. Fletcher. *Supreme Discomfort: The Divided Soul of Clarence Thomas*. New York: Doubleday, 2007.

Nixon, Richard M. *RN: The Memoirs of Richard Nixon*. New York: Grosset & Dunlap, 1978.

Thomas, Clarence. *My Grandfather's Son: A Memoir*. New York: Harper, 2007.

♦ Web Sites

"Grutter v. Bollinger (02-241) 539 U.S. 306 (2003): Opinion of the Court." Cornell University Law School "Legal Information Institute" Web site. http://www.law.cornell.edu/supct/html/02-241.ZO.html.

"The History of Affirmative Action Policies." In Motion Magazine Web site. http://www.inmotionmagazine.com/aahist.html.

Questions for Further Study

1. Compare this document with A. Leon Higginbotham: "An Open Letter to Justice Clarence Thomas from a Federal Judicial Colleague." Higginbotham was highly skeptical of Thomas's appointment to the Supreme Court, arguing that the new justice might set back the cause of civil rights. Do you think that Thomas confirmed Higginbotham's fears with his decision in *Grutter v. Bollinger*?

2. What is your opinion of the type of race-based admissions policy that was the bone of contention in this case? Do you believe such a policy is fair? Would you agree with Thomas that such a policy potentially stigmatizes African Americans?

3. Thomas uses quotations from the abolitionist Frederick Douglass and Justice John Marshall Harlan's dissent in the 1896 case *Plessy v. Ferguson*, which created the legal basis for Jim Crow segregation. What did Thomas gain from using these figures and their words in buttressing his argument?

4. Both the entry and the document make reference to the 1978 case *Regents of the University of California v. Bakke*. How did the outcome of *Grutter v. Bollinger* differ from that of *Bakke*? What might have changed in the social and legal environment to account for any difference?

5. The word *diversity* is often used in academic, business, and other environments to refer to the notion that all student bodies, workplaces, and the like benefit from the presence of people of various races and ethnicities. Do you believe this is true? How would you respond to the argument that historically black colleges lack racial diversity?

Essential Quotes

"The majority upholds the Law School's racial discrimination not by interpreting the people's Constitution, but by responding to a faddish slogan of the cognoscenti."

"The Constitution abhors classifications based on race, not only because those classifications can harm favored races or are based on illegitimate motives, but also because every time the government places citizens on racial registers and makes race relevant to the provision of burdens or benefits, it demeans us all."

Concurrence/Dissent in *Grutter v. Bollinger*

Full text of Justice Clarence Thomas's dissent

Justice Thomas, with whom Justice Scalia joins as to Parts I–VII, concurring in part and dissenting in part.

Frederick Douglass, speaking to a group of abolitionists almost 140 years ago, delivered a message lost on today's majority:

"[I]n regard to the colored people, there is always more that is benevolent, I perceive, than just, manifested towards us. What I ask for the negro is not benevolence, not pity, not sympathy, but simply *justice*. The American people have always been anxious to know what they shall do with us.... I have had but one answer from the beginning. Do nothing with us! Your doing with us has already played the mischief with us. Do nothing with us! If the apples will not remain on the tree of their own strength, if they are worm-eaten at the core, if they are early ripe and disposed to fall, let them fall! ... And if the negro cannot stand on his own legs, let him fall also. All I ask is, give him a chance to stand on his own legs! Let him alone! ... [Y]our interference is doing him positive injury." What the Black Man Wants: An Address Delivered in Boston, Massachusetts, on 26 January 1865, reprinted in 4 The Frederick Douglass Papers 59, 68 (J. Blassingame & J. McKivigan eds. 1991) (emphasis in original).

Like Douglass, I believe blacks can achieve in every avenue of American life without the meddling of university administrators. Because I wish to see all students succeed whatever their color, I share, in some respect, the sympathies of those who sponsor the type of discrimination advanced by the University of Michigan Law School (Law School). The Constitution does not, however, tolerate institutional devotion to the status quo in admissions policies when such devotion ripens into racial discrimination. Nor does the Constitution countenance the unprecedented deference the Court gives to the Law School, an approach inconsistent with the very concept of " strict scrutiny."

No one would argue that a university could set up a lower general admission standard and then impose heightened requirements only on black applicants. Similarly, a university may not maintain a high admission standard and grant exemptions to favored races. The Law School, of its own choosing, and for its own purposes, maintains an exclusionary admissions system that it knows produces racially disproportionate results. Racial discrimination is not a permissible solution to the self-inflicted wounds of this elitist admissions policy.

The majority upholds the Law School's racial discrimination not by interpreting the people's Constitution, but by responding to a faddish slogan of the cognoscenti. Nevertheless, I concur in part in the Court's opinion. First, I agree with the Court insofar as its decision, which approves of only one racial classification, confirms that further use of race in admissions remains unlawful. Second, I agree with the Court's holding that racial discrimination in higher education admissions will be illegal in 25 years. See *ante*, at 31 (stating that racial discrimination will no longer be narrowly tailored, or "necessary to further" a compelling state interest, in 25 years). I respectfully dissent from the remainder of the Court's opinion and the judgment, however, because I believe that the Law School's current use of race violates the Equal Protection Clause and that the Constitution means the same thing today as it will in 300 months.

body contains a "critical mass" of underrepresented minority students. Attaining "diversity," whatever it means, is the mechanism by which the Law School obtains educational benefits, not an end of itself. The Law School, however, apparently believes that only a racially mixed student body can lead to the educational benefits it seeks. How, then, is the Law School's interest in these allegedly unique educational "benefits" *not* simply the forbidden interest in "racial balancing," *ante*, at 17, that the majority expressly rejects?

A distinction between these two ideas (unique educational benefits based on racial aesthetics and race for its own sake) is purely sophistic—so much so that the majority uses them interchangeably. Compare *ante*, at 16 ("[T]he Law School has a compelling interest in attaining a diverse student body"), with *ante*, at 21 (referring to the "compelling interest in securing the *educational benefits* of a diverse student body" (emphasis added)). The Law School's argument, as facile as it is, can only be understood in one way: Classroom aesthetics yields educational benefits, racially discriminatory admissions policies are required to achieve the right racial mix, and therefore the policies are required to achieve the educational benefits. It is the *educational benefits* that are the end, or allegedly compelling state interest, not "diversity." But see *ante*, at 20 (citing the need for "openness and integrity of the educational institutions that provide [legal] training" without reference to any consequential educational benefits).

One must also consider the Law School's refusal to entertain changes to its current admissions system that might produce the same educational benefits. The Law School adamantly disclaims any race-neutral alternative that would reduce "academic selectivity," which would in turn "require the Law School to become a very different institution, and to sacrifice a core part of its educational mission." Brief for Respondents Bollinger et al. 33–36. In other words, the Law School seeks to improve marginally the education it offers without sacrificing too much of its exclusivity and elite status.

The proffered interest that the majority vindicates today, then, is not simply "diversity." Instead the Court upholds the use of racial discrimination as a tool to advance the Law School's interest in offering a marginally superior education while maintaining an elite institution. Unless each constituent part of this state interest is of pressing public necessity, the Law School's use of race is unconstitutional. I find each of them to fall far short of this standard.

III

◆ A

A close reading of the Court's opinion reveals that all of its legal work is done through one conclusory statement: The Law School has a "compelling interest in securing the educational benefits of a diverse student body." *Ante*, at 21. No serious effort is made to explain how these benefits fit with the state interests the Court has recognized (or rejected) as compelling, see Part I, *supra*, or to place any theoretical constraints on an enterprising Court's desire to discover still more justifications for racial discrimination. In the absence of any explanation, one might expect the Court to fall back on the judicial policy of *stare decisis*. But the Court eschews even this weak defense of its holding, shunning an analysis of the extent to which Justice Powell's opinion in *Regents of Univ. of Cal. v. Bakke*, (1978), is binding, *ante*, at 13, in favor of an unfounded wholesale adoption of it.

Justice Powell's opinion in *Bakke* and the Court's decision today rest on the fundamentally flawed proposition that racial discrimination can be contextualized so that a goal, such as classroom aesthetics, can be compelling in one context but not in another. This "we know it when we see it" approach to evaluating state interests is not capable of judicial application. Today, the Court insists on radically expanding the range of permissible uses of race to something as trivial (by comparison) as the assembling of a law school class. I can only presume that the majority's failure to justify its decision by reference to any principle arises from the absence of any such principle. See Part VI, *infra*.

◆ B

Under the proper standard, there is no pressing public necessity in maintaining a public law school at all and, it follows, certainly not an elite law school. Likewise, marginal improvements in legal education do not qualify as a compelling state interest.

1. While legal education at a public university may be good policy or otherwise laudable, it is obviously not a pressing public necessity when the correct legal standard is applied. Additionally, circumstantial evidence as to whether a state activity is of pressing public necessity can be obtained by asking whether all States feel compelled to engage in that activity. Evidence that States, in general, engage in a certain activity by no means demonstrates that the activity constitutes a pressing public necessity, given the expansive role of government in today's society. The fact that some fraction of the States reject a particular enterprise, however, creates a presumption that the enterprise itself is not a compelling state interest. In this sense, the absence of a public, American Bar Association (ABA) accredited, law school in Alaska, Delaware, Massachusetts, New Hampshire, and Rhode Island, see ABA–LSAC Official Guide to ABA-Approved Law Schools (W. Margolis, B. Gordon, J. Puskarz, & D. Rosenlieb, eds. 2004) (hereinafter ABA–LSAC Guide), provides further evidence that Michigan's maintenance of the Law School does not constitute a compelling state interest.
2. As the foregoing makes clear, Michigan has no compelling interest in having a law school at all,

much less an *elite* one. Still, even assuming that a State may, under appropriate circumstances, demonstrate a cognizable interest in having an elite law school, Michigan has failed to do so here.

This Court has limited the scope of equal protection review to interests and activities that occur within that State's jurisdiction. The Court held in *Missouri ex rel. Gaines v. Canada*, (1938), that Missouri could not satisfy the demands of "separate but equal" by paying for legal training of blacks at neighboring state law schools, while maintaining a segregated law school within the State. The equal protection "obligation is imposed by the Constitution upon the States severally as governmental entities—each responsible for its own laws establishing the rights and duties of persons within its borders. It is an obligation the burden of which cannot be cast by one State upon another, and no State can be excused from performance *by what another State may do or fail to do*. That separate responsibility of each State within its own sphere is of the essence of statehood maintained under our dual system." *Id.*, at 350 (emphasis added).

The Equal Protection Clause, as interpreted by the Court in *Gaines*, does not permit States to justify racial discrimination on the basis of what the rest of the Nation "may do or fail to do." The only interests that can satisfy the Equal Protection Clause's demands are those found within a State's jurisdiction.

The only cognizable state interests vindicated by operating a public law school are, therefore, the education of that State's citizens and the training of that State's lawyers. James Campbell's address at the opening of the Law Department at the University of Michigan on October 3, 1859, makes this clear:

"It not only concerns *the State* that every one should have all reasonable facilities for preparing himself for any honest position in life to which he may aspire, but it also concerns *the community* that the Law should be taught and understood.... There is not an office *in the State* in which serious legal inquiries may not frequently arise.... In all these matters, public and private rights are constantly involved and discussed, and ignorance of the Law has frequently led to results deplorable and alarming.... [I]n the history of *this State*, in more than one instance, that ignorance has led to unlawful violence, and the shedding of innocent blood." E. Brown, Legal Education at Michigan 1859–1959, pp. 404–406 (1959) (emphasis added).

The Law School today, however, does precious little training of those attorneys who will serve the citizens of Michigan. In 2002, graduates of the University of Michigan Law School made up less than 6% of applicants to the Michigan bar, Michigan Lawyers Weekly, available at http://www.michiganlawyersweekly.com / barpassers0202.cfm, barpassers0702.cfm (all Internet materials as visited June of Sweezy to free speech. See, *e.g.*, *id.*, at 265 ("For a citizen to be made to forgo even a part of so basic a liberty as his political autonomy, the subordinating interest of the State must be compelling"). Still, claiming that the United States Reports "need not be burdened with proof," Justice Frankfurter also asserted that a "free society" depends on "free universities" and "[t]his means the exclusion of governmental intervention in the intellectual life of a university." *Id.*, at 262. According to Justice Frankfurter: "[I]t is the business of a university to provide that atmosphere which is most conducive to speculation, experiment and creation. It is an atmosphere in which there prevail 'the four essential freedoms' of a university—to determine for itself on academic grounds who may teach, what may be taught, how it shall be taught, and who may be admitted to study.'" *Id.*, at 263 (citation omitted).

In my view, "[i]t is the business" of this Court to explain itself when it cites provisions of the Constitution to invent new doctrines–including the idea that the First Amendment authorizes a public university to do what would otherwise violate the Equal Protection Clause. The majority fails in its summary effort to prove this point. The only source for the Court's conclusion that public universities are entitled to deference even within the confines of strict scrutiny is Justice Powell's opinion in *Bakke*. Justice Powell, for his part, relied only on Justice Frankfurter's opinion in *Sweezy* and the Court's decision in *Keyishian v. Board of Regents of Univ. of State of N. Y.*, (1967), to support his view that the First Amendment somehow protected a public university's use of race in admissions. *Bakke*, 438 U.S., at 312. *Keyishian* provides no answer to the question whether the Fourteenth Amendment's restrictions are relaxed when applied to public universities. In that case, the Court held that state statutes and regulations designed to prevent the "appointment or retention of 'subversive' persons in state employment," 385 U.S., at 592, violated the First Amendment for vagueness. The statutes covered all public employees and were not invalidated only as applied to university faculty members, although the Court appeared sympathetic to the notion of academic freedom, calling it a "special concern of the First Amendment." *Id.*, at 603. Again, however, the Court did not relax any independent constitutional restrictions on public universities.

I doubt that when Justice Frankfurter spoke of governmental intrusions into the independence of universities, he was thinking of the Constitution's ban on racial discrimination. The majority's broad deference to both the Law School's judgment that racial aesthetics leads to educational benefits and its stubborn refusal to alter the status quo in admissions methods finds no basis in the Constitution or decisions of this Court.

♦ B

1. The Court's deference to the Law School's conclusion that its racial experimentation leads to educational benefits will, if adhered to, have serious collateral consequences. The Court relies heavily on social science evidence to justify its deference. See *ante*, at 18–20; but see also Rothman, Lipset, & Nevitte, Racial Diversity Reconsidered, 151 Public Interest 25 (2003) (finding that the racial mix of a student body produced by racial discrimination of the type practiced by the Law School in fact hinders students' perception of academic quality). The Court never acknowledges, however, the growing evidence that racial (and other sorts) of heterogeneity actually impairs learning among black students. See, *e.g.*, Flowers & Pascarella, Cognitive Effects of College Racial Composition on African American Students After 3 Years of College, 40 J. of College Student Development 669, 674 (1999) (concluding that black students experience superior cognitive development at Historically Black Colleges (HBCs) and that, even among blacks, "a substantial diversity moderates the cognitive effects of attending an HBC"); Allen, The Color of Success: African-American College Student Outcomes at Predominantly White and Historically Black Public Colleges and Universities, 62 Harv. Educ. Rev. 26, 35 (1992) (finding that black students attending HBCs report higher academic achievement than those attending predominantly white colleges).

   At oral argument in *Gratz v. Bollinger*, *ante*, counsel for respondents stated that "most every single one of [the HBCs] do have diverse student bodies." Tr. of Oral Arg. in No. 02–516, p. 52. What precisely counsel meant by "diverse" is indeterminate, but it is reported that in 2000 at Morehouse College, one of the most distinguished HBC's in the Nation, only 0.1% of the student body was white, and only 0.2% was Hispanic. College Admissions Data Handbook 2002–2003, p. 613 (43d ed. 2002) (hereinafter College Admissions Data Handbook). And at Mississippi Valley State University, a public HBC, only 1.1% of the freshman class in 2001 was white. *Id.*, at 603. If there is a "critical mass" of whites at these institutions, then "critical mass" is indeed a very small proportion.

   The majority grants deference to the Law School's "assessment that diversity will, in fact, yield educational benefits," *ante*, at 16. It follows, therefore, that an HBC's assessment that racial homogeneity will yield educational benefits would similarly be given deference. An HBC's rejection of white applicants in order to maintain racial homogeneity seems permissible, therefore, under the majority's view of the Equal Protection Clause. But see *United States v. Fordice*, 748 (1992) (Thomas, J., concurring) ("Obviously, a State cannot maintain ... traditions by closing particular institutions, historically white or historically black, to particular racial groups"). Contained within today's majority opinion is the seed of a new constitutional justification for a concept I thought long and rightly rejected—racial segregation.

2. Moreover one would think, in light of the Court's decision in *United States v. Virginia*, (1996), that before being given license to use racial discrimination, the Law Schoolwould be required to radically reshape its admissions process, even to the point of sacrificing some elements of its character. In *Virginia*, a majority of the Court, without a word about academic freedom, accepted the all-male Virginia Military Institute's (VMI) representation that some changes in its "adversative" method of education would be required with the admission of women, *id.*, at 540, but did not defer to VMI's judgment that these changes would be too great. Instead, the Court concluded that they were "manageable." *Id.*, at 551, n. 19. That case involved sex discrimination, which is subjected to intermediate, not strict, scrutiny. *Id.*, at 533; *Craig v. Boren*, 197 (1976). So in *Virginia*, where the standard of review dictated that greater flexibility be granted to VMI's educational policies than the Law School deserves here, this Court gave no deference. Apparently where the status quo being defended is that of the elite establishment—here the Law School—rather than

a less fashionable Southern military institution, the Court will defer without serious inquiry and without regard to the applicable legal standard.

◆ C

Virginia is also notable for the fact that the Court relied on the "experience" of formerly single-sex institutions, such as the service academies, to conclude that admission of women to VMI would be "manageable." 518 U.S., at 544–545. Today, however, the majority ignores the "experience" of those institutions that have been forced to abandon explicit racial discrimination in admissions.

The sky has not fallen at Boalt Hall at the University of California, Berkeley, for example. Prior to Proposition 209's adoption of Cal. Const., Art. 1, §31(a), which bars the State from "grant[ing] preferential treatment … on the basis of race … in the operation of … public education," Boalt Hall enrolled 20 blacks and 28 Hispanics in its first-year class for 1996. In 2002, without deploying express racial discrimination in admissions, Boalt's entering class enrolled 14 blacks and 36 Hispanics. University of California Law and Medical School Enrollments, available at http://www.ucop.edu/acadadv/datamgmt/ lawmed/ law-enrolls-eth2.html. Total underrepresented minority student enrollment at Boalt Hall now exceeds 1996 levels. Apparently the Law School cannot be counted on to be as resourceful. The Court is willfully blind to the very real experience in California and elsewhere, which raises the inference that institutions with "reputation[s] for excellence," *ante*, at 16, 26, rivaling the Law School's have satisfied their sense of mission without resorting to prohibited racial discrimination.

V

Putting aside the absence of any legal support for the majority's reflexive deference, there is much to be said for the view that the use of tests and other measures to "predict" academic performance is a poor substitute for a system that gives every applicant a chance to prove he can succeed in the study of law. The rallying cry that in the absence of racial discrimination in admissions there would be a true meritocracy ignores the fact that the entire process is poisoned by numerous exceptions to "merit." For example, in the national debate on racial discrimination in higher education admissions, much has been made of the fact that elite institutions utilize a so-called "legacy" preference to give the children of alumni an advantage in admissions. This, and other, exceptions to a "true" meritocracy give the lie to protestations that merit admissions are in fact the order of the day at the Nation's universities. The Equal Protection Clause does not, however, prohibit the use of unseemly legacy preferences or many other kinds of arbitrary admissions procedures. What the Equal Protection Clause does prohibit are classifications made on the basis of race. So while legacy preferences can stand under the Constitution, racial discrimination cannot. I will not twist the Constitution to invalidate legacy preferences or otherwise impose my vision of higher education admissions on the Nation. The majority should similarly stay its impulse to validate faddish racial discrimination the Constitution clearly forbids.

In any event, there is nothing ancient, honorable, or constitutionally protected about "selective" admissions. The University of Michigan should be well aware that alternative methods have historically been used for the admission of students, for it brought to this country the German certificate system in the late 19th century. See H. Wechsler, The Qualified Student 16–39 (1977) (hereinafter Qualified Student). Under this system, a secondary school was certified by a university so that any graduate who completed the course offered by the school was offered admission to the university. The certification regime supplemented, and later virtually replaced (at least in the Midwest), the prior regime of rigorous subject-matter entrance examinations. *Id.*, at 57–58. The facially race-neutral "percent plans" now used in Texas, California, and Florida, see *ante*, at 28, are in many ways the descendents of the certificate system.

Certification was replaced by selective admissions in the beginning of the 20th century, as universities sought to exercise more control over the composition of their student bodies. Since its inception, selective admissions has been the vehicle for racial, ethnic, and religious tinkering and experimentation by university administrators. The initial driving force for the relocation of the selective function from the high school to the universities was the same desire to select racial winners and losers that the Law School exhibits today. Columbia, Harvard, and others infamously determined that they had "too many" Jews, just as today the Law School argues it would have "too many" whites if it could not discriminate in its admissions process. See Qualified Student 155–168 (Columbia); H. Broun & G.

Britt, Christians Only: A Study in Prejudice 53–54 (1931) (Harvard).

Columbia employed intelligence tests precisely because Jewish applicants, who were predominantly immigrants, scored worse on such tests. Thus, Columbia could claim (falsely) that "'[w]e have not eliminated boys because they were Jews and do not propose to do so. We have honestly attempted to eliminate the lowest grade of applicant [through the use of intelligence testing] and it turns out that a good many of the low grade men are New York City Jews.'" Letter from Herbert E. Hawkes, dean of Columbia College, to E. B. Wilson, June 16, 1922 (reprinted in Qualified Student 160–161). In other words, the tests were adopted with full knowledge of their disparate impact. Cf. *DeFunis v. Odegaard*, 335 (1974) (*per curiam*) (Douglas, J., dissenting).

Similarly no modern law school can claim ignorance of the poor performance of blacks, relatively speaking, on the Law School Admissions Test (LSAT). Nevertheless, law schools continue to use the test and then attempt to "correct" for black underperformance by using racial discrimination in admissions so as to obtain their aesthetic student body. The Law School's continued adherence to measures it knows produce racially skewed results is not entitled to deference by this Court. See Part IV, *supra*. The Law School itself admits that the test is imperfect, as it must, given that it regularly admits students who score at or below 150 (the national median) on the test. See App. 156–203 (showing that, between 1995 and 2000, the Law School admitted 37 students—27 of whom were black; 31 of whom were "underrepresented minorities"—with LSAT scores of 150 or lower). And the Law School's *amici* cannot seem to agree on the fundamental question whether the test itself is useful. Compare Brief for Law School Admission Council as *Amicus Curiae* 12 ("LSAT scores ... are an effective predictor of students' performance in law school") with Brief for Harvard Black Law Students Association et al. as *Amici Curiae* 27 ("Whether [the LSAT] measure[s] objective merit.... is certainly questionable").

Having decided to use the LSAT, the Law School must accept the constitutional burdens that come with this decision. The Law School may freely continue to employ the LSAT and other allegedly merit-based standards in whatever fashion it likes. What the Equal Protection Clause forbids, but the Court today allows, is the use of these standards hand-in-hand with racial discrimination. An infinite variety of admissions methods are available to the Law School. Considering all of the radical thinking that has historically occurred at this country's universities, the Law School's intractable approach toward admissions is striking.

The Court will not even deign to make the Law School try other methods, however, preferring instead to grant a 25-year license to violate the Constitution. And the same Court that had the courage to order the desegregation of all public schools in the South now fears, on the basis of platitudes rather than principle, to force the Law School to abandon a decidedly imperfect admissions regime that provides the basis for racial discrimination.

VI

The absence of any articulated legal principle supporting the majority's principal holding suggests another rationale. I believe what lies beneath the Court's decision today are the benighted notions that one can tell when racial discrimination benefits (rather than hurts) minority groups, see *Adarand*, 515 U.S., at 239 (Scalia, J., concurring in part and concurring in judgment), and that racial discrimination is necessary to remedy general societal ills. This Court's precedents supposedly settled both issues, but clearly the majority still cannot commit to the principle that racial classifications are *per se* harmful and that almost no amount of benefit in the eye of the beholder can justify such classifications.

Putting aside what I take to be the Court's implicit rejection of *Adarand*'s holding that beneficial and burdensome racial classifications are equally invalid, I must contest the notion that the Law School's discrimination benefits those admitted as a result of it. The Court spends considerable time discussing the impressive display of *amicus* support for the Law School in this case from all corners of society. *Ante*, at 18–19. But nowhere in any of the filings in this Court is any evidence that the purported "beneficiaries" of this racial discrimination prove themselves by performing at (or even near) the same level as those students who receive no preferences. Cf. Thernstrom & Thernstrom, Reflections on the Shape of the River,

46 UCLA L. Rev. 1583, 1605–1608 (1999) (discussing the failure of defenders of racial discrimination in admissions to consider the fact that its "beneficiaries" are underperforming in the classroom).

The silence in this case is deafening to those of us who view higher education's purpose as imparting knowledge and skills to students, rather than a communal, rubber-stamp, credentialing process. The Law School is not looking for those students who, despite a lower LSAT score or undergraduate grade point average, will succeed in the study of law. The Law School seeks only a façade—it is sufficient that the class looks right, even if it does not perform right.

The Law School tantalizes unprepared students with the promise of a University of Michigan degree and all of the opportunities that it offers. These overmatched students take the bait, only to find that they cannot succeed in the cauldron of competition. And this mismatch crisis is not restricted to elite institutions. See T. Sowell, Race and Culture 176–177 (1994) ("Even if most minority students are able to meet the normal standards at the 'average' range of colleges and universities, the systematic mismatching of minority students begun at the top can mean that such students are generally overmatched throughout all levels of higher education"). Indeed, to cover the tracks of the aestheticists, this cruel farce of racial discrimination must continue—in selection for the Michigan Law Review, see University of Michigan Law School Student Handbook 2002–2003, pp. 39–40 (noting the presence of a "diversity plan" for admission to the review), and in hiring at law firms and for judicial clerkships—until the "beneficiaries" are no longer tolerated. While these students may graduate with law degrees, there is no evidence that they have received a qualitatively better legal education (or become better lawyers) than if they had gone to a less "elite" law school for which they were better prepared. And the aestheticists will never address the real problems facing "underrepresented minorities," instead continuing their social experiments on other people's children.

Beyond the harm the Law School's racial discrimination visits upon its test subjects, no social science has disproved the notion that this discrimination "engender[s] attitudes of superiority or, alternatively, provoke[s] resentment among those who believe that they have been wronged by the government's use of race." *Adarand*, 515 U.S., at 241 (Thomas, J., concurring in part and concurring in judgment). "These programs stamp minorities with a badge of inferiority and may cause them to develop dependencies or to adopt an attitude that they are 'entitled' to preferences." *Ibid.*

It is uncontested that each year, the Law School admits a handful of blacks who would be admitted in the absence of racial discrimination. See Brief for Respondents Bollinger et al. 6. Who can differentiate between those who belong and those who do not? The majority of blacks are admitted to the Law School because of discrimination, and because of this policy all are tarred as undeserving. This problem of stigma does not depend on determinacy as to whether those stigmatized are actually the "beneficiaries" of racial discrimination. When blacks take positions in the highest places of government, industry, or academia, it is an open question today whether their skin color played a part in their advancement. The question itself is the stigma—because either racial discrimination did play a role, in which case the person may be deemed "otherwise unqualified," or it did not, in which case asking the question itself unfairly marks those blacks who would succeed without discrimination. Is this what the Court means by "visibly open"? *Ante*, at 20.

Finally, the Court's disturbing reference to the importance of the country's law schools as training grounds meant to cultivate "a set of leaders with legitimacy in the eyes of the citizenry," *ibid.*, through the use of racial discrimination deserves discussion. As noted earlier, the Court has soundly rejected the remedying of societal discrimination as a justification for governmental use of race. *Wygant*, 476 U.S., at 276 (plurality opinion); *Croson*, 488 U.S., at 497 (plurality opinion); *id.*, at 520–521 (Scalia, J., concurring in judgment). For those who believe that every racial disproportionality in our society is caused by some kind of racial discrimination, there can be no distinction between remedying societal discrimination and erasing racial disproportionalities in the country's leadership caste. And if the lack of proportional racial representation among our leaders is not caused by societal discrimination, then "fixing" it is even less of a pressing public necessity.

The Court's civics lesson presents yet another example of judicial selection of a theory of political representation based on skin color—an endeavor I have previously rejected. See *Holder v. Hall*, 899 (1994) (Thomas, J., concurring in judgment). The majority appears to believe that broader utopian goals justify the Law School's use of race, but "[t]he Equal Protection Clause commands the elimination of racial barriers, not their creation in order to satisfy our theory as to how society ought to be organized." *DeFunis*, 416 U.S., at 342 (Douglas, J., dissenting).

VII.

As the foregoing makes clear, I believe the Court's opinion to be, in most respects, erroneous. I do, however, find two points on which I agree.

♦ A

First, I note that the issue of unconstitutional racial discrimination among the groups the Law School prefers is not presented in this case, because petitioner has never argued that the Law School engages in such a practice, and the Law School maintains that it does not. See Brief for Respondents Bollinger et al. 32, n. 50, and 6–7, n. 7. I join the Court's opinion insofar as it confirms that this type of racial discrimination remains unlawful. *Ante*, at 13–15. Under today's decision, it is still the case that racial discrimination that does not help a university to enroll an unspecified number, or "critical mass," of underrepresented minority students is unconstitutional. Thus, the Law School may not discriminate in admissions between similarly situated blacks and Hispanics, or between whites and Asians. This is so because preferring black to Hispanic applicants, for instance, does nothing to further the interest recognized by the majority today. Indeed, the majority describes such racial balancing as "patently unconstitutional." *Ante*, at 17. Like the Court, *ante*, at 24, I express no opinion as to whether the Law School's current admissions program runs afoul of this prohibition.

♦ B

The Court also holds that racial discrimination in admissions should be given another 25 years before it is deemed no longer narrowly tailored to the Law School's fabricated compelling state interest. *Ante*, at 30. While I agree that in 25 years the practices of the Law School will be illegal, they

are, for the reasons I have given, illegal now. The majority does not and cannot rest its time limitation on any evidence that the gap in credentials between black and white students is shrinking or will be gone in that timeframe. In recent years there has been virtually no change, for example, in the proportion of law school applicants with LSAT scores of 165 and higher who are black. In 1993 blacks constituted 1.1% of law school applicants in that score range, though they represented 11.1% of all applicants. Law School Admission Council, National Statistical Report (1994) (hereinafter LSAC Statistical Report). In 2000 the comparable numbers were 1.0% and 11.3%. LSAC Statistical Report (2001). No one can seriously contend, and the Court does not, that the racial gap in academic credentials will disappear in 25 years. Nor is the Court's holding that racial discrimination will be unconstitutional in 25 years made contingent on the gap closing in that time.

Indeed, the very existence of racial discrimination of the type practiced by the Law School may impede the narrowing of the LSAT testing gap. An applicant's LSAT score can improve dramatically with preparation, but such preparation is a cost, and there must be sufficient benefits attached to an improved score to justify additional study. Whites scoring between 163 and 167 on the LSAT are routinely rejected by the Law School, and thus whites aspiring to admission at the Law School have every incentive to improve their score to levels above that range. See App. 199 (showing that in 2000, 209 out of 422 white applicants were rejected in this scoring range). Blacks, on the other hand, are nearly guaranteed admission if they score above 155. *Id.*, at 198 (showing that 63 out of 77 black applicants are accepted with LSAT scores above 155). As admission prospects approach certainty, there is no incentive for the black applicant to continue to prepare for the LSAT once he is reasonably assured of achieving the requisite score. It is far from certain that the LSAT test-taker's behavior is responsive to the Law School's admissions policies. Nevertheless, the possibility remains that this racial discrimination will help fulfill the bigot's prophecy about black underperformance—just as it confirms the conspiracy theorist's belief that "institutional racism" is at fault for every racial disparity in our society.

I therefore can understand the imposition of a 25-year time limit only as a holding that the deference the Court pays to the Law School's educational judgments and refusal to change its admissions policies will itself expire. At that point these policies will clearly have failed to "'eliminat[e] the [perceived] need for any racial or ethnic'" discrimination because the academic credentials gap will still be there. *Ante*,

Document Text

at 30 (quoting Nathanson & Bartnika, The Constitutionality of Preferential Treatment for Minority Applicants to Professional Schools, 58 Chicago Bar Rec. 282, 293 (May–June 1977)). The Court defines this time limit in terms of narrow tailoring, see *ante*, at 30, but I believe this arises from its refusal to define rigorously the broad state interest vindicated today. Cf. Part II, *supra*. With these observations, I join the last sentence of Part III of the opinion of the Court.

For the immediate future, however, the majority has placed its *imprimatur* on a practice that can only weaken the principle of equality embodied in the Declaration of Independence and the Equal Protection Clause. "Our Constitution is color-blind, and neither knows nor tolerates classes among citizens." *Plessy v. Ferguson*, 559 (1896) (Harlan, J., dissenting). It has been nearly 140 years since Frederick Douglass asked the intellectual ancestors of the Law School to "[d]o nothing with us!" and the Nation adopted the Fourteenth Amendment. Now we must wait another 25 years to see this principle of equality vindicated. I therefore respectfully dissent from the remainder of the Court's opinion and the judgment.

Glossary

Amicus Curiae: Latin for "friend of the court," referring to briefs submitted by outside parties or groups in support of one position or the other

Equal Protection Clause: the section of the Fourteenth Amendment to the Constitution that states that "no state shall … deny to any person within its jurisdiction the equal protection of the laws"

Frederick Douglass: the preeminent nineteenth-century American abolitionist and former slave

inter alia: Latin for "among other things"

intermediate scrutiny: a legal test that requires a law or policy to further an important government interest in a way that is substantially related to that interest

Justice Frankfurter: Felix Frankfurter, a twentieth-century justice who was an advocate of judicial restraint

Justice Powell: Lewis Franklin Powell, a twentieth-century justice known as a moderate

per curiam: referring to a decision issued "by the court" rather than a particular justice or group of justices

stare decisis: Latin for "to abide by decided cases," referring to the principle of following judicial precedent

strict scrutiny: a test applied by the courts to a law or policy requiring the government to show a compelling interest in the regulation and that the regulation is narrowly tailored to achieve that interest

President George W. Bush meets with President-elect Obama in the Oval Office on November 10, 2008. By White House photo by Eric Draper [Public domain], via Wikimedia Commons

Barack Obama: "A More Perfect Union"

"What we have already achieved gives us hope — the audacity to hope — for what we can and must achieve tomorrow."

Overview

Obama gave what may have been the best speech of his presidential campaign at a time when his quest for the Democratic nomination was in peril. On March 13, 2008, the ABC evening newscast showed video clips from sermons that the Reverend Jeremiah Wright gave to his congregation at the Trinity United Church of Christ in Chicago after the attacks of September 11, 2001. Wright fulminated against American racism as well as U.S. foreign policy, alleging that both bore responsibility for the terrorist strikes in New York City and Washington, D.C. In one clip, he thundered, "God damn America." Within hours, cable news programs and Internet sites were saturated with his remarks.

The outrage over Wright's incendiary statements quickly created political problems for Obama. Wright was not only Obama's pastor but also a spiritual mentor of his for two decades. It was from one of Wright's sermons that Obama learned the phrase "the audacity of hope," which he incorporated into his keynote address at the 2004 Democratic convention and used as the title of the book he published in 2006, in which he explained the political ideas that would be central to his campaign for president. Critics questioned Obama's judgment and even his values, wondering how he could have such a close relationship with someone who held such extreme opinions. Some political observers argued that the inflammatory views of Obama's African American minister would add to his problems in winning support among working-class white voters, a critical constituency for any Democratic presidential nominee. Those voters had helped Senator Hillary Rodham Clinton win the Ohio primary in early March and surge to a lead in the polls in Pennsylvania, the state that would hold the next primary on April 22.

Obama decided to deal with the Wright controversy by giving an address on race, a topic about which he had been considering a speech for months. He wrote the address mainly by himself in three days and decided to deliver it at a place symbolizing shared American values, the National Constitution Center in Philadelphia.

About the Author

Barack Hussein Obama was born in Honolulu on August 4, 1961, and spent most of his youth in Hawaii. His father, who came to the United States from Kenya to pursue higher education, left the family when Obama was two years old and eventually returned to the country of his birth; Obama's parents divorced in 1964. His mother, Stanley Ann Dunham, later married an Indonesian who was studying at the University of Hawaii. In 1967 the family moved to Jakarta, and Obama became familiar with Indonesian culture and society. His mother supplemented his formal schooling with tutorials in African American history. She also made her son get up at 4 am five days each week to take English lessons before going to school.

In 1971 Obama returned to Hawaii to live with his maternal grandparents and attend an elite private academy, the Punahou School. During the Christmas season that year, his mother and father joined him for an extended visit. This two-week family reunion provided Obama with his only memories of his father; he never saw his father again before an automobile accident in Kenya took his life in 1982.

Like many adolescents, Obama, who went by the name "Barry," engaged in what he called "a fitful interior struggle" to establish his own identity (Obama, *Dreams from My Father*, p. 76). The role models he discovered and the advice he received provided limited help, as he was the son of an African father and a white mother, living in a state where most people were Asian Americans or Pacific Islanders. Obama became politically active while attending Occidental College, in Los Angeles, California, and participated in demonstrations against the South African practice of apart-

Preamble to the U.S. Constitution.

heid. He engaged in lengthy discussions with friends about politics, learned that he had a talent for public speaking, and became "Barack" instead of "Barry." In 1981, after two years at Occidental, he transferred to Columbia University, where he earned a bachelor's degree in political science in 1983.

After working for two years in New York, Obama became a community organizer in African American neighborhoods of Chicago's South Side in 1985. Concluding that he needed additional training to do his work more effectively, he enrolled in Harvard Law School. In 1990 he was elected editor of the *Harvard Law Review*, becoming the first African American to hold that position. After graduating in 1991, Obama returned to Chicago and, the following year, married Michelle Robinson, also a graduate of Harvard Law. He worked for a law firm that took on many civil rights cases and also taught constitutional law at the University of Chicago Law School.

In 1996 Obama won the first of two consecutive terms in the Illinois Senate, representing a district encompassing Hyde Park on Chicago's South Side. After an unsuccessful bid for election to the U.S. Congress in 2000, he regained his seat in the Illinois Senate in 2002. During that campaign, he spoke out against going to war with Iraq. In the Illinois primary in March 2004, he defeated six rivals to secure the Democratic nomination for the U.S. Senate. In November he won the Senate seat by the widest margin in Illinois history.

In the Senate, Obama served on the Foreign Relations Committee and sponsored ethics reform legislation, but he soon began considering a run for the presidency. He declared his candidacy on February 10, 2007, in Springfield, Illinois. During most of 2007 polls showed that Obama was far behind the front-runner for the Democratic nomination, Senator Hillary Rodham Clinton of New York. Obama, however, campaigned tirelessly, built an extensive and remarkably effective political organization, raised large amounts of money from small donors by relying on the Internet, and emphasized that he stood for "change," especially the ending of the war in Iraq. After a long and close battle with Clinton in early 2008, Obama accumulated a majority of the delegates through the last primaries and caucuses in early June. He accepted the Democratic nomination for president when the party held its national convention in Denver at the end of August. On November 4, Obama defeated the Republican nominee, Senator John McCain of Arizona, by winning 52.9 percent of the popular vote and 365 electoral votes. On January 20, 2009, he took the oath of office as the forty-fourth president of the United States.

Explanation and Analysis of Documents

Obama took the title of this speech from the prologue to the Constitution, a document that embodies the principles of liberty, justice, and equal citizenship but which left unresolved the future of slavery. As Obama explains, the American people have struggled with slavery and its legacies as they have sought "a more perfect union." He affirms his belief that Americans past and present have narrowed the "gap between the promise of our ideals and the reality of their time" and uses his life story as a testament to that progress. Much as he did in his keynote address, Obama relies on his distinctive history to explain why he believes "that this nation is more than the sum of its parts—that out of many, we are truly one."

Despite his emphasis on unity, Obama acknowledges that his campaign could never avoid the issue of race, which has produced contradictory judgments—that he is "either too black' or not black enough,'" that he has won primaries because or in spite of being African American.

He connects the Wright controversy to "a particularly divisive turn" in the discussion of race and makes absolutely clear that he rejects Wright's "profoundly distorted" views about endemic white racism and radical Islam. Yet he also maintains that the excerpts from Wright's sermons cobbled together "in an endless loop on the television and YouTube" amount to a caricature of a complicated, if imperfect man. Speaking with a mixture of sympathy and sadness, Obama then recounts how Wright introduced him to Christianity and explained "our obligations to love one another" and to care for those in need. Wright's sermons inspired parishioners, as Obama shows in quoting a passage from his book *Dreams from My Father*, a memoir of his early life in Hawaii and Chicago. Obama maintains that Wright and his church represent "the kindness and cruelty, the fierce intelligence and the shocking ignorance, the struggles and successes, the love and yes, the bitterness and bias that make up the black experience in America." As someone who struggled to establish his own identity as an African American, Obama asserts that he can "no more disown" Wright than he could "the black community" or his white grandmother. He explains, "These people are a part of me. And they are a part of America, this country that I love."

Obama goes on to maintain that the Wright controversy reflects "the complexities of race in this country that we've never really worked through—a part of our union that we have yet to perfect." The bitterness that Wright expressed is rooted in inequalities with a long history. Drawing on the novelist William Faulkner, who emphasized that the past was part of the present, Obama recounts the ways that legalized discrimination, segregated schools, and lack of economic opportunity "continue to haunt us." While many African Americans "overcame the odds" to secure "a piece of the American Dream," others still suffer from a "legacy of defeat," which gives rise to public and private anger, expressed at the kitchen table or in the pulpit at church. According to Obama, that anger has a counterpart in the resentment of some white citizens over such issues as affirmative action and welfare. Anxieties about the future arising from "stagnant wages" and vanishing job opportunities only exacerbate these discontents. The result, Obama concludes, is the "racial stalemate we've been stuck in for years."

Obama acknowledges that neither a single election nor a single candidate—even himself—can close these racial divisions, but he asserts that the American people "have no choice" but to "continue on the path of a more perfect union." He speaks as someone whose own heritage makes him familiar with the hopes and fears of both black and white people, and he implores his fellow citizens to acknowledge the shortcomings of their society while recognizing what Wright did not fully appreciate—that "the true genius of this nation" is that "America can change." As he did in his keynote address, he emphasizes the biblical injunction to care for one another. He also frames the choice faced by the American people as he did almost four years earlier: They can embrace either a politics of cynicism or a politics of hope. The former means that nothing will change, while the latter promises to advance issues—education, health care, job opportunities, veterans benefits—that can improve the lives of all Americans. Despite his broadly ideological tone, he is, of course, making a case for his own presidential candidacy.

Obama closes with a hopeful account about a young white woman, Ashley Baia, whose story of persistence and achievement inspired an elderly African American man in South Carolina. Obama says that he is confident that voters will come together and say "not this time" to efforts to play blacks and whites against each other or to concentrate on distractions rather than major issues. Instead, he predicts, they will continue on the course of perfecting the union that began with the framing of the Constitution in Philadelphia.

Obama earned widespread praise for his compassionate, courageous, and calm discussion of an issue that often produces sensationalist commentary. He also strengthened his claim that he was a candidate who could transcend the usual partisan or cultural divisions and promote reconciliation by elevating the discussion of critical issues. The speech helped dampen the Wright controversy but did not end it. In late April, Wright gave a series of addresses and interviews in which he repeated some of his earlier extreme statements. Obama once more denounced Wright's assertions and finally broke all ties with his former pastor.

Impact

As she battled Barack Obama for the Democratic nomination for president, Senator Hillary Rodham Clinton insisted that her opponent offered speeches instead of solutions and eloquence instead of experience. He was a proven orator but an untested leader. Words, she asserted, mattered much less that skill at enacting programs and implementing policies. Obama responded, "Don't tell me words don't matter. 'I have a dream'—just words?… We have nothing to fear but fear itself'—just words? Just speeches?" (Zeleny, p. 12). Obama succinctly implied that Martin Luther King, Jr., and Franklin D. Roosevelt were able to bring change in part because of their exceptional ability to inspire and uplift. Their words as well as their deeds had profound and lasting effects.

Obama, in turn, owed much of his success in his campaign for president to his remarkable talent for using words to kindle hope and nurture desire for change. He told stories of unlikely achievement—often from his own life—to encourage Americans to believe that they could still realize their individual dreams while working together to reform the nation's society and politics. He balanced appeals for innovation with calls for rededication to traditional values of service and responsibility. His words, too, indeed helped to bring change, as he became the first African American president. Obama's most important legacy will be his achievements in office—his ability to make his administration's deeds match his words. By the time he took the presidential oath, he had already shown that he knew how to use stirring oratory to accomplish great things and to inspire his fellow citizens to hope for much more.

Further Reading

♦ Article
Zeleny, Jeff. "An Obama Refrain Bears Echoes of a Governor's Speeches." *New York Times*, February 18, 2008, p. 12.

♦ Books
Mendell, David. *Obama: From Promise to Power*. New York: Amistad, 2007.

New York Times editors. *Obama: The Historic Journey*. New York: Callaway, 2009.

Olive, David. *An American Story: The Speeches of Barack Obama: A Primer*. Toronto: ECW Press, 2008.

Thomas, Evan. *"A Long Time Coming": The Inspiring, Combative 2008 Campaign and the Historic Election of Barack Obama*. New York: PublicAffairs, 2009.

♦ Web Sites
Pilkington, Ed. "Obama Inauguration: Words of History ... Crafted by 27-Year-Old in Starbucks." Guardian Web site. http://www.guardian.co.uk/world/2009/jan/20/barack-obama-inauguration-us-speech.

"'The Speech': The Experts' Critique." New York Times Web site. http://roomfordebate.blogs.nytimes.com/2009/01/20/the-speech-the-experts-critique/?scp=3&sq=safire&st=cse.

———Chester Pach

Time Line

1961	August 4	■ Barack Obama is born in Honolulu, Hawaii.
1983	May 17	■ Obama graduates from Columbia University.
1990	February 6	■ Obama is elected editor of the *Harvard Law Review*, becoming the first African American to hold that position in the publication's 104-year history.
1996	November 5	■ Obama wins the first of three terms in the Illinois Senate.
2002	October 2	■ Speaking in Chicago, Obama declares that he opposes war with Iraq.
2004	July 27	■ At the Democratic National Convention in Boston, at which John Kerry is nominated for president, Obama gives the keynote address.
	November 2	■ Obama is elected to the U.S. Senate from Illinois.
2007	February 10	■ Obama announces his candidacy for the presidency in Springfield, Illinois.
2008	March 18	■ At the National Constitution Center in Philadelphia, Pennsylvania, Obama gives a speech on race in the United States entitled "A More Perfect Union."
	June 3	■ At the conclusion of the last primaries and caucuses, Obama asserts that he has enough delegates to win the Democratic presidential nomination over Hillary Rodham Clinton.
	August 28	■ In a speech at Invesco Field in Denver, Colorado, titled "The American Promise," Obama accepts the Democratic nomination for president.
	November 4	■ Obama is elected the forty-fourth president of the United States.
2009	January 20	■ President Obama delivers his inaugural address.

Essential Quotes

"We cannot solve the challenges of our time unless we solve them together—unless we perfect our union by understanding that we may have different stories, but we hold common hopes; that we may not look the same and we may not have come from the same place, but we all want to move in the same direction—towards a better future for our children and our grandchildren."

"I have asserted a firm conviction—a conviction rooted in my faith in God and my faith in the American people—that working together we can move beyond some of our old racial wounds, and that in fact we have no choice if we are to continue on the path of a more perfect union."

"What we have already achieved gives us hope—the audacity to hope—for what we can and must achieve tomorrow."

Questions for Further Study

1. Barack Obama has often been compared to John F. Kennedy because of his relative youth and idealism. Compare Obama's Inaugural Address with Kennedy's. What common ideals do they address? How are the two speeches different?

2. A common theme that runs through Obama's speeches is that his personal background and ancestry are different from those of the typical American politician. Explain why Obama stressed these differences and whether they contributed to his victory in the presidential election and his ability to govern.

3. Obama often makes specific reference to ordinary people in his speeches; that is, rather than talking in general about "workers" or "mothers," he identifies a particular person or refers to people living in a particular town. Comment on this rhetorical device and whether you believe it is effective.

4. Obama makes frequent reference to the Founding Fathers, the Constitution, the Declaration of Independence, the Revolutionary War, and other people and events from American history. What purpose do you believe he has in doing so?

5. Both Barack Obama and George W. Bush had to deal with terrorist threats from groups such as al Qaeda in the wake of the terrorist attacks of September 11, 2001. Compare Obama's positions on these matters with President Bush's as expressed in the Bush's address to the nation following the attacks and his Second Inaugural Address.

"A More Perfect Union"

Full text of Barack Obama's speech, "A More Perfect Union"

"We the people, in order to form a more perfect union."

Two hundred and twenty one years ago, in a hall that still stands across the street, a group of men gathered and, with these simple words, launched America's improbable experiment in democracy. Farmers and scholars; statesmen and patriots who had traveled across an ocean to escape tyranny and persecution finally made real their declaration of independence at a Philadelphia convention that lasted through the spring of 1787.

The document they produced was eventually signed but ultimately unfinished. It was stained by this nation's original sin of slavery, a question that divided the colonies and brought the convention to a stalemate until the founders chose to allow the slave trade to continue for at least twenty more years, and to leave any final resolution to future generations.

Of course, the answer to the slavery question was already embedded within our Constitution—a Constitution that had at its very core the ideal of equal citizenship under the law; a Constitution that promised its people liberty, and justice, and a union that could be and should be perfected over time.

And yet words on a parchment would not be enough to deliver slaves from bondage, or provide men and women of every color and creed their full rights and obligations as citizens of the United States. What would be needed were Americans in successive generations who were willing to do their part—through protests and struggle, on the streets and in the courts, through a civil war and civil disobedience and always at great risk—to narrow that gap between the promise of our ideals and the reality of their time.

This was one of the tasks we set forth at the beginning of this campaign—to continue the long march of those who came before us, a march for a more just, more equal, more free, more caring and more prosperous America. I chose to run for the presidency at this moment in history because I believe deeply that we cannot solve the challenges of our time unless we solve them together—unless we perfect our union by understanding that we may have different stories, but we hold common hopes; that we may not look the same and we may not have come from the same place, but we all want to move in the same direction—towards a better future for our children and our grandchildren.

This belief comes from my unyielding faith in the decency and generosity of the American people. But it also comes from my own American story.

I am the son of a black man from Kenya and a white woman from Kansas. I was raised with the help of a white grandfather who survived a Depression to serve in Patton's Army during World War II and a white grandmother who worked on a bomber assembly line at Fort Leavenworth while he was overseas. I've gone to some of the best schools in America and lived in one of the world's poorest nations. I am married to a black American who carries within her the blood of slaves and slaveowners—an inheritance we pass on to our two precious daughters. I have brothers, sisters, nieces, nephews, uncles and cousins, of every race and every hue, scattered across three continents, and for as long as I live, I will never forget that in no other country on Earth is my story even possible.

It's a story that hasn't made me the most conventional candidate. But it is a story that has seared into my genetic makeup the idea that this nation is more than the sum of its parts—that out of many, we are truly one.

Throughout the first year of this campaign, against all predictions to the contrary, we saw how hungry the American people were for this message of unity. Despite the temptation to view my candidacy through a purely racial lens, we won commanding victories in states with some of the whitest populations in the country. In South Carolina, where the Confederate Flag still flies, we built a powerful coalition of African Americans and white Americans.

This is not to say that race has not been an issue in the campaign. At various stages in the campaign, some commentators have deemed me either "too black" or "not black enough." We saw racial tensions bubble to the surface during the week before the South Carolina primary. The press has scoured every exit poll for the latest evidence of racial polarization, not just in terms of white and black, but black and brown as well.

And yet, it has only been in the last couple of weeks that the discussion of race in this campaign has taken a particularly divisive turn.

On one end of the spectrum, we've heard the implication that my candidacy is somehow an exercise in affirmative action; that it's based solely on the desire of wide-eyed liberals to purchase racial reconciliation on the cheap. On the other end, we've heard my former pastor, Reverend Jeremiah Wright, use incendiary language to express views that have the potential not only to widen the racial divide, but views that denigrate both the greatness and the goodness of our nation; that rightly offend white and black alike.

I have already condemned, in unequivocal terms, the statements of Reverend Wright that have caused such controversy. For some, nagging questions remain. Did I know him to be an occasionally fierce critic of American domestic and foreign policy? Of course. Did I ever hear him make remarks that could be considered controversial while I sat in church? Yes. Did I strongly disagree with many of his political views? Absolutely—just as I'm sure many of you have heard remarks from your pastors, priests, or rabbis with which you strongly disagreed.

But the remarks that have caused this recent firestorm weren't simply controversial. They weren't simply a religious leader's effort to speak out against perceived injustice. Instead, they expressed a profoundly distorted view of this country—a view that sees white racism as endemic, and that elevates what is wrong with America above all that we know is right with America; a view that sees the conflicts in the Middle East as rooted primarily in the actions of stalwart allies like Israel, instead of emanating from the perverse and hateful ideologies of radical Islam.

As such, Reverend Wright's comments were not only wrong but divisive, divisive at a time when we need unity; racially charged at a time when we need to come together to solve a set of monumental problems—two wars, a terrorist threat, a falling economy, a chronic health care crisis and potentially devastating climate change; problems that are neither black or white or Latino or Asian, but rather problems that confront us all.

Given my background, my politics, and my professed values and ideals, there will no doubt be those for whom my statements of condemnation are not enough. Why associate myself with Reverend Wright in the first place, they may ask? Why not join another church? And I confess that if all that I knew of Reverend Wright were the snippets of those sermons that have run in an endless loop on the television and You Tube, or if Trinity United Church of Christ conformed to the caricatures being peddled by some commentators, there is no doubt that I would react in much the same way

But the truth is, that isn't all that I know of the man. The man I met more than twenty years ago is a man who helped introduce me to my Christian faith, a man who spoke to me about our obligations to love one another; to care for the sick and lift up the poor. He is a man who served his country as a U.S. Marine; who has studied and lectured at some of the finest universities and seminaries in the country, and who for over thirty years led a church that serves the community by doing God's work here on Earth—by housing the homeless, ministering to the needy, providing day care services and scholarships and prison ministries, and reaching out to those suffering from HIV/AIDS.

In my first book, *Dreams From My Father*, I described the experience of my first service at Trinity:

> People began to shout, to rise from their seats and clap and cry out, a forceful wind carrying the reverend's voice up into the rafters.... And in that single note—hope!—I heard something else; at the foot of that cross, inside the thousands of churches across the city, I imagined the stories of ordinary black people merging with the stories of David and Goliath, Moses and Pharaoh, the Christians in the lion's den, Ezekiel's field of dry bones. Those stories—of survival, and freedom, and hope—became our story, my story; the blood that had spilled was our blood, the tears our tears; until this black church, on this bright day, seemed once more a vessel carrying the story of a people into future generations and into a larger world. Our trials and triumphs became at once unique and universal, black and more than black; in chronicling our journey, the stories and songs gave us a means to reclaim memories that we didn't need to feel shame about ... memories that all people might study and cherish—and with which we could start to rebuild.

That has been my experience at Trinity. Like other predominantly black churches across the country, Trinity embodies the black community in its entirety—the doctor and the welfare mom, the model student and the former gang-banger. Like other black churches, Trinity's services are full of raucous laughter and sometimes bawdy humor. They are full of dancing, clapping, screaming and shouting that may seem jarring to the untrained ear. The church contains in full the kindness and cruelty, the fierce intelligence and the shocking ignorance, the struggles and successes, the love and yes, the bitterness and bias that make up the black experience in America.

And this helps explain, perhaps, my relationship with Reverend Wright. As imperfect as he may be, he has been like family to me. He strengthened my faith, officiated my wedding, and baptized my children. Not once in my conversations with him have I heard him talk about any ethnic group in derogatory terms, or treat whites with whom he interacted with anything but courtesy and respect. He contains within him the contradictions—the good and the bad—of the community that he has served diligently for so many years.

I can no more disown him than I can disown the black community. I can no more disown him than I can my white grandmother—a woman who helped raise me, a woman who sacrificed again and again for me, a woman who loves me as much as she loves anything in this world, but a woman who once confessed her fear of black men who passed by her on the street, and who on more than one occasion has uttered racial or ethnic stereotypes that made me cringe.

These people are a part of me. And they are a part of America, this country that I love.

Some will see this as an attempt to justify or excuse comments that are simply inexcusable. I can assure you it is not. I suppose the politically safe thing would be to move on from this episode and just hope that it fades into the woodwork. We can dismiss Reverend Wright as a crank or a demagogue, just as some have dismissed Geraldine Ferraro, in the aftermath of her recent statements, as harboring some deep-seated racial bias.

But race is an issue that I believe this nation cannot afford to ignore right now. We would be making the same mistake that Reverend Wright made in his offending sermons about America—to simplify and stereotype and amplify the negative to the point that it distorts reality.

The fact is that the comments that have been made and the issues that have surfaced over the last few weeks reflect the complexities of race in this country that we've never really worked through—a part of our union that we have yet to perfect. And if we walk away now, if we simply retreat into our respective corners, we will never be able to come together and solve challenges like health care, or education, or the need to find good jobs for every American.

Understanding this reality requires a reminder of how we arrived at this point. As William Faulkner once wrote, "The past isn't dead and buried. In fact, it isn't even past." We do not need to recite here the history of racial injustice in this country. But we do need to remind ourselves that so many of the disparities that exist in the African-American community today can be directly traced to inequalities passed on from an earlier generation that suffered under the brutal legacy of slavery and Jim Crow.

Segregated schools were, and are, inferior schools; we still haven't fixed them, fifty years after *Brown v. Board of Education*, and the inferior education they provided, then and now, helps explain the pervasive achievement gap between today's black and white students.

Legalized discrimination—where blacks were prevented, often through violence, from owning property, or loans were not granted to African-American business owners, or black homeowners could not access FHA mortgages, or blacks were excluded from unions, or the police force, or fire departments—meant that black families could not amass any meaningful wealth to bequeath to future generations. That history helps explain the wealth and income gap between black and white, and the concentrated pockets of poverty that persists in so many of today's urban and rural communities.

A lack of economic opportunity among black men, and the shame and frustration that came from not being able to provide for one's family, contributed to the erosion of black families—a problem that welfare policies for many years may have worsened. And the lack of basic services in so many urban black neighborhoods—parks for kids to play in, police walking the beat, regular garbage pick-up and building code enforcement—all helped create a cycle of violence, blight and neglect that continue to haunt us.

This is the reality in which Reverend Wright and other African-Americans of his generation grew up. They came of age in the late fifties and early sixties, a time when segregation was still the law of the land and opportunity was systematically constricted. What's remarkable is not how many failed in the face of discrimination, but rather how many men and women overcame the odds; how many were able to make a way out of no way for those like me who would come after them.

But for all those who scratched and clawed their way to get a piece of the American Dream, there were many who didn't make it—those who were ultimately defeated, in one way or another, by discrimination. That legacy of defeat was passed on to future generations—those young men and increasingly young women who we see standing on street corners or languishing in our prisons, without hope or prospects for the future. Even for those blacks who did make it, questions of race, and racism, continue to define their worldview in fundamental ways. For the men and women of Reverend Wright's generation, the memories of humiliation and doubt and fear have not gone away; nor has the anger and the bitterness of those years. That anger may not get expressed in public, in front of white co-workers or white friends. But it does find voice in the barbershop or around the kitchen table. At times, that anger is exploited by politicians, to gin up votes along racial lines, or to make up for a politician's own failings.

And occasionally it finds voice in the church on Sunday morning, in the pulpit and in the pews. The fact that so many people are surprised to hear that anger in some of Reverend Wright's sermons simply reminds us of the old truism that the most segregated hour in American life occurs on Sunday morning. That anger is not always productive; indeed, all too often it distracts attention from solving real problems; it keeps us from squarely facing our own complicity in our condition, and prevents the African-American community from forging the alliances it needs to bring about real change. But the anger is real; it is powerful; and to simply wish it away, to condemn it without understanding its roots, only serves to widen the chasm of misunderstanding that exists between the races.

In fact, a similar anger exists within segments of the white community. Most working- and middle-class white Americans don't feel that they have been particularly privileged by their race. Their experience is the immigrant experience—as far as they're concerned, no one's handed them anything, they've built it from scratch. They've worked hard all their lives, many times only to see their jobs shipped overseas or their pension dumped after a lifetime of labor. They are anxious about their futures, and feel their dreams slipping away; in an era of stagnant wages and global competition, opportunity comes to be seen as a zero sum game, in which your dreams come at my expense. So when they are told to bus their children to a school across town; when they hear that an African American is getting an advantage in landing a good job or a spot in a good college because of an injustice that they themselves never committed; when they're told that their fears about crime in urban neighborhoods are somehow prejudiced, resentment builds over time.

Like the anger within the black community, these resentments aren't always expressed in polite company. But they have helped shape the political landscape for at least a generation. Anger over welfare and affirmative action helped forge the Reagan Coalition. Politicians routinely exploited fears of crime for their own electoral ends. Talk show hosts and conservative commentators built entire careers unmasking bogus claims of racism while dismissing legitimate discussions of racial injustice and inequality as mere political correctness or reverse racism.

Just as black anger often proved counterproductive, so have these white resentments distracted attention from the real culprits of the middle class squeeze—a corporate culture rife with inside dealing, questionable accounting practices, and short-term greed; a Washington dominated by lobbyists and special interests; economic policies that favor the few over the many. And yet, to wish away the resentments of white Americans, to label them as misguided or even racist, without recognizing they are grounded in legitimate concerns—this too widens the racial divide, and blocks the path to understanding.

This is where we are right now. It's a racial stalemate we've been stuck in for years. Contrary to the claims of some of my critics, black and white, I have never been so naive as to believe that we can get beyond our racial divisions in a single election cycle, or with a single candidacy—particularly a candidacy as imperfect as my own.

But I have asserted a firm conviction—a conviction rooted in my faith in God and my faith in the American people—that working together we can move beyond some of our old racial wounds, and that in fact we have no choice if we are to continue on the path of a more perfect union.

For the African-American community, that path means embracing the burdens of our past without becoming victims of our past. It means continuing to insist on a full measure of justice in every aspect of American life. But it also means binding our particular grievances—for better health care, and better schools, and better jobs—to the larger aspirations of all Americans—the white woman struggling to break the glass ceiling, the white man whose been laid off, the immigrant trying to feed his family. And it means taking full responsibility for own lives—by demanding more from our fathers, and spending more time with our children, and reading to them, and teaching them that while they may face challenges and discrimination in their own lives, they must never succumb to despair or cynicism; they must always believe that they can write their own destiny.

Ironically, this quintessentially American—and yes, conservative—notion of self-help found frequent expression in Reverend Wright's sermons. But what my former pastor too often failed to understand is that embarking on a program of self-help also requires a belief that society can change.

The profound mistake of Reverend Wright's sermons is not that he spoke about racism in our society. It's that he spoke as if our society was static; as if no progress has been made; as if this country—a country that has made it possible for one of his own members to run for the highest office in the land and build a coalition of white and black; Latino and Asian, rich and poor, young and old—is still irrevocably bound to a tragic past. But what we know—what we have seen—is that America can change. That is the true genius of this nation. What we have already achieved gives us hope—the audacity to hope—for what we can and must achieve tomorrow.

In the white community, the path to a more perfect union means acknowledging that what ails the African-American community does not just exist in the minds of black people; that the legacy of discrimination—and current incidents of discrimination, while less overt than in the past—are real and must be addressed. Not just with words, but with deeds—by investing in our schools and our communities; by enforcing our civil rights laws and ensuring fairness in our criminal justice system; by providing this generation with ladders of opportunity that were unavailable for previous generations. It requires all Americans to realize that your dreams do not have to come at the expense of my dreams; that investing in the health, welfare, and education of black and brown and white children will ultimately help all of America prosper.

In the end, then, what is called for is nothing more, and nothing less, than what all the world's great religions demand—that we do unto others as we would have them do unto us. Let us be our brother's keeper, Scripture tells us. Let us be our sister's keeper. Let us find that common stake we all have in one another, and let our politics reflect that spirit as well.

For we have a choice in this country. We can accept a politics that breeds division, and conflict, and cynicism. We can tackle race only as spectacle—as we did in the OJ trial—or in the wake of tragedy, as we did in the aftermath of Katrina—or as fodder for the nightly news. We can play Reverend Wright's sermons on every channel, every day and talk about them from now until the election, and make the only question in this campaign whether or not the American people think that I somehow believe or sympathize with his most offensive words. We can pounce on some gaffe by a Hillary supporter as evidence that she's playing the race card, or we can speculate on whether white men will all flock to John McCain in the general election regardless of his policies.

We can do that.

But if we do, I can tell you that in the next election, we'll be talking about some other distraction. And then another one. And then another one. And nothing will change.

That is one option. Or, at this moment, in this election, we can come together and say, "Not this time." This time we want to talk about the crumbling schools that are stealing the future of black children and white children and Asian children and Hispanic children and Native American children. This time we want to reject the cynicism that tells us that these kids can't learn; that those kids who don't look like us are somebody else's problem. The children of America are not those kids, they are our kids, and we will not let them fall behind in a 21st century economy. Not this time.

This time we want to talk about how the lines in the Emergency Room are filled with whites and blacks and Hispanics who do not have health care; who don't have the power on their own to overcome the special interests in Washington, but who can take them on if we do it together.

This time we want to talk about the shuttered mills that once provided a decent life for men and women of every race, and the homes for sale that once belonged to Americans from every religion, every region, every walk of life. This time we want to talk about the fact that the real problem is not that someone who doesn't look like you might take your job; it's that the corporation you work for will ship it overseas for nothing more than a profit.

This time we want to talk about the men and women of every color and creed who serve together, and fight together, and bleed together under the same proud flag. We want to talk about how to bring them home from a war that never should've been authorized and never should've been waged, and we want to talk about how we'll show our patriotism by caring for them, and their families, and giving them the benefits they have earned.

I would not be running for President if I didn't believe with all my heart that this is what the vast majority of Americans want for this country. This union may never be perfect, but generation after generation has shown that it can always be perfected. And today, whenever I find myself feeling doubtful or cynical about this possibility, what gives me the most hope is the next generation—the young people whose attitudes and beliefs and openness to change have already made history in this election.

There is one story in particularly that I'd like to leave you with today—a story I told when I had the great honor of speaking on Dr. King's birthday at his home church, Ebenezer Baptist, in Atlanta.

There is a young, twenty-three year old white woman named Ashley Baia who organized for our campaign in Florence, South Carolina. She had been working to organize a mostly African-American community since the beginning of this campaign, and one day she was at a roundtable discussion where everyone went around telling their story and why they were there.

And Ashley said that when she was nine years old, her mother got cancer. And because she had to miss days of work, she was let go and lost her health care. They had to file for bankruptcy, and that's when Ashley decided that she had to do something to help her mom.

She knew that food was one of their most expensive costs, and so Ashley convinced her mother that what she really liked and really wanted to eat more than anything else was mustard and relish sandwiches. Because that was the cheapest way to eat.

She did this for a year until her mom got better, and she told everyone at the roundtable that the reason she joined our campaign was so that she could help the millions of other children in the country who want and need to help their parents too.

Now Ashley might have made a different choice. Perhaps somebody told her along the way that the source of her mother's problems were blacks who were on welfare and too lazy to work, or Hispanics who were coming into the country illegally. But she didn't. She sought out allies in her fight against injustice.

Anyway, Ashley finishes her story and then goes around the room and asks everyone else why they're supporting the campaign. They all have different stories and reasons. Many bring up a specific issue. And finally they come to this elderly black man who's been sitting there quietly the entire time. And Ashley asks him why he's there. And he does not bring up a specific issue. He does not say health care or the economy. He does not say education or the war. He does not say that he was there because of Barack Obama. He simply says to everyone in the room, "I am here because of Ashley."

"I'm here because of Ashley." By itself, that single moment of recognition between that young white girl and that old black man is not enough. It is not enough to give health care to the sick, or jobs to the jobless, or education to our children.

But it is where we start. It is where our union grows stronger. And as so many generations have come to realize over the course of the two-hundred and twenty one years since a band of patriots signed that document in Philadelphia, that is where the perfection begins.

Glossary

demagogue: a political leader who gains support by appealing to passions or prejudices

Depression: the Great Depression, the economic collapse that began in 1929 and persisted throughout the 1930s

endemic: native to

FHA: Federal Housing Administration

Katrina: reference to a 2005 hurricane that caused massive destruction along the Gulf Coast, including catastrophic flooding in the city of New Orleans

OJ trial: reference to the highly publicized 1995 trial of the former football star and actor O. J. Simpson for murdering his ex-wife and her male friend

Patton: General George S. Patton, the charismatic but controversial leader of U.S. Army troops in Europe during World War II

William Faulkner: American novelist, author of Requiem for a Nun, from which the quote is taken; more accurately, the quote is "The past is never dead. It's not even past."

"We the people …": the opening words of the U.S. Constitution

Sign for "colored" waiting room at a Greyhound bus terminal in Rome, Georgia, 1943. Esther Bubley [Public domain], via Wikimedia Commons

U.S. Senate Resolution Apologizing for the Enslavement and Racial Segregation of African Americans

"The Congress acknowledges the fundamental injustice, cruelty, brutality, and inhumanity of slavery and Jim Crow laws."

Overview

On June 18, 2009, the U.S. Senate passed a resolution apologizing for slavery and racial segregation, including the "Jim Crow" laws that underpinned the nation's division along racial lines from the end of Reconstruction to the 1960s. The resolution was concurrent within Congress, meaning that the same resolution was passed by the U.S. House of Representatives.

Explanation and Analysis of Document

The resolution reviews the tragic history of slavery and racial segregation and asserts that a federal apology for past injustices committed against African Americans can be a way to help the nation bind its racial wounds. Notably, the resolution sidesteps calls for monetary reparations to be paid to the descendants of slaves. The resolution is nonbinding, meaning that it does not have the force of law; as phrased in the eighteenth and final clause, it is a "sense of the Congress" resolution that expresses a sentiment about something but has no legal effect. For this reason, it was not necessary for the Senate to forward the resolution to the president for his signature. While many political observers believed that such an apology was long overdue and welcomed it, others found it to be "too little, too late" and asserted that its only value was symbolic. Moreover, the apology renewed the contentious debate over the issue of reparations—that is, monetary payments to atone for past wrongs—for the descendants of slaves.

The resolution ends with a formal disclaimer. It states first that nothing in the resolution "authorizes or supports any claim against the United States." This means that the Senate was not explicitly or implicitly acknowledging any right to reparations on the part of African Americans. A fear was that an acknowledgment of culpability would lead to renewed and increased demands for monetary or other forms of reparations and that the resolution, with its acknowledgment of guilt, would serve as a prominent exhibit in such demands. The second part of the disclaimer notes that the resolution in no way "serves as a settlement of any claim against the United States."

Audience

An apology to African Americans on the part of the federal government was regarded by some as long overdue. The Senate, along with the House of Representatives, arguably hoped that with the election of Barack Obama as president, the resolution could help usher in a period of racial reconciliation. In this sense, the audience was the entire nation. Clearly, African Americans, to whom the government was apologizing, were the primary focus of the intended audience. All of the major sponsors of the resolution were white, so one hope was certainly that African Americans could take some satisfaction in official recognition of past wrongs on the part of largely white legislators. The resolution also had an international audience; as other nations were recognizing the ill effects of past actions, sentiment was growing that the United States should do so as well.

Impact

As with most official apologies to groups that have been victimized, the nature of the impact lies in the eye of the beholder. The Senate resolution is almost exclusively symbolic, as it has no legal force, nor does it propose any concrete action. Certainly many African Americans were gratified that the federal government finally recognized its culpability for slavery and Jim Crow. But many observers regarded

Freedmen voting in New Orleans, 1867. [Public domain], via Wikimedia Commons

the apology as a flimsy manifestation of "white guilt." According to this view, issuing the apology allowed some to buy racial reconciliation on the cheap, while the apology did nothing to change history, nor did it do anything to alter the position of American Americans in modern society. Thus for some, the apology was merely a gesture, an act of political theater, or a manifestation of what has been called "political correctness"—the notion that there are certain "correct" opinions to be held as much for show as for substance.

The Senate's apology did have one important effect, in that it renewed the debate about reparations for African Americans—particularly because the resolution evades the notion that it supports calls for reparations. To some observers, the apology seems to outright reject any prospect of reparations. To other observers, though, the apology is vague on this issue and leaves open the possibility of reparations sometime in the future. For example, Senator Roland Burris, an Illinois Democrat, stated on the Senate floor that the "disclaimer in no way would eliminate future actions that may be brought before this body that may deal with reparations."

The reparations movement can be said to have begun during the Civil War, when General William Tecumseh Sherman issued Special Field Order No. 15, which promised forty acres and a mule to free blacks in the Sea Islands around Charleston, South Carolina. Sherman's order, while initially providing a refuge for freedpeople, ultimately had little effect, for much of the land was reclaimed by white owners, and many of the blacks who had settled on the land were eventually removed by the army and the Freedmen's Bureau. Although in 1893 Henry McNeal Turner organized a convention that called for remedies for African Americans, including reparations—which he calculated to be $49 billion—the movement for reparations died during the Jim Crow era.

Such demands, however, have been renewed in recent years by such figures as Representative John Conyers, Jr., of Michigan; the Nation of Islam leader Louis Farrakhan; and the Green Party presidential candidate Ralph Nader. Additionally, various organizations, such as the American Bar Association, have called for congressional investigations into the issue of reparations. According to polls taken early in the 2000s, just over half of African Americans supported some sort of cash reparations, as did about one in ten whites. One of the arguments that has been made in support of reparations—in addition to the obvious one that slavery and its aftermath were gross injustices that deprived African Americans of the ability to accumulate wealth—is that the government provided reparations to Japanese Americans for their internment in World War II, and African Americans are no less deserving. The response has been that the World War II internment was the direct result of federal mandate, but slavery was conducted by private individuals.

Some efforts have been made to calculate just how much the United States would owe the descendants of slaves. One estimate, based on payment for some 222 million hours of forced labor, compounded at 6 percent, would lead to a total of $97 trillion dollars, money that the government, of course, does not have. Even more modest proposals have led to estimates that reparations would cost Americans not of African descent tens of thousands of dollars apiece. Numerous other objections to reparations have been made: that the government has provided implicit reparations through a range of government welfare-type programs and affirmative action programs that benefit African Americans; that it would be difficult, if not impossible, to determine who would have a valid claim to descent from a slave; that some African Americans themselves owned slaves; that the majority of whites in the South—and the vast majority in the North—were not slave owners; that slavery in America could not have existed without the complicity of African and Muslim slave traders; that many thousands of whites died in the Civil War, leaving their descendants bereft, in part to end slavery; that millions of immigrants to the United States arrived long after slavery ended and thus should not be obligated to make any sacrifices; and that far from contributing to America's accumulated wealth, slavery was most prevalent in the nation's poorest states—while those states where slavery ended early, such as Massachusetts, New York, and Pennsylvania, became the nation's richest states. Thus, the Senate's apology inadvertently—or perhaps deliberately—renewed the long-simmering debate over the question of what America owes, if anything, to the descendants of slaves and what, if anything, can ever be done to atone for the evils of slavery and Jim Crow.

Further Reading

♦ Books

Gibney, Mark, ed. *The Age of Apology: Facing Up to the Past*. Philadelphia: University of Pennsylvania Press, 2009.

Horowitz, David. *Uncivil Wars: The Controversy over Reparations for Slavery*. San Francisco, Calif.: Encounter Books, 2002.

Martin, Michael T., and Marilyn Yaquinto, eds. *Redress for Historical Injustices in the United States: On Reparations for Slavery, Jim Crow, and Their Legacies*. Durham, N.C.: Duke University Press, 2007.

Nobles, Melissa. *The Politics of Official Apologies*. New York: Cambridge University Press, 2008.

Salzberger, Ronald P., and Mary C. Turck, eds. *Reparations for Slavery: A Reader*. Lanham, Md.: Rowman & Littlefield, 2004.

Smith, Nick. *I Was Wrong: The Meanings of Apologies*. New York: Cambridge University Press, 2008.

Tavuchis, Nicholas. *Mea Culpa: A Sociology of Apology and Reconciliation*. Stanford, Calif.: Stanford University Press, 1991.

Walters, Ronald W. *The Price of Racial Reconciliation*. Ann Arbor: University of Michigan Press, 2009.

♦ Web Sites

Becker, Bernie. "Senate Approves Slavery Apology, with Reparations Disclaimer." *New York Times*, April 9, 2009. http://thecaucus.blogs.nytimes.com/2009/06/18/senate-approves-slavery-apology-with-reparations-disclaimer/.

"Black Activists Call Senate Slavery Apology 'Useless'; Say It Will Empower the Call for Reparations." National Center for Public Policy Research Web site. http://www.nationalcenter.org/P21PR-Reparations_062209.html.

Flaherty, Peter, and John Carlisle. *The Case against Slave Reparations*. National Legal and Policy Center Web site. http://www.nlpc.org/pdfs/Final_NLPC_Reparations.pdf.

Kane, Eugene. "Senate Apology on Slavery Lacks Sincerity." *Milwaukee Journal Sentinel* JSOnline Web site. http://www.jsonline.com/news/milwaukee/48636877.html.

Williams, Walter E. "Senate Slavery Apology." Human Events Web site. http://www.humanevents.com/article.php?id=32596.

———Michael J. O'Neal

Essential Quotes

"Whereas Africans forced into slavery were brutalized, humiliated, dehumanized, and subjected to the indignity of being stripped of their names and heritage."

"Whereas the system of de jure racial segregation known as 'Jim Crow', which arose in certain parts of the United States after the Civil War to create separate and unequal societies for Whites and African-Americans, was a direct result of the racism against people of African descent that was engendered by slavery."

"Whereas an apology for centuries of brutal dehumanization and injustices cannot erase the past, but confession of the wrongs committed and a formal apology to African-Americans will help bind the wounds of the Nation that are rooted in slavery and can speed racial healing and reconciliation."

"The Congress acknowledges the fundamental injustice, cruelty, brutality, and inhumanity of slavery and Jim Crow laws."

"Nothing in this resolution authorizes or supports any claim against the United States; or serves as a settlement of any claim against the United States."

Questions for Further Study

1. Why do you think it took so long for a U.S. government body to apologize for slavery and segregation?

2. What is your reaction to the Senate's apology? Do you regard it as something that can lead to racial reconciliation? Or do you see it as an empty gesture?

3. What is your position with regard to reparations for African American descendants of slavery? What arguments support the view that reparations should be paid? What are the arguments against reparations?

4. In recent years there have been many such apologies for colonialism, imperialism, genocide, and other ills and abuses of the past. What accounts for these many apologies from governments and other institutions? Do you think these apologies accomplish anything?

5. Representative Steve Cohen, a sponsor of the concurrent apology in the U.S. House of Representatives, was involved in a close 2008 reelection race in his Tennessee district, which is a majority black district. Do you think that political considerations may have motivated his sponsorship of the apology? Why or why not?

U.S. Senate Resolution Apologizing for the Enslavement and Racial Segregation of African Americans

Full text of the resolution

Concurrent Resolution

Apologizing for the enslavement and racial segregation of African-Americans.

1. Whereas during the history of the Nation, the United States has grown into a symbol of democracy and freedom around the world;
2. Whereas the legacy of African-Americans is interwoven with the very fabric of the democracy and freedom of the United States;
3. Whereas millions of Africans and their descendants were enslaved in the United States and the 13 American colonies from 1619 through 1865;
4. Whereas Africans forced into slavery were brutalized, humiliated, dehumanized, and subjected to the indignity of being stripped of their names and heritage;
5. Whereas many enslaved families were torn apart after family members were sold separately;
6. Whereas the system of slavery and the visceral racism against people of African descent upon which it depended became enmeshed in the social fabric of the United States;
7. Whereas slavery was not officially abolished until the ratification of the 13th amendment to the Constitution of the United States in 1865, after the end of the Civil War;
8. Whereas after emancipation from 246 years of slavery, African-Americans soon saw the fleeting political, social, and economic gains they made during Reconstruction eviscerated by virulent racism, lynchings, disenfranchisement, Black Codes, and racial segregation laws that imposed a rigid system of officially sanctioned racial segregation in virtually all areas of life;
9. Whereas the system of de jure racial segregation known as " Jim Crow," which arose in certain parts of the United States after the Civil War to create separate and unequal societies for Whites and African-Americans, was a direct result of the racism against people of African descent that was engendered by slavery;
10. Whereas the system of Jim Crow laws officially existed until the 1960s—a century after the official end of slavery in the United States—until Congress took action to end it, but the vestiges of Jim Crow continue to this day;
11. Whereas African-Americans continue to suffer from the consequences of slavery and Jim Crow laws—long after both systems were formally abolished—through enormous damage and loss, both tangible and intangible, including the loss of human dignity and liberty;
12. Whereas the story of the enslavement and de jure segregation of African-Americans and the dehumanizing atrocities committed against them should not be purged from or minimized in the telling of the history of the United States;
13. Whereas those African-Americans who suffered under slavery and Jim Crow laws, and their descendants, exemplify the strength of the human character and provide a model of courage, commitment, and perseverance;
14. Whereas on July 8, 2003, during a trip to Gorée Island, Senegal, a former slave port, President George W. Bush acknowledged the continuing legacy of slavery in life in the United States and the need to confront that legacy, when he stated that slavery "was … one of the greatest crimes of history.… The racial bigotry fed by slavery did not end with slavery or with segregation. And many of the issues that still trouble America have roots in the bitter experience of other times. But however long the journey, our destiny is set: liberty and justice for all";
15. Whereas President Bill Clinton also acknowledged the deep-seated problems caused by the continuing legacy of racism against African-Americans that began with slavery, when he initiated a national dialogue about race;
16. Whereas an apology for centuries of brutal dehumanization and injustices cannot erase the past, but confession of the wrongs committed and a

Document Text

formal apology to African-Americans will help bind the wounds of the Nation that are rooted in slavery and can speed racial healing and reconciliation and help the people of the United States understand the past and honor the history of all people of the United States;

17. Whereas the legislatures of the Commonwealth of Virginia and the States of Alabama, Florida, Maryland, and North Carolina have taken the lead in adopting resolutions officially expressing appropriate remorse for slavery, and other State legislatures are considering similar resolutions; and
18. Whereas it is important for the people of the United States, who legally recognized slavery through the Constitution and the laws of the United States, to make a formal apology for slavery and for its successor, Jim Crow, so they can move forward and seek reconciliation, justice, and harmony for all people of the United States: Now, therefore, be it
    a. Resolved by the Senate (the House of Representatives concurring), That the sense of the Congress is the following:
    (i) Apology for the enslavement and segregation of african-americans—The Congress—
    (1) acknowledges the fundamental injustice, cruelty, brutality, and inhumanity of slavery and Jim Crow laws;
    (2) apologizes to African-Americans on behalf of the people of the United States, for the wrongs committed against them and their ancestors who suffered under slavery and Jim Crow laws; and
    (3) expresses its recommitment to the principle that all people are created equal and endowed with inalienable rights to life, liberty, and the pursuit of happiness, and calls on all people of the United States to work toward eliminating racial prejudices, injustices, and discrimination from our society.
    (ii) Disclaimer—Nothing in this resolution—
    (1) authorizes or supports any claim against the United States; or
    (2) serves as a settlement of any claim against the United States.

Passed the Senate June 18, 2009.
Attest:
Nancy Erickson,
Secretary.

Glossary

Black Codes: nineteenth-century local and state laws that limited the civil rights and liberties of African Americans

de jure: Latin for "by law"

Jim Crow: the informal name given to the legal and social systems that kept African Americans in a subservient position in the late nineteenth and early twentieth centuries

national dialogue about race: a reference to President Bill Clinton's 1998 Initiative on Race

Reconstruction: the period after the Civil War when the rebellious states of the Confederacy were readmitted to the Union

The New Jim Crow cover. By Source (WP:NFCC#4), Fair use, https://en.wikipedia.org/w/index.php?curid=53261603

MICHELLE ALEXANDER: *THE NEW JIM CROW*

"Rather than rely on race, we use our criminal justice system to label people of color 'criminals' and then engage in all the practices we supposedly left behind."

Overview

In 2016, the United States imprisoned the largest proportion of its population of any nation-state in the world. Around 2.3 million prisoners were held for variable crimes, about 453 out of every 100,000 people – and about 22% of the entire imprisoned population in the world. Of that prison population, more than a third of them were African Americans, even though blacks make up only 12% of the US population as a whole. Around the same time, a prominent civil rights lawyer and law school professor, Michelle Alexander, published a book suggesting a logic behind these incarceration rates. *The New Jim Crow: Mass Incarceration in the Age of Colorblindness* (2010) opened up a nationwide debate on the prison system in the US, because Alexander's thesis posited that incarceration was a new way of keeping the African-American population in the US disenfranchised and impoverished, a new form of "Jim Crow" segregation. In her introduction, Alexander described the process by which she came to this conclusion.

Context

In 1971, President Richard Nixon held a press conference during which he referred to the abuse of illicit drugs as "public enemy number one", and declared that his administration was launching a "war on drugs". At approximately the same time, the civil rights movement had inspired the most ambitious campaign yet towards full integration of African-Americans into the mainstream of American society: black students would be driven by bus across towns and cities to attend better public schools and make integration a reality. Nixon's opposition to desegregation busing and his "war on drugs" could be read as an attack on the status of African-Americans in US society, as poverty, poor education and drugs plagued black neighborhoods.

By the end of the 1970s, busing had all but died as an effort at education, and in the 1980s, the "war on drugs" escalated. Under the Reagan administration, Vice President George HW Bush led an initiative attacking drug use in American communities. To the general public, the campaign was as innocuous as First Lady Nancy Reagan's famous admonition to children to "Just Say No" to drugs. Yet over the next twenty years, laws applied to drug abuse and distribution became more and more stringent. Federal law enforcement became heavily involved in policing inner city neighborhoods where many blacks lived. The CIA even admitted in 1998 that it allowed Nicaraguan drug cartels to distribute cocaine in these areas, and users would often be arrested by local police.

Aggressive enforcement of drug laws across the United States led inevitably to a greater level of incarceration of African-Americans due to the freer circulation of illicit drugs in their communities. No one would argue that the use and distribution of cocaine, heroin and other drugs should be anything less than wrong, and that distributors of the drugs preyed on African-American communities. But the criminalization of users and distributors seemed an easy way of waging a "war on drugs", treating a symptom as opposed to the cause: the demand for drugs and their easy inflow throughout American life. And while the laws as written did not seem discriminatory on paper, in practice, far more blacks were incarcerated for drug crimes – and over time, other crimes – that other populations in the US.

By 2011, the United Nations' Global Commission on Drug Policy produced a report on the global "War on Drugs". Its executive summary opened by stating "The global war on drugs has failed, with devastating consequences for individuals and societies around the world. Fifty years after the initiation of the UN Single Convention on Narcotic Drugs, and years after President Nixon launched the US government's war on drugs, fundamental reforms in national and global drug control policies are urgently needed."

One reason for this failure was that, like the opposition to busing, the "war on drugs" could be viewed as a substitute for a war on African-American life in the US. This assault on integration was far more insidious, however. Michelle Alexander began research into the justice system in the United States believing that it was largely indiscriminate. As she related in the introduction to her book, *The New Jim Crow*, she had a very different opinion of how the "war on drugs" worked, and subsequently, the entire justice system.

About the Author

Michelle Alexander was born October 7, 1967 and grew up in Oregon; she eventually received her law degree from Stanford University and became an attorney with the American Civil Liberties Union. She focused on the problem of racial profiling amongst police officers, thus beginning her association with causes related to the justice system and racial discrimination. In an interview, she described an encounter with a black man at the Oakland California branch of the ACLU whose life had been destroyed by a plea bargain he was advised to take on a drug conviction, and how he had no means to stop the later police harassment he experienced as a black man in the city. The encounter led to her conception of the thesis that went into her book. She also led a campaign against racial profiling known as the Driving While Black or Brown (DWB) Campaign.

Alexander clerked for Supreme Court Justice Harry Blackmun and on the United States Court of Appeals for the D.C. Circuit. She held numerous positions at law schools around the country, including Stanford, her alma mater, Ohio State, and a position at the Union Theological Seminary. In 2005, she received a Soros Justice Fellowship, with which she did the research that went into *The New Jim Crow*. She appeared in at least two documentaries discussing the prison system and its role in oppressing African-Americans, and wrote numerous op-ed pieces for American newspapers like the *New York Times*.

Explanation and Analysis of the Document

Alexander's introduction opens with an example: of Jarvious Cotton, an African-American Mississippi man who was convicted and served a sentence for murder. After parole, according to Mississippi law, felons who committed murders are no longer eligible to vote – along with felons who commit the crimes of rape, bribery, theft, arson, fraud, perjury, forgery, embezzlement or bigamy. Conservative commentators on Alexander's book often turned this argument against her, believing that the issue with Cotton's disenfranchisement was more about Mississippi law discriminating against him for committing a felony (some of them nonviolent) as opposed to discriminating against him for being black. It might be allowed that Alexander's point was more about Cotton's disenfranchisement as opposed to the reasons why – he had served his time in prison but was still being punished for his crime in a fashion that mirrored the disenfranchisement, and murder, of his ancestors in Mississippi.

Alexander's conclusion is that "In each generation, new tactics have been used for achieving the same goals—goals shared by the Founding Fathers. Denying African Americans citizenship was deemed essential to the formation of the original union. Hundreds of years later, America is still not an egalitarian democracy." What she believes is that other means have been used to discriminate against races, and one of them is the criminalization of black men – "Rather than rely on race, we use our criminal justice system to label people of color 'criminals' and then engage in all the practices we supposedly left behind." While her point is clear, she might have found a better example than Jarvious Cotton to make it under these circumstances, since anyone convicted of murder would be labeled by society as a criminal.

She then goes into how she came to reach these conclusions over the course of her career as a civil rights lawyer. Alexander states that, during her time working with the ACLU, she would not have believed "that something akin to a racial caste system currently exists in the United States." The election of Barack Obama in 2008 would seem to have put the idea to rest. But upon her leaving an election night party, she was disturbed by seeing "[a] black man… on his knees in the gutter, hands cuffed behind his back, as several police officers stood around him talking, joking, and ignoring his human existence … What did the election of Barack Obama mean for him?"

Alexander believed that the real problems in the African-American community were certainly not over, but improving as the United States made "racial progress". What blacks needed was affirmative action, further integration and especially better access to quality education. Yet while rushing to catch a bus in Oakland, she saw a sign for a radical group meeting stating "The Drug War Is the New Jim Crow." She considered the comparison "absurd", but as her focus as a lawyer and advocate changed from employment discrimination to criminal justice reform, the comparison seemed apt. "By the time I left the ACLU, I had come to suspect that I was wrong about the criminal justice system. …I came to see that mass incarceration in the United States had, in fact, emerged as a stunningly comprehensive and well-disguised system of racialized social control that functions in a manner strikingly similar to Jim Crow."

Audience

Alexander's book was aimed at policymakers, but also at a discerning and informed general public. It was published by the New Press, a nonprofit group that focused on manuscripts directed at the public interest, books that "promote and enrich public discussion and understanding of the issues vital to our democracy and to a more equitable world." More than once, however, the book was criticized for not having a bibliography, thus making it somewhat more difficult to figure out where Alexander got her sources. Yet it was reviewed in many journals with large circulations and it reached its audience, becoming the focus of discussion that the New Press tended to publish.

Impact

The New Jim Crow: Mass Incarceration in the Age of Colorblindness touched off a major public debate on the nature of criminal justice in the United States. Michelle Alexander traveled the country lecturing on the book's thesis and accepted position with Ohio State University and the Union Theological Seminary in New York City. Readers found her assertions on the drug war startling, such as that whites using cocaine tended to be given opportunities to accept drug counseling and detoxification whereas blacks using crack were often thrown in prison. Alexander compared such justice to poll taxes or literacy tests or segregation laws from an earlier era. Furthermore, convicted felons entered an "underworld of legalized discrimination", by which they could be excluded from jobs, kept from voting, watched in neighborhoods and isolated from mainstream society. "The nature of the criminal justice system has changed. It is no longer concerned primarily with the prevention and punishment of crime, but rather with the management and control of the dispossessed."

Most critics argued that Alexander's case was overstated, though many still agreed with some of its premises. The biggest criticism was of her alleged overemphasis on the "war on drugs" – most felony convictions since 2000 have been for violent crimes as opposed to drug crimes. Yet others acknowledged that a third of black men were likely to spend time in prison at least once in their lifetimes, and as Alexander's statistics showed, the majority would then spend the rest of their lives disenfranchised from the political and economic system in America.

The most detailed response came from John Pfaff, a law professor at Fordham University, who wrote *Locked In: The True Causes of Mass Incarceration? and How to Achieve Real Reform* (2017). Besides noting Alexander's overemphasis on the "war on drugs", Pfaff provided statistical analysis to assert that the majority of prisoners in state prison systems had been convicted of violent crimes; only 16% were related to drug offenses, and of that group, 95% had committed some other violent offense. Those convicted strictly of drug-related crimes tended to be in federal prisons for running large, often international drug cartels. Nonviolent drug offenders only amounted to 1% of the state prison population. Also, the focus on police enforcement of law and arrests avoided discussing the role of prosecutors, who often chose charges based on the possibility of obtaining a conviction at some level of the criminal justice system.

Regardless of response, Michelle Alexander's book provided statistics and arguments toward a public debate over the nature of the American criminal justice system, particularly in regard to race. Answers to its arguments by critics and supporters alike would not exist without the book's thesis to challenge viewpoints.

Further Reading

♦ Books

Alexander, Michelle. *The New Jim Crow: Mass Incarceration in the Age of Colorblindness*. New York: the New Press, 2010.

Forman, James Jr. *Locking Up Our Own: Crime and Punishment in Black America*. New York: Farrar Straus and Giroux, 2017.

Hinton, Elizabeth. *From the War on Poverty to the War on Crime: The Making of Mass Incarceration in America*. Cambridge, MA: Harvard University Press, 2016.

Pfaff, John. *Locked In: The True Causes of Mass Incarceration? and How to Achieve Real Reform*. New York: Basic Books, 2017.

♦ Web Sites

Nellis, Ashley. "The Color of Justice: Racial and Ethnic Disparity in State Prisons". The Sentencing Project (2016) http://www.sentencingproject.org/publications/color-of-justice-racial-and-ethnic-disparity-in-state-prisons/ [accessed August 6, 2017].

"Racial Disparities in Criminal Justice". American Civil Liberties Union https://www.aclu.org/issues/mass-incarceration/racial-disparities-criminal-justice [accessed August 6, 2017].

War on Drugs: Report of the Global Commission on Drug Policy (2011) https://www.scribd.com/ fullscreen/56924096?access_key=key-xoixompyejnky70a9mq [accessed August 6, 2017].

———*David Simonelli*

Time Line

1971	June	■ President Richard Nixon declares "war on drugs"
1982		■ Reagan Administration renews the "war on drugs"
1994		■ first habitual offender laws ("three strikes") passed in US and applied to people with three felony convictions; places many drug offenders in prison for life
2010		■ publication of Michelle Alexander's *The New Jim Crow*
2011	June	■ publication of "War on Drugs: Report of the Global Commission on Drug Policy"
2017	February	■ publication of John Pfaff's *Locked In: The True Causes of Mass Incarceration? and How to Achieve Real Reform*

Essential Quotes

"In each generation, new tactics have been used for achieving the same goals—goals shared by the Founding Fathers. Denying African Americans citizenship was deemed essential to the formation of the original union. Hundreds of years later, America is still not an egalitarian democracy."

"Rather than rely on race, we use our criminal justice system to label people of color 'criminals' and then engage in all the practices we supposedly left behind."

"We have not ended racial caste in America; we have merely redesigned it."

"By the time I left the ACLU, I had come to suspect that I was wrong about the criminal justice system. …I came to see that mass incarceration in the United States had, in fact, emerged as a stunningly comprehensive and well-disguised system of racialized social control that functions in a manner strikingly similar to Jim Crow."

The New Jim Crow

Excerpt from the introduction to Michelle Alexander's The New Jim Crow

Jarvious Cotton cannot vote. Like his father, grandfather, great-grandfather, and great-great-grandfather, he has been denied the right to participate in our electoral democracy. Cotton's family tree tells the story of several generations of black men who were born in the United States but who were denied the most basic freedom that democracy promises—the freedom to vote for those who will make the rules and laws that govern one's life. Cotton's great-great-grandfather could not vote as a slave. His great-grandfather was beaten to death by the Ku Klux Klan for attempting to vote. His grandfather was prevented from voting by Klan intimidation. His father was barred from voting by poll taxes and literacy tests. Today, Jarvious Cotton cannot vote because he, like many black men in the United States, has been labeled a felon and is currently on parole.

Cotton's story illustrates, in many respects, the old adage "The more things change, the more they remain the same." In each generation, new tactics have been used for achieving the same goals—goals shared by the Founding Fathers. Denying African Americans citizenship was deemed essential to the formation of the original union. Hundreds of years later, America is still not an egalitarian democracy. The arguments and rationalizations that have been trotted out in support of racial exclusion and discrimination in its various forms have changed and evolved, but the outcome has remained largely the same. An extraordinary percentage of black men in the United States are legally barred from voting today, just as they have been throughout most of American history. They are also subject to legalized discrimination in employment, housing, education, public benefits, and jury service, just as their parents, grandparents, and great-grandparents once were.

What has changed since the collapse of Jim Crow has less to do with the basic structure of our society than with the language we use to justify it. In the era of colorblindness, it is no longer socially permissible to use race, explicitly, as a justification for discrimination, exclusion, and social contempt. So we don't. Rather than rely on race, we use our criminal justice system to label people of color "criminals" and then engage in all the practices we supposedly left behind. Today it is perfectly legal to discriminate against criminals in nearly all the ways that it was once legal to discriminate against African Americans. Once you're labeled a felon, the old forms of discrimination—employment discrimination, housing discrimination, denial of the right to vote, denial of educational opportunity, denial of food stamps and other public benefits, and exclusion from jury ser vice—are suddenly legal. As a criminal, you have scarcely more rights, and arguably less respect, than a black man living in Alabama at the height of Jim Crow. We have not ended racial caste in America; we have merely redesigned it.

I reached the conclusions presented in this book reluctantly. Ten years ago, I would have argued strenuously against the central claim made here—namely, that something akin to a racial caste system currently exists in the United States. Indeed, if Barack Obama had been elected president back then, I would have argued that his election marked the nation's triumph over racial caste—the final nail in the coffin of Jim Crow. My elation would have been tempered by the distance yet to be traveled to reach the promised land of racial justice in America, but my conviction that nothing remotely similar to Jim Crow exists in this country would have been steadfast.

Today my elation over Obama's election is tempered by a far more sobering awareness. As an African American woman, with three young children who will never know a world in which a black man could not be president of the United States, I was beyond thrilled on election night. Yet when I walked out of the election night party, full of hope and enthusiasm, I was immediately reminded of the harsh realities of the New Jim Crow. A black man was on his knees in the gutter, hands cuffed behind his back, as several police officers stood around him talking, joking, and ignoring his human existence. People poured out of the building; many stared for a moment at the black man cowering in the street, and then averted their gaze. What did the election of Barack Obama mean for him?

Like many civil rights lawyers, I was inspired to attend law school by the civil rights victories of the 1950s and 1960s. Even in the face of growing social and political opposition to remedial policies such as affirmative action, I clung to the notion that the evils

Document Text

of Jim Crow are behind us and that, while we have a long way to go to fulfill the dream of an egalitarian, multiracial democracy, we have made real progress and are now struggling to hold on to the gains of the past. I thought my job as a civil rights lawyer was to join with the allies of racial progress to resist attacks on affirmative action and to eliminate the vestiges of Jim Crow segregation, including our still separate and unequal system of education. I understood the problems plaguing poor communities of color, including problems associated with crime and rising incarceration rates, to be a function of poverty and lack of access to quality education—the continuing legacy of slavery and Jim Crow. Never did I seriously consider the possibility that a new racial caste system was operating in this country. The new system had been developed and implemented swiftly, and it was largely invisible, even to people, like me, who spent most of their waking hours fighting for justice.

I first encountered the idea of a new racial caste system more than a decade ago, when a bright orange poster caught my eye. I was rushing to catch the bus, and I noticed a sign stapled to a telephone pole that screamed in large bold print: The Drug War Is the New Jim Crow. I paused for a moment and skimmed the text of the flyer. Some radical group was holding a community meeting about police brutality, the new three-strikes law in California, and the expansion of America's prison system. The meeting was being held at a small community church a few blocks away; it had seating capacity for no more than fifty people. I sighed, and muttered to myself something like, "Yeah, the criminal justice system is racist in many ways, but it really doesn't help to make such an absurd comparison. People will just think you're crazy." I then crossed the street and hopped on the bus. I was headed to my new job, director of the Racial Justice Project of the American Civil Liberties Union (ACLU) in Northern California.

When I began my work at the ACLU, I assumed that the criminal justice system had problems of racial bias, much in the same way that all major institutions in our society are plagued with problems associated with conscious and unconscious bias. As a lawyer who had litigated numerous class-action employment-discrimination cases, I understood well the many ways in which racial stereotyping can permeate subjective decision-making processes at all levels of an organization, with devastating consequences. I was familiar with the challenges associated with reforming institutions in which racial stratification is thought to be normal—the natural consequence of differences in education, culture, motivation, and, some still believe, innate ability. While at the ACLU, I shifted my focus from employment discrimination to criminal justice reform and dedicated myself to the task of working with others to identify and eliminate racial bias whenever and wherever it reared its ugly head.

By the time I left the ACLU, I had come to suspect that I was wrong about the criminal justice system. It was not just another institution infected with racial bias but rather a different beast entirely. The activists who posted the sign on the telephone pole were not crazy; nor were the smattering of lawyers and advocates around the country who were beginning to connect the dots between our current system of mass incarceration and earlier forms of social control. Quite belatedly, I came to see that mass incarceration in the United States had, in fact, emerged as a stunningly comprehensive and well-disguised system of racialized social control that functions in a manner strikingly similar to Jim Crow.

Copyright 2010, 2012 by Michelle Alexander. This excerpt originally appeared in The New Jim Crow: Mass Incarceration in the Age of Colorblindness, *published by The New Press. Reprinted here with permission.*

Cover of an early edition of "Jump Jim Crow" sheet music (c. 1832) Edward Williams Clay [Public domain], via Wikimedia Commons.

Shelby County v. Holder

"Not only do States retain sovereignty under the Constitution, there is also a 'fundamental principle of equal sovereignty' among the States."

Overview

Shelby County v. Holder is a U.S. Supreme Court case decided in 2013. The parties to the case were Shelby County, Alabama, and Eric Holder, the attorney general of the United States at the time. At issue were two key provisions of the Voting Rights Act (VRA) of 1965, a law passed to prohibit racial discrimination in voter registration and election laws. One of the provisions was Section 5, which required jurisdictions to obtain federal preclearance before making any changes in their voting laws or procedures to ensure that those changes would not have the effect of discriminating against voters on the basis of race. The other was Section 4(b), which provided a coverage formula to determine which jurisdictions were required to obtain federal preclearance based on a history of racial discrimination at the polls. As of 2008, the preclearance provisions largely applied to states throughout the South, as well as to Alaska, Arizona, and most of Virginia, as well as selected counties and townships in various states, among them North Carolina, Florida, California, and South Dakota. In its 5–4 decision, the Court held that the preclearance formula was based on outdated information that was no longer pertinent. Thus, it imposed on the affected jurisdictions an unconstitutional burden by violating the principles of federalism and the equal sovereignty of the states. In the view of many Court observers, the Court's decision effectively gutted the VRA.

Context

The U.S. Constitution gives each state the authority to determine voter qualifications and voting procedures. In the wake of the Civil War, however, it was apparent that in some states, various obstacles were depriving African Americans of their voting rights, among them literacy tests, poll taxes, property-ownership requirements, proofs of good moral character, the ability to read and interpret documents, and the like. In response, the Fifteenth Amendment, ratified in 1870, affirmed that "the right of citizens of the United States to vote shall not be denied or abridged by the United States or by any State on account of race, color, or previous condition of servitude." To put teeth into the amendments, Congress passed a series of Enforcement Acts in the 1870s to grant the federal government authority to intervene in states where African Americans were being denied their right to vote. The Supreme Court, however, ruled that various provisions of the acts were unconstitutional, and in time Congress repealed many of the acts' provisions. In a 1903 case, *Giles v. Harris,* the Court ruled that the judiciary did not have the authority to force states to register minorities to vote.

The issue lay dormant through much of the twentieth century until the civil rights movement gathered steam in the 1950s and 1960s, putting pressure on Congress to pass legislation to protect the voting rights of minorities. In response, Congress passed the Civil Rights Act of 1957 and the Civil Rights Act of 1960. This legislation, however, proved unequal to the task, for various legal standards made it extremely difficult for the U.S. Justice Department to litigate claims of voter discrimination. Additionally, the Justice Department found local officials unwilling to cooperate with federal investigations into charges of voter discrimination. The Civil Rights Act of 1964 contained voter protections, but again the act as it pertained to voting rights proved ineffective and difficult to enforce. Congress responded with the Voting Rights Act of 1965.

The VRA prohibited "voter denial," that is, preventing a person from casting a ballot or from having that ballot counted, particularly through imposition of a "test or device," such as literacy tests, that had the effect of discriminating against classes of voters. It also prohibited "voter dilution," referring to efforts to diminish the strength or effectiveness of a vote by, for example, gerrymandering voting districts. But the act also contained two key provisions that would be challenged in *Shelby County.* The first of these was Section

S. 1564–10

Sec. 17. Nothing in this Act shall be construed to deny, impair, or otherwise adversely affect the right to vote of any person registered to vote under the law of any State or political subdivision.

Sec. 18. There are hereby authorized to be appropriated such sums as are necessary to carry out the provisions of this Act.

Sec. 19. If any provision of this Act or the application thereof to any person or circumstances is held invalid, the remainder of the Act and the application of the provision to other persons not similarly situated or to other circumstances shall not be affected thereby.

John W. McCormack
Speaker of the House of Representatives.

Hubert H. Humphrey
Vice President of the United States and President of the Senate.

APPROVED
AUG – 6 1965

Lyndon B. Johnson

Last page of Voting Rights Act of 1965. By 89th United States Congress (http://www.ourdocuments.gov) [Public domain], via Wikimedia Commons

5, which required covered jurisdictions—those with a history of voter discrimination—to obtain "preclearance" from the federal government before enacting any changes in its voting requirements or procedures. This provision required the jurisdiction to demonstrate that any proposed change did not have the effect of discriminating against racial minorities. If the jurisdiction was unable to do meet this burden, the change would not be allowed to take effect. The other provision, Section 4(b), consisted of a "coverage formula" that was to be used to determine which "political subdivisions" would require preclearance. Essentially, the coverage formula consisted of two prongs. First, the jurisdiction made use of a "test or device" to qualify voters: educational requirements, literacy tests, tests of moral character, or requirements that a person be vouched for before voting. Additionally, this provision prohibited the use of English-only registration and election materials when a jurisdiction had a significant population of a non-English-speaking minority group. The second prong of the coverage formula applied to any jurisdiction where half of its eligible citizens were not registered to vote or did not vote in recent presidential elections; the specifics of this provision evolved as time passed and further national elections were held.

When the VRA came up for reauthorization, Shelby County brought suit against the U.S. attorney general asking for a permanent injunction against enforcement of these provisions of the act, arguing that they were unconstitutional. Both the district court and the U.S. Court of Appeals upheld the constitutionality of the provisions. The U.S. Supreme Court agreed to hear the case on appeal, and on June 25, 2013, the Court issued its decision. By a 5–4, the Court struck down Section 4(b), holding that it exceeded the enforcement powers of Congress under the Fourteenth and Fifteenth Amendments to the Constitution. The Court reasoned that the formula violates the constitutional principal of federalism and that it treats states in a disparate fashion on the basis of decades-old conditions that have "no logical relationship to the present day." The Court did not rule on the constitutionality of Section 5, for without a coverage formula, Section 5 was rendered moot.

About the Author

The Court's decision in *Shelby County v. Holder* was written by Chief Justice John Roberts. Joining him in the majority opinion were Justices Antonin Scalia, Anthony Kennedy, Clarence Thomas, and Samuel Alito; the majority was generally regarded as the more conservative wing of the Supreme Court. Dissenting were Justices Ruth Bader Ginsburg, Stephen Breyer, Sonia Sotomayor, and Elena Kagan, generally thought of as the Court's more liberal wing. Roberts was born in Buffalo, New York, on January 27, 1955, although his family later settled in Indiana. He attended Harvard University, then graduated from Harvard Law School in 1979. In the years that followed, he held various clerkship positions, including one for Supreme Court Justice William Rehnquist; he also worked in private practice. From 2003 to 2005 he was a judge for the U.S. District Court of Appeals for the District of Columbia. President George W. Bush nominated him to the U.S. Supreme Court to replace Justice Sandra Day O'Connor after her retirement, but before Roberts's confirmation hearings, Chief Justice Rehnquist died. Accordingly, President Bush nominated Roberts to the chief justice position. On September 29, 2005, he took his seat, the youngest chief justice in a century.

Explanation and Analysis of the Document

Justice Roberts begins with a historical overview, examining not only the Voting Rights Act of 1965 but also the Fifteenth Amendment, which guaranteed to all citizens, including African Americans, the right to vote. He discusses the "covered" jurisdictions of the VRA, the "tests or devices" that had the effect of denying African Americans the right to vote, and the concept of "preclearance," requiring a jurisdiction that wanted to enact a change in voting requirements or procedures to obtain federal approval, which it could obtain only if it could prove that the change did not have "the purpose [nor] the effect of denying or abridging the right to vote on account of race or color." He notes that both Sections 4 and 5 of the VRA were intended to be temporary, and in fact they needed to be reauthorized at various points in the intervening years; as part of that reauthorization, various jurisdictions were added to Section 5. The coverage formula contained in Section 4(b), however, remained unchanged. After summarizing the history of the case in the district court and the U.S. Court of Appeals, Roberts turns to the constitutional issues raised.

At issue are the Supremacy Clause of Constitution (Article VI, Section 2) and the Tenth Amendment to the Constitution. This amendment has proven to be a knotty one, for it has to do with the balance between the powers delegated to the federal government and those retained by the states. Under the Constitution, states retain sovereignty, giving them broad authority to enact laws, including election laws. The federal government will presumably intervene only when a state law runs counter to the Constitution. Further, the Constitution requires that states be treated equally; states cannot be subjected to disparate treatment by the federal government. Roberts then states that "the Voting Rights Act sharply departs from these basic principles." He explains that the circumstances that existed at the time of the passage of the VRA warranted federal intervention, for the "blight of racial discrimination in voting" had "infected the electoral process in parts of our country for nearly a century." He further notes that the coverage formula at that time made sense. However, he writes: "Nearly 50 years later, things have changed dramatically."

Roberts goes on to note, first, that the "tests and devices" that inhibited black voter participation are things of the past. Further, he provides data to show that black voter registration is very much on a par with white voter registration in the covered states. In 1965, for example, 69 percent of whites but only 19 percent of blacks were registered to vote in Alabama, one of the covered jurisdictions. In 2004, 73.8 percent of whites and 72.9 percent of blacks were registered, a gap of less than 1 percent. Despite these significant improvements on the ground, the relevant provisions of the VRA were reauthorized as if nothing had changed. Roberts notes that "the bar that covered jurisdictions must clear has been raised even as the conditions justifying that requirement have dramatically improved." He goes on to state: "Coverage today is based on decades-old data and eradicated practices. The formula captures States by reference to literacy tests and low voter registration and turnout in the 1960s and early 1970s." Roberts acknowledges the historical argument: that for decades, a system of Jim Crow laws disenfranchised African Americans, particularly in the South. He argues, however, that history did not end in 1965 and that the law as it stands keeps "the focus on decades-old data relevant to decades-old problems, rather than current data reflecting current needs." He concludes: "Our country has changed, and while any racial discrimination in voting is too much, Congress must ensure that the legislation it passes to remedy that problem speaks to current conditions."

Audience

The audience for any U.S. Supreme Court decision is likely to be fourfold. The first, of course, includes the parties to the suit, in this case Shelby County, Alabama, and the attorney general of the United States—and, by extension, the U.S. Justice Department. The second audience will include other jurisdictions that are affected by the Voting Rights Act and by the Court's decision—and even those that are not covered but that are contemplating changes in the voter registration process. The third includes members of the public who are Court watchers and who are interested in Supreme Court decisions in general and those pertaining to civil rights in particular. A fourth includes law school teachers and constitutional scholars, who will likely cite this case in examinations of voting laws, civil rights issues, constitutional issues, federalism, and the like.

Impact

After the Court's ruling, several states that had been affected by the preclearance provision of the VRA—and several that had not—changed voter registration procedures in their states. Among the changes was removal of online voter registration, early voting, Sunday voting, same-day (i.e., election day) registration, preregistration for those about to turn age eighteen, and "Souls to the Polls" programs designed to allow congregations at African American churches to vote as a community of faith after church services. Also, various states proposed tougher voter identification laws and took firm steps to purge ineligible voters from their registration rolls. One such state was Wisconsin, which passed a voter ID law that was challenged by the American Civil Liberties Union and the Advancement Project (a civil rights organization), which argued that the law would disproportionately affect minority voters. In a broader sense, many observers, including the nation's president at the time, Barack Obama, along with civil rights activists, condemned the ruling, calling it a setback in the ongoing struggle for civil rights. In 2014, a bill to remedy the defects of the VRA, titled the Voting Rights Amendment Act of 2014, was proposed in Congress, but the bill died in the Senate and House Judiciary Committees. A later bill, the Voting Rights Amendment Act of 2015, similarly died in committee.

Further Reading

Barnes, Robert. "Supreme Court Stops Use of Key Part of Voting Rights Act," *Washington Post*, June 25, 2013.

Bullock, Charles S. III, Ronald Keith Gaddie, and Justin J. Wert, eds. *The Rise and Fall of the Voting Rights Act*. Norman, OK: University of Oklahoma Press, 2016.

Davidson, Chandler. *Quiet Revolution in the South: The Impact of the Voting Rights Act, 1965–1990*. Princeton, NJ: Princeton University Press, 1994.

Gillette, William. *The Right to Vote: Politics and the Passage of the Fifteenth Amendment*. Baltimore, MD: Johns Hopkins Press, 1969.

Liptak, Adam. "Supreme Court Invalidates Key Part of Voting Rights Act," *New York Times*, June 25, 2013, p. A1

Supreme Court of the United States, *Shelby County, Alabama v. Holder, Attorney General*, https://www.supremecourt.gov/opinions/12pdf/12-96_6k47.pdf .

U.S. Department of Justice. "About Section 5 of the Voting Rights Act," https://www.justice.gov/crt/about-section-5-voting-rights-act.

——*Michael J. O'Neal, PhD*

Time Line		
1870	February 3	■ The Fifteenth Amendment to the Constitution is ratified.
1903	April 27	■ *Giles v. Harris*, U.S. Supreme Court case in which the Court held that the judiciary did not have the authority to force states to register minorities to vote.
1960	May 6	■ Civil Rights Act of 1960 signed into law
1964	July 2	■ Civil Rights Act of 1964 signed into law
1965	August 6	■ Voting Rights Act of 1965 signed into law
2013	*June 25*	■ *U.S. Supreme Court issues its decision in Shelby County v. Holder*

Essential Quotes

"Not only do States retain sovereignty under the Constitution, there is also a 'fundamental principle of equal sovereignty' among the States."

"In 1966, we found these departures from the basic features of our system of government justified. The 'blight of racial discrimination in voting" had "infected the electoral process in parts of our country for nearly a century.'"

"There is no valid reason to insulate the coverage formula from review merely because it was previously enacted 40 years ago. If Congress had started from scratch in 2006, it plainly could not have enacted the present coverage formula. It would have been irrational for Congress to distinguish between States in such a fundamental way based on 40-year-old data, when today's statistics tell an entirely different story."

Questions for Further Study

1. What constitutional arguments does Roberts use in the decision to strike down provisions of the Voting Rights Act?

2. What fundamental changes in voting patterns does Roberts use in his analysis?

3. What historical developments are relevant to Roberts's analysis of the issues raised by this case?

SHELBY COUNTY V. HOLDER

Extracts from the court opinion.

SUPREME COURT OF THE UNITED STATES

No. 12–96

SHELBY COUNTY, ALABAMA, PETITIONER v. ERIC H. HOLDER, Jr., ATTORNEY GENERAL, et al.

on writ of certiorari to the united states court of appeals for the district of columbia circuit

[June 25, 2013]

Chief Justice Roberts delivered the opinion of the Court.

The Voting Rights Act of 1965 employed extraordinary measures to address an extraordinary problem. Section 5 of the Act required States to obtain federal permission before enacting any law related to voting—a drastic departure from basic principles of federalism. And §4 of the Act applied that requirement only to some States—an equally dramatic departure from the principle that all States enjoy equal sovereignty. This was strong medicine, but Congress determined it was needed to address entrenched racial discrimination in voting, "an insidious and pervasive evil which had been perpetuated in certain parts of our country through unremitting and ingenious defiance of the Constitution." *South Carolina v. Katzenbach*, 383 U. S. 301, 309 (1966) . As we explained in upholding the law, "exceptional conditions can justify legislative measures not otherwise appropriate." Id., at 334. Reflecting the unprecedented nature of these measures, they were scheduled to expire after five years. See Voting Rights Act of 1965, §4(a), 79Stat. 438.

Nearly 50 years later, they are still in effect; indeed, they have been made more stringent, and are now scheduled to last until 2031. There is no denying, however, that the conditions that originally justified these measures no longer characterize voting in the covered jurisdictions. By 2009, "the racial gap in voter registration and turnout [was] lower in the States originally covered by §5 than it [was] nationwide." *Northwest Austin Municipal Util. Dist. No. One v. Holder*, 557 U. S. 193 –204 (2009). Since that time, Census Bureau data indicate that African-American voter turnout has come to exceed white voter turnout in five of the six States originally covered by §5, with a gap in the sixth State of less than one half of one percent. See Dept. of Commerce, Census Bureau, Reported Voting and Registration, by Sex, Race and Hispanic Origin, for States (Nov. 2012) (Table 4b).

At the same time, voting discrimination still exists; no one doubts that. The question is whether the Act's extraordinary measures, including its disparate treatment of the States, continue to satisfy constitutional requirements. As we put it a short time ago, "the Act imposes current burdens and must be justified by current needs." Northwest Austin, 557 U. S., at 203.

I

♦ **A**

The Fifteenth Amendment was ratified in 1870, in the wake of the Civil War. It provides that "[t]he right of citizens of the United States to vote shall not be denied or abridged by the United States or by any State on account of race, color, or previous condition of servitude," and it gives Congress the "power to enforce this article by appropriate legislation."

"The first century of congressional enforcement of the Amendment, however, can only be regarded as a failure." Id., at 197. In the 1890s, Alabama, Georgia, Louisiana, Mississippi, North Carolina, South Carolina, and Virginia began to enact literacy tests for voter registration and to employ other methods designed to prevent African-Americans from voting. *Katzenbach*, 383 U. S., at 310. Congress passed statutes outlawing some of these practices and facilitating litigation against them, but litigation remained slow and expensive, and the States came up with new ways to discriminate as soon as existing ones were struck down. Voter registration of African-Americans barely improved. Id., at 313–314.

Inspired to action by the civil rights movement, Congress responded in 1965 with the Voting Rights Act. Section 2 was enacted to forbid, in all 50 States, any "standard, practice, or procedure . . . imposed or applied . . . to deny or abridge the right of any citizen of the United States to vote on account of race or

Document Text

color." 79Stat. 437. The current version forbids any "standard, practice, or procedure" that "results in a denial or abridgement of the right of any citizen of the United States to vote on account of race or color." 42 U. S. C. §1973(a). Both the Federal Government and individuals have sued to enforce §2, see, e.g., *Johnson v. De Grandy*, 512 U. S. 997 (1994), and injunctive relief is available in appropriate cases to block voting laws from going into effect, see 42 U. S. C. §1973j(d). Section 2 is permanent, applies nationwide, and is not at issue in this case.

Other sections targeted only some parts of the country. At the time of the Act's passage, these "covered" jurisdictions were those States or political subdivisions that had maintained a test or device as a prerequisite to voting as of November 1, 1964, and had less than 50 percent voter registration or turnout in the 1964 Presidential election. §4(b), 79Stat. 438. Such tests or devices included literacy and knowledge tests, good moral character requirements, the need for vouchers from registered voters, and the like. §4(c), id., at 438–439. A covered jurisdiction could "bail out" of coverage if it had not used a test or device in the preceding five years "for the purpose or with the effect of denying or abridging the right to vote on account of race or color." §4(a), id., at 438. In 1965, the covered States included Alabama, Georgia, Louisiana, Mississippi, South Carolina, and Virginia. The additional covered subdivisions included 39 counties in North Carolina and one in Arizona. See 28 CFR pt. 51, App. (2012).

In those jurisdictions, §4 of the Act banned all such tests or devices. §4(a), 79Stat. 438. Section 5 provided that no change in voting procedures could take effect until it was approved by federal authorities in Washington, D. C.—either the Attorney General or a court of three judges. Id., at 439. A jurisdiction could obtain such "preclearance" only by proving that the change had neither "the purpose [nor] the effect of denying or abridging the right to vote on account of race or color." Ibid.

Sections 4 and 5 were intended to be temporary; they were set to expire after five years. See §4(a), id., at 438; Northwest Austin, supra, at 199. In *South Carolina v. Katzenbach*, we upheld the 1965 Act against constitutional challenge, explaining that it was justified to address "voting discrimination where it persists on a pervasive scale." 383 U. S., at 308.

In 1970, Congress reauthorized the Act for another five years, and extended the coverage formula in §4(b) to jurisdictions that had a voting test and less than 50 percent voter registration or turnout as of 1968. Voting Rights Act Amendments of 1970, §§3–4, 84Stat. 315. That swept in several counties in California, New Hampshire, and New York. See 28 CFR pt. 51, App. Congress also extended the ban in §4(a) on tests and devices nationwide. §6, 84Stat. 315.

In 1975, Congress reauthorized the Act for seven more years, and extended its coverage to jurisdictions that had a voting test and less than 50 percent voter registration or turnout as of 1972. Voting Rights Act Amendments of 1975, §§101, 202, 89Stat. 400, 401. Congress also amended the definition of "test or device" to include the practice of providing English-only voting materials in places where over five percent of voting-age citizens spoke a single language other than English. §203, id., at 401–402. As a result of these amendments, the States of Alaska, Arizona, and Texas, as well as several counties in California, Florida, Michigan, New York, North Carolina, and South Dakota, became covered jurisdictions. See 28 CFR pt. 51, App. Congress correspondingly amended sections 2 and 5 to forbid voting discrimination on the basis of membership in a language minority group, in addition to discrimination on the basis of race or color. §§203, 206, 89Stat. 401, 402. Finally, Congress made the nationwide ban on tests and devices permanent. §102, id., at 400.

In 1982, Congress reauthorized the Act for 25 years, but did not alter its coverage formula. See Voting Rights Act Amendments, 96Stat. 131. Congress did, however, amend the bailout provisions, allowing political subdivisions of covered jurisdictions to bail out. Among other prerequisites for bailout, jurisdictions and their subdivisions must not have used a forbidden test or device, failed to receive preclearance, or lost a §2 suit, in the ten years prior to seeking bailout. §2, id., at 131–133.

We upheld each of these reauthorizations against constitutional challenge. See *Georgia v. United States*, 411 U. S. 526 (1973); *City of Rome v. United States*, 446 U. S. 156 (1980); *Lopez v. Monterey County*, 525 U. S. 266 (1999).

In 2006, Congress again reauthorized the Voting Rights Act for 25 years, again without change to its coverage formula. Fannie Lou Hamer, Rosa Parks, and Coretta Scott King Voting Rights Act Reauthorization and Amendments Act, 120Stat. 577. Congress also amended §5 to prohibit more conduct than before. §5, id., at 580–581; see *Reno v. Bossier Parish School Bd.*, 528 U. S. 320, 341 (2000) (Bossier II); *Georgia v. Ashcroft*, 539 U. S. 461, 479 (2003). Section 5 now forbids voting changes with "any discriminatory purpose" as well as voting changes that diminish the ability of citizens, on account of race, color, or language minority status, "to elect their preferred candidates of choice." 42 U. S. C. §§1973c(b)–(d).

Shortly after this reauthorization, a Texas utility district brought suit, seeking to bail out from the Act's coverage and, in the alternative, challenging the Act's constitutionality. See Northwest Austin, 557 U. S., at 200–201. A three-judge District Court explained that only a State or political subdivision was eligible to seek bailout under the statute, and concluded that the utility district was not a political subdivision, a term that encompassed only "counties, parishes, and voter-registering subunits." *Northwest Austin Municipal Util. Dist. No. One v. Mukasey*, 573 F. Supp. 2d 221, 232 (DC 2008). The District Court also rejected the constitutional challenge. Id., at 283.

We reversed. We explained that " 'normally the Court will not decide a constitutional question if there is some other ground upon which to dispose of the case.' " Northwest Austin, supra, at 205 (quoting *Escambia County v. McMillan*, 466 U. S. 48, 51 (1984) (per curiam)). Concluding that "underlying constitutional concerns," among other things, "compel[led] a broader reading of the bailout provision," we construed the statute to allow the utility district to seek bailout. Northwest Austin, 557 U. S., at 207. In doing so we expressed serious doubts about the Act's continued constitutionality.

We explained that §5 "imposes substantial federalism costs" and "differentiates between the States, despite our historic tradition that all the States enjoy equal sovereignty." Id., at 202, 203 (internal quotation marks omitted). We also noted that "[t]hings have changed in the South. Voter turnout and registration rates now approach parity. Blatantly discriminatory evasions of federal decrees are rare. And minority candidates hold office at unprecedented levels." Id., at 202. Finally, we questioned whether the problems that §5 meant to address were still "concentrated in the jurisdictions singled out for preclearance." Id., at 203.

Eight Members of the Court subscribed to these views, and the remaining Member would have held the Act unconstitutional. Ultimately, however, the Court's construction of the bailout provision left the constitutional issues for another day.

♦ B

Shelby County is located in Alabama, a covered jurisdiction. It has not sought bailout, as the Attorney General has recently objected to voting changes proposed from within the county. See App. 87a–92a. Instead, in 2010, the county sued the Attorney General in Federal District Court in Washington, D. C., seeking a declaratory judgment that sections 4(b) and 5 of the Voting Rights Act are facially unconstitutional, as well as a permanent injunction against their enforcement. The District Court ruled against the county and upheld the Act. 811 F. Supp. 2d 424, 508 (2011). The court found that the evidence before Congress in 2006 was sufficient to justify reauthorizing §5 and continuing the §4(b) coverage formula.

The Court of Appeals for the D. C. Circuit affirmed. In assessing §5, the D. C. Circuit considered six primary categories of evidence: Attorney General objections to voting changes, Attorney General requests for more information regarding voting changes, successful §2 suits in covered jurisdictions, the dispatching of federal observers to monitor elections in covered jurisdictions, §5 preclearance suits involving covered jurisdictions, and the deterrent effect of §5. See 679 F. 3d 848, 862–863 (2012). After extensive analysis of the record, the court accepted Congress's conclusion that §2 litigation remained inadequate in the covered jurisdictions to protect the rights of minority voters, and that §5 was therefore still necessary. Id., at 873.

Turning to §4, the D. C. Circuit noted that the evidence for singling out the covered jurisdictions was "less robust" and that the issue presented "a close question." Id., at 879. But the court looked to data comparing the number of successful §2 suits in the different parts of the country. Coupling that evidence with the deterrent effect of §5, the court concluded that the statute continued "to single out the jurisdictions in which discrimination is concentrated," and thus held that the coverage formula passed constitutional muster. Id., at 883.

Judge Williams dissented. He found "no positive correlation between inclusion in §4(b)'s coverage formula and low black registration or turnout." Id., at 891. Rather, to the extent there was any correlation, it actually went the other way: "condemnation under §4(b) is a marker of higher black registration and turnout." Ibid. (emphasis added). Judge Williams also found that "[c]overed jurisdictions have far more black officeholders as a proportion of the black population than do uncovered ones." Id., at 892. As to the evidence of successful §2 suits, Judge Williams disaggregated the reported cases by State, and concluded that "[t]he five worst uncovered jurisdictions . . . have worse records than eight of the covered jurisdictions." Id., at 897. He also noted that two covered jurisdictions—Arizona and Alaska—had not had any successful reported §2 suit brought against them during the entire 24 years covered by the data. Ibid. Judge Williams would have held the coverage formula of §4(b) "irrational" and unconstitutional. Id., at 885.

We granted certiorari. 568 U. S. ___ (2012).

II

In Northwest Austin, we stated that "the Act imposes current burdens and must be justified by current needs." 557 U. S., at 203. And we concluded that "a departure from the fundamental principle of equal sovereignty requires a showing that a statute's disparate geographic coverage is sufficiently related to the problem that it targets." Ibid. These basic principles guide our review of the question before us. [1]

◆ A

The Constitution and laws of the United States are "the supreme Law of the Land." U. S. Const., Art. VI, cl. 2. State legislation may not contravene federal law. The Federal Government does not, however, have a general right to review and veto state enactments before they go into effect. A proposal to grant such authority to "negative" state laws was considered at the Constitutional Convention, but rejected in favor of allowing state laws to take effect, subject to later challenge under the Supremacy Clause. See 1 Records of the Federal Convention of 1787, pp. 21, 164–168 (M. Farrand ed. 1911); 2 id., at 27–29, 390–392.

Outside the strictures of the Supremacy Clause, States retain broad autonomy in structuring their governments and pursuing legislative objectives. Indeed, the Constitution provides that all powers not specifically granted to the Federal Government are reserved to the States or citizens. Amdt. 10. This "allocation of powers in our federal system preserves the integrity, dignity, and residual sovereignty of the States." *Bond v. United States*, 564 U. S. ___, ___ (2011) (slip op., at 9). But the federal balance "is not just an end in itself: Rather, federalism secures to citizens the liberties that derive from the diffusion of sovereign power." Ibid. (internal quotation marks omitted).

More specifically, " 'the Framers of the Constitution intended the States to keep for themselves, as provided in the Tenth Amendment, the power to regulate elections.' " *Gregory v. Ashcroft*, 501 U. S. 452 –462 (1991) (quoting *Sugarman v. Dougall*, 413 U. S. 634, 647 (1973) ; some internal quotation marks omitted). Of course, the Federal Government retains significant control over federal elections. For instance, the Constitution authorizes Congress to establish the time and manner for electing Senators and Representatives. Art. I, §4, cl. 1; see also *Arizona v. Inter Tribal Council of Ariz., Inc.*, ante, at 4–6. But States have "broad powers to determine the conditions under which the right of suffrage may be exercised." *Carrington v. Rash*, 380 U. S. 89, 91 (1965) (internal quotation marks omitted); see also Arizona, ante, at 13–15. And "[e]ach State has the power to prescribe the qualifications of its officers and the manner in which they shall be chosen." *Boyd v. Nebraska ex rel. Thayer*, 143 U. S. 135, 161 (1892) . Drawing lines for congressional districts is likewise "primarily the duty and responsibility of the State." *Perry v. Perez*, 565 U. S. ___, ___ (2012) (per curiam) (slip op., at 3) (internal quotation marks omitted).

Not only do States retain sovereignty under the Constitution, there is also a "fundamental principle of equal sovereignty" among the States. Northwest Austin, supra, at 203 (citing *United States v. Louisiana*, 363 U. S. 1, 16 (1960) ; *Lessee of Pollard v. Hagan*, 3 How. 212, 223 (1845); and *Texas v. White*, 7 Wall. 700, 725–726 (1869); emphasis added). Over a hundred years ago, this Court explained that our Nation "was and is a union of States, equal in power, dignity and authority." *Coyle v. Smith*, 221 U. S. 559, 567 (1911) . Indeed, "the constitutional equality of the States is essential to the harmonious operation of the scheme upon which the Republic was organized." Id., at 580. Coyle concerned the admission of new States, and *Katzenbach* rejected the notion that the principle operated as a bar on differential treatment outside that context. 383 U. S., at 328–329. At the same time, as we made clear in Northwest Austin, the fundamental principle of equal sovereignty remains highly pertinent in assessing subsequent disparate treatment of States. 557 U. S., at 203.

The Voting Rights Act sharply departs from these basic principles. It suspends "all changes to state election law—however innocuous—until they have been precleared by federal authorities in Washington, D. C." Id., at 202. States must beseech the Federal Government for permission to implement laws that they would otherwise have the right to enact and execute on their own, subject of course to any injunction in a §2 action. The Attorney General has 60 days to object to a preclearance request, longer if he requests more information. See 28 CFR §§51.9, 51.37. If a State seeks preclearance from a three-judge court, the process can take years.

And despite the tradition of equal sovereignty, the Act applies to only nine States (and several additional counties). While one State waits months or years and expends funds to implement a validly enacted law, its neighbor can typically put the same law into effect immediately, through the normal legislative process. Even if a noncovered jurisdiction is sued, there are important differences between those proceedings and preclearance proceedings; the preclearance proceeding "not only switches the burden of proof to the supplicant jurisdiction, but also applies substantive standards quite different from those governing the rest of the nation." 679 F. 3d, at 884 (Williams, J., dissenting) (case below).

All this explains why, when we first upheld the Act in 1966, we described it as "stringent" and "potent." Katzenbach, 383 U. S., at 308, 315, 337. We recognized that it "may have been an uncommon exercise of congressional power," but concluded that "legislative measures not otherwise appropriate" could be justified by "exceptional conditions." Id., at 334. We have since noted that the Act "authorizes federal intrusion into sensitive areas of state and local policymaking," Lopez, 525 U. S., at 282, and represents an "extraordinary departure from the traditional course of relations between the States and the Federal Government," Presley v. Etowah County Comm'n, 502 U. S. 491 –501 (1992). As we reiterated in Northwest Austin, the Act constitutes "extraordinary legislation otherwise unfamiliar to our federal system." 557 U. S., at 211.

◆ B

In 1966, we found these departures from the basic features of our system of government justified. The "blight of racial discrimination in voting" had "infected the electoral process in parts of our country for nearly a century." Katzenbach, 383 U. S., at 308. Several States had enacted a variety of requirements and tests "specifically designed to prevent" African-Americans from voting. Id., at 310. Case-by-case litigation had proved inadequate to prevent such racial discrimination in voting, in part because States "merely switched to discriminatory devices not covered by the federal decrees," "enacted difficult new tests," or simply "defied and evaded court orders." Id., at 314. Shortly before enactment of the Voting Rights Act, only 19.4 percent of African-Americans of voting age were registered to vote in Alabama, only 31.8 percent in Louisiana, and only 6.4 percent in Mississippi. Id., at 313. Those figures were roughly 50 percentage points or more below the figures for whites. Ibid.

In short, we concluded that "[u]nder the compulsion of these unique circumstances, Congress responded in a permissibly decisive manner." Id., at 334, 335. We also noted then and have emphasized since that this extraordinary legislation was intended to be temporary, set to expire after five years. Id., at 333; Northwest Austin, supra, at 199.

At the time, the coverage formula—the means of linking the exercise of the unprecedented authority with the problem that warranted it—made sense. We found that "Congress chose to limit its attention to the geographic areas where immediate action seemed necessary." Katzenbach, 383 U. S., at 328. The areas where Congress found "evidence of actual voting discrimination" shared two characteristics: "the use of tests and devices for voter registration, and a voting rate in the 1964 presidential election at least 12 points below the national average." Id., at 330. We explained that "[t]ests and devices are relevant to voting discrimination because of their long history as a tool for perpetrating the evil; a low voting rate is pertinent for the obvious reason that widespread disenfranchisement must inevitably affect the number of actual voters." Ibid. We therefore concluded that "the coverage formula [was] rational in both practice and theory." Ibid. It accurately reflected those jurisdictions uniquely characterized by voting discrimination "on a pervasive scale," linking coverage to the devices used to effectuate discrimination and to the resulting disenfranchisement. Id., at 308. The formula ensured that the "stringent remedies [were] aimed at areas where voting discrimination ha[d] been most flagrant." Id., at 315.

◆ C

Nearly 50 years later, things have changed dramatically. Shelby County contends that the preclearance requirement, even without regard to its disparate coverage, is now unconstitutional. Its arguments have a good deal of force. In the covered jurisdictions, "[v]oter turnout and registration rates now approach parity. Blatantly discriminatory evasions of federal decrees are rare. And minority candidates hold office at unprecedented levels." Northwest Austin, 557 U. S., at 202. The tests and devices that blocked access to the ballot have been forbidden nationwide for over 40 years. See §6, 84Stat. 315; §102, 89Stat. 400.

Those conclusions are not ours alone. Congress said the same when it reauthorized the Act in 2006, writing that "[s]ignificant progress has been made in eliminating first generation barriers experienced by minority voters, including increased numbers of registered minority voters, minority voter turnout, and minority representation in Congress, State legislatures, and local elected offices." §2(b)(1), 120Stat. 577. The House Report elaborated that "the number of African-Americans who are registered and who turn out to cast ballots has increased significantly over the last 40 years, particularly since 1982," and noted that "[i]n some circumstances, minorities register to vote and cast ballots at levels that surpass those of white voters." H. R. Rep. No. 109–478, p. 12 (2006). That Report also explained that there have been "significant increases in the number of African-Americans serving in elected offices"; more specifically, there has been approximately a 1,000 percent increase since 1965 in the number of African-American elected officials in the six States originally covered by the Voting Rights Act. Id., at 18.

The following chart, compiled from the Senate and House Reports, compares voter registration numbers from 1965 to those from 2004 in the six originally covered States. These are the numbers that were before Congress when it reauthorized the Act in 2006:

	1965			2004		
	White	Black	Gap	White	Black	Gap
Alabama	69.2	19.3	49.9	73.8	72.9	0.9
Georgia	62.[6]	27.4	35.2	63.5	64.2	-0.7
Louisiana	80.5	31.6	48.9	75.1	71.1	4.0
Mississippi	69.9	6.7	63.2	72.3	76.1	-3.8
South Carolina	75.7	37.3	38.4	74.4	71.1	3.3
Virginia	61.1	38.3	22.8	68.2	57.4	10.8

See S. Rep. No. 109–295, p. 11 (2006); H. R. Rep. No. 109–478, at 12. The 2004 figures come from the Census Bureau. Census Bureau data from the most recent election indicate that African-American voter turnout exceeded white voter turnout in five of the six States originally covered by §5, with a gap in the sixth State of less than one half of one percent. See Dept. of Commerce, Census Bureau, Reported Voting and Registration, by Sex, Race and Hispanic Origin, for States (Table 4b). The preclearance statistics are also illuminating. In the first decade after enactment of §5, the Attorney General objected to 14.2 percent of proposed voting changes. H. R Rep. No. 109–478, at 22. In the last decade before reenactment, the Attorney General objected to a mere 0.16 percent. S. Rep. No. 109–295, at 13.

There is no doubt that these improvements are in large part because of the Voting Rights Act. The Act has proved immensely successful at redressing racial discrimination and integrating the voting process. See §2(b)(1), 120Stat. 577. During the "Freedom Summer" of 1964, in Philadelphia, Mississippi, three men were murdered while working in the area to register African-American voters. See *United States v. Price*, 383 U. S. 787, 790 (1966) . On "Bloody Sunday" in 1965, in Selma, Alabama, police beat and used tear gas against hundreds marching in support of African-American enfranchisement. See Northwest Austin, supra, at 220, n. 3 (Thomas, J., concurring in judgment in part and dissenting in part). Today both of those towns are governed by African-American mayors. Problems remain in these States and others, but there is no denying that, due to the Voting Rights Act, our Nation has made great strides.

Yet the Act has not eased the restrictions in §5 or narrowed the scope of the coverage formula in §4(b) along the way. Those extraordinary and unprecedented features were reauthorized—as if nothing had changed. In fact, the Act's unusual remedies have grown even stronger. When Congress reauthorized the Act in 2006, it did so for another 25 years on top of the previous 40—a far cry from the initial five-year period. See 42 U. S. C. §1973b(a)(8). Congress also expanded the prohibitions in §5. We had previously interpreted §5 to prohibit only those redistricting plans that would have the purpose or effect of worsening the position of minority groups. See Bossier II, 528 U. S., at 324, 335–336. In 2006, Congress amended §5 to prohibit laws that could have favored such groups but did not do so because of a discriminatory purpose, see 42 U. S. C. §1973c(c), even though we had stated that such broadening of §5 coverage would "exacerbate the substantial federalism costs that the preclearance procedure already exacts, perhaps to the extent of raising concerns about §5's constitutionality," Bossier II, supra, at 336 (citation and internal quotation marks omitted). In addition, Congress expanded §5 to prohibit any voting law "that has the purpose of or will have the effect of diminishing the ability of any citizens of the United States," on account of race, color, or language minority status, "to elect their preferred candidates of choice." §1973c(b). In light of those two amendments, the bar that covered jurisdictions must clear has been raised even as the conditions justifying that requirement have dramatically improved.

We have also previously highlighted the concern that "the preclearance requirements in one State [might] be unconstitutional in another." Northwest Austin, 557 U. S., at 203; see *Georgia v. Ashcroft*, 539 U. S., at 491 (Kennedy, J., concurring) ("considerations of race that would doom a redistricting plan under the Fourteenth Amendment or §2 [of the Voting Rights Act] seem to be what save it under §5"). Nothing has happened since to alleviate this troubling concern about the current application of §5.

Respondents do not deny that there have been improvements on the ground, but argue that much of this can be attributed to the deterrent effect of §5, which dissuades covered jurisdictions from engaging in discrimination that they would resume should §5 be struck down. Under this theory, however, §5 would be effectively immune from scrutiny; no matter how "clean" the record of covered jurisdictions, the argument could always be made that it was deterrence that accounted for the good behavior.

The provisions of §5 apply only to those jurisdictions singled out by §4. We now consider whether that coverage formula is constitutional in light of current conditions.

III

◆ A

When upholding the constitutionality of the coverage formula in 1966, we concluded that it was "rational in both practice and theory." Katzenbach, 383 U. S., at 330. The formula looked to cause (discriminatory tests) and effect (low voter registration and turnout), and tailored the remedy (preclearance) to those jurisdictions exhibiting both.

By 2009, however, we concluded that the "coverage formula raise[d] serious constitutional questions." Northwest Austin, 557 U. S., at 204. As we explained, a statute's "current burdens" must be justified by "current needs," and any "disparate geographic coverage" must be "sufficiently related to the problem that it targets." Id., at 203. The coverage formula met that test in 1965, but no longer does so.

Coverage today is based on decades-old data and eradicated practices. The formula captures States by reference to literacy tests and low voter registration and turnout in the 1960s and early 1970s. But such tests have been banned nationwide for over 40 years. §6, 84Stat. 315; §102, 89Stat. 400. And voter registration and turnout numbers in the covered States have risen dramatically in the years since. H. R. Rep. No. 109–478, at 12. Racial disparity in those numbers was compelling evidence justifying the preclearance remedy and the coverage formula. See, e.g., Katzenbach, supra, at 313, 329–330. There is no longer such a disparity.

In 1965, the States could be divided into two groups: those with a recent history of voting tests and low voter registration and turnout, and those without those characteristics. Congress based its coverage formula on that distinction. Today the Nation is no longer divided along those lines, yet the Voting Rights Act continues to treat it as if it were.

◆ B

The Government's defense of the formula is limited. First, the Government contends that the formula is "reverse-engineered": Congress identified the jurisdictions to be covered and then came up with criteria to describe them. Brief for Federal Respondent 48–49. Under that reasoning, there need not be any logical relationship between the criteria in the formula and the reason for coverage; all that is necessary is that the formula happen to capture the jurisdictions Congress wanted to single out.

The Government suggests that Katzenbach sanctioned such an approach, but the analysis in Katzenbach was quite different. Katzenbach reasoned that the coverage formula was rational because the "formula . . . was relevant to the problem": "Tests and devices are relevant to voting discrimination because of their long history as a tool for perpetrating the evil; a low voting rate is pertinent for the obvious reason that widespread disenfranchisement must inevitably affect the number of actual voters." 383 U. S., at 329, 330.

Here, by contrast, the Government's reverse-engineering argument does not even attempt to demonstrate the continued relevance of the formula to the problem it targets. And in the context of a decision as significant as this one—subjecting a disfavored subset of States to "extraordinary legislation otherwise unfamiliar to our federal system," Northwest Austin, supra, at 211—that failure to establish even relevance is fatal.

The Government falls back to the argument that because the formula was relevant in 1965, its continued use is permissible so long as any discrimination remains in the States Congress identified back then—regardless of how that discrimination compares to discrimination in States unburdened by coverage. Brief for Federal Respondent 49–50. This argument does not look to "current political conditions," Northwest Austin, supra, at 203, but instead relies on a comparison between the States in 1965. That comparison reflected the different histories of the North and South. It was in the South that slavery was upheld by law until uprooted by the Civil War, that the reign of Jim Crow denied African-Americans the most basic freedoms, and that state and local governments worked tirelessly to disenfranchise citizens on the basis of race. The Court invoked that history—rightly so—in sustaining the disparate coverage of the Voting Rights Act in 1966. See Katzenbach, supra, at 308 ("The constitutional propriety of the Voting Rights Act of 1965 must be judged with reference to the historical experience which it reflects.").

But history did not end in 1965. By the time the Act was reauthorized in 2006, there had been 40 more years of it. In assessing the "current need[ ]" for a preclearance system that treats States differently from one another today, that history cannot be ignored. During that time, largely because of the Voting Rights Act, voting tests were abolished, disparities in voter registration and turnout due to race were erased, and African-Americans attained political office in record numbers. And yet the coverage formula that Congress reauthorized in 2006 ignores these developments, keeping the focus on decades-old data relevant to decades-old problems, rather than current data reflecting current needs.

The Fifteenth Amendment commands that the right to vote shall not be denied or abridged on account of race or color, and it gives Congress the power to enforce that command. The Amendment is not designed to punish for the past; its purpose is to ensure a better future. See *Rice v. Cayetano*, 528 U. S. 495, 512 (2000) ("Consistent with the design of the Constitution, the [Fifteenth] Amendment is cast in fundamental terms, terms transcending the particular controversy which was the immediate impetus for its enactment."). To serve that purpose, Congress—if it is to divide the States—must identify those jurisdictions to be singled out on a basis that makes sense in light of current conditions. It cannot rely simply on the past. We made that clear in Northwest Austin, and we make it clear again today.

♦ C

In defending the coverage formula, the Government, the intervenors, and the dissent also rely heavily on data from the record that they claim justify disparate coverage. Congress compiled thousands of pages of evidence before reauthorizing the Voting Rights Act. The court below and the parties have debated what that record shows—they have gone back and forth about whether to compare covered to noncovered jurisdictions as blocks, how to disaggregate the data State by State, how to weigh §2 cases as evidence of ongoing discrimination, and whether to consider evidence not before Congress, among other issues. Compare, e.g., 679 F. 3d, at 873–883 (case below), with id., at 889–902 (Williams, J., dissenting). Regardless of how to look at the record, however, no one can fairly say that it shows anything approaching the "pervasive," "flagrant," "widespread," and "rampant" discrimination that faced Congress in 1965, and that clearly distinguished the covered jurisdictions from the rest of the Nation at that time. *Katzenbach*, supra, at 308, 315, 331; Northwest Austin, 557 U. S., at 201.

But a more fundamental problem remains: Congress did not use the record it compiled to shape a coverage formula grounded in current conditions. It instead reenacted a formula based on 40-year-old facts having no logical relation to the present day. The dissent relies on "second-generation barriers," which are not impediments to the casting of ballots, but rather electoral arrangements that affect the weight of minority votes. That does not cure the problem. Viewing the preclearance requirements as targeting such efforts simply highlights the irrationality of continued reliance on the §4 coverage formula, which is based on voting tests and access to the ballot, not vote dilution. We cannot pretend that we are reviewing an updated statute, or try our hand at updating the statute ourselves, based on the new record compiled by Congress. Contrary to the dissent's contention, see post, at 23, we are not ignoring the record; we are simply recognizing that it played no role in shaping the statutory formula before us today.

The dissent also turns to the record to argue that, in light of voting discrimination in Shelby County, the county cannot complain about the provisions that subject it to preclearance. Post, at 23–30. But that is like saying that a driver pulled over pursuant to a policy of stopping all redheads cannot complain about that policy, if it turns out his license has expired. Shelby County's claim is that the coverage formula here is unconstitutional in all its applications, because of how it selects the jurisdictions subjected to preclearance. The county was selected based on that formula, and may challenge it in court.

{ED: Is suggest deleting the portion of the decision that I've lined out. It wanders into the weeds and is not necessary to the central decision.}

******

Striking down an Act of Congress "is the gravest and most delicate duty that this Court is called on to perform." *Blodgett v. Holden*, 275 U. S. 142, 148 (1927) (Holmes, J., concurring). We do not do so lightly. That is why, in 2009, we took care to avoid ruling on the constitutionality of the Voting Rights Act when asked to do so, and instead resolved the case then before us on statutory grounds. But in issuing that decision, we expressed our broader concerns about the constitutionality of the Act. Congress could have updated the coverage formula at that time, but did not do so. Its failure to act leaves us today with no choice but to declare §4(b) unconstitutional. The formula in that section can no longer be used as a basis for subjecting jurisdictions to preclearance.

Our decision in no way affects the permanent, nationwide ban on racial discrimination in voting found in §2. We issue no holding on §5 itself, only on the coverage formula. Congress may draft another formula based on current conditions. Such a formula is an initial prerequisite to a determination that exceptional conditions still exist justifying such an "extraordinary departure from the traditional course of relations between the States and the Federal Government." Presley, 502 U. S., at 500–501. Our country has changed, and while any racial discrimination in voting is too much, Congress must ensure that the legislation it passes to remedy that problem speaks to current conditions.

The judgment of the Court of Appeals is reversed. It is so ordered.

◆ **Notes**

1 Both the Fourteenth and s were at issue in Northwest Austin, see Juris. Statement i, and Brief for Federal Appellee 29–30, in *Northwest Austin Municipal Util. Dist. No. One v. Holder*, O. T. 2008, No. 08–322, and accordingly *Northwest Austin* guides our review under both Amendments in this case.

Glossary

"covered" jurisdictions: states or political subdivisions that had maintained a test or device as a prerequisite to voting that had the effect of discriminating against minority groups

preclearance: a provision of the Voting Rights Act of 1965 requiring political subdivisions that wanted to enact a change in voting requirements or procedures to obtain authorization from the federal government

test or device: any requirement used to prevent minorities from registering to vote or from voting, including such requirements as poll taxes and literacy tests.

Protest march in response to the Jamar Clark shooting, Minneapolis, Minnesota. Fibonacci Blue from Minnesota, USA - Justice for Jamar Response Action. [CC BY 2.0 (http://creativecommons.org/licenses/by/2.0)], via Wikimedia Commons

Movement for Black Lives—Vision for Black Lives

"Together, we demand an end to the wars against Black people."

Overview

In July 2015, a coalition of African-American community groups gathered at Cleveland State University to link their efforts together and found a larger, umbrella organization whose numbers could not be easily ignored by government. The result in 2016 was the Movement for Black Lives. Over the course of its assembly between 2015 and 2016, leaders and members of MBL wrote up a manifesto of sorts, a platform of demands defined by the problems that brought the demands about and the solutions the MBL expected to effect. The resulting platform became known over social media as the Vision for Black Lives, and was generally associated by the public with one of the smaller groups contained within the Movement for Black Lives, called Black Lives Matter.

Context

In February 2012, a 17-year-old African-American boy named Trayvon Martin was shot and killed while walking through a Sanford, Florida neighborhood by a neighborhood watch captain, George Zimmerman. In the subsequent trial, Zimmerman was acquitted of murder and manslaughter, even though the only thing that aroused his suspicions on Trayvon was the fact that Trayvon was black and wearing a sweatshirt with the hood on his head.

The verdict outraged many Americans but in particular African-Americans. The Trayvon Martin episode focused attention on encounters around the United States between black people and the police. Sadly, a whole series of similar killings was exposed to public scrutiny in the next few years as a result: Eric Garner in Staten Island in July 2014, Michael Brown in Ferguson, Missouri in August 2014, Tamir Rice in Cleveland in November 2014, Sandra Bland in Hempstead, Texas in July 2015, Philando Castile in St. Paul, Minnesota in July 2016, and many more. Worse, in most of these incidents, the police officers involved received no serious punishment, if any – some were not even indicted.

After the Trayvon Martin verdict, three female activists, Patrisse Cullors, Alicia Garza and Opal Tometi, came together to create a community action initiative they referred to as Black Lives Matter. Numerous other black organizations that opposed police violence and injustice against blacks were created at the same time, but Black Lives Matter had a catchy hashtag in the era of social media, righteously stated, easily remembered and widely spread on the internet. Cullors, Garza and Tometi also developed a more wide-ranging agenda, stated in a manifesto on the BLM website, addressing issues of gender, economic, and educational inequality. While its ideas were somewhat polarizing, the most important point of the manifesto was that it saw police brutality as a symptom of a larger cause, the disenfranchisement of African-Americans in mainstream American culture and politics, and thus held a larger appeal to the activist community as a whole.

Black Lives Matter was one of many activist groups that came together in July 2015 at Cleveland State University, to combine their forces for the purposes of advocacy. More than 50 different groups, some older than the Trayvon Martin episode but most newer, came together under a title chosen based on the notoriety of Black Lives Matter: the Movement for Black Lives. Over 1500 attendees came together to "strategize ways for the Movement for Black Lives to hold law enforcement accountable for their actions on a national level". For three days, the participants held panels and discussions on the problems of African-American life in the United States. Over the course of the next year, the groups worked out a lasting structure.

Yet even though they shared many of the same goals, there were many differences of opinion on what the Movement for Black Lives should be about. Was it largely about the police brutality that had cost so many young lives? Or was it, as Black Lives Matter had declared, largely about the lasting problem of discrimination, with antecedents in the centuries of slavery? The result was a free-floating constitutional convention, with the identification of problems and proposed solutions, which resulted in a platform for

Protest march in response to the shooting of Philando Castile, St. Paul, Minnesota on July 7, 2016. By Fibonacci Blue from Minnesota, USA [CC BY 2.0 (http://creativecommons.org/licenses/by/2.0)], via Wikimedia Commons

the Movement for Black Lives. As spread through social media, it came to have the name Vision for Black Lives.

About the Author

Since the Vision for Black Lives is a manifesto hoping to direct future legislation – a constitution – like any constitution, it had many authors. The platform was produced by a coalition of the leaders of approximately 50 black activist groups. Naturally, so many different groups had vastly different agendas, and the year's worth of negotiations over the platform was heated and conflictual. Black Lives Matter and its platform led the way in terms of structure, but also important was the Black Panthers' Ten-Point Program, dating from the 1960s and articulating much the same vision. Other groups involved in the design of the platform included the Black Youth Project 100, the Dream Defenders, the Ella Baker Center for Human Rights, the National Black Food and Justice Alliance, the Center for Media Justice, Mothers Against Police Brutality and dozens of others. Importantly, not every group involved in the negotiations signed off on the platform. One was Campaign ZERO, a group focused mostly on reforming the criminal justice system. Their members wanted to demand that police wear body cameras and walk beats in communities as opposed to simply driving through them. The Movement for Black Lives opposed body cameras as simply another way of discriminating against African-American communities, since such cameras were not considered necessary in white communities. On the other hand, Campaign ZERO's policy vision was accepted by the Democratic National Convention in its platform in 2016.

Explanation and Analysis of the Document

The Vision for Black Lives opens with a statement of purpose. The organizations aver that African-Americans have always had to demonstrate for and seized their own political rights as laid out in the US Constitution, and the time has come to do it once again. Violence against black communities has given them common cause with each other and with other oppressed groups in the United States, including "those who are women, queer, trans, femmes, gender nonconforming, Muslim, formerly and currently incarcerated, cash poor and working class, disabled, undocumented, and immigrant". In articulating their vision, the movement asserts that its ideas are universal and international, and that their hope is to provide a blueprint for future legislation, though they recognize that they might not achieve many of their aims anytime soon.

The platform is divided then into six demands – "End the War on Black People", "Reparations", "Invest-Divest", "Economic Justice" "Community Control", and "Political Power". Each of these demands is spelled out in a numbered list of specific outcomes the group wants to achieve.

Importantly, the outcomes are followed by sections called "What is the Problem?" and "What is the Solution?" One of the running complaints in the press about Black Lives Matter was that few people knew exactly what the group stood for, other than an end to police brutality. Furthermore, many people implied that the term "Black Lives Matter" was a denial that other lives mattered as much to the organization, a misinterpretation that was explicitly denied in their own manifesto – the point was that, amongst all the other people struggling to succeed in the United States, "black lives matter, too". Here, in the Movement for Black Lives' platform, there would be no mistaking exactly what was meant by the idea that "black lives matter". If future policymakers were to agree with the platform, they must adhere to the goal of achieving the six demands, for the reasons spelled out, and with the hope of achieving the suggested solutions.

♦ END THE WAR ON BLACK PEOPLE

The platform calls for the establishment of a fair justice system, an improved education system, an end to capital punishment (which was inordinately discriminatory toward black convicts) and a revamping of the prison system, the end of surveillance of black neighborhoods and the like. An interesting inclusion in all the demands is the expectation that discrimination against transgendered, queer and gender nonconforming African-Americans will come to an end too. Both the Black Lives Matter platform and the Vision for Black Lives recognize the unique difficulties faced by LGBTQ groups within the African-American community, and explicitly acknowledged those difficulties in their statements of purpose. In their statement of the problem, the authors note that repairing the problem with black crime is connected to repairing the state of black education – "Zero-tolerance policies — a combination of exclusionary disciplinary policies and school-based arrests — are often the first stop along the school-to-prison pipeline and play a key role in pushing students out of the school system and funneling them into jails and prisons." This is especially true of black girls, who often have been abused and have few outlets for their issues when their schools practice zero tolerance. In summary, the solutions involve incorporating care and consideration into the practices of schooling and juvenile justice, such that "we would save hundreds of millions of dollars annually and provide the opportunity for our children to outlive their mistakes."

♦ REPARATIONS

Perhaps the most well-known and least understood part of the platform was the demand for reparations to be paid to African-Americans in retribution for the evils of slavery and discrimination. Most white Americans recoiled from the concept, including 57% of those polled in the weeks near the 2016 Democratic National Convention. Yet it was not nearly as outlandish as Americans seemed to think it was in world history. The German government long provided restitution to Holocaust survivors; the Truth and Reconciliation

Committee in South Africa occasionally awarded reparations to those families damaged in the era of apartheid; and the government in Cambodia has tried to accommodate the victims of Pol Pot's communist purge in the 1970s. Likewise, many people mistook reparations to mean cash payouts to make up for the abuses inflicted on the ancestors of those African-Americans alive today. In point of fact, as the solutions point out, reparations in the Visions for Black Lives amounts to the provision of equal opportunity to all through free public education at all levels and for all societies – a program actually adopted by Democratic Senator Bernie Sanders in his campaign for president in 2016.

♦ INVEST-DIVEST
In this demand, the platform calls for economic backing of the principles of the earlier demands. Money and investment should be poured into education and employment, health and safety, and taken out of programs involving criminalization and incarceration.

♦ ECONOMIC JUSTICE
More comprehensively, the platform calls for a reconstructed economy that includes "collective ownership, not merely access." Most of these demands would be familiar to any liberal on the American political spectrum. The movement called for restructuring tax codes to take more money from the rich and less from the poor, the encouragement of black businesses and entrepreneurship, better environmental regulations, the breaking up of large banks, corporations and trade deals, and the provision of low-interest loans to the African-American community. Most controversial might have been the call to end the Trans-Pacific Partnership, an initiative of then-President Barack Obama which was meant to lower prices in the American marketplace through increased competition with East Asian goods, but which was widely perceived as simply handing jobs over to those same East Asian companies while putting American companies out of business. In essence, this demand called in general for wealth redistribution from the rich to the poor through the tools of government taxation and programs.

♦ COMMUNITY CONTROL
This demand addresses the considered problem of democratization, a growing issue in the twenty-first century. Perception grew amongst both conservatives and liberals that the tools of government were increasingly in the hands of the wealthy and the powerful, interest groups with money who distorted politics for their own ends. The Movement for Black Lives called for greater control over education, police departments, and budgeting in government in general. Interestingly, the solutions in this section address the specific issue of police brutality, while ignoring the larger question of who retained power in government.

♦ POLITICAL POWER
The platform ends with a call for the removal of the power of money in elections and expansion of the right to vote for African-Americans, in particular ending laws directed at "voter fraud' in many states. The problem of voter fraud was a sham – the number of fraudulent votes numbered less than 1000 in any given election across the entire United States, yet efforts to combat it through the demand for drivers' licenses, bills and other identification methods specifically targeted blacks because they were often too poor to have such identification. The demand also calls for net neutrality and universal access to the internet as an information source, treating the internet as if it were another utility in a home. Most controversial, the movement called for the "release of all political prisoners held in the U.S." and an investigation into the FBI's campaigns against the Black Panthers and other African-American political organizations in the 1970s. "Political prisoners" likely included Mumia Abu-Jamal, an accused murderer of a Philadelphia policeman who was then serving a life sentence in a Pennsylvania state prison.

Audience

The obvious audience for the Vision for Black Lives was the African-American community itself. The platform was meant to be a rallying point, a rebirth of the unity of the civil rights movement, and a basis for future legislation. Likewise, the platform's date of issuance was no mistake: a week before the 2016 Democratic National Convention. The convention did not adopt the platform as a basis for running its campaign – the concept of reparations was very unpopular – but the leaders of the Movement for Black Lives did not expect immediate success. Over time, the more cohesive that the black community became behind the Vision for Black Lives, the likelier they would be to exercise political power in the voting booth, and also with the political parties and the government.

Impact

The Movement for Black Lives and Black Lives Matter became well known in US culture, though less so for the Vision for Black Lives and more for the useful social media hashtag #BlackLivesMatter. Still, many other interest groups read the platform and commented favorably or unfavorably on its tenets. Though there is nothing in the platform discussing Israel, many Israel advocacy groups accused the movement of being anti-Semitic based on later statements condemning Israel's role in the conflict with Palestinians. On the other hand, several other minority advocacy groups endorsed the platform, especially in light of the continued exposure of police violence in the years following its issue. Professional athletes such as football player Colin Kaepernick and basketball player LeBron James demonstrated and made public statements in favor of the Movement's program. Other groups identified with the Movement's desire to promote the democratization of

American politics and the reduction in the power of corporate money in government.

Further Reading

◆ **Books**

Lebron, Christopher J. *The Making of Black Lives Matter: A Brief History of an Idea.* New York: Oxford University Press, 2017.

Camp, Jordan T. and Christina Heatherton, editors. *Policing the Planet: Why the Policing Crisis Led to Black Lives Matter.* New York: Verso, 2016.

D'Angelo, Raymond and Herbert Douglas, editors. *Taking Sides: Clashing Views in Race and Ethnicity.* New York: McGraw-Hill Education, 2017.

Liu, Eric. *You're More Powerful Than You Think: A Citizen Guide to Making Change Happen.* New York: Public Affairs, 2017.

◆ **Web Sites**

Cullors, Patrice, Opal Tometi, and Alicia Garza. *Black Lives Matter.* Haki Creatives http://blacklivesmatter.com/ [accessed August 3, 2017].

The Movement for Black Lives. https://policy.m4bl.org/ [accessed August 3, 2017].

——David Simonelli

Time Line		
2012	February	■ Trayvon Martin is shot in Sanford, Florida by George Zimmerman
2013	July 13	■ Zimmerman acquitted of murder and manslaughter charges
2014	July	■ Eric Garner strangled to death by police in New York City
2014	August	■ Michael Brown of Ferguson, Missouri shot and killed by police
2014	November	■ Tamir Rice shot and killed by police in Cleveland
2015	July	■ Sandra Bland found dead by hanging in jail cell in Hempstead, Texas National Convening of the Movement for Black Lives at Cleveland State University
2016	July	■ Philando Castile shot and killed by police in St. Paul, Minnesota
		■ Platform of Movement for Black Lives published, referred to as Vision for Black Lives
		■ Democratic National Convention held in Philadelphia

Essential Quotes

"Together, we demand an end to the wars against Black people."

"Zero-tolerance policies — a combination of exclusionary disciplinary policies and school-based arrests — are often the first stop along the school-to-prison pipeline and play a key role in pushing students out of the school system and funneling them into jails and prisons."

"We demand **reparations for past and continuing harms.** The government, responsible corporations and other institutions that have profited off of the harm they have inflicted on Black people — from colonialism to slavery through food and housing redlining, mass incarceration, and surveillance — must repair the harm done."

"We demand **investments in the education, health and safety of Black people,** instead of investments in the criminalizing, caging, and harming of Black people. We want investments in Black communities, determined by Black communities, and **divestment from exploitative forces** including prisons, fossil fuels, police, surveillance and exploitative corporations."

"We demand a world where those most impacted in our **communities control the laws, institutions, and policies that are meant to serve us** – from our schools to our local budgets, economies, police departments, and our land – while recognizing that the rights and histories of our Indigenous family must also be respected."

"We demand **independent Black political power and Black self-determination** in all areas of society. We envision a remaking of the current U.S. political system in order to create a real democracy where Black people and all marginalized people can effectively exercise full political power."

Movement for Black Lives—Vision for Black Lives

Full text of the Black Lives Matter platform

Black humanity and dignity requires Black political will and power. Despite constant exploitation and perpetual oppression, Black people have bravely and brilliantly been the driving force pushing the U.S. towards the ideals it articulates but has never achieved. In recent years we have taken to the streets, launched massive campaigns, and impacted elections, but our elected leaders have failed to address the legitimate demands of our Movement. We can no longer wait.

In response to the sustained and increasingly visible violence against Black communities in the U.S. and globally, a collective of more than 50 organizations representing thousands of Black people from across the country have come together with renewed energy and purpose to articulate a common vision and agenda. We are a collective that centers and is rooted in Black communities, but we recognize we have a shared struggle with all oppressed people; collective liberation will be a product of all of our work.

We believe in elevating the experiences and leadership of the most marginalized Black people, including but not limited to those who are women, queer, trans, femmes, gender nonconforming, Muslim, formerly and currently incarcerated, cash poor and working class, disabled, undocumented, and immigrant. We are intentional about amplifying the particular experience of state and gendered violence that Black queer, trans, gender nonconforming, women and intersex people face. There can be no liberation for all Black people if we do not center and fight for those who have been marginalized. It is our hope that by working together to create and amplify a shared agenda, we can continue to move towards a world in which the full humanity and dignity of all people is recognized.

While this platform is focused on domestic policies, we know that patriarchy, exploitative capitalism, militarism, and white supremacy know no borders. We stand in solidarity with our international family against the ravages of global capitalism and anti-Black racism, human-made climate change, war, and exploitation. We also stand with descendants of African people all over the world in an ongoing call and struggle for reparations for the historic and continuing harms of colonialism and slavery. We also recognize and honor the rights and struggle of our Indigenous family for land and self-determination.

We have created this platform to articulate and support the ambitions and work of Black people. We also seek to intervene in the current political climate and assert a clear vision, particularly for those who claim to be our allies, of the world we want them to help us create. We reject false solutions and believe we can achieve a complete transformation of the current systems, which place profit over people and make it impossible for many of us to breathe.

Together, we demand an end to the wars against Black people. We demand that the government repair the harms that have been done to Black communities in the form of reparations and targeted long-term investments. We also demand a defunding of the systems and institutions that criminalize and cage us. This document articulates our vision of a fundamentally different world. However, we recognize the need to include policies that address the immediate suffering of Black people. These policies, while less transformational, are necessary to address the current material conditions of our people and will better equip us to win the world we demand and deserve.

We recognize that not all of our collective needs and visions can be translated into policy, but we understand that policy change is one of many tactics necessary to move us towards the world we envision. We have come together now because we believe it is time to forge a new covenant. We are dreamers and doers and this platform is meant to articulate some of our vision. The links throughout the document provide the stepping-stones and roadmaps of how to get there. The policy briefs also elevate the brave and transformative work our people are already engaged in, and build on some of the best thinking in our history of struggle. This agenda continues the legacy of our ancestors who pushed for reparations, Black self-determination and community control; and also propels new iterations of movements such as efforts for reproductive justice, holistic healing and reconciliation, and ending violence against Black cis, queer, and trans people.

Document Text

DEMANDS

♦ END THE WAR ON BLACK PEOPLE

We demand an **end to the war against Black people**. Since this country's inception there have been named and unnamed wars on our communities. We demand an end to the criminalization, incarceration, and killing of our people. This includes:

1. An immediate end to the criminalization and dehumanization of Black youth across all areas of society including, but not limited to; our nation's justice and education systems, social service agencies, and media and pop culture. This includes an end to zero-tolerance school policies and arrests of students, the removal of police from schools, and the reallocation of funds from police and punitive school discipline practices to restorative services.
2. An end to capital punishment.
3. An end to money bail, mandatory fines, fees, court surcharges and "defendant funded" court proceedings.
4. An end to the use of past criminal history to determine eligibility for housing, education, licenses, voting, loans, employment, and other services and needs.
5. An end to the war on Black immigrants including the repeal of the 1996 crime and immigration bills, an end to all deportations, immigrant detention, and Immigration and Custom Enforcement (ICE) raids, and mandated legal representation in immigration court.
6. An end to the war on Black trans, queer and gender nonconforming people including their addition to anti-discrimination civil rights protections to ensure they have full access to employment, health, housing and education.
7. An end to the mass surveillance of Black communities, and the end to the use of technologies that criminalize and target our communities (including IMSI catchers, drones, body cameras, and predictive policing software).
8. The demilitarization of law enforcement, including law enforcement in schools and on college campuses.
9. An immediate end to the privatization of police, prisons, jails, probation, parole, food, phone and all other criminal justice related services.
10. Until we achieve a world where cages are no longer used against our people we demand an immediate change in conditions and an end to all jails, detention centers, youth facilities and prisons as we know them. This includes the end of solitary confinement, the end of shackling of pregnant people, access to quality healthcare, and effective measures to address the needs of our youth, queer, gender nonconforming and trans families.

♦ What is the problem?

- Across the country, Black children attend under-resourced schools where they are often pushed off of an academic track onto a track to prison. Zero-tolerance policies — a combination of exclusionary disciplinary policies and school-based arrests — are often the first stop along the school-to-prison pipeline and play a key role in pushing students out of the school system and funneling them into jails and prisons.
- Each year more than three million students are suspended from school — often for vague and subjective infractions such as "willful defiance" and "disrespect" — amounting to countless hours of lost instructional time. As a result, Black students are denied an opportunity to learn and punished for routine child and adolescent behaviors that their white peers are often not disciplined for at all.
- For Black youth, the impact of exclusionary school discipline is far reaching – disengaging them from academic and developmental opportunities and increasing the likelihood that they will be incarcerated later in life. In addition, current research emphasizes the need to examine the unique ways in which Black girls are impacted by punitive zero-tolerance policies. There are higher disciplinary disparities between Black girls and white girls than disciplinary disparities between Black boys and white boys; yet, Black girls have historically been overlooked in the national discourse around youth impacted by the school-to-prison pipeline.
- Black youth are also more likely to experience higher rates of corporal punishment. According to the Office of Civil Rights (OCR) at the U.S. Department of Education, Black students constitute 17.1 percent of the nationwide student population, but 35.6 percent of those paddled. In addition, while girls are paddled less than boys, Black girls are more than twice as likely to be paddled than white girls. In the 13 states that paddle more than 1,000 students per year,

Black girls are 2.07 times as likely as white girls to be beaten.
- Outside of schools, young Black people are criminalized in ways that limit their life chances at every point. 2010 data shows that while Black youth comprised 17 percent of all youth, they represented 31 percent of all arrests. These disparities persist even as juvenile "crime" rates have fallen. Among youth arrests, young Black people are more likely to be referred to a juvenile court than their white peers, and are more likely to be processed (and less likely to be diverted). Among those adjudicated delinquent, they are more likely to be sent to solitary confinement. Among those detained, Black youth are more likely to be transferred to adult facilities. The disparities grow at almost every step, stealing the dignity of young Black people and forcing them onto lifelong pathways of criminalization and diminished opportunity.
- For Black girls, the U.S.'s failure to address gender-based violence, which they experience at greater levels than any other group, is paramount to the criminalization they experience. In fact, sexual abuse is one of the primary predictors of girls' entry into the juvenile justice system, with girls often being routed to the system specifically because of their victimization. For instance, girls who are victims of sex trafficking are often arrested on prostitution charges. The punitive nature of this system is ill-equipped to support young girls through the violence and trauma they've experienced, which further subjects them to sexual victimization and a lifelong path of criminalization and abuse.
- There is a critical need for a coordinated strategy in local communities that addresses rampant racial disparities in the application of zero-tolerance policies and criminalization practices that impact Black boys and girls. Fortunately, a powerful grassroots movement, led primarily by youth and parents of color, has taken shape across the country to address these harmful policies — but much more work remains.
- Tens of thousands of youth under the age of 21 are currently incarcerated for offenses ranging from truancy to more serious charges. Every crime bill passed by Congress throughout the 1980s and 1990s included new federal laws against juvenile crimes and increased penalties against children. Similar trends can be seen throughout state legislation. There is mounting research that children under the age of 23 do not have fully-developed brains and that the cheapest, most humane, and most cost-effective way to respond to juvenile crime is not incarceration, but programs and investments that strengthen families, increase stability and provide access to educational and employment opportunities. Prosecuting youth with crimes is not only cruel; but it also permanently disadvantages them with a criminal record, which makes completing their education, getting a job, finding housing and growing up to be contributing members of society unfairly difficult.

♦ **What does this solution do?**
- Advances a grassroots organizing strategy at the local and state level that centers the work of ending the criminalization of Black youth through a racial and gender justice framework — led and informed by youth and parents.
- Addresses state-sanctioned violence that stems from over-policed schools and the deprivation of resources to public schools.
- Opens resources for alternative practices like restorative justice as a way to train students, parents and staff to deal with interpersonal conflict. Restorative justice practices are used as an alternative to zero-tolerance policies by helping to build stronger school communities through: 1) Developing effective leadership; 2) Building trust, interconnection and deeper relationships amongst students, parents, teachers and staff; 3) Providing methods to address misbehavior in away that gets to the root cause of conflicts and holds individuals accountable; 4) Repairing harm in a way that maintains the integrity of the community and doesn't further isolate offenders.
- By ending the practice of charging youth with misdemeanors and limiting the ability to charge them with felonies we would save hundreds of millions of dollars annually and provide the opportunity for our children to outlive their mistakes.

...

♦ **REPARATIONS**
We demand **reparations for past and continuing harms**. The government, responsible corporations and other institutions that have profited off of the harm they have inflicted on Black people — from

colonialism to slavery through food and housing redlining, mass incarceration, and surveillance — must repair the harm done. This includes:

1. Reparations for the systemic denial of access to high quality educational opportunities in the form of full and free access for all Black people (including undocumented and currently and formerly incarcerated people) to lifetime education including: free access and open admissions to public community colleges and universities, technical education (technology, trade and agricultural), educational support programs, retroactive forgiveness of student loans, and support for lifetime learning programs.
2. Reparations for the continued divestment from, discrimination toward and exploitation of our communities in the form of a guaranteed minimum livable income for all Black people, with clearly articulated corporate regulations.
3. Reparations for the wealth extracted from our communities through environmental racism, slavery, food apartheid, housing discrimination and racialized capitalism in the form of corporate and government reparations focused on healing ongoing physical and mental trauma, and ensuring our access and control of food sources, housing and land.
4. Reparations for the cultural and educational exploitation, erasure, and extraction of our communities in the form of mandated public school curriculums that critically examine the political, economic, and social impacts of colonialism and slavery, and funding to support, build, preserve, and restore cultural assets and sacred sites to ensure the recognition and honoring of our collective struggles and triumphs.
5. Legislation at the federal and state level that requires the United States to acknowledge the lasting impacts of slavery, establish and execute a plan to address those impacts. This includes the immediate passage of H.R.40, the "Commission to Study Reparation Proposals for African-Americans Act" or subsequent versions which call for reparations remedies.

♦ **What is the problem?**
- Education in the U.S. has always been a subversive act for Black people. During enslavement we were legally barred from the most basic forms of education including literacy. Post-Civil War, and even after the *Brown v. Board of Education (1954)* decision, Black people have been locked into segregated institutions that are underfunded, under resourced and often face severe health risk because of the decrepit conditions of their school buildings.
- The current racial equity gap in education has roots that date back to enslavement. In fact, recent studies suggest that racial educational inequalities may be the most (measurable) enduring legacy of slavery. The same study also verified ongoing income inequality correlated to counties where slavery was prevalent.
6. The cradle-to-college pipeline has been systematically cut off for Black communities. According to the National Center for Education Statistics, 23 states spend more per pupil in affluent districts than in high-poverty districts that contain a high concentrations of Black students; and the U.S. Department of Education's Office of Civil Rights shows persistent and glaring opportunity gaps and racial inequities for Black students. Black students are less likely to attend schools that offer advanced coursework, less likely to be placed in gifted and talented programs, more likely to attend schools with less qualified educators, and employ law enforcement officers but no counselors.
- Public universities, colleges, and technical education remain out of reach for most in the United States and policies to help students cover costs continue to shift towards benefiting more affluent families.
- Funding cuts across the country are forcing individual students' tuition and fees to cover more operating costs than ever at public colleges and universities. At City University of New York (CUNY), the largest city public university system in the U.S., tuition and fees cover over 50 percent of the operating budget. Since right before the recession, government funding for higher education has significantly fallen. 47 states spent less in 2014-2015 on per student funding than they did at the start of the recession.
- Financial aid is not sufficiently covering the basic needs of students attending public universities and colleges, leaving many of them struggling to eat and pay for housing, transportation, daycare and healthcare. A Wisconsin Hope Lab survey showed half of all students surveyed were

struggling with food and housing insecurity, 20 percent didn't have money to eat and 13 percent were homeless.
- Access to education — from university, to college, to community schools, to continuing adult education, to agricultural training — is essential to ensure that our communities can thrive. In addition to college age students, the ability to access lifelong education is essential to the political, economic and cultural health of our nation.
- The rising costs of higher education and exploitative and predatory lending practices of private and for-profit institutions make Black students more likely to drop-out, and leave them and their families stuck with debilitating and crippling debt. U.S. student loan debt nearly totals $1.3 trillion, with close to $900 billion in federal student loans, and more than 7 million borrowers in default.
- Historically Black Colleges and Universities continue to play a critical role in offering Black students, especially from low-income communities, access to higher education in an environment where they are supported and able to thrive. However, federal and state funding systematically underfunds Historically Black Colleges and Universities (HBCU's) compared to Predominantly White Institutions (PWI). Since the recession, deep state funding cuts have disproportionately affected HBCU's, putting the future of many in jeopardy, and impairing their ability to offer high-quality educational opportunities to their students.

♦ **What does this solution do?**
- We seek complete open access for all to free public university, college and technical education programs (including technology, trade and agricultural) as well as full-funding for lifelong learning programs that support communities and families. We also seek the forgiveness of all federal student loans. Policies shall apply to all and should focus on outreach to communities historically denied access to education including undocumented, incarcerated and formerly incarcerated people.
- Cover all living costs, including but not limited to housing, transportation, childcare, healthcare, and food for students attending public universities, colleges, and technical educational programs (including technology, trade, and agricultural).
- Fully fund and provide open access to K-12, higher education, technical educational programs (including technology, trade, and agricultural), educational support programs and lifelong learning programs to every individual incarcerated in local, state, and federal correctional facilities (juvenile and adult).
- Provide full access to all undocumented people to state and federal programs that provide aid to cover the full costs, including living costs, to attend public universities, and colleges, technical educational programs, and lifelong learning programs.
- Increased federal and state investments in all Historically Black Colleges (HBCUs).

...

♦ **INVEST-DIVEST**
We demand **investments in the education, health and safety of Black people**, instead of investments in the criminalizing, caging, and harming of Black people. We want investments in Black communities, determined by Black communities, and **divestment from exploitative forces** including prisons, fossil fuels, police, surveillance and exploitative corporations. This includes:
1. A reallocation of funds at the federal, state and local level from policing and incarceration (JAG, COPS, VOCA) to long-term safety strategies such as education, local restorative justice services, and employment programs.
2. The retroactive decriminalization, immediate release and record expungement of all drug related offenses and prostitution, and reparations for the devastating impact of the "war on drugs" and criminalization of prostitution, including a reinvestment of the resulting savings and revenue into restorative services, mental health services, job programs and other programs supporting those impacted by the sex and drug trade.
3. Real, meaningful, and equitable universal health care that guarantees: proximity to nearby comprehensive health centers, culturally competent services for all people, specific services for queer, gender nonconforming, and trans people, full bodily autonomy, full reproductive services,

mental health services, paid parental leave, and comprehensive quality child and elder care.
4. A constitutional right at the state and federal level to a fully-funded education which includes a clear articulation of the right to: a free education for all, special protections for queer and trans students, wrap around services, social workers, free health services (including reproductive body autonomy), a curriculum that acknowledges and addresses students' material and cultural needs, physical activity and recreation, high quality food, free daycare, and freedom from unwarranted search, seizure or arrest.
5. A divestment from industrial multinational use of fossil fuels and investment in community-based sustainable energy solutions.
6. A cut in military expenditures and a reallocation of those funds to invest in domestic infrastructure and community well-being.

♦ **What is the problem?**
- Reinvestment of federal grants (JAG, COPS and VOCA) to education, employment and restorative justice services in Black communities most impacted by the mass incarceration and crime.
- In the last few decades, the federal government has thrown billions of dollars at state and local governments to fund quickly expanding police forces and jails. Since Sept. 11, the Department of Homeland Security (DHS) alone has given between $30 billion and $40 billion in direct grants to state and local law enforcement, as well as other first responders. The federal government doled out an additional $376 million to state and local law enforcement in 2013 through the Edward Byrne Memorial Justice Grant program. That was down from more than $1 billion in 1998. And of course there is the estimated $5 billion worth of surplus military equipment that the has gone to local law enforcement, 20 college campuses and over 20 school districts through the Department of Defense's (DOD)1033 P These funds are given with little or no oversight and there is no accountability mechanism.
- Moreover, there is no evidence that the massive spending on incarceration reduces crime rates or keeps communities safer. Studies do show that jobs and education make communities stronger and keep them safer. Investments in community based drug and mental health treatment, education, universal pre-K, and other social institutions can make communities safer while improving life outcomes for all. Children who do not participate in the preschool programs are 70 percent more likely to be arrested for a violent crime by age 18. And youth who participate in summer job programs in Chicago saw a 43 percent decrease in arrests over a 16-month period. Studies show that jobs and education do not just make communities stronger — they make them safer.

♦ **What does this solution do?**
- The federal government should reallocate funding currently dedicated to policing and incarceration and instead invest those funds in long-term safety strategies such as educational, community restorative justice and employment programs that have been shown to improve community safety.

...

♦ **ECONOMIC JUSTICE**
We demand **economic justice for all** and a reconstruction of the economy to ensure Black communities have collective ownership, not merely access. This includes:
1. A progressive restructuring of tax codes at the local, state, and federal levels to ensure a radical and sustainable redistribution of wealth.
2. Federal and state job programs that specifically target the most economically marginalized Black people, and compensation for those involved in the care economy. Job programs must provide a living wage and encourage support for local workers centers, unions, and Black-owned businesses which are accountable to the community.
3. A right to restored land, clean air, clean water and housing and an end to the exploitative privatization of natural resources — including land and water. We seek democratic control over how resources are preserved, used and distributed and do so while honoring and respecting the rights of our Indigenous family.
4. The right for workers to organize in public and private sectors especially in "On Demand Economy" jobs.
5. Restore the Glass-Steagall Act to break up the large banks, and call for the National Credit

Union Administration and the US Department of the Treasury to change policies and practices around regulation, reporting and consolidation to allow for the continuation and creation of black banks, small and community development credit unions, insurance companies and other financial institutions.

6. An end to the Trans-Pacific Partnership and a renegotiation of all trade agreements to prioritize the interests of workers and communities.

7. Through tax incentives, loans and other government directed resources, support the development of cooperative or social economy networks to help facilitate trade across and in Black communities globally. All aid in the form of grants, loans or contracts to help facilitate this must go to Black led or Black supported networks and organizations as defined by the communities.

8. Financial support of Black alternative institutions including policy that subsidizes and offers low-interest, interest-free or federally guaranteed low-interest loans to promote the development of cooperatives (food, residential, etc.), land trusts and culturally responsive health infrastructures that serve the collective needs of our communities.

9. Protections for workers in industries that are not appropriately regulated including domestic workers, farm workers, and tipped workers, and for workers — many of whom are Black women and incarcerated people— who have been exploited and remain unprotected. This includes the immediate passage at the Federal and state level of the Domestic Workers Bill of Rights and extension of worker protections to incarcerated people.

♦ **What is the problem?**
- There is a desperate need to replace the current practice of collecting revenue in regressive ways with a more just system for collecting taxes.
- Across the United States, there are major political obstacles to raising any kind of revenue, along with a false perception of who pays and how this has changed over time.
- As with most injustices in our economic and political systems, regressive taxation has hit Black people, low-income people, and people of color the hardest.
- Many municipalities have increasingly decreased the use of progressive taxation and instead resorted to privatization and new fees and higher sales taxes in order to maintain bare-boned public infrastructure with minimal social support. As a result, residents are being forced to pay more for public services like trash collection, access to water, sewage, public property maintenance, and parking meters.
- Across the country, low-income people, disproportionately Black and other people of color, pay proportionally more in state and local taxes than the wealthy: In the ten states with the most regressive tax structures, the poorest fifth pay up to seven times as much in state and local taxes and fees as the wealthiest residents, as a percentage of their income.
- The wealth gap between white and Black households keeps growing, with the average white family now owning over 7.5 times as much wealth as the average Black family. Tax breaks for homeowners, retirement savings, employer-sponsored health insurance, and capital gains contribute to widening this gap.
- When states are not shifting the cost of public services onto poorer residents, they cut services all together, which affects poorer communities the most. Many municipalities, oftentimes with majority Black populations, have increased public school class sizes, shortened school days, closed vital city offices, reduced public transportation, reduced affordable housing assistance, cut essential health care programs, and eliminated public sector jobs.
- As the wealthiest Americans and powerful corporations continue to evade their fair share of taxes, many public services, programs and initiatives that could increase racial and economic justice go underfunded or unfunded.

♦ **What does this solution do?**
- Progressive taxes on income to raise revenue more equitably:
- Raise marginal tax rates for high earners, specifically the top percentile (the top 1% have seen their effective tax rate reduced to around 20 percent, down from 90 percent in the 1960s). Begin by raising the top marginal rate first to 50 percent and then gradually up to 80 percent.
- Remove income caps on payroll taxes that fund social security and unemployment insurance.

- Raise corporate income taxes, especially on large corporations and end tax deferral for foreign income of multinational corporations.
- Taxes on wealth to reduce the wealth inequality:
- Increase taxes on capital to the point where they are higher than taxes on labor, as wealth inequality is greater than income inequality. Specifically:
  Increase capital gains tax
  Create anti-speculation tax on property transfers
  Increase estate tax
  Have states shift to an income-sensitized property tax that focuses on homes above a certain threshold and second homes
  Impose a wealth tax (on tangible and financial assets)
- Remove harmful tax breaks and tax undesirable activities instead:
- Taxing "bads" not "goods": shift from sales taxes to taxing externalities such as environmental damage, and make this approach income-sensitized to hold low-income people harmless.
- Create a financial transaction tax on the trading of stocks, bonds, derivatives and currencies.
- Assess and eliminate tax expenditures such as mortgage reduction for homes sold above a specified price threshold, health insurance exemption, investment-based retirement accounts, etc., and instead support wealth-building by households who don't yet hold such assets.
- Make low-wage employer pay penalty fees or levy a payroll tax rate proportional to wage disparity.
- Expand the earned income tax credit.
- Provide a universal child tax credit.
- Create mechanisms for sharing tax revenues between neighboring localities to reduce tax flight and segregation.

...

♦ COMMUNITY CONTROL

We demand a world where those most impacted in our **communities control the laws, institutions, and policies that are meant to serve us** – from our schools to our local budgets, economies, police departments, and our land – while recognizing that the rights and histories of our Indigenous family must also be respected. This includes:

1. Direct democratic community control of local, state, and federal law enforcement agencies, ensuring that communities most harmed by destructive policing have the power to hire and fire officers, determine disciplinary action, control budgets and policies, and subpoena relevant agency information.
2. An end to the privatization of education and real community control by parents, students and community members of schools including democratic school boards and community control of curriculum, hiring, firing and discipline policies.
3. Participatory budgeting at the local, state and federal level.

♦ What is the problem?

- Across the country, there are more 200 entities involved in direct oversight of local law enforcement agencies. However, despite national trends in the disproportionate impact of lethal force, excessive force, sexual assault and misconduct by law enforcement on the Black community — in conjunction with the lack of discipline of officers or effective measures to deter these force incidents — there remains no national standards for powers and features of civilian oversight of law enforcement.
- Sexual assault is the second most commonly reported form of police misconduct, but the majority of departments have no policy or measures in place to prevent, detect or ensure accountability for this form of police violence disproportionately affecting Black women, cis and trans, gender nonconforming, and queer people. Accountability for police sexual harassment, assault, and violence is usually solely the responsibility of police departments and prosecutors, preventing many survivors from coming forward or obtaining justice.
- In 30 states, state law in fact makes it impossible to change the contractual bargaining power to hire and terminate police.
- These functions and powers should apply to civilian oversight entities overseeing law enforcement practices in the both patrol and custody settings including local jails, hold cells, and detention centers.
- Lack of empowered civilian oversight with the above features creates significant roadblocks to law enforcement transparency and accountability and prevents any means for communities

most impacted by lethal force, excessive force and misconduct to effectively reduce other types of violence .
- Federal law enforcement agencies also inflict violence, and have almost no accountability to the most impacted communities.
- Restorative justice and other community based safety measures across the country are being used by communities who aspire for real community safety and reject police violence as being capable of ever delivering safety.

◆ **What does this solution do?**
- By requiring all civilian oversight agencies to retain the power to hire and fire officers, determine disciplinary action in cases of misconduct related to excessive and lethal force, determine the funding of agencies, set and enforce policies, and retain concrete means of retrieving information — such as subpoena power — from law enforcement and third parties as it pertains to circumstances involving excessive, sexual and lethal force; communities will be able significantly to reduce the number of Black people impacted by police violence.

...

◆ **POLITICAL POWER**
We demand **independent Black political power and Black self-determination** in all areas of society. We envision a remaking of the current U.S. political system in order to create a real democracy where Black people and all marginalized people can effectively exercise full political power. This includes:
1. An end to the criminalization of Black political activity including the immediate release of all political prisoners and an end to the repression of political parties.
2. Public financing of elections and the end of money controlling politics through ending super PACs and unchecked corporate donations.
3. Election protection, electoral expansion and the right to vote for all people including: full access, guarantees, and protections of the right to vote for all people through universal voter registration, automatic voter registration, pre-registration for 16-year-olds, same day voter registration, voting day holidays, Online Voter Registration (OVR), enfranchisement of formerly and presently incarcerated people, local and state resident voting for undocumented people, and a ban on any disenfranchisement laws.
4. Full access to technology including net neutrality and universal access to the internet without discrimination and full representation for all.
5. Protection and increased funding for Black institutions including Historically Black Colleges and Universities (HBCU's), Black media and cultural, political and social formations.

◆ **What is the problem?**
While the criminal justice system has managed to create a pipeline from schools to prisons for Black and Brown communities, it has also been used as a tool of the state to delegitimize and neutralize people's movements throughout history.

The criminalization of freedom movements and activists has resulted in the incarceration of hundreds of people, many of whom are recognized as legitimate freedom fighters. Black communities have been disproportionately targeted by the state and have become political prisoners incarcerated in local, state and federal prisons. The FBI's Counter Intelligence Program (COINTELPRO) outlined the purpose, objectives, methods and tools used to criminalize freedom movements.

Today, direct victims of COINTELPRO (and similar law enforcement initiatives) remain exiled and incarcerated, while indirectly Black communities remain under surveillance by all levels of law enforcement with the intention of preventing the growth of another nationwide movement.

The tradition of surveillance and harassment of activists and freedom movements, has fostered fear, mistrust and suspicion in movement spaces that would otherwise function effectively.

◆ **What does this solution do?**
We are calling for the release of all political prisoners held in the U.S. and the removal of legitimate freedom fighters from the International Terrorists list. Additionally, we call on Congress to hold hearings on the impact of COINTELPRO as the Church Committee hearings in 1975 did not offer remedies to individuals and communities negatively impacted by this government initiative.

...

Missouri Highway Patrol Captain Ronald Johnson was asked to take over policing of Ferguson, as a tactical shift to reduce the violence. Jamelle Bouie - BY 2.0 (http://creativecommons.org/licenses/by/2.0)], via Wikimedia Commons.

INVESTIGATION OF THE FERGUSON POLICE DEPARTMENT—REPORT SUMMARY

"Our investigation indicates that this disproportionate burden on African-Americans cannot be explained by any difference in the rate at which people of different races violate the law."

Overview

In August 2014, a suspect in a local convenience store shoplifting incident, Michael Brown, was shot and killed in Ferguson, Missouri, by police office Darren Wilson. Brown was black; Wilson was white. The shooting prompted many protests in Ferguson, and because of its highly charged racial nature, it was investigated by the FBI and the US Department of Justice, which wrote up a pair of reports. The first exonerated Officer Wilson of any civil rights violations, but the second report, excerpted here, produced a damning study of the city of Ferguson's racial biases and poor priorities when it came to law enforcement.

Context

At somewhere around noon on Saturday, August 9 2014, eighteen year old Michael Brown and an acquaintance, Dorian Johnson, were walking down the middle of a street in Ferguson, Missouri, a suburb of St. Louis. Ferguson police officer Darren Wilson asked the two men to move over to the sidewalk, but soon realized they were suspects in a shoplifting incident that had happened up the road. Accounts differ as to what happened next – Wilson claimed Brown attacked him and reached to his waistband as if going for a gun, while Johnson said Wilson assaulted Brown. Whatever happened, officer Wilson shot Michael Brown seven times, killing him.

Almost immediately, demonstrators, most of them African-American, took to the streets of Ferguson to protest Brown's death. Since the death of Trayvon Martin in Florida two years earlier, the US news media and politicians had been sensitive to the poor relations between most black communities and their local police force. Most significantly, the death of so many African-Americans at the hands of the police led to the formation of Black Lives Matter, a community activist organization dedicated to asserting black rights in society and on the streets of the United States' cities. Often labeled a racist, terrorist group by those who did not know or understand the group's agenda, the presence of Black Lives Matter prompted counter-demonstrations and occasional violence. The governor of Missouri, Jay Nixon, first called in the Missouri state police, then his own National Guard to police the streets of Ferguson and keep the peace. President Obama, offering a gesture of concern, sent Attorney General Eric Holder to Ferguson to assess the problem there and file a report.

Three months later, Wilson faced a grand jury in defense of his actions on August 9. Twelve jurors, 9 white and 3 black, decided there was not enough evidence to bring charges against Wilson; a US Department of Justice investigation decided the same thing – neither of them acclamations of innocence, but rather a testament to the contradictory accounts offered by witnesses. Wilson gave his version of events, but was not cross-examined by the prosecutor, St. Louis district attorney Robert McCulloch. Neither did McCulloch recommend any charges to the grand jury necessary to bring Wilson to court, angering the African-American community. McCulloch's father had been shot and killed by a black man in 1965, and the perception was that McCulloch was reluctant to prosecute a cop.

Protests arose in the African-American community in Ferguson immediately upon Brown's death, and continued past the grand jury investigation. But they did not gain momentum until March 2015, when Attorney General Holder and the Department of Justice released their report from a second investigation, into alleged racial bias in the Ferguson Police Department. The report alleged that the Ferguson police performed prejudicially toward the black community, and sparked even more protests, not just in Ferguson but around the United States, in response to police brutality toward African-Americans.

About the Author

The actual report writers for the Department of Justice remain anonymous. The report was delivered by Attorney General Eric Holder and his assistant, Acting Assistant Attorney General Vanita Gupta, director of the Civil Rights Division of the Department of Justice and thus responsible for most of the report. The US Department of Justice is designed specifically for such purposes, to be an unbiased reporter and prosecutor against crimes against the constitution and federal law. In the case of Ferguson, Missouri, the report's authors meant to offer disinterested direction for reform of the police department.

Explanation and Analysis of the Document

The actual report issued by the Department of Justice was 102 pages long; the portion here is the report summary, the first six pages, which condenses the rest. The report immediately speaks on the reasons why its issuance was necessary—"This investigation has revealed a pattern or practice of unlawful conduct within the Ferguson Police Department that violates the First, Fourth, and Fourteenth Amendments to the United States Constitution, and federal statutory law." The next paragraph is self-explanatory.

> Ferguson's law enforcement practices are shaped by the City's focus on revenue rather than by public safety needs. This emphasis on revenue has compromised the institutional character of Ferguson's police department, contributing to a pattern of unconstitutional policing, and has also shaped its municipal court, leading to procedures that raise due process concerns and inflict unnecessary harm on members of the Ferguson community. Further, Ferguson's police and municipal court practices both reflect and exacerbate existing racial bias, including racial stereotypes. Ferguson's own data establish clear racial disparities that adversely impact African-Americans. The evidence shows that discriminatory intent is part of the reason for these disparities. Over time, Ferguson's police and municipal court practices have sown deep mistrust between parts of the community and the police department, undermining law enforcement legitimacy among African-Americans in particular.

♦ Focus on Generating Revenue

The rest of the summary goes into each charge in detail. The report notes that Ferguson's emphasis on generating revenue through fines and fees is notable, and apparently excessive. Policemen and the court system were expected to produce money through writing tickets, levying fines, charging court fees, and the like. Policemen received pressure to produce fine money from the city council, delivered through the office of the police chief.

♦ Police Practices

The result of the focus on revenue was a focus on "aggressive enforcement of Ferguson's municipal code". In other words, police officers hoped citizens would break laws that would result in fines, and emphasized the enforcement of such fines over safety, trust and cooperation. "Productivity" in levying fines led to promotions. Most of all, police tended to look upon the African-American community in Ferguson not "as constituents to be protected than as potential offenders and sources of revenue." This emphasis created a combative climate, where police officers under pressure tended to interpret almost any citizen as potentially resisting arrest, particularly if they complain about their treatment by police, which violates the First and Fourth Amendments to the Constitution. As an example, the report offers the story of a 32-year-old black man who was harassed by a policeman while resting in his car after playing basketball, and ended up losing both his driver's license and his job as a result.

♦ Municipal Court Practices

Once revenue generation reached the level of the courtroom in Ferguson, the fines only went up. The report states that "[t]his has led to court practices that violate the Fourteenth Amendment's due process and equal protection requirements." Especially egregious was that the court issued arrest warrants for missing court appearances or not paying fines like parking or traffic tickets – a good way of making the amounts of those fines rise. Worse, violators lost their licenses by virtue of state law, and could not get them returned unless they paid fines in full, no matter how large, and all at one time as opposed to making payments. Despite recognition on the part of the City Council and the court that such practices were harmful to an impoverished community, the practice continued. Again, the report provides an example, of an African-American woman who parked her car illegally in 2007 and, eight years later, still owed money on the ticket and even spent almost a week in jail.

♦ Racial Bias

Above all, these practices were all highly prejudicial to Ferguson's largely poor African-American population. In a series of striking statistics, the report notes that blacks accounted for two-thirds of the town's population, but nearly all of the town's vehicle stops, citations and arrests. Cars with black drivers were searched entirely disproportionately in comparison to how police officers tended to find contraband – whites were 26% more likely to be carrying something illegal in their cars. Blacks received more fines, largely for silly offenses like jaywalking or being angry about a traffic stop, and speeding was assessed largely by eye with black drivers as opposed to a radar gun. Almost all arrests that required the use of force were against African-Americans, especially with the use of dogs. Once in court, African-Americans had a case dismissed far less often than whites and compounded their fines, resulting in further arrest warrants. As the report states, "[O]ur investigation has revealed that these disparities occur, at least in part, because of unlawful bias against and stereotypes about African-Americans." Then it cites emails in which such sentiments of bias were expressed by city officials at all levels.

◆ **Community Distrust**

The natural result of these law enforcement practices was a lack of trust on the part of the African-American community towards the Ferguson police force. Despite the city's efforts to claim that any public complaints come from "outside agitators", the report found that distrust of the police and the courts among the African-American community in Ferguson was very real. Aggressive and unlawful police practices, examples of discrimination based on race and a refusal to admit the city's role in the problem had made the problem worse, coupled with a withdrawal from community policing efforts like walking a beat in a neighborhood. "As a consequence of these practices, law enforcement is seen as illegitimate, and the partnerships necessary for public safety are, in some areas, entirely absent." To fix the problem, the city of Ferguson needed to admit the problem, account for its law enforcement practices, pay its police better and reorient law enforcement in Ferguson.

Audience

The US Department of Justice's report on Ferguson police department was meant for public consumption, and it clearly had an impact on the interested public. It was read often enough that it was published as a book by the New Press in 2016. Yet the most important audience was the city of Ferguson itself and its public officials. The report was meant to expose the problems in the city's police practices and offer solutions, and it was taken as such by the city's officials.

Impact

At the press conference held in conjunction with the release of the report, Eric Holder referred to the report as "searing", and noted that the then-current protests in March 2015 were long in the making. The next day, Police Chief Tom Jackson resigned from the Ferguson Police Department. There was some sense that Ferguson might simply dismantle its police force altogether rather than reforming it, but this notion was dismissed fairly quickly. Peaceful demonstrations picked up momentum in light of the report, and more city officials were fired or resigned in its wake. In the week after the report's issue, however, two St. Louis County police officers were shot and injured during the demonstrations. On the one year anniversary of Michael Brown's death, a man at a protest was injured in a gunfight with police, emphasizing the urgency of addressing the problem. In response, the Department of Justice announced its intention to impose a solution on Ferguson if the city council did not act sooner. The Missouri legislature even voted to reduce the size of fines allowed to be issued in St. Louis County, the county where Ferguson sat, only to have the law overturned by the Missouri Supreme Court.

In May 2015, a black police official from Miami Florida named Delrish Moss succeeded Tom Jackson as Ferguson's police chief. Protests calmed over time, and the Justice Department negotiated with the Ferguson city council. Yet police reform was not forthcoming. A year and a half after Michael Brown's death, the Justice Department filed a lawsuit against the city of Ferguson, claiming that there had been no reforms accepted since the report was issued. The lawsuit stepped up negotiations, and in March 2016, Ferguson accepted the report' recommendations – to end the emphasis on revenue, punish police misconduct, and repair its relationship with the African-American community. Ironically, the community's top concern with the implementation of the report's recommendations were its costs – costs that had previously been met in part by the very fines the report sought to end.

In the years following Michael Brown's death, the Ferguson city council saw a turnover of elected officials, with more African-Americans sitting on the council. African-Americans were recruited to the police force, and the emphasis on revenue generation ended.

Further Reading

◆ **Books**

United States Department of Justice, *Federal Reports on Police Killings: Ferguson, Cleveland, Baltimore, and Chicago.* Brooklyn, NY: Melville House, 2017.

United States Department of Justice Civil Rights Division. *The Ferguson Report: Department of Justice Investigation of the Ferguson Police Department.* New York: New Press, 2015.

Lebron, Christopher J. *The Making of Black Lives Matter: A Brief History of an Idea.* New York: Oxford University Press, 2017.

Camp, Jordan T. and Christina Heatherton, editors. *Policing the Planet: Why the Policing Crisis Led to Black Lives Matter.* New York: Verso, 2016.

——David Simonelli

Time Line

2014	August 9	■ Michael Brown shot and killed by Officer Darren Wilson in Ferguson, Missouri
2014	August 10-18	■ Demonstrators protest Brown's shooting; some protests turn violent, and Governor Jay Nixon calls out the Missouri National Guard to police a curfew on Ferguson; protests continue, peacefully, through the next several months
2014	August 18	■ Attorney General Eric Holder sent to Ferguson to prepare report for Obama Administration
2014	August 20	■ Grand jury convened to decide whether charges will be pressed against Officer Wilson
2014	November	■ Grand jury decides, based on evidence, not to indict Officer Wilson for murder or civil rights violations; US Department of Justice report concurs with grand jury, citing lack of evidence for civil rights violations
2015	March	■ Second Department of Justice report condemns institutional racism inherent in Ferguson Police Department; Police Chief Tom Jackson resigns post
2015	May	■ Jackson replaced by Delrish Moss, African-American officer
		■ Missouri legislature passes law limiting revenue St Louis suburbs can collect from traffic fines and ticketing; later struck down by Missouri Supreme Court
2016	February	■ Department of Justice issues lawsuit calling for reform in Ferguson law enforcement; after initially balking at costs, Ferguson City Council accepts report's recommendations in March

Essential Quotes

"This investigation has revealed a pattern or practice of unlawful conduct within the Ferguson Police Department that violates the First, Fourth, and Fourteenth Amendments to the United States Constitution, and federal statutory law."

"Ferguson's law enforcement practices are shaped by the City's focus on revenue rather than by public safety needs. This emphasis on revenue has compromised the institutional character of Ferguson's police department."

"Ferguson's law enforcement practices overwhelmingly impact African-Americans. Data collected by the Ferguson Police Department from 2012 to 2014 shows that African-Americans account for 85% of vehicle stops, 90% of citations, and 93% of arrests made by FPD officers, despite comprising only 67% of Ferguson's population."

"Our investigation indicates that this disproportionate burden on African-Americans cannot be explained by any difference in the rate at which people of different races violate the law. Rather, our investigation has revealed that these disparities occur, at least in part, because of unlawful bias against and stereotypes about African-Americans."

Summary of the Report

I. REPORT SUMMARY

The Civil Rights Division of the United States Department of Justice opened its investigation of the Ferguson Police Department ("FPD") on September 4, 2014. ...This investigation has revealed a pattern or practice of unlawful conduct within the Ferguson Police Department that violates the First, Fourth, and Fourteenth Amendments to the United States Constitution, and federal statutory law. ...

Ferguson's law enforcement practices are shaped by the City's focus on revenue rather than by public safety needs. This emphasis on revenue has compromised the institutional character of Ferguson's police department, contributing to a pattern of unconstitutional policing, and has also shaped its municipal court, leading to procedures that raise due process concerns and inflict unnecessary harm on members of the Ferguson community. Further, Ferguson's police and municipal court practices both reflect and exacerbate existing racial bias, including racial stereotypes. Ferguson's own data establish clear racial disparities that adversely impact African-Americans. The evidence shows that discriminatory intent is part of the reason for these disparities. Over time, Ferguson's police and municipal court practices have sown deep mistrust between parts of the community and the police department, undermining law enforcement legitimacy among African-Americans in particular.

Focus on Generating Revenue

The City budgets for sizeable increases in municipal fines and fees each year, exhorts police and court staff to deliver those revenue increases, and closely monitors whether those increases are achieved. City officials routinely urge Chief Jackson to generate more revenue through enforcement. In March 2010, for instance, the City Finance Director wrote to Chief Jackson that "unless ticket writing ramps up significantly before the end of the year, it will be hard to significantly raise collections next year. ... Given that we are looking at a substantial sales tax shortfall, it's not an insignificant issue." Similarly, in March 2013, the Finance Director wrote to the City Manager: "Court fees are anticipated to rise about 7.5%. I did ask the Chief if he thought the PD could deliver 10% increase. He indicated they could try." The importance of focusing on revenue generation is communicated to FPD officers. Ferguson police officers from all ranks told us that revenue generation is stressed heavily within the police department, and that the message comes from City leadership. The evidence we reviewed supports this perception.

Police Practices

The City's emphasis on revenue generation has a profound effect on FPD's approach to law enforcement. Patrol assignments and schedules are geared toward aggressive enforcement of Ferguson's municipal code, with insufficient thought given to whether enforcement strategies promote public safety or unnecessarily undermine community trust and cooperation. Officer evaluations and promotions depend to an inordinate degree on "productivity," meaning the number of citations issued. Partly as a consequence of City and FPD priorities, many officers appear to see some residents, especially those who live in Ferguson's predominantly African-American neighborhoods, less as constituents to be protected than as potential offenders and sources of revenue.

This culture within FPD influences officer activities in all areas of policing, beyond just ticketing. Officers expect and demand compliance even when they lack legal authority. They are inclined to interpret the exercise of free-speech rights as unlawful disobedience, innocent movements as physical threats, indications of mental or physical illness as belligerence. Police supervisors and leadership do too little to ensure that officers act in accordance with law and policy, and rarely respond meaningfully to civilian complaints of officer misconduct. The result is a pattern of stops without reasonable suspicion and arrests without probable cause in violation of the Fourth Amendment; infringement on free expression, as well as retaliation for protected expression, in violation of the First Amendment; and excessive force in violation of the Fourth Amendment.

Document Text

Even relatively routine misconduct by Ferguson police officers can have significant consequences for the people whose rights are violated. For example, in the summer of 2012, a 32-year-old African-American man sat in his car cooling off after playing basketball in a Ferguson public park. An officer pulled up behind the man's car, blocking him in, and demanded the man's Social Security number and identification. Without any cause, the officer accused the man of being a pedophile, referring to the presence of children in the park, and ordered the man out of his car for a pat-down, although the officer had no reason to believe the man was armed. The officer also asked to search the man's car. The man objected, citing his constitutional rights. In response, the officer arrested the man, reportedly at gunpoint, charging him with eight violations of Ferguson's municipal code. One charge, Making a False Declaration, was for initially providing the short form of his first name (e.g., "Mike" instead of "Michael"), and an address which, although legitimate, was different from the one on his driver's license. Another charge was for not wearing a seat belt, even though he was seated in a parked car. The officer also charged the man both with having an expired operator's license, and with having no operator's license in his possession. The man told us that, because of these charges, he lost his job as a contractor with the federal government that he had held for years.

Municipal Court Practices

Ferguson has allowed its focus on revenue generation to fundamentally compromise the role of Ferguson's municipal court. The municipal court does not act as a neutral arbiter of the law or a check on unlawful police conduct. Instead, the court primarily uses its judicial authority as the means to compel the payment of fines and fees that advance the City's financial interests. This has led to court practices that violate the Fourteenth Amendment's due process and equal protection requirements. The court's practices also impose unnecessary harm, overwhelmingly on African-American individuals, and run counter to public safety.

Most strikingly, the court issues municipal arrest warrants not on the basis of public safety needs, but rather as a routine response to missed court appearances and required fine payments. In 2013 alone, the court issued over 9,000 warrants on cases stemming in large part from minor violations such as parking infractions, traffic tickets, or housing code violations. Jail time would be considered far too harsh a penalty for the great majority of these code violations, yet Ferguson's municipal court routinely issues warrants for people to be arrested and incarcerated for failing to timely pay related fines and fees. Under state law, a failure to appear in municipal court on a traffic charge involving a moving violation also results in a license suspension. Ferguson has made this penalty even more onerous by only allowing the suspension to be lifted after payment of an owed fine is made in full. Further, until recently, Ferguson also added charges, fines, and fees for each missed appearance and payment. Many pending cases still include such charges that were imposed before the court recently eliminated them, making it as difficult as before for people to resolve these cases.

The court imposes these severe penalties for missed appearances and payments even as several of the court's practices create unnecessary barriers to resolving a municipal violation. The court often fails to provide clear and accurate information regarding a person's charges or court obligations. And the court's fine assessment procedures do not adequately provide for a defendant to seek a fine reduction on account of financial incapacity or to seek alternatives to payment such as community service. City and court officials have adhered to these court practices despite acknowledging their needlessly harmful consequences. In August 2013, for example, one City Councilmember wrote to the City Manager, the Mayor, and other City officials lamenting the lack of a community service option and noted the benefits of such a program, including that it would "keep those people that simply don't have the money to pay their fines from constantly being arrested and going to jail, only to be released and do it all over again."

Together, these court practices exacerbate the harm of Ferguson's unconstitutional police practices. They impose a particular hardship upon Ferguson's most vulnerable residents, especially upon those living in or near poverty. Minor offenses can generate crippling debts, result in jail time because of an inability to pay, and result in the loss of a driver's license, employment, or housing.

We spoke, for example, with an African-American woman who has a still-pending case stemming from 2007, when, on a single occasion, she parked her car illegally. She received two citations and a $151 fine, plus fees. The woman, who experienced financial difficulties and periods of homelessness over several years, was charged with seven Failure to Appear offenses for missing court dates or fine payments on her parking tickets between 2007 and 2010. For each Failure to Appear, the court issued an arrest warrant and imposed new fines and fees. From 2007 to 2014, the woman was arrested twice, spent six days in jail, and paid $550 to the court for the events stemming from this single instance of illegal parking. Court records show that she twice attempted to make partial payments of $25 and $50, but the court returned those payments, refusing to accept anything less than payment in full. One of those payments was later accepted, but only after the court's letter rejecting payment by money order was returned as undeliverable. This woman is now making regular payments on the fine. As of December 2014, over seven years later, despite initially owing a $151 fine and having already paid $550, she still owed $541.

Racial Bias

Ferguson's approach to law enforcement both reflects and reinforces racial bias, including stereotyping. The harms of Ferguson's police and court practices are borne disproportionately by African-Americans, and there is evidence that this is due in part to intentional discrimination on the basis of race.

Ferguson's law enforcement practices overwhelmingly impact African-Americans. Data collected by the Ferguson Police Department from 2012 to 2014 shows that African-Americans account for 85% of vehicle stops, 90% of citations, and 93% of arrests made by FPD officers, despite comprising only 67% of Ferguson's population. African-Americans are more than twice as likely as white drivers to be searched during vehicle stops even after controlling for non-race based variables such as the reason the vehicle stop was initiated, but are found in possession of contraband 26% less often than white drivers, suggesting officers are impermissibly considering race as a factor when determining whether to search. African-Americans are more likely to be cited and arrested following a stop regardless of why the stop was initiated and are more likely to receive multiple citations during a single incident. From 2012 to 2014, FPD issued four or more citations to African-Americans on 73 occasions, but issued four or more citations to non-African-Americans only twice. FPD appears to bring certain offenses almost exclusively against African-Americans. For example, from 2011 to 2013, African-Americans accounted for 95% of Manner of Walking in Roadway charges, and 94% of all Failure to Comply charges. Notably, with respect to speeding charges brought by FPD, the evidence shows not only that African-Americans are represented at disproportionately high rates overall, but also that the disparate impact of FPD's enforcement practices on African-Americans is 48% larger when citations are issued not on the basis of radar or laser, but by some other method, such as the officer's own visual assessment.

These disparities are also present in FPD's use of force. Nearly 90% of documented force used by FPD officers was used against African-Americans. In every canine bite incident for which racial information is available, the person bitten was African-American.

Municipal court practices likewise cause disproportionate harm to African-Americans. African-Americans are 68% less likely than others to have their cases dismissed by the court, and are more likely to have their cases last longer and result in more required court encounters. African-Americans are at least 50% more likely to have their cases lead to an arrest warrant, and accounted for 92% of cases in which an arrest warrant was issued by the Ferguson Municipal Court in 2013. Available data show that, of those actually arrested by FPD only because of an outstanding municipal warrant, 96% are African-American.

Our investigation indicates that this disproportionate burden on African-Americans cannot be explained by any difference in the rate at which people of different races violate the law. Rather, our investigation has revealed that these disparities occur, at least in part, because of unlawful bias against and stereotypes about African-Americans. We have found substantial evidence of racial bias among police and court staff in Ferguson. For example, we discovered emails circulated by police supervisors and court staff that stereotype racial minorities as criminals, including one email that joked about an abortion by an African-American woman being a means of crime control.

City officials have frequently asserted that the harsh and disparate results of Ferguson's law enforcement system do not indicate problems with police or court practices, but instead reflect a pervasive lack of "personal responsibility" among "certain segments" of the community. Our investigation has found that the practices about which area residents have complained are in fact unconstitutional and unduly harsh. But the City's personal-responsibility refrain is telling: it reflects many of the same racial stereotypes found in the emails between police and court supervisors. This evidence of bias and stereotyping, together with evidence that Ferguson has long recognized but failed to correct the consistent racial disparities caused by its police and court practices, demonstrates that the discriminatory effects of Ferguson's conduct are driven at least in part by discriminatory intent in violation of the Fourteenth Amendment.

Community Distrust

Since the August 2014 shooting death of Michael Brown, the lack of trust between the Ferguson Police Department and a significant portion of Ferguson's residents, especially African-Americans, has become undeniable. The causes of this distrust and division, however, have been the subject of debate. Police and other City officials, as well as some Ferguson residents, have insisted to us that the public outcry is attributable to "outside agitators" who do not reflect the opinions of "real Ferguson residents." That view is at odds with the facts we have gathered during our investigation. Our investigation has shown that distrust of the Ferguson Police Department is longstanding and largely attributable to Ferguson's approach to law enforcement. This approach results in patterns of unnecessarily aggressive and at times unlawful policing; reinforces the harm of discriminatory stereotypes; discourages a culture of accountability; and neglects community engagement. In recent years, FPD has moved away from the modest community policing efforts it previously had implemented, reducing opportunities for positive police-community interactions, and losing the little familiarity it had with some African-American neighborhoods. The confluence of policing to raise revenue and racial bias thus has resulted in practices that not only violate the Constitution and cause direct harm to the individuals whose rights are violated, but also undermine community trust, especially among many African-Americans. As a consequence of these practices, law enforcement is seen as illegitimate, and the partnerships necessary for public safety are, in some areas, entirely absent.

Restoring trust in law enforcement will require recognition of the harms caused by Ferguson's law enforcement practices, and diligent, committed collaboration with the entire Ferguson community. At the conclusion of this report, we have broadly identified the changes that are necessary for meaningful and sustainable reform. These measures build upon a number of other recommended changes we communicated verbally to the Mayor, Police Chief, and City Manager in September so that Ferguson could begin immediately to address problems as we identified them. As a result of those recommendations, the City and police department have already begun to make some changes to municipal court and police practices. We commend City officials for beginning to take steps to address some of the concerns we have already raised. Nonetheless, these changes are only a small part of the reform necessary. Addressing the deeply embedded constitutional deficiencies we found demands an entire reorientation of law enforcement in Ferguson. The City must replace revenue-driven policing with a system grounded in the principles of community policing and police legitimacy, in which people are equally protected and treated with compassion, regardless of race.

"The Gerry-mander" first appeared in this cartoon-map in the Boston Gazette, 26 March 1812. Staff of Boston Gazette - Boston Gazette, 26 March 1812. [Public domain], via Wikimedia Commons

Cooper v. Harris

"Uncontested evidence in the record shows that the State purposefully established a racial target: African-Americans should make up no less than a majority of the voting-age population."

Overview

On May 22, 2017 the Supreme Court of the United States issued its opinion in *Cooper v. Harris*, a suit involving a challenge to the redrawing of voting districts in North Carolina on the basis of a violation of the Voting Rights Act of 1965. The Court upheld the lower Federal court's ruling that the North Carolina state legislators had illegally packed districts with African-American voters, which in turn reduced the influence of African-American voters in other North Carolina districts.

Context

A number of redistricting cases have come before the United States Supreme Court alleging violations of the Voting Rights Act. The majority of the cases have involved states in the southern United States, including Alabama, Virginia and North Carolina, which have a long history of voter suppression and utilizing redistricting (gerrymandering) as a means of diluting and minimizing the impact of African-American and Latino votes. *Cooper v. Harris* is the latest gerrymandering case heard by the Supreme Court in an attempt to provide guidance and to further shape federal law under the Voting Rights Act.

In 1993 the Supreme Court enumerated a general rule in another North Carolina gerrymandering case, *State v. Reno*, in which it held that race could not normally be the predominant factor considered in redistricting, as that would be a violation of the Equal Protection Clause of the U.S. Constitution. However, the Court concluded that race could be one of many factors considered in order to ensure compliance with the Voting Rights Act. If race was deemed to be a predominant factor in the redistricting, then a stringent level of review called strict scrutiny was applied which then required the state in question to show that the redistricting plan served a "compelling interest" and was "narrowly tailored" to meet that interest. *Shaw v. Reno* came before the Supreme Court in 1996 and in that case the Court established that the Voting Rights Act was considered to be a "compelling interest" under the strict scrutiny standard.

In this latest challenge to a redistricting plan by the North Carolina legislature, Justice Elena Kagan, writing for the Court majority, held that race was a predominant factor in drawing the districts. However, North Carolina lacked a strong basis in evidence for believing that it needed a minority-dominated district in order to avoid any liability under Section 2 of the Voting Rights Act. Rather, Kagan's opinion held that racial gerrymandering, rather than political gerrymandering, was the predominant factor in drawing the other district as a minority-dominated district.

The case arises from two North Carolina congressional districts, District 1 and District 12 which have a long legislative history before the Supreme Court. The two districts have been the basis of four earlier racial gerrymandering cases at the Court. In 2016 a three-judge federal district court in North Carolina invalidated both districts, holding that the state legislators had illegally packed the districts with African-American voters, which had the effect of reducing the influence of African-American voters in other districts. District 1 has been likened to an octopus in its geographical shape, with a body that starts at the North Carolina/Virginia border with tentacles that stretch out west, south and east. District 12 is more serpentine in shape; as the court noted it "begins in the south-central part of the State (where it takes in a large part of Charlotte) and then travels northeast, zig-zagging much of the way to the State's northern border."

The Supreme Court granted certiorari to hear the matter and upheld the district court decision by a 5-3 decision, in a major ruling on racial gerrymandering. Justice Kagan wrote for the majority. Justice Clarence Thomas wrote a concurring opinion. Justice Samuel Alito filed an opinion concurring in the judgment in part and dissenting in part, in which Chief Justice John Roberts and Justice Anthony Kennedy joined. Justice Gorsuch took no part in the consideration or decision of the case.

About the Author

Elena Kagan is an Associate Justice on the Supreme Court. She was born on April 28, 1960 in New York City. Kagan studied history at Princeton before attending Harvard Law School, where she was supervising editor of the *Harvard Law Review*. Kagan was a law clerk for Judge Abner Mikva of the U.S. Court of Appeals for the District of Columbia Circuit after which she served as a law clerk for Justice Thurgood Marshall. She moved into the private sector working as an associate for the Washington D.C. law firm Williams & Connolly.

In 1991 Kagan began teaching at the University of Chicago Law School and by 1995 was a tenured professor of law. Kagan began working as associate counsel for President Bill Clinton later that year and spent four years working in the White House, first as Deputy Assistant to the President for Domestic Policy before taking the role of Deputy Director of the Domestic Policy Council.

President Clinton nominated Kagan to serve on the U.S. Court of Appeals D.C. Circuit. Her nomination languished in the Senate Judiciary Committee and, in 1999 Kagan returned to academia, beginning as a visiting professor at Harvard Law before eventually becoming Dean of Harvard Law in 2003. When President Barack Obama, a fellow Harvard alumnus, won the 2008 presidential election, Kagan was selected as solicitor general. She was confirmed in that position by the Senate on March 19, 2009, becoming the first woman to serve as solicitor general of the United States. Two months after being confirmed, President Obama nominated Kagan to replace Justice John Paul Stevens on the Supreme Court after his retirement. Kagan was confirmed by the Senate in a 63-37 vote, making her the fourth woman to sit on the Supreme Court. Kagan was also the youngest Justice at 50 years old and the only one without previous experience as a sitting judge.

During her tenure on the Supreme Court, Kagan sided with the majority on two landmark Supreme Court rulings. First, she was one of six justices to uphold a critical component of the 2010 Affordable Care Act (Obamacare) in *King v. Burwell*. That decision allowed the federal government to keep providing subsidies to Americans who purchased healthcare insurance through exchanges regardless of whether they were operated by state or federal government. Second, Kagan again joined the majority in a 5-4 ruling in *Obergefell v. Hodges* that made same sex marriage legal in all 50 states.

Explanation and Analysis of the Document

In the majority opinion, Justice Kagan noted that the crux of a racial gerrymandering case amounts to answering two questions. The first is whether race was the predominant factor behind the state legislature's decision to move particular voters in or out of a particular district. The second question is, if race was the predominant factor, can the state show that it had "good reasons" to believe that the Voting Rights Act would be violated if the legislature did not use race to draw the districts?

The Supreme Court's inquiry into the first question is limited because it can only review the district court's findings of fact to determine if they are clearly wrong, a very high threshold. Thus, a district court's factual findings on whether race was the predominant factor will not be overturned if the findings are "plausible", even if the justices might reach a different conclusion. In analyzing the first question, Kagan noted that before drawing the boundary lines for District 1, the gerrymandering map "purposefully established a racial target: African-Americans should make up no less than a majority of the voting-age population." Kagan noted that in fulfilling this goal, the gerrymandering plan resulted in a "district with stark racial borders. Within the same counties, the portions that fall inside District 1 have black populations two to three times larger than the portions placed in neighboring districts." Kagan concluded that the federal district court was not clearly wrong in finding that "race predominated in drawing District 1."

Regarding the second question in the analysis, Kagan found the state did not have "good reasons" to believe that it had to either consider race or risk violating the Voting Rights Act with its redistricting plan. To the contrary, the opinion concludes that the state provided "no reason" to show that it needed to increase the number of African-American voters in District 1 because the district had consistently been electing minority members of Congress.

The state attempted to argue that race wasn't a factor but, rather, that party affiliation was a predominant factor and many Democrats happened to be African-American. The district court had concluded that although race and party affiliation were closely aligned, it was race that was the predominant factor. Kagan's opinion acknowledged it was not an easy task for the district court to make the determination on whether race was a predominant factor in drawing the redistricting maps but that the Supreme Court had to find the district court's determination to be "clearly wrong" in its determination, and that in the instant case it was not.

Thus, the majority concluded that race was a predominant factor; that the district wrong was not "clearly wrong" in making that finding; and, that the state failed to make any showing of a "good reason" demonstrating the Voting

Rights Act would be violated if race had not been used to draw the redistricting map.

Justices Alito, Chief Justice Roberts, and Justice Kennedy disagreed with the majority opinion about District 12 being invalidated. Justice Thomas provided the needed fifth vote to uphold the district court's invalidating of District 12, somewhat surprising as he traditionally is regarded as a more conservative jurist.

In his opinion, Justice Alito concurred in part with Kagan's opinion, and dissented in part as well. Hew believed that the challengers to the racial gerrymandering should have been required to provide their own redistricting map, stating that an alternative map "is a logical response to the difficult problem of distinguishing between racial and political motivations when race and political party preference closely correlate." Alito further asserted that the majority opinion risked confusing "a political gerrymander for a racial gerrymander" and that the opinion "invades a traditional domain of state authority."

Audience

As with all Supreme Court cases, the audience for the opinions in Cooper v. Harris amounted to any concerned citizen of the United States. It is said that the Supreme Court amends the constitution every time it rules on a case, and Cooper v. Harris was no different. Following the ruling, all state legislatures were put on notice that racial gerrymandering would be heavily scrutinized by the Supreme Court.

Impact

Although *Cooper v. Harris* did not definitively create new law on the issue, its interpretation of state legislature motives in drawing up redistricting maps in coordination with the Voting Rights Act was regarded as a major ruling on racial gerrymandering. Particularly, *Cooper* made clear that the Supreme Court took a common-sense approach to the idea that legislatures that utilize race in drawing districts, even if race is used as a proxy for political affiliation, would be seen as highly suspect. It provided guidance and a road map for what challengers to redistricting needed to prove in order to establish that race was a predominant factor in the drawing of districts.

Further Reading

◆ Articles

Michael Kent Curtis, "Using the Voting Rights Act to Discriminate: North Carolina's Use of Racial Gerrymanders, Two Racial Quotas, Safe Harbors, Shields, and Inoculations to Undermine Multiracial Coalitions and Black Political Power," *Wake Forest Law Review*, 51 (2016): 421-492.

"The Future of Majority-Minority Districts in Light of Declining Racially Polarized Voting," *Harvard Law Review*, 116 (2003): 2208-2229.

◆ Books

Daley, David. *Ratf**ked : The True Story Behind the Secret Plan to Steal America's Democracy.* New York: Liveright Publishing Corp., 2016.

Grofman, Bernard, editor. *Race and Redistricting in the 1990s.* New York: Agathon Press, 1998.

◆ Web Sites

Cooper v. Harris, 137 S.Ct. 1455 (2017). Justia: US Supreme Court https://supreme.justia.com/cases/ federal/us/581/15-1262/ [accessed August 3, 2017].

Shaw v. Reno, 113 S.Ct. 2816 (1993). Justia: US Supreme Court https://supreme.justia.com/cases/ federal/us/509/630/ [accessed August 3, 2017].

—— *Michele McBride Simonelli, Esq., Ohio Seventh District Court of Appeals*

Time Line		
1965	August	■ Voting Rights Act of 1965 passed
1993	April	■ Supreme Court case *State v. Reno* holds that race may be used to redraw districts, but only in compliance with the Voting Rights Act
2000		■ After the 2000 census is completed, Districts 1 and 12 in North Carolina are redrawn with white pluralities
2016	February	■ US Fourth Circuit Court of Appeals rules that districts must be redrawn
2017	May	■ US Supreme Court upholds Circuit Court ruling in *Cooper v. Harris*

Essential Quotes

"Uncontested evidence in the record shows that the State purposefully established a racial target: African-Americans should make up no less than a majority of the voting-age population."

"The result is a district with stark racial borders. Within the same counties, the portions that fall inside District 1 have black populations two to three times larger than the portions placed in neighboring districts."

"Applying a clear error standard, we uphold the District Court's conclusions that racial considerations predominated in designing both District 1 and District 12. ...For District 1, we further uphold the District Court's decision that [section] 2 of the V[oting] R[ights] A[ct] gave North Carolina no good reason to reshuffle voters because of their race. We accordingly affirm the judgment of the District Court."

Questions for Further Study

1. 1. What is the Voting Rights Act of 1965 and how has it impacted voting rights in the United States?

2. 2. Utilizing the Supreme Court's analysis, how might a state legislature ensure that redistricting plans are not utilizing race as a predominant factor?

3. 3. How is congressional redistricting a state issue, as the concurring opinion noted? How is it a federal issue?

COOPER V. HARRIS

Extracts from Supreme Court Opinion.

JUSTICE KAGAN delivered the opinion of the Court.

The Constitution entrusts States with the job of designing congressional districts. But it also imposes an important constraint: A State may not use race as the predominant factor in drawing district lines unless it has a compelling reason. In this case, a three-judge District Court ruled that North Carolina officials violated that bar when they created two districts whose voting-age populations were majority black. Applying a deferential standard of review to the factual findings underlying that decision, we affirm.

I

♦ A

The Equal Protection Clause of the Fourteenth Amendment limits racial gerrymanders in legislative districting plans. It prevents a State, in the absence of "sufficient justification," from "separating its citizens into different voting districts on the basis of race." .... When a voter sues state officials for drawing such race-based lines, our decisions call for a two-step analysis.

First, the plaintiff must prove that "race was the predominant factor motivating the legislature's decision to place a significant number of voters within or without a particular district." ...

Second, if racial considerations predominated over others, the design of the district must withstand strict scrutiny. ...The burden thus shifts to the State to prove that its race-based sorting of voters serves a "compelling interest" and is "narrowly tailored" to that end. ...

Two provisions of the VRA—§2 and §5—are involved in this case. ... Section 2 prohibits any "standard, practice, or procedure" that "results in a denial or abridgement of the right . . . to vote on account of race." §10301(a). .... Section 5, at the time of the districting in dispute, worked through a different mechanism. Before this Court invalidated its coverage formula, see Shelby County v. Holder, ... that section required certain jurisdictions (including various North Carolina counties) to pre-clear voting changes with the Department of Justice, so as to forestall "retrogression" in the ability of racial minorities to elect their preferred candidates, Beer v. United States....

When a State invokes the VRA to justify race-based districting, it must show (to meet the "narrow tailoring" requirement) that it had "a strong basis in evidence" for concluding that the statute required its action. ... Or said otherwise, the State must establish that it had "good reasons" to think that it would transgress the Act if it did not draw race-based district lines. .... That "strong basis" (or "good reasons") standard gives States "breathing room" to adopt reasonable compliance measures that may prove, in perfect hindsight, not to have been needed. ...

♦ B

This case concerns North Carolina's most recent redrawing of two congressional districts, both of which have long included substantial populations of black voters. In its current incarnation, District 1 is anchored in the northeastern part of the State, with appendages stretching both south and west (the latter into Durham). District 12 begins in the south-central part of the State (where it takes in a large part of Charlotte) and then travels northeast, zig-zagging much of the way to the State's northern border. ... The design of that "serpentine" district, we held, was nothing if not race-centric, and could not be justified as a reasonable attempt to comply with the VRA.

The next year, the State responded with a new districting plan, including a new District 12—and residents of that district brought another lawsuit alleging an impermissible racial gerrymander. A District Court sustained the claim twice, but both times this Court reversed. ... Racial considerations, we held, did not predominate in designing the revised District 12. Rather, that district was the result of a political gerrymander—an effort to engineer, mostly "without regard to race," a safe Democratic seat. ...

The State redrew its congressional districts again in 2001, to account for population changes revealed in the prior year's census. Under the 2001 map, which went unchallenged in court, neither District 1 nor District 12 had a black voting-age population (called a "BVAP") that was a majority of the whole: The former had a BVAP of around 48%, the latter a BVAP of around 43%. .... Nonetheless, in five successive general elections conducted in those reconfigured districts, all the candidates preferred by most African-American voters won their contests—and by some handy margins. In District 1, black voters' candidates of choice garnered as much as 70% of the total vote, and never less than 59%. ...

Another census, in 2010, necessitated yet another congressional map—(finally) the one at issue in this case. ...

The new map (among other things) significantly altered both District 1 and District 12. The 2010 census had revealed District 1 to be substantially underpopulated: To comply with the Constitution's one-person-one-vote principle, the State needed to place almost 100,000 new people within the district's boundaries. ... Rucho, Lewis, and Hofeller chose to take most of those people from heavily black areas of Durham, requiring a fingerlike extension of the district's western line. ... With that addition, District 1's BVAP rose from 48.6% to 52.7%. ...District 12, for its part, had no need for significant total-population changes: It was overpopulated by fewer than 3,000 people out of over 730,000. ... Still, Rucho, Lewis, and Hofeller decided to reconfigure the district, further narrowing its already snakelike body while adding areas at either end—most relevantly here, in Guilford County. ... Those changes appreciably shifted the racial composition of District 12: As the district gained some 35,000 African-Americans of voting age and lost some 50,000 whites of that age, its BVAP increased from 43.8% to 50.7%. ...

... a three-judge District Court held both districts unconstitutional. All the judges agreed that racial considerations predominated in the design of District 1... all rejected the State's argument that it had a "strong basis" for thinking that the VRA compelled such a race-based drawing of District 1's lines. ... the court explained that the State had failed to put forward any reason, compelling or otherwise, for its attention to race in designing that district.

The State filed a notice of appeal, and we noted probable jurisdiction. McCrory v. Harris, 579 U. S. ___ (2016).

II

We address at the outset North Carolina's contention that a victory it won in a very similar state-court lawsuit should dictate (or at least influence) our disposition of this case. As the State explains, the North Carolina NAACP and several other civil rights groups challenged Districts 1 and 12 in state court immediately after their enactment, charging that they were unlawful racial gerrymanders. ... By the time the plaintiffs before us filed this action, the state trial court, in Dickson v. Rucho, had rejected those claims... The North Carolina Supreme Court then affirmed that decision by a 4–3 vote, applying the state-court equivalent of clear error review. ...In this Court, North Carolina makes two related arguments based on the Dickson litigation: first, that the state trial court's judgment should have barred this case altogether, under familiar principles of claim and issue preclusion; and second, that the state court's conclusions should cause us to conduct a "searching review" of the decision below, rather than deferring (as usual) to its factual findings. ....

The State's preclusion theory rests on an assertion about how the plaintiffs in the two cases are affiliated. ...

But North Carolina never satisfied the District Court that the alleged affiliation really existed. ... Because of those unresolved "factual disputes," the District Court denied North Carolina's motion for summary judgment. ...

That conclusion defeats North Carolina's attempt to argue for claim or issue preclusion here. We have no basis for assessing the factual assertions underlying the State's argument any differently than the District Court did. Nothing in the State's evidence clearly rebuts Harris's and Bowser's testimony that they never joined any of the Dickson groups. We need not decide whether the alleged memberships would have supported preclusion if they had been proved. It is enough that the District Court reasonably thought they had not.

...

III

With that out of the way, we turn to the merits of this case, ... We uphold both conclusions.

◆ A

Uncontested evidence in the record shows that the State's mapmakers, in considering District 1, purposefully established a racial target: African-Americans should make up no less than a majority of the voting-age population. ... Senator Rucho and Representative Lewis were not coy in expressing that goal. They repeatedly told their colleagues that District 1 had to be majority-minority, so as to comply with the VRA. ... Dr. Hofeller testified multiple times at trial that Rucho and Lewis instructed him "to draw [District 1] with a [BVAP] in excess of 50 percent." ...

Hofeller followed those directions to the letter, such that the 50%-plus racial target "had a direct and significant impact" on District 1's configuration. ...

Faced with this body of evidence...the District Court did not clearly err in finding that race predominated in drawing District 1. Indeed, as all three judges recognized, the court could hardly have concluded anything but. ...

◆ B

The more substantial question is whether District 1 can survive the strict scrutiny applied to racial gerrymanders. ...

This Court identified, in Thornburg v. Gingles, three threshold conditions for proving vote dilution under §2 of the VRA...First, a "minority group" must be "sufficiently large and geographically compact to constitute a majority" in some reasonably configured legislative district. ... Second, the minority group must be "politically cohesive." ... And third, a district's white majority must "vote sufficiently as a bloc" to usually "defeat the minority's preferred candidate." ... ...If a State has good reason to think that all the "Gingles preconditions" are met, then so too it has good reason to believe that §2 requires drawing a majority-minority district. ...But if not, then not.

Here, electoral history provided no evidence that a §2 plaintiff could demonstrate the third Gingles prerequisite—effective white bloc-voting. ... In the lingo of voting law, District 1 functioned, election year in and election year out, as a "crossover" district, in which members of the majority help a "large enough" minority to elect its candidate of choice. ...

The State counters that, in this context, past performance is no guarantee of future results... So, North Carolina contends, the question facing the state mapmakers was not whether the then-existing District 1 violated §2. Rather, the question was whether the future District 1 would do so if drawn without regard to race. And that issue, the State claims, could not be resolved by "focusing myopically on past elections."

... The prospect of a significant population increase in a district only raises—it does not answer—the question whether §2 requires deliberate measures to augment the district's BVAP. (...State must carefully evaluate whether a plaintiff could establish the Gingles preconditions—including effective white bloc-voting—in a new district created without those measures. We see nothing in the legislative record that fits that description.

...Over and over in the legislative record, Rucho and Lewis cited Strickland as mandating a 50%-plus BVAP in District 1. ... In effect, they concluded, whenever a legislature can draw a majority-minority district, it must do so— even if a crossover district would also allow the minority group to elect its favored candidates. ...

That idea, though, is at war with our §2 jurisprudence— Strickland included. Under the State's view, the third Gingles condition is no condition at all, because even in the absence of effective white bloc-voting, a §2 claim could succeed in a district (like the old District 1) with an under 50% BVAP. But this Court has made clear that unless each of the three Gingles prerequisites is established, "there neither has been a wrong nor can be a remedy." ...

In sum: Although States enjoy leeway to take race-based actions reasonably judged necessary under a proper interpretation of the VRA, that latitude cannot rescue District 1. ... But neither will we approve a racial gerrymander whose necessity is supported by no evidence and whose raison d'être is a legal mistake. Accordingly, we uphold the District Court's conclusion that North Carolina's use of race as the predominant factor in designing District 1 does not withstand strict scrutiny.

IV

We now look west to District 12, making its fifth (!) appearance before this Court. This time, the district's legality turns, and turns solely, on which of two possible reasons predominantly explains its most recent reconfiguration. The plaintiffs contended at trial that the General Assembly chose voters for District 12, as for District 1, because of their race; more particularly, they urged that the Assembly intentionally increased District 12's BVAP in the name of ensuring preclearance under the VRA's §5. But North Carolina declined to mount any defense ...The mapmakers drew their lines, in other words, to "pack" District 12 with Democrats, not African-Americans. After hearing evidence supporting both parties' accounts, the District Court accepted the plaintiffs'.

... In Shaw II, for example, this Court emphasized the "highly irregular" shape of then-District 12 in concluding that race predominated in its design. ... But such evidence loses much of its value when the State asserts partisanship as a defense, because a bizarre shape—as of the new District 12—can arise from a "political motivation" as well as a racial one...

...

... we uphold the District Court's finding of racial predominance respecting District 12. The evidence offered at trial, including live witness testimony subject to credibility determinations, adequately supports the conclusion that race, not politics, accounted for the district's reconfiguration. And no error of law infected that judgment...the District Court had no call to dismiss this challenge just because the plaintiffs did not proffer an alternative design for District 12 as circumstantial evidence of the legislature's intent.

♦ A

Begin with some facts and figures, showing how the redistricting of District 12 affected its racial composition. ...

As the plaintiffs pointed out at trial, Rucho and Lewis had publicly stated that racial considerations lay behind District 12's augmented BVAP. ... Thus, the District Court found, Rucho's and Lewis's own account "evince[d] intentionality" as to District 12's racial composition: Because of the VRA, they increased the number of African-Americans. ....

Hofeller confirmed that intent ...Before the redistricting, Hofeller testified, some black residents of Guilford County fell within District 12 while others fell within neighboring District 13. The legislators, he continued, "decided to reunite the black community in Guilford County into the Twelfth." ..."[M]indful that Guilford County was covered" by §5, Hofeller explained, the legislature "determined that it was prudent to reunify [the county's] African-American community" into District 12. ... It would "avoid the possibility of a [VRA]charge" that would "inhibit preclearance." ...

...

... Congressman Mel Watt ...recounted a conversation he had with Rucho in 2011 ..., Rucho said that "his leadership had told him that he had to ramp the minority percentage in [District 12] up to over 50 percent to comply with the Voting Rights Law." ...In the court's view, Watt's account was of a piece with all the other evidence—including the redistricters' on-the-nose attainment of a 50% BVAP—indicating that the General Assembly, in the name of VRA compliance, deliberately redrew District 12 as a majority-minority district. ...

The State's contrary story—that politics alone drove decision making—came into the trial mostly through Hofeller's testimony. Hofeller explained that Rucho and Lewis instructed him, first and foremost, to make the map as a whole "more favorable to Republican candidates." ...In part of his testimony, Hofeller further stated that the Obama-McCain election data explained (among other things) his incorporation of the black, but not the white, parts of Guilford County then located in District 13. ...

The District Court, however, disbelieved Hofeller's asserted indifference to the new district's racial composition. The court recalled Hofeller's contrary deposition testimony—his statement (repeated in only slightly different words in his expert report) that Rucho and Lewis "decided" to shift African-American voters into District 12 "in order to" ensure preclearance under §5...Right after asserting that Rucho and Lewis had told him "[not] to use race" in designing District 12, Hofeller added a qualification: "except perhaps with regard to Guilford County." ... As the District Court understood, that is the kind of "exception" that goes pretty far toward swallowing the rule. ...

Finally, an expert report by Dr. Stephen ... looked at the six counties overlapping with District 12.... The question he asked was: Who from those counties actually ended up in District 12? The answer he found was: Only 16% of the region's white registered voters, but 64% of the black ones. ... Those stark disparities led Ansolabehere to conclude that "race, and not party," was "the dominant factor" ....

The District Court's assessment that all this evidence proved racial predominance clears the bar of clear error review. The court emphasized that the districting plan's own architects had repeatedly described the influx of African-Americans into District 12 as a §5 compliance measure, not a side-

Document Text

effect of political gerrymandering...—that Watt told the truth when he recounted Rucho's resolve to hit a majority-BVAP target; and conversely that Hofeller skirted the truth (especially as to Guilford County) when he claimed to have followed only race-blind criteria in drawing district lines. We cannot disrespect such credibility judgments. ...

♦ B

The State mounts a final, legal rather than factual, attack on the District Court's finding of racial predominance. When race and politics are competing explanations of a district's lines, argues North Carolina, the party challenging the district must introduce a particular kind of circumstantial evidence: "an alternative [map] that achieves the legislature's political objectives while improving racial balance." ...

....

A plaintiff's task... is simply to persuade the trial court—without any special evidentiary prerequisite—that race (not politics) was the "predominant consideration in deciding to place a significant number of voters within or without a particular district." ...that burden of proof, we have often held, is "demanding." ... And because that is so, a plaintiff will sometimes need an alternative map, as a practical matter, to make his case. But in no area of our equal protection law have we forced plaintiffs to submit one particular form of proof to prevail. ...Nor would it make sense to do so here. ...

...

V

Applying a clear error standard, we uphold the District Court's conclusions that racial considerations predominated in designing both District 1 and District 12. For District 12, that is all we must do, because North Carolina has made no attempt to justify race-based districting there. For District 1, we further uphold the District Court's decision that §2 of the VRA gave North Carolina no good reason to reshuffle voters because of their race. We accordingly affirm the judgment of the District Court.

It is so ordered.

JUSTICE GORSUCH took no part in the consideration or decision of this case.

Glossary

gerrymandering: purposefully dividing a geographical region into electoral districts with intent to allow one political party to have a majority of sympathetic voters

judicial review: a constitutional doctrine which allows a court to review legislative or executive acts to determine whether they are constitutional

strict scrutiny: the highest level of judicial review, applied by the Supreme Court to a law that is alleged to violate equal protection rights under the U.S. Constitution and to determine if the law is narrowly tailored to serve a compelling state interest

Voting Rights Act of 1965: a landmark federal law that seeks to prohibit racial discrimination in voting

Teachers' Activity Guides

The following activity guide corresponds to the National History Standards as published by the National Center for History in the schools. The documents in *Milestone Documents in African American History* relate to most, though not all, of the eras and standards found in the National History Standards.

Era 2: Colonization and Settlement (1585–1763)

Standard 1: Why the Americas attracted Europeans, why they brought enslaved Africans to their colonies, and how Europeans struggled for control of North America and the Caribbean

Focus Question: What factors converged in the New World to make slavery a viable institution?

- Ask students to think about this question: Why did African slavery turn out to be a more viable labor option than either Native Americans or indentured servants in the southern colonies? Have students create a T-chart that lists the pros and cons of using all three groups as a source of labor in the plantation economy of the South.
- John Rolfe, of the Jamestown colony in Virginia, provides the first official record of the coming of Africans to America in a letter to Sir Edwin Sandys, which forms part of the *Record of the Virginia Company of London*. In that letter, referring to the arrival of a Dutch man-of-war under the direction of "Captain Jope," he says only, "He brought not anything but 20 and odd Negroes, which the Governor and Cape Merchant bought for victuals (whereof he was in great need as he pretended) at the best and easiest rate they could." This mention seems quite unimportant, except that in this letter Rolfe also describes the establishment of new plantations and the division of land under a new system. Have students research the headright system of land distribution used in the colonies. Based on their understanding of the system, have students write an essay that explains how the headright system created a need for labor that resulted in the use of indentured servants and eventually slaves.
- Explain how race served as a contributing factor to the rise of slavery. Reflect on how the color of one's skin is viewed in popular culture and compare and contrast traditional and contemporary connotations.

Standard 3: How the values and institutions of European economic life took root in the colonies and how slavery reshaped European and African life in the Americas

Focus Question: What role did religion play in the early resistance to the institution of slavery during the colonial period?

- Have students use John Woolman's essay *Some Considerations on the Keeping of Negroes* (1754) and "A Minute against Slavery, Addressed to Germantown Monthly Meeting" (1688) to create a list of arguments against slavery that emerged prior to the Declaration of Independence.
- After students research the Quakers in colonial America, have them create a Wiki where each student can add information that explains the Quaker impact on the origin and philosophy of passive resistance, or moral suasion, in the early abolitionist movement. What Quaker doctrines were brought to the movement? Entries on the Wiki should provide evidence of events, speeches, and other documentation as support.
- Ask students to read Virginia's Act XII: Negro Women's Children to Serve according to the Condition of the Mother (1662) and Virginia's Act III: Baptism Does Not Exempt Slaves from Bondage (1667). After the students summarize the main points of each act, have the class debate the role of religion in the creation of these legal rulings. What reasons did the colonial governments have for issuing these decrees? Were they really religious or were they economic decrees?
- How could religion be used to both support and refute slavery? Have students write a persuasive essay or present a persuasive speech supporting either side using information from the documents of this era as support.

Era 3: Revolution and the New Nation (1754–1820s)

Standard 1: The causes of the American Revolution, the ideas and interests involved in forging the Revolutionary movement, and the reasons for the American victory

Focus Question: In what ways were the ideas of the Declaration of Independence a contradiction to the realities of slavery?

- Just six months after the signing of the Declaration of Independence, Prince Hall and seven other African

Americans petitioned the Massachusetts General Court (1777) to free all slaves. Ask students to read the petition and find examples in his petition of the ideas and principles used in the Declaration of Independence. Students should then create a poster that Hall might have used to promote his petition to the court.

- Conduct a class discussion about the content of Lord Dunmore's Proclamation of 1775. Ask students to speculate on the colonial reaction to it. Ask students to decide which colonies would have supported it and which would have opposed it. Finally, have students assess whether the Proclamation affected the intent of the Declaration of Independence one year later to deal with the issue of slavery.
- Lord Dunmore's Proclamation, among others, led to the formation of several black regiments in the British army, among them Dunmore's Ethiopian Regiment. Black Loyalists served in a variety of positions for the British during the Revolution. Have the students research the Black Loyalists and write a brief history of their service.
- Have students read the "Act to Prohibit the Importation of Slaves" and reflect on the role of law and how laws have an impact in both positive and negative ways.

Standard 2: The impact of the American Revolution on politics, economy, and society

Focus Question: What effect did the American Revolution have on the abolition movement in the colonies?

- Ask students to read Pennsylvania's Act for the Gradual Abolition of Slavery (1780) and lead a discussion on how this was an important step in the growth of the abolitionist movement. Have students create a time line of dates when other American colonies abolished slavery and of other important legislation that encouraged the end of slavery as the United States added territories. The last item on the time line should be the Thirteenth Amendment (1865).
- Provide students with the text of Thomas Jefferson's *Notes on the State of Virginia* (1784) and Benjamin Banneker's Letter to Thomas Jefferson (1791). Tell students to think about whether Benjamin Banneker had read Jefferson's notes before he wrote to him regarding emancipation in 1791. Have students write a response from Jefferson to Banneker.

Standard 3: The institutions and practices of governments created during the Revolution and how they were revised between 1787 and 1815 to create the foundation of the American political system based on the U.S. Constitution and the Bill of Rights

Focus Question: How did the U.S. Constitution and the Bill of Rights address the issue of slavery in the new nation?

- Despite being created from the Northwest Ordinance of 1787, which banned slavery, Ohio's Black Code (1804) seemed to violate the spirit of the Ordinance as well as that of the Constitution and the Bill of Rights regarding free men. Have students research the provisions of the Northwest Ordinance and outline the examples of violations in the Black Code of Ohio to the spirit of that document and the Constitution and Bill of Rights.
- The Fugitive Slave Act was enacted by the U.S. Congress in 1793. Ask students to read it and write a letter to the editor in which they discuss the provisions in the Bill of Rights that would have been violated if they had been applied to slaves in 1793.
- The word *slavery* is not used in the Constitution (1787) until the addition of the Thirteenth Amendment in 1865. Slavery, however, is discussed in the text of the Constitution and in several of the amendments. Divide the class into small groups and have the groups compete to see which group can find the five instances where slavery shaped the content of the document without being mentioned by name.

Era 4: Expansion and Reform (1801–1861)

Standard 2: How the Industrial Revolution, increasing immigration, the rapid expansion of slavery, and the westward movement changed the lives of Americans and led toward regional tensions

Focus Question: How did slavery influence debate over sectionalism and states' rights?

- Ask students to read and compare the Fugitive Slave Act of 1793 with the Fugitive Slave Act of 1850. When they have finished, have the students create a Venn diagram to record their comparison. Then discuss as a class the role western expansion played in the changes between the two acts.
- Organize a class debate on the constitutional, political, and moral issues involved with ending the slave trade in 1808. Provide the students with Peter William's "Oration on the Abolition of the Slave Trade" (1808) and Solomon Northup's description of a slave auction in *Twelve Years a Slave* (1853) as starting points for gathering arguments for each side.

Standard 3: The extension, restriction, and reorganization of political democracy after 1800

Focus Question: How did the rapid growth of slavery after 1800 affect the lives of African Americans, both slave and free?

- Divide the class into groups and assign each group one of the documents of David Walker, William Wells Brown, John S. Rock, Henry Brown, Martin Delany, Frederick Douglass, or others. Have each group give a short multimedia presentation that summarizes each document. Then ask the students to consider

the common themes found in the writings of African Americans prior to the Civil War. What are their goals, dreams, and complaints? Consider the audience for each document when comparing the themes. What differences can be found in these documents' approach to the issue of freedom for African Americans? Have each student summarize their conclusions in an essay.
- Ask students to read Harriet Jacob's *Incidents in the Life of a Slave Girl* (1861), an autobiographical account of her life, including her time as a fugitive slave living in the North. Have students choose an incident from the narrative and draw an illustration for that event. Remind students to write an appropriate caption.
- Have groups of students analyze the court cases *State v. Mann* (1830), *United States v. Amistad* (1841), *Prigg v. Pennsylvania* (1842), *Roberts v. City of Boston* (1850), and *Dred Scott v. Sandford* (1857), along with other cases found in research, to create a time line of decisions regarding slavery or the lives of African Americans between 1801 and 1861. Then ask the students to review the time line and determine how the courts helped or hindered the rights of African Americans during this time. What principles seemed to guide the judges and justices in these cases?

Standard 4: The sources and character of cultural, religious, and social reform movements in the antebellum period

Focus Question: What ideas and principles drove the abolition movement in the antebellum period?

- Have students assess the role of religion in the abolition movement by researching online and in these volumes and adding information that they find about churches, denominations, and religious leaders' role in the abolition movement to a class Wiki on the subject.
- After reading *The Confessions of Nat Turner* (1831), have students evaluate the impact of his slave rebellion by writing an 1831 newspaper editorial taking the position that he either helped or hurt the cause of abolition with his actions or his words.
- Have students discuss the importance of education and what role it played in Douglass' journey to freedom.

Era 5: Civil War and Reconstruction (1850–1877)

Standard 1: The causes of the Civil War

Focus Question: Was slavery really the cause of the Civil War?

- Ask students to support the argument that John Brown's raid on the federal arsenal at Harpers Ferry, Virginia, was really the first salvo in the Civil War by reading it and other accounts of the raid and comparing it with the account of the only survivor of the trials and executions following the raid, Osborne P. Anderson, in *A Voice from Harper's Ferry* (1861). Then provide students with the lyrics of "The John Brown Song," (available at http:www.loc.gov/teachers/lyrical/songs/docs/john_ brown_trans.pdf) Have students research the song's history and report on the impact of the song on the Civil War.
- Have students read the revised Virginia Slave Code from 1860. Lead a class discussion about the message sent to the federal government and to the supporters of the abolition movement in these revisions. Have students rank the revisions in order of importance to Virginians as they anticipated the coming of a crisis.

Standard 2: The course and character of the Civil War and its effects on the American people

Focus Question: How did the Civil War affect the lives of African Americans, both free and slave?

- Have students conduct research to provide examples of the contributions and participation by African Americans on the side of the Confederacy and the Union during the course of the war. Ask students to write a short story or a poem or create a comic book that tells the story of a heroic African American during the Civil War.
- Have students read Abraham Lincoln's Emancipation Proclamation (1863). On the computer, have students run the text of the document through Wordle (or a similar program) to create a word cloud that emphasizes the most important terms in the document. Then have students analyze the document, in an essay or poster, in terms of Lincoln's audience, timing, and purpose in issuing it.

Standard 3: How various Reconstruction plans succeeded or failed

Focus Question: Other than ending slavery, what did the period of Reconstruction achieve?

- Ask students to research the origin of the Ku Klux Klan. Instruct them to find out how the Ku Klux Klan arose and became a powerful source of intimidation in the South despite the passage of the Ku Klux Klan Act of 1871. Discuss with students the goals and provisions of the act. Have students speculate on why the legislation failed and what impact it had on the future of race relations.
- Assign one of the sections of the Black Code of Mississippi (1865) to groups of students. Ask the students to create a flier that could be used to educate African Americans in Mississippi on the rules to be instituted in that section. Remind students that literacy rates were very low and to be creative in designing the message. When all the fliers are completed, post them around the classroom and have student groups attempt to interpret them.

- Set up a mock committee hearing and have students reenact the testimony of the seven African American participants who testified in 1866 before the Joint Committee on Reconstruction on Atrocities in the South against Blacks. Some students can play the part of those testifying. and others can take the role of the committee members. Then conduct a class discussion using the following questions: What concerns did the seven African Americans who testified have about the state of southern society and the future of African Americans in the region? What did they propose for the direction of Reconstruction? What might have happened if their concerns had been addressed?
- Ask students to read and outline the major changes to the U.S. Constitution as listed in the Thirteenth, Fourteenth, and Fifteenth Amendments—known collectively as the Reconstruction Amendments. Create a graphic organizer for students to list the provisions of each amendment and then have students review the amendments to establish the reason that they were not enforced for nearly a century. Have students record that information on the organizer.
- Have students read Henry McNeal Turner's Speech on His Expulsion from the Georgia Legislature (1868), George White's Farewell Address to Congress (1901), and Richard Harvey Cain's speech "All That We Ask Is Equal Laws, Equal Legislation, and Equal Rights" (1874). All were African American legislators during or immediately after Reconstruction. Then tell students to research the statistics on the number of African Americans who served in state legislatures and the U.S. Congress between 1865 and 1900. What problems did the trio foresee for post-Reconstruction America? How did their speeches reflect the frustration of the end of Reconstruction for African Americans? Ask students to write essays that address these questions and provide evidence of their statistical research within the essay.
- Review with the class the facts of the 1876 Supreme Court case *United States v. Cruikshank*. Ask students to read Chief Justice Morrison R. Waite's opinion of the Court. Help students define the concept of "dual citizenship." Discuss with the class how it effectively blocked enforcement of the Fourteenth Amendment (1868). Then have students research the main provisions of the Civil Rights Act of 1964 and the Voting Rights Act of 1965, which finally overturned this ruling. Have them explain how those two pieces of historic legislation ended the idea of dual citizenship.

Era 6: The Development of the Industrial United States (1870–1900)

Standard 2: Massive immigration after 1870 and how new social patterns, conflicts, and ideas of national unity developed amid growing cultural diversity

Focus Question: Did the new immigration after the Civil War help or hinder the efforts of African Americans to achieve economic and social parity?

- Have students compare and contrast the views of Booker T. Washington (in his Atlanta Exposition Address of 1895) and W. E. B. Du Bois (in "Of Mr. Booker T. Washington and Others," from *The Souls of Black Folk*, written in 1903) on the path that African Americans should take toward gaining equality with whites in the United States. Organize a class debate that utilizes the words of the two African American leaders to argue whether economic or political rights should be fought for first and the ways in which to go about gaining parity with whites.
- Consider both sides of the "separate but equal" doctrine in the *Plessy v. Ferguson* (1896) Supreme Court case. Was the decision in *Plessy* inevitable once the Court backed away from vigorous federal implementation of the Fourteenth and Fifteenth Amendments in the case of *United States v. Cruikshank* (1873)? Have students read the opinion of the court for both cases. Ask students to write an essay that argues that the interpretation of the Fourteenth Amendment in *Cruikshank* can be seen in the *Plessy* decision.
- How did John E. Bruce believe that African Americans should strive to achieve equality? Contrast his view, as set forth in "Organized Resistance Is Our Best Remedy" (1889), with the ideas of the civil rights movement led by Martin Luther King, Jr., in the 1960s. Instruct students to read the Bruce speech and several of King's essays and speeches, including "Letter from Birmingham Jail" and "I Have a Dream." Have students create a chart that lists the principles and actions on which the two agreed and the points on which they differed. Then ask students to brainstorm the ways history might have changed if African Americans had chosen to follow Bruce's plan.

Standard 3: The rise of the American labor movement and how political issues reflected social and economic changes

Focus Question: How were African Americans included in the rising organized labor movement of the late 1800s?

- In his letter to the editor, "In the Lion's Mouth" (1891), John L. Moore of the Colored Farmers' National Alliance and Cooperative Union says that he believes that only the protected right to vote will help African Americans achieve equality. Ask students to read the letter. Then have them research the Populist and Progressive movements to find out if any of his proposals were included in the platforms of the two movements. How many of his proposals are part of today's electoral process?
- In his speech "The Present Relations of Labor and Capital" (1886), the African American newspaper editor and civil rights and labor organizer T. Thomas For-

tune argued that class conflict, not strictly race, was the source of the African American struggle in the years after the Civil War. Why did he think that white racism and an exploitative economic system acted together to subjugate blacks? The speech was printed in his newspaper, the *New York Freeman*. Ask students to write a letter to the editor based on an assigned persona (labor organizer, robber baron, African American factory worker, African American sharecropper, or southern landowner, for example). Letters should take the point of view of the assigned persona and address directly the points of Fortune's speech.

Era 7: The Emergence of Modern America (1890–1930)

Standard 1: How Progressives and others addressed problems of industrial capitalism, urbanization, and political corruption

Focus Question: In what ways did the failure of the Progressive movement to address the needs of African Americans and other minorities lead to more racial tension in the United States in the 1920s? • Ask students to define lynching and trace its legal history in the United States. Discuss with students the arguments of Ida B. Wells-Barnett, in "Lynch Law in America" (1900), and the NAACP, in *Thirty Years of Lynching* (1919), in their pleas to make lynching a crime. • Have students prepare a written defense for the statement that African American women had the most difficult status in American society. Allow students to use the documents of Mary Church Terrell in "The Progress of Colored Women" (1898) and Alice Moore Dunbar-Nelson in "The Negro Woman and the Ballot" (1927) to support their position. What specific problems were unique to African American women? Have students post responses to an online discussion board created by the teacher and respond to the posts of other students. • Ask students to determine why the Supreme Court case *Guinn v. United States* (1915) failed to improve voting rights for African Americans. Tell them to analyze the opinion to draw their conclusions. Discuss with students the various methods used by southern states to disenfranchise African American voters.

Standard 2: The changing role of the United States in world affairs through World War I

Focus Question: Why did World War I not result in any gains in the fight for equality for African American?

- Have students research the Brownsville raid of 1906. Then have students consult Theodore Roosevelt's Brownsville Legacy Special Message to the Senate (1906). Ask them to evaluate his message based on what was discovered in the research. Have them respond to the following questions in a classroom discussion: Does it appear that he got all sides of the story? Was he given accurate information? Did he have any reason to distort the facts? Do you think that the Brownsville raid had an impact on the decision to keep the military segregated in World War I?
- What arguments in Monroe Trotter's Protest to Woodrow Wilson (1914) could have been used to support desegregation during wartime to bolster mobilization efforts? Using Glogster or other online poster-making programs, have students create posters that could be used in a campaign to persuade Wilson to desegregate the federal government during World War I.

Standard 3: How the United States changed from the end of World War I to the eve of the Great Depression

Focus Question: Why were the 1920s a time of great change for African Americans despite the failure of the Progressive movement and World War I to further their cause of equality?

- Discuss with students the ongoing debate over the goals African Americans should focus on in their struggle for equality— political or economic, segregation or integration, assimilation or maintenance of a distinct culture. Have students create a list of the principles that encompassed black nationalism and alternative movements that emerged in the early twentieth century. Instruct them to use the documents of W. E. B. Du Bois, Marcus Garvey, Cyril Briggs, the Niagara Movement, and William Pickens to compile the list of ideas on both sides of the debate.
- After they have created the list of principles, have students sort them into two categories based on whether the principle supports integration into white society or separatism (creation of a separate society).
- Ask students to decide which approach they think they would have supported during the 1920s and what they think different groups of Americans would have supported. Tell students to defend their decision using facts from the reading and other research.
- Ask students to draw or use UMapper to create an illustrated map of the Harlem described by James Weldon Johnson in his article "Harlem: The Culture Capital" (1925). Illustrations should include pictures of buildings, people, and artifacts that help describe the Harlem Renaissance.

Era 8: The Great Depression and World War II (1929–1945)

Standard 1: The causes of the Great Depression and how it affected American society

Focus Question: Did the severe economic downturn of the Great Depression lead to increased instances of racism in the United States?

- Have students review Chapter 2 of Haywood Patterson's book *Scottsboro Boy* (1950). Discuss instances of

racial hostility that he witnessed during his trials. What role did racial prejudice play in the legal processes? Ask students to write a short newspaper article as if they had interviewed him in jail.
- Ask students why they think the NAACP chose to focus on educational inequality rather than political or economic inequality during the 1930s. Tell students to read Charles Hamilton Houston's "Educational Inequalities Must Go" (1935) and look for indications that the Great Depression might have played a role in the NAACP's decision.
- Invite students to create a cartoon or storybook presentation (hand drawn or using computer software) of the events surrounding Marian Anderson's 1939 Easter Sunday concert at the Lincoln Memorial in Washington, D.C., as recounted in her autobiography, *My Lord, What a Morning* (1956). Remind students to address how her treatment was representative of the times and the legal reasons that prevented her from performing at Constitution Hall.

Standard 2: How the New Deal addressed the Great Depression, transformed American federalism, and initiated the welfare state **Focus Question**: Why can it be argued that the New Deal was not a "good deal" for African Americans?

- Have students make a list of the problems that John P. Davis saw, program by program, with the New Deal, in terms of its effect on African Americans, in "A Black Inventory of the New Deal" (1935).
- Next, instruct students to read Robert C. Weaver's essay "The New Deal and the Negro: A Look at the Facts" (1935) and make a list of the ways Weaver saw the New Deal helping the plight of African Americans.
- Finally, ask students to research statistics on poverty, homelessness, and unemployment for African Americans between 1933 and 1940. Then have students debate whether Davis or Weaver was most accurate in his assessment of the effect of the New Deal.

Standard 3: The causes and course of World War II, the character of the war at home and abroad, and its reshaping of the U.S. role in world affairs

Focus Question: What steps did minorities use to secure an end to segregation in the defense industries and the military during World War II?

- Have students read the union organizer A. Philip Randolph's 1941 article "Call to Negro America to March on Washington." Ask students to research Executive Order 8802, issued by President Franklin Roosevelt. Discuss whether the order was a satisfactory reason for the cancellation of the march on Washington, D.C., called for by Randolph. Discuss with students Randolph's role in the 1963 March on Washington.
- Ask students to write an essay about whether Mary McLeod Bethune's speech "What Does American Democracy Mean to Me?" is a good example of the frustration of African Americans regarding racial inequality and injustice in 1940. Remind students to draw on their knowledge of the Great Depression and the New Deal and its impact on minorities and women to support their essay and her points.

Era 9: Postwar United States (1945 to early 1970s)

Standard 3: Domestic policies after World War II

Focus Question: Did President Harry Truman improve the legacy of the New Deal in the area of minority rights?

- Have students outline the answers that the President's Commission on Civil Rights report *To Secure These Rights* (1947) provided to the four questions it posed for its investigation.
- Then have students decide which question from the civil rights report was addressed by President Truman's Executive Order 9981(1948) and discuss why the president chose this area to address first. Instruct students to research the history of segregation in the military to add to the understanding of this order.

Standard 4: The struggle for racial and gender equality and for the extension of civil liberties

Focus Question: What impact did the civil rights movement have on society in the 1950s and 1960s and beyond?

- Ask students to analyze what made the civil rights movement of the 1950s and 1960s different from prior attempts to achieve voting rights and end segregation. Students should focus their analysis on the goals, strategies, leadership, and support for the movement.
- Divide the class into groups to read the Supreme Court's decisions in *Sweatt v. Painter* (1950), *Brown v. Board of Education* (1954), *Bond v. Floyd* (1966), *South Carolina v. Katzenbach* (1966), and *Loving v. Virginia* (1967). Have each group present a short summary of each decision regarding civil rights. Discuss as a class what message the nearly unanimous decisions sent to those in southern states resisting the upholding of the Fourteenth and Fifteenth Amendments within their borders. Have a class discussion concerning why the decisions in these cases were not enough to force southern states to uphold the amendments.
- Have students read the Moynihan Report issued by the Department of Labor in 1965 and the Kerner Commission Report from 1968. What points do they both make? Where do they differ? Which was more accurate? Ask students to create a Venn diagram to log their answers to those questions. Then have students log on to an online discussion board set up by the teacher to respond to the following question: Was the Kerner

Commission Report optimistic or pessimistic about the future of race relations and minority status in the United States? Assess its accuracy forty years later.
- Ask students to compare in an essay the themes in Martin Luther King, Jr.'s 1967 speech "Beyond Vietnam: A Time to Break the Silence" with his earlier works, such as the "Letter from Birmingham Jail" and "I Have a Dream" speech. Suggest that students look at the Kerner Commission Report to help formulate reasons for the change.
- Ask students to summarize the main provisions of the Civil Rights Act of 1964 and the points made by John F. Kennedy's in his Civil Rights Address of 1963. Then lead a class discussion about whether, if Kennedy had still been alive, he would have felt that the proposals in his Civil Rights Address had been achieved.
- Despite the passage of the Civil Rights Act of 1964 and the Voting Rights Act of 1965, some African Americans felt that the civil rights movement was too conservative and moved too slowly. Have students read Malcolm X's speech "After the Bombing" (1965) and Stokely Carmichael's "Black Power" (1966), along with Eldridge Cleaver's essay "Education and Revolution" (1969). Ask students to write a letter from one of the men to Martin Luther King, Jr., defending his point of view about the direction of the movement.

Era 10: Contemporary United States (1968 to the present)

Standard 2: Economic, social, and cultural developments in contemporary United States

Focus Question: What issues have been important to African Americans since the passage of the landmark civil rights legislation of the middle 1960s?

- Ask students to use Shirley Chisholm's speech "The Black Woman in Contemporary America" (1974) to decide whether she thought that African American women were part of the women's rights movement of the 1970s. Ask students to record their responses on a teacher-created online discussion board.
- Have students debate whether Angela Davis believed that African Americans in prison are political prisoners based on her comments in the essay "Political Prisoners, Prison, and Black Liberation" (1971). Remind each side that they must provide evidence from her essay in their arguments.
- Ask students to trace the message about race relations in the documents of these major African American political figures in each of the following decades: Thurgood Marshall (1970s), Jesse Jackson (1980s), and Colin Powell (1990s). Have students create a chart to organize the similarities and differences in their messages. Then have students research the progress made by African Americans in each decade in economic, political, educational, and social equality. Have them make charts and graphs to show the progress in numerical terms.
- Instruct students to conduct research into the life, career, and philosophy of Supreme Court Justice Clarence Thomas. Create a Wiki space for students to add information as they find it about him. Then have students use the Wiki information and his written opinion to determine why he dissented in the affirmative action case of *Grutter v. Bollinger* in 2003.
- African American athletes have been important figures in the ongoing quest for equality in the United States. Have students analyze the messages about race relations presented in Jesse Owens's *Blackthink: My Life as Black Man and White Man* (1970) and Jackie Robinson's *I Never Had It Made* (1972). Then have students create for each athlete a 30-second public service announcement for radio that expresses his message about race relations.
- In 2009, the first African American president, Barack Obama, was inaugurated. Ask students to read his speech "A More Perfect Union" (2008) and his Address to the NAACP Centennial Convention (2009). Then have students create a chart that identifies the issues regarding race as he sees them and examine his proposals to tackle each issue.
- I What does Michelle Alexander describe as the direct origins and residual effects of America's "racial caste system"? Depict her descriptions in any kind of artistic form.

LIST OF DOCUMENTS BY CATEGORY

Correspondence

John Rolfe's Letter to Sir Edwin Sandys (1619/1620)
"A Minute against Slavery, Addressed to Germantown Monthly Meeting" (1688)
Benjamin Banneker's Letter to Thomas Jefferson (1791)
John L. Moore's "In the Lion's Mouth" (1891)
Martin Luther King, Jr.: "Letter from Birmingham Jail" (1963)
A. Leon Higginbotham, Jr.: "An Open Letter to Justice Clarence Thomas from a Federal Judicial Colleague" (1991)

Essays, Reports, and Tracts

John Woolman's *Some Considerations on the Keeping of Negroes* (1754)
Thomas Jefferson's *Notes on the State of Virginia* (1784)
Samuel Cornish and John Russwurm's First *Freedom's Journal* Editorial (1827)
David Walker's *Appeal to the Coloured Citizens of the World* (1829)
William Lloyd Garrison's First *Liberator* Editorial (1831)
First Editorial of the *North Star* (1847)
Thomas Morris Chester's Civil War Dispatches (1864)
Anna Julia Cooper's "Womanhood: A Vital Element in the Regeneration and Progress of a Race" (1886)
Ida B. Wells-Barnett's "Lynch Law in America" (1900)
W. E. B. Du Bois: *The Souls of Black Folk* (1903)
Thirty Years of Lynching in the United States (1919)
Cyril Briggs's *Summary of the Program and Aims of the African Blood Brotherhood* (1920)
Walter F. White: "The Eruption of Tulsa" (1921)
James Weldon Johnson's "Harlem: The Culture Capital" (1925)
Alain Locke's "Enter the New Negro" (1925)
Alice Moore Dunbar-Nelson: "The Negro Woman and the Ballot" (1927)
Walter F. White's "U.S. Department of (White) Justice" (1935)
John P. Davis: "A Black Inventory of the New Deal" (1935)
Robert Clifton Weaver: "The New Deal and the Negro: A Look at the Facts" (1935)
Charles Hamilton Houston's "Educational Inequalities Must Go!" (1935)
A. Philip Randolph's "Call to Negro America to March on Washington" (1941)
To Secure These Rights (1947)
Moynihan Report (1965)
Kerner Commission Report Summary (1968)
Eldridge Cleaver's "Education and Revolution" (1969)
Angela Davis's "Political Prisoners, Prisons, and Black Liberation" (1971)
FBI Report on Elijah Muhammad (1973)
Final Report of the Tuskegee Syphilis Study Ad Hoc Advisory Panel (1974)
One America in the 21st Century (1999)
Michelle Alexander: *The New Jim Crow* (2010)

Manifestos, Petitions, and Proclamations

Lord Dunmore's Proclamation (1775)
Petition of Prince Hall and Other African Americans to the Massachusetts General Court (1777)
Martin Delany: *The Condition, Elevation, Emigration, and Destiny of the Colored People of the United States* (1852)
Emancipation Proclamation (1863)
Niagara Movement Declaration of Principles (1905)
Louis Farrakhan's Million Man March Pledge (1995)

Legal Opinions

State v. Mann (1830)
United States v. Amistad (1841)
Prigg v. Pennsylvania (1842)
Roberts v. City of Boston (1850)
Dred Scott v. Sandford (1857)
United States v. Cruikshank (1876)
Civil Rights Cases (1883)
Plessy v. Ferguson (1896)
Guinn v. United States (1915)
Sweatt v. Painter (1950)
Brown v. Board of Education (1954)
South Carolina v. Katzenbach (1966)
Bond v. Floyd (1966)
Loving v. Virginia (1967)
Clay v. United States (1971)
Clarence Thomas's Concurrence/Dissent in *Grutter v. Bollinger* (2003)
Cooper v. Harris (1971)

Legislation

Virginia's Act XII: Negro Women's Children to Serve according to the Condition of the Mother (1662)
Virginia's Act III: Baptism Does Not Exempt Slaves from Bondage (1667)

Pennsylvania: An Act for the Gradual Abolition of Slavery (1780)
Slavery Clauses in the U.S. Constitution (1787)
Fugitive Slave Act of 1793
Ohio Black Code (1804)
Fugitive Slave Act of 1850
Virginia Slave Code (1860)
Black Code of Mississippi (1865)
Thirteenth Amendment to the U.S. Constitution (1865)
Fourteenth Amendment to the U.S. Constitution (1868)
Fifteenth Amendment to the U.S. Constitution (1870)
Ku Klux Klan Act (1871)
Act in Relation to the Organization of a Colored Regiment in the City of New York (1913)
Civil Rights Act of 1964
U.S. Senate Resolution Apologizing for the Enslavement and Racial Segregation of African Americans (2009)

Military Orders

War Department General Order 143 (1863)
William T. Sherman's Special Field Order No. 15 (1865)

Narratives

The Confessions of Nat Turner (1831)
Narrative of the Life of Henry Box Brown, Written by Himself (1851)
Twelve Years a Slave: Narrative of Solomon Northup (1853)
Harriet Jacobs's *Incidents in the Life of a Slave Girl* (1861)
Osborne P. Anderson: *A Voice from Harper's Ferry* (1861)
Haywood Patterson and Earl Conrad's *Scottsboro Boy* (1950)
Marian Anderson's *My Lord, What a Morning* (1956)
Jesse Owens's *Blackthink: My Life as Black Man and White Man* (1970)
Jackie Robinson's *I Never Had It Made* (1972)

Presidential/Executive Documents

Emancipation Proclamation (1863)
Theodore Roosevelt's Brownsville Legacy Special Message to the Senate (1906)
Executive Order 9981 (1948)
John F. Kennedy's Civil Rights Address (1963)
Barack Obama's Inaugural Address (2009)
Barack Obama's Address to the NAACP Centennial Convention (2009)

Speeches/Addresses

Richard Allen: "An Address to Those Who Keep Slaves, and Approve the Practice" (1794)
Prince Hall: *A Charge Delivered to the African Lodge* (1797)
Peter Williams, Jr.'s "Oration on the Abolition of the Slave Trade" (1808)
Henry Highland Garnet: "An Address to the Slaves of the United States of America" (1843)
William Wells Brown's "Slavery As It Is" (1847)
Sojourner Truth's "Ain't I a Woman?" (1851)
Frederick Douglass's "What to the Slave Is the Fourth of July?" (1852)
John S. Rock's "Whenever the Colored Man Is Elevated, It Will Be by His Own Exertions" (1858)
Frederick Douglass: "Men of Color, To Arms!" (1863)
Henry McNeal Turner's Speech on His Expulsion from the Georgia Legislature (1868)
Richard Harvey Cain's "All That We Ask Is Equal Laws, Equal Legislation, and Equal Rights" (1874)
T. Thomas Fortune: "The Present Relations of Labor and Capital" (1886)
John Edward Bruce's "Organized Resistance Is Our Best Remedy" (1889)
Josephine St. Pierre Ruffin's "Address to the First National Conference of Colored Women" (1895)
Booker T. Washington's Atlanta Exposition Address (1895)
Mary Church Terrell: "The Progress of Colored Women" (1898)
George White's Farewell Address to Congress (1901)
Monroe Trotter's Protest to Woodrow Wilson (1914)
William Pickens: "The Kind of Democracy the Negro Expects" (1918)
Marcus Garvey: "The Principles of the Universal Negro Improvement Association" (1922)
Mary McLeod Bethune's "What Does American Democracy Mean to Me?" (1939)
Ralph J. Bunche: "The Barriers of Race Can Be Surmounted" (1949)
Roy Wilkins: "The Clock Will Not Be Turned Back" (1957)
George Wallace's Inaugural Address as Governor (1963)
John F. Kennedy's Civil Rights Address (1963)
Malcolm X: "After the Bombing" (1965)
Stokely Carmichael's "Black Power" (1966)
Shirley Chisholm: "The Black Woman in Contemporary America" (1974)
Thurgood Marshall's Equality Speech (1978)
Jesse Jackson's Democratic National Convention Keynote Address (1984)
Colin Powell's Commencement Address at Howard University (1994)
Barack Obama: "A More Perfect Union" (2008)
Barack Obama's Inaugural Address (2009)
Barack Obama's Address to the NAACP Centennial Convention (2009)

Testimony

Testimony before the Joint Committee on Reconstruction on Atrocities in the South against Blacks (1866)
Fannie Lou Hamer's Testimony at the Democratic National Convention (1964)
Anita Hill's Opening Statement at the Senate Confirmation Hearing of Clarence Thomas (1991)

Acknowledgments

Schlager Group gratefully acknowledges the permission granted to reproduce the copyright material in this book. Every effort has been made to trace copyright holders and to obtain their permission for the use of copyright material. The publisher apologizes for any errors or omissions in the list below and would be grateful if notified of any corrections that should be incorporated in future reprints or editions of this set.

Colin Powell's Commencement Address at Howard University: Reprinted courtesy of General Colin L. Powell, USA (Ret.).

Henry McNeal Turner's Speech on His Expulsion from the Georgia Legislature: From *Lift Every Voice and Sing: African American Oratory, 1787–1900*, ed. Philip S. Foner and Robert James Branham. Tuscaloosa: University of Alabama Press, 1998. Reprinted courtesy of the University of Alabama Press.

Jesse Owen's Blackthink: My Life as Black Man and White Man: From *Blackthink* by Jesse Owens and Paul G. Neimark. Copyright © 1972 by Jesse Owens and Paul G. Neimark. Reprinted by permission of HarperCollins Publishers.

Marian Anderson's My Lord, What a Morning: "Easter Sunday," copyright (c) 1956, renewed 1984 by Marian Anderson, from *My Lord, What a Morning* by Marian Anderson. Used by permission of Viking Penguin, a division of Penguin Group (USA) Inc.

Martin Luther King, Jr.: Reprinted by arrangement with The Heirs to the Estate of Martin Luther King Jr., c/o Writers House as agent for the proprietor New York, NY. • "Letter from a Birmingham Jail": Copyright 1967 Dr. Martin Luther King Jr; copyright renewed 1991 Coretta Scott King

Malcolm X: "After the Bombing": Reprinted courtesy of the family of Malcolm X. Malcolm X™ is a trademark of the Family of Malcolm X / www.CMGWorldwide.com.

Excerpt from *The New Jim Crow*, copyright 2010, 2012 by Michelle Alexander. Reprinted by permission of The New Press. www.thenewpress.com

INDEX

Volume numbers are indicated before each page number.

A

Abernathy, Ralph 3:1196
A. Leon Higginbotham: "An Open Letter to Justice Clarence Thomas from a Federal Judicial Colleague" 4:1534
A. Philip Randolph's "Call to Negro America to March on Washington" 3:905, 3:1001, 3:1014, 3:1063, 3:1102
Act for the Gradual Abolition of Slavery 1:56, 1:83, 1:90, 1:144–145, 1:153
Act in Relation to the Organization of a Colored Regiment in the City of New York 3:865, 3:873
Act of March 3, 1819, Relative to the Slave Trade 1:270, 1:272, 1:279
Act to Regulate Black and Mulatto Persons. See Ohio Black Code.
Adams, Abigail 1:75
Adams, John 1:75, 1:96, 1:99, 1:108, 1:111
Adams, John Quincy 1:269, 1:272, 1:284, 1:286, 1:306, 2:555
affirmative action 2:585, 2:762, 3:1011, 4:1472, 4:1489, 4:1490, 4:1492–1493, 4:1525, 4:1527–1530, 4:1532–1533, 4:1547, 4:1552, 4:1554, 4:1561, 4:1568, 4:1572–1573.
See also Clarence Thomas's Concurrence/Dissent in *Grutter v. Bollinger.* 4:1523, 4:1529
African Blood Brotherhood for African Liberation and Redemption 3:927, 3:929, 3:932
Agricultural Adjustment Act 3:995–996, 3:1005, 3:1008
Agricultural Adjustment Administration 3:997–998, 3:1002, 3:1010, 3:1016
Alain Locke's "Enter the New Negro" 3:957
Ali, Muhammad 4:1383–1384
Alice Moore Dunbar-Nelson: "The Negro Woman and the Ballot" 3:985
Allen, Richard 1:99, 1:153, 1:156
  "An Address to Those Who Keep Slaves, and Approve the Practice" 1:153, 1:159
American Anti-Slavery Society 1:196, 1:211, 1:244–245, 1:267, 1:303, 1:307, 1:315, 1:318, 1:325, 1:329, 1:335, 1:406, 2:453, 2:456, 2:479, 3:834
American Colonization Society 1:51, 1:55–56, 1:208, 1:211–212, 1:303, 1:307, 1:391, 1:405–406, 1:411, 1:415, 2:451, 2:522, 2:592
American Equal Rights Association 2:604, 2:777, 2:783

American Federation of Labor 2:689, 2:725, 3:809, 3:1005, 3:1015, 3:1017, 3:1063–1064, 3:1096, 4:1490
American and Foreign Anti-Slavery Society 1:209, 1:303
American Missionary Association 3:820, 3:828, 3:901, 3:903
American Revolution. See Revolutionary War.
American Society for Colonizing the Free People of Color. See American Colonization Society. 1:208
American Woman Suffrage Association 2:604, 2:735, 2:738, 2:777, 2:783, 2:786, 2:789
Anderson, Marian
  My Lord, What a Morning 3:1059, 3:1060–1061, 3:1159
Anderson, Osborne P.
  A Voice from Harper's Ferry 2:491–492, 2:496
Angela Davis's "Political Prisoners, Prisons, and Black Liberation" 4:1395
Anita Hill's Opening Statement at the Senate Confirmation Hearing of Clarence Thomas 4:1489, 4:1497
Anna Julia Cooper's "Womanhood: A Vital Element in the Regeneration and Progress of a Race" 2:695, 3:905
Anthony, Susan B. 1:379, 2:583, 2:604, 2:735, 2:777, 2:780–781, 2:783, 2:786, 2:789, 3:985
Anti-Lynching Crusaders 3:986–987, 3:989, 3:992, 3:994
Articles of Confederation 1:95, 1:114, 1:186, 1:282, 1:301, 2:435, 2:445–446, 2:601, 2:629, 2:634
Ashley, James M. 2:555, 2:556
Association of Southern Women for the Prevention of Lynching 3:911, 3:915
Atlanta Compromise. See Booker T. Washington's Atlanta Exposition Address. 1085
Attucks, Crispus 1:74, 1:114, 2:453, 2:507–508, 3:821, 3:833, 3:1069

B

Back to Africa movement 1:405, 1:410, 2:717–718, 3:928, 3:960
Banneker, Benjamin
  Letter to Thomas Jefferson 1:99–100, 1:135, 1:138, 1:141, 3:880
Barack Obama: "A More Perfect Union" 4:1545
Bates, Daisy 4:1461–1462, 4:1467, 4:1469
Baumfree, Isabella. See Truth, Sojourner. 1:380
Beecher, Philemon 1:172–173
Benezet, Anthony 1:87, 1:153, 1:198, 1:205–206
Benjamin Banneker's Letter to Thomas Jefferson 1:135, 1:141, 3:880

Berkeley, Sir William 1:13, 1:15–16, 1:18
Bethune, Mary McLeod 3:1055-1057, 4:1461
    "What Does American Democracy Mean to Me?"
        3:1055, 3:1057, 3:1064, 3:1096, 4:1461, 4:1467,
        4:1469
Bill of Rights 1:96, 1:148, 1:173, 2:583, 2:585
Bingham, John A. 2:565, 2:582, 2:603–604
Black Cabinet 3:995, 4:1007, 4:1009, 4:1055, 4:1059, 4:1064
Black Code of Mississippi 2:543, 2:547, 2:617
Black Codes.
    See also Black Code of Mississippi, Ohio Black
        Code 1:171, 1:177, 1:379, 2:557, 2:564, 2:581,
        2:583–585, 2:590, 2:611–612, 2:617, 2:635, 2:637,
        3:806, 3:937, 4:1404, 4:1564–1565
Black, Hugo 2:585, 2:605, 4:1281–1282, 4:1381
Black Muslims. See Nation of Islam. 4:1231, 4:1235,
    4:1393, 4:1431, 4:1435, 4:1447
black nationalism 1:405, 1:409–410, 2:453, 2:458, 2:687,
    2:750, 3:841, 3:927–933, 3:952, 3:1005, 3:1041,
    3:1043–1044, 3:1091, 4:1234, 4:1237, 4:1265,
    4:1432–1433, 4:1439, 4:1451, 4:1504
Black Panther Party 1:410, 4:1261–1262, 4:1265, 4:1275,
    4:1326, 4:1351, 4:1354, 4:1366, 4:1377, 4:1397,
    4:1405, 4:1407, 4:1411
Black Power 1:410, 2:456, 2:458, 2:721, 2:750,
    3:872, 3:905, 3:929, 3:933, 3:949, 3:1042, 3:1199,
    4:1261–1262, 4:1263, 4:1265, 4:1268, 4:1269–1274,
    4:1298, 4:1305, 4:1326, 4:1329, 4:1339,
    4:1365–1366, 4:1375–1377, 4:1387, 4:1434, 4:1516
Bleeding Kansas 1:112, 2:424, 2:437, 2:479, 2:484, 2:491
Bond, Julian 4:1245, 1246, 1248, 1262, 1352
Bond v. Floyd 4:1245–1247, 4:1250–1251, 4:1253
Booker T. Washington's Atlanta Exposition Address 2:691,
    2:747, 2:754, 3:826, 3:840, 3:1091
Boston Tea Party 1:75
Bradley, Joseph P. 2:623, 2:651
Briggs, Cyril 3:928-929
    *Summary of the Program and Aims of the African Blood
        Brotherhood* 3:927–929, 3:931, 3:934
Brooke, Edward W. 8:810
Brotherhood of Sleeping Car Porters 2:725, 3:959, 3:971,
    3:1001, 3:1056, 3:1063–1065
Brown II 3:1150, 3:1174, 4:1148
Brown v. Board of Education 3:904, 3:1021–1022, 3:1024,
    3:1034, 3:1088, 3:1095, 3:1098, 3:1145–1147,
    3:1150, 3:1155, 3:1173, 3:1195, 3:1198
Brown, Henry Billings 2:757–758, 2:766, 3:1114
Brown, Henry "Box" 1:345, 1:367, 1:368, 1:369,
    1:370–371, 2:466,
    *Narrative of the Life of Henry Box Brown, Written by
        Himself* 1:367–368, 1:369
Brown, H. Rap 4:1262, 4:1377
Brown, John 1:244–245, 1:252, 1:255, 1:357, 1:388–389,
    2:424–425, 2:455–456, 2:458, 2:465–466, 2:479,
    2:491–493, 2:500, 2:504–506, 2:508, 3:821, 3:830,
    4:1398, 4:1403, 4:1405.
    See also Osborne P. Anderson: *A Voice from Harpers Ferry*.

Brown, William Wells 1:165, 1:303, 1:308, 1:325, 1:371,
    1:427, 1:821
    Clotel; or, The President's Daughter 1:326
    *Narrative of William W. Brown, a Fugitive Slave.
        Written by Himself*
    "Slavery As It Is" 1:325, 1:331
Brownsville attack 3:854
Bryan, George 1:83, 1:87
Buchanan, James 1:359, 2:437, 2:439
Buffalo Soldiers 1:523, 3:849, 3:1503, 3:1507
Bunche, Ralph 3:995–996, 3:1009, 3:1064, 3:1083–1085
    "The Barriers of Race Can Be Surmounted" 3:1083,
        3:1087–1088, 3:1091
Bureau of Refugees, Freedmen, and Abandoned Lands.
    See Freedmen's Bureau. 2:534, 2:546, 2:579, 2:611,
    4:1324,
Bush, George H. W. 4:1475, 4:1487, 4:1489, 4:1495,
    4:1503, 4:1519–1520, 4:1532,
Bush, George W. 4:1385, 4:1416, 4:1501, 4:1503,
    4:1550, 4:1564, 4:1577
Butler, Benjamin 2:521–522, 2:530, 2:593, 2:635

C

Cain, Richard Harvey 2:635, 2:637, 2:640–641
    "All That We Ask Is Equal Laws, Equal Legislation, and
        Equal Rights" 2:635, 2:639
Carlos, John 4:1365–1366
Carmichael, Stokely 2:458, 4:1262, 4:1352, 4:1433,
    4:1516
    "Black Power" 3:872, 3:933, 4:1304, 4:1387, 4:1516
Cato's Rebellion. See Stono Rebellion. 1:251, 3:821
Catt, Carrie Chapman 2:781
Charles Hamilton Houston's "Educational Inequalities
    1:347, 3:1019, 3:1020–1021, 4:1056, 4:1114, 4:1119,
    4:1159
    Must Go!" 1:347, 3:1019, 3:1024, 4:1180
Chase, Salmon P. 1:146, 1:284, 2:533, 2:556, 2:624
Chester, Thomas Morris 2:519, 2:521, 2:539, 3:857,
    3:872, 3:905
    Civil War Dispatches 2:539, 3:857, 3:872
Chisholm, Shirley 2:785, 4:1352, 4:1458, 4:1463
    "The Black Woman in Contemporary America"
Cinqué, Joseph 1:306, 1:313
Civil Rights Act (1866) 2:557, 2:565, 2:567, 2:582, 2:595,
    2:649, 4:1323
Civil Rights Act (1870) 2:612
Civil Rights Act (1871). See Ku Klux Klan Act. 2:584,
    2:586, 2:612–613
Civil Rights Act (1875) 2:613, 2:615, 2:639–640,
    2:643, 2:649, 2:651–652, 2:654–655, 3:759,
    3:986, 4:1113
Civil Rights Act (1957) 4:1289, 4:1575
Civil Rights Act (1960) 4:1289, 4:1575, 4:1579
Civil Rights Act (1964) 2:655, 3:1024, 4:1301, 4: 1302,
    4:1327, 4:1331, 4:1579, 4:1177, 4:1210, 4:1230,
    4:1246, 4:1248

Civil Rights Cases 2:585, 2:615, 2:643, 2:649, 2:651, 2:655, 2:657, 2:758–759, 2:761, 2:767, 2:768, 3:818, 3:1114
Civilian Conservation Corps 3:1009
Clarence Thomas's Concurrence/Dissent in *Grutter v. Bollinger* 4:1523
Clay, Cassius. *See* Ali, Muhammad. 4:1379, 4:1384
Clay, Henry 1:303, 1:405, 2:435
Clay v. United States 4:1379, 4:1381, 4:1382, 4:1383
Cleaver, Eldridge 4:1402, 4:1265, 4:1351
    "Education and Revolution" 2:721, 3:933, 4:1351, 4:1354, 4:1357, 4:1402
Clinton, Bill 4:1496
Clinton, Hillary Rodham 4:1523, 4:1546–1547, 4:1549
Code of Virginia. See Virginia Slave Code. 2:463, 2:465
Cohen, Steve 4:1563
cold war 3:1000, 3:1074, 3:1076, 3:1080, 3:1096, 3:1099, 3:1102, 3:1115, 3:1173, 3:1175, 3:1176–1177, 3:1186, 3:1209, 3:1210, 3:1211, 4:1253, 4:1300, 4:1367, 4:1432, 4:1433, 4:1520
Colin Powell's Commencement Address at Howard University 5:1501, 5:1506
    Colored Farmers' National Alliance 2:723, 2:727, 2:729–730
Colored Women's League of Washington 2:735, 2:737, 2:777, 2:779
Committee against Jim Crow in Military Service and Training 3:1063, 3:1064, 3:1065, 3:1067
Commonwealth v. Jennison 1:108
Communism 3:927, 3:930, 3:940, 3:959, 3:1041–1042, 3:1066, 3:1115, 3:1173, 3:1175–1176, 3:1183, 3:1186, 3:1191, 4:1254, 4:1300, 4:1311, 4:1398, 4:1433
Compromise of 1850 1:304, 1:309,1: 316, 1:355, 1:387, 1:391, 2:424, 2:437,2:439, 2:491, 2:715. *See also* Fugitive Slave Act of 1850.
Compromise of 1877 2:626, 2:640, 3:806, 3:818, 3:1125
Confessions of Nat Turner 1:251–254, 1:255, 1:258
Confiscation Acts 2:513
Congress of Industrial Organizations 3:1064, 3:1096, 4:1490
Congress of Racial Equality 3:1218, 3:1220
Congressional Reconstruction. *See* Radical Reconstruction. 2:544, 2:591, 2:603
Connor, Eugene "Bull" 3:1196–1197, 4:1230
Conspiracy of 1741 1:38, 1:251
Constitution (U.S.) 2:511, 2:513, 2:543, 2:553. *See also* Fifteenth Amendment to the U.S. Constitution, Fifth
    2:608, 2:609, 2:657, 2:777, 3:883, 3:886
    Amendment to the U.S. Constitution, First
    Amendment to the U.S. Constitution, Fourteenth 2:657, 3:1019, 3:1113, 4:1315
    Amendment to the U.S. Constitution, Nineteenth 3:901, 3:902, 3:904
    Amendment to the U.S. Constitution, Thirteenth 1:367, 1:381, 2:543, 2:657
    Amendment to the U.S. Constitution

Constitutional Convention 1:86, 1:451, 2:544, 2:601, 2:638, 4:1294, 4:1584
Continental congress 1:66, 1:69, 1:78, 1:96, 1:183, 395, 3:1191
convict lease system 2:781, 2:788
Conyers, John, Jr. 4:1560
Coolidge, Calvin 4:1433
Cooper, Anna Julia 2:458, 2:695, 2:697
    "Womanhood: A Vital Element in the Regeneration and Progress of a Race" 2:695, 2:697
Cornish, Samuel 1:207, 1:209
Crisis, The 3:995, 3:999, 3:1019, 4:1035
Crummel, Alexander 1:196, 1:405, 2:698, 2:699, 3:830
Crusades 1:21
Cuffe, Paul 1:405, 3:821
Cyril Briggs's *Summary of the Program and Aims of the African Blood Brotherhood* 3:931

D

Daughters of the American Revolution 3:1159, 3:1167
David Walker's *Appeal to the coloured Citizens of the Word* 1:99, 1:158, 1:200, 1:234
Davis. Angela 4:1352, 4:1395, 4:1397, 4:1399
    "Political Prisoners, Prisons, and Black Liberation" 4:1398
Davis, Jefferson 2:530, 2:576, 2:586, 3:820
Davis, John P. 3:996, 3:1008, 3:1010–1011
    "A Black Inventory of the New Deal" 3:995–996, 3:997, 3:999, 3:1002, 3:1008
Delany, Martin R. 1:165, 1:316, 1:319, 2:458, 2:708, 3:933
    The Condition, Elevation, Emigration, and Destiny of the Colored People of the United States 1:405, 1:407, 1:458, 4:1432
De Priest. Oscar Stanton 3:810
Dixiecrats 3:1095
Douglass. Frederick 1:155, 1:212, 1:245, 1:304, 1:308, 1:315, 1:318
    First Editorial of the *North Star* 1:212
    "What to the Slave Is the Fourth of July?" 1:155, 1:328, 1:330
    "Men of Color. To Arms!" 2:526
    Narrative of the Life of Frederick Douglass, an American Slave, Written by Himself 1:315, 1:317
Douglass' Monthly 1:320
Douglas, Stephen A. 1:356, 2:478
Douglas, William O. 4:1381, 4:1382
Dred Scott v. Sandford 1:110, 1:112, 1:182, 1:281, 1:284, 1:387, 2:424, 2:435–436, 2:439, 2:440–441, 2:451, 2:453–454, 2:479, 2:603, 2:649, 2:653, 2:680, 2:716, 2:717, 2:757
Du Bois, W. E. B. 1:165, 1:407, 2:697, 2:738, 2:750, 2:782, 3:876, 3:958, 3:976, 3:999, 3:1008, 4:1398, 4:1405, 4:1434
    The Souls of Black Folk 2:782, 3:817, 3:818, 3:819, 3:820, 3:822, 3:823, 3:838, 3:875, 3:959, 3:1083, 3:1085, 3:1087.
See also Crisis, The.

Dunbar-Nelson, Alice Moore 3:985, 3:986
"The Negro Woman and the Ballot" 3:985, 3:988, 3:992
Dunbar, Paul Laurence 3:979, 3:986, 3:996, 3:1008, 3:1060
Dyer, Leonidas C. 3:986. *See also* Dyer bill.
Dyer bill 3:985, 3:992

E

Eisenhower, Dwight D. 3:1174, 3:1184, 3:1210, 4:1281, 4:1284, 4:1332, 4:1503
Eldridge Cleaver's "Education and Revolution" 2:721, 4:1363
Emancipation Proclamation 1:356, 1:359, 2:467–468, 2:511–517, 2:519, 2:534–535, 2:546, 2:553, 2:555, 2:559, 2:565, 2:569, 2:578–579, 2:581, 2:581, 2:603, 2:687, 2:777, 3:973, 3:986, 4:1371, 4:1377
Emergency Education Program 3:1011
Emergency Relief Appropriations Act 3:1008, 3:1010
Enforcement Acts 2:605, 2:611, 2:615, 2:617, 2:624–625, 2:637, 2:640, 3:806, 4:1575 *See also* Ku Klux Klan Act 1:177, 2:584, 2:595, 2:611, 2:617, 2:622, 2:637, 2:651, 3:818
Equal Employment Opportunity Commission 3:1097, 3:1100, 4:1346, 4:1489, 4:1492, 4:1532
Evers, Medgar
Executive Order 8802 3:1057, 3:1064–1065, 3:1067, 3:1073
Executive Order 9981 2:523, 3:872, 3:1057, 3:1065, 3:1067, 3:1073, 3:1074–1077, 3:1081, 3:1095, 3:1114, 3:1146, 4:1315, 4:1414

F

Fair Employment Practices Commission 3:1067, 3:1096
Fair Housing Act 3:1024
Fannie Lou Hamer's Testimony at the Democratic National Convention 3:1217, 3:1225, 4:1266
Fanon, Frantz 4:1263, 4:1265, 4:1268
Fard, Wallace D. 4:1230
Farrakhan, Louis 1:405, 4:1436, 4:1450–1451, 4:1472, 4:1473, 4:1514, 4:1516
Million Man March Pledge 4:1439, 4:1511, 4:1517
Faubus, Orval 3:1174, 4:1229
FBI Report on Elijah Muhammad 4:1431, 4:1435, 4:1439, 4:1449
Federal Council on Negro Affairs. *See* Black Cabinet. 3:1055
Federal Emergency Relief Agency 3:1009
Fifteenth Amendment to the U.S. Constitution 2:601, 2:609, 2:777, 3:883–886
Fifth Amendment to the U.S. Constitution 2:438
Fifty-fourth Massachusetts Volunteer Infantry 2:519, 2:648
Fillmore, Millard 1:144, 1:148, 1:358–359, 2:391
Final Report of the Tuskegee Syphilis Study Ad Hoc Advisory Panel 4:1447, 4:1451

First Editorial of the *North Star*. *See also* 1:315, 1:321
Douglass, Frederick. 1:155, 1:245, 1:304, 1:307–308, 1:316–320, 1:325, 1:328, 1:355, 1:369, 1:371, 1:387–389, 1:394–395, 1:405–406, 1:409, 2:424, 2:426, 2:441, 2:453, 2:455, 2:477, 2:479, 2:481, 2:491–492, 2:515, 2:654, 2:700, 2:779, 2:781, 2:793, 3:821, 3:830, 3:838–839, 3:875, 3:900, 3:903, 3:907, 3:1198, 4:1264, 4:1271, 4:1276, 4:1535, 4:1543
First Great Awakening 1:23, 1:52, 1:55
Force Act 2:612, 3:1035
Fortune, T. Thomas 1:165, 2:685, 2:687, 2:693, 2:793
"The Present Relations of Labor and Capital" 2:685–687, 2:689, 2:693
Fourteenth Amendment to the U.S. Constitution 1:345, 2:565, 2:581, 2:587, 2:716, 3:1019, 3:1113, 4:1315
Franklin, Benjamin 1:86–87, 1:96, 1:109, 1:154, 1:210, 1:341, 2:613, 4:1417, 4:1426
Franklin, John Hope 2:639, 3:941, 4:151, 4:1519, 4:1524
Frederick Douglass: "Men of Color, To Arms!"
Frederick Douglass' Paper. *See also* North Star.
Frederick Douglass's "What to the Slave Is the Fourth of July?" 1:330
Free Soil Party 1:175, 2:556
Freedmen's Bureau 2:534, 2:537–538, 2:557, 2:563–567, 2:570–571, 2:579, 2:581, 2:584, 2:590–591, 2:611–613, 2:717, 3:806, 4:1323, 4:1324, 4:1560
Freedom Riders 3:1195, 3:1197, 4:1230
Freedom Summer 3:1217–1220, 4:1474, 4:1586
Freedom Vote initiative 3:1218
Freedom's Journal 1:155, 1:207–211, 1:214–215, 1:218, 1:318
Freemasonry 1:161–163, 1:165
Frémont, John C. 2:437, 2:512
French and Indian War 1:52, 1:55, 3:865
French Revolution 1:164, 1:233, 1:314, 2:555, 2:688, 2:693, 3:955, 4:1397
Fugitive Slave Act of 1793 1:99, 1:143–148, 1:151, 1:269, 1:281–283, 1:285, 1:287, 1:301, 1:328, 1:355–357, 1:360, 1:387, 2:466, 2:477, 2:484
Fugitive Slave Act of 1850 1:111, 1:149, 1:176–177, 1:287, 1:304, 1:308, 1:342, 1:355, 1:357–359, 1:361, 1:367, 1:387, 1:390, 2:426, 2:465–466, 2:480, 2:491, 2:653, 1:668. *See also* Compromise of 1850.

G

Gage, Frances Dana 1:379, 1:381–382, 1:385
Gage, Thomas 1:75, 1:78
Garland, Charles 3:1019
Garnet, Henry Highland, 1:302–304, 1:307–308, 1:310, 1:405, 1:410
"An Address to the Slaves of the United States of America" 1:303, 1:307–308, 1:310
Garrison, William Lloyd 1:157–158, 1:221, 1:237, 1:243, 1:248, 1:254, 1:303, 1:307–308, 1:315–319, 1:325–326, 1:328–330, 1:338, 1:342, 1:381, 1:390, 1:392, 2:451, 2:454–455, 2:491, 2:515, 2:521
First *Liberator* Editorial 1:158, 1:243, 1:248

Garvey, Marcus 1:405, 1:410, 2:686–687, 2:717–718, 2:750, 3:900–901, 3:927–929, 3:931, 3:937, 3:949, 3:958, 3:960, 3:972, 3:999, 3:1005, 4:1230, 4:1404, 4:1411, 4:1432.
  "The Principles of the Universal Negro Improvement Association". *See also* Universal Negro Improvement Association. 3:949, 3:953
George H. White's Farewell Address to Congress 2:643, 3:805
George Wallace's Inaugural Address as Governor 3:1183, 3:1187
Grant, Ulysses S. 1:317, 1:381–382, 2:512, 2:521, 2:534, 2:535, 2:556, 2:563–564, 2:591, 2:603–604, 2:612–613, 2:621, 2:623, 2:651, 2:716–717, 2:733, 3:854
Gray, Thomas Ruffin 1:251–252
Great Depression 2:481, 2:585, 2:750, 3:819, 3:824, 3:949, 3:959, 3:961, 3:971–973, 3:995–998, 3:1001, 3:1005, 3:1007, 3:1021–1022, 3:1025, 3:1031, 3:1041, 3:1055, 3:1063, 3:1075, 3:1126–1127, 4:1414, 4:1433
Great Migration 2:792, 3:810, 3:900, 3:902, 3:904, 3:927, 3:958, 3:960, 3:975, 3:1084, 3:1087
Great Society 4:1297–1298, 4:1301, 4:1325–1327, 3:1330
Greeley, Horace 2:424, 2:441, 2:477, 2:479
Grutter v. Bollinger. See Clarence Thomas's Concurrence/Dissent in *Grutter v. Bollinger.* 4:1523, 4:1529
Guinn v. United States 2:605, 3:842, 3:883–888, 3:891

H-I

Haitian Revolution 1:164, 1:208, 1:210, 1:221
Hall, Prince 1:73, 1:75–82, 1:157, 1:161–163, 1:165, 1:168, 1:218
  A Charge Delivered to the African Lodge 1:161–163, 1:168
  Petition of Prince Hall and Other African Americans to the Massachusetts General Court 1:73, 1:75, 1:82
Hamer, Fannie Lou 3:1217–1219, 3:1222, 3:1225, 4:1474, 4:1482, 4:1582
  Testimony at the Democratic National Convention 3:1217, 3:1225
Hamilton, Alexander 1:96, 1:109, 1:114, 1:121
Harlan, John Marshall 2:651, 2:653, 2:757–758, 2:760, 2:770, 3:1114, 4:1381–1382
Harlem Renaissance 3:817, 3:931, 3:939, 3:957–959, 3:961, 3:971–974, 3:987–989, 3:996 3:1007, 3:1033, 3:1041–1045, 4:1313
Harpers Ferry raid. *See* Brown, John. 2:495
Harriet Jacobs's *Incidents in the Life of a Slave Girl* 2:477–485
Harrisburg Eight 4:1399, 4:1410
Hayes, Rutherford B. 1:388, 2:626, 2:651, 3:806, 3:808, 3:818, 3:1125
Haymarket Riot 2:687, 2:689
Haywood Patterson and Earl Conrad's *Scottsboro Boy* 3:1037, 3:1125
Henderich, Gerhard 1:31, 1:34

Henry Highland Garnet "An Address to the Slaves of the United States of America" 1:303, 1:310
Henry McNeal Turner's Speech on His Expulsion from the Georgia Legislature 2:589, 2:596
Higginbotham, A. Leon 4:1534
  "An Open Letter to Justice Clarence Thomas from a Federal Judicial Colleague"
Hill, Anita 4:1489–1490, 4:1492–1493, 4:1497
  Opening Statement at the Senate Confirmation Hearing of Clarence Thomas 4:1489, 4:1497
Ho Chi Minh 4:1265, 4:1275, 4:1300, 4:1307, 4:1309, 4:1313
Hoover, J. Edgar 3:1195, 4:1265, 4:1298, 4:1301, 4:1328, 4:1354, 4:1404, 4:1409, 4:1431, 4:1433, 4:1435, 4:1449
Houston, Charles Hamilton 3:1019–1021, 3:1056, 3:1114, 4:1145–1146
  "Educational Inequalities Must Go!" 1:347, 3:1019–1020, 3:1023–1024, 4:1026
Howe, Julia Ward 2:735
Hughes, Langston 3:821, 3:957–958, 3:960–961, 3:972, 3:976, 3:996, 3:1041, 4:1306
Humphreys, Benjamin Grubb 2:544
Ickes, Harold 3:995, 3:998, 3:1009, 3:1159
Ida B. Wells-Barnett's "Lynch Law in America" 2:791
Initiative on Race. *See* One America in the 21st Century. 4:1519, 4:1521
International Labor Defense 3:1125–1127, 3:1129, 3:1140

J

Jackie Robinson's *I Never Had It Made* 4:1413, 4:1416, 4:1418
Jackson, Andrew 1:269, 4:284
Jackson, Jesse 1:165, 4:1434, 4:1472, 4:1476
  Democratic National Convention Keynote Address 4:1434, 4:1471, 4:1472, 4:1476, 4:1480, 4:1513, 4:1216–1217, 4:1219–1220, 4:1549, 3:928
Jacobs, Harriet 2:479-482
  Incidents in the Life of a Slave Girl 2:477–481, 2:485
James Weldon Johnson's "Harlem: The Culture Capital" 3:963, 3:971–974, 3:976
Japanese internment (World War II) 3:941, 4:1147
Jefferson, Thomas 1:95-96, 1:111, 1:135-137
  Notes on the State of Virginia 1:56, 1:66, 1:76, 1:84, 1:86, 1:94–95, 1:98–99, 1:102, 1:136–139, 1:156, 1:158, 1:219, 2:464, 3:1190–1191, 3:1193
Jesse Jackson's Democratic National Convention Keynote Address 3:928, 4:1217–1220, 4:1266, 4:1366, 4:1472, 4:1473, 4:1520, 4:1549
Jesse Owens's *Blackthink: My Life as Black Man and White Man* 4:1365–1366, 4:1421
Jim Crow 4:1513, 4:1553, 4:1559, 4:1560–1565, 4:1567–1568, 4:1572–1573, 4:1478
John P. Davis: "A Black Inventory of the New Deal" 3:995, 3:996–997, 3:999, 3:1002, 3:1014, 3:1059
John R. Kennedy's Civil Rights Address 3:1208
John Rolfe's Letter to Sir Edwin Sandys 1:1, 1:4, 1:18

Johnson, Andrew 1:235, 2:537, 2:543, 2:546, 2:556–557, 2:563, 2:569, 2:581, 2:603, 2:613–615, 3:806, 4:1324
Johnson, James Weldon 3:842, 3:878, 3:911, 3:938, 3:957, 3:971-974, 3:1019, 3:1033
    "Harlem: The Culture Capital" 3:842, 3:878, 3:923, 3:938, 3:939, 3:952, 3:957–958, 3:960, 3:963, 3:970–973, 3:976, 3:1033
Johnson, Lyndon B. 3:1147, 3:1161, 3:1221
John S. Rock's "Whenever the Colored Man Is Elevated, It Will Be by His Own Exertions" 2:459, 2:461, 3:1001
John Woolman's *Some Considerations on the Keeping of Negroes* 1:34, 1:51, 1:53, 1:158
Joint Committee on National Recovery 3:1064
Josephine St. Pierre Ruffin's "Address to the First National Conference of Colored Women" 2:458, 2:700, 2:702, 2:733–738, 2:743

K

Kansas-Nebraska Act 1:342, 1:359, 2:424, 2:437–438, 2:441, 2:453, 2:456, 2:478, 2:482, 2:491, 2:582, 2:716
Kennedy, John F. 1:98, 3:1177, 3:1197, 3:1209-1210, 4:1298, 4:1317, 4:1529
    Civil Rights Address 3:1009, 3:1161, 3:1177, 3:1184, 3:1196–1197, 3:1209, 3:1211, 4:1325, 4:1327, 4:1330, 4:1338, 4:1347
Kerner Commission Report Summary 4:1325, 4:1327–1330
Kerner, Otto, Jr. 4:1327
King, Martin Luther, Jr. 4:1328, 4:1330, 4:1332, 4:1366, 4:1404, 4:1420
    "Beyond Vietnam: A Time to Break Silence" 4:1251, 4:1266, 4:1297, 4:1301
    "I Have a Dream" 3:1196, 3:1199, 4:1230
    "Letter from Birmingham Jail" 3:1196, 3:1199, 4:1230
Kitchin, William W. 3:808
Korean War 1:75, 3:870, 3:1075–1076, 3:1077, 3:1115
Ku Klux Klan Act 2:584, 2:611, 2:618, 2:622, 2:637, 2:651, 3:818

L

Ladies' Anti-Slavery Society 1:387–388,
Lee, Robert E. 1:317, 1:381, 2:493, 2:495, 2:512, 2:519, 2:533–534, 2:544, 2:563–565, 2:586, 2:716, 3:862, 3:1187, 3:1193
Legal Defense and Education Fund 3:1114
Liberator 1:157, 1:243–245, 1:247–249, 1:254, 1:303, 1:307, 1:315, 1:317, 1:319, 1:325, 1:329–330, 1:340, 1:340, 1:381, 1:390, 2:453–455, 2:491, 2:521, 2:534, 3:931, 3:964, 4:1299–1300, 4:1307–1308, 4:1506
    See also Garrison, William Lloyd. 1:157, 1:237, 1:243, 1:248, 1:254, 1:303, 1:307–308, 1:315–319, 1:325–326, 1:328–330, 1:338, 1:342, 1:381, 1:390, 1:392, 1:403, 2:451, 2:454–455, 2:491, 2:515, 2:521
Liberty Party 1:245, 1:303–304, 1:307, 1:306, 1:318, 1:320, 1:329

Lincoln, Abraham 1:108, 1:113, 1:138, 1:245
    See also Emancipation Proclamation, Gettysburg Address. 1:356, 1:359, 2:467–468, 2:511, 2:512–515, 2:517, 2:519, 2:534, 2:535, 2:546, 2:553, 2:555, 2:557, 2:565, 2:578, 2:581, 2:584, 2:603, 2:687, 2:777, 3:973, 3:986, 4:1371,
Lindbergh kidnapping law 3:1034
Little Rock Arkansas school desegregation crisis
Locke, Alain 3:957–959, 3:961, 3:971, 3:972–974, 3:1041
    "Enter the New Negro" 3:957–959, 3:961, 3:964
Lodge, Henry Cabot 2:723
Lord Dunmore's Proclamation 1:65, 1:67, 1:71
Louis Farrakhan's Million Man March Pledge 4:1511, 4:1514, 4:1517
Loving v. Virginia 4:1248, 4:1315–1319, 4:1321

M

Madison, James 1:303
Malcolm X: "After the Bombing" 4:1229
Malcolm X 4:1229-1231
    "After the Bombing"
March on Washington for Jobs and Freedom (1963) 3:1063, 3:1065, 3:1160
Marcus Garvey: "The Principles of the Universal Negro Improvement Association" 3:949
Marian Anderson's *My Lord, What a Morning* 3:1059, 3:1167
Marshall, John 1:48, 1:269, 1:284, 2:651, 2:653, 2:657, 2:757, 2:758, 2:760, 2:770, 3:1114, 3:1153, 4:1382
Martin Delany: *The Condition, Elevation, Emigration, and Destiny of the Colored People of the United States* 1:405
Martin Luther King, Jr.: "Beyond Vietnam: A Time to Break Silence" 4:1297
Martin Luther King, Jr.: "I Have a Dream" 2:749, 4:1247
Martin Luther King, Jr.: "Letter from Birmingham Jail" 3:1195–1196
Marx, Karl 2:689, 4:1357, 4:1397, 4:1398
Mary Church Terrell: "The Progress of Colored Women" 2:777
Mary McLeod Bethune's "What Does American Democracy Mean to Me?" 3:1055
Mason, James Murray 1:356
Massachusetts Anti-Slavery Society 1:303, 1:307, 1:316, 1:317, 1:329, 1:388
McCarthy, Joseph 3:820, 3:1098, 4:1398
McKay, Claude 3:928, 3:931–932, 3:957, 3:958, 3:960, 3:967, 3:972, 3:976
McLaurin v. Board of Regents 3:1021, 3:1023
McLean, John 1:269, 1:281, 1:284, 2:439, 2:440
Messenger, The 1:9, 1:67, 2:527, 2:530, 2:597, 2:717, 3:985, 3:988, 3:989, 3:1017, 3:1065, 3:1066, 4:1434, 4:1435, 4:1440, 4:1441, 4:1514
Mexican-American War 1:304, 1:316, 1:319, 2:423, 2:424, 2:437, 2:439, 2:453, 2:454, 2:477, 2:535
Middle Passage 1:123, 1:195
Million Man March 4:1511, 4:1513–1514, 4:1517, 4:1439

Mississippi Freedom Democratic Party 3:1217, 3:1218
Mississippi Plan 3:806, 3:809
Missouri Compromise 1:173, 1:199, 1:267, 1:269, 2:423–424, 2:435, 2:436, 2:437, 2:438, 2:439, 2:440, 2:453, 2:477–478, 2:715
Missouri ex rel. Gaines v. Canada 3:1020, 3:1023, 3:1114, 3:1116, 3:1122, 3:1145–1146, 3:1156, 4:1537
Mondale, Walter 4:1471, 4:1473
Monroe Trotter's Protest to Woodrow Wilson 3:875, 3:881
Montgomery bus boycott 3:1024, 4:1298, 4:1299, 4:1315
Moore, John L. "In the Lion's Mouth" 2:723
Morris, Gouverneur 1:109, 1:184
Morris, Robert 1:342, 1:343, 1:345
Moskowitz, Henry 3:819, 3:823
Mott, Lucretia 1:245, 1:380, 2:735, 2:777, 2:780, 3:985
Moynihan, Daniel Patrick 4:1459
Moynihan Report 4:1459, 4:1466
Muhammad, Elijah. *See also* FBI Report on Elijah Muhammad 4:1431, 4:1433, 4:1435, 4:1437, 4:1440, 4:1449
Muhammad, Khalid Abdul 4:1504, 4:1505
Muhammad, Wallace Fard. *See* Fard, Wallace D. 4:1431, 4:1434, 4:1436, 4:1437, 4:1450
Murray, John. 4th Earl of Dunmore 1:65, 1:66, 1:153
Murray v. Maryland 3:1114

N

Narrative of the Life of Henry Box Brown, Written by Himself 1:367–369
Nash, Diane 4:1461–1462, 4:1467
Nat Turner's Rebellion. *See Confessions of Nat Turner.*
Nation Industrial Recovery Act 3:995–996, 3:1008, 3:1010
Nation of Islam 1:409, 1:410, 3:949, 4:1229–1230, 4:1231–1232, 4:1234, 4:1379–1380, 4:1382, 4:1389, 4:1431, 4:1436, 4:1440, 4:1442, 4:1450, 4:1472, 4:1511, 4:1513–1514, 4:1560
National Advisory Commission on Civil Disorders. *See* Kerner Commission Report Summary. 4:1325, 4:1327, 4:1329–1330
National American Woman Suffrage Association 2:604, 2:777, 2:783, 2:786
National Association for the Advancement of Colored People 2:735, 2:749, 2:761–780, 3:819, 3:820, 3:837, 3:875, 3:883, 3:899, 3:900, 3:909, 3:1056, 3:1064, 3:1095, 3:1096, 3:1125, 3:1127, 3:1145, 3:1159, 3:1169, 4:1221, 4:1434, 4:1462, 4:1489, 4:1490, 4:1511
National Association of College Women 2:777, 2:779, 2:783
National Association of Colored Women 2:697, 2:700, 2:735, 2:738, 2:777, 2:781, 2:788, 3:986, 3:1055
National Conference of Colored Women 2:700, 2:733, 2:735–736, 2:743
National Congress of Mothers 2:780

National Council of Negro Women 3:1055–1056, 3:1096, 4:1467
National Equal Rights League 3:838
National Federation of Afro-American Women 2:733, 2:735, 2:737, 2:777, 2:779
National Independent Equal Rights League 3:875–876, 3:878
National Negro Congress 3:996–997, 3:999–1000, 3:1005, 3:1008, 3:1056, 3:1063, 3:1064, 3:1065
National Recovery Administration 3:996–997, 3:998, 3:1008–1009
National Urban League 3:875, 3:971, 3:973, 3:999, 3:1007, 3:1011, 3:1056, 3:1096
National Woman Suffrage Association 2:604, 2:777, 2:783
Negro Family: The Case for National Action. See The Moynihan Report.
New Deal 1:371, 2:481, 3:911, 3:995–1000, 3:1002, 3:1004, 3:1007–1012, 3:1015–1017, 3:1034, 3:1063–1065, 3:1075, 3:1086, 3:1099, 3:1115, 3:1161
New England Anti-Slavery Society 1:218, 1:214, 2:453
New Negro Movement 3:928, 3:931, 3:957
Newton, Huey P. 4:1265, 4:1326, 4:1351, 4:1352, 4:1354
Niagara Movement Declaration of Principles. 3:837, 3:845
Nineteenth Amendment to the U.S. Constitution 3:901–902, 3:904, 3:989
Nixon, Richard M. 3:849, 3:1210, 4:1317
Nkrumah, Kwame 3:949, 4:1232, 4:1240, 4:1263
North Star. See also Frederick Douglass' Paper 1:388
Northup, Solomon 1:355, 2:423–426,
 Twelve Years a Slave: Narrative of Solomon Northup 2:423, 2:426, 2:430
Northwest Ordinance 1:145, 1:171–172, 1:282, 1:303, 2:435, 2:438, 2:555

O

Obama, Barack 3:810, 3:1163, 4:1397, 4:1520, 4:1545-1548
 "A More Perfect Union" 4:1545
O'Connor, Sandra Day 4:1530, 4:1577
Ohio Black Code 1:171, 1:173, 1:175, 1:177, 1:179
One America in the 21st Century 4:1519, 4:1521, 4:1523, 4:1524
Opden Graff, Abram 1:30–31
Opden Graff, Derick 1:30
Operation PUSH 4:1472, 4:1477
Opportunity: A Journal of Negro Life 3:958
Organization of Afro-American Unity 4:1231, 4:1234–1235, 4:1239, 4:1434
Osborne P. Anderson: *A Voice from Harper's Ferry* 2:491
Ovington, Mary 3:819, 3:823
Owens, Jesse 3:1163, 4:1365-1369
 Blackthink: My Life as Black Man and White Man 4:1365, 4:1371, 4:1421

P-Q

Paine, Thomas 1:87, 1:93, 1:401
Palestine Accords 3:1083
Pan-Africanism. 2:697, 2:700, 3:821, 3:838, 3:900, 3:949, 3:972, 3:1042
Parks, Rosa 3:1195, 3:1197, 4:1229, 4:1582
Pastorius, Francis Daniel 1:30, 1:36
Pathways to One America in the 21st Century: Promising Practices for Racial Reconciliation
Patterson, Haywood 3:1127
   Scottsboro Boy 3:1125, 3:1126, 3:1127
Pearson v. Murray 3:1022–1023
Penn, William 1:29
Pennsylvania: An Act for the Gradual Abolition of Slavery 1:56, 1:83, 1:145, 1:153
Pennsylvania personal liberty law 1:281–282, 1:356
Personal liberty laws 1:143, 1:147, 1:355, 1:357, 1:359, 1:387, 2:423, 2:477
Petition of Prince Hall and Other African Americans to the Massachusetts General Court 1:139, 1:166
Pickens, William 3:899-904
   "The Kind of Democracy the Negro Expects" 3:899, 3:901, 3:1069
Pierce, Franklin 1:359
Pittsburgh Anti-Slavery Society 1:406
Plessy v. Ferguson. *See also* separate-but-equal doctrine. 1:345, 1:346, 2:558, 2:585, 2:605, 2:651, 2:757, 2:758, 2:762, 2:764, 2:779, 2:792, 3:806, 3:840, 3:842, 3:1083, 3:1114, 3:1145, 3:1148
Pocahontas 1:3–4, 1:14, 4:1316
Poor, Salem 1:86, 1:163, 3:821, 3:829
Populist movement 2:725, 2:727, 3:850, 3:883
Post, Amy 2:477, 2:479
Powell, Colin 4:1501
Powhatan Confederacy 1:1, 1:3–4
President's Commission on Civil Rights 3:1067
Prigg v. Pennsylvania 1:143, 1:148, 1:269, 1:281, 1:358, 2:439
Prince Hall Freemasonry. *See* Freemasonry. 1:161–162
Prince Hall: A Charge Delivered to the African Lodge
Progressive movement 2:735, 3:961
Prosser, Gabriel 1:217, 1:251, 3:821
Public Works Administration 3:998, 3:1003, 3:1009
Quakers 1:29–33, 1:36, 1:51–56, 1:86–87, 1:107, 1:114, 1:125, 1:137, 1:153, 1:183, 1:305, 2:451, 2:477, 4:1264, 4:1273

R

Racial Integrity Act 4:1316–1317, 4:1322
Radical Reconstruction 2:563, 2:566–567, 2:589–591
Radical Republicans 2:513, 2:537, 2:556, 2:563–567, 2:582–584, 2:591, 2:593, 2:611, 2:614, 2:649, 3:806, 3:817
Ralph J. Bunche: "The Barriers of Race Can Be Surmounted" 3:1083

Randolph, A. Philip 4:1264, 4:1395, 4:1398, 4:1405, 4:1416, 4:1471–1472, 4:1489, 4:1520, 4:1532
   "Call to Negro America to March on Washington" 3:1063
Randolph, Edmund 1:109
Reagan, Ronald 4:1264, 4:1395, 4:1398, 4:1405, 4:1416, 4:1471–1472, 4:1489, 4:1520, 4:1532
Reconstruction. *See also* Radical Reconstruction 2:563, 2:566–567, 2:589–591, 2:653 3:805
Reconstruction Acts 2:590, 2:611, 2:621, 2:637, 2:640, 3:806, 3:817
Reconstruction Amendments. *See* Fourteenth Amendment to the U.S. Constitution, Fifteenth Amendment to the U.S. Constitution, Thirteenth Amendment to the U.S. Constitution
Red Summer of 3:938
Regents of the University of California v. Bakke 4:1529
Religious Society of Friends. *See* Quakers 1:29
Resettlement Administration 3:1010
Reverend John L. Moore's "In the Lion's Mouth"
Revolutionary War 1:68, 1:70, 1:75–76, 1:95–96, 1:135, 1:140, 1:161–162, 1:163, 1:165–196, 1:207, 1:217, 2:519, 2:725, 3:821, 3:833, 3:953, 3:1060, 3:1080, 4:1550
Richard Allen: "An Address to Those Who Keep Slaves, and Approve the Practice" 1:153, 1:159
Richard Harvey Cain's "All That We Ask Is Equal Laws, Equal Legislation, and Equal Rights" Speech 2:635
Robert Clifton Weaver: "The New Deal and the Negro; A Look at the Facts" 3:1007, 3:1015, 3:1059
Roberts v. City of Boston 1:341, 1:348, 2:759, 2:767, 3:1148
Robeson, Paul 3:1160, 4:1432, 4:1434
Robinson, Jackie 4:1413-1416
   I Never Had It Made 4:1413, 4:1416, 4:1418
Robinson, Marius, 1:379, 1:380, 1:382–383, 1:385
Rock, John S. 2:453-454
   "Whenever the Colored Man Is Elevated, It Will Be by His Own Exertions" 2:451
Rolfe, John 1:2-4, 1:14, 4:1316
   Letter to Sir Edwin Sandys 1:1, 1:8, 1:14, 1:15, 1:18, 1:26
Roosevelt, Eleanor 3:1036, 3:1067, 3:1159–1165
Roosevelt, Franklin D. 3:1037, 3:1057, 3:1096, 3:1170, 4:1281, 4:1367, 4:1487, 4:1547
Roosevelt, Theodore 2:747, 3:852-855
   Brownsville Legacy Special Message to the Senate 3:849
Roosevelt's Four Freedoms 3:1095, 3:1096
Roy Wilkins: "The Clock Will Not Be Turned Back" 3:1173
Ruffin, Josephine St. Pierre 2:733-738
   "Address to the First National Conference of Colored Women" 2:702, 2:733
Ruffin, Thomas 1:235
   State v. Mann 2:240-243

Rush, Benjamin 1:86–87
Russwurm, John 1:207–1:209, 1:319
Rustin, Bayard 3:1063

S

Salem, Peter 1:86, 1:163, 3:833
Salem Female Anti-Slavery Society 1:325–326, 1:329
Samuel Cornish and John Russwurm's First *Freedom's Journal* Editorial 1:207, 1:214
Sandys, Edwin 1:1, 1:4–5, 1:10–11, 1:14–15, 1:18
Seale, Bobby 4:1265, 4:1326, 4:1351
Second Great Awakening 1:316
Selma-to-Montgomery march 3:1161, 3:1200, 4:1263, 4:1276, 4:1474
Seneca Falls Convention 2:604, 2:606, 2:733, 2:777, 2:780, 2:789
separate-but-equal doctrine. 2:779, 3:1114, 3:1116–1117, 3:1119, 4:1229 See also Brown v. Board of Education, Plessy v. Ferguson.
Seven Years' War 1:55
Shaw, Lemuel 1:342, 1:345
Shays's Rebellion 1:76, 1:78, 1:114, 1:163
Shelley v. Kraemer 3:886, 3:1099, 3:1114, 3:1116, 3:1122, 3:1146, 4:1323
Sherman, William Tecumseh 2:521, 2:533, 2:535, 4:1560
  Special Field Order No. 15 2:533–538, 2:540, 4:1560
Shillady, John R. 3:910–911, 3:917
Shirley Chisholm: "The Black Woman in Contemporary America" 4:1459
Sipuel v. Board of Regents 3:1020, 3:1023, 3:1114, 3:1116, 3:1122
Slaughter-House Cases 1:345–346, 2:558, 2:583, 2:585, 2:615, 2:624, 2:625, 2:629, 2:640, 2:652–653, 2:766–767, 4:1323
Slavery Clauses in the U.S. Constitution 1:107, 1:116
Smith, Alfred E. 1:987, 1:989
Smith, Tommie 4:1365–1366, 4:1377
Socialism 3:931, 3:959–960, 3:1055, 3:1065, 3:1202, 4:1263, 4:1265, 4:1351, 4:1397
Sojourner Truth: "Ain't I a Woman?" 1:379, 1:385, 2:697, 3:1224
Soledad Brothers 4:1399, 4:1408, 4:1411
Somerset Case 1:74
South Carolina v. Katzenbach 2:605–606, 4:1279, 4:1281–1284, 4:1286–1287, 4:1581–1582
Southern Christian Leadership Conference 3:1197, 3:1200, 3:1218–1220, 4:1230, 4:1247, 4:1298–1299, 4:1301, 4:1306, 4:1434, 4:1472
Southern Tenant Farmers Union 3:996, 3:998–999, 3:1064
Spanish-American War 2:523, 3:820, 3:824, 3:829, 3:850, 3:853, 3:857, 3:865–866
Stanton, Edwin 2:519, 2:534, 2:567
Stanton, Elizabeth Cady 2:606
State v. Mann 1:233–238, 1:240
Stevens, Thaddeus 2:564–565, 2:582–583, 2:649

Stokely Carmichael's "Black Power" 3:872, 3:905, 3:933, 4:1304, 4:1387, 4:1516
Stone, Lucy 2:604, 2:735, 2:777, 2:780, 2:783, 2:786, 2:789
Stono Rebellion 1:183, 1:251, 3:821, 3:834
Storey, Moorfield 3:911
Story, Joseph 1:269, 1:284, 1:287, 1:356, 2:439
  Prigg v. Pennsylvania 1:281
  United States v. Amistad 1:287
Stowe, Harriet Beecher 1:233, 2:237, 2:424, 2:439, 2:479, 2:491, 2:715–716, 2:721, 3:960
  Uncle Tom's Cabin 1:316, 1:387, 2:477, 2:491, 2:715, 3:960
Student Nonviolent Coordinating Committee 3:1218, 4:1245, 4:1247, 4:1253, 4:1261, 4:1269, 4:1273, 4:1433–1434, 4:1469
Submarginal Land Purchase Program 3:1008, 3:1010
Subsistence Homestead program 3:998, 3:1010
Sumner, Charles 1:342–345, 2:454, 2:555–556, 2:564, 2:583, 2:613, 2:635, 2:638, 2:649, 2:651, 2:767
Sweatt v. Painter 1:347, 3:1021, 3:1023, 3:1025, 3:1113–1117, 3:1120, 3:1156

T

Tacky's War 1:251
Taft, William Howard 2:749, 3:849, 3:853, 3:858, 3:880
Tammany Hall 3:867–868
Taney, Roger. See also *Dred Scot v. Sandford*.
Taylor, Zachary 2:437
Tennessee Valley Authority 3:996, 3:998, 3:1004, 3:1008, 3:1010
Ten-Point Program (Black Panthers) 4:1593
Terrell, Mary Church 2:697, 2:736, 2:777-780, 4:1461
  "The Progress of Colored Women" 2:777, 4:1464
Testimony before the Joint Committee on Reconstruction on Atrocities in the South against Blacks 2:563, 2:570
Theodore Roosevelt's Brownsville Legacy Special Message to the Senate 3:849
Thirteenth Amendment to the U.S. Constitution 1:317, 1:367, 1:381, 2:543, 2:553, 2:561, 2:657, 2:716
Thirty Years of Lynching in the United States, 2:792, 3:909, 3:911, 3:917
Thomas Jefferson's *Notes on the State of* Virginia 1:56, 1:95, 1:102
Thomas Morris Chester's Civil War Dispatches 2:519, 2:539, 3:857, 3:872, 3:905
Thomas, Clarence 4:1489-1490, 4:1529-1533
  Concurrence/Dissent in *Grutter v. Bollinger* 4:1529, 4:1535
Thomas, Norman 3:1019
Three-fifths Compromise 1:108, 1:144, 1:303
Thurgood Marshall's Equality Speech 4:1532
Thurmond, Strom 3:1095
Tillman, Benjamin 2:726

To Secure These Rights 1:230, 2:631, 3:1067, 3:1075, 3:1095, 3:1096, 3:1099, 3:1100, 3:1103
Toussaint-Louverture, François-Dominique 1:164
Trotter, William Monroe 2:689, 3:838
    Protest to Woodrow Wilson 3:875, 3:878, 3:881
Truman, Harry 2:523, 3:870, 3:939, 3:1036, 3:1057, 3:1065, 3:1067, 3:1075, 3:1081, 3:1114, 4:1315, 4:1317
Truman Doctrine 3:1096
Trumbull, Lyman 2:555, 2:556
Truth, Sojourner 1:379-382, 1:385
T. Thomas Fortune: "The Present Relations of Labor and Capital" 2:685
Tubman, Harriet 2:492, 3:1127
Tulsa Race Riot: A Report by the Oklahoma Commission to Study the Tulsa Race Riot of 1921 3:941
Ture, Kwame, *See* Carmichael, Stokely. 4:1262
Turner, Henry McNeal 2:591-592, 2:593, 4:1560
    Speech on His Expulsion from the Georgia Legislature 2:589, 2:596
Turner, Nat. *See also Confessions of Nat Turner.* 1:253
Tuskegee Airmen 4:1503, 4:1507
Tuskegee Syphilis Study. See also Final Report of the Tuskegee Syphilis Study Ad Hoc Advisory Panel 4:1447, 4:1452, 4:1455
Twelve Years a Slave: Narrative of Solomon Northup 2:423, 2:426, 2:430
Twenty-fourth Amendment to the U.S. Constitution 3:809, 3:810
Tyler, John 1:391, 1:437

U

Underground Railroad 1:304–305, 1:308, 1:316, 1:326, 1:359, 1:367–368, 1:370, 1:406, 2:465–468, 2:496, 2:519, 2:565, 2:577, 4:1403
United States v. Amistad 1:267, 1:274
United States v. Cruikshank 2:615, 2:621, 2:623–624, 2:629, 2:640, 2:651, 2:653, 2:676, 3:818, 3:1097
Universal Negro Improvement Association 1:410, 2:717–718, 3:900–901, 3:929, 3:931, 3:938, 3:949, 3:953–954, 3:958, 3:999, 4:1230, 4:1411, 4:1432. *See also* Garvey, Marcus
U.S. Colored Troops 2:493, 2:527, 2:529, 2:536–537, 2:591
U.S. Commission on Civil Rights 3:1067, 3:1100, 4:1284
U.S. Senate Resolution Apologizing for the Enslavement and Racial Segregation of African Americans 4:1559, 4:1564

V

Van Buren, Martin 1:269, 1:271, 2:437
Vesey, Denmark, 1:218, 1:234, 1:251, 1:267, 2:821
Vietnam War 3:1196–1197, 4:1229–1230, 4:1245, 4:1246, 4:1248–1249, 4:1261–1262, 4:1264–1265, 4:1296, 4:1297, 4:1299–1301, 4:1325, 4:1330, 4:1379, 4:1383, 4:1399, 4:1416, 4:1248, 4:1433

Vinson, Frederick M. 3:1146–1147
Virginia Company of London 1:1, 1:4, 1:13, 1:15, 1:21–23
Virginia House of Burgesses 1:1, 1:13, 1:15, 1:65–67, 3:1183
Virginia House of Delegates 1:23. *See also* Virginia House of Burgesses
Virginia Slave Code 2:463, 2:468, 2:472
Virginia's Act III: Baptism Does Not Exempt Slaves from Bondage 1:21, 1:27
Virginia's Act XII: Negro Women's Children to Serve according to the Condition of the Mother 1:13, 1:16, 1:19, 1:65
Voting Rights Act (1965) 2:605, 2:727, 2:810, 2:842, 2:887, 3:1024, 3:1177, 3:1195, 3:1197, 3:1199, 3:1221, 4:1246, 4:1248, 4:1278–1283, 4:1287–1289, 4:1292–1293, 4:1297–1298, 4:1301, 4:1315, 4:1325, 4:1326–1327, 4:1475, 4:1485, 4:1532, 4:1575, 4:1577–1578, 4:1581–1589, 4:1617–1619

W—X—Y—Z

Wagner–Van Nuys bill 3:1035
Waite, Morrison J. 2:623
Walker, David 1:99, 1:211, 1:217–218, 1:223, 1:234, 1:308, 1:405, 2:821
    Appeal to the Coloured Citizens of the World 1:99, 1:211, 1:217–218, 1:234, 1:308, 3:821
Wallace, George 1: 589, 3:1183, 3:1187, 3:1209, 4:1229, 4:1264, 4:1373
    Inaugural Address as Governor 3:1183, 3:1187
Walter F. White: "The Eruption of Tulsa" 3:937, 3:944
Walter F. White's "U.S. Department of (White) Justice" 3:1031–1033, 3:1036, 3:1038
War on Poverty 4:1297–1299, 4:1301, 4:1325, 4:1326
Warren, Earl 3:1024, 3:1117, 3:1145, 3:1146–1148, 4:1248, 4:1281, 4:1315, 4:1317
Washington, Booker T. 1:165, 1:408, 2:451, 2:455–456, 2:687, 2:689, 2:718–719, 2:738, 2:747–748, 2:754–754, 2:780–782, 2:792, 3:817–824, 3:828, 3:830, 3:832, 3:837–841, 3:852–853, 3:875, 3:878, 3:899–902, 3:938, 3:957, 3:973, 3:976, 3:1060, 3:1083–1084, 4:1329
    Atlanta Exposition Address 2:456, 2:738, 2:747, 2:749, 2:754, 2:782, 3:840, 3:875, 3:1084–1085
Washington, George 1:75, 1:86, 1:96, 1:110, 1:143, 1:145, 1:157, 1:161, 1:306, 1:390, 1:405, 2:494, 3:865, 3:953, 3:1060, 3:1184, 3:1191, 4:1433, 4:1484, 4:1501
Washington, Madison 1:306, 1:313
Watts riot 4:1349
Weaver, Robert Clifton 3:1007–1008, 3:1015, 3:1059
    "The New Deal and the Negro: A Look at the Facts" 3:1007–1009, 3:1015
W. E. B. Du Bois: *The Souls of Black Folk* 2:782, 2:817–820, 3:822–823, 3:827–828, 3:838, 3:875, 3:959, 3:1083, 3:1085, 3:1087
Wells-Barnett, Ida B. 2:779, 2:791–795, 2:798
    "Lynch Law in America" 2:791, 2:793, 2:795, 2:798

Western New York Anti-Slavery Society 1:326
Wheatley, Phillis 1:74, 1:77, 2:779–780, 3:821
Whipper, William 1:319
White, Edward 3:883, 3:886
White, George H. 3:805, 3:807, 3:810, 3:813
    Farewell Address to Congress 3:805, 3:813
White, Walter F. 3:924, 3:937, 3:941, 3:944, 3:1031
    "The Eruption of Tulsa" 3:937, 3:944
    "U.S. Department of (White) Justice" 3:1031–1033, 3:1036, 3:1038
White House Conference on Negro Women and Children 1:13, 1:15–16, 1:19, 1:65, 3:1055–1056, 3:1096, 4:1467
Wilberforce, William 1:125, 1:198, 1:205, 1:392
Wilkins, Roy 3:999, 3:1172–1173, 3:1175, 3:1221, 4:1327, 4:1428, 4:1434
    "The Clock Will Not Be Turned Back" 3:1173, 3:1182
William Lloyd Garrison's First *Liberator* Editorial 1:243, 1:248
William Pickens: "The Kind of Democracy the Negro Expects" 3:899
William T. Sherman's Special Field Order No. 15 2:533, 2:537–538
William Wells Brown's "Slavery As It Is" 1:325, 1:332, 1:372
Williams, Peter, Jr. 1:115, 1:195–196, 1:202
    "Oration on the Abolition of the Slave Trade" 1:195, 1:202

Wilmot Proviso 1:319
Wilson, James F. 2:555–556
Wilson, Stanyarne 2:808
Wilson, Woodrow 2:614, 3:853, 3:875–876, 3:878, 3:881, 3:899, 3:902, 3:904, 3:912, 3:928–929, 3:938, 3:985, 3:996, 3:1099, 3:1175
Woolman, John 1:51–53, 1:55, 1:58, 1:87, 1:153, 1:198, 2:451, 2:453
    Some Considerations on the Keeping of Negroes 1:51, 1:53, 1:58, 2:451
Works Progress Administration slave narratives 1:371
World War I 2:522–523, 2:614, 2:735, 3:840, 3:853, 3:865, 3:870, 3:877–878, 3:899–901, 3:904, 3:927–928, 3:930, 3:938, 3:958, 3:961, 3:971–972, 3:975, 3:987, 3:999, 3:1021, 3:1031, 3:1065–1066, 3:1075, 3:1096, 4:1245, 4:1248, 4:1317, 4:1328, 4:1433
World War II 2:523, 2:655, 3:820, 3:901, 3:904, 3:911, 3:939, 3:941, 3:1009, 3:1023, 3:1055–1057, 3:1063, 3:1065–1067, 3:1073–1075, 3:1086, 3:1088, 3:1095, 3:1098–1099, 3:1100, 3:1114, 3:1149, 4:1238, 4:1245, 4:1248, 4:1315, 4:1327, 4:1328, 4:1414–1415, 4:1433–1434, 4:1503, 4:1520, 4:1551, 4:1561
Wright, Jeremiah 4:1545, 4:1552
Wynne, Robert 1:13, 1:15–16
Young, Andrew 2:810